CONTENTS

(re)Tracing
AFRICA

A Multidisciplinary Study of African History, Societies, and Culture

SECOND EDITION

Salome C. Nnoromele
Ogechi E. Anyanwu

Kendall Hunt
publishing company

Kendall Hunt
publishing company

www.kendallhunt.com
Send all inquiries to:
4050 Westmark Drive
Dubuque, IA 52004-1840

ISBN 978-1-4652-7063-4

This book is dedicated to our African/African-American Studies (AFA) students,
at Eastern Kentucky University, whose interest in African studies and abundant curiosity
about the continent inspired the AFA faculty to produce a textbook aimed
at addressing their questions.

LIST OF CONTRIBUTORS

Lady Jane Acquah is a Ph.D. student at the University of Texas at Austin. She studies religion, specifically, Islam in West Africa. Her research is about the trajectory between politics and religion with the Ahmadiyya Muslim Movement in Ghana as her focus. She has an M. Phil in history from the University of Cape Coast, Ghana.

Aje-Ori Agbese is an assistant professor at The University of Texas Pan American's department of communication. Her research interests include Nigerian media history, African media and politics, global mass media, intercultural communication, Nigerian movies, and women and the media. She is the author of several journal articles and two books: *The Role of the Press and Communication Technology in Democratization: The Nigerian Story, 2006; and The Role of Intercultural Communication in Conflict Resolution: A Look at African Immigrant Fathers and their U.S.-born Children, 2009*. Prior to becoming an educator, she worked in different capacities in public relations, journalism, and social organizations in Nigeria and the United States.

Richard Aidoo is an assistant professor of Politics in the Department of Politics and Geography at Coastal Carolina University, Conway, South Carolina. His main research and teaching interests include international relations, the political economy of sub-Saharan African countries, Sino-Africa relations, African foreign policy issues, and trade and aid issues in the developing world. He has contributed on economic development issues in Africa, and some of his works appear in *Journal of Modern African Studies, Africa Today, Africa Insight, and African and Asian Studies*.

Ogechi Emmanuel Anyanwu is an associate professor of history at Eastern Kentucky University. He received his Ph.D. in African history at Bowling Green State University, Ohio. He also holds a Masters degree in International Affairs and Diplomacy and a Bachelor of History degree, both from Nigeria. Prior to joining Eastern Kentucky University, he had worked for many years at Imo State University as an assistant lecturer in the department of history and international studies (2000–2003), an executive assistant to the Vice-Chancellor (1998–2000), and an administrative officer in the Institute for Continuing Education Program (1996–1998). Dr. Anyanwu's research interests and focus have been on education, religion, and law in Africa. He is the author of *The Politics of Access: University Education and Nation Building in Nigeria, 1948–2000* (Calgary: University of Calgary Press, 2011). His articles have appeared in several refereed national and international journals. His most recent articles include "The Anglo-American-Nigerian Collaboration in Nigeria's Higher Education Reform: The Cold War and Decolonization, 1948–1960," *Journal of Colonialism and Colonial History* 11, no.3 (Winter 2010), 1–26, "Experiment with Mass University Education in Post-Civil War Nigeria, 1970–1979," *Journal of Nigerian Studies* 1, no. 1 (Fall 2010), 1–36; and "Challenging the Status Quo: Alan Pifer and Higher Education Reform in Colonial Nigeria," *History of Education* 42, no. 1 (2013): 70–91. He is the editor-in-chief of *Journal of Retracing Africa* (JORA), a joint publication of Eastern Kentucky University and Bepress.

Ukachukwu D. Anyanwu, B.A. (Hon.), M.A., Ph.D. (History), is Professor of History of Development with emphasis on Igbo and Nigerian society at Imo State University, Owerri, Nigeria. His publications include *Local Government Democracy in Nigeria* (Okigwe: Whythem, 1996); co-editor of *Igbo and the Tradition of Politics* (Enugu: Fourth Dimension; 1993); *Agriculture and Modernity in Nigeria* (New York: Tri Atlantic Book, 1998), and co-editor of *Perspectives on the Nigerian Civil War* (Owerri: Imo State University Press, 2010) and

Themes on Igbo Culture, History and Development (Lagos: UBA OND, 2010). Dr. Anyanwu was former deputy Vice-Chancellor of Imo State University and current director of the university's Centre for Igbo Studies.

Lekan Badru is the executive director of HealthInsignia Inc, a private, nonprofit 501c3 organization established to help Nigeria's medical personnel with primary health-related services in keeping up to date with technological knowledge in healthcare management. He has written scholarly articles and presented papers on issues of economic development, debt crises, gender politics, and foreign policy in Africa, with primary focus on Nigeria. He received a Master's degree in Political Science, with specialization in International Relations and Foreign Policy, from the University of Louisville, Kentucky, in 2006, where he was given a graduate teaching and research scholarship.

E. Kwadwo O. Beeko is currently an Adjunct Assistant Professor at the University of Pittsburgh, where he lectures at the Department of Africana Studies and the Department of Music. He possesses a Bachelor of Music Education (B.Ed. Mus.) from the University of Cape Coast, Ghana; a Master of Philosophy in Music (M.Phil. Mus.) from the University of Ghana; and a Doctoral Degree (Ph.D.) in Ethnomusicology from the University of Pittsburgh. His publication include *Creative Processes in Akan Musical Cultures: Innovations within Tradition*, VDM-Verlag Dr. Muller Aktiengesell Schaft & Co., KG, Germany, 2009 (originally, a Ph.D. Dissert., 2005); "Towards a New Stylistic Identity: An Analytical Overview of Ghanaian Contemporary Choral Music," in *Composition in African and the Diaspora*, Vol.2, edited by Akin Euba and Cynthia Tse Kimberlin (Centre for Intercultural Musicology (C.I.M.), London: MRI Press, 2010; "The Dual-Relationship Concept of Right-Ownership in Akan Musical Tradition: A Solution for the Individual and Communal Rights-Ownership Conflicts in Music Tradition;" in *International Journal of Cultural Property* (2011) 18: 1–28; and "Historical and Intellectual Determination of Identity: The Case of Kwabena Nketia's Akan Solo Pieces," in *The Life and Works of Emeritus J. H. Kwabena Nketia*, University of Ghana, Legon, to be published in 2011. Other works he is currently working on for future publication include "Reviving Tradition, Engaging Modernity: Style and Aesthetics in Ghanaian (Neo)-Pentecostal-Charismatic Church Musical Practices," and "Modes of Cultural Representation: Koo Nimo's Sung-Tales as Rhetoric, Innuendo, and Double-entendre."

Samuel Ezeanyika is a senior lecturer/research fellow in Political/Social Economy in the Unit of Development Studies, Department of Political Science and Public Administration, Evan Enwerem University, PMB 2000, Owerri, Imo State, Nigeria. He is also the Director of Development Studies Research Group (DESREG), located in Evan Enwerem University, Owerri. He has written extensively on political economy, international economic relations, and democracy. He also has considerable research interests and field work exposure covering poverty alleviation and livelihood approaches; rural nonfarm economy in Africa; social capital, community development, and cultural norms in Africa; poverty and environment among rural households in Africa; social networks, institutions and sustainable development in Africa; social economics and social network analysis in Africa's rural communities. He is a member of three editorial boards and the Editor-in-Chief of *African Journal of Communication and Development*.

Steve Hess is a Ph.D. candidate in political science at Miami University and is currently completing his dissertation, which explores the institutional sources of authoritarian resilience and breakdown in the cases of China, Taiwan, Kazakhstan, and the Philippines. Beyond the dissertation, his primary research interests center on revolutions and other forms of contentious politics in East Asia and the former Soviet Union. This work has appeared in published form in journals such as *Asian Survey, Problems of Post-Communism*, and *Central Asian Survey*. Steve has previously worked as a staff member for both the Central Asian Studies Society and the Center for Asian Democracy and as a volunteer in the United States Peace Corps in China. Recently, he has accepted a tenure-track position to teach political science at the University of Bridgeport in Connecticut that will commence upon the completion of his degree at Miami.

Michael O. Kasongo is an Associate Professor of History at Kentucky State University. He received his Ph. D. from the University of Kentucky. Previously, he served as an Adjunct Professor of African/African-American Studies at Eastern Kentucky University. He has authored three books, *Born to be a Preacher and a Teacher: The Life Story of Michael O. Kasongo* (Author House, 2008), *History of the Methodist Church in*

Central Congo (University Press of America, 1998), and *La Traduction du Mot Grâce dans la Langue des Ana-Mongo* (Lodja, 1972).

Timothy G. Kiogora was an associate professor at Eastern Kentucky University. He earned a joint Diploma in the Arts (1973) at St. Paul's College/ Makerere University before proceeding to Southern Methodist University in Dallas, Texas, where he obtained a Master's Degree in Ethics/Religious Studies in 1976. Dr. Kiogora also received a University of Denver Ph.D. in Social Ethics/African Studies in 1988. His research focused on ways in which some postcolonial African leaders engaged indigenous humanitarian hermeneutics in developing social-ethical approaches to political governance. Kiogora taught at the Universities of Denver (1982–1984), Nairobi, Kenya (1989–1993), and Eastern Kentucky University (1994–2012). Among his published essays in books are *Amnesty in Africa: Ethical Aberration or Usable Public Policy Instrument in Moral Dimensions in African Christianity* (Nairobi: Initiatives Press, 1993) and "Hermeneutics of Black Theology" in *Initiation into Theology* (Pretoria, S. Africa: J. Van Schaick Publishers, 1997) and *Good Governance and Development in Peacemaking and Democratization in Africa: Theoretical Perspectives and Church Initiatives* (Nairobi: East African Educational Publishers, 1996).

Michael Mwenda Kithinji is an assistant professor of history at the University of Arkansas, Fort Smith. He received his Ph.D. in history from Bowling Green State University, Ohio, in 2009. He also has a Masters degree from Saint Cloud State University, Minnesota, and a bachelor's degree from the University of Nairobi in Kenya. His research specialization is in colonial and postcolonial African history. Some of his publications include "Higher Order Thinking in Planning Social Studies Lessons: An Examination of Teachers' Uses of Source Documents," *The History Teacher*; "A Tug of War: Moi versus the World Bank and the Transformation of University Education in Kenya," OFO: *Journal of Transatlantic Studies*; and "An Imperial Enterprise: The Making and Breaking of the University of East Africa, 1949–1969," *Canadian Journal of African Studies* (forthcoming).

Ida Kumoji-Ankrah is an Associate Professor in the Department of Art and Design at Eastern Kentucky University, where she currently teaches graphic design. As an educator, designer, and artist, her research explores topics based on cross-cultural design, African art and symbols, African textile design, typography, interactive design, branding in Africa, and African oral/digital storytelling. Ida earned her B.A. in Fine Arts from St. Catherine University, and M.F.A. in Graphic Design from University of Minnesota. Ida has research publications in books, journals, and magazines and has presented at various conferences. She is also actively engaged in exhibiting her work in galleries and museums and working with clients on commissioned design projects. To date, she has been in over ninety juried and invitational exhibitions nationally and internationally. Her work is also in public and private collections, such as Women's Center (University of Minnesota), St. Catherine University, National Institution of Museum of Tetovo, Macedonia, and Visual Arts Center, Washington Pavilion of Arts and Science Visual Arts Education Collection.

Chukwunenye Clifford Njoku is a Ph.D. student in the Department of International Relations and Strategic Studies at the University of Malaya, Malaysia. He holds a Masters degree in African History (University of Malaya) and a Bachelor of Public Administration obtained at Abia State University, Uturu, Nigeria. He has previously headed various departments in banking operations with Savannah Bank of Nigeria PLC. Njoku's research interests and focus have been on comparative politics, multicultural studies of Africa and Asia. He is the author of *Idols of Nations Amidst the Gospel in the 21st Century, A Call to Depopulate Hell, A Voice from Asia* (Kuala Lumpur: Akitiara Corporation Sdn Bhd, 2008); *Bowel of Mercy: The Burden of a Compassionate Heart* (Kuala Lumpur: Akitiara Corporation Sdn Bhd, 2009). He has four forthcoming articles.

Aloysius Mom Njong is a senior lecturer at the Faculty of Economics and Management, University of Dschang-Cameroon. He currently heads the Department of Economic Policy and Analysis. He holds a Ph.D. in Development Economics, and his current research areas include growth, poverty, inequality, and distributive issues. Dr Njong is a Fulbright alumnus under the Scholar-in-Residence Program at Huston-Tillotson University, Texas State, USA. He has published widely in journals such as *The International Journal of Public-Private Partnerships*; Sheffield Hallam University, UK; *African Journal of Economic Policy*; Oxford Poverty and Human

Initiative Working Paper Series; *Journal of Education Administration and Policy Studies*; and *European Journal of Social Sciences*.

Emmanuel N. Ngwang is a 1986 graduate of Oklahoma State University with a Ph.D. in American Literature, and a Professor of English and Foreign Languages at Claflin University, where he teaches Postcolonial Literary Theory, Literature, and Drama. Before joining the faculty of Claflin University, he taught in several universities since 1982: University of Yaoundé, Cameroon (1987–1997); Kentucky State University (1997–2003); and Mississippi Valley State University from 2003–2010. He has published and presented research papers on postcolonial, African, and modern dramatic literature and feminism. Some of his recent publications include "Arrah's Existential Dilemma: A Study of Anne Tanyi-Tang's Arrah" in *Cameroon Literature in English: Critical Essays* (2010), "Spaces, Gender, and Healing in Alice Walker's *The Color Purple* and Mariama Ba's *So Long a Letter*" in *New Urges in Postcolonial Literature: Widening Horizons* (2009), "Re-Configuration of Colonialism or the Negation of the Self in Postcolonial Cameroon in Bole Butake's Plays" in *Reconceiving Postcolonialism: Visions and Revisions* (2009), "Buchi Emecheta's *Destination Biafra*: A Feminist (Re-)Writing of the Nigerian Civil War" in *Journal of African Literature: International Research on African Literature and Culture (JAL:IRCALC)* (2008), "In Search of Cultural Identity or a Futile Search for Anchor: Africa in Selected African American Literary Works" in *Identities and Voices. ALIZES (TRADE WINDS, 2007)*; "Literature as Politics: Revisiting Bole Butake's *Lake God and Other Plays*" in *The Literary Griot: International Journal of African-World Expressive Culture* (2002), and "Female Empowerment and Political Change: A Study of Bole Butake's *Lake God, The Survivors, and And Palm Wine Will Flow*" in *ALIZE (TRADE WINDS): A Journal of English Studies* (2004) (University of La Reunion, France).

Salome C. Nnoromele, co-editor of the anthology, is the Director of the African/African-American Studies and Professor of English at Eastern Kentucky University. She received her undergraduate degree from the University of Utah. Her master's and doctorate degrees are from the University of Kentucky. She is the co-author of *Journeys Home: An Anthology of Contemporary African Diasporic Experience*, the author of *Life Among the Ibo Women of Nigeria*, and several other books and articles on African culture and literature. Her teaching and research interests focus on the intersections of race, gender, and politics in nineteenth-century British literature, African literatures and cultures, and intercultural African diasporic experiences. She is the Managing Editor of *Journal of Retracing Africa* (JORA), a joint publication of Eastern Kentucky University and Bepress.

Patrick C. Nnoromele is Associate Professor in the Department of Philosophy and Religion and Chaplain for the Chapel of Meditation at Eastern Kentucky University. He received a Bachelor of Theology from ECWA Theological Seminary at Igbaja, Nigeria, a Bachelor of Arts from William Jennings Bryan College in Dayton, Tennessee. His Masters of Arts in Political Philosophy is from Wayne State University, Detroit Michigan; and he holds a Ph. D. in American Pragmatism and Philosophy of Religion from the University of Utah. Prior to coming to Eastern Kentucky University in 1994, he taught at the University of Kentucky and Cedarville University, OH. His research interests include African philosophy and religion and teaching pedagogies, especially in relationship to qualitative analysis and critical thinking in enhancement of learning and student success.

Abdoulaye Saine is Professor of African Studies and International Political Economy in the Department of Political Science at Miami University, Oxford, Ohio. He has written widely on the military in politics, democracy, and democratization in West Africa. Some of his recent publications include *The Paradox of Third-Wave Democratization in Africa: The Gambia under AFPRC-APRC Rule, 1994–2008* (Lexington Books/Roman & Littlefield Publishers, Lanham, MD, 2009), and a co- edited volume, *Elections and Democratization in West Africa, 1990–2009* (Africa World Press, Trenton, NJ, 2011). He is co-author (along with Steven Hess and Richard Aidoo), "Taming the Dragon: Outlining an African Response to Growing Chinese Engagement," in the March 2011 issue of *Africa Insight* and has a forthcoming book on *Cultures and Traditions of The Gambia* (Greenwood Press). Saine's current research interests focus on globalization, Africa-China economic relations, Islam, and the U.S.-led War on Terror.

Lovetta A. Thompson was an Adjunct Professor of African/African-American Studies at Eastern Kentucky University. She received her Master's Degree in Pan-African Studies from the University of Louisville. Her

Bachelor of Arts degree is from the University of Kentucky. Her research interests examine the ways in which postwar reconstruction programs effectively address the root causes of war and violence in postcolonial Africa, with special emphasis on Sierra Leone, West Africa.

Kenneth White was an Assistant Professor of Social Work in academia. His current position is Facilitator for Presbyterian Response to Haiti. In collaboration with the Haitian government, Non-governmental Organizations (NGOs), religious and charitable organizations, and others, he works to address the needs of the many thousands left homeless and/or orphaned due to the earthquake. Four major areas of his work in Haiti include connecting with others to build permanent homes, reconstructing schools, ensuring food security, and addressing community health. Dr. White's publications include "Scourge of Racism: Genocide in Rwanda," *Journal of Black Studies* (May 8, 2007) and "Hinduism: Racial-Religious Oppression of the Dalits (Africans) of India," *Journal of Black Studies*. His areas of interest and/or research include human rights and genocidal studies; racial, gender, heterosexual, religious, and disability microaggressions; cultural competent social work practice; and phases of identity development. He has traveled extensively and lived in several countries, including Sierra Leone.

ACKNOWLEDGMENTS

The idea for this project came from the students and faculty members for AFA 201 (The African Experience) at Eastern Kentucky University. Even though there are many books about Africa, our students and faculty felt the collective need for a book that offered a more comprehensive analysis of the continent, one that transcended the Western world's cyclical attitude of presenting Africa as a place lacking in meaningful development and trapped in a primordial existence. Our students demanded a book that would showcase the vibrancy of the African continent, its history, transformation, and challenges. Our teachers wanted a book that would enable them to present a balanced view of the continent. This book fulfil their wishes.

We are grateful to these cohorts of students and faculty for insisting that such a book is an imperative if we must begin to step away from the misinformation and ignorance that cloud any discussion of Africa in the Western world and beyond. We specially thank our beloved colleague and friend, Dr. Timothy Kiogora, who had served on the Advisory Board for the first edition of this book but went home to his ancestors on December 31, 2012. We miss his friendship and constructive feedback at all levels of this project. We thank all the faculty members at Eastern Kentucky University who teach the course on The African Experience (AFA 201) for providing invaluable feedback that has been incorporated into the production of this second edition. We are indebted to Ms. Evelyn Jones, the office assistant for the African/African-American Studies at Eastern Kentucky University, for providing much needed organizational support.

We also express our deep gratitude to the chapter contributors for continuing to entrust us with their manuscripts and assisting us in making this dream come true. Their expertise in varying fields of African studies and their commitment to retracing Africa's history and providing a more accurate and diversified view of the continent is appreciated. Finally, we thank our individual families for their love, understanding, and support throughout the entire process of working on this project. We are grateful.

Dr. Salome C. Nnoromele, Eastern Kentucky University
Dr. Ogechi E. Anyanwu, Eastern Kentucky University

PREFACE

Centuries of scholarship on Africa produced in the Western world have been largely filled with myths, stereo-types, and misconceptions about the African continent and its people. Although many books have been written to correct the negative image of the continent, the misrepresentations and mischaracterization of Africa have continued to dominate conversations surrounding past and current events in the region. *(Re)tracing Africa* provides readers with a holistic perspective on the region by reconstructing the social, political, economic, and cultural experiences of African societies during the precolonial, colonial, and postcolonial periods. Similar to the first edition, this second edition is thematically organized in five parts, and with a total of twenty-three chapters. The book presents Africa from the many perspectives of the humanistic and social science disciplines and, therefore, helps readers to understand Africa in its totality. Beside the addition of two more chapters, and the revision of existing chapters, this second edition contains a list of electronic and print resources for further reading and exploration of various aspects of the African experience that both students and teachers will find particularly useful.

In Part I, the authors examine the geography of the African continent, the centralized and decentralized states that emerged and flourished in precolonial Africa as well as the inexcusable historical and contemporary misrepresentation of Africa, especially in the West. Part II focuses on precolonial African indigenous religion, the growth and practice of Islam in Africa, women in traditional and modern Africa, and the development of education from the precolonial period to the present. The diverse and dynamic literary, art, and musical tradi-tions of African societies are explored in Part III. Essays in Parts II and III effectively underscore the centrality of African social institutions and practices in the collective and dynamic experiences of African peoples.

No understanding of the African experience is complete without a reexamination of the continent's encounters with Europe, particularly from the fifteen century to the mid-twentieth century. As all the six chapters in Part IV reveal, Africa's destiny and geo-political landscape have been fundamentally impacted by the transatlantic slave trade and the subsequent voluntary African immigration to America, European colonial rule (and all the atrocities committed during that period, notably genocide), Pan-African movement, and the infamous discriminatory policy dubbed apartheid.

Overcoming the legacy of colonialism and pursuing sociopolitical and economic transformation of Africa have preoccupied the attention of Africa's policymakers since independence. All the six chapters in Part V of this book demonstrate that although remarkable progress has been made in Africa since independence, the commitment to build strong, united, and vibrant nations in various countries has been threatened by preventable human rights violations, wars and conflicts, leadership crisis, and limited flow of foreign direct investment. More importantly, they show how internal factors interacted with external forces to dictate con-temporary problems and challenges facing Africa.

Written in clear, accessible language by both accomplished and emerging Africanists in diverse fields such as history, government, education, economics, sociology, philosophy, religion, art, and literature, *(Re)tracing Africa* is a welcome and significant addition to a growing body of scholarship dedicated to deconstructing long-held Eurocentric, sensational narratives about Africa and Africans. The various essays in this book pro-vide detailed background information to help readers appreciate the diversity of African history, cultures, and societies. By emphasizing interdisciplinary analysis of the historical and contemporary issues surrounding African development, as well as treating topics often neglected in the mainstream books on African studies, this book provides a compelling and refreshing insights into the missing voices in African studies, thereby promot-ing a better, more comprehensive, and balanced understanding of the continent.

This book is ideal for undergraduate and graduate students seeking to expand their knowledge of the entirety of the African experience. Scholars teaching early Africa, colonial Africa, and modern Africa will find this book particularly useful. For general readers (including, but not limited to, some ill-informed media personalities in the West reputed for spreading stereotypes about Africa) who are interested in having a comprehensive knowledge of the richness, diversity, troubles, and potentials of the continent, this book is a must-read, as it is broadly conceived to meet their needs.

CHAPTER 1

The Map of Africa

Robert Stock

The Anglo-Irish satirist Jonathan Swift, writing in the early 18th century, commented on the prevalent ignorance about Africa and the African people:

> So geographers in Afric maps
> With savage pictures fill their gaps,
> And o'er uninhabitable downs
> Place elephants for want of towns.

A century later, Africa remained, in the public mind, "darkest Africa"— a mysterious and virtually unknown continent. Even now, in the 21st century, Africa remains the least-known continent. The names of African countries are often in the news, but people generally know too little about these countries to give meaning to what they read and hear. Where is Mali? Is Malawi a different place? Is it Ghana or Guyana that is in Africa? What was the former name of Burkina Faso? Is Equatorial Guinea a part of Guinea? Simple questions such as these are difficult even for college-educated Westerners.

Africa covers a vast territory. At its widest from west to east and at its longest from north to south, the distance is almost the same: approximately 7,500 km. To put this into context, the distance from Los Angeles to New York is 4,470 km. Or, if you prefer, with a surface area of 24.6 million km^2, Africa south of the Sahara is about three times the size of the continental United States.

Just as Africa has occupied a relatively small part of the consciousness of most Westerners, it has also been portrayed on world maps in a way that makes it seem smaller than it actually is. The widespread use of the Mercator and other scale-distorting projections has contributed to misperceptions about the relative sizes of landmasses. Because distortion within a Mercator projection increases markedly with distance from the equator, places at higher latitudes, such as Greenland and Canada, appear much larger than places of comparable size nearer the equator. For example, although Greenland appears to be roughly the same size as Africa on a Mercator projection, it is actually only 7.3% as large, or slightly smaller than the Democratic Republic of the Congo.

THE POLITICAL MAP

The contemporary political map of Africa south of the Sahara bears little resemblance to that of 120 years ago, when the scramble to carve up the continent among European imperialist powers was in full swing. What is important at this point is to recognize that African borders are recent and often unrelated to either cultural/political realities or natural features.

Another unfortunate colonial legacy is the extreme fragmentation of the political map. In all, there are 47 independent states, some of which are too small to be considered economically viable. The small sizes and national populations of the majority of African states (Table 1.1) are continuing constraints on development. Certain states have shapes that are unusual and unhelpful. The Gambia is the most extreme example; it extends 325 km along the Gambia River and is no more than 30 km wide. In addition, except for a short coastline, The Gambia is completely surrounded by Senegal.

Table 1.1 Countries of Africa South of the Sahara

Country	Capital	Area (1,000 km²)	Population (1,000)	Per capita income ($PPP)[a]	Human development index, 2011
Angola	Luanda	1,246	13,134	4,872	0.486
Benin	Porto Novo	113	6,272	1,364	0.427
Botswana	Gaborone	600	2,005	13,049	0.633
Burkina Faso	Ouagadougou	274	11,535	1,141	0.331
Burundi	Bujumbura	28	6,356	368	0.316
Cameroon	Yaoundé	475	14,876	2,031	0.482
Cape Verde	Praia	4	427	3,402	0.568
Central African Republic	Bangui	623	3,717	707	0.343
Chad	N'Djamena	1,284	7,885	1,105	0.328
Comoros	Moroni	2	706	1,079	0.433
Congo (Dem. Rep.)	Kinshasa	2,345	50,948	280	0.286
Congo (Republic)	Brazzaville	342	3,018	3,066	0.533
Côte d'Ivoire	Yamoussoukro	322	16,013	1,387	0.400
Djibouti	Djibouti	22	632	2,335	0.429
Equatorial Guinea	Malabo	28	457	17,608	0.537
Eritrea	Asmara	94	3,659	536	0.349
Ethiopia	Addis Ababa	1,130	62,908	971	0.363
Gabon	Libreville	267	1,230	12,249	0.674
The Gambia	Banjul	11	1,303	1,282	0.353
Ghana	Accra	239	19,306	1,584	0.541
Guinea	Conakry	246	8,154	863	0.344
Guinea-Bissau	Bissau	36	1,199	994	0.353
Kenya	Nairobi	583	30,669	1,492	0.509
Lesotho	Maseru	30	2,035	1,664	0.450
Liberia	Monrovia	111	2,913	265	0.329
Madagascar	Antananarivo	587	15,970	824	0.480
Malawi	Lilongwe	118	11,308	753	0.400
Mali	Bamako	1,240	11,351	1,123	0.359

Table 1.1. (*continued*)

Country	Capital	Area (1,000 km²)	Population (1,000)	Per capita income ($PPP)[a]	Human development index, 2011
Mauritania	Nouakchott	1,031	2,665	1,859	0.453
Mozambique	Maputo	802	18,292	898	0.322
Namibia	Windhoek	824	1,757	6,206	0.625
Niger	Niamey	1,267	10,832	641	0.295
Nigeria	Abuja	924	113,862	2,069	0.459
Rwanda	Kigali	26	7,609	1,133	0.429
São Tomé e Príncipe	São Tomé	1	138	1,792	0.509
Senegal	Dakar	196	9,421	1,708	0.459
Sierra Leone	Freetown	72	4,405	737	0.336
Somalia	Mogadishu	638	8,778	—	—
South Africa	Pretoria	1,221	42,800	9,469	0.619
South Sudan	Juba	239	9,243	—	—
Sudan	Khartoum	728	34,557	1,894[b]	0.408
Swaziland	Mbabane	17	925	4,484	0.522
Tanzania	Dodoma	945	35,119	1,328	0.466
Togo	Lomé	57	4,527	798	0.435
Uganda	Kampala	236	23,300	1,124	0.446
Zambia	Lusaka	753	10,421	1,254	0.430
Zimbabwe	Harare	391	12,627	376	0.376

Note. Data sources: United Nations Development Programme (UNDP). *Human Development Report 2011*. New York: Oxford University Press, 2011. World Bank. *World Development Report 2011*. Washington, DC: World Bank, 2011.

[a] 2011 per capita income, adjusted to reflect purchasing power parity in 2005.

[b] Data for Sudan are for the country prior to the secession of South Sudan (July, 2011).

Africa's Evolving Political Map

One of the ongoing tasks for those involved in African studies is to "relearn" the map periodically. For example, the former Republic of Sudan was divided on July 9, 2011, resulting in the formation of the new country of South Sudan with its capital at Juba. South Sudan's achievement of independence was but the final step in a complex process of armed struggle, negotiation, and finally self-determination—a process that commenced in the 1950s with the formation of the first armed movements dedicated to the establishment of an independent South Sudanese state. A peace accord, signed by the South Sudan Liberation Army and the government of Sudan in 2005, provided the region with greater autonomy within a united Sudan and an opportunity to determine its future through a referendum on independence. This referendum took place in January 2011; 99% of eligible voters (in South Sudan, as well as South Sudanese living in the northern part of the country and abroad) voted in favor of independence. However, even as South Sudan has achieved its long-standing desire for independence, the new country's exact borders remain in limbo, as the oil-rich border region of Abyei continues to be in dispute.

Changes to place names or administrative structures also occur occasionally (see Table 1.2). In several cases, name changes at independence or after independence represent a decision to replace colonial names with ones more historically and culturally relevant.

Table 1.2 Some Important Postindependence Changes to the Map of Africa

Countries renamed at time of independence

New name	Former name
Botswana	Bechuanaland
Djibouti	French Somaliland
Ghana	Gold Coast
Lesotho	Basutoland
Malawi	Nyasaland
Zambia	Northern Rhodesia
Zimbabwe	Rhodesia

Countries renamed since independence

New name	Former name
Benin	Dahomey
Burkina Faso	Upper Volta
Zaíre (1971–1997)	Congo-Kinshasa
Democratic Republic of the Congo (1997–present)	Zaire
Tanzania	Tanganyika and Zanzibar

Name changes to capital cities

New name	Former name	Country
Banjul	Bathurst	The Gambia
Harare	Salisbury	Zimbabwe
Kinshasa	Léopoldville	Dem. Rep. Congo
N'Djamena	Fort Lamy	Chad
Maputo	Lorenço Marques	Mozambique

New capital city established

New capital	Old capital	Country
Abuja	Lagos	Nigeria
Dodoma	Dar es Salaam	Tanzania
Lilongwe	Zomba	Malawi
Yamoussoukro	Abidjan	Côte d'Ivoire

South Africa has changed hundreds of place names since the end of the apartheid era, replacing English and Afrikaans names with names derived from African languages. New metropolitan administrative regions have also been established, amalgamatin adjoining cities or joining suburban entities with some of the country's largest cities. For example, several cities in the East Rand area have been amalgamated to form Ekurhuleni; the newly created metropolitan are centered on Pretoria is called Tshwane; and the new urban region centered on Durban is known as eThekwini. There has been some confusion about these new names, which are not identical (either spatially or politically) to the cities located at their cores. Although these names are widely used colloquially by black South Africans in place of the "white/colonial" city names, at this writing they have not been officially approved. As such, the original, still-official names for these cities have been used throughout this book.

Several countries have also relocated their capital cities. In each case, the change has been justified as a means of bringing government closer to the people by abandoning colonial seats of government for smaller, more centrally located places.

Africa's Landlocked States

Sixteen African states are landlocked. Most of these states share a common legacy of colonial indifference and neglect. Countries such as Mali, Niger, and Chad served as labor reserve areas from which workers were recruited for the plantations and mines of more prosperous colonies. The (relative) exceptions to this pattern of colonial neglect are Uganda, once described by Winston Churchill as the "pearl of Africa," and Southern and Northern Rhodesia (now Zimbabwe and Zambia, respectively), which were prosperous centers of mining and commercial agriculture. Ethiopia joined the ranks of Africa's landlocked states in 1993 after its coastal province of Eritrea, annexed in 1954, succeeded in gaining its independence after three decades of armed struggle.

With the notable exception of Botswana, Africa's landlocked states continue to be very poor and undeveloped. Six of them have adjusted per capita incomes (adjusted for purchasing power parity [PPP], to reflect the relative cost of living; see below, p. 25) of less than $1,000. They also tend to have small populations; only Ethiopia and Uganda have more than 20 million people. However, their greatest source of vulnerability results from a perpetual dependence on neighboring states for an outlet to the sea. This problem is exacerbated by the frequent absence of reasonable transportation linkages. Six of the landlocked states have no railroads, and even where linkages exist, political tensions between neighbors or within neighboring states may preclude the use of these railroads.

The situation of South Sudan provides an extreme example of the vulnerability of landlocked states. South Sudan has considerable reserves of petroleum that will be critical to its future development as a modern nation. However, the established routes for the export of its petroleum run through Sudan to Port Sudan, located on the Red Sea. After struggling for several decades to gain independence from Sudan, the South Sudanese are deeply distrustful of the intentions of the Sudanese state. One year after South Sudan became independent, there was still no agreement on terms for the shipment of South Sudanese goods through Sudan. In the absence of such an agreement, Sudan has confiscated a portion of the oil passing through its territory as a transportation levy, and has moved to stop the shipment of oil from South Sudan.

South Sudan hopes to reduce its vulnerability by developing a new export route that would link it to the Kenyan coast. However, this route would take years to develop, and some economists have said that it would not be economically viable. As long as it has only one viable export route—particularly one that lies through its hostile neighbor, Sudan—South Sudan will remain highly vulnerable and unable to consolidate its independence.

LEVELS OF DEVELOPMENT

Maps are powerful tools for displaying and analyzing spatial distributions, such as variations in wealth and the quality of life. Although Africa south of the Sahara is very poor as a whole, extreme variations of wealth and development exist across the continent. There are significant differences between the most and least developed countries in income, economic diversity, and quality of life. There are also large differences within each country—between urban and rural areas, and between the rich and the poor.

There is no universally accepted measure of development, in part because development is multidimensional and in part because there are disagreements about what development entails. The most widely used measure is per capita gross national income (GNI). Many analysts now prefer to use per capita incomes that have been adjusted to reflect differences in the cost of living in different countries in place of nominal (unadjusted) per capita incomes. Unless otherwise stated, the income data cited in this book will be given in the form of per capita GNI (PPP), in U.S. dollars. Keep in mind that although variations in per capita GNI are certainly important, aggregate national income data do not show how wealth is distributed in a society, or whether available wealth has been used to improve productivity or the quality of life.

Africa is not uniformly poor. Indeed, per capita GNIs (PPPs) vary considerably (see Table 1.1). The $13,049 nominal per capita GNI (PPP) of Botswana is 47 times that of the Democratic Republic of the Congo, which at $280 has the continent's second lowest per capita GNI (PPP). However, the majority of countries have very low incomes: All 15 countries in the world with a per capita GNI (PPP) of less than $1,000 are located in Africa south of the Sahara. Only 3 of the 34 countries worldwide with per capita incomes below $2,000 are not located in Africa.

Another widely used measure is the human development index (HDI) (see Table 1.1 and Figure 1.8). In the *Human Development Report*, published under the auspices of the United Nations Development Programme (UNDP), the HDI is described as an index of the range and quality of options available to people to shape their own destinies. The index is calculated annually by using measures of life expectancy, education, and per capita income; these variables are combined according to a methodology described in the report. The HDI scores for 2011 emphasize the continuing underdevelopment of Africa, compared even to the most disadvantaged countries in other parts of the world. There are 15 African countries with lower scores than Afghanistan, which has the lowest HDI rating outside Africa. Of 30 countries that were given the lowest HDI ratings in 2011, 28 were located in Africa south of the Sahara. The lowest HDI, 0.286, was assigned to the Democratic Republic of the Congo.

The HDI is a serious attempt to move beyond the limitations of per capita GNI. However, with another mix of variables or with a different weighting of variables, somewhat different results would emerge. Thus care should be exercised in drawing conclusions based on the proportional size of HDI scores for different countries or on the ranking of countries when their HDI scores are fairly similar. Nevertheless, this index is useful for focusing attention on broad differences in levels of national development and for identifying countries whose people are the most disadvantaged.

Measures such as GNI and HDI have another major weakness—namely, that they provide only national aggregate measures of development. National scores may be quite misleading for African countries where there are very large differences in income and human welfare among regions or social groups within a country. We need to keep in mind several weaknesses in national statistics. For example, economic data generally ignore or underestimate the value of women's work and of subsistence production. Some statistical measures of development also reflect Western cultural and economic biases.

The use of national aggregate measures also helps to perpetuate a vision of development as occurring naturally within the bounded territories of nation-states. When development is conceived at a national scale, the rich diversity of resources and of development responses at the local level does not receive appropriate attention. Nor are the many ways in which development is facilitated through connections that link diverse places—urban and rural, North and South—given due consideration. Robinson's *Development and Displacement* (see "Further Reading") expands upon these important ideas. These and other issues related to the meaning of development and its implementation as policy are discussed further in Chapter 3.

REGIONAL AND POLITICAL GROUPINGS

One approach to the definition of groupings of countries is membership in regional economic and political organizations based on shared culture and history. The most important political organization linking African states is the African Union, founded in 2002 as the successor to the Organization of African Unity (OAU). All African states, with the exception of Western Sahara, are members. Among the continent's 11 regional political—economic organizations, two stand out: the Economic Community of West African States (ECOWAS), which links 15 countries in West Africa; and the Southern African Development Community (SADC), composed of 12 states in southern Africa plus Mauritius and Seychelles. The SADC came together initially with the objective of reducing the member states' dependence on South Africa. Following the abolition of apartheid, South Africa joined and became "first among equals" in SADC.

In addition to groups defined by membership in an organization, regional groupings are often defined on the basis of geographical proximity and perceived similarity. Figure 1.9 shows some of the commonly used informal regional groupings of countries in Africa south of the Sahara. Note that there is no single defining characteristic, and also that there is less than complete agreement on which countries should be included in each group.

The term *West Africa* commonly refers to countries west of the Cameroon—Nigeria border, an important physical and cultural dividing line in the continent. *The Sahel* countries form a significant subregion within West Africa characterized by desert-margin environments and (especially in recent years) recurring drought. *East Africa* consists of Kenya, Tanzania, Uganda, Rwanda, and Burundi, the members of the East African Community. The new nation of South Sudan is also included because of its long-standing ties—demographic, social, and political—to Uganda and Kenya. Since the end of apartheid, *southern Africa* has become a meaningful grouping for the first time. Previously, there had been a group referred to as the *Frontline States*, defined by their proximity to South Africa and opposition to apartheid. Other informal regional groupings include the four countries of the *Horn of Africa* (Ethiopia, Eritrea, Somalia, and Djibouti) and the states of *west central Africa* (anchored by Cameroon to the north and the Democratic Republic of the Congo to the south).

THE PHYSICAL MAP

At first glance, the physical map of Africa looks rather uninteresting. The coastline of the continent is often straight and uncomplicated, with only a few identifiable seas, gulfs, and other adjoining bodies of water. Topographically, the vast, gently undulating plateaus create an impression of uniformity, especially when there are no great mountain ranges such as the Himalayas to catch one's eye.

A closer inspection, however, reveals considerable variety in Africa's topography. For example, there are escarpments up 2,000 m in elevation fringing the southeast African coast; the escarpment known as the Drakensberg Mountains in South Africa is especially spectacular. Then there is the world's largest rift valley system, extending from southern Mozambique through eastern Africa to the Red Sea and beyond. And \??\ this list can be added the magnificent volcano peaks, notably Mounts Kenya, Kilima\??\ jaro, Elgon, Meru, and Cameroon, which arise between 4,000 m and almost 6,000 \??\ above sea level.

Another significant feature is the half dozen major river systems that together drain some four-fifths of Africa south of the Sahara (Figure 1.10). Four rivers stand out the Nile, the Congo, the Niger, and the Zambezi. Others of regional note are the Orange, the Limpopo, the Kasai, the Ubangi, the Benue, the Volta, and the Senegal.

Because the coastline is regular and has very few substantial indentations, Africa has few good natural harbors. Historically the scarcity of harbors, along with the presence of escarpments and major rapids near the mouths of many rivers, impeded early European attempts to explore and exploit the continent.

Becoming familiar with the locations of prominent physical features as well as other elements of the African map is not a particularly important end in itself. However, familiarity does provide a basis for interpreting specific issues and situations, each of which occurs in a particular context that is spatial, environmental, social, political, and economic. Thus the maps in this chapter serve to establish the spatial context for our study of the geography of Africa south of the Sahara.

FURTHER READING

Thematic and regional atlases address diverse aspects of the geography of Africa. The first Griffiths volume is a useful general source, while the others listed below are more specialized in nature.

Griffiths, I. L. L. *An Atlas of African Affairs*, 2nd ed. London: Routledge, 1994.

There are several excellent historical atlases of Africa:

Ajayi, J. F. A., and M. Crowder. *Historical Atlas of Africa*. London: Longman, 1985.

Fage, J. D. *An Atlas of African History*. New York: Africana, 1980.

Freeman-Grenville, G. S. P. *New Atlas of African History*. Englewood Cliffs, NJ: Prentice-Hall, 1991.

Griffiths, I. L. L. *Africa on Maps Dating from the Twelfth to the Eighteenth Century*. Leipzig, Germany: Editions Leipzig, 1968.

McEvedy, C. *Penguin Atlas of African History*. New York: Penguin USA, 1996.

For a fascinating study of fact and fiction in early maps of Africa, see the following source:

Bassett, T. J., and P. W. Porter. "From the best authorities: The Mountains of Kong in the cartography of West Africa." *Journal of African History*, vol. 32 (1991), pp. 367–414.

Here are two useful series of atlases, each volume of which pertains to a particular country:

Barbour, K. M., J. O. C. Oguntoyinbo, J. O. C. Onyemelukwe, and J. C. Nwafor. *Nigeria in Maps*. New York: Africana, 1982. (Other volumes in the series deal with Sierra Leone [1972], Malawi [1972], Tanzania [1971], Zambia [1971], and Liberia [1972].)

Les Atlas Jeune Afrique: République Centraficaine. Paris: Editions Jeune Afrique, 1984. (The Jeune Afrique atlas series also includes volumes on Africa [1973], Congo [1977], Niger [1980], and Senegal [1980].)

The following are examples of thematic atlases on Africa:

Bossard, L., ed. *Regional Atlas on West Africa*. Paris: Organisation for Economic Co-operation and Development (OECD), 2009.

Christopher, A. J. *The Atlas of Changing South Africa*, 2nd ed. New York: Routledge, 2001.

Food and Agriculture Organization of the United Nations (FAO). *Atlas of African Agriculture*. Rome: FAO, 1986.

Murray, J. *Cultural Atlas of Africa*, 2nd rev. ed. London: Fitzhenry & Whiteside, 2002.

Norwich, I. *Norwich's Maps of Africa: An Illustrated and Annotated Carto-Bibliography*, 2nd ed. Norwich, VT: Terra Nova Press, 1997.

For ideas on African underdevelopment in global perspective, see the following sources:

Robinson, J. *Development and Displacement*. Oxford: Oxford University Press, 2002.

Smith, D. *The State of the World Atlas*, 6th ed. London: Penguin, 1999.

INTERNET SOURCES

The following sites provide access to national maps for African countries:

The Map Library. www.maplibrary.org/stacks/africa/index.php

Northwestern University. *Africa Base Map*. www.library.northwestern.edu/africana/map/

Several university libraries have websites devoted to their Africa collections:

University of Texas Libraries. *Perry-Castañeda Library Map Collection: Africa Maps*. www.lib.utexas.edu/maps/africa.html

Stanford University Library offers a comprehensive listing of sites related to African maps: Stanford University Library *Africa South of the Sahara: Maps*. http://library.stanford.edu/depts/ssrg/africa/map.html

CHAPTER 2

The Rise and Fall of States and Empires in Precolonial Africa

Lady Jane Acquah

INTRODUCTION

States, kingdoms, and empires in Africa date back to antiquity. As Molefi Asante, a historian, has noted, "No continent has ever had as many viable kingdoms and empires for as long a time as the continent of Africa."[1] This chapter is not so much concerned with the specific civilizations, kingdoms, and states that developed in Africa as with the elements that made it possible for them to rise and fall at different times. Among the factors that contributed to the emergence of precolonial states, empires, and kingdoms in Africa are agriculture, religion, trade, leadership, environment, technology, and invader groups. The following factors, among others, account for their collapse: environmental degradation, warfare, political disputes, economic decline, slave trade, and foreign interventions. Using a geographical and regional approach (North Africa, East Africa, Central Africa, South Africa, and West Africa), we shall consider the circumstances that influenced state formation and their collapse in Africa.

THE RISE AND FALL OF STATES AND EMPIRES IN NORTH AFRICA

The Nile River, the longest river in the world, is responsible for the rise of states and empires in North Africa. The Nile consists of two main rivers: the White Nile, which flows from the highlands of Uganda, and the Blue Nile, which flows from the Ethiopian highlands. Together, they merge with the Atbara River in Sudan to join the Indian Ocean on the East African coast. From June to September, high rainfall in the Ethiopian highlands causes the Blue Nile to flood its banks, carrying with it rich silts that it deposits at the banks of the river. This natural phenomenon provides 18, 250 kilometers of arable land along the banks of the Nile from Aswan to the Delta.[2]

The Nile attracted people fleeing from the desiccation of the Sahara to settle along its banks. This led to important developments in food production and trade, giving rise to a population explosion and consequently the rise of states and empires such as ancient Egypt, Nubian kingdoms of Kush, Meroe, and Napata (all in modern Sudan) in North Africa. The navigable nature of the river enabled shipbuilding, which facilitated trade. The Nile valley abounded in limestone, sandstone, and granite, which were utilized in the stone architecture, monuments, and pyramids of ancient Egypt. The importance of the Nile in the thriving of North African states cannot be overemphasized.

Agriculture contributed to the emergence of states and empires in North Africa.[3] The annual Nile flood fertilized the cultivable land, thus making available land for farming and rich pasture for animals. Agriculture was the basis of the Egyptian civilization. The Egyptians planted cereals like millet, sorghum, and barley; and reared sheep, goats, and cattle. The Egyptians invented complex irrigation systems such as the shaduf, "a pole

Map showing North African precolonial states. Courtesy of University of Texas at Austin Library, http://www.lib.utexas.edu/maps/historical/shepherd_1911/shepherd-c-004.jpg

on a fulcrum with counter-weight on one end and a water-bucket on the other, to raise water into the fields" and the sagia (an ox-drawn watershed) to produce food throughout the year.[4] The introduction of iron implements from Meroe (Northern Sudan) helped to revolutionize agriculture in Egypt. A food supply of different diets was guaranteed, leading to a population explosion. The availability of food had the effect of granting spare time to build permanent settlements, develop skills such as writing, metalworking (bronze, copper, and gold), fine arts, religious practices, and science (mathematics and astrology). It also encouraged the emergence of an aristocratic class that controlled surpluses and trade, and who became those upon whom people depended for favors. Egyptian society became stratified. Food sufficiency guaranteed labor for military service and building projects such as the pyramids, canals, and roads. Accordingly, villages expanded into towns and states, which in turn expanded into kingdoms and empires.

Trade was a very important factor in the development of states and empires in North Africa. North African states engaged in regional and international trade with the Mediterranean World, the Near East and Asia. The initial trading activities started with the exchange of surplus food and other products for goods that people lacked. Over time, this trade expanded to other areas, utilizing the Nile and land routes into the African hinterland. Rulers who could control trade routes and the flow of goods grew powerful and influential. They imposed taxes and tributes on merchants, thus accruing wealth to expand their states. The kingdoms of Kush, founded by the Nubians in the eleventh century, emerged because of the ability of their rulers to control the trade that passed through their territory to the Red Sea and Indian Ocean seaports. Kush grew so powerful that it was able to conquer and rule Egypt in 730 BCE and created the 25th (or Ethiopian) dynasty, which lasted for sixty years.[5] Ancient Egypt had the advantage of controlling the gold mines in the eastern desert, the ebony and ivory trade in Nubia, and the copper mines in the Sinai region, in addition to trading with Punt (Somalia) and Arabia for spices, incense, and perfumes. Morocco traded with the Sudanese empires and East African states using the city of Sijilmasa as its main entrepot for gold and salt from Taghaza.[6] Trade brought tax revenue, new technology, and access to luxury goods. This made rulers of states wealthy, and with wealth came the expansion of states into empires.

Effective and dynamic leadership is a necessity for a viable state. The abundance of food and the development of trade required leaders to control surpluses and ensure the safety of trade routes, goods, and merchants, in addition to keeping the various classes of society in order. In ancient Egypt, Narmer (Menes) unified the forty-two city-states of Upper and Lower Egypt into one formidable kingdom in 3100 BCE by creating the position of the Pharaoh through the invocation of religion. To prevent the authority of the Pharaoh from being usurped by other enthusiasts, Narmer established a royal family and succession by primogeniture (a system whereby the eldest child, especially the male child, inherits the throne from his father). In the Kushite kingdom, Kashta and Piankhy are the two able kings attributed with the successful conquest of Egypt, thus enabling Kush to be independent and even rule over Egypt, for a time.[7] In general, leaders gained the trust of their followers and were able to lead their armies to war, broker peace, and to expand their territory.

Religion was another component that greatly influenced the rise and sustainability of precolonial states in North Africa. African indigenous religion and Islam influenced the rise of leaders and, subsequently, the rise of states and empires. In African indigenous religion, the leader occupied the crucial position as the nexus between the people, the gods, and their ancestors in addition to having the power to interpret natural occurrences such as death, disease, famine, harvest, and rainfall. Due to this religious quality, his or her political authority is hardly challenged. For instance, the ancient Egyptians worshipped a pantheon of gods. Narmer introduced an innovation in the belief system of Lower and Upper Egypt by marrying these gods and producing a monotheist religion. Of the multiplicity of gods, the outstanding one was Osiris—son of the god Re or Amon Re—who was murdered by his brother Seth. The inability of Osiris's wife, Isis, to resurrect her husband left him as god of the underworld.[8] Narmer legitimized his rule by claiming family ties to these gods, thereby invoking divine approval for his leadership.

Islam also helped tremendously in the founding and prospering of states and empires. Through religious persecutions, missionary work, and trade, Islam crossed the Arabian Peninsula to the African continent beginning in the seventh century. Islamic traditions and schools flourished due to this contact, constituting the driving force behind the revivals that occurred thereafter. In North Africa, some of the Sanhaja Berbers converted to Islam. In the eleventh century, Abdullah ibn Yasin, a Muslim theologian, founded the al-Murabitun Movement (the name of which was corrupted by the Spanish to Almoravid). Ibn Yasin's movement attracted many followers who shared his ardor to spread Islam. With the alliance of the Lamtuna Berbers who wanted political dominance and economic control in the Sudan, he waged several jihads resulting in the creation of the Moroccan empire.[9] Ibn Yasin's jihad spread Islam as far as the Sudan, and with it, trade. In the twelfth century, Abu Abdullah Muhammad ibn Tumart founded the al-Muwahhidun (Almohad) movement to reform Islam. The Almohad conquered the Moroccan capital of Marrakesh and established their empire. Religion held the state together and facilitated trade through which ideas were disseminated. Arabic became the principal language of trade in addition to religion. Merchants from the Middle East and Far East felt confident and safe as they shared the same religion with the North African traders.

Immigration to North Africa also engendered the rise of states. By the beginning of the ninth century, Islam and trade had brought merchants, artisans, and religious scholars from Asia, Arabia, and Europe to settle in North Africa. In addition, political and religious persecutions carried out by Spain in the fifteenth century forced several groups, mostly scholars and farmers, to emigrate into Tunisia and Morocco. These groups of people joined and mixed with the Moroccan empire. Desertification of the Sahara also forced settlers from the Sudan and Chad into the area of "Aswan to the Batn al-hajar (Belly of Stones)."[10] These migrants intermarried with the indigenous people to create the foundations of the Nubian kingdom (Sudan). The importance of these migrant groups in the founding of states and empires was that they served as vehicles through which ideas of iron technology, literature, religion, and luxury goods flowed into North Africa.

The states and empires in North Africa, however, declined over time. One of the major causes of the decline of states, empires, and kingdoms in North Africa was political instability. This was caused by overexpansion, succession disputes, invasion, political rivalry, and corruption. Ancient Egypt suffered succession disputes when the position of the Pharaohs weakened, making it possible for outside forces to invade.[11] Vassal states such as Kush were able to wrest their independence from and even conquer their former master.[12] The Moroccan empire of the Almoravids expanded beyond their means to govern. Their wars of expansion into Europe (Spain) in the twelfth century cost many lives and strained the resources of the state.[13] Additionally, since the foundation of the empire was based on religious revivalism, the theologians and Imams in charge of administration were unable to keep the diverse fabric of the empire intact.[14] This paved the way for local chiefs to grow powerful and oppress their subjects by overtaxing them. The imposition of "non-Quranic taxes" on Andalusia created discontent among the Muslim populace.[15] The Almohad Empire began to weaken when succession disputes between the two brothers, Umar and Abu Ya'qub Yusuf occurred in 1143.[16] From the seventeenth century onward, political rivalry between local lords and religious elites for power escalated into incessant wars, thus weakening the states.[17]

Invasions and wars also led to the demise of North African states and empires. Ancient Egypt became an easy target when the government and internal security weakened. Egypt underwent a series of conquests that shrunk its power base: Kush in 715 BCE, Assyria in 691 BCE, Persia in 526 BCE, Greece in 333 BCE, Rome from 168 BCE to 31 BCE, Arabs in 639 CE, Philistine in 1227 BCE, and the Mamluk Turks in 1250 BCE. Invasion from a revived Egypt in 1502 ended the Nubian state. Kush collapsed in the fourth century CE from attacks by nomadic groups from Axum.[18] These wars and invasions disrupted society, weakened governments, destroyed trade, and cost lives.

Another important element that conditioned the collapse of states and empires was environmental degradation. In order to sustain the economic activity of metal production in the Nubian kingdom of Meroe, for instance, hardwood trees were cut to use as fuel to smelt iron, copper, and bronze.[19] The constant felling of trees over the years without replacing them led to deforestation and subsequently a change in the rainfall pattern. Droughts caused by environmental and climatic change adversely affected the economy of North Africa. The Nile, the lifeline of Egypt especially, and North Africa generally, reduced in size. This affected agriculture and the livelihood of the people, hence the weakening of states.

The decline of economic activities also spelled the doom of North African states. The Almohad empire depended on trade with Europe and the Sahara; when peace in the Sahara was disturbed through warfare, trade was disrupted. The new sea route, which diverted trade from Asia to Europe through the Atlantic Ocean, reduced the volume of trade in North Africa. This reduced the revenues that flowed into the coffers of North African states and empires, contributing to their demise.

The advent of colonialism from the nineteenth century ended the age of North African empires. European imperialists struggled with African states for political and economic control. With the use of advanced weapons, African collaborators, and treachery, European powers, especially France and Britain, succeeded in dividing North African states among themselves.

THE RISE AND FALL OF EAST AND CENTRAL AFRICAN STATES AND EMPIRES

Agriculture laid the foundation for many states, kingdoms, and empires in East and Central Africa. In the first century BCE, plantain and banana were introduced from Southeast Asia through trade with Indonesia, Malaysia, and India to Bantu settlers in east Africa, who in turn spread these as they migrated inland.[20] In the seventeenth century, the Portuguese also brought new crops such as maize and cassava to central Africa. These crops adapted to the soil and did not need intensive labor to cultivate them. The Bantu introduced iron tools to the region and helped to transform agricultural practices. Aksum grew coffee, finger millet (Eleusine coracana), ensete (Ensete edulis), noog oil plant, wheat, barley, sorghum, and teff (Eragrostis tef), which became a staple crop of east Africa. Coastal peoples fished for shellfish to be used as beads, food, perfume, and shells; sharks, and barracudas.[21] The success of farming and fishing practices led to abundance of food and the development of trade. Between 1100 and 1350, pastoralism increased, especially after the introduction of the Zebu cattle (Bos indicus), a drought-resistant species from India.[22]

Crop production and the domestication of animals such as cattle, sheep, and goats guaranteed an abundance of food which led to population explosion. This resulted in increased competition for land for agriculture and pasture for grazing. The Ila and Tonga in Zambia, for instance, increasingly sought new land to farm.[23] The availability of food also spared people in the villages time to specialize in crafts, arts, and military services. Cattle created wealth, political hegemony, and enabled leaders to control trade routes for iron tools, salt, dried fish, and bark cloth. Areas like Sofala, the Rufiji Delta, Pemba Island, Mombasa, Malindi, Tana Delta, Lamu Archipelago, and Juba in East Africa all started as agricultural communities producing crops, rearing animals, and fishing. As merchant ships sailed to these coastal towns to acquire food supplies, fresh water, and to sell their merchandise, these otherwise small farming communities expanded into states and grew wealthy. By the sixteenth and seventeenth centuries, abundance of food had allowed kingdoms like Bunyoro (Uganda), Buganda (Uganda), Rwanda, Burundi, Kongo, Luba, and Lunda (Congo) to grow.

The influx of foreigners into east and central Africa enabled also the development of states and empires. Through a change in demography and the infusion of new ideas about kingship, governance, technology in agriculture (irrigation and terracing), architecture, mineral extraction, weaponry, warfare, and the art of writing, existing indigenous states and practices gave way to formidable states and empires such as the Luba, Lunda, and Kongo. The Luo-Bito invaders from east Africa conquered the Chwezi rulers of the Kitara states and established their rule. The Luo legitimized their rule by adopting some of the Chwezi royal paraphernalia such as royal drums, and copper objects such as official spears and the cone-shaped beaded crown.[24] Migrants from Saba in Arabia in the northeast coast of Africa, between the eighth and third centuries BCE mingled with the indigenes to found Aksum.[25] The Luba invaded the petty villages in the Congo grassland and unified them to found the states of Katanga and Kongo in modern Congo. The Lunda invaders founded the Akimbo kingdom around 1700. Bantu migrants flowed into east, central, and southern Africa, spreading root crops like banana and iron and changing the face of agriculture in these areas. These groups intermingled to found states and empires.[26]

Interregional and international trade via the Indian Ocean, Red Sea, and Atlantic Ocean played a key role in the rise of states and empires in east and central Africa. From October to April, "lanteen-rigged" dhows and merchant ships used the northeast monsoon winds to sail from the Red Sea, Asia, and the Persian Gulf to the Swahili coast and returned upon the April–October southwest monsoon winds with African goods. Imported goods to the Swahili coast included glass beads, Chinese porcelain, Cambodian jars, and spindle whorls. The East African coastal states traded with India, Yemen, China, Persia, and the rest of Africa, exporting slaves, gold, ivory, ebony, ambergris, sandalwood, and tortoise shells.

East African coastal towns and agricultural villages such as Sofala, Kilwa, Ungwana, Manda, Lamu, Mombasa, Mafia, Kisiwani, and Zanzibar, which had navigable rivers and shorelines with natural harbors, became distribution centers that consequently helped in their expansion into independent states with centralized government. This necessitated strong, permanent, and spacious buildings for accommodation and storage of goods. As the East African coastal towns grew bigger, they attracted people from the African interior, Arabia, and Asia. Gradually, cultures and people mixed to create the Swahili culture. Kilwa was the most prosperous of the Swahili states because it had its own coin mintage. It had customs officials who regulated trade by imposing import and export taxes on all goods that entered or left its territory. For instance, a tax of one elephant tusk was levied on every seven tusks bought. The funds generated went into the maintenance of the royal court and the state military.

Trade in the forest was carried on paths and rivers such as Congo, Kesai, Kavango, Senkuru, Zambezi, and lakes Malawi, Kisale, Bangweului, Mweni, making it easy for goods, people, and ideas to be exchanged between central Africa and other parts of the continent. Control of the trade routes meant the right to tax, exact tribute, and control the price of goods such as guns, ammunition, and cotton cloths imported through the Indian Ocean trade. King Mutesa of Kongo controlled Lake Victoria with his navies composed of canoes and raided the neighbors for ivory and cattle. The Bemba sold salt, ivory, slaves, and fish to Swahili Arabs, thereby growing powerful enough to unify numerous villages in the eighteenth century.[27] Through the regulation of trade and wars of conquest, the Bemba expanded their territory. The Kongo expanded when central Africa was drawn into the Atlantic trade in the fifteenth century. Using ports such as Duala and Benguela, they sold slaves, copper, and ivory to the Portuguese. Iron and copper products such as farm tools, weapons, and jewelry from Malawi, Sanga, and Kongo were exchanged for slaves and ivory. Iron encouraged the establishment of permanent military organizations, enabling states to conquer weaker neighbors and expand their frontiers. Trade led to the introduction of new ideas, tastes, and diets that transformed the lifestyle of the people. Towns expanded into large trading centers while clientele states developed to provide trade goods such as ivory, gold, slaves, and agricultural produce in exchange for protection. Thus, a complex relationship of interdependence led to the rise of centralized states and empires such as Kongo, Luba, and Loango, all in present-day Congo.

Religion (Christianity, Islam, and African indigenous religion) influenced states to expand into empires and kingdoms. Christianity was believed to have been introduced by two shipwrecks, *Frumentius* and *Aedesius*, to the Aksumite empire of Ethiopia in the fourth century.[28] The conversion of the Aksumite king, Exana, to Christianity, made it a state religion, thus marrying Ethiopia to the civilizations of the Christian world. Literature in the Geez language and trade in foreign goods propelled Ethiopia into the limelight and supported the development of an indigenous version of Christianity, the Coptic Church. Islam entered the African continent through East Africa in the seventh century and rapidly spread. Through trade, Arab merchants settled in East Africa. Mixing with the indigenes and different cultures, the Swahili culture emerged. In central Africa, the development of African religious cults gained such prominence that they sanctioned political power. The Luba invented divine kingship headed by the *balopwe*, who was revered as the living representative of their dead ancestors and the custodian of their shrines.[29] The divine status of Luba kings warranted their veneration after their death in shrines set up in their respective villages. The Lunda learned this practice from the Luba. The Mbundu farmers who founded Ndongo (in Angola) developed a rain and fertility cult, which gradually transformed into the religious and political authority.[30] Headed by the custodian of the Lunga (spiritual objects) shrine, the priests' power over rain gave them the right to tax the community. The effect of religion and the political leaders it produced closed all avenues for the leadership to be challenged. This ensured the security and stability of the states, hence their growth.

Leadership was one other deciding factor that enabled states and empires to rise in Africa. Kalal Ilunga, a Luba, founded the Sanga state and instituted succession by primogeniture.[31] Another Luba, Cibunda Ilunga, also founded Lunda by marrying the Lunda queen, Rweeji.[32] He established a "perpetual" kingship, whereby the new king adopts the entire family of the deceased ruler thus severing all familial relations with his family. This guaranteed unity and loyalty to the state. The availability of strong leadership empowered the military, promoted trade, and expanded territories. These factors worked interdependently to forge villages and hamlets into states.

East and Central African states and empires also gradually declined. Political instability caused by wars, internal disturbances, and Portuguese interferences in the politics of the states and empires paved the way for the demise of some east and central African states. Axum degenerated after 700 CE due to religious upheavals between the Muslims in the eastern and northern parts of the kingdom, and the Christians in the south and west. Internecine warfare, succession disputes, and conflicts over trade caused political unrest among the Swahili states. Sofala and Kilwa clashed over gold and ivory from Great Zimbabwe, Pate and Lamu competed over the control of the trade in the Tana Delta, and Malindi and Mombasa struggled for the control of trade with Mijikenda in the hinterlands and agricultural products from Pemba.[33] Some states and empires expanded beyond their ability to govern. The successors of Kalonga Mzura of Malawi did not have the military power to control the vast empire; consequently, by 1763, the empire began to degenerate, creating conditions for tributary states to throw off the yoke of vassalage.[34]

Foreign intervention from European countries like Portugal contributed in no small way to the collapse of East and Central African states and empires. Portuguese activities undermined the authority of African rulers. This prompted two reactions from the African states: either they entered into alliance with the invaders against their local enemies as Malindi did against Mombasa, or they accepted a tributary status with respect to Portugal. Kilwa and Zanzibar paid tribute in 1502 and 1503, respectively, but when they defaulted, the Portuguese attacked Mombasa and Kilwa in 1505, Brava in 1506, and Mombasa again in 1529.[35] The apogee of this unrest was the city-states' invitation of the Omani Arabs to come to their aid against the Portuguese. Through solidarity of Islam, the Omani Arabs responded to the call by ousting the Portuguese from the coast in 1729 and replacing European dominance with their own. This war cost human lives, destruction of property, and the disruption of trading activities. The Portuguese invaded the Kongo kingdom in 1665 and paved the way for its decline by installing their own puppet monarchs. Portugal interfered in the politics of Bunyoro, and the British succeeded in exiling Kabarega to the Seychelles Island in 1899.

The decline in trade crippled the east African city-states and empires in the interior. The Portuguese interference in commercial activities weakened the states by cutting off their sources of wealth. Beginning in the fifteenth century, the Portuguese disrupted trade in the Indian Ocean by issuing passports to all merchant ships for the purpose of keeping records and taxing them.[36] Some merchants refused to acquire the passports, because it meant paying taxes to the Portuguese, thereby reducing their profits. The Portuguese patrolled the Indian Ocean and Red Sea with their warships and attacked merchant ships that did not possess the passports. Consequently, the number of merchant ships that sailed to the east African coast declined. The prestige of the states dwindled.

The introduction of the trans-Atlantic slave trade contributed to the fall of states and empires in east and central Africa. The lucrative trade in human beings gradually replaced the trade in goods such as gold, ivory, cotton cloth, aromatics, and spices. As early as the 1700s, the central African states and empires felt the impact of this trade. In addition to warfare, the slave trade was responsible for reducing human populations and other trading activities. Insecurity and mass flight from towns adversely affected socio-economic and political developments. The introduction of guns and ammunition through the Indian and Atlantic Ocean trade to African states had a two-edge repercussion on Africans. While it assisted the expansion of towns and villages into states and empires, it also contributed to their collapse. The new weapons made warfare more gruesome, intensified slave raiding and increased the volume of the trade in humans. It is estimated that East Africa imported about one million guns, four million pounds of gunpowder, and millions of rounds of ammunition between 1885 and 1902.[37] The lack of peace and unity was an advantage to the Europeans when they began the colonization of Africa.

Climatic changes also contributed to the fall of east African states and empires. In the sixteenth century, East Africa suffered a devastating drought that dried up most of its rivers, desiccated those that remained, and fostered land erosion.[38] The rains, which normally fell from April–May to September, afforded East Africans the luxury of planting and harvesting crops twice a year. Moreover, the farming techniques of terracing and irrigating the Ethiopian mountains depended on this rainfall pattern. Thus, the change devastated agriculture; plants and animals equally suffered. Only teff could be grown annually. The failure of crops, the death of livestock, and the scarcity of water and food culminated in famine and disease that ravaged the towns and states of its people. The severity of this environmental disaster caused several villagers to abandon their homes and relocate close to rivers. One consequence of this was interstate and ethnic wars between the Swahili, Mijikenda, Somali and Oromo pastoralist groups over farmlands, pasture, and water resources.[39]

THE RISE AND FALL OF STATES AND EMPIRES IN SOUTHERN AFRICA

Agriculture supported the development of states and empires in southern Africa. The San and Khoikhoi hunter-gatherers transformed into a nomadic group by acquiring cattle and sheep from their neighbors. From their livestock, the pastoralists had meat, milk, butter, and hides, which they exchanged with their agricultural neighbors for iron products, pottery, crops, wild game, fruits, berries, and honey. The animals became the basis of their wealth in a system where they could be "exchanged, invested and inherited," and used to contract marriage alliances.[40] By 1000 CE, Bantu agro-pastoralists from the Great Lakes region migrated and settled in the savanna grassland south of the Limpopo. These were the Nguni, Shona, and Sotho-Tswana groups. They grew sorghum, millet, cowpeas, and beans and kept goats, sheep, cattle; fished, and hunted for meat. More importantly, they possessed iron, which helped in food production as well as warfare. Food sufficiency led to population explosion, forcing humans and livestock, especially, cattle, to compete for space, farmland, water resources, and pasture. This sparked off a series of southward and westward expansions bringing them into contact with the San and Khoikhoi. The expansion forced stronger communities to annex weaker ones into states. The availability of food helped the Mwana Mutapa, Mapungubwe, Great Zimbabwe, and Zulu empires to grow.

Trade played a crucial role in the rise of precolonial southern African states and empires. By 1000 CE, the Nguni, Shona, and Sotho-Tswana village clusters were trading with Central, West, and East African states in foodstuffs, ivory, iron, copper, gold, and salt. Mapungubwe traded in iron products and gold in the Indian Ocean trade and procured glass beads, porcelain, and cloth. This brought wealth and prestige to the kings and facilitated the kingdom's rise to prominence. The rise of Great Zimbabwe was facilitated by its strategic position close to the Sabi River and its trade links with the Swahili traders at the east African coast. This allowed the ruler to control trade goods and routes and to impose taxes that swelled up the state's coffers and subsequently expanded into a viable political entity. The Mwana Mutapa kingdom (1450–1760) also thrived on revenues from the gold and ivory trade with the East African coastal states. Changa, the king of Guniuswa, traded with the Swahili coastal towns, exporting ivory and gold and importing Indian cotton goods, Persian and Chinese porcelain and pottery. A clientele relationship developed between the actual producers of the gold and ivory and the middlemen who forwarded them to the ports. Through a series of cordial relationships, vassal and tributary relations, and wars of conquests, towns grew wealthy and expanded into empires.

Wars of conquests helped states to emerge. Leaders embarked on wars of expansion to gain control of trade routes, trade goods, rivers, mineral resources, and land. In the fifteenth century, the Shona, led by Mutota of the Rozui clan, waged wars against their neighbors and incorporated them into an empire that bore his title, Mwana Mutapa, "lord of the plundered lands."[41] When he died in 1450, Mutota's empire covered modern Zambia and Zimbabwe. Beginning in 1790, the threat of Dutch farmers forced Dingiswayo, a Mtetwa Nguni, to embark on a series of wars to unite the villages and tribes. Shaka the Zulu, who succeeded him, created the Zulu empire to achieve Nguni unification.

Military organization was one unique factor that aided some empires in South Africa to rise. One such development was the new military structure introduced by Shaka. He reorganized the Nguni military by regimenting the fighting forces into age-sects. His greatest innovation was the inventions of two new weapons, the *asagai* and the long iron-tipped spear. These weapons ensured that when the soldier threw the long spear, he always had the *asagai* to continue fighting. His military forces went through long arduous training sessions and lived in military camps away from civilian settlements. The fighting machines that Shaka created were fearless warriors. The success of their warfare was the expansion of the Nguni ethnic groups to form the Zulu empire by 1825.

The collapse of southern African states can be attributed to political volatility caused by foreign interference in local politics, succession disputes, and persistent fighting. The relationship between the African states and European countries, especially Portugal, was that of trade and friendly coexistence in return for annual tributes to the African sovereign states. However, beginning from the seventeenth century, this was invalidated when the Portuguese in the hinterland grew more independent of their commanders at Mombasa. They refused to pay their tribute in addition to constantly interfering in local politics. Kaparize exercised punitive action against them for failing to pay their tribute. In 1628–1629, the Portuguese responded by attacking the Mwana Mutapa with a force of thirty thousand Africans and two hundred and fifty Portuguese, deposing the king, and installing a stooge.[42] They continually interfered in the new Mwana Mutapa's political affairs. The Portuguese pitched one state against another by supporting them in their local rivalries and providing them with guns and ammunition. In 1917, the Portuguese deposed the last of the Mwana Mutapas, Chioko, and colonized them.

Succession disputes contributed to the decline of the Mwana Mutapa kingdom. After the death of Matope, there were many contesters to the throne. The kingdom disintegrated into fragments. This instability created the opportunity for some powerful vassal rulers like Changa and Togwa, who had grown rich from trade, to seize their independence. In 1490, the kingdom split into two, Mwana Mutapa in the north and Great Zimbabwe in the south. The Zwangendeba Nguni, fleeing from the Zulu wars of conquest, plundered Great Zimbabwe in the 1800s, killing many and instilling such terror in the people that many deserted their towns. This marked the demise of Great Zimbabwe. The Zulu empire suffered a series of defeats, British interference, and disintegration, all culminating in its demise.

Lack of unity and collaboration among states is the underlying factor that prevented them from fighting off foreign interferences. The Mwana Mutapa seized the opportunity created by the Portuguese attacks on their neighbors to cripple the Urozui (Karanga) when the latter were occupied with a war with the Portuguese in the east. The Mwana Mutapa attacked the Urozui in the west as opposed to allying with them to fight the Portuguese.

The disruption of trade weakened the economies of the states and empires. The Portuguese sought to take over the commercial activities in the interior. To do this successfully, they sought the permission of the rulers to build trading stations at Tete, Sena, Dambarare, Masapa, Luanze, and Bokoto. These trade posts enabled the Portuguese to directly deal with the clientele, thus breaking the cartel of the Mwana Mutapa rulers. Not only was the rulers' source of wealth cut, but their authority was also undermined. Furthermore, the Portuguese wars with the Mwana Mutapa crippled trade because several people died in the expedition and most survivors fled. The states therefore declined and remained at the mercy of the European powers.

The introduction of the slave trade and its impact on societies weakened the states and kingdoms in southern Africa. The trade depopulated states like Ndongo, Matamba, Mbundu, Ovimbundu, and Imbangala. By the close of the nineteenth century, the once-vibrant empires and kingdoms of southern Africa were nothing but pale shadows of their former selves. Basil Davidson sums up Portuguese activities in Africa as:

> . . . Arriving in the name of Christian civilization, the Portuguese had brought misery and ruin, whether by their ceaseless claim, demand for captives or by their many wars of conquest. Disunited, with the strong among them preying on the weak, African states lost their independence. And, with it, much of the vigor of their own civilization.[43]

THE RISE AND FALL OF STATES IN WEST AFRICA

Trade was one of the prominent factors that conditioned the flourishing of states and empires in precolonial West Africa. The most important trade that linked West Africa with other parts of the continent was the Trans-Saharan trade, which began in 1000 BCE. The introduction of camel in the fourth century BCE by Arabs into the western Sudan increased the volume of the trade. The ancient empires of Ghana, Mali, Songhay, the Hausa states, Kanem-Bornu, Asante, Oyo, and Dahomey were all strategically positioned to engage in trade. They all benefited from playing the intermediary role in the trade between the North Africans, the Indian Ocean, and the Atlantic Ocean. These empires at different times controlled the trade routes that carried gold from south of the Sahara and salt from the northern part of the Sahara.[44]

States strove to control territories with resources for trade. Ancient Ghana conquered the copper mines at Taghaza and Mali and expanded its influence to the gold and salt mines and copper mines at Takedda. Rulers imposed taxes on the goods that passed through their territories. For instance, "each donkey-load of salt" that entered ancient Ghana attracted a tax of a gold dinar while a tax of two gold dinars was levied on "each donkey-load of salt" that left the empire.[45] The Sudanese empires exported dried fruits, leather tassels, wheat, sheep, cattle, honey, and imported red and blue blouses, gum Arabic, cowries, shells, copper, ivory, and pearls. The wealth gained afforded the rulers the funds to purchase lavish goods such as guns, ammunition and horses and to keep elaborate courts. Villages and small towns expanded their territories, grew powerful, established schools, specialized in arts and crafts, and gradually emerged into states and empires.

The advent of Europeans added another impetus to the rise of states in the forest regions. The trans-Atlantic trade assisted previously small villages to grow rich and powerful as well as expand their frontiers into towns and cities. In the Niger Delta region of modern Nigeria, rivers such the Niger, Benin, and Cross, with natural harbors for ships to anchor and offload merchandise, was the center of trade between the Europeans (British, Portuguese, Dutch, and French) and the indigenes. In the sixteenth century, coastal communities like the Igbo, Edo, Jekri, Ibibio, and Efik expanded their villages into states due to the middlemen position they played in the trade between the hinterland and the Europeans. The Asante of modern Ghana exported kolanuts, gold, elephant tusks, animal skins, and other forest products to the Sudan through the trans-Saharan trade, and gold and slaves to the Atlantic coast. In addition, they played the middlemen for goods entering Asante from the Atlantic coast and leaving to the Sudan. In 1701, the Asante conquered Denkyira to gain direct access to the trade at the coast with the Europeans. The Atlantic trade was also the main premise on which the Asante fought the coastal towns of the Assin and Fante for direct access to European goods, especially guns and ammunition.[46] Trade and economic activities brought enormous wealth thus empowering rulers for expansion.

Leadership influenced the rise of states in precolonial West Africa. A recognized leader whose authority was obeyed by all the sections of the society was necessary for governance, trade, peace, and safety of people and their properties. Sundiata Keita (a Mandingo warrior) of ancient Mali provided good leadership and led his warriors to expand their territory in 1230. Under his leadership, his soldiers were employed in farms to produce food, but it could also be inferred that it was to occupy the soldiers. The Yoruba prince, Ewuare (1450–1480), united the Benin villages and towns and instituted succession by primogeniture.[47] In Kano, the Saifawa dynasty united a number of agro-pastoralist autocratic states into the Kano state.[48] The Hausa States, originally a number of enclosed villages known as *Birni*, came together under the leadership of the *Sarki*. Osei Tutu and his legendary priest, Okomfo Anokye, united the seven lineage-villages of the Asante into the Asante union with the Oyoko clan as the royal lineage. These leaders embarked on wars of expansion and successfully evolved into formidable empires and kingdoms.

Food production is another element in the evolution of states in West Africa. The foundations of the economy and political development of the Sudanese states were farming and animal rearing. The savanna climates of the Sudan supported pastoralists and farmers. The Niger River and Lake Chad facilitated agriculture. Audaghost cultivated dates, wheat, millet, vines, and gourds, and kept cattle, pigs, and sheep because the area had water in abundance. The Songhay Empire constituted three groups of people: Gow (hunters), Sorko (fishermen), and Mossi (farmers). These socioeconomic groups ensured food sufficiency. The Oyo cultivated yams, and fished to supplement their diet. The abundance of food helped the Oyo communities to specialize in brass work, iron-smelting, terracotta, and cloth weaving. The Asante of Ghana, living in the forest zone of West Africa that is watered by Lake Bosomtwi, the Pra and Ofin rivers, were mainly farmers who supplemented their food with fishing and hunting. Through the Atlantic trade, the Portuguese introduced new food crops (cassava, cocoyam, maize) from the New World. These new crops were most suitable to the forest soil and changed the diets of the people. Fulani nomads in the Senegal valley provided milk, meat, and manure to refertilize the land of their farming neighbors in the symbiotic relationship that existed between them. The availability of food led to population explosion, competition for land and water, movement of people, and the founding of towns. Leadership became a necessity, society begun to be stratified, and specialization in arts, crafts, and metalworking flourished to make empires like Mali, Songhay, and Asante.

Religion was an important factor in the rise of states in West Africa. African traditional religion and Islam were the two religions that occasioned the rise of states. The spiritual and political head of the Oni of Ife, for instance, united the Oyo villages in the seventeenth century. The cult of Oduduwa, a hero god, sanctioned the office of the Oni and other state rulers, thereby creating a binding relationship between states, and religion.[49] In Asante, Okomfo Anokye, a legendary priest, united the seven Asante towns into a union by conjuring the golden stool from the sky. The golden stool, according to the legend, embodied the souls of all the Asante. This engendered great loyalty to the stool and monarch that was unprecedented in the history of the people.

Islamic revivalism in the eighteenth century created states and empires in West Africa. In the eighteenth century, the Islamized Fulani in Futa Jallon waged a series of holy wars for some fifty years at the end of which they established a theocratic state led by the Imam with the political title of Almamy.[50] The Futa Toro and Bondu regions in the Senegal Valley saw the rise of similar theocratic states in the eighteenth century. The Sokoto empire was the creation of Uthman dan Fodio, a Muslim Fulani Torodbe of the Maliki school from Futa Toro, who waged jihads to spread and reform Islam beginning in 1804. The jihads paved the way for the extensive spread of Islam in West Africa, and encouraged Arab traders and missionaries to travel into the interior and find their way into the courts of the Asante empire, Hausaland, and other states as diplomats, clerics, accountants, spiritual leaders, and the founders of Islamic schools.

Incessant wars also conditioned the rise of states and kingdoms. In the fourteenth century, the Bulala forced the Kanem to flee their homes. The Kanem founded the Bornu empire by subduing the So, who inhabited east of Lake Chad where they fled.

One of the causes of the collapse of the precolonial states in West Africa was political instability caused by succession disputes, interstate rivalries, and European interference. Ancient Mali suffered from this canker after the reign of Mansa Musa, who is famous for his pilgrimage to Mecca. Mansa Maghan, the successor of Mansa Musa, could not keep a firm hold on his kingdom, thus encouraging their vassals and neighbors to invade or secede. The Fulbe, the Mossi and Tuareg in Upper Senegal, resiliently forayed Malian territory. The reign of Mansa Suleyman offered a strong governmental interlude for Mali, but after his death in 1359, the empire of Mali was set on a degeneration trail beginning with the escape of two Songhay princes in 1363.[51] The Songhai Empire also went through a series of ineffective rulers after the death of Askia Mohammed in 1538. When the empire weakened, secession from vassal states became a common occurrence. Kanem Bornu's sovereign power collided with the rising power of the Hausa states over the control of trade routes. These political rivalries disrupted economic activities. The Sokoto caliphate became so big that it could not be administered adequately; consequently, it suffered systemic revolts from their subjects. All these weakened the states and kingdoms.

Invasion by foreign forces and wars between the precolonial African states also contributed, and in some cases, caused the demise of the states and empires. Religion, economic, and political reasons were the forces behind these invasions and wars. Religion and economic reasons were behind the Almoravid invasion of ancient Ghana beginning in 1062. The Almoravid wanted to spread Islam to the 'pagan' empire of Ghana in addition to controlling trade. The Ghana capital of Kumbi Saleh fell to the Almoravids in 1077. The Almoravid occupation of Ghana ushered in a period of instability and secession by vassal states like Tekrur, Mali, and Songhay. Geared by the obsession to find and control the gold mines that produced the gold in the trans-Saharan trade, Mawlay Ahmed al-Mansur, the sixth Saadian sultan of Morocco, commissioned Judar Pasha, a Spaniard, to invade Songhay. In 1585, the Moorish army seized control of Taghaza salt mines, breaking Songhai monopoly on the trade in salt, capturing Gao and Timbuktu in 1591, and taking control of the state. This occupation led to a period of political instability caused by internecine fighting among the Moorish army, Songhay princes for succession, vassal states fighting for their freedom, and the neighboring states such as the Fulbe and Tuareg who took advantage of the anarchic situation to expand their territory. All these affected trade and weakened the states.

Interstate wars were contributory factors to the demise of West African empires. The importation of firearms from Arab merchants and Europeans revolutionized warfare, made it bloodier, and more violent. The Hausa States suffered relentless attacks from Songhai in the west and Bornu in the east. In the seventeenth and eighteenth centuries, interstate wars became rampant: Zamfara against Kebbi, Gobir against Zamfara, and Kano against Katsina.[52] The Kwararafa (Jukun) from the Benue river valley raided the Hausa states and Bornu kingdom for slaves. The Uthman dan Fodio army clashed with all the Hausa states: Zaria (1804), Katsina (1805), Gobir (1808), and Bornu (1818).[53] These wars weakened the states and made their collapse easy.

The breakdown of economic activities contributed in no small way to the collapse of precolonial West African states. Since trade (local and long-distance or international) helped these empires and states to rise, the destruction or reduction of it affected their economies adversely, thus leading to their gradual decline. The diversion of the gold trade from Audaghost to the Niger and Taghaza through the Sahara caused the decline of the trans-Saharan trade. The intensification of the slave trade depopulated states and caused insecurity. The abolition of the slave trade in the early 1800s also diminished the livelihood and the source of wealth for most West African states like Asante, Dahomey, and the Oyo.

From the nineteenth century onwards, various European nations such as Britain, Portugal, and France begun to interfere directly in the local politics of West African states. Settling among the African people as traders and missionaries, they increasingly interfered in trade and politics, especially after the abolition of the slave trade. The British pushed into the interior of modern Ghana, upsetting the power base of the Asante. States like Dahomey and Oyo all lost their sovereignty to European countries.

CONCLUSION

States, kingdoms, and empires are not new to the African continent. Factors such as trade, religion, leadership, food production, wars of conquest, and the presence of invading groups worked interdependently to cause states, kingdoms, and empires to rise. These states and empires developed complex political organizations, sociocultural institutions, undertook complex architectural projects such as the pyramids of Egypt, stone ruins of Great Zimbabwe, and stelae and obelisks of Ethiopia, and developed their own written languages like the Geez of Meroe and hieroglyphics of Egypt. All these developments were indigenous to the African continent. These states, empires, and kingdoms collapsed at different times due to a number of factors: decline in economic activities, political instability, the slave trade, foreign interference in African affairs, and ultimately the colonization of Africa by Europeans.

ENDNOTES

1 Molefi Kete Asante, *The History of Africa: The quest for eternal harmony* (New York: Routledge, Taylor & Francis Group, 2007), 93.

2 John Reader, *Africa: A biography of the continent* (New York: Alfred A. Knopf, 1998), 193.

3 For more information on agriculture in North Africa, see Peter Mitchell, *African connections: Archaeological perspectives on Africa and the wider world* (New York: Altamira Press, 2005), 33–63.

4 Robert O. Collins and James M. Burns, *A history of sub-Saharan Africa* (Cambridge, UK: Cambridge University Press, 2007), 26.

5 J. D. Fage, *A history of Africa* (London: Hutchinson & Co. Ltd, 1978), 37.

6 E. W. Boville, *The golden trade of the Moors* (2nd ed.) (Oxford, UK: Oxford University Press, 1970), 68.

7 Derek A. Welsby, *The Kingdom of Kush: The Napatan and Meroetic empires* (London: British Museum Press, 1996), 16.

8 Glenn Perry, *The History of Egypt* (Connecticut: Greenwood Press, 2004), 23; for a better understanding of ancient Egyptian religion, see Wendy Christensen, *Empire of ancient Egypt* (New York: Infobase Publishing, 2009), 109–130.

9 C. R. Pennell, *Morocco: From Empire to Independence* (Oxford, UK: Oneworld Publications, 2003), 40; J. Devisse and I. Hrbek, "the Almoravids" in *General History of Africa: Africa from the seventh to the eleventh century*, Vol. III, ed. Ivan Hrbek (Paris: UNESCO, 1992), 176–189; Philip C. Naylor, *North Africa: A history from antiquity to the present* (Austin: University of Texas Press, 2009), 89–108.

10 Collins and Burns, *A history of Sub-Saharan Africa*, 27.

11 The Hyksos, Hittites, Philistines, Assyrians, Persians, and Berber tribes took turns in invading and ruling Egypt at different times. See Glen E. Perry, *The history of Egypt* (Westport, Connecticut: Greenwood Press, 2004), 23–38; Reader, *Africa*, 197.

12 Reader, *Africa*, 197.

13 C. R. Pennell, *Morocco: From empire to independence* (Oxford, UK: One World Publications, 2003), 48.

14 Ibid., 47.

15 Ibid., 48.

16 Ibid., 53.

17 Ibid., 59.

18 Stanley Burstein (Ed.), *Ancient African civilization: Kush and Axum* (Princeton, NJ: Markus Wiener Publishers, 1998), 9.

19 Reader, *Africa*, 198–199.

20 For a detailed discussion of the Bantu, see Roland Oliver, "The Problem of the Bantu Expansion" in *Papers in African Prehistory*, ed. J.D. Fage and R. A. Oliver (London: Syndics of the Cambridge University Press, 1970), 141–156.

21 Chapurukha Kusimba, *The rise and fall of Swahili states* (Walnut Creek, CA: AltaMira Press, 1999), 126.

22 Collins and Burns, *A history of sub-Saharan Africa*, 119.

23 Basil Davidson, *A history of East and Central Africa to the late nineteenth century* (New York: Doubleday & Company, 1969), 221.

24 Davidson, *A history of East and Central Africa*, 49.

25 Collins and Burns, *A history of sub-Saharan Africa*, 66.

26 For more information, see Collins and Burns, 142–150; S. Lwanga-Lunyiigo and J. Vansina, "The Bantu-speaking peoples and their expansion" in *General history of Africa*. Vol. III. Edited by Muhammad Fasi and Ivan Hrbek (London: J. Currey; Berkeley, CA: University of California Press; Paris: Unesco, 1990), 140–162.

27 David Birmingham, "The forest and the savanna of Central Africa," in *The Cambridge History of Africa*, Vol.5 c. 1790 – c.1870, ed. J. D. Fage, John E. Flint, and Roland Anthony Oliver (Cambridge, UK: Cambridge University Press, 1976), 247–248.

28 Tekle Tsadik Mekouria, "Christian Axum," in *General history of Africa: Ancient civilizations of Africa*, Vol. II, ed. G. Mokhtar (Paris: UNESCO, 1990), 224–235.

29 Alexander Ives Bortolot, "Kingdoms of the Savanna: The Luba and Lunda Empires," in *Heilbrunn timeline of art history* (New York: The Metropolitan Museum of Art, 2000–). www.metmuseum.org/toah/hd/luba/hd_luba.htm (October 2003). Accessed 6/1/2011.

30 Elizabeth Allo Isichei, *A history of African societies to 1870* (Cambridge, UK: Cambridge University Press, 1997), 109–110.

31 Robert Collins, *A History of Sub-Saharan Africa*, 145.

32 Ibid., 147.

33 Kusimba, *The rise and fall of Swahili states*, 158.

34 Davidson, *A History of East and Central Africa*, 246.

35 Ibid., 112.

36 For details, see Edward A. Alpers, *Ivory and Slaves: Changing patterns of international trade in East Central Africa* (Berkeley: University of California Press, 1975), 39–68.

37 Davidson, *A history of East and Central Africa*, 220.

38 Kusimba, *The rise and fall of Swahili States*, 156.

39 Ibid.

40 Robert Collins, *Central and South African history* (Princeton, NJ: M. Wiener Publishers, 1990), 161.

41 Collins, *Central and South African history*, 11, 60.

42 Davidson, *A History of East and Central Africa*, 261–4.

43 Ibid., 280.

44 John G. Jackson, *Introduction to African Civilizations* (Secaucus, NJ: Citadel Press, 1970), 202.

45 Ibid., 204.

46 Elizabeth Isichei, *History of West Africa since 1800* (New York: Africana Publishing Company, 1977), 63–64.

47 Roberto O. Collins and James M. Burns. *A history of sub-Saharan Africa* (Cambridge, UK: Cambridge University Press, 2007), 135.

48 E. V. Boville, *The golden trade of the Moors*, 2nd ed (Oxford, UK: Oxford University Press, 1970), 223.

49 Collins and Burns, *A History of sub-Saharan Africa*, 132–133.

50 Boville, *The Golden Trade*, 229.

51 Jackson, *Introduction to African Civilizations* (Secaucus, NJ: Citadel Press, 1970), 212.

52 Boville, *The Golden Trade*, 225.

53 Ibid., 230.

REVIEW QUESTIONS

1. Identify and discuss all the factors responsible for the rise and fall of states and empires in Africa.
2. Discuss the role of the Nile River in the rise of the kingdoms and states of North Africa.
3. How did trade and food production help in the rise of precolonial African states?
4. In what ways did the contact between Europe, Asia, and Africa affect political developments in the continent?
5. In what ways did contact with Europe lead to the demise of African kingdoms and empires?

Writing prompt

Precolonial African states emerged gradually over the centuries. Do you think they would have perfected their systems of government and social and cultural institutions to fit into the twenty-first century without colonization and the creation of "modern" nations?

CHAPTER 3

The Social Construction of Africa and Africans in Western Mass Media

Abdoulaye Saine, Richard Aidoo, and Steve Hess

Comprehending the social construction of Africa in Western mass media as "The Dark Continent" must begin at the philosophical, scientific, and literary traditions that spawned them in nineteenth- and twentieth-century Europe and America. In them, we find a power-driven epistemology created for a specific purpose and designed to serve specific hegemonic political and economic agendas. This Western image of Africa and Africans helped to justify and legitimize African enslavement, colonization and current marginalization in the global political economy. In both post–Cold War and post-9/11 international systems, Western powers and the United States, in particular, have used terms and metaphors such as "Globalization," the "Axis of Evil," "War on Terror," "Clash of Civilizations," and "End of History" as an excuse to carry out an overarching mission of completely recolonizing the world. The use of the Dark Continent to describe Africa is for the most part motivated by hegemonic economic and political interests. It rationalizes, as well as helps maintain, domination of Africans by Westerners. These metaphors and images, like earlier ones framed around the Dark Continent, derive from political and economic interests, which seek to preserve U.S. and European hegemony through the acceptance of "democracy," "human rights," and a neo-liberal economic order to simultaneously "save" and dominate non-Western populations.

IMAGES OF AFRICA AND AFRICANS IN WESTERN MASS MEDIA

In discussing the representation of Africa in Western media, it is important to analyze and deconstruct the history, persistence, and the ideological power of the metaphor of Africa as the Dark Continent. This metaphor identifies and incorporates an entire continent as "Other" in a way that reaffirms Western dominance and reveals hostile and Eurocentric presumptions of Africa and Africans in travel accounts, news reports, and academic writing. Therefore, in order to understand this metaphor and the explicit framing of Africa and Africans as the "Other," we must look to the European and Euro-American discourses on Africa during the nineteenth century, which constructed and represented the land and its peoples to the Western public as racially inferior and savage.[1]

While the use of the metaphor, Dark Continent, has been discredited in the academic literature, generally, it continues to play a key role in the contemporary framing of Africa and Africans in the mass media. The term was first used by European explorers around the nineteenth century to describe a continent that they knew so little about. It was not so much an issue of darkness, per say, but European ignorance of the continent, its peoples and cultures. As a consequence, what the Dark Continent metaphor and others like it succeed at doing is homogenizing and flattening places and peoples and denying the actualities and specificities of social and economic processes that transformed Africa. In doing so, these metaphors obscure a nuanced examination of European and Euro-American cultural and economic hegemony in Africa.[2] In the end, the Dark Continent metaphor legitimizes the status quo and perpetuates unequal relations of power and exploitation. The pre-occupation of Europeans to "civilize" or "uplift" the "beastly" or "noble" "savages" in nineteenth- and early twentieth-century Africa did not represent a high ethical stance, but instead served a political and economic purpose—that of quieting and normalizing a population.[3]

What is remarkable about the Dark Continent metaphor is that it negates Africa. Consequently, Western construction of Africa and the so-called Third World assumes a privileged viewpoint, conceived of as existing within itself, beyond history-making and political play. In the various metaphors of Africa and the Third World, for example, the Self versus Other dichotomy is very apparent. It assumes the position of an "Enlightened" Europe versus the "Dark" Continent, "modern" Europe as opposed to "traditional" Africa; "rational" Europeans in contrast to "irrational" and "superstitious" Africans, "progressive" Europe versus "backward" Africa. In other words, Europe is constructed as the ideal that all must follow and the standard by which all else is measured. Within this ideological worldview, the "Third World," is therefore perceived in contrast to the "First World," as a disruption, a deviation, an anomaly, which must be checked and brought under control, if history is to be played out according to plan, and if progress is to be achieved.[4] Put in another way, each side of this dichotomy comprises a particular identity, with the "Third-World" identity defined in relation to the original identity of the first. The Western attitude of racial superiority over Africans and other peoples was initially a mere cultural bias, supported loosely by a Eurocentric orthodox biblical ideology. But it gradually grew into a formidable two-pronged historical reality: slavery and formal colonialism on one hand, and academic expressions of white superiority and racial separateness on the other. The academic expressions were made by prominent European scholars such as Immanuel Kant and Friedrich Hegel, for example. Kant explained the emergence of different races in relation to different natural causes affecting them in different geographical regions of the world. According to Kant, "the constitution of the soil (moisture or drought), and food, also, induce a hereditary difference or strain among animals of one and the same stock and race, especially in stature, proportion of limbs (plump or lanky), and also in the temperament."[5] In his view, such differences could readily be observed among distinct human races. For Kant, the original human species was white. The black race, he believed, had emerged as a result of humid heat bearing on the skin of the original species.[6] He also believed that it was possible to demonstrate that Native Americans and blacks were a spiritually decadent race among other members of the human stock who had "no feeling beyond the trifling."[7] Hegel, often depending on historical accounts constructed by European explorers and missionaries, argued that "History" was a process of change through the intervention of reason in the world. Through reason, human beings knew and transformed its reality in a continuous dialectical manner. From these transformations, culture was born.[8] For Hegel, culture was rooted in reason and dialectics. He implied, consequently, that where there was "no culture," there was no reason. In Africa, as Hegel contended,

> Life is not a manifestation of dialectical reason but of a succession of contingent happenings and surprises. Africans live in a state of innocence. They are unconscious of themselves, as in the natural and primitive state of Adam and Eve in the biblical paradise before the emergence of reason and will. Africans are intractable. The condition in which they live is incapable of any historical development or culture. They have no reason and because they lack reason, they also lack development and culture. They have no history in the true sense of the word.[9]

The writings and ideas of Kant and Hegel can be understood in context. The eighteenth century was a period of cultural revitalization and power consolidation in Europe. This revitalization and consolidation often took the form of self-comparison with other peoples in the areas of culture and history. Africa was a ready example to be framed as the opposite of the desirable heights which Europe sought to attain. In anthropology, philosophy, and religion, Africa was described as utterly inferior to Europe.[10] Consequently, Europe and Africa have been envisioned as separate worlds with a deep and abiding gulf between them, and their differences are constructed as being so irreconcilable that the gulf can never be bridged.[11] European literature of the twentieth century and later reflects the same story and themes. The works of Joseph Conrad, Somerset Maugham, Laurens Van der Post, Joyce Cary, and Graham Greene, to name a few, assign the Africans to a lower social order, as a people unable to reason or cope with abstractions and incapable of mastering the subtle complexities essential to civilization.[12] Perhaps the greatest virtue attributed to the "savage" Africans was their presumed "acceptance" of a subordinated place in the scheme of things.

This scheme of the social order was envisioned by the imperial British as manifesting itself in a manner in which, properly reflecting the "natural order," the supposed superior British and the supposed inferior African played out their complementary roles. These attitudes are revealed in various European colonial policies—British "indirect-rule" popularized by Lord Lugard in colonial Nigeria; French "assimilation" policy in Senegal and other French colonies; and a hybrid of the two in Portuguese-dominated colonies of Guinea Bissau, Angola, and Mozambique. In these systems, African individuals were not lauded for their capacity to serve as autonomous decision makers but rather as functionaries within social structures imposed by Europeans from the outside. Throughout their history in Africa, the Europeans saw themselves as benefactors. Many Western statesmen and commentators discussing Africa to this day still resist seeing themselves as self-seeking conquerors, preferring instead to see themselves as noble benefactors with purely altruistic purposes.[13]

Philosophers, anthropologists, and early naturalists, including Charles Darwin, subscribed to this European distorted worldview regarding Africa, and assisted in creating a pseudo-scientific justification for Eurocentric racism. They did this by inventing the concept of the "negro." The "negro" was/ is conceived as being less than human. It is a "thing" rather than a person. It has no history, no civilization, or culture and thus, it has no humanity. It follows, then, that during the time of colonization and the transatlantic slave trade, Europeans were not slaughtering and raping a people, only "savages."[14] The invention of the "negro" appears to have been necessary in order to provide justification for European supremacy in the "Age of Enlightenment" and today. In sum, the European and Euro-American dominated "scientific" and "social-scientific" communities fashioned a body of knowledge in which Europeans were considered superior and Africans inferior. In doing so, they were then able to rationalize the "inhumanity" of the Negro. It is ideas such as these that gave rise to the "Tuskegee Experiment" where "white scientists" and "physicians" like the Nazis injected syphilis into healthy black men or failed to treat the infected, even after the discovery of penicillin.[15]

Both historical and ethnographic data, however, presented a picture of Africa and Africans that was at variance with the metaphor of the Dark Continent. When early European explorers encountered, not discovered, the stone walls and ruins of Great Zimbabwe in the late 1800s, they were hard put to explain its origin. In their view, the ruins were remains of structures too complex and advanced in building technique and design to be a product of native African builders. The ruins of Great Zimbabwe, as well as Egypt of Antiquity, empires of Ghana, Mali, and Songhay were often explained away by pseudo-history as the remains of some biblical empire.[16] According to Sheik Anta Diop, many scientists during the period loathed associating black people with the human race, much less with civilization. Consequently, science bowed before race prejudice and truth recoiled in panic.[17]

Even the highly regarded third edition of the *Encyclopedia Britannica* in 1798, under the entry "Negroes" referred to black people as "the unhappy race" and described their behavior as characterized by "idleness, treachery, revenge, cruelty, impudence, stealing, lying, profanity, debauchery, nastiness, and intemperance," which are said to have extinguished the principles of natural law and to have silenced the reproofs of conscience.[18] "The 'Negro' was also looked upon as a stranger to every sentiment of compassion, and an awful example of the corruption of man when left to himself."[19] In sum, the identification of Africa as the Dark Continent was socially constructed. These representations, the late Edward Said argued, point to the "politics of hegemonic power-relations between the colonizer and the colonized."[20] This is where we must begin to understand Africa's construction in the Western mass media in Europe and the United States.

After four centuries of Western writing on Africa, many of these beliefs have been toned down considerably, especially in the writings of modern-day academics. The empires of Europe and, with them, the colonial administrators are no more. For the most part, Africa is no longer the great "unknown" waiting to be discovered. It has become yet another part of the so-called Third World where people struggle against the vestiges of slavery, colonialism, neocolonialism, and underdevelopment.[21] Why then do many of these stereotypes continue to appear so often on TV, and in newspapers and film today?

The answer may lie in the image residues of Africa and Africans from earlier times that remain embedded in modern Western discourse on Africa. In the first set of images, Africa is represented as a monolith, a continent riveted by civil war, famine, and hunger, where fly-infested children with distended bellies roam the bush in search of food and water. In the second image, the African is lewd and a "beastly savage." Finally, there is the supposedly positive, but still inaccurate image of Africa: of the proud and exotic peoples and wildlife coexisting in the Serengeti in an almost perfect state of nature. The long-term dominance of these categories of images or variations of them account for their acceptance in European and Euro-American literary and media traditions as the only appropriate ways to conceive and write about Africa. Authenticity and acceptance are mostly assured when TV and/or newspaper reports evoke these images. These images add both color and vitality to what are otherwise, dull narratives.[22] Films, like *Tarzan*, for instance, have familiarized Westerners with an Africa composed of old notions of the Dark Continent. And in the face of these images, reality has little chance of being accepted. With few exceptions, no matter how different in style, form, or content, all the books and the films based on these images present the same Western fantasy and distortion of Africa.[23]

Tragically, it is this oversimplification in the mass media that continues to inform the West about Africa. People who would otherwise be predisposed to distrust what they do not understand readily embrace inaccurate, shorthand explanations of a continent and peoples they know little about. The preponderance of Western-born and educated reporters, editors, writers, and producers ensure that inaccurate Western images and viewpoints prevail in news reporting. Although many journalists genuinely try to be objective in their interpretations of events, few can erase or escape their political socialization or deny their culture and the voice that a subconscious bias lends it. Given the inordinate influence of the Western mass media, negative images of Africa, however unrepresentative or dishonest, only reinforce ancient stereotypes.[24] In fact, a process of cognitive consistency, which is based on the notion that humans, by and large, tend to resist change and prefer stability, perpetuates established images and stereotypes. Cognitive consistency is thus the subconscious effort human beings often make to avoid potentially contradictory perceptions.[25]

WHAT PURPOSE DO THESE CONSTRUCTED IMAGES OF AFRICA SERVE?

Robert Cox has eloquently argued in relation to neo-Realist international relations theory "that theory is always for someone and for some purpose."[26] In other words, European scientific and social theories of the nineteenth century constructed the world from a specific social and political position and were not independent.[27] There is, Cox argues, "no such thing as theory in itself, divorced from a standpoint in time and space."[28] When a theory so represents itself, it is important to examine it as an ideology and to lay bare its concealed perspective.[29] Second, critical theorists, post-modernists, neo-Marxists as well as Standpoint feminists have been concerned about the relationship between power and knowledge. Foucault, in particular, opposed the notion that knowledge is immune from the workings of power. Instead, he argued that power in fact produces knowledge. Power requires knowledge and knowledge relies on and often reinforces existing power relations.[30] Thus, there is no "truth" that exists outside of power.

Consequently, the metaphors and images that have come to define Africa and Africans in contemporary Western mass media, like their intellectual precursors of earlier times, have, by and large, served Western colonial and imperial interests in Africa and elsewhere. Although, over the last three hundred years, the worldview has shifted from a parochial and conservative Christian worldview to a relatively more secular and liberal one, deep-seated negative perceptions of Africa remain. Western images of Africa continue to distort and caricature Africa's reality.[31] However, the distortion of Africa and Africans is not unique. Other entities, such as Arabs and Muslims, Native Americans, Asians, women, and native populations of Australia and New Zealand have been similarly used to serve the interests of empire.

Contemporary images, commentaries and assessments attempting to describe or explain the "African crisis" since the 1980s have resurfaced following the end of the Cold War. Assessing his stint on the continent, George Alagiah, a former Africa correspondent for the BBC, conceded that Western television pictures painted Africa as a faraway place where good people go hungry, bad people run the government, and chaos and anarchy are the norm. To illustrate his point, Alagiah recounts an instance toward the end of his stint. While covering a famine in southern Sudan, he filed two reports to be broadcasted consecutively on BBC's national news. The first described the situation on the ground and the second made a deliberate effort to explain the causes of the famine. The first film had the most impact, as letters from viewers reflected people's feeling of genuine sorrow "for the poor souls of southern Sudan," with little attention paid to why the famine occurred. Alagiah, therefore, concluded that "to get people in British living rooms to identify with the frazzled aid worker as she tries to cope with a humanitarian disaster is easy. To get people to see that the crisis is part of the convulsive process of post-colonial political realignment is more difficult."[32] Africa is once more constructed in ways that mimic old Western notions and images. This would have been amusing today were it not for the tragic events that unfolded in Rwanda in 1994 and in the Sudan and the Democratic Republic of Congo, where millions have died. As in Rwanda in the 1990s, the crisis in Darfur in the mid-2000s led to the death and daily displacement of thousands while the debate over the meaning of "genocide" continued. Brian Steidle, a former U.S. Marine officer, cogently presents this situation in a recent award-winning documentary, *The Devil Came on Horseback*. In this documentary, Steidle struggles to call attention to the ongoing Darfur conflict and also solicit help from Washington and the West to quell the atrocities. Even though the documentary taps into the often-used images of bodies burnt and blackened, corpses stacked like cordwood, and rape victims recounting their tales of horror, more disparaging and discouraging are the reactions of the West (particularly Washington) to the situation in Darfur. In addition to revealing some of the warped perceptions of Africa and its problems, this documentary highly underscores the weight that is given to issues of concern on the continent.[33]

Even those Americans who would be hard pressed to name a few African countries and their capitals are apt to throw their hands in despair and conclude that the continent is a "lost cause."[34] This is because many Americans have come to know Africa mostly by its wars and tragedies, and more recently by the activities of terrorists' organizations like Al Shabaab, Al Qaeda, and Boko Haram. They overlook recent success stories of African countries in settings as diverse as Ghana, Senegal, Tanzania, and Cape Verde in generating robust economic growth, reducing poverty, and reconstructing effective democratic institutions.[35] For instance, Liberia's recovery from a tragic history of ethnic conflict, exclusionary politics, and authoritarian rule from the 1980s to producing Africa's first elected woman president—Ellen Johnson Sirleaf—and being ranked among the Top Ten most improved nations in the 2009 World Bank's Doing Business Survey[36] is almost unknown. One flagrant case of Afro-pessimism is the book by Keith Richburg, *Out of America*, a soul-searching account of an African American journalist who spent three years covering conflicts in Somalia, Rwanda, Liberia, and Zaire.[37] In the end, Richburg distances himself from his African roots and declares:

> Excuse me if I sound cynical, jaded. I'm beaten down, and I'll admit it. And it's Africa that has made me feel this way. I feel for her suffering. I empathize with her pain, and now, from afar, I still recoil in horror whenever I see yet another television picture of another tribal slaughter, another refugee crisis. But most of all I think: Thank God my ancestor got out, because now, I am not one of them. In short, thank God that I am American.[38]

Richburg is not alone. Others, for example George Ayitteh, an African resident in the United States, have also expressed similar views.[39] Many journalists and scholars alike attribute Africa's current crisis to its geography, "a case of bad latitude."[40] As tempting as it can be to give into pessimism over Africa, Afro-pessimists make two fundamental mistakes. The first error has to do with the assumption that Africa, the world's second largest continent, three times larger than the United States and home to as many as one billion people, is incapable of change, just as philosophers and anthropologists of earlier centuries had argued. The second mistake is focusing on Africa's tragedies and wars as its defining character while simultaneously overlooking the continent's real progress in education, health, the economy, and democratic governance. They further compound these errors, argues Howard French, an African American, and author of *A Continent for the Taking: The Tragedy and Hope of Africa*, by overlooking one of Africa's greatest assets—African Americans and their ancestral ties to the United States, who represent the wealthiest and potentially politically influential group of African descent in the world.[41] Finally, Afro-pessimist observations about Africa are driven fundamentally by what Patrick Chabal calls "politics of the mirror," that is, the tendency of today's many Western commentators to frame their observations of Africa using assumptions that govern beliefs about their own societies. Chabal sums this up well when he argues:

> First we have perennially been disappointed in that the reality of Africa has never matched our expectations. Second, and more ominously, we have failed to look at Africa as it is. . . rather than as we imagine it to be. Third, and as a result, we have confined Africa to the dustbin of history; that is, as a continent the history of which we cannot be expected to understand and on which we eventually "give up."[42]

Relegation of Africa to the dustbin of history by the mass media and some scholars has important implications for U.S. foreign policy toward African states and peoples. While Americans should take pride in the transformative role the United States played in Europe, Japan, South Korea, and other Asian countries, and to some extent in Latin America following World War II, one is forced to notice that only Africa has been left out of the party. But why, French asks, has Africa been left out in the cold? French contends that:

> We have been told that the continent holds no strategic interests for the United States. It is because rather than embracing the continent as a promising and lucrative new frontier for investment, we have been told, in the words of former U.S. Senator Jesse Helms, that Africa is a "rat hole" into which we throw vast sums of aid money only to see it disappear.[43]

The economic data says, otherwise, however. Since the 1990s, each major region of Africa boasted as much trade with the United States as all the constituents of the former Soviet Union combined. Today, the continent is the source of about 18 percent of U.S. oil imports. This figure is expected to rise to 25 percent in the next decade or two.[44] This is not to mention the extractive mineral industries that provide inputs for U.S. and other Western industries.

French, in fact, argues that he is convinced that:

> Africa's isolation and our [American] stinginess toward the continent is related to the very same long-term discrimination and disdain that Americans of African descent have battled against from their earliest days on this continent. And one of the most costly and insidious results of the transatlantic slave trade was the near total disconnect between Africans and African Americans which continues to this day.[45]

In his book, *The Ties that Bind: African American Consciousness of Africa*, Bernard Magubane takes up the theme of "near total disconnect" to interrogate "the nature and meaning of white hegemony, and the image of Africa to which blacks in the Western World were exposed during the age of imperialism." This, Magubane argues, is of particular import in the development of the black's self-image in the New World because white ideas about blacks, he contends, did not arise from a vacuum, but had certain economic and political determinants.[46] Perhaps, it is in this context that one can understand Keith Richburg's perceptions and representations of Africa in his book *Out of America*. In this regard, there is remarkable continuity and consistency in the past and contemporary assumptions and images of Africa. BBC reports on the raging war in the Democratic Republic of Congo have told of indiscriminate killings and rising cannibalism among rebel militias that allegedly cook and eat their victims.[47] A variation of this story is that of a white explorer left to boil in a huge pot as savage Africans mill around in anticipation of their white-flesh dinner.[48] Are these news reports a figment of the European imagination or reality? Hammond and Jablow, in their book, *The Africa That Never Was*, contend that reported instances of cannibalism in Africa were mere fabrication. Yet, paradoxically, the BBC, CNN, and in particular the *New York Times* are also good sources of news and sometimes provide excellent coverage of events unfolding in Africa. Jeffrey Sachs has, among others, used the *New York Times* as a platform from which to inform the world about Africa and to serve as an advocate for African causes. Journalists and scholars that take the time to do painstaking research can often deliver a good product. However, many others are content to essentialize the continent and its diverse peoples and cultures as a monolith to fit a particular genre and in order to conform to the prevalent Western view of Africa and Africans.

Another example is the framing of HIV/AIDS in some academic circles. Part of the academic literature on the incidence of HIV/AIDS today might well have been lifted from the anthropological literature of the nineteenth century of the highly sexed African male and female. Take this example by the late William Rushing:

> Most groups in Africa have a sex-positive culture. Sex is viewed as a part of courtship and a form of recreation; the relations between lovers are viewed as affairs between friends. The men tend to be "womanizers," premarital sex for females is accepted as is female adultery. Polygamous sexual relations are thus widespread for the married no less than the unmarried. This is the hallmark of a sex-positive culture. It also facilitates the spread of HIV.[49]

In the medical arena, the different patterns of AIDS infection exhibited by African countries have resulted in the development of a plethora of research on AIDS in the continent that resembles earlier narrow-minded colonial efforts to understand patterns of TB and syphilis.[50] Often, explanations of the different patterns invariably lay blame on the peculiarities of African customs, traditions, and behaviors that relate to issues of sexuality and reproduction at the expense of other significant factors as the colonial historical context, poverty, dependency, and underdevelopment.[51]

CONCLUSION

Images and descriptions of Africa in the popular press and some academic research suggest that the African continent is a troubled land where corruption, ethnic warfare, poverty, hunger, environmental destruction, and pestilence prevail. Some have even suggested that Africa is a lost cause, asserting that the continent should be "written off" by international development organizations. This may, in fact, account for the lack of a concerted global effort to end the war in the Democratic Republic of Congo where approximately three million people have died compared to the overwhelmingly positive tsunami response in Asia. Meanwhile, commercial tour operators also hawk the region as a place of high adventure and excitement. Even quasi-scholarly publications such as the *National Geographic* magazine often promote a vision of a primitive or wild Africa or both.[52] What these popular and commercial descriptions hold in common is the level of superficiality and one-sidedness. Yes, as elsewhere, bad things do happen in Africa, and there is beautiful scenery to be seen, but this is only one part of a varied and very complex picture. It is the apparent willingness, perhaps laziness and ignorance of many popular commentators to provide a more nuanced view of an enormous continent that is often frustrating to Africans and many Africanists alike.[53]

Africa is, after all, a place of extraordinarily diverse, vibrant, and dynamic cultures. Since the early 1990s, specifically, no other continent has seen more dramatic improvements in human rights, political freedoms, and economic development—from the overthrowing of apartheid in South Africa to the revitalization of economies in countries such as Ghana, Senegal, and Uganda. Although environmental threats are real, African societies have proven their capacity to use resources in a sustainable fashion that meets their material needs without compromising the environment for future generations. The importance of human relations, family, and good neighborliness in many African societies also stands in stark contrast to the more closed and individualistic tendencies in a number of Western settings.[54] Therefore, the construction of Africa as the Dark Continent in Western mass media both today and in the past has been more myth than reality. Also, one unfortunate reality is that with the existence of the World Wide Web, present and past negative reflections of the image of Africa and Africans will continue to spread widely, extending beyond generations.

While the explicit portrayal of Africa as the barbaric Dark Continent has been rejected in contemporary academic and popular discourse in the West, the image has reemerged in new metaphors in the post-colonial era. These portrayals have continued to negate Africa, emphasize its violence, poverty, and instability, and draw the conclusion that the continent and its peoples are either a complete "lost cause" or cannot be redeemed without the help and altruism of the West. As suggested by the findings of critical theorists, from Robert Cox to Michel Foucault, the self-sustaining nature of these images is rooted not in their objective truth but rather the purpose they serve in furthering the interests of those who wield power. The social construction of Africa, in other words, has little to do with concrete conditions on the continent. In fact, dozens of African countries, such as Ghana or Botswana, have in recent decades achieved unprecedented levels of stability, marked solid economic growth, major gains in political development, and major gains in rooting out poverty. This reality, however, is masked by the pervasiveness of a well-entrenched image of Africa in Western mass media, fostered in the interest of maintaining a U.S. and European-centric global political order.

ENDNOTES

1 Lucy Jarosz, "Constructing the Dark Continent: Metaphor as Geographic Representation," *Geografiska Annaler,* 74 (1992): 105–115.

2 Ibid.

3 D.S. Johnson, "Constructing the Periphery in Modern Global Politics," in *The International Political Economy*, eds. C. Murphy and R. Tooze (Boulder, CO: Lynne Rienner Publishers, 1991), 156.

4 Ibid., 154.

5 Immanuel Kant, "On the Different Races of Man," in *Race and the Enlightenment: A Reader*, ed. Emmanuel Chukwudi Eze (Oxford, UK: Blackwell, 2001), 40.

6 Ibid., 48.

7 Ibid., 49.

8 D.A. Masolo, *African Philosophy in Search of Identity* (Bloomington: Indiana University Press, 1994), 4.

9 G.W.F. Hegel, *Lectures on the Philosophy of World History* (Cambridge, UK: Cambridge University Press, [1975] 1989).

10 Masolo, *African Philosophy*, 4.

11 Dorothy Hammond and Alta Jablow, *The Africa That Never Was* (Prospect Heights, IL: Waveland Press, 1992), 124.

12 Joseph Conrad, *Heart of Darkness* (Boston: Bedford Books, [1902] 1996); Somerset Maugham, "The Explorer," in *The Works of Somerset Maugham: Nine Novels in One Volume* (Houston, TX: Halcyon Press Ltd.; [1908] 2009); Laurens Van der Post, *The Dark Eye in Africa* (New York: Morrow, 1955); Joyce Cary, *Mister Johnson* (New York: Harper, 1951); Graham Greene, *The Heart of the Matter* (New York: Viking Press, 1948).

13 Hammond and Jablow, *The Africa That Never Was*, 132.

14 Errol Henderson, *Afrocentrism and World Politics: Toward a New Paradigm* (Westport, CT: Praeger, 1995), 31.

15 Ibid., 39.

16 Hammond and Jablow, *The Africa That Never Was*, 16.

17 Henderson, *Afrocentrism*, 29.

18 *Encyclopaedia Britannica*, 3rd Edition (Edinburg: A. Bell and C. Macfarquhar, 1798).

19 Paul Gordon Lauren, *Power and Prejudice: The Politics and Diplomacy of Racial Discrimination* (Boulder: Westview Press, 1998). 22.

20 Jarosz, "Constructing the Dark Continent, 106.

21 Hammond and Jablow, *The Africa That Never Was*, 124; Jarosz, "Constructing the dark continent," 106.

22 Hammond and Jablow, *The Africa That Never Was*, 8.

23 Ibid., 13.

24 Mir Zohair Husain, *Global Islamic Politics* (New York, Boston: Longman, 2003), 307.

25 Ibid., 311.

26 Robert Cox, "Social forces, states, and world orders: Beyond international relations theory," in *Approaches to World Order*, eds. Robert Cox and Timothy Sinclair (New York: Cambridge University Press, 1996), 87.

27 Steve Smith, "Reflectivist and constructivist approaches to international theory," in *The Globalization of World Politics: An Introduction to International Relations*, eds. John Baylis and Steve Smith, eds. (Oxford, UK: Oxford University Press, 2001), 224–249.

28 Cox, "Social forces," 87.

29 Smith, "Reflectivist and Constructivist Approaches," 235.

30 Ibid., 240.

31 Husain, *Global Islamic Politics*, 304.

32 George Alagiah, "New light on the dark continent," *The Guardian* (London), 3 May 1999, Media Section 4–5; and see Alex Thomson. *An Introduction to African Politics* (London and New York: Routledge, 2010), 2.

33 *The devil came on horseback,* Documentary directed by Annie Sundberg and Ricki Stern, 2007. Also, see Brian Steidle and Gretchen Steidle Wallace, *The devil came on horseback: Bearing witness to the genocide in Darfur* (New York: Public Affairs, 2007).

34 Howard French, "The hope of Africa, beyond war and disaster there is plenty," *The Crisis* (December 2004), 12–14.

35 Steven Radelet, "Success stories from 'Emerging Africa,' *Journal of Democracy* 21:4 (October 2010): 87–102.

36 Ellen Johnson Sirleaf, "Introduction" in Steven Radelet, *Emerging Africa: How 17 Countries are Leading the Way* (Washington DC: Center for Global Development, 2010).

37 Keith Richburg, *Out of America: A Black Man Confronts Africa* (New York: Basic Books, 1997).

38 Jeff Popke, "The politics of the mirror: On geography and Afro-Pessimism,"*African Geographical Review* (2001), and reprinted in *Taking Sides: Clashing Views on Controversial African Issues*, ed. W. Mosley (Guilford, CT: McGraw Hill/ Duskin, 2004), 10.

39 George Ayittey, *Africa in Chaos* (New York: St. Martin's Press, 1998).

40 Jeffrey Sachs and Andrew Warner, "Sources of slow growth in African economies," *Journal of African Economies* 6:3 (1997), 335–376.

41 French, "The Hope of Africa," 13.

42 Popke, "The Politics of the Mirror," 11.

43 French, "The Hope of Africa," 14.

44 Ibid., 14.

45 Ibid.

46 Bernard Makhosezwe Magubane, *The Ties that Bind: African American Consciousness of Africa* (Trenton: Africa World Press, 1989), 15.

47 BBC News, "UN condemns DR Congo cannibalism," last modified January 15, 2003 http://news.bbc.co.uk/2/hi/africa/2661365.stm.

48 David F. Salisbury, "Brief history of cannibal controversies," *Exploration,* last modified August 15, 2001, http://exploration.vanderbilt.edu/news/news_cannibalism_pt2.htm.

49 William Rushing, *The AIDS Epidemic: Social Dimensions of an Infectious Disease* (Boulder, CO: Westview Press, 1995).

50 Joseph Oppong and Ezekiel Kalipeni, "A cross-cultural perspective on AIDS in Africa: A response to Rushing, in *Taking Sides: Clashing Views on Controversial African Iissues*, ed. William Mosley (Guilford, CT: McGraw-Hill/ Dushkin, 2004), 255.

51 Ibid.

52 William Mosley, "Interpreting African Issues: Commentators, scholars, and policymakers," in *Taking Sides: Clashing Views on Controversial African Issues* (Guilford, CT: McGraw-Hill/ Duskin, 2004), xiii–xxi.

53 Ibid., xiv.

54 Ibid.

REVIEW QUESTIONS

1. What are the prevailing images of Africa and Africans in contemporary Western mass media? What similarities do these current images share with images of Africa during the colonial era?
2. According to the social constructivist framework applied in this essay, how are images of the African "Other" created and sustained? Why is it difficult for westerners to resist stereotypical images and perceptions of Africa and Africans?
3. What is the relationship between the concrete realities of life in Africa and the images of Africa that are promoted in Western mass media?
4. Are constructions of Africans unique and/or comparable to other constructions of the "Other" in the Middle East and Latin America?
5. In what ways are women/gender constructed? Provide a comparative analytical survey that highlights both images of similarities and differences.

Writing Prompt

Instead of seeing Africa as the "economic basket case" of the world, what would a more nuanced picture or description of Africans look like? Cite some examples from recent current events and developments in the region that support your position.

CHAPTER 4

How We Learn

Curtis Keim

In the 1970s, scholars of Africa realized that American high school textbooks were filled with stereotypes about Africa. With the coming of independence for African countries in the 1960s and with the American civil rights movement, the most glaring myths had disappeared. But less obvious myths persisted. In a 1978 study, *Africa in Social Studies Textbooks*, Astair Zekiros and Marylee Wiley detailed the extent to which our public schools were perpetuating myths and inaccuracies about Africa. They noted that most textbooks were written by "'armchair' authors who rely on weak sources for their own information." Thus, no matter what the textbook authors were discussing, they tended to make Africans look like the Africa they imagined rather than the one that existed.[1] Fortunately, several decades later our textbooks are much better.

On the other hand, schools have only a modest influence on how we think about Africa. Despite improved texts, by the time students get to college, most still have outdated ideas about the continent. Even college graduates may not have corrected their misconceptions of Africa. In a 1996 study of preservice social studies teachers, 82 percent thought there were tigers in Africa, 94 percent believed wild animals were common everywhere on the continent, 74 percent understood most Africans to be illiterate, and 93 percent were convinced that more kinds of diseases exist in Africa than in Asia and South America. Respondents commonly used stereotypical "African words" such as *tribe* (90 percent), *primitive* (69 percent), *cannibals* (60 percent), and *savages* (60 percent). Modern Africa was largely misunderstood.

A 2007 survey asked American college students studying in several African countries to describe their attitudes toward Africa before and during their time there. When asked what they had *expected* to find in Africa, they provided words much like the ones described in Chapter 1, especially *poor, dangerous, hot, underdeveloped, violent, tribal,* and *spiritual*. When they described how they felt *after* spending time in Africa, they emphasized words such as *beautiful, diverse, friendly, culture misunderstood, developing, changing,* and *vibrant*. Words such as *dangerous* and *underdeveloped* did not disappear entirely, but overall the students' perceptions were significantly more positive.[2]

Both teachers and students are bombarded with mistaken images of Africa in our everyday culture, so it is not surprising that they often mistake Africa for what it is not. Correcting these errors is not a losing battle, but it *is* an up-hill one. If readers of textbooks and teachers of classes are wearing tinted glasses, even the most accurate texts will appear to be the same color as the glasses. What is the tint of these glasses? "Americana," the hue of our cultural heritage. Thus, to know how Americans learn about Africa, we must look at the more general culture in which our glasses get manufactured.

TELEVISION CULTURE

One way to study how we learn about Africa is to examine *popular culture,* the ordinary information we get from television, magazines, movies, novels, and other common sources. This approach leads us first to television because it is our most pervasive everyday source of ideas about practically everything. In sheer numbers of programs, Africa is actually better represented on television than many other areas of the world. Regrettably, however, the shows do not provide a very accurate view of Africa, in part because of the large number of nature programs. This is actually an improvement over television a decade ago when the nature shows were joined by cartoons that featured Africa, such as *George of the Jungle, Johnny Quest,* and frequent reruns of *Mickey Mouse* and *Pop-eye* episodes made in the 1940s and 1950s. Most of the cartoon images of Africa were stereotyped presentations of ferocious large animals, lost treasure protected by evil genies and geniuses, and hungry cannibals. Fortunately, after about 2000 these cartoons mostly disappeared and were replaced by action cartoons that rarely use Africa as a setting.

Today's nature shows still tend to portray Africa as a place filled with wild animals, park rangers, and naturalists who battle against poachers and encroaching agriculture. By featuring carnivores, the programs also use Africa to emphasize "survival of the fittest" motifs. Yet most Africans never see wild animals because they live in towns or in parts of the continent where the human population is dense. Furthermore, the relationships in nature are vastly more complex than those symbolized by the few large animals that nature programs favor.

As stations on cable and satellite television have multiplied, so have programs on African *people.* The number of programs is not great, but from time to time the Learning Channel, the Discovery Channel, the History Channel, Black Entertainment Television, the Africa Channel, and other stations show Africa-related ethnographies and documentaries. For example, I recently watched an excellent show on ABC about the Abayudaya Jews of rural Uganda and a PBS *Nova* episode on how termites affect a village in northern Cameroon. What is still lacking, however, is a serious understanding of how people currently live in Africa. Today, 40 percent of Africans live in cities, and most rural Africans are deeply connected to cities in one way or another. Why, then, do shows about African culture rarely show a city scene, middle-class Africans, a paved road, or a farmer producing a crop that will be sold in a town or eventually reach us? One reason is that urban documentaries are more difficult to film than those about life in rural areas. Most African elites live in cities and don't like reporters and filmmakers prying into their affairs.

Perhaps a more significant reason for television's preference for rural over urban Africa is our ongoing romance with the exotic. We consider nature and the life of people with less contact with modern cultures more interesting and more enlightening than studies of everyday modern African life. Thus, despite greater television access to Africa as a result of the cable revolution, the televised image of Africa remains drastically incomplete. This is not to say that no good documentaries have been made on African urban life. For example, British directors Kim Longinotto and Florence Ayisi have made *Sisters in Law,* the powerful story of Beatrice Ncuba and Vera Ngassa, a judge and a state prosecutor, in the town of Kumba, Cameroon. This film, aired on PBS's *Independent Lens,* presents a positive, complex picture of the lives of contemporary urban women. But such films are rare.

If we can't find a whole picture of Africa on most television shows, we should be able to turn to television news to find out about contemporary Africa. Yet here the picture is even bleaker. What usually prompts the infrequent appearances of Africa in the news or in news documentaries is a war, coup, drought, famine, flood, epidemic, or accident. Such events certainly occur, but they are not the essence of Africa or of any other part of the world. To be fair, despite the problems, our reporters are providing more context for such news events than ever before. Cable News Network (CNN), for example, occasionally runs stories produced by African reporters. And television coverage of the transition to majority rule in South Africa included a great deal about the history and life of South Africans. Since that time, however, South Africa has almost disappeared from the news except for occasional reports of trouble.

Of course, charges that news reportage is biased are common for all areas of the world including American cities. Defenders of television news say that reporters have too little time to provide background and that Americans don't want to watch it anyway. Increasingly, news programs border on entertainment. We want our emotions aroused, but not so much that we actually might feel compelled to think deeply or take some kind of action. Moreover, news from Africa is expensive. If all this is true, the point here should be that we learn what we want to learn and that we like our picture of Africans the way it is now.

THE PRINT MEDIA

Newspapers provide about the same coverage of Africa as television news does and for the same reasons. Unless you subscribe to a world-class paper such as the *New York Times,* the *Christian Science Monitor,* or the *Washington Post,* you are likely to find no more than a couple of column inches of space devoted to Africa *per week.* And the stories tend to be of two kinds, "trouble in Africa" and "curiosities from Africa." The "trouble in Africa" reporting usually follows a pattern. At any given time, only a handful of American reporters cover Africa south of the Sahara, a region containing a population more than twice as large as that of the United States. These reporters either are based in one of the big cities, such as Johannesburg (South Africa), Nairobi (Kenya), or perhaps Abidjan (Côte d'Ivoire), or are visiting these cities. They report on local events, and, if trouble arises in a neighboring country, they fly in, get the story, and fly out, or they collect what information they can from where they are. News about Congo, Nigeria, or Zimbabwe might be broadcast from Abidjan. It sounds authentic because it comes from Africa, but it might as well be from the United States, which has equally good or better communications with most African cities. When there is a big story, reporters flock to it, stay for a while, then leave. And because reporters rarely speak local languages or have well-developed local contacts, the result is shallow reporting. In many cases, we hear nothing from a country for months or years, and then it appears in the news once or even every day for a couple of weeks before disappearing until trouble occurs again.

Charlayne Hunter-Gault—a longtime observer of Africa, reporter for the *New York Times,* correspondent for PBS, and now Special Africa Correspondent for National Public Radio—makes the point well in her book *New News Out of Africa.* She writes that

> the perception throughout Africa is that foreign media are only interested in stories that fit the old journalistic maxim "If it bleeds, it leads." Much of the shallow coverage of death, disaster, disease, and despair for which foreign media treatments of Africa are criticized derives from what is called "parachute journalism"—dropping in for a brief look at a situation, then flying back out without taking the time to delve deeply into the background or put a story in context.[3]

If we try to put a positive spin on reporting about "trouble in Africa," we might concede that our reporting is about the best we can hope for, considering the difficult conditions under which reporters must work. We are badly served, however, because our news is superficial, sensationalist, and infrequent.

In some cases, it is also clearly biased. In a study of media coverage of the civil war in Angola, for example, Elaine Windrich found that reporters tended to accept uncritically the US government position concerning our ally Jonas Savimbi. In the context of the Cold War, this was considered acceptable, but the American public was clearly duped. Savimbi was actually a tyrant and a liar, and we eventually had to drop him in favor of his enemies. Everyone, especially Angolans, would have been better served had reporting been more thorough and fair.

Ironically, bias in media coverage can also be found in the desire of some reporters to treat Africa well. Ugandan journalist Charles Onyango-Obbo observes that in the 1990s younger liberal Western journalists began reporting on what they termed a "new breed" of African rulers who they supposed would bring democracy, honesty, and development to African governments and economies. In producing such reports, the journalists glossed over the undemocratic and dishonest features of the new regimes, thus allowing the new rulers to believe that the West would look the other way if they acted badly. "Africa, the continent," Onyango-Obbo concludes,

> is a collection of nations that are pretty much like others elsewhere in the world, struggling with successes and with failures, and there should be no special type of journalism reserved for its coverage. The patronizing reporting one witnesses today is as bad as the condescending work of the past. What the African continent needs is good journalism, one that tells the stories as they are reported and observed. What has happened to coverage of Africa in the Western media today offers the latest proof that there is no alternative to this proven approach.[4]

Items also appear regularly in newspapers that can be characterized as "curiosities from Africa." Weeks go by in my local paper without any substantial news from Africa, and then the paper (not a bad paper, actually) includes a front-page story about "newest version of Nigeria-based rip-off targets dog lovers," a scam luring people to send money to buy or rescue purebred puppies that don't exist.[5] Is this news about Africa? Yes, Is it interesting? Kind of. Does it give us perspective on what is happening in Africa? Not much. Is it useful? Somewhat. Is it the most important news from Africa? Not at all. Once again, however, we should remind ourselves that there has been progress. In this case, the story about puppies was not about curiosities of African village life, but about Africans living in cities with everyday access to modern tools such as the Internet.

After television and newspapers, we can examine popular magazines. We should do better here if only because our magazines offer more space to devote to pondering what is going on in the world. Indeed, journals such as the *New Yorker,* the *Atlantic Monthly, Current History, Discover, Vanity Fair,* and the *World and I* have published thoughtful, unbiased articles about Africa in the last few years. Once again, progress. Yet the number of "trouble in Africa" articles outweighs the number of articles that help us to see Africans as real people attempting to solve their problems in rational ways, even if the solutions might be different from the ones we would choose.

Most Americans read less sophisticated fare as a daily diet. In more popular magazines, most articles about Africa are of the "African safari" genre. A few wild animals, a few natives, a camp, a curio market, a little art, a gourmet meal, and you're home. For example, *SmartMoney* advertises that "South Africa has it all: gorgeous scenery, fascinating cultures, rhino-filled game reserves—and, best of all, a weak [currency]." In *Outside,* a blurb for an article quotes a safari brochure as promising "unfiltered Africa, an extremely rare, hard-core, expeditionary safari in the oldest style." In also notes that when the author of the article arrived in Zimbabwe, he experienced "fabled wildlife, and mutiny on the veld." Yet other themes include "celebrity goes to Africa," "curious customs." and "African agony." These views of Africa not only evoke stereotypes we already hold but reinforce them as well.

National Geographic

One very popular magazine, *National Geographic*—with an astounding global circulation of nearly eight million—is America's picture window on the world. What are we likely to see through this window? The editorial policy of the magazine since its early days has been to avoid controversy and print "only what is of a kindly nature . . . about any country or people."[6] That policy, still followed a century later, directs the organization toward wild animals and ethnography and away from the social, political, and economic conditions in which Africans live. Countries such as Congo (Kinshasa) and Malawi were featured in the 1970s and 1980s, but in the 1990s most African countries became unsuitable for *National Geographic*. As conditions worsened in Africa, it was increasingly difficult to be kind to modern Africa, at least from the American perspective, and the frequency of *National Geographic* articles dealing with individual African countries declined correspondingly. There are 1990s articles set in Congo and Malawi, but they treat Congo River travel and Lake Malawi water life, much safer topics than the countries themselves.

A 1996 article about Eritrea demonstrates the point: Eritrea could be featured because, as a brand-new country, it was considered full of hope. Likewise, the magazine's 1993 treatment of the life of blacks in South Africa came long after the world had chosen sides on the issue, which made the subject safe and, to my eye, exploited the situation by printing gripping photographs. This is an example of what has been termed "development pornography." We are asked only to *look* at others' misery, not do anything about it or even understand it.

In the 1990s and after, *National Geographic* continued to run articles on Africa, but they tended to feature animals. The exceptions tend to be "trouble in Africa" articles that, for example, warn against environmental deterioration, describe problems with oil extraction, and decry violence. Although often useful, these articles, even taken as a whole, offer a distorted picture of Africa. A 1997 article on Central Africa provides a brief but generally accurate analysis of the history of the civil wars in Rwanda and Burundi. Yet most readers would be unable to decipher the implications of the article's points because the author provides little background on post-independence international influence and competition in Africa. A 2003 article on national parks in Gabon rightly praises Gabon's conservation efforts but is entitled "Saving Africa's Eden," thus stereotyping Africa's environment as both idyllic and prehistoric. (Also see Chapter 4.) "Curse of the Black Gold," a 2007 piece, deals with the problems of the oil industry in the Niger Delta and appears to take the side of Africans by pointing to the failure of aid programs and the neglect of international companies such as Shell. However, the article ends on a pessimistic note, giving no suggestions for action and claiming that there are "no answers in sight."[7] This statement effectively tells the reader not to look for answers and not to act, reaffirming the stereotype of Africa as a hopeless place.

In a 2004 article on modern Johannesburg, "City of Hope and Fear," the author focuses on fear and violence in this South African city.[8] The article stands out because only a year later the magazine's sister publication, *National Geographic Traveler,* included an article on Johannesburg, "Brash and Brilliant," that celebrates "Jo'burg" as a tourist destination.[9] Although portions of South Africa do have high rates of violent crime, as do portions of the United States, journalist Charlayne Hunter-Gault, quoted earlier, chastises the media for focusing on the violence of Johannesburg:

> Many people say that they want to visit Africa for the adventure, for some of the world's greatest natural wonders, and because it is the last best place to see animals not in a zoo. Many tell me they are making plans to go there, especially to South Africa, whose struggle against apartheid engaged so many of them. Then, in the next breath, they express concern about the reports of crime they've heard. One caller shared with me the report his son came back with that "everyone" in South Africa carries a gun, which was news to me, a Johannesburg resident of almost ten years.[10]

National Geographic, our window on the world, is rarely a place to get a balanced picture of Africa. This magazine calls itself scientific, yet avoids controversy, thriving on beautiful photography and safe topics. It would have to take such an approach to be so widely accepted in the United States and indeed in the world. Is this publication then useless? No, beauty and safety have their places, and, like our other media, *National Geographic* is improving. Forty years ago *National Geographic* would not have published on topics such as environmental degradation and oil extraction, as it does today. But even if the magazine doesn't actively exploit, it does reinforce our stereotypes and confuse us by asserting that beauty, safety, and bland analysis are somehow equal to science and geography.

MOVIES

Movies, too, teach us our African stereotypes. Whether oldies such as *The African Queen, Mogambo,* and *Tarzan the Ape Man,* or newer pictures such as *The Constant Gardener* and *The Last King of Scotland,* there are dozens of such "African" feature films, and each tells a story that seems to be about Africa but in which Africa only provides an exotic background. One funny movie, *The Gods Must Be Crazy,* a South African shoestring production that has become popular as a video and DVD release, is an exception because of its many scenes featuring African actors. However, it is full of South African white stereotypes of hunter-gatherers, Bantu villagers, Cuban revolutionaries, African dictators, and white damsels in distress—pure entertainment. There is nothing wrong with entertainment, of course, except that this is where we pick up our ideas about Africa. One of my students informed me that in high school he was tested on the content of *The Gods Must Be Crazy,* which his teacher had considered an authoritative source on African life. Africa has appeared more recently in such feature films as *Blood Diamond, Tears of the Sun,* and *Lord of War.* However, as their titles suggest, these movies perpetuate myths of Africa as remote, exotic, and full of violence and disease. All three films echo Leonardo DiCaprio's line in *Blood Diamond*: "God left this place a longtime ago."

Tears of the Sun, an action film, is an example of how difficult it is to portray *Africa* as savage while portraying *Africans* as civilized. The premise of the film is that the Navy SEAL commando played by Bruce Willis delves into war-torn Nigeria to extract an American doctor from the cross fire—the war being flippantly explained in terms of "tribal hatred," as if that phrase is enough to encompass the whole array of causes for war and to silence any hopes of remediation. However, despite its stereotypical basis, the film treats its African characters with relative dignity. African refugees in *Tears of the Sun* arm and defend themselves, and two of them have personalities that are as well developed as those of the white characters. Thus the film's image of Africans as rational, functional human beings conflicts with its overall message that African wars are caused by ancient, "tribal" rivalries and cannot be ended by rational means.

Lord of War tells the story of an international arms dealer and features Africa only in its second half. The movie represents Africa as a heart of darkness, the geographic equivalent of the Nicholas Cage character's descent into human depravity in the arms trade. Dialogue from the movie reinforces this idea: the main (white) character refers to the outskirts of Monrovia as "the edge of hell." Individual characters are also shallow: African men are all members of a corrupt and licentious governing elite, and the women are hypersexual and mute. The film gives the sense that Africa is a place even a hardened international arms dealer finds unsettling. Gratuitous images of violence, such as a dead man lying unattended in the street beside a hotel, reinforce this image.

Lord of War also evokes African remoteness. In one scene the central character is forced to make an emergency landing and unload his cargo of AK-47s before an Interpol agent catches him. He does so by offering the contents of his plane to a crowd of poor villagers, who strip the plane not only of its contents but of its structure as well, dismantling it for scrap materials.

Blood Diamond, the most offensive of the three films, damages the image both of the continent and of the individual African. Solomon, the film's only significant African character, is hollow, unintelligent, and aggressively instinctual. During a scene in which he and the character played by Leonardo DiCaprio are hiding from passing trucks of militants, Solomon thinks he spots his missing son and cries out, alerting the enemy to their presence. He does not seem to realize his mistake even the following day, after a sharp rebuke from DiCaprio. Later, in another chaotic fighting scene (instigated once again by an act of stupidity), in which everyone is using firearms, Solomon picks up a shovel to bash in the head of the man who kidnapped his son.

In *Blood Diamond*, the whites are always the ones scheming, plotting, dealing, and above all, *thinking*. The film's Africans never so much as protest at the injustices of their society, let alone fight back. Solomon, apparently motivated by little more than animal instinct to protect his son, is unable to think through his actions. Dialogue also makes ample use of the abbreviation TIA (for "This is Africa") to dismiss anything violent or distressing that occurs, implying that in Africa, misery is the only way of life.

While it is no longer acceptable to create a film set in Africa that does not feature Africans or that makes overtly racist statements without encasing them in the dialogue of unsavory characters, Hollywood stereotyping of Africa has become veiled rather than growing less prevalent. Fortunately, several contemporary films from international producers offer more enlightened perspectives. *The Constant Gardener*, *The Last King of Scotland*, and *Hotel Rwanda* are particularly good, though each has its problems. These problems are small, however, compared to those of films produced entirely by Americans.

AMUSEMENT PARKS

Busch Gardens Africa in Tampa, Florida, is another prime example of how we learn about Africa and also how this learning process is changing. In the 1970s the park was called Busch Gardens: The Dark Continent. At that time, a poster advertising the park depicted a white family in an African environment, the husband in a safari suit and pith helmet holding a chimpanzee and pointing to some off-poster sight, and the wife looking on passively. His children also following his gaze, from the back of an elephant. An Arab or Swahili guide in flowing robes looks on, while three barely visible black African men dressed in loincloths carry the family's luggage.

Twenty years later, this racist and sexist poster is no longer used. As a result of protests, Busch Gardens has tried to change its "Dark Continent" image. Now the park focuses instead on neutral images: the large animal park, replicas of African houses, African-made tourist art, and rides that have mildly African themes. Nostalgia for nineteenth-century stereotypes persists, however, and thus there are endless inconsistencies. The idea of Ubanga Banga Bumper Cars in the section called The Congo would be hilarious except for the underlying message this stereotypical "African" name sends about Africa. It is strange to think of the Dolphin Theater and Festhaus restaurant being in Timbuktu, a town on the southern edge of the Sahara Desert. The park's Stanleyville area is named after the violent white conqueror of the Congo River, Henry Morton Stanley, and the colonial town that bore his name. Modern Congolese found the name odious enough to change it to Kisangani. And the real Kisangani doesn't have warthogs, orangutans, or a barbecue smokehouse. The conflicts with reality go on and on, but to anyone who knows little about Africa, these inconsistencies aren't readily apparent.

Busch Gardens claims to offer a chance to "immerse yourself in the culture of the African continent as you experience its majestic wildlife." How is observing wildlife equal to participation in anyone's culture? Moreover, how does Busch Gardens' silly version of African culture represent the complexity of African realities? Instead, Busch Gardens Africa teaches Americans damaging stereotypes about Africa. Perhaps in another twenty years we will look back at this version of Busch Gardens as a misguided and misinformed (if not racist) approach to both Africa and entertainment.

Another amusement pack, Disney World in Orlando, has become a global pilgrimage destination. When I visited, I was reminded of Africa at several turns (literally) as I took the Jungle River Cruise in boats named after real rivers and places in the Congo rain forest (not jungle): Bomokandi Bertha, Wamba Wanda, and so on. It was all fun and a bit hokey, of course, and the site's designers included elephants and a pygmy war camp. But pygmies don't have war camps—they are more like conservationists than soldiers—and Africa is certainly more than elephants, jungles, and riverboats.

The boat trip guides have a rollicking time telling jokes during the trip. For example:

On the left, a friendly group of native traders. Ukka Mucka Lucka . . . Ubonga Swahili Ungawa . . . Wagga Kuna Nui Ka. . . . It's a good thing I speak their language. [*Turns to guest*] They want to trade their coconurs for your [*wife/child/husband*]. . . . I think we should hold out for at least four.

This is my good friend Sam, who runs the Cannibal Cafe. The last time I talked to Sam was at his cafe. I told him that I didn't like his brother very much. He told me, "Next time, have the salad."[11]

These couldn't be funny if our culture hadn't put Dark Continent images in our heads before the trip.

In 1998 Disney expanded its treatment of Africa with Animal Kingdom, an animal theme park located near Disney World. The African Savannah section of the park is set up to give visitors the sense that they are in a genuinely natural environment. There are, for example, no fences between the visitors and the animals. The illusion of real wilderness is made possible by hidden moats around the predators that give the impression that carnivores and herbivores are living in the same space. They are not, of course, because it would be too costly to allow lions to eat gazelles. Besides, viewing real predatory activity would upset most tourists.

But to merely experience nature is not considered entertaining enough. As one brochure puts it, "The imagination of Disney is going to take you on a journey into the masteries, marvels and thrills of the ever-unfolding story of animals." Indeed, Disney advertises that the park tells the story of *all* animals, "real, imaginary and extinct."[12]

Participants in the Kilimanjaro Safari, which visits a recreated African savanna, buy tickets from a window in a building that looks like a decayed colonial-era outpost. Conquest nostalgia is sold here. And visitors are escorted in buses outfitted to give the feeling of a "real" safari. Further, as visitors pass certain points, underground sensors trigger events in the fashion of similar tours at Disney World and Disneyland. This is wild nature on demand. And there is a story line: you are hot on the trail of a group of poachers.

In Disney's topsy-turvy world, fictional animals compete with real ones, entertainment competes with understanding, and corporate profits compete with what is termed scientific research. Captivity promotes wildness, we're told, while African complexity is further reduced to stereotypes. And the hunt for poachers models Disney's other enterprises, which from their founding in the 1950s have epitomized the Western dream of the conquest and management of nature through science and technology.

San Diego Zoo's Wild Animal Park offers the same conquest nostalgia as the parks described above. In a children's storytelling arena, a live "Dr. Livingston" entertains visitors in the evening. The park's "Journey into Africa" tour claims to represent an authentic Africa. The website reads, "As you approach your tour vehicle, you start getting a sense of this place called Africa. . . . Lift-up flaps, maps, and cultural artifacts establish a 'sense of place.'" What is this sense of place? It can hardly be a sense of the whole, complex continent of Africa. Rather, it is a canned production designed to echo the safari mythology of our own culture.

The zoo clearly feels it needs to transform seeing African animals into an African adventure, and what better way to do that than to evoke African stereotypes that the visitor can connect with? Journey into Africa includes "the heart of Africa" (a colonial phrase), which turns out to be "its amazing diversity of species." You enter the "Nairobi Village" through a portal that simulates "the ceremonial chamber of a Ugandan king," and you visit the "Mombasa Lagoon," modeled on a "Congo fishing village." The allusions to an Africa filled with villagers, tribes, nonmodern political organizations, and animals go on and on.

A more positive example is Lowry Park Zoo in Tampa, Florida. A smaller park, Lowry does not attempt to compete with the entertainment and advertising strategies of nearby Busch Gardens and Animal Kingdom. It features an "Ituri Forest" region, designed to mimic the tropical rain forest habitat in the northern Congo River

Basin. Concerned only with animals, the zoo makes no pretensions of showing African culture to its visitors, nor does it make overtly stereotypical statements about Africa.

CELEBRITIES

Is it possible that celebrity attention to Africa's problems could actually reinforce our stereotypes about the continent? This generation's celebrity attention to Africa began in earnest in 1985, when stars Bob Geldof, Bobby Shriver, and others organized the first LiveAid concert, an international event mounted with the intention of raising funds to fight AIDS and poverty in Africa. Since then, additional concerts and a steady stream of celebrity visitors (among them Bono, Mia Farrow, Angelina Jolie, Brad Pitt, Madonna, Guy Ritchie, Jessica Lange, Oprah Winfrey, and Simon Cowell) have helped call attention to many African issues. Some of these celebrities have been criticized in the media for seeking publicity at Africa's expense. And Jolie and Pitt were accused of "celebrity colonialism" for effectively using the government of Namibia to provide privacy and security so they could have a special birthing experience in what she called "the cradle of human kind." Narcissism is certainly alive and well.

Nigerian novelist Uzodinma Iweala says that while Africans appreciate help, the continent does not need to be saved. Celebrities and others use Africa not only to call attention to themselves but also as a prop in their fantasy worlds:

> My mood is dampened every time I attend a benefit whose host runs through a litany of African disasters before presenting a (usually) wealthy, white person, who often proceeds to list the things he or she has done for the poor, starving Africans. Every time a well-meaning college student speaks of villagers dancing because they were so grateful for her help, I cringe. Every time a Hollywood director shoots a film about Africa that features a Western protagonist, I shake my head—because Africans, real people though we may be, are used as props in the West's fantasy of itself. And not only do such depictions tend to ignore the West's prominent role in creating many of the unfortunate situations on the continent, they also ignore the incredible work Africans have done and continue to do to fix those problems.

Many have doubted the sincerity of celebrity efforts to help Africa, but it might be more useful to examine the effect of these efforts rather than their motives. In Chapter 6 I discuss the overall effectiveness of American efforts to help Africa. Our purpose here is to ask whether celebrities teach us stereotypes about Africa. Michael Holman, former editor of the *Financial Times,* a British newspaper, suggests that "celebrity aid" reinforces stereotypes by promoting gift giving rather than deep analysis of African problems. If we continue to see African problems as susceptible to redress only through aid, we will continue to see Africans as helpless and inferior. What message, for example, is sent when celebrities make high-profile adoptions from Africa? That Africa has no future? Holman suggests that celebrities could do the most good for Africa if they would abandon stereotypical help-for-poor-Africans strategies and focus on starting debates about questions that matter. Things might really be different, says Holman, if Madonna, who adopted a child from Malawi, would, say,

> respond to the fact that the diaspora of Africa's educated is swollen by 60,000 a year. This has led to the bizarre, outrageous situation that more doctors who were trained in Malawi are practicing in England's second city of Birmingham than in Malawi itself. If one of Malawi's main exports is health professionals, that is not in itself a bad thing—what is unacceptable is that there is no organised replenishment.

Holman doubts that the celebrities' "armies of advisers and publicists and sponsors" would permit such statements. What do you think? I believe that intelligent entertainment celebrities (that's not necessarily an oxymoron) could help spark much-needed debates and still remain celebrities. For now, celebrities tend to reinforce Dark Continent stereotypes and thus keep us from addressing real issues concerning how the world—the one inhabited by both Africans and Americans—is structured.

OTHER SOURCES

The other places where we learn our ideas about Africa are too numerous to discuss here. How about children's books, place mats in restaurants, Africa-themed resorts, billboards, and computer games? I've seen Africa used in exotic, inaccurate, and sometimes offensive ways in each of these examples.

My impression is that children's authors are ahead of many others in our culture in trying to portray Africa accurately. Nonetheless, there are matters to pay attention to. Yulisa Amadu Maddy, a Sierra Leonean theater artist and director and novelist, has taken an interest in American children's literature related to Africa. He notes that although children's books today intend to capture the positive spirit of Africa, they still contain mistakes that confuse readers and insult Africans. In *The Market Lady and the Mango Tree,* for example, a greedy market lady claims a mango tree that grows in the marketplace as her personal property and refuses to give mangoes to children unless they pay. She buys a Mercedes Benz with her profits and then begins selling her mangoes to a jelly factory at such a high price that the villagers cannot afford them. In the end, the market lady's guilty conscience makes her sell the car and give the mangoes to children free of charge. It is a good story, meant to reinforce community values and favor children, except that it portrays the market lady as a stereotypical rich, power-hungry African elite and the village as responding in helpless, un-African ways. There are no doubt greedy people in Africa, but this shore book—despite its positive intentions and excellent illustrations—gives a distorted picture of reality. Says Maddy, "No one in his or her right mind, no matter how greedy, would claim a mango tree in the marketplace as private property."[13]

Maddy also notes that in Ann Grifalconl's *Flyaway Girl,* east and west are confused; a mask and a food item from West Africa are associated with the Maasai of East Africa. In Paul Geraughty's *The Hunter,* African ivory poachers are blamed for killing elephants when, in fact, Western demand for ivory should also be blamed. Frequently, adds Maddy, stories based on African folktales rely on biased colonial sources that modified the folktales to make Western moral points, not African ones.[14]

Another study of children's literature asks whether books about South Africa give children a realistic picture. Linda Labbo and Sherry Field took a selection of American books to South Africa to ask teachers there what they thought. In general, the teachers were impressed and wished that their own students had access to the materials, but they also found that books about children and African animals or about village life could easily give a mistaken impression of life in South Africa. Most South Africans live in cities, and very few have money to visit game parks or private game farms, practically the only places to find wild animals. The South African teachers also suggested that when American students read about village life, they should read several books so as to begin to understand the variety of South African cultures.

Churches and missionaries also play a role in reinforcing the idea of Africans as primitives. Missionaries returning from Africa often communicate to churches in the West that non-Christian Africans need fundamental change because they are culturally, if not biologically, primitive. Ironically, missionaries themselves are often more respectful of African cultures than parishioners in the United States. Those parishioners who give money for African causes frequently want to feel that they are converting or helping poor, unenlightened savages in the old-fashioned missionary mode. The refrain of a 1998 Christian song entitled "Please Don't Send Me no Africa" encapsulates such an attitude toward the continent:

> Please don't send me to Africa
> I don't think I've got what it takes
> I'm just a man, I'm not a Tarzan
> Don't like lions; gorillas, or snakes
> I'll serve you here in suburbia
> In my comfortable, middle-class life
> But please don't send me out into the bush
> Where the natives are restless at night[15]

This sentiment, "Please don't send me to Africa," appears also in sermons and other church literature to represent a significant sacrifice. But while intended to satirize the faintness of Christian hearts; it does a severe disservice to Africa. Africa is mistaken as a wild, distant place where animals and restless natives abound and discomfort is standard.

And museums? It's remarkable that we continue the nineteenth-century practice of putting animals and "native" peoples in the same museum, the "natural history" museum. In the American Museum of Natural History in New York, the Field Museum in Chicago, the National Museum of Natural History in Washington, D.C., and many others, the implication is that premodern African cultures belonged to the history of nature rather than the history of civilization. Moreover, such treatment implies that animals and Africans can be considered separately from ourselves in our understanding of the world. Aware of these problems, natural history museum curators do what they can to overcome them.

Art museums pose a somewhat different problem. Art curators must help us understand that what we consider art is not a universal category appreciated in the same way by all humans. When we see a display of African art—in which masks and statues are usually overrepresented—we see something entirely different than what most Africans themselves do. I might add that curators in both art and natural history museums are frequently ahead of their advertising departments in teaching us about Africa. Curators are often trained as specialists in African studies. Publicists, by contrast, are trained to attract an audience, so they often play on exotic and stereotypical aspects that reflect public interest in Africa. They are correct in assuming that the public is interested in the exotic. But because museums are also committed to accuracy, exhibits since the 1990s and their advertising have displayed much less stereotyping.

Corporate advertising also uses Africa to sell products. Exxon Mobil, Dow, Snapple, Coca-Cola, Honda, Microsoft, and IBM, for example, have recently produced ads depicting their products in association with Africa. Some of these ads are shown in Chapter 10. Advertisers easily pick up on our stereotypes and use them to convince us to buy. Moreover, they educate us about what our culture already "knows" about Africa.

Once you are aware of the ways we commonly treat Africa, you will soon (and perhaps frequently) see Africa treated stereotypically in everyday life. I hope you will also begin to think about why our stereotypes persist. Few such treatments are conscious attempts to make Africa look bad. Far from it. Despite American racism, or perhaps because of it, we are probably more sensitive to this question than most other people in the world. At least in the public sphere, we make explicit efforts to avoid derogatory allusions to Africa or Africans. Therefore, such unintended stereotypical references are all the more indicative of how we see the world. Clearly, they indicate that our belief in an Africa full of animals, "the bush," and desperate people is so embraced by Americans that we do not even see it as derogatory. The problem, of course, is that such views become self-perpetuating. Even if we want to avoid portraying Africa in stereotypical terms, we are bound to do so because we have few other models of Africa to which we can compare these images.

ENDNOTES

1. Astair Zekiros, with Marylee Wiley, *Africa in Social Studies Text books*, Bulletin no.9550 (Madison: Wisconsin Department of Public Instruction, 1978), 4. An article by Wiley contains most of the same ideas and is easier to locate: "Africa in Social Studies Textbooks", *Social Education* November–December 1982: 492–497,548–552.

2. See, for example, Elisabeth Gaynor Ellis, Anthony Esler, and Burton F. Beers, *World History: Connections to Today, the Modern Era* (Englewood Cliffs, NJ: Prentice-Hall, 2004).

3. Kim Longinotco and codirected by Florence Ayisi, *Sisters in Law* (London: Vixen Films, 2007), 104 minutes, Pidgin with subtitles, film information at www.pbs.org/ independentlens/sistersinlaw/; WLLTV; *Independent Lens* (Allentown-Bethlehem-Easton, PA; broadcast November 27, 2007) available for purchase or rent at www.wmm. com/ filmcatalog/ pages/c645.shtm.

4. Elaine Windrich, "Media Coverage of the Angolan War," *Africa Today* Spring 1992: 89–100.

5. Charles Onyango-Obbo, "Seeking Balance in a Continent Portrayed by Its Extremes," *Nieman Reports* Fall 2004: 6–8.

6. David Colker, "Cuddly Puppy Just a Figment of Seamster's Imagination," Morining *Call* (Allentown, PA), 30 May 2007, A1, A3.

7. James B. Steward, "The Smart Traveler," *SmartMolney* October 1996: 169.

8. Philip Gourevitch, "Wondering Where the Lions Are," *Outside* October 1996: 74. Gourevitch is an informed observer of Africa. The promotion for his article uses stereotypes to hype what is actually a fair critique of the safari experience.

9. Bernard Block, "Romance and High Purpose: *The National Geographic*," *Wilson Library Bulletin* January 1994: 333–337.

10. Robert Caputo, "Zaire River," *National Geographic* November 1990: 5–35; Peter Reinthal. "The Living Jewels of Lake Malawi," *National Geographic* May 1991: 42–51.

11. Tom O'Neill, "Curse of the Black Gold—Hope and Betrayal in the Niger Delta," *National Geographic* May 2007: 88–117.

12. Peter Goodwin, "Johannesburg: City of Hope and Fear," *National Geographic* April 2004: 58–77.

13. Hamilton Wende, "Brash and Brilliant," *National Geographic Traveler* March 2005: S9.

14. Charlayne Hunter-Gault, "Changing the Rules in Africa," OUP Blog, 20 July 2006, http://blog.oup.com/2006/07/changing-the_ru (27 September 2007).

15. Sean Rouse, "Jungle Cruise Jokes," www.csua.berkeley.edu/~yoda/disneyland/jungle.htm (4 October 2007). For more on the Jungle River Cruise, visit http://en.wikipedia.org/wiki/Jungle_Cruise (5 October 2007).

CHAPTER 5

African Indigenous Religion

Patrick C. Nnoromele

When one utters the word, "religion," the unassuming listener in any culture or tradition seems to know what the speaker is trying to convey. However, scholars suggest that the concept of "religion" is quite complex and elusive as to defy any possibility of arriving at any satisfactory definition. In his book, *The Verities of Religious Experience*, William James argued that part of the problem of defining religion comes as a result of the concept being too large for any one definition to contain all of its varying aspects.[1] For we live in a religiously saturated world. Every imaginable culture has a religion of some sort. Therefore, a meaningful definition of such a concept requires at a minimum a reasonable degree of consistency and coherence across cultural lines. In other words, we need a definition that is broad enough to provide us with a coherent understanding of religion by which to measure modern depictions of it. Thus far, it has proven difficult to come up with any definition of religion that is not subject to counter examples.

The other problem in defining *religion* is that, when people commence with the academic study of religion, they find it extremely difficult to leave behind ideas from the respective religions or cultures in which they are raised. A clear example of this is found in Henry Fielding's novel, *Tom Jones*. In this novel, Henry Fielding declares through of one his characters, Thwakum: "When I mention religion, I mean the Christian religion, not only the Christian religion, but the Protestant religion; and not only the Protestant religion, but the Church of England."[2] Thus, religion for Thwakum, as is for many others, becomes the function of the cultural context within which one is raised. This attitude may help to explain why, even though numerous studies have been conducted on African peoples, cultures, and histories, the African worldview of religion is still the least understood in the Western world.

Admittedly, religion is not an African concept. As demonstrated by socio-linguistic studies of Africa, the term is noticeably absent among many ethnic groups in Africa that characteristically practice certain forms of spirituality, beliefs, and rituals often viewed as religious. The absence of the term *religion* in many African languages, and the ambiguous nature of the concept in general, have unfortunately led some scholars to wonder if indigenous Africans can be said to have a religion. Such scholars like Benjamin C. Ray argued that "religion is a late-comer to the scholarly discourse about Africa."[3] According to him, it was not until the late colonial period of the 1950s that some scholars began to use the term, *religion*, to characterize *African Religion* in a positive way.[4] However, the issue is not about when the academic discourse of *religion* came to Africa. Nor is it about whether some African communities have a term for this human exercise called religion. The fact is that religion, like culture, is a human activity. It is difficult to think of a people without it. Africans are a people. They have a culture and are inherently religious.

An analysis of the linguistic root of the *word religion* might help elucidate the concept and our understanding. The term is believed to come from two Latin words, *re* meaning *"again"* and *lig* meaning "join" or "connect."[5] When one combines both words, *re* and *lig,* we have *relig,* which means "to reconnect" or "to join again."

According to Michael Molloy, "If this derivation is correct, then the word *religion* suggests the joining of our natural, human world to the sacred world."[6] In his book, *Religion Without Revelation*, John Huxley, a biologist, puts it this way: "Religion [is] a way of life founded upon the apprehension of the sacredness in existence."[7] With this working definition in mind, one can conclude without fear of self-contradiction that Africans do indeed have and practice what the academic world calls *religion*. This chapter, therefore, encapsulates what is most significant about African Indigenous religion, providing valuable insights on how it compares and/or differs from other dynamic religions, most especially Western Christianity. It also identifies the basic doctrinal tenets of African Indigenous religion and addresses some of its misconceptions. By establishing what is common to major religions of the world, and stressing the existential thrust of African Indigenous religion, its commitment to life now and hereafter, the chapter challenges the marginalization of African Indigenous religion and presents it as a credible religious institution in the world today. It also questions the logic of some Western-trained elites who think that African Indigenous religion needs to conform to the European theological precepts to be credible.

WHAT AFRICAN RELIGION IS NOT

The verities of African religion never change, but the academic perspective of it seems to be in constant flux. This is partly the reason some scholars tend to mischaracterize the tenets of the religion. Hope and Woodward succinctly state, "no religions have been more confused in the minds of Western people than the religions of Africa."[8] What then is the African Indigenous religion? In order to address this question, it seems more appropriate to begin with a discussion of what African Indigenous religion is not.

A number of existing literature on African religion display several misconceptions about the religion. Some of these misconceptions have their foundation on anthropological studies carried out by two European scholars, Edward B. Tylor and Herbert Spencer during the nineteenth century. In his book, *Primitive Culture*, Tylor erroneously argued that religion originated from the perception of "primitive" peoples who thought that there were impalpable realities, a life force called spirit or soul in every living organism, such as trees, animals, humans, and so on. This view was popularized by his immediate disciples, and Tylor gave it the name Animism—derived from the Latin word, *anima*, meaning "soul." Drawing from Tylor's conclusion, Margaret Trowel, writing on the religion of the African, expressed it in these words: "Every tree or stone, every snake or wild beast, may contain some spirit or other ancestor returning to live again in whom they choose."[9] This type of anthropological approach to the study of African Indigenous religion has led many people in the Western world to misperceive and mislabel African religion as Animism.

Animism, which is the attribution of a measure of conscious life to a variety of entities, is a *part* of the doctrine of African indigenous religious systems, but it does not constitute the whole religion. In African religion, there is a general recognition that the cosmos contains infinite number of spirits. These spirits are believed to be impalpable and invisible to human eyes. However, they are the source of life in anything they inhabit. Thus, if a tree is alive, it is because it is en-souled by the spirit. Life, therefore, is defined as the presence of spirit in a body; while death is the absence or departure of the spirit from the body. Animism, no doubt, is part and parcel of African Indigenous religion. But Animism does not wholly define African Indigenous religion.

African religion is also wrongly characterized as *Ancestor Worship or Veneration*. Africans do not worship their ancestors, but they do show them respect. Often, this makes itself manifest in certain forms of rituals or practices that are incorrectly perceived by non-practitioners of the religion as Ancestor Worship. Community, in the African worldview is made up of two main groups, the *Living-human* and the *Living-dead*. When any human dies, he or she moves to a different taxonomy of the community, namely the *Living-dead*. However, they are still part of this one unitary whole Africans call community. It is this model of community that Edwin Smith, perhaps, was trying to convey when he said: "The African community is a single, continuing unit, conscious of no distinction . . . between its members still *here* on earth and its members now *there* wherever it may be."[10] Physical death, in African religious perspective, does not mean the annihilation of the *personal self*. Rather, it is a transition into the kingdom of the gods or spirit beings. In other words, the physically deceased person becomes a *spirit*.

As spirit, the individual acquires some special attributes unavailable to corporeal beings in their mortal states. They acquire "enhanced powers associated with their new status."[11] Their power and knowledge far exceed that of ordinary men and women; and, as such, they play significant roles in the life of their communities. They take active interests in the well-being of their living family members as well as the society as a whole. These ancestors are believed to communicate their wishes to the living in varying ways, such as in dreams or through diviners. They are also believed to possess the power to bless and to inflict pain or even death upon any human member of the community as the ultimate punishment for certain misconducts. Hence, ancestor spirits, as part of the community, are both feared and highly venerated or respected. Their living family members give them gifts in form of offerings and sacrifices. The respect for ancestors evident in African Indigenous religion is common to several Asian religions, like Taoism, Buddhism, and Confucianism. One would be hard pressed to find any academic study of these religions that depicts them as Ancestor Worship. Likewise, African religion is not Ancestor Worship.

African Indigenous religion is often also misconstrued as "paganism." The term "paganism" is actually derived from a Latin word, "Paganus," and was used for a nature-based religion whose followers lived primarily in the countryside.[12] Sometimes, a pagan is also defined as "one who has little or no religion."[13] The fact is that however one looks at the issue, African religion does not fit into either category or definition. While African religion is noted for its reverential attitude toward the natural world, including humans, animals, trees, sun, moon, land, and so on, the whole religion is not nature-based and therefore, cannot be called paganism. The question then is: if African religion is not animism, ancestor worship, or paganism, what then constitutes African Indigenous religion? There may not be any satisfactory response to this vital question. For African Indigenous religion is so complex and syncretistic that it escapes any precise definition or description. However, there are several essential attributes of the religion.

ESSENTIAL TENETS OF AFRICAN INDIGENOUS RELIGION

African Indigenous religion is a faith without a founder. It has no holy books or sacred writings to define acceptable doctrinal standards. It also has no "systematic theology" like some other world religions. However, the African concept of the Divine with all its pragmatic attributes is overwhelmingly evident in the expressive cultural mediums of proverbs, folklores, songs, chants, arts, myths, as well as beliefs and traditions. Even though African religion has no holy book or treatise, the collective principles expressed in their oral traditions are as authentic to Africans as the Bible is to the Christians or the Holy Qur'an to the Muslims. For instance, proverbs, according to the *Encyclopedia of Religion and Ethics,* are "short wise sayings which have come into common use." They are "the wisdom of many and the wit of one; the experience and wisdom of several ages gathered and summed up in one expression."[14] Proverbs are highly cherished among the Africans. The Zulu people say that without proverbs, language would be but a skeleton without flesh or a body without a soul. The Igbos of Nigeria describe proverbs as "vegetables for eating words." The Yorubas view them as "horses for chasing missing words." Africans use proverbs to convey their views of God. African proverbs provide us with significant insights into the people's convictions or ideas of God. Here are some examples of the African view of God expressed in proverbial terms. "The plant protected by God is never hurt by the wind"; "God goes above any shield." These expressions are found among the Banyarwanda groups of Uganda and the Congo.[15] Similar expressions of God in proverbs saturate many other African groups.

In the book, *African studies,* Ernest Gray put together hundreds of parables from the Nyanja people that create further insights to the ubiquitous nature and varying characteristics of the Supreme God and the created deities.[16] Here is another example: "God needs no pointing out to a child." In other words, the reality of God is so obvious that even a child needs no instruction or guidance to affirm its being. In the African theistic view, the world is filled with evidence of the reality of the divinities. It is everywhere just like the wind, as expressed by another proverb of the Nyanja people: "If you would tell God, tell the wind." Scholars recognize that, at times, arriving at the exact meaning of African proverbs may seem problematic. As Emil Torday affirms: "He is a bold man who presumes to be able to distinguish between hard facts and figures of speech. . . ."[17] Therefore, one must handle proverbs with much care. However, they still remain our most valuable source of information on the African beliefs about God, more especially for a religion without a written holy book that documents its theological doctrines. In addition to proverbs, myths play a unique role in the African account of creation and the origin of God and humanity. African religion draws on the metaphors of these myths to explain the beginning of the world, the cycle of nature, and the wheel of birth, death, and rebirth.

Custodians of African religion such as the elders, priests, and priestesses are important vehicle in the process of transmission. African religious stipulations are passed on orally from one generation to another. Its doctrinal tenets are written in the individual hearts of its practitioners; and the people are able to apply their beliefs to various situations as the need warrants. Thus, African Indigenous religion is a cultural heritage, a people's way of life. In a sense, it embraces Paul Tillich's definition of religion, which says: "Religion is the substance of culture, and culture the substance of religion."[18] African Indigenous religion is simply "*life*." For any African, to be is to be religious. Religion pervades the totality of existence. One of the distinguished scholars of African indigenous religions expressed it in these words:

> [African religions] permeate all the departments of life. There is no formal distinction between the sacred and the secular, between the religious and the non-religious, between the spiritual and the material areas of life. Wherever the African is, there is his religion: he carries it to the fields where he is sowing seeds or harvesting a new crop; he takes it with him to the beer party or to attend a funeral ceremony; and if he is educated, he takes religion with him to the examination room at school or in the university; if he is a politician, he takes it to the house of parliament. *Although many African languages do not have a word for religion as such* (my emphasis), it nevertheless accompanies the individual from long before his birth to long after his death.[19]

African Indigenous religion also embodies the four essential characteristics evident in the world's major religions: (1) Beliefs: These are patterns of religious thought that determine proper or right behaviors in any given situation. (2) Religious officials: This refers to the overseers of religious matters who serve as oracles, elders, kings, and diviners. In other major religions of the world, they are called rabbis, imams, prophets, priests, pastors and many other names. (3) Religious ceremonies: These refer to the expression of the practitioner's beliefs in concrete or practical terms. A few examples of such ceremonies are rituals, offerings, gifts, worship, and prayer. (4) Religious objects and places: These are primary objects of religious worship and holy places for religious events. Some are in forms of masks, shrines, or hills. In other religions, worship places are called temples, synagogues, churches, mosques, just to name a few. The place of worship in African indigenous religion is called a shrine. Africans build their shrines wherever they need to communicate with their god or gods. As such, shrines can be found inside people's houses, outside in family compounds, near rivers, on large community lands, at marketplaces, essentially anywhere. Shrines can be elaborate or simple, depending on the need or desire of the builder.

THE CONCEPT OF GOD OR THE DIVINE IN AFRICAN RELIGION

Discourse on African religion has always included a question of whether African indigenous worldview embraces a concept of God or the divine. In his book, *African Ideas of God: A Symposium*, Edwin William Smith reported that during his attendance at a dinner hosted by the Acting-Governor of the Anglo-Egyptian Sudan during the nineteenth century, a fellow guest, the eminent biographer Emil Ludwig, asked him during a religious conversation: "How can the untutored African conceive God?" Smith, who had been a missionary to Africa, responded by saying that "there was no need to persuade Africans of the existence of God: they are sure of it."[20] Like Ludwig, there are many scholars even today within the Western tradition who doubt that Africans have a concept of God. But the fact is that the belief in God for the African is as old as the African Indigenous religion itself. Prior to Western influence on Africa, there was no African atheist. According to Biblical history, Egypt is on record as an ancient African culture that enslaved the Hebrews and exposed them to the idea of many gods of the Egyptians. After their emancipation, the Hebrews believed that God issued them the Decalogue containing ten stipulations commonly called "The Ten Commandments." God, in the Decalogue, spoke of what the Jews believed to be his unique relationship with them, and then issued the first commandment, which said:

> I am the Lord your God, who brought you out of the house of bondage. You shall have no other gods before me. You shall not make for yourself a carved image—any likeness of anything that is in heaven above, or that is in the earth beneath, or that is in the water under the earth. You shall not bow down to them. For I, the Lord your God, am a jealous God. . . .[21]

In the Ten Commandments, there is no law that says: Thou shall not be an atheist. The reason for the absence is unmistakable. In Africa then, where the Hebrews lived for generations, there were no known atheists. Therefore, they could not be tempted to succumb to something without being exposed to it. The Egyptian culture, like other cultures in Africa, was saturated with pantheon of gods. Moses, growing up in such an environment, was fully aware of it. Hence, when God sent him to deliver the Hebrews from Egyptian bondage, he was curious to ask "which God" was sending him on this mission.[22] The view of God within Africa is so fundamental that scholars of African religion provide several reasons to explain the origin and the development of the concept of God within African communities and their worldview.

THE ORIGIN OF THE AFRICAN BELIEF IN GOD

It is suggested that one of the catalysts that led the Africans to the belief in God is the realization of their own limitations as humans. This concern has its foundation on their anxieties about the origin and nature of the Cosmos. Who created the universe? Who, if anyone, is in charge of nature? The people's inability to control adverse forces of nature in their environment was unmistakable. For example, they could not prevent things like draughts, hurricanes, lightning, or sicknesses. Death was the most dramatic. They could not refuse to die when death struck. The logical inference drawn from this is the existence of some Being or Beings superior to humans who created the cosmos and is ultimately in charge of its operations and all natural phenomena. This being the Africans called God: *Chineke* (Igbo of Nigeria); *Nyame* (Asante of Ghana); *Nzambi* (Bacongo of Uganda); *Amma* (Dogon of Mali). Each of the more than one thousand African ethnic groups has its own name for God. Thus, the notion of God, who is expressed as a "Supreme Being" was introduced to explain the origin of the Cosmos, its continuity and operations.

Another concern that might have led Africans to the belief in God is the question about their own mortality or immortality. They wanted to know whether there is an element of the "Self" that continued to exist beyond the physical annihilation or bodily death. They wondered if bodily destruction is the end of one's life. Probably, there was also the problem of "Self," attempting to address such issues as: Who or what am I? What is this thing I call "Me" or "My-Self"? Am I just a mortal body? Or is there an element or component of the "Self" or "Me" that is incorporeal? Responses, or lack thereof, to these enigmatic and inexorable questions also led Africans to postulate the reality of a Spirit Being or God. Thus, in attempting to come to terms with the transience of life as they knew it, and the many puzzling questions about life and the universe, Africans came to believe that there must be a supreme being or beings, non-transient and in control of the universe.

THE AFRICAN MONOTHEISTIC/POLYTHESITIC VIEW OF THE DEITY(IES)

The African concept of God is complex, rich, and varied. It contains both monotheistic and polytheistic elements. Hence, the intellectual study of the African view of God within the academic circle generally leads to unavoidable disagreements. Part of the problem is mostly that of interpretation. Many academic writers on African Indigenous religion invariably succumb to the temptation of interpreting and translating the African theistic view from the Western patterns of religious expressions. The tendency to understand the principles of African concept of God through the lenses of other world religions has often resulted in misrepresentations and misunderstanding of the African religious view. This conflation of the African view of God is keenly evident in the following description attributed to the African theistic worldview:

> The belief that there is a supreme High God who created the world and then withdrew from active participation in it is common in polytheistic religions around the world. This belief is shared by many African people. Although most African religions are polytheistic in their day-to-day practices, there is a common belief that beyond all of the minor gods, spirits, and ancestors there is one High God who created and governs the universe. When early anthropologists and missionaries discovered this fact, some concluded that Africans had originally been monotheistic but had lapsed into polytheism. . . . In many African religions, the High God appears as a creator who did his work and then retired to some distant place. It is often believed that this god has little contact with the world and its daily operation. . . .[23]

When scholars say that the African view of God is polytheistic, they are correct. Africans recognize varying gods and goddesses in their religious belief systems. Many African communities have deities responsible for differing aspects of the cosmos and the natural world. Examples include the god of storm, the god of draught, the god of lightning, the earth goddess, and gods of the sea and mountains, to mention a few. When scholars also argue that Africans believe in the existence of "one High God who created and governs the universe," they are correct as well. The African religious belief system contains elements of both polytheism and monotheism. But the claim that "Africans had originally been monotheistic but had lapsed into polytheism" is wholly incorrect and practically mistaken for the following reasons. One, there is no evidence showing that the African polytheistic view of God is a "lapse" from their monotheistic concept of God. Two, the concept of a "High God" or "Supreme Deity" who created the cosmos and then retired to the inner alcove of the heavens with little or no contacts with the world and its daily operations is conceptually Western, not African. The view of a detached, transcendent God or Deity of the natural universe as found in other religions like Judaism and Christianity is un-African and utterly irrelevant to the African experience. Moreover, it conflates the African view of the cosmos and fails to appreciate the basis for the introduction of the notion of the Supreme God into African theistic worldview.

Unlike most cultures' view of God, the African religious belief system is simultaneously polytheistic and monotheistic. In African Indigenous religion, the concept of a Supreme God was a logical necessity that serves two primary purposes: to explain the *origin* of the Cosmos and to account for its *continuity*. Perhaps this is why the Africans address the Supreme Being as the Maker, Creator, Sustainer, Ruler, and Governor of the Universe. The following song from the Karanga people of Zimbabwe metaphorically portrays the Supreme Being as the "Great Spirit" or "Great Pool":

> Great Spirit. . . Waters of the pool that turn Into misty rain when stirred. Vessel overflowing with oil. . . Thou bringest forth the shoots That they stand erect. . . Thou givest of rain to mankind. . . .[24]

In this song, the Supreme God who is the Great Spirit in the African belief system is acknowledged as the creator or giver of rain or water, which is a metaphor for life. For without water, there would be no life of any form on the planet earth. Life and growth of any living organism are ultimately the effects of this gift from the Supreme Being. As a result, water or river is generally considered sacred and used for purification rites among varying religious groups in many places in Africa.

Africans believe in the existence of the one Supreme or High God who created the universe. Some argue, as John Mbiti points out, that God made the heavenly part of the Cosmos first; then standing on it, He created the earth. Yet others believe that the entire Cosmos was created in one act.[25] Still some maintain that God is actively creating new lives and new things. Hence, for this group, creation is not a divine act of a remote past. Rather, it is a constant process without end. While African religious thought might be ambiguous in terms of how the Supreme God created the Universe, it remains clear about the continued and active participation of the Supreme Being in the world he created. The African Supreme God has not "retired to a distant place," but still governs and sustains the constancy of the enormous Cosmos. One can say that this Being is the "glue" that holds the universe in place and keeps it running. For the Supreme God who created this gigantic Cosmos actively sustains and keeps it from disintegration.

In addition to the Supreme God, the African religious thought also recognizes "smaller" deities. These deities take care of the minor, but important, day-to-day activities or operations of the physical world. In some African societies, like the Nuer People of southern Sudan or the Yoruba people of Nigeria, these deities are believed to have played some roles in the creation of some things in the cosmos. The African belief in the concept of God originated from the pragmatic concerns of the people and the existential environment in which they found themselves. These concerns are so varied in their respective manifestations that they do not only mandate the introduction of a Supreme God but also other gods and their active involvement in the resolution of the problems that gave rise to the concept. In other words, the Africans introduced the notion of Divinity into their belief systems to explain the origin and continued existence of the Universe. But most importantly, it was a means of receiving help in their personal and co-operate existence. In his book, *Africa and Christianity*, Westermann expressed it in these words:

> [The introduction of God into African religion] has its origin. . . in a feeling of incapacity and in an obstinate desire to overcome it; it is a search for help and comfort, a means of maintaining and

strengthening life in the midst of a thousand dangers, and a way of conquering the fear which shoots its arrows from every hidden ambush. Man is weak, and what he needs is increased strength. . . the absorbing question for him is how to acquire some of the power so that it may serve for his own salvation or that of the group. . . .[26]

Hence, the African monotheistic and polytheistic views are acquiescent. They maintain that the Supreme God is uncreated or self-existing. For instance, in the Batammaliba creation myth, *Kuiye* the Creator of the universe is said to be "always there, no one could form this deity."[27] *Kuiye*, who is believed to be both male and female (or better, gender-neutral), created itself, the earth, and formed humans. He also created other deities (lesser gods and goddesses) to serve as intermediaries between Him and the world. These created deities are respectively addressed as gods or goddesses of the sun, drought, moon, hurricane, thunder, rain, fertility, harvest, and so on. The African Supreme God did not abandon the Cosmos after creation to let it function by its own mechanism. The African Supreme God and other gods are imminently involved directly and indirectly in the believers' lives, their world, and daily operations. This is, to the Africans, the reason for God and the essence of African Indigenous religion. For, as Edwin William Smith puts it, "if the essence of religion is a sense of dependence upon supersensible powers who are able and willing to help, then we are in the presence of religion."[28]

The African concept of *Divinity* is quite different from the Judeo-Christian understanding or concept of God. First, under the Western concept, God is always articulated in masculine terms like "father," "man" with several *divine* attributes. African deities are not all males. There are female deities like the earth goddess or mother earth. Both males and females also serve in the roles of diviners and mediums. Priests and priestesses are equally respected in their roles as conveners of the wills of the deities to their communities. Second, in the Western conceptual scheme, God possesses the intrinsic attributes of being omnipresence, omnipotence, omniscience, transcendence, and immanence. But in the African modes of thought, it is conceptually difficult to achieve some of these attributes without pragmatic self-contradiction. For the notion of God, to the Africans, is not an abstract concept, but a pragmatic one. Hence, the African attitude is primarily a matter of existential commitment to the daily aspects of living rather than academic study of theism.

Some African scholars, such as John S. Mbiti, for instance, have argued that the African philosophical view recognizes the omnipresence of the Supreme God. "Life itself is an indication of God's omnipresence."[29] This type of claim by Mbiti and others seems to embody a serious, but obtuse logical implication. If the presence of *life* on earth is an indication of God's omnipresence, one would be logically compelled to ask, if the reality or presence of *death* (which is part and parcel of human experience like life) means the absence of God's omnipresence. The point is that the move to extract such intrinsic attribute is not only unnecessary, it seems logically dubious. The African theistic view does not need to conform to the Judeo-Christian point of view to be credible. Moreover, the African view was decades in place before the advent of Christianity. Even though the notion of "Transcendent Deity" may offer a philosophically significant way of thinking about God in the abstract, it lacks theological significance in African theism. As T.C. Young correctly expressed, such effort is like trying "to colour that idea in non-indigenous tints, or interpret it upon a canvas too large—often much too large—for the original, indigenous frame."[30] Moreover, to the African, deities do not need to be omnipresent, omnipotent, and all transcendent to meet the daily realities of life. The deities know enough and have power enough to bring about positive changes in their respective spheres of operations. This is the ideal structure of African Indigenous religion, but its specific details are numerous and varied. Just as W.R.C. Horton accurately points out, the primary concern of the African Indigenous religion is not about conceptual description of the ultimate grounds of all existence, but an attempt to explain and influence the workings of the peoples' everyday world by ascertaining the constant principles that underlie the chaos and flux of human experience.[31] In other words, religion or theism to the African is all about survival and the well-being of their present existence and hereafter.

THE PERSONAL GOD OR CHI

In addition to the Supreme God and many other gods of the Africans, several African societies also believe in the concept of the personal god or "Chi." Among the Igbo people of Nigeria, for instance, each individual is said to have a personal god or *Chi*. Here are some proverbs reflecting such belief: "Nwata n'amu elu, Chi ya achiri uche n'aka," meaning: "While a child is learning how to climb, his *Chi's* (personal god) heart beats fast." "Ofu nne n'amu, ma ofu Chi adaghi eke," meaning: "Two people can come from the same mother, but no two people can have identical *Chi (god) or are the same.*" "Onye kwe Chi ye ekwe," meaning: "If a person says yes, his/her personal god *(Chi)* says yes, too." Thus, for the Igbos whose population is in millions and rapidly growing, there are at least as many personal gods as there are the Igbo people.

RITUALS IN AFRICAN RELIGION

Africans believe that both the Supreme Being and the lesser gods demand utmost respect and obedience from humans. The Supreme Being has the power to inflict pain and suffering on humans for violations of the natural order of things. Even though the powers of the lesser gods are limited to their area of operation or jurisdiction, their powers, nonetheless, supersede that of mortal men and women. Their actions are irrevocable by mere humans, and they often act as they please. Therefore, humans pray to the gods for protection of life and property, and they offer them offerings and sacrifices to appease them. Thus, the African conceptual dependence upon the powers of the Supreme Being and the "lesser" deities in maintaining their daily activities and life is inherently exhibited in the rituals of sacrifice, gift-giving, and prayers. The rituals offer them a significant avenue of validating the genuineness of their faith or idea of divinity.

Sacrifice is a primary means of ensuring good relationships with the gods. During community conflicts, the assistance of the deities is constantly solicited by differing groups for victory over their enemies. They offer sacrifices of fowls, goats, lizards, or other animals to ask for protection. If they believe the gods are angry with them, they offer sacrifices to appease them. They also consult oracles and mediums to know the expectations of the gods for good harvests, health, fertility, and other things. In some cases, the practitioners may give offerings, rather than sacrifice, contingent upon what the gods want. For in African Indigenous religion, as John Mbiti accurately points out, there is a difference between *sacrifice* and *offering.* Sacrifice entails shedding of blood, mainly of animals, but offerings do not require blood.[32] In offering, gifts are given in forms of fabrics, artifacts, money, cola-nuts, food, drinks, or crops. In addition, offering times also offer occasions for celebration—singing, dancing, and feasting to the praises and adorations of the gods, including the Supreme God. Sacrifices are often solemn occasions, mostly in an effort to appease the gods, to ask for favor, or to right a wrong.

Additionally, part of the duties of the deities is to enforce religious precepts. Offenders are directly punished by the gods. Punishments may include some form of natural disasters, such as floods, drought or famine, diseases, and even death. Hence, in times of such calamities, the religious Africans turn to the Supreme God in prayer through the smaller gods, who serve as intermediaries between them and the Supreme God. Prayers are often accompanied by some form of sacrifice, gifts, or libations. This religious practice is evident in this prayer by the Gikuyu of Kenya:

> You who make mountains tremble and rivers flood; we offer you this sacrifice that you may bring us rain. People and children are crying; sheep, goats and cattle are crying. . . . We beseech you to accept this, our sacrifice, and bring prosperity.[33]

Africans also pray to the deities as a show of respect and in acknowledgment of their respective areas of operations or jurisdiction. Take for example this prayer by the Ashanti people to the Earth goddess:

> Earth, while I am yet alive, It is upon you that I put my trust. Earth who receives my body, We are addressing you, And you will understand.[34]

The African gods are believed to have power enough to bring about positive changes in their respective spheres of operations. Africans turn to them in acts of prayer and devotion just about any time and in any place. They do not hesitate to appeal to their gods in times of great crises or to thank them in times of prosperity. The gods are part and parcel of the community and immanently engaged in the affairs of the people.

THE ROLE OF ARTS IN AFRICAN INDIGENOUS RELIGION

In African Indigenous religion, as in many other religions, God is spirit. Since spirits are wholly impalpable, the Africans ethnographically try to represent the Supreme God and other deities in different forms of art, such as masks, drawings, charms, symbols, carved objects, dance-staff, wooden images, or sculptures of assorted types, just to mention a few. "Art," it has been said, "is a direct measure of a man's spiritual vision."[35] Vision, according to a Bambara proverb, is the mother of art.[36] Art also is a form of expression, as Benedetto Croce accurately noted.[37] In the Western conceptual scheme, arts are primarily for aesthetic consumption. But in African belief systems, it is mainly a religious attempt to connect with the spirit beings, commonly called divinities, in order to convert their powers into a force that works for the human good. Thus, most African arts are closely associated with their religion.

Since the deities in African religion are spirits, and spirits cannot be perceived through the physical senses, it is only logical for the Africans to create varying forms of art as avenues of effective communication with the spirit beings. As J. Cornet puts it, arts "allow men to enter into contact with [deities of different mystical forms] in order to appeal to their kindness or appease their wrath."[38] This is the basic motif of many African arts. It is what gave rise to the numerous statues, sacred objects of varying kinds in African Indigenous religion that some European scholars of African religion unwittingly described as African gods. These arts are not African gods. Africans do not worship arts or inanimate objects. Religious arts, symbols, and objects offer Africans a tangible way of representing the invisible Deities/Gods/Spirits they worship. They enable the African religious believers to make truth-claims about their gods. Such truth-claims are aptly expressed in the words of this African song:

> O world invisible, we view thee, O world intangible, we know thee, O world unknowable, we know thee, Inapprehensible, we clutch thee![39]

Sometimes, people have difficulties in comprehending certain "truths" unless they are represented in palpable or concrete fashion. The concept of "God" or the "deities" is one prime example of this fact. Hence, African traditional religion is saturated with varying art forms, ritual objects, symbols, shrines, masks, and clothes anchored in utilitarian values and relevance for their daily existence.

CONCLUSION

African Indigenous religion is as complex and as varied as the peoples who practice it. As most things African, their cultural and religious practices, of course, have their foundation on the central concept of *community*. Community is the fabric of the African philosophy and the hub of their religious and cultural values. Simply put, African religion is a communal religion, the belief in personal god notwithstanding. Practically and sociologically speaking, it is more of a family, group, or ethnic religion than individual religion. The Africans believe that one is because others exist. In their philosophy of religion, there is no such thing "as absolutely independent existence." The gods, the ancestors, and the living are intrinsic constituents of the functional community. They all play important roles in the survival and sustenance of the community.

Its variance from major world religions, especially, Western Christianity, has resulted in much of its tenets being misunderstood. Most scholars inadvertently fail to recognize the fact that the African view of the divine is both monotheistic and polytheistic; it is not one or the other, as is the case with most of the world religions. For, within their theistic stance, Africans recognize both Supreme God and the lesser gods as being simultaneously responsible for the reality of the existential needs of humankind. Hence, the historic attempt to derive the essential attributes of the Christian monotheistic concept from the African monotheistic/polytheistic view is simply unperceptive. It is like trying to dress up the African Supreme God and the deities with the Western monotheistic attires. It won't work; the clothes won't fit.

Africans are an intrinsically religious people. Spirituality and religious rituals pervade all aspects of their existence and view of their natural world and their place in it. Hence, any meaningful understanding of African peoples must take in stock their religious views. And, any deliberate and useful analysis of the African indigenous religious thought must approach it on its own terms. African Indigenous religion is as old as the African continent itself and one of the oldest surviving world religions. It is not a derivative of other religions or a lesser form of other religions. Its tenets reveal the sophisticated, complex, and intellectual reasoning of the African peoples as they contemplate the nature of their existence, their relationship to their natural world, the cosmos, and other sentient and non-sentient beings that made up the universe.

ENDNOTES

1   William James, *The Varieties of Religious Experience* (New York: Longman, 1902), 53.

2   Henry Fielding, *The History of Tom Jones, A Foundling* (New York: Literary Guild of America, 1948), 41.

3   Benjamine Ray, *African Religions: Symbol, Ritual, and Community*, 2nd edition (Upper Saddle River, NJ: Prentice Hall, 1999), xi.

4   Ibid.

5   *Webster's New World Dictionary*, 2nd edition (New York: William Collins, 1972).

6   Michael Molloy, *Experiencing the World's Religions Tradition, Challenge, and Change* (Mountain View, CA: Mayfield Publishing Company, 2002), 6.

7   Julian Huxley, *Religion Without Revelation* (New York: Macmillan, 1991), 33.

8   Lewis M. Hopfe and Mark R. Woodward, *Religions of the World,* 7th edition (Upper Saddle River, NJ: Prentice Hall, 1998), 55.

9   Margaret Trowel, *African Tapestry* (London: Faber & Faber Publishing, 1957), 126.

10 T. Cullen Young, "The Ideas of God in Northern Nyasaland," in *African Ideas of God: A Symposium*, Edwin William Smith, ed. (University Park: Pennsylvania State University, Edinburgh House Press, 1961), 39.

11 Ibid.

12 Michael Molloy, ed., *Experiencing the World's Religious Tradition: Tradition, Challenge, and Change*, 460.

13 *Merriam Webster's Collegiate Dictionary*, 10th edition (Springfield, MA: Merriam-Webster, 1995).

14 Edwin William Smith, *African Ideas of God: A Symposium* (University Park: Pennsylvania State University, Edinburgh House Press, 1950), 4.

15 J. A. Kelso, "Proverbs," *Encyclopedia of Religion and Ethics*, vol. 1 (Edinburgh: T&T Clark Publishing, 1918), 415.

16 E. Gray, "Some Proverbs of the Nyanja People," in *African Studies* (Johannesburg, South Africa: University of the Witwatersrand, September, 1944), 101.

17 Smith, *African Ideas of God: A Symposium*, 10.

18 Paul Tillich, "Between Mountain and Plain," *Time* (October 20, 1952), 33.

19 John S. Mbiti, *African Religion and Philosophy*, 2nd edition (Portsmouth, NH: Heinemann Publishers, 2006), 2.

20 Smith, *African Ideas of God: A Symposium*, 1.

21 Exodus 20: 1–5.

22 Exodus 3: 13–14.

23 Lewis M. Hopfe & Mark R. Woodward, *Religions of the World,* 7th edition (Upper Saddle River, NJ Prentice Hall, 1998), 56–57.

24 Smith, *African Ideas of God: A Symposium*, 127.

25 See John S. Mbiti, *Introduction to African Religion*, 32.

26 D. Westermann, *Africa and Christianity* (London: Oxford University Press, 1937), 84.

27 Suzanne Preton Blier, *The Anatomy of Architecture: Ontology and Metaphor in Batammaliba Architectural Expression* (New York: Cambridge University Press, 1987), 37.

28 Smith, *African Ideas of God: A Symposium*, 26.

29 Mbiti, Concepts of God in Africa, 5.

30 Smith, *African Ideas of God: A Symposium*, 2.

31 W. R. C. Horton, "Ritual Man in Africa," *Africa, 34* (1964). See also his "African Traditional Thought and Western Science," *Africa 37, no 1* (1967): 50–71.

32 John S. Mbiti, *Introduction to African Religion* (Oxford, UK: Heinemann Educational Books, 1989), 57–59.

33 J. Kenyatta, *Facing Mount Kenya* (London: Heinemann, 1938), 247.

34 Geoffery Parrinder, *African Traditional Religion* (Chicago: Hutchinson House, 1954), 48.

35 Herbert Edward Read, *The Meaning of Art* (London, Faber and Faber, 1972), 84.

36 Ibid

37 Ibid

38 J. Cornet, *Art of Africa: Treasures from the Congo*, translated by B. Thompson (New York: Phaiden Publishers, 1971).

39 E. Bolaji Idowu, *OLODUMARE: God in Yoruba Belief* (London: Longman Group Limited, 1970), 65.

REVIEW QUESTIONS

1. What is religion? Given what you know of religion, do you think Africans have a religion? If your answer is "Yes," what is it? If your answer is "No," why not?
2. Discuss some of the reasons that may have led to the African conception of God or the Divine.
3. Based on your study of African Indigenous religion, list and carefully describe the advantages one may derive in studying other religions of the world than one's own.
4. Describe the African view of ancestors and their role within the community.
5. What is paganism? And what is Aimism? In your opinion, what do you think is the reason why some people construe African Indigenous religion as paganism and/or animism?
6. List and explain the common tenets of African Indigenous Religion.

Writing Prompt

Carefully describe the concepts of monotheism and polytheism. In what ways is African theistic thought both monotheistic and polytheistic?

CHAPTER 6

Islam and Islamic Revivalism in Africa

Ogechi Emmanuel Anyanwu

With a population estimated at 1.6 billion, representing twenty-three percent of the world's population, Islam is one of the key world religions.[1] Membership of the religion has surged in the last four decades, making it the fastest growing religion. Founded in Saudi Arabia in the 7th century by prophet Mohammed and making inroads into North Africa shortly afterwards, Islam has reshaped the sociocultural, economic and political history of Africa. Africa houses the second largest adherents of the Islamic faith. About half of the continent's 1 billion people identify with the religion. Before the establishment of colonial rule in Africa, Islam was crucial in the emergence and demise of states and empires, the creation of new identities, and the promotion of social solidarity along religious lines. Christian and Western cultural values European powers imposed on African societies during the colonial period challenged the essence of Islamic and indigenous African religions resulting in different degrees of changes. The need to remain faithful to their faith in the face of radical social changes occasioned by colonialism and Christianization of the continent found expression in the stout resistance Muslim societies posed against European conquest and administration of their societies in the early 1900s.

Postcolonial African countries inherited Western-styled political, economic, social, and judicial institutions forced on them by European colonial powers. Leaders of newly independent African countries mostly maintained those institutions. Most of them were Western educated and thus operated within similar frameworks—sometimes against the wishes of more conservative, culturally sensitive African individuals and groups. Instability was unavoidable. Islamic beliefs and practices had united Muslim communities in a collective conscience during the precolonial period. Colonialism threatened that unity. Efforts by Islamic communities in mostly pluralistic and secular postcolonial African countries to revive the precolonial Islamic principles, law, and traditions have reshaped social interaction, and caused tension, conflict, and violence in many countries in Africa. Existing works on Islam in Africa have not fully captured the significant place of Islam in the making and remaking of Africa.[2] This chapter analyzes the history of complex interactions, conflicts, and accommodation that ensued when Islamic traditions encountered both Africa's indigenous civilizations and European Christian values. It argues that the history of Islam in Africa can only be fully understood and appreciated in the context of several processes—trade, migration, Islamic law, colonial approach to Islam, and nation building in multicultural modern Africa. By approaching the study of Islam in Africa from a standpoint that incorporates the multiple forces that shaped its rise, challenges, survival, and revival at different historical periods, this chapter provides a good introduction to understanding the significance of Islam in the socioeconomic and political transformation of modern Africa.

THE BIRTH AND SPREAD OF ISLAM

Islam, an Arabic word that means submission to the will Allah (God), emerged in Saudi Arabia in 610 AD. According to Islamic tradition, God sent an angel to reveal to Prophet Muhammad a set of divine guidelines for humans. The Koran (also spelt Quran), the Islamic sacred book, contains those religious stipulations. Muslims believe that Angel Gabriel dictated the 114 chapters of the Koran to Prophet Mohammed who memorized the words and later dictated them to his companions. The Koran contains guidelines that govern every aspect of Muslims' life, from civil matters to criminal offenses. It shapes politics, law, economy, and sociocultural relations among Muslims. At different times and places, the practice of Islam has been adapted to reflect local sensibilities and cultures.

Unlike Christians who believe that Jesus is the son of God, adherents of the Islamic faith, known as Muslims, believe that Prophet Muhammad was the last and greatest of all prophets chosen by God. There are two sects within Islam: Sunnis and Shias (also known as Shiites). These two sects share more in common but differ on the line of leadership succession following the death of Prophet Mohammed in 632 A.D. The dispute lay at the heart of the opposing theological identities of these sects. The Sunni group is the largest sect in Islam, constituting more than 87% of Muslims. The sect acknowledges the legitimacy of the first three successors of Prophet Muhammad. The Shia group, on the other hand, accepts the fourth successor of the Prophet, Ali—Muhammad's son-in-law—as the true Islamic leader.[3]

Despite the differences between the two major Islamic groups, they are united around the five fundamental tenets of Islamic theology. The declaration of faith called Shahada is the first pillar of Islam. It is expressed in these words: "There is no God but Allah, and Mohammad is the prophet of Allah."[4] This pillar represents the cornerstone of Islam's monotheistic attribute. It is also an acknowledgment that God, like in Christianity and indigenous African religions, is the creator of the universe, the ruler, sustainer, and provider of humankind. The second pillar of Islam is prayer, known as Salat. Whether a prayer is offered as a personal devotion or a collective activity, its observance five times a day is expected of a true Muslim. The ritual of washing of face, hands, and feet typically precedes daily prayers offered at daybreak, noon, mid-afternoon, dusk, and before bedtime. Ibn Battuta, a North African Arab traveler, who visited many African kingdoms during the 14th century observed the dedication with which Muslims followed their religious obligations. According to him, most Muslims he encountered "meticulously observe the times of prayer and attendance to them, so also it is with regard to their congregational services. . . . When it is Friday, if a man does not come early to the Mosque he will not find a place to pray because of the numbers of the crowd."[5]

The third pillar of Islam expects Muslims to embark on an annual pilgrimage to Mecca, the birthplace of Prophet Mohammed. Known in Arabic as Hajj, and encouraged by the Koran, going on an annual pilgrimage reaffirms Muslims' faith in their religion and thus promotes social cohesion among believers. Pilgrimage holds a religious significance to Muslims. It reenacts the events in 622 AD when, compelled by adversaries—and fearing for his life—Prophet Mohammed fled from the holy city of Mecca to Medina. The honorific titles of Haji and Hajjah are respectively given to men and women who travel to Mecca on a religious pilgrimage. The fourth pillar of Islam is fasting observed during the month of Ramadan. Fasting is considered important largely because it redirects the minds of Muslims from worldly desires such as food and thus allows them to give undivided attention to spiritual things. It is a cleansing and sacrificial act expected to invite God's favor on the participants. The fifth pillar of Islam is Zakat which encourages collective responsibility for the good of all people, especially the less fortunate. Muslims are expected to contribute about 2.5% of their annual wealth to help the needy. While contribution is regulated by the state in some countries, collection is decentralized in others. A committee is usually charged with the responsibility to distribute the funds collected to the needy.

The spread of Islam in many African societies during the early years of its emergence was rapid. A number of factors account for it. The first was the ability of Islam to accommodate indigenous religious practices of African societies. Unlike European Christian missionaries who largely dismissed Africa's indigenous religions and sought to supplant it with Christian beliefs, Islam shared similar beliefs with African peoples thus facilitating the process of accommodation.[6] The initial tolerant nature of Islam was such that most African converts continued to observe some indigenous religious practices while aligning with the basic principles of Islamic faith as stipulated in the five pillars of Islam. Before Islam came to Africa, well-established religious beliefs and practices had flourished in the continent. The belief in the supernatural and the spiritual world had underpinned indigenous African religions for generations. Similar beliefs and cultural practices shared by Muslims made Africans receptive to Islamic teachings. Both Islam and indigenous African religions believe in the spirit world, venerate ancestors, permit polygamy, and accept mystical powers and divination as legitimate religious practices. However the similarities in beliefs which inspired the accommodating attitudes of Islam to indigenous African religions before the 10th century was eventually swept aside by the emergence of reformist movement that used violence to enforce stricter Islamic practices.

The second factor responsible for the spread of Islam was its emphasis on educating adherents. Like Christianity, education was crucial in the spread and consolidation of Islam. Wherever Islam gained prominence, libraries and schools were built. From Egypt to Mali, Islamic centers of learning emerged as vehicles for consolidating the Islamic religion. Koranic schools provided an opportunity for adherents to read and recite the Koran since it is a religious duty. Other centers of learning dubbed Madrassas equally provided the opportunity to combine religious instructions with secular learning in mathematics, architecture, astronomy, and philosophy. The first known Madrassa was established in Egypt in 1005 A.D. It had a library, and teachers taught different subjects. Students studied the Qur'an, Islamic law, logic, grammar, and rhetoric. With time, the curriculum was expanded to include subjects like mathematics, philosophy, history, politics, ethics, music, metaphysics, medicine, astronomy and chemistry.[7] Some of these Madrassas were institutions of higher learning. There was the Al-Azhar University in Egypt, the University of Fez in Morocco, and the University of Timbuktu in Mali. The emergence of these institutions emphasizing mostly religious instruction testifies "to the standard of education achieved in Africa before the colonial intrusion."[8] The role of Muslim elite in the spread of the religion is remarkable. Arab and African Islamic scholars and clerics travelled across the Islamic societies, empires, and states to share their religious ideas and enrich the practice of Islamic religion and law. The influence of Muslim scholarship was prominent in all branches of learning.[9]

The spread of Islam to Africa before the 10th century was slow, peaceful, and partial. Seldom did Muslims force non-believers to accept Islam. Holy War described by Prophet Mohammed was only allowed as a defense of faith rather than as a tool of conversion. Inward spiritual struggle and outward physical struggle are two commonly recognized meanings of Jihad. Both are expected of Muslims in fulfilment of their Islamic faith. The first involves attempts to become a better Muslim by observing the commandments Koran stipulates. The second involves waging a war in response to persecution and oppression. Such wars, dubbed holy wars, are usually fought when the Islamic faith is threatened.[10] The concept of jihad, however, has been interpreted by fanatics to include waging wars against non-believers for rejecting Islamic teachings, especially since the 18th century. This led to the rise and fall of many kingdoms in precolonial Africa such as Ghana, Mali, and Sokoto. The perverted interpretation of jihad by violent extremists groups in postcolonial Africa has caused them to justify attacks on non-believers as worthy responses to perceived religious percussion.

Islam reached Africa through the east and from the north and the major agents in the spread of Islam in the continent were Arab traders, Berbers, and missionaries.[11] The benefits that came with trade connections with Arab Muslim merchants, its commitment to charity, and its theological similarities and tolerance of indigenous African religious beliefs made Islam very attractive to both lower and upper class peoples in Africa.

ISLAM IN NORTH AFRICA

North Africa's close proximity to Saudi Arabia, the birthplace of Islam, facilitated the spread of the religion to the area shortly after its founding. Centuries of interactions had existed between North Africa and the Arabian Peninsula. The geographical barriers posed by the vast Sahara, the Red Sea, and the Indian Ocean did little to prevent trade from flourishing between the two areas. Consequently, well-established Arab communities existed in North Africa before the birth of Islam. Seven years after the death of Prophet Mohammed in 639, Islam penetrated much of North Africa, also known as the Maghreb. Thus Egypt, a country where Christianity was the main religion centuries before the birth of Islam, became the first country in Africa to come under Islamic influence. Many centuries, however, would pass before the majority of the population would become Muslims—although a small Christian population still exists in Egypt, called the *Coptic* Christians.

Once Islam was established in Egypt, it constituted the pathway through which it expanded to other areas in North Africa. Arab traders introduced Islamic religion to Tunisia, Algeria and Morocco, and the predominantly Berber-speaking people of North Africa in turn embraced it. The Berbers were the original inhabitants of North Africa and were highly instrumental in the spread of Islam to many parts of Africa. The Berbers are found in many areas across the Sahara and Sahel regions of Africa. They played a significant role not only in the religious realm but also in African politics. They were the backbone of an Arab fighting force and the Almoravid movement. Led by a Berber scholar, Abdallah Ibn Yasin, the Almoravids or al-murabitun (men of the monastery), later came to preach a strict adherence to Islamic law and believed in waging 'jihad' (Islamic holy war) against the infidel (unbeliever).[12] The Berbers also spread the religion southwards along the Nile River valley into Sudan and Ethiopia. Centuries of resistance to the religion by Christian populations in Nubia (northeast Sudan) gave way to the conversion to Islam of most of northern Sudan and Eritrea in the 15th century. With the spread of Islam, Arabs increasingly began to dominate the politics of host communities thus ensuring that North Africa remains the only region in the continent that is both predominantly Islamic and Arabic. Many North African countries such as Egypt, the Sudan, Libya, Tunisia, Algeria, and Morocco still have Arabic as their official language.

ISLAM AND WEST AFRICAN STATES

More than a thousand years before the introduction of Islam in Africa, the Berber speaking peoples of North Africa had traded salt and other commodities for gold and ivory from both the savannah and forest regions of West Africa. The conversion of many Berber traders by the 12th century meant that the spread of Islam would follow trade routes. Trade between West Africa and North Africa across the Sahara Desert had existed since the classical age, but from the 5th century, camels and horses facilitated trade by making transportation across the desert easier. Although the Berber traders did not set out to convert West Africans, they observed their religious practices during their business trips. With time, Muslim scholars and clerics joined the traders to West Africa and soon after became useful to non-Muslim local rulers who benefited from their knowledge of law, governance, and administration. For years, Islam was an elitist religion, accepted mostly by merchants and the privileged few who had trade dealings with Muslim traders. When the traditional African rulers accepted Islam, they in turn became instrumental in the eventual spread of the religion among the general populace.

The spread of Islam in West Africa focused initially on the Sudanic empires, such as Ghana, but later spread to other areas in the region. Gold, found in large quantities in Ghana, underpinned the trans-Saharan trade that flourished even after the decline of the empire in the first half of the 13th century. By the 11th century, Islam had been firmly established in Ghana, playing a key role in government, administration, and law. It brought population and religious diversity and influenced social and legal institutions of the empire. As al-Bakri, a Spanish Muslim geographer wrote in 1094, "Ghana consists of two towns. One of these towns, which is inhabited by Muslims, is large and possesses twelve mosques, in which they assemble for Friday prayer. There are salaried imams and muezzins, as well as jurists and scholars."[13] Although the king of Ghana never converted to Islam, he engaged the services of Muslim jurists and administrators. He demonstrated his sensitivity and respect for cultural and religious identities by allowing different religious and cultural groups to greet him in accordance to their unique belief systems. According to al-Bakri, "When the people who profess the same religion as the king approach him they fall on their knees and sprinkle dust on their heads, for this is their way of greeting him. As for the Muslims, they greet him only by clapping their hands."[14]

With the collapse of Ghana in the 13th century, the Mali Empire consolidated interactions with the Islamic world. Sundiata, one of the rulers of Mali, not only converted to Islam but also extensively used Muslim administrators for the empire. Another ruler of Mali, Mansa Musa, popularized Islam in the region by embarking on a pilgrimage to Mecca in 1324, a visit that highlighted the empire's wealth due to gold. The visit also resulted in the empire's embrace of Muslim architecture and the emergence of Timbuktu as a famous center of Islamic scholarship. Al-Mu'ammar provided Ibn Khaldun an account of Mansa Musa's hajj:

> We used to keep the Sultan company during his progress, I and Abu Ishaq al-Tuwayjin, to the exclusion of his viziers and chief men, and converse to his enjoyment. At each halt he would regale us with rare foods and confectionery. His equipment and furnishings were carried by 12,000 private slave women, wearing gowns of brocade and Yemeni silk.[15]

Whether in Ghana, Mali and other West African states and kingdoms, Islam was initially an elitist religion practiced mostly by the upper class before it gradually spread to the masses. The lower class people, just like their leaders, continued to combine their indigenous African religious practices with Islamic beliefs. With time, Islamic religious zealots with a strict interpretation of Islamic teachings embarked on religious revivalist movements designed to stamp out any indigenous religious practices that contradict Islamic principles. Nowhere in Africa was this movement more pronounced and consequential than in West Africa.

ISLAMIC REVOLUTIONS IN WEST AFRICA

The Fulbe or Fulani Muslim leaders were at the center of the Islamic jihads that swept across states in West Africa between the mid-18th and early 19th century. Found mostly in West Africa, the Fulanis are one of the largest ethnic groups in Africa. Mostly nomadic people, the Fulani people were united by a common language, Fulfulde, and religion, Islam. Although the largest movement they led occurred in Sokoto (present-day northern Nigeria), Islamic movements began in Guinea.

The Fulani people had settled in the highlands of Futa Jallon (present day Guinea) from the early 16th century. The menace their herding activities posed to crops led to a tense relationship with indigenous farmers who restricted their movement to safeguard their farmlands. Local rulers equally imposed taxes on them. Dissatisfied with their treatment, united by their newfound faith in Islamic religion, and assisted by Muslim traders, the Fulani launched a rebellion against the rulers (who they described as 'pagans') and farmers in 1725. The rebellion resulted in the establishment of a theocratic state of Futa Jalon where Islamic law prevailed. The success of the Islamic jihad in Futa Jalon inspired similar movement in Futa Toro (present day Senegal). In the 1760s and 1770s, Muslim Fulani and Tukolor embarked on similar jihads and successfully established an Islamic state in Futa Toro.

Before the imposition of colonial rule, Islam had become the primary religion of most states and kingdom in West Africa, influencing politics, law, and society. The series of Islamic jihads that swept the area led to the further spread of the religion and the establishment of Muslim theocratic states in Futa Jallon and Futa Toro. Islam and indigenous African religions were flexible and accommodating. Africans who accepted Islam continued to observe practices dictated by their indigenous religions. The syncretic religious practices of Islamic West African societies presented a big problem for the future by giving Islamic reformists a reason to wage jihads to stamp out what was perceived as tainted Islamic practices. As early as the 14th century, Muslims dominated the ruling class of Hausa city-states such as Gobir, Katsina, Kano, Zazzau, Zamfara, and Kebbi in modern day Nigeria. The need to purify the worship of Islam led to efforts by Muslim clerics to embark on reformist movement aimed at applying the Islamic law of Shariah and upholding a theocratic political system.

The jihad in Hausa states aimed at terminating "syncretism, polytheism, and corruption among Northern Nigeria's Hausa/Fulani peoples," and by doing so, "the jihadists united Muslims under the Sokoto Caliphate in a collective conscience by adopting Shari'ah to adjudicate civil and criminal cases."[16] Usman dan Fodio, a Fulani scholar, military strategist and religious leader led the jihad. Exploiting the fears and grievances of Fulani pastoralists, Usman dan Fodio successfully waged a jihad in 1804 that overthrew the king of Gobir. Subsequent decades of Islamic wars saw the conquest of other Hausa city-states and the reorganization and administration of the conquered territories under an Islamic leader, caliph, who ruled a new state called the Sokoto Caliphate.[17] From 1804 when the Sokoto Caliphate was established to 1906 when the British established a new state called the Northern Protectorate (later Northern Nigeria), the Sokoto Caliphate was the largest state in West Africa since the 16th century. In line with Fodio's dream, "Shari'ah [Islamic law] regulated all aspects of Muslims' lives, both civil and criminal, and it was applied to all the conquered territories, imposing a collective conscience based on Islamic religion."[18] Islamic education thrived. In 1900 when the British established the Protectorate of Northern Nigeria, there were, according to Lord Lugard, about 250,000 students in the 20,000 Koranic schools in the area.[19]

Another Islamic state that emerged during the period of Islamic revivalism in West Africa was the Mandinka Empire located on the eastern part of Futa Jalon. At the height of its power in the late 19th century, the Mandinka Empire was the third largest empire in West Africa following Sokoto and Futa Toro empires. Samori Toure founded the empire. He was a wealthy trader, trading gold and cattle for weapons from the coast which led to the establishment of a modern army. He and his army conquered surrounding kingdoms between 1865 and 1875 and established an effective political environment that facilitated trade and ensured economic prosperity. Besides, his conversion to Islam strengthened his kingdom as Islamic education and law largely formed the basis for social and political life.[20]

EAST AFRICAN CITY STATES AND ISLAM

Before the birth of Islam, centuries of interactions had existed between East Africa and Arabia, Persia, India, and China through the Indian Ocean. Unlike North Africa, East Africa did not witness far-reaching Islamic conversion. Like West Africa, Islam was limited to the privileged few who had commercial relations with Arab merchants. The date Islam entered East Africa is unclear but by the 8th century, Islam had made its way to the region. The possible directions through which Islam entered East Africa were the Arab Peninsula, which is about fifty miles away from East Africa, dubbed the Horn of Africa. Egypt was another direction since it was the first African country that converted to Islam. Somalia was another possible route because the port of Zeila had been a key commercial center in the 10th century when the political center of Islam shifted from Mecca to Baghdad. There is also an oral tradition suggesting that Islam came to East Africa from Shiraz in Persia. According to a local Kilwa chronicle, Islam came from Persia:

> Then came Sultan Ali bin Selimani the Shirazi, that is, the Persian. He came with his ships, and brought his goods and his children. One child was called Fatima, the daughter of Sultan Ali: we do not know the names of the other children. They came with Musa bin Amrani the Beduin; they disembarked at Kilwa, that is to say, they went to the headman of the country, the Elder Mrimba, and asked for a place in which to settle at Kisiwani. This they obtained. And they gave Mrimba presents of trade goods and beads. Sultan Ali married Mrimba's daughter. He lived on good terms with the people.[21]

Further, a 10th century account of a Persian sailor, Buzurg Ibn Shahriyar captures the early influence of Islam in East Africa. According to the account,

> A group of Persian sailors were shipwrecked off what is present day Mozambique. They were taken to the court of a local king who helped them resume their journey. Before they went they tricked the king into boarding their ship. They then kidnapped him and sold him into slavery in Oman. Years later, after many adventures the king succeeds in reclaiming his throne. By this time he has converted to Islam. By chance the sailors who originally kidnapped him turn up at his court. They are amazed and terrified to find him back in power. But he forgives them, saying they were the instrument of his becoming a Muslim.[22]

Islam did not make significant inroads in the northeastern part of Africa. Even though the surrounding kingdoms in the north, west, and east of Ethiopian kingdom had converted to Islam by the 19th century, Ethiopia remained a Christian kingdom. Trade between coastal East African city-states and Arab traders had gone on for centuries but it was only between the 17th and the 19th centuries that Islam gained ground in those states.[23] Muslim Arab traders settled in the coastal regions of east Africa. Unlike in West Africa, they had minimal contacts with Africans in the interiors areas of the region largely because they used African intermediaries to conduct their trade with locals inland. Goods such as gold and ivory from the interior made their way to the coast in exchange for cloth, glassware and other commodities the Arabs imported. Closer interactions between Arab traders and locals in the interior came in the late 18th and 19th centuries with the establishment of coconut and sugar plantation by the Arabs along the coast and coastal islands. The survival and profitability of these plantations depended on the availability of cheap labor. Thus began a systematic importation of slaves from the interior of east Africa in which Arab traders visited and established close relationship with African kingdoms in the interior and in the process spread Islam.

The complex and continuous commingling of East Africans with Arabs led to the emergence of a distinct identity. The increase in intermarriages between Arabs and East Africans and the long years of association ensured that the indigenous African peoples and cultures coalesced with Arabic civilization to produce a new culture called Swahili, and a new language called Kiswahili, which is a mixture of Arabic-indigenous African language. Kiswahili, which emerged as a consummation of centuries of contacts, remains a tool for a literate culture and communication. The language remains a regional language of numerous communities in East Africa. Millions speak the language in Tanzania, Kenya, and Congo (DRC). Governments in those countries recognize Kiswahili as their official language. It is also spoken by a vast majority of people in Uganda while spoken by small groups in Burundi, the Comoros, Rwanda, northern Zambia, Malawi, and Mozambique.[24]

In the 15th century, the Portuguese first challenged Arab domination of trade in East Africa, especially in the coastal kingdom of Kilwa. Although further spread of Islam ebbed with the establishment of colonial rule in much of East Africa by the late 19th century, attempts at Christianization of the region met with limited success.

ISLAM IN SOUTHERN AFRICA

Compared to other regions in Africa, the introduction Islam into Southern Africa was recent. The impetus was the desire for cheap labor by the Dutch after occupying the southernmost tip of Africa, known as the Cape of Good Hope, in the 1650s. Engaged in agriculture and increasingly concerned with the unreliable supply of slave labor by the African inhabitants, the Dutch began importing slaves and servants from Malaysia, Indonesia, Madagascar, and western India from the 17th century. Many of the slaves imported were Moslems and their descendants maintained their Islamic identity. When the British annexed the territory in the early 1800s, they established sugar plantations in the province of Natal leading to the second wave of importation of mostly Muslim slaves from South East Asia.[25] In the 1860s, Indians came to South Africa and settled in Transvaal and Natal bringing their Muslim faith with them and converting about 13,000 indigenous South Africans.[26]

Even though Christianity remains the dominant religion in Southern Africa, Muslim minorities still play an important role in the religious politics and history of the region. Unlike Muslims in other regions in Africa, the Muslim communities in Southern Africa scarcely follow strict adherence to Islamic law. In South Africa, for instance, two competing forces have emerged since the collapse of apartheid in 1994. The conservative group pushes for greater adherence to Islamic law, polygyny, and greater divorce rights for men and inheritance as stipulated by the Koran. The more liberal element, on the other hand, insists on respect for the principle of non-discrimination as provided by the new post-apartheid South African constitution.[27] Dialogue between the two groups continues to shape the inter-faith scene in post-apartheid South Africa.

COLONIALISM AND ISLAM

While Islam was shaping the politics, society, and economy of various African peoples in the interior, the Atlantic slave trade dominated the economy of African coastal regions. European slave traders made limited attempts to penetrate the interiors of Africa. Following the abolition of the trade in 1807, Africa witnessed increased encroachment of European traders, explorers, missionaries, and consuls who came to enforce the ban on the slave trade, introduce "legitimate trade," map out Africa, and expose Africans to the "blessings" of Christianity and European civilization. Establishing effective control of African territories in European spheres of influence was a vital precondition for exploiting the peoples' natural resources. Colonial rule was inevitable. Led by Britain and France—and joined by Germany, Italy, Belgium, Portugal, and Spain—European powers embarked on murderous campaigns from the 1880s to annex African territories. The exercise received official European endorsement at the Berlin Conference of 1884–5, which provided the legal and political framework for the occupation of Africa.[28]

The conquest of African societies was widely resisted. Resistance in Islamic areas was fiercer and prolonged. Muslims believed that they were engaged in a holy war to defend their faith against infidels for which fighting to death was a worthy cause. Their unwillingness to submit or cooperate with the British invaders was evident in the letter Abd al-Rahmanthe, the Sultan of Sokoto, wrote to Lord Lugard: "I do not consent that any one from you should ever dwell with us. I will never agree with you. I will have nothing ever to do with you. Between us and you there are no dealings except as between Muslims and Unbelievers: war, as God Almighty has enjoined on us. There is no power and no strength save in God Most High."[29] Many Muslims considered the fight to keep their faith against the potential social changes colonial rule represented as a divine duty. Elsewhere in Africa, Samori Toure, founder of the Mandinka Empire, an Islamic state in present-day Guinea, organized his army of about 35,000 to wage a prolonged, bloody resistance against French colonial occupation from 1882 until his capture in 1898.

Stiff resistance Muslim societies posed against colonial presence dictated European accommodating administrative policies. To keep the peace after the conquest of Muslim societies, colonial powers surprisingly entrenched Islamic faith among adherents and even created the conditions that encouraged its consolidation and spread. Three factors accounted for this scenario. First, in the Islamic areas, the powers and legitimacy of Islamic local leaders received official endorsement under the indirect rule policy of colonial administration practiced by virtually all colonial powers in one form or the other. Eager to keep the peace, facilitate effective colonial administration, and guarantee the cooperation of mostly conservative Muslim leaders, colonial powers preserved the autocratic and theocratic powers of Islamic political structures. Christian missionary work in those areas suffered as colonial government restricted evangelization, especially in Sudan, Senegal, and Nigeria. For instance, at the inauguration of the Protectorate of Northern Nigeria on January 1, 1900, Lord Lugard, a British soldier and colonial administrator, pledged to honor the agreement he had with the Muslim leaders that he would prevent Christian missionary work in the area.[30]

Colonial residents in the Muslim northern Nigeria were quick in condemning missionary activities in their provinces and even recommending that they cease their operations. P. Lonsdale, the resident of Bauchi Province, "doubted the measure of tolerance exhibited by missionaries . . . [insisting] "that a spirit of narrow-mindedness, accompanied by poor education, exists in the case of many new arrivals in the missionary ranks to this country."[31] According to E.C. Duff, the resident of Kaduna Province, "within my personal experience where Christin Missions have been established in or near Muslim centers the result has led to constant administrative difficulties." Duff feared that if the feeling persists that the work of missionaries "was an administrative act of government," it would be "a source of grave potential danger to the administration."[32] Guy N. Vertue, the resident of Maiduguri Province, feared that if the spread of Christianity in predominantly Muslim areas continued, it would shatter "the foundation on which the administrative policy has been built—'acting as a disintegrating force it will tend to draw a part of the community away from its traditional customs' thus causing friction and disturbance."[33] Born out of necessity, the pro-Islamic attitude of colonial powers remained in force for much of the colonial period with minor changes.[34] Because missionaries dominated the provision of Western education, southern Nigeria, just as in southern Sudan, where they operated freely enjoyed an educational advantage. Since Christianity was synonymous with Western education, Muslims naturally resisted it. Even when the colonial government established experimental schools in the Muslim North, the pace of growth was slow. The tension arising from the educational disadvantaged status of the North has been at the center of the social and political policies and crisis that dominate the history of postcolonial Nigeria.[35]

Second, the establishment of colonial rule brought more opportunities for trade as different commodities brought from Europe diversified the economy. As many commercial cities emerged, Muslim traders travelled outside their predominantly Islamic areas and in the process spread Islam to their host communities. In Nigeria, Hausa traders from the north spread Islam to neighboring Yourbaland. In Senegal, Islamic brotherhoods, such as the Mourides, were influential agents in the spread of Islam in many communities. Third, unlike Christianity, Islam attracted more followers because many of its practices parallel African indigenous customs such as polygamy, respect for ancestors and belief in spirits. By respecting African religious beliefs, Islamic teachings were easily welcomed by more Africans. The only advantage Christianity had in colonial Africa was the dominant control of education by Christian missionary bodies. Missionary-controlled schools insisted on religious instruction. Because Western education became the route to social mobility in the colonial society and afterwards, demand for it in non-Islamic areas was high. More importantly, those who obtained it dominated colonial and postcolonial political, economic, and social institutions.

Although European powers gave much independence in local affairs to Muslim communities, they established native courts to regulate the administration of justice. Those courts were established to "Administer native law and custom prevailing in the area of their jurisdiction and might award any type of punishment recognized, thereby, except mutilation, torture or any other which is repugnant to natural justice and humanity."[36] Restricting the type of punishment that native courts could award was the cornerstone of the British "repugnancy test system." Only punishment that passed the test survived. For instance, this provision gave colonial powers the authority to invalidate and deny enforcement of any customary or Islamic laws that fell outside the prescribed judicial boundaries. Islamic law of Shariah that supported, for instance, stoning to death for adultery, were not enforced. Therefore, Muslims increasingly felt that the totality of their religion and law was sacrificed. Meaningful revival of the totality of Islamic principles during the colonial period was unsuccessful. Independence of African countries in the years before and after the 1960s, especially Muslim areas, presented a new opportunity.

ISLAM AND THE CHALLENGE OF NATION BUILDING

During the colonial period, the political, sociocultural, and judicial systems and practices in Africa witnessed significant changes. Virtually all newly independent Africans leaders were western-educated and sought to maintain the European model bequeathed to their countries. The need to reassert their cultural and religious identities found expression in Islamic revivalism in postcolonial Africa. Such revivalism in pluralistic and secular countries often came in direct conflict with the existing order. Using the principles of Islamic faith to hold their leaders accountable has been a common feature of Muslim societies in Africa. The anti-government movements in North Africa between 2010 and 2013 demonstrate Muslims' active participation in their government. Such efforts achieved limited success because due to the Cold War politics, the United States and the Soviet Union supported dictatorial regimes that suppressed freedom of speech and violated human rights of Africans. Post-Cold War Africa had witnessed increasing intensity in the revival of Islamic religion. Known as the Arab spring, a series of violent and non-violent revolutionary protests swept through much of African countries such as Tunisia, Egypt, Libya, Sudan, Algeria, Mauritania, Western Sahara, and Djibouti. Predominantly Muslim population in these countries rose up against their governments to express dissatisfaction with the prevailing dictatorship, corruption, moral decay, human rights abuses, poverty, among other things. Beside the overthrow and killing of the Libyan leader, Muammar Gaddafi, and the pledge by the Sudanese president, Omar al-Bashir not to contest in the 2015 election, other notable outcomes of these protests were the resignation of Tunisian president, Zine El Abidine Ben Ali, and Egyptian president, Hosni Mubarak, and their replacement with Islamist-led governments. As Lapidus puts it, "The contemporary world-wide wave of Islamic revivalist movements is a direct response to the global changes that constitute modernity."[37]

Unlike countries mentioned above, Mali is a country where tension from those who use Islam to justify terror is evident. In 2012, the National Movement for the Liberation of Azawad led by the Tuareg, a Berber people, and assisted by violent extremist groups, resulted in declaring independence of Azaward, an area in northern Mali. When Ansar Dine and Al-Qaeda in the Islamic Maghreb (AQIM), took control of Azawad from the Tuareg with the intent of implementing Islamic law, and the government had difficulty containing the threat, the French intervened and defeated the rebels. The threat posed to normal life in northern Mali and the prevailing fear and uncertainty belies many centuries of religious tolerance and Islamic learning that specially typify the ancient city of Timbuktu. Although the nine-month occupation of northern Mali ended in 2013, "Few of the things a city needs in order to function – electricity, fuel, banks, marketplaces, and basic government services such as the town hall or judiciary – are fully up and running."[38]

Efforts at reviving complete Islamic practices by more moderate individuals and groups within Muslim societies, as the experience of peaceful religious coexistence in Senegal shows, were often overshadowed by the activities of a few who were dedicated to using violence to advance their selfish agenda while claiming to be acting in the name of Islam.[39] Islamic religion, like Christianity, does not endorse violence. Peaceful and violent people are found in every religion. Their choice of peace or violence is less about their religion and more about their politics, interests, agenda, and fears. The fifteen countries in Africa with more than fifty percent of their population professing Islam have not witnessed unrests, conflicts or war different from other predominantly Christian countries in Africa or elsewhere.[40] Using perverted interpretation of Islamic faith to justify acts of violence has been a noticeable trend in the domestic politics of many postcolonial African states. In East Africa, Al-Shabaab, a militant group based in Somalia, and intent on enforcing strict adherence to Islamic law, has continued to launch attacks in Somalia, Kenya and Uganda since the early 2006.[41] Remarkable among its activities was the deadly attack on the Westgate Mall in Nairobi, Kenya that resulted in fatalities in 2013. After a four-day standoff with Kenyan security officials, more than 60 people were dead. Since 2007, al-*Shabaab* "has carried out nearly 550 terrorist attacks, killing more than 1,600 and wounding more than 2,100."[42] Countries like Cameroon and Chad have equally witnessed attacks linked to violent extremists acting in the name of Islam.[43]

Nowhere is the trend of violent extremism more pronounced and consequential than in Nigeria, the most populous country in Africa with the largest Muslim population on the continent. Indirect rule system of administration adopted by the British in administering their colonies such as Nigeria meant that Muslim communities kept much of their Islamic culture, traditions, and law intact throughout the colonial period. At independence,

British common law formed the basis for the country's criminal justice system. For the conservative Muslims, Nigeria's independence in 1960s was in a sense a loss of independence for the Muslim north as they lost the considerable autonomy they enjoyed during the colonial period. Efforts to revive Islamic law to govern both criminal and civil aspects of the Muslims' justice system lacked intensity and momentum due to Nigeria's unstable domestic scene evident in the Nigeria-Biafra War (1967–1970) and the violent and dictatorial climate created by the military governments (1966–1979, 1983–1999) dominated by more liberal Muslim military leaders. With the return of democratic rule in 1999, and the emergence of a Christian from the South as the country's president, Islamic revival gathered momentum. Between 1999 and 2002, twelve states in the North adopted the Islamic law of Shariah to govern both criminal and civil aspects of their justice system in violation of the country's constitution. The international outcry that came when some women were convicted of adultery and hastily sentenced to death by stoning led to the softening of Islamic law in Nigeria since 2005.[44]

Frustrated by the widespread corruption of the Muslim political elite in the North, dismayed by a high level of unemployment, inequality, and poverty, and mistaking Nigeria's Western styled political and judicial system as a major source of Nigeria's problems, a militant group emerged in 2002. It is called the Congregation of the People of Tradition for Proselytism and Jihad or Boko Haram. Founded by Mohammed Yusuf in 2002 and based in the northeastern part of Nigeria, Boko Haram, a Hausa word that means, "Western education is evil," called for the establishment of an Islamic state under Islamic law. According to Andrew Walker, "Boko Haram is an Islamic sect that believes politics in northern Nigeria has been seized by a group of corrupt, false Muslims. It wants to wage a war against them, and the Federal Republic of Nigeria generally, to create a "pure" Islamic state ruled by sharia law."[45] The indiscriminate killings committed by this group against innocent civilians in the name of God represent a disturbing but unsurprising perversion of Islamic religion. The acts overshadow the work of the vast majority of Muslims dedicated to peace, and further perpetuate the stereotypes of Islam as a violent religion. Between 2002 and 2014, more than 12,000 innocent people lost their lives due to attacks linked to this militant group whose ideas are incompatible not only with secular societies in Nigeria but also mainstream Muslims.[46] The increasing sophistication and regularity of attacks by Boko Haram and the transnational posture the organization has assumed, was captured by the U.S. Department of State report:

> Boko Haram (BH) maintained a high operational tempo in 2013 and carried out kidnappings, killings, bombings, and attacks on civilian and military targets in northern Nigeria, resulting in numerous deaths, injuries, and destruction of property in 2013. The number and sophistication of BH's attacks are concerning, and while the group focuses principally on local Nigerian issues and actors, there continue to be reports that it has financial and training links with other violent extremists in the Sahel region. Boko Haram, along with a splinter group commonly known as Ansaru, has also increasingly crossed Nigerian borders to neighboring Cameroon, Chad, and Niger to evade pressure and conduct operations.[47]

What initially gave rise to the emergence of Boko Haran were local concerns. But between 2012 and 2014, the sect became more or less a criminal enterprise bent on irrational killings of innocent civilians in Nigeria. One of the highlights of its activities was the kidnapping of more than 200 young Muslim and Christian students at gunpoint while they were sleeping in their dormitories at the Government Girls Secondary School in Chibok, Borno state on April 14, 2014. Boko Haram threatened to sell them into slavery or force them to marry members of the group. A man claiming to be the leader of the group, Abubakar Shekau, released a video tape in which he stated: "I abducted your girls. I will sell them in the market, by Allah. There is a market for selling humans. Allah says I should sell. He commands me to sell. I will sell women. I sell women."[48]

Local and international analysts and observers, both Muslims and non-Muslims, agree that the activities of Boko Haran violate the tenets of Islam they claim to preserve. Arsalan Iftikhar, an international human rights lawyer, and adjunct professor of religious studies at DePaul University in Chicago made a simple but powerful indictment of the sect by asking its members to "pick up a Quran and bring back our girls."[49] Nigeria's former military head of state, General Muhammadu Buhari, insisted that "misguided persons masquerading as adherents of Islam" committed the acts. As he rightly stated, "It is clear from what they profess that they are not followers of God. They do not mean well for our country and her citizens. I am a Muslim. I am versed in the teaching of Christianity, and I understand both religions seek peaceful co-existence of all humanity."[50]

In the wake of the global campaign to rescue the kidnapped girls, dubbed, "# Bring Back the Girl," Western countries led by the United States pledged to provide military assistance to Nigeria in their efforts to combat the threat of Boko Haran. External support in the fight against violent extremist groups under the guise of Islamic vanguard ushers in a tricky and uncertain future for Nigeria. If there is any lesson from the recent experience of external support in combating extremists groups in Yemen, Iraq, Afghanistan, and Pakistan, it is that such campaigns hardly guarantee sustainable peace and stability. Rather it could play into the hands of extremists dedicated to exploiting Western involvement to recruit militants, attract more funding, and thus prolonging the conflict. Given the inability of Nigerian government to contain the menace posed by the group and the public pressure to see immediate result, Western involvement seemed inevitable.

CONCLUSION

The history of Africa since the 7th century is incomplete without analyzing the role Islam played. Islam shaped the direction of African politics, economy, and culture since its spread to the continent. The five pillars of Islam served as a yardstick to measure compliance to Islamic faith. The misguided minority who use Islam to justify violent acts against both innocent Muslims and non-Muslims have also been faithful to their faith in terror. The tendency to confuse Muslims who use their misinterpretation of the Koran to serve their selfish, radical, and violent interests with the Islamic religion itself has unfortunately led to prejudice, fear, hatred, and discrimination against Muslims in the Western world, often dubbed *Islamophobia*.[51] Separating the two is crucial in order to appreciate the contributions Islam has made to African civilization in particular and world history in general. As this chapter has shown, understanding the history of Islam in Africa is crucial in appreciating the religious and cultural diversity of the continent. It also provides a useful window into understanding the problems and promise of Africa.

Mindless killing of those considered heretics or infidels in the name of God has been a disturbing reality in the history of religions. Attempts by those who use religion to justify violent acts have often led to the deaths of unintended targets. As shown in the attacks in Nigeria, Kenya, and other African countries, innocent Muslim non-targets are victims too. The difficulty in differentiating Muslims from non-Muslim targets echoes the Catholic inquisition that led to indiscriminate slaughter of both Catholics and Cathars in 1209. The Cathars, a Christian dualist movement that thrived mostly in France, rejected the authority of the pope. Pope Innocent 111, who considered the group heretical and a threat to the Catholic faith, launched series of attacks against them. As the attack on Beziers towns began, a soldier asked Arnaud Amalric, a French monk, who was the Pope's official representative during the crusade, how to determine which townspeople were Catholics and which were Cathars. The response of the Catholic abbot remains a chilling reminder of the inanity of religious extremism. He said, "Kill them! The Lord knows those who are his own."[52] By the time the crusade was over, the Catholic army had killed about 20 thousand men, women, and children in the town and burned the town to the ground. In the next two decades of the Cathars Crusades, as many as one million people died in religious conflicts.[53]

Violent extremism in the name of God is inescapable. It is not unique to one religion. It does not diminish, however, the commitment of all religions to peace. The dreadfulness of religious extremism derives from the disquieting reality that decent people could easily commit and excuse irrational crimes supposedly in the name of God. As Steven Weinberg writes, "With or without religion, good people can behave well and bad people can do evil; but for good people to do evil—that takes religion."[54]

ENDNOTES

1 See Pew Research Center, *Mapping the Global Muslim Population: A Report on the Size and Distribution of the World's Muslim Population* (Washington, D.C.: Pew Research Center, 2009). See also Pew Research Center, *The Global Religious Landscape: A Report on the Size and Distribution of the World's Major Religious Groups as of 2010* (Washington, D.C.: Pew Research Center, 2012).

2 See the following books for detailed discussion on the various aspects of Islamic history in Africa: J. Spencer Trimingham, *History of Islam in West Africa* (London: Oxford University Press, 1962); Nehemia Levtzion and Randall L. Pouwels, eds., *The History of Islam in Africa* (Athens: Ohio University Press, 2000); David Robinson, *Muslim Societies in African History* (London: Cambridge University Press, 2004); Bruce S. Hall, *A History of Race in Muslim West Africa, 1600–1960* (London: Cambridge University Press, 2011); John Hanson, *Migration, Jihad, and Muslim authority in West Africa: The Futanke Colonies in Karta* (Bloomington : Indiana University Press, 1996); Lamin O Sanne, *The Jakhanke Muslim Clerics: A Religious and Historical Study of Islam in Senegambia* (Lanham, MD.: University Press of America, 1989); Ghislaine Lydon, On Trans-Saharan trails: Islamic law, trade networks, and cross-cultural exchange in nineteenth-century Western Africa (Cambridge; New York: Cambridge University Press, 2009).

3 *Mapping the Global Muslim Population.*

4 Etienne Dinet and Sliman Ben Ibrahim, *The Life of Mohammad the Prophet of Allah* (Paris: Paris Book Club, 1918).

5 See Peter N. Stearns, ed., *World History in Documents: A Comparative Reader*, 2nd edition (New York: New York University Press, 2008), 149–150.

6 No one form of religious belief or practice is necessarily superior to another. Christin missionaries who spread Christianity in Africa in the 19th century believed in the superiority of their religion. They thus required African peoples to forsake their beliefs and embrace the Christian God and his son as the only route to earning eternal life after death. Islam did not make similar claims. By identifying with some of the indigenous African religious practices, Islam gained increased acceptance in the continent.

7 Munir D. Ahmad, "Muslim Education Prior to the Establishment of Madrasah," *Islamic Studies* 26, no. 4 (1987): 321–348.

8 Walter Rodney, *How Europe Underdeveloped Africa* (Washington, D.C.: Howard University Press, 1981), 240.

9 For instance, Al Kwarizmi's book, *The Calculation of Integration and Equation*, enriched modern mathematical knowledge. Al Idrisi's maps, drawn in the 12th century, left a legacy in modern geography. Scholars, writers, and travelers such as Ibrahim ibn Yaqub (9th century), Ibn Jubair (12th century) and Ibn Battuta (14 century) have left lasting impact in modern knowledge. In Timbuktu, the Shaykh Bay Al-Kunti's library was a major center of Islamic research in law and religion for much of Sub-Saharan Africa in the 1930s.

10 Rudolph Peters, *Islam and Colonialism: The Doctrine of Jihad in Modern History* (The Hague; New York: Mouton, 1979), 118; Diane Morgan, *Essential Islam: A Comprehensive Guide to Belief and Practice* (Santa Barbara, Calif.: Praeger/ABC-CLIO, 2010), 87.

11 Levtzion and Pouwels, 1.

12 Michael Brett and Elizabeth Fentress, *The Berbers* (Oxford, UK; Cambridge, USA: Blackwell, 1996).

13 Al-Bakri, cited in J. F. P. Hopkins, trans., N. Levtzion and J. F. P. Hopkins, eds., *Corpus of Early Arabic Sources for West African History* (Cambridge: Cambridge University Press, 1981), 79.

14 Ibid., 80.

15 Ibid.

16 Ogechi E. Anyanwu, "Enforcing Shari'ah Law in Nigeria: Women, Justice, and Muslims' Collective Conscience," *The American Journal of Islamic Social Sciences* 26, no. 3 (2009): 27.

17 Islam also spread to neighboring Yorubaland and Nupe.

18 Ogechi E. Anyanwu, "Crime and Justice in Post-colonial Nigeria: The Justifications and Challenges of Islamic Law of Sharia," *Journal of Law and Religion* XXI, no. 2 (2005–2006): 324.

19 K. O. Dike, "Development of Modern Education in Nigeria," in *The One and the Many: Individual in the Modern World*, ed. J. N. Brookes (New York: Harper & Row, 1962), 237.

20 T. A. Osae, S. N. Nwabara, and A. T. O. Odunsi, *A Short History of West Africa, A.D. 1000 to the present* (New York: Hill and Wang, 1973).

21 G S P Freeman-Grenville, *The East African Coast: Select Documents from the first to the earlier Nineteenth Century* (Oxford: Clarendon Press, 1962).

22 Ibid.

23 Viera Pawlikova-Vilhanová, "Rethinking the Spread of Islam in Eastern and Southern Africa," *Asian & African Studies* 19, Issue 1 (February 2010): 134–167.

24 Derek Nurse, *Thomas J Hinnebusch, and Gérard Philipson, Swahili and Sabaki: A Linguistic History* (Berkeley: University of California Press, 1993).

25 For more information, see Ephraim Mandivenga, "The Role of Islam in Southern Africa," in Religion and Politics in Southern Africa, Carl Fredrik Hallencreutz and Mai Palmberg, eds. (Uppsala: Scandinavian Institute of African Studies, 1991).

26 Rosemary Ridd, "South Africans," in *Muslim Peoples: A World Ethnographic Survey*, 2nd ed., Weekes, Richard V., ed. (Westport, CT: Greenwood Press, 1984).

27 Farid Esack, Qur'an, *Liberation and Pluralism: An Islamic Perspective of Interreligious Solidarity Against Oppression* (Oxford, England: Oneworld Publications, 1997).

28 For more information, see Adu Boahen, *African Perspectives on Colonialism* (Baltimore: Johns Hopkins University Press, 1987).

29 F. D. Lugard, *Collected Annual Report for Northern Nigeria*, 1900–1911 (London: HMSO, N.D), 159.

30 Dike, 238.

31 CO 583, "Missionary Activities in Northern Province," Dispatches, Vol. 2, Nigerian 1919.

32 Ibid.

33 Ibid.

34 For more on the politics of religion during the colonial period, see E. A. Ayandele, *Missionary Impact on Modern Nigeria 1842–1914: A Political and Social Analysis* (New York: Humanities Press, 1967); Andrew Barnes, "Evangelization Where It Is Not Wanted: Colonial Administrators and Missionaries in Northern Nigeria during the First Third of the Twentieth Century," *Journal of Religion in Africa* XXV, no. 4 (1995): 412–41.

35 For more information, see Ogechi E. Anyanwu, *The Politics of Access: University Education and Nation Building in Nigeria, 1948–2000* (Calgary: University of Calgary Press, 2011).

36 The Native Courts Proclamation of 1900 as cited in E. A. Keay and S. S. Richardson, *The Native Customary Courts of Nigeria* (London: Sweet and Maxwell, 1966), 22.

37 Ira M. Lapidus, "Islamic revival and Modernity: The Contemporary Movements and the Historical Paradigms," Journal *of the Economic and Social History of the Orient* 40, No. 4 (1997): 444.

38 "Islamist insurgency in Mali casts long shadow over Timbuktu," July, 2013, accessed January 10, 2014, http://www.theguardian.com/global-development/2013/jul/01/islamist-insurgency-mali-timbuktu.

39 Such religious extremism, however, is not unique to Islam. As Steven Weinberg rightly states, "I could point out endless examples of the harm done by religious enthusiasm, through a long history of pogroms, crusades, and jihads. In our century, it was a Muslim zealot who killed Sadat, a Jewish zealot who killed Rabin, and a Hindu zealot who killed Gandhi. No one would say that Hitler was a Christian zealot, but it is hard to imagine Nazism taking the form it did without the foundation provided by centuries of Christian anti-Semitism." See Steven Weinberg, "A Designer Universe," *The New York Review of Books*, October 21, 1999, 47.

40 Those predominantly Muslim countries include: Algeria, Comoros, Djibouti, Egypt, The Gambia, Libya, Mali, Mauritania, Morocco, Nigeria, Senegal, Somalia, Sudan, and Tunisia.

41 "Designation of Al-Shabaab," *U.S. State Department*, March 18, 2008, accessed May 1, 2014, http://web.archive.org/web/20080319184009/http://www.state.gov/r/pa/prs/ps/2008/mar/102338.htm; "Al-Shabab attacks Somali Presidential Palace," *Aljazeera*, February 22, 2014, accessed May 14, 2014, http://www.aljazeera.com/news/africa/2014/02/somali-presidential-hq-attacked-al-shabab-201422112586270319.html; "Al-Shabab launch suicide raid on Somali hotel," *Aljazeera*, March 19, 2014, accessed May 14, 2014, http://www.aljazeera.com/news/africa/2014/03/al-shabab-suicide-bomb-attack-somali-hotel-201431813415994401.html.

42 START, National Consortium for the Study of Terrorism and Responses to Terrorism, *Background Report: Al-Shabaab Attack on Westgate Mail in Kenya* (College Park, MD: University of Maryland, 2007), 1.

43 U.S. Department of State, *Country Reports on Terrorism 2013* (Washington, D.C.: United States Department of State Publication, 2014).

44 See Anyanwu, "Crime and Justice in Post-colonial Nigeria."

45 Andrew Walker, *What is Boko Haram, United States Institute of Peace Special Report, June 2012* (Washington, D.C.: United States Institute of Peace, 2012), accessed May 10, 2014, http://www.usip.org/sites/default/files/SR308.pdf.

46 Ibid.

47 *Country Reports on Terrorism 2013*, 7.

48 Aminu Abubakar and Josh Levs, " 'I will sell them,' Boko Haram leader says of kidnapped Nigerian girls," *CNN*, May 6, 2014, accessed May 10, 2014, http://www.cnn.com/2014/05/05/world/africa/nigeria-abducted-girls/

49 Arsalan Iftikhar, "Hey Boko Haram, pick up a Quran and bring back our girls," *CNN*, May 6, 2014, accessed May 10, 2014, http://religion.blogs.cnn.com/2014/05/06/hey-boko-haram-pick-up-a-quran/comment-page-2/.

50 Emmanuel Aziken, "Buhari to Boko Haram: You're Bigots Masquerading as Muslims," *Vanguard Newspaper*, May 8, 2014, accessed May 10, 2014, http://www.vanguardngr.com/2014/05/buhari-boko-haram-youre-bigots-masquerading-muslims/#sthash.vgD4cwHy.dpuf.

51 For more information, see Imhoff, Roland and Recker, Julia, "Differentiating Islamophobia: Introducing a new scale to measure Islamoprejudice and Secular Islam Critique," *Political Psychology* 33, no. 6 (December 2012): 811–824.

52 Walker L. Wakefield, *Heresy, Crusade and Inquisition in Southern France, 1100–1250* (Berkeley: University of California Press, 1974), 197.

53 See M. D. Costen, *The Cathars and the Albigensian Crusade* (Manchester, U.K.: Manchester University Press, 1997).

54 Weinberg, 47.

REVIEW QUESTIONS

1. Discuss the Islamic revolutions that swept through West Africa in the 18th and 19th centuries. What were the causes and consequences of those Islamic movements?
2. Discuss the factors responsible for the spread of Islam in East Africa.
3. Why was Egypt the first country in Africa to convert to Islam? What role did Egypt and its peoples play in the spread of Islam to other regions in Africa?
4. Discuss the differences and similarities in the spread of Islam in North Africa, West Africa, East Africa, and Southern Africa.

Writing Prompt

Islam is a religion of peace. Do you agree? How has *Islamophobia* manifested and thrived in the Western world. Compare the violence that dominated the history of Islam, especially in postcolonial Africa, with the Christian religious crusades in Europe during the middle ages.

CHAPTER 7

Women in Africa

Aje-Ori Agbese

Who is an African woman? Obviously, an African woman is a woman from Africa, right? But the answer is not that simple. Google has 195 million answers. While some define African women along sociopolitical and economic lines, implying she is a submissive victim in a lost battle against male domination, economic hardship, health issues, and politics, others define her by her physical attributes, a woman with little or too much clothing, whose hairstyles range from braids to afros with a demure, submissive look. Other times she looks quite savage. African women like Nigeria's Ngozi Okonjo-Iweala and Olufunmilayo Falusi Olopade, Sudan's Iman, Zimbabwe's Thandi Newton, and Kenya's Wangari Maathi are also defined by their achievements in entertainment, science, literature, economics, business, and beauty. Apparently, an African woman is many things to many people. For Runoko Rashidi, an African woman is a "queen, goddess, scholar, diplomat, scientist, icon, prophet and freedom fighting warrior."[1] But do these adjectives apply to every woman in Africa?

The problem with the term *African women* is that it is broad and leaves room for generalizations and stereotypes. For instance, books titled "African women" suggest that the experiences and issues discussed in the text are applicable to all women in Africa. However, the information mostly often only applies to women from one country, region, or ethnic group in Africa. With fifty-five countries, and thousands of ethnic groups, it is impossible to suggest that all African women have one identity, perform the same roles, share the same racial experience, undergo the same economic and sociopolitical issues, or have the same history. A woman from Senegal and one from Egypt have different experiences that are further compounded by language, ethnicity, race, religion, and region within those countries. For instance, Makinde defines a Yoruba woman as "a mother, a wife, a daughter, a priestess, or even a witch."[2] Could a Zulu woman be defined this way too? As Cheryl Johnson-Odim puts it, women in Africa "have several identities, each of which has meaning for their lives" and these identities change with time.[3] Bottom line, the major thing African women have in common is "femaleness."[4] Therefore, the phrase women in Africa will be used in this chapter because women on the continent do not commonly self-identify as African women when you meet them. They self-identify by country, state, or ethnicity. This chapter explores what it meant and still means to be a woman in Africa, and by using specific examples in order not to generalize the experiences of one group to all, it makes a significant contribution in dispelling commonly held stereotypes and prejudices about women in Africa.

PLACING WOMEN IN AFRICAN HISTORY

Telling the story of women in Africa is a daunting task. Recent anthropological and genetic studies suggest a woman in Africa gave birth to all of humanity more than one million years ago.[5] Yet, for a long time women were absent from African historiography. One reason for this, according to Margaret Strobel, is that written African records were few.[6] Those that were found in many societies did not include women probably because men kept such records. Romans, Greeks, and Arabic travelers wrote some of the earliest records scholars found but their accounts of women in Africa were tainted with their prejudices. According to Coquery Vidrovitch, these explorers', travelers' and missionaries' accounts stereotyped women as "princesses, chiefs' mothers, slaves, concubines."[7] Missionaries presented them as having "pagan attitudes—bare breasts, an often exaggerated sexual freedom, polygamy."[8] Nevertheless, several sub-Saharan cultures preserved the history of women in "non-written sources" like "proverbs, folktales, and myths of origins."[9] Swazi women used folk songs, called *umtsimba* songs, at traditional ceremonies to describe and discuss gender and power relations.[10] Songs also tell us that matrilineal societies, where authority and inheritance come through women, were commonly accepted in Africa. Polyandry, where women had multiple husbands, was also common in parts of Kenya, Tanzania, Cameroun, and Nigeria.[11] There is also evidence that women in some parts of Africa kept and passed on oral and written records of their societies. There are examples among the Yoruba, where older women and queen mothers kept such records. For instance, "In Dahomey, the most secret traditions were transmitted by women."[12] Such accounts have provided information to understand gender issues in traditional African societies. Another reason for the lack of records is that like many cultures in the world, the history of women in Africa was affected by interactions with other cultures and events. The best way to describe women in Africa, therefore, is to examine the periods that defined their lives. These are precolonial, colonial, independent (or postcolonial), and contemporary Africa.

WOMEN IN PRECOLONIAL AFRICA

Precolonial Africa covers the enormous landscape and diverse societies that existed for more than 2,000 years before Europeans colonized the continent in the nineteenth century. Oral and some written accounts tell stories of women that in many ways challenge the stereotypes that exist about the contributions women made to Africa's past. Take the economy, for instance.

Since farming was the earliest form of economy, women in Africa were part of farming communities. Their major responsibility was gathering food (especially grains) and devising ways to farm and store food. In East, Central, and present-day South Africa, around 8,000 BCE, women gathered all kinds of food, including "protein-rich food such as termites, caterpillars, and locusts."[13] Women in some precolonial African societies also owned land and made a living for themselves and their families through agriculture. In matrilineal cultures, women owned land until they moved away. In patrilineal ones, land belonged to men but women got or used land as secondary users through their fathers, husbands, brothers, or other male relatives. A woman used the land as long as she maintained good relations with her male relatives. In much of East Africa, where women were secondary users of land, women could farm and benefit from the produce. But for women who wanted to own land without marriage or kinship in these areas, there were other options. In Buganda (in Uganda), widows, divorcees, or women who were tired of marriage got land from a male relative or chief by doing favors for their families like chores, babysitting, or pledging their allegiance.

In communities with livestock, women owned cattle, as exemplified by the Luos in Uganda and Kenya, which was and still is a great indicator of wealth in eastern and southern Africa. Yoruba women were also the keepers of livestock in their various communities. It is important to point out that division of labor was quite equal in nomadic cultures like those of the San and Mbuti. Women in Africa also participated in trading, be it in minerals, food, livestock, clothing, or slaves. In some societies, though, trading was limited to the upper class because it had foreign policy implications.

Politically, women actively participated in government and political affairs in precolonial Africa. Women are represented in African history as warriors, queens, cabinet members, and counselors. However, each ethnic group or kingdom differed in how women were involved. While some societies built women into the political structure, others had systems where women inherited power. Examples abound of women like Queen Amina of Zaria who took over from her mother at age sixteen. Famed for her bravery and military conquests, Amina invented the earthen walls that other Hausa kingdoms copied to fortify their cities. The Yoruba kingdom also included an *Iyalode* who headed a council of women called *Obinrin Ilu*. The *Iyalode* and her officials maintained law and order, participated in decision making, and even settled disputes in various communities.[14] The *Ilu* could also call for the *Oba* (king) to commit suicide or resign when he failed in his duties. Even the Oba's wives were not left out and offered advice and guidance.

Another example is found in the kingdom of Dahomey (present-day Benin), where the king had an army of well-trained women until the nineteenth century. These amazons of Black Sparta played an active role when France invaded Dahomey in 1890 and 1892.[15] Queen Anna Nzingha (or Njinga), whose territories extended from present-day Angola to The Democratic Republic of Congo, is reserved a place in history with her military prowess that kept the Portuguese at bay for more than forty years and her efforts to end the Atlantic slave trade. One of the strongest rulers of Kenya was Mwana Mkisi, a woman. Burkina Faso still celebrates its warrior queen, Iyennegi, who defended the Mossi and its lands in late 100 CE. Queen mothers were also very powerful as exemplified by the Asante *aasantehemaa* in Ghana. Some political systems also allowed for dual leadership like in Onitsha where the *Obi* had a female counterpart, the *Omu*. With the *Otu Ogene*, her cabinet, she presided over women's affairs, trade, and even set prices. Evidence suggests that in these societies, men did not feel threatened by women in powerful positions because they believed the women earned their positions through age, kinship, or merit. But not all African societies were that open. Where women were prevented from openly participating in government, they used loopholes in the system to acquire and maintain some level of power.

Indirectly, women were important in building political alliances and loyalty through marriage in precolonial Africa.[16] Kingdoms in Uganda and Benin grew through such unions. Although women's influence reduced as governments became more centralized in Africa, marriage remains an important way of forging alliances. Women were also influential when they gave birth (reproductive power) or as concubines.[17] According to Makinde, "By becoming a mother, a woman is promoted to the esteemed position in which she can be referred to as a precious stone. Therefore, it is a tragedy for a Yoruba woman not to have a child."[18] Children were considered economic assets and an extension of the family. As caregivers, it was through women that children learned what was expected of them, proper behavior, and relational skills. In Somalia, Burundi and Tanzania, mothers were celebrated as the first schools of life.[19] In Cameroon, among the Bamileke people, a woman who had twins was called *magne* and thought to be blessed by God. A *magne* was a peacekeeper, one who reconciled differences wherever she went.[20] But the reproductive function of women was also a disadvantage in some regard. Women were valued when they had children, but barren women faced divorce or neglect. But some societies provided such women with an alternative. The commonest form was woman-to-woman marriage where a woman could marry another woman.[21] Although the women did not have a sexual relationship (and so were not lesbians), the female husband retained control over her wife and the children she had either through the female husband's husband or someone else. This way, she could indirectly produce children for her husband. This option was also available to rich or postmenopausal women in several African societies including the Ijaw, Nupe, Ekiti, Bunu, Akoko, Zulu, Kikuyu, Nandi, Fon, and Dinka.[22]

Other indirect methods of influencing policy can also be found among the Igbos in Nigeria. If the king of Onitsha did not perform his duties, a naked woman sat on his throne and he was removed.[23] Among the Yoruba, women's groups punished men who abused their wives in humiliating ways. It was not uncommon to tie the hands and feet of abusive husbands and let them "roll down a rocky hill."[24] Women in parts of sub-Saharan Africa also asserted their rights by sitting on men (to humiliate them) or exposing their breasts (believed to bring a curse on men). Women could also influence policy through age. In some societies, postmenopausal women received more respect and were seen as equal or almost equal to men. Since women were often secluded during menstruation, menopause gave them an edge to participate openly.

Women were also a political force through women's groups or collectives that were formed to encourage financial, political, and emotional independence.[25] Such "women's indigenous cultural, socio-economic, development, mutual support and informal sector groupings are important associational formations that are vital in local governance, economic empowerment, local participation and social cushions in the community."[26] These groups were quite active and influential in trade, government and even in the fight against colonialism.

Another way women participated in society was through religion. African religions are full of goddesses and deities who performed various roles. Egypt had Au set (Isis), the eternal savior of mankind, and Menos, who created writing. Goddesses like Ethiopia's Buk and the Yorubas' Yemoja protected women and made them fertile. Women were priestesses, mediums, healers and diviners who mediated between the spirit world and the community.[27] The African belief in a spiritual influence meant female diviners were constantly consulted to find solutions to problems like poverty, illness, or miscarriages.[28] Such women were powerful as they "could say and do many things when possessed by a spirit that would otherwise be completely unacceptable (and for which they might even be punished were the spirit not speaking through them)."[29] For instance, Charwe from

Zimbabwe, under spiritual possession, led a revolt against the British in 1896. In all, precolonial Africa provides diverse examples on the lives of women. Although not all African societies favored or even involved women, there is ample evidence that contradicts the common belief about Africa that women had no place in society. European invasion and the subsequent establishment of colonial rule in all African societies (except Liberia and Ethiopia) undermined the role of women in Africa.

WOMEN IN COLONIAL AFRICA

Whenever two cultures meet, the consequences are usually mixed. However, colonization was not a chance meeting of cultures but the forceful integration of several cultures to one. In 1885, through the Berlin Act, European nations laid siege to Africa and thus began the official colonial history of Africa.[30] The goal was to make Africa more like Europe. The result was a crisis that benefitted Europe. Colonialism changed the political, economic, and social fabric of many African societies in many ways. Some people have argued that colonialism gave women in Africa greater freedom in marriage, choice, women's rights, economic opportunities, and the right to divorce.[31] However, evidence suggests colonization did more harm to women than good. It reduced or eradicated women's authority and opportunities to participate in their nation's social, economic and political agendas.

European colonizers arrived in Africa with a mindset that women were beneath men. As Carol Christ puts it, "Colonial thinkers perceived colonial cultures as feminine, thus justifying their conquest of them, while at the same time reinscribing the domination of masculine over feminine both at home and abroad."[32] For the British, "The Victorian mind-set situated men and women differently in social, political, and economic relations. Men were expected to be in the public sphere and women in the private."[33] Europeans needed to control women because they were the ""gateway" to the African population, and potential competitors of European women."[34] In Zimbabwe, Europeans encouraged single women to stay in the cities to meet "the sexual needs of African men and, thus, deter them from desiring white women. White women, for their part, were anxious to keep their husbands away from single African women, so they refused to hire them as domestic workers and urged the colonial state to force them to carry passes."[35] Working with conservative men in Africa, Europeans made traditional customs that benefitted men into law. The laws redefined bride price as giving men autonomy over wives and in some cases, made divorce difficult for women because it demanded repayment. It was colonization, not patrilineal African traditions, that permanently gave land rights to men. In British colonies, gender discrimination was legalized.

In societies where the traditional system matched the British mindset, colonial rule deepened the gender gap. A good example is found in northern Nigeria where the Fulani Jihad brought Fulani interpretations of the Qur'an to the region in 1810.[36] Believing Hausa culture gave women too much freedom, Fulani leaders removed women from political positions and secluded them using Sha'ria law and the purdah system, whereby women did not go out before sundown and wore veils. Muslim writers and historians also removed women's contributions to Hausaland, which produced Queen Amina of Zaria and Tawa of Gobir. Women were heavily secluded under Islam and lost their public rights to a great degree.[37] When the British arrived, they made no move to reinstate women in prominent roles and even further excluded women from their writings except in writings on marriage and divorce customs.[38] The British use of indirect rule in Northern Nigeria ensured Fulani leaders and their policies toward women remained intact. According to Imam, "to argue for women's political rights or possibilities of leadership" in the region was framed as "anti-tradition, un-Islamic, and anti-Northern."[39] Women's groups like the *Bori* spirit possession cult, under which women performed leadership roles in precolonial Hausaland, were outlawed under colonial rule.[40] Interestingly, *Karuwanci*, whereby single women made a living through sex, was not outlawed.[41] When the British left Nigeria, northern women were behind their peers in the south. While southern women voted in 1954 and 1959, northern women could not vote until universal suffrage was granted to Nigerians in 1976.[42] As a result, northern women voted in the 1979 elections.

In addition, women were also displaced with the introduction of European capitalism.[43] For instance, in emphasizing a cash crop economy, women were displaced from agricultural trade, a role originally reserved for women in many precolonial societies. In British colonies, agricultural officers gave information and seeds to only men.[44] While men learned new ways and tools of agriculture and trade, women did not. Women were refused credit and where they received any, they were given products that took forever to sell. In some parts of Africa, women had to compete with businessmen from East India and Europe. To counter these measures, women, especially in West Africa, created women associations that provided financial support and goods. In some cases, a few women established business empires that flourished after independence. When Europeans observed the influence women collectives had on trade, they even pushed for their power to be "nipped in the bud."[45] Colonialism also affected women psychologically. Foreigners raped and harassed women sexually. For example, to control the stream of Africans coming to Bulawyo in Zimbabwe, the British built "bachelor hostels" and single-room accommodations for men.[46] To stay in the city, women had to marry, prostitute, or play house (wives without bride price).

Colonial rule did not use laws and force alone. It also used God. Under the auspices of colonialism, early Christian missionaries in Africa pushed the belief that a good woman in God's eyes was submissive and married.[47] Missionaries propagated the ideal that "women should stay at home, submit to the will of colonial officials and their husbands and essentially renounce their economic and social privileges."[48] Her Christian Godly role was defined as child bearer. While men were part of the church hierarchy, women were not. While missionaries adopted male rituals to Africanize Christianity, women's rituals were considered "dirty."[49] While African customs provided safeguards for women dealing with issues like barrenness, Christianity stigmatized such women.[50] Missionaries preached that a woman who could not have children was not a real woman. They also pushed for monogamous marriages and told men to relinquish their other wives. Despite these, some missionaries allowed female education in the early twentieth century that was often restricted to home economics and courses on their obligatory roles and duties in African society.[51] Teachers resisted educating them beyond "female topics" and the occasional math or foreign language class. When parents asked for more courses for their daughters in Queen's College in Nigeria, for instance, the principal replied that, "The character of girls' education should be of a particular kind. It is almost universally agreed that it should not be a copy of that which is given to boys."[52] Nevertheless, women learned reading, writing, and new ways of doing house chores that lessened their load. Not long afterwards, women actively participated in promoting Christianity and even used it to fight colonization in parts of southern and central Africa like Dona Beatriz (Kimpa Vita) of Congo did.[53] Women also used other means to fight colonization.

One of the strongest forms of resistance in the colonial era was women collectives. The earliest account of women collectively fighting colonial policies that were inimical to their position was by South African women in 1913 when they demonstrated against pass laws. In the 1920s, Kikuyu women in Kenya used songs to protest labor rules. Colonial administrators also taxed women through trade, food, animals, and other regulations. The issue of taxes was an especially sore topic for women because it threatened their identity as women, which was tied to their trades, farms, and families.[54] In places like Abeokuta in Nigeria, the British started taxing women in 1918. However, while women had to pay taxes from the age of 15, which the British considered marriageable age, men were taxed from the age of 16 (18 by other accounts). Women who did not pay these taxes were often humiliated in different ways, including being stripped, beaten, or searched.[55] Two of the most studied cases of women collectively fighting colonial rule were the Aba Women's Riots of 1929 to 1930 and the Abeokuta Women's Union of 1946.

Under the Abeokuta Women's Union (formerly Abeokuta Ladies Club), led by Funmilayo Ransome-Kuti, the women appealed to the Alake of Egbaland (the sole native authority) to stop a new food tax. Instead, he increased their taxes in October 1946. In reaction, the women first hired a certified accountant to check the Alake's treasury. This revealed that £24,706 was carelessly spent. Further investigations revealed other abuses by the Alake, such as sexual harassment of women, leasing lands he did not own to foreign firms, and ignoring the medical needs of women. All these the Abeokuta Women's Union (AWU) publicized, through the press, and in 1947 more than 10,000 women demonstrated outside the Alake's palace from November 29 to 30. Following the demonstration, they were promised that the allegations would be investigated and the tax suspended. That did not happen. Several women were arrested. On December 8, more than 10,000 women again amassed in front of the palace to protest and ask for the release of the arrested women. They left, with the arrested women, on December 10. The AWU also petitioned the British government and in 1948, following protests and petitions, the Alake was exiled to Oshogbo in the interest of peace.[56] The tax system was reformed, to the relief of the women. These collectives were examples of early women's movements in Africa. Women were killed in the process, others exiled. In some countries, women's groups kept the momentum and worked with men to end colonial rule.

Overall, the lives of women in the colonial era differed depending on the traditional and religious system in place when the Europeans came. However, colonization did not greatly benefit women in Africa and actually laid the foundation for how women would be treated in postcolonial Africa.

WOMEN IN POSTCOLONIAL AFRICA

Africans began fighting for independence at different times. The first revolt against European control actually began before the Berlin conference with the Urabi revolt in Egypt in 1881. In other parts of the continent, the fight for independence received a great boost from the exposure and participation of Africans in events like World War II and Africans studying abroad. Many of the early leaders of West Africa, such as Nnamdi Azikiwe and Kwame Nkrumah, studied in the United States and learned about self-determination. While some Africans went to war for independence, others used intellectual and diplomatic methods. Women in Africa were not left out as they also fought for independence in different capacities. As Madam Pelewura said to the men who attended a rally against British control of food prices and taxes, "Tell me of that thing which men can undertake alone without the help of womenfolk?"[57]

Starting in the 1890s, women led movements against colonization and European invasion in Zimbabwe, Kenya, Rwanda, Congo, Nigeria, Senegal, and others.[58] As Johnson-Odim reveals in her work, "Through boycotts, marches, sit-ins, labor stoppages, refusals to pay taxes, mass demonstrations, attacks on symbols of colonial authority, collective ridicule, and in other ways," women in Africa "were active participants in protests against colonizers and those indigenes who supported and/or represented them."[59] Some of these women were jailed, exiled, or killed for their efforts. Others, like Funmilayo Ransome-Kuti of Nigeria, were not allowed to travel abroad and garner support for their efforts. The efforts of women combined with those of men to produce successful waves of decolonization beginning in the 1950s. However, despite their contributions, the nationalist movements of the "1930s through the 1950s did not always admit women as full partners."[60] Since colonial Africa removed or criminalized aspects of African culture that favored women in many respects, one could argue that postcolonial Africa is truly a combination of colonial Africa and colonially defined traditional Africa, one that privileged men and more or less dismissed women. It appears that to keep the status quo, men in Africa "needed to believe that traditional" societies "did not value women, and so they reinvented tradition. In some communities women were discouraged from participating in politics on the basis that traditional society did not include them in such fields."[61] Men in Africa were not alone in this mindset though because colonialism had globally created a patriarchy that recreated "all women in the image of the Western woman, who found herself in a male-dominated society."[62] But there could have been other reasons.

Women in Africa were not often educated in political matters during colonization. They were probably not conversant with the ways of running a central government in the new era. Another explanation could be that women in postcolonial Africa were not wealthy enough to participate in politics. Colonial rules involving taxes, savings, inheritance, and the like made it difficult for many women to store wealth during colonization. Tripp also suggests that following independence, women's groups' major concern was not political but more focused on improving "religious, welfare and domestic concerns."[63]

Nevertheless, as the newly independent nations of Africa struggled to define themselves, the future of women in these countries seemed dim. Few countries acknowledged the rights of women in their constitutions. Those that created a place for women in such documents did not enforce them. According to Fallon, "Women's primary concerns, such as health, education, discrimination, low wages, land tenure, and conditions of the informal sector, never became priorities for the government. Many women are also excluded from the formal economy and receive an unequal distribution of resources and access to employment."[64] This was worsened by the economic and political instability that affected many countries. By the late 1960s, leaders in many countries had turned their countries into personal kingdoms where they and they alone made decisions.[65] Democratic principles were replaced with paternalistic autocracy.[66] Soon, military coups became "the institutionalized method for changing governments in postcolonial Africa."[67] Military officers instigated coups frequently, citing corruption, dictatorship, ethnic wars, and party squabbles. Military regimes across the continent largely ignored women and their issues. In Nigeria, a military government even blamed market women for high prices and inflation in the 1980s.[68] Soldiers were sent to the market to beat women and make them reduce prices. Jerry Rawlings' Provisional National Defense Council also saw market women as enemies of progress. Violence against women, such as rapes and beating (domestic violence) also increased in some countries, but were not considered crimes.[69] This attitude has remained in some African countries and has become law in others. For instance, Nigeria's penal code allows a man to beat his wife as long as he does not cause permanent injury. In Ghana, where women accounted for 10 percent of its parliament under Nkrumah, no woman was part of the Ghanaian government in 1990.[70]

By the 1980s, Africa was the only continent whose population grew but its food production reduced.[71] To make matters worse, several leaders received Structural Adjustment Program (SAP) loans from the International Monetary Fund and World Bank that carried stipulations for development. SAP policies in many African countries actually worsened the situation of women. In Zambia, for instance, devaluing the currency put things further beyond the reach of women, who are among the poorest groups in society.[72] Importation of products brought cheap goods into countries where women headed the local production of such goods like cloth and food. Jean Due and Christina Gladwin state that SAP specifically worsened the lives and incomes of women in agriculture in Africa because its policies were "too macroeconomic in scope" and ignored "the reality of life at the village and household level, where male-female power relationships affect who gets access to the means of production and who controls the surplus or profit that results from added incentives to produce."[73]

Although most women in Africa were marginalized and silenced through all this, there were a few women who made an impact in postcolonial Africa. One reason for this is the international women's and feminist movements. In the 1970s and 1980s, female scholars in Africa were actively participating in the global scene on women's rights. Groups like the Association of African Women for Research and Development, formed in 1977, had "an agenda for African feminism" using research and activism.[74] International meetings and documents like the Convention on the Elimination of All Forms of Discrimination against Women (CEDAW) in 1979 also raised awareness and created resolutions to empower women and bring them into the nation-building process. There were also examples of strong women leaders in countries like Britain, where Margaret Thatcher was prime minister from 1975 to 1987. India's Indira Gandhi was the first woman to head a democracy when she came to power in 1967 and again in 1971. Who could forget Israel's Golda Meir or The Philippines' Corazon Aquino? These women showed that women could actively and effectively contribute to nation-building. Women writers in Africa also used novels and poetry to describe the situation of women on the continent. Women like Tsitsi Dangarembga, Buchi Emecheta, Ama Ata Aidoo, and Helen Ovbiagele challenged such notions and spoke from a woman's perspective. Through literature, they explored polygamy, inheritance, politics, healthcare, wife inheritance, romance, and other issues. Such works challenged the male-dominated African works that presented women as "symbols or instruments for the male hero," misrepresented or ignored them.[75]

Men also needed the support of women in politics. Women in some countries formed political parties and participated in elections. But once the election was over, the men did not let them in. By the late 1980s, military governments like those of Ibrahim Babangida of Nigeria found a way to appropriate women's participation to stay in power. In September 1987, Babangida's wife, Maryam, took a stand on the "unappreciated" and "marginal position" of women in Nigeria.[76] Believing that women in the rural areas were lagging behind, she created the Better Life for Rural Women program to "empower rural women socially, economically and politically through adult education and training in fields of education, agriculture, public health, arts and crafts and food processing."[77] The government created a National Commission for Women to supervise the program. The program created several opportunities for women and even brought gender cultural issues like wife inheritance, female circumcision (or genital mutilation), and widowhood rites to media and national attention. For her efforts, Babangida was awarded the Africa Prize in Leadership in 1991. However, this organization and similar ones were conservative and did not ruffle "the feathers of the male-dominated state by taking up issues on women's rights vis-à-vis men, such as equality and equal representation."[78] This is probably because such organizations were the creations of the wives and daughters of men in power. They gave women opportunities and silenced them at the same time. Nevertheless, women persisted in finding a voice. That voice became louder in the 1990s following events like the 1995 World Conference on Women in Beijing and the political transitions to democracy that swept Africa in the 1990s.

WOMEN IN CONTEMPORARY AFRICA

The political transitions that swept Africa in the 1990s were in response to Africa's need to move from authoritarian, single-party and military rule to democracy through multiparty elections. A major event that pushed the need was the National Conference in Benin in 1990 that ended General Kerekou's 18-year dictatorship.[79] A second event was Nelson Mandela's release from prison in 1990 and South Africa lifting its ban on black politics. Africans also watched Eastern Europeans actively protest their economic and political situations. Before long, Africans were actively demanding change and several countries, especially in sub-Saharan Africa, instituted multiparty elections. For women, this marked a new chapter.

When some countries returned to civilian rule, they also redefined women's participation. Women found new opportunities with foreign nongovernmental and educational institutions providing funding and training women who were interested in politics and activism.[80] The Beijing conference "encouraged women's organizations to hold their governments accountable to their various commitments to improving women's status."[81] In Nigeria, Olusegun Obasanjo's government made seven of his 48 ministers women. In Liberia, Ellen Johnson-Sirleaf ran for president in 1997. Women's rights organizations and nongovernmental organizations also formed to address issues like sexual and reproductive rights, rape, widowhood rites, disabled women, economic empowerment, and more. Other groups, including religious organizations, worked to provide women with healthcare information and facilities, legal aid, education, and business training. Women also became more involved in mass communication. Tripp puts these changes down to the creation of "autonomous organizations" that challenged the strangling hold the government had on women's groups following the post-independence era.[82] By autonomously creating associations that went beyond trade, welfare or domestic interests, women could "freely select their own leaders, create their own agendas and pursue their own sources of funding," and challenge the system.[83] By the twenty-first century, women in Africa were recording a number of accomplishments. Johnson-Sirleaf became the first female Liberian president in 2005, the first woman to lead an African country. Constantia Pandeni was the first woman to lead the Mineworkers Union of Namibia in 2001. In 2003, Sarah Jubril and Mojisola Adekunle Obasanjo ran for the Nigerian presidency. In Uganda, women were heading financial institutions like the stock exchange, law societies, chamber of commerce, and more. In 2008, Rwanda topped the world by having the most women in parliament. As of 2010, women accounted for 56 percent of Rwanda's parliament and are in the top ministries.[84] Rwandan women can now own land and when they marry have the option to join their properties with their husbands' or retain them. They also have access to contraception and a hotline for rape.

Internationally, women in Africa are making strides. Kenya's Wangari Maathi was the first woman from the continent to win the Nobel Peace prize and increase awareness on women and the environment. Others like Nigeria's Ngozi-Okonjo-Iweala are working at the World Bank and restructuring global economies. In entertainment, more women are challenging the media images of women in Africa. South Africa's Charlize Theron won the Oscar for best actress in 2004. In 2009, Oprah Winfrey named Nigerian actress Genevieve Nnaji one of the 100 most famous people in the world.[85] Women in Africa are also redefining fashion, science, medicine, business, politics, music, literature, and global activism in different capacities.

Telecommunications and mass media have also allowed women in Africa to organize nationally, internationally and globally. More women are speaking out against events and using the Internet and film to mobilize present issues. Women play dominant roles in the Nigerian film industry as producers, writers and directors. Emem Isong, for instance, has written and/or produced more than sixty movies since 1994.

CONCLUSION

The future seems brighter for women in Africa, although many are still working to reclaim their voices in some countries. Cultural traditions like early marriage, polygamy, domestic violence and female genital mutilation are still problems that women are fighting to end. Some countries have been successful in getting the government to criminalize such acts in their countries, but have not been as successful in getting the police and the courts to enforce the laws. Maternal mortality rates are still high in Africa, as is poverty. About 40 percent of all deaths from unsafe abortion practices happen in Africa and HIV/AIDS is a growing problem for women and children in Botswana, South Africa, Uganda, Lesotho, and Kenya.[86] In some countries, women have been their own enemy. In 2008, Nigeria's chairperson for the Nigerian Senate's Committee on Women, Senator Ufot Ekaette, introduced a bill against indecent dressing. According to the proposal, women from the age of 14 who wear clothes that expose their "breast, laps, belly and waist . . . and any part of her body from two inches below her shoulders downwards to the knee" will be arrested.[87] One of the effects of this proposed bill was the murder, through rape, of Grace Ushang for wearing the khaki pants that are part of the National Youth Corp uniform in 2009.[88] But change is coming in different ways. The revolts in Tunisia, Libya, and Egypt will shed light on women's involvement in political and social change in the twenty-first century. Overall, women in Africa are doing something, passively or actively, about their lives as they have always done. The future alone will tell if the present trend of involvement will continue or be derailed with another major global event.

ENDNOTES

1 Runoko Rashidi, "The African Woman as Heroine: Great Black Women in History," www.cwo.com/~lucumi/women. html (accessed March 25, 2011).

2 Taiwo Makinde, "Motherhood as a Source of Empowerment of Women in Yoruba Culture," *Nordic Journal of African Studies* 13, no. 2 (2004): 165.

3 Cheryl Johnson-Odim, "Women and Gender in the History of Sub-Saharan Africa," in *Women's History in Global Perspective*, vol. 3, ed. Bonnie G. Smith (Chicago: University of Illinois Press, 2005), 9.

4 Catherine Coquery-Vidrovitch, *African Women: A Modern History* (Boulder, CO: Westview Press, 1997), 1.

5 Yafet Tewelde, "Women of Africa: The Key to Civilization," www.bycav.com/node/25 (accessed December 14, 2009).

6 Margaret Strobel, "African Women History," *The History Teacher* 15, no. 4 (1982): 509–522.

7 Coquery Vidrovitch, *African women,* 3.

8 Ibid.

9 Johnson-Odim, "Women and Gender in the History of sub-Saharan Africa," 11.

10 Nonhlanhla Dlamini, "Gendered Power Relations, Sexuality and Subversion in Swazi Women's Folk Songs Performed during Traditional Marriage Rites and Social Gatherings," Muziki: *Journal of Music Research in Africa,* 6 no. 2 (2009), 133–144.

11 Polyandry existed in different forms in these societies. In some, like those of Northern Nigeria and Northern Cameroon, marriage was for life. There was no divorce. So a woman who left her husband was still married to him and could return whenever she wished and have children for him, even if she remarried. However, she could only live with one husband at a time. The children from these marriages were legitimate. In some cases, women could have lovers outside their marriage. If she did not marry the man, children from that union were considered illegitimate. For the Bashilele of the Democratic Republic of Congo, polyandry was practiced through a woman who came from another village through seduction, force, or arranged marriage. She was considered the wife of the village (called *ngalababola* or *hohombe*), a prestigious position. She could have sex with all the men in the village and live with up to five husbands, whom she catered to. However, she had the right to reduce the number. The Bashileles used polyandry to form alliances with other communities or villages. Today, polyandry is illegal in many African countries, and Christianity and Islam have rejected it too. However, in countries where traditional customs are still respected, couples can get away with polyandry like the Irigwe in Nigeria and the Masai in Kenya by using traditional marriage rites.

12 Coquery Vidrovitch, *African women,* 4.

13 Johnson-Odim, 18.

14 Bolanle Awe, "The Iyalode in the Traditional Yoruba Political System" in *Sexual Stratification: A cross-cultural view,* ed. Alice Schlegel (New York: Columbia University Press, 1977), 144–160.

15 For more information, read Stanley B. Alpern, *Amazons of Black Sparta: The Women Warriors of Dahomey* (New York: New York University Press, 1998).

16 Johnson-Odim, "Women and Gender."

17 All the kings of the Songhai empire in West Africa were children of concubines.

18 Taiwo Makinde, "Motherhood as a Source of Empowerment of Women in Yoruba Culture," 167.

19 Miriam Agatha Chinwe Nwoye, "Role of Women in Peace Building and Conflict Resolution in African Traditional Societies: A Selective Review," www.afrikaworld.net/afrel/chinwenwoye.htm (accessed March 12, 2011).

20 UNESCO, *Women and Peace in Africa.* Paris: UNESCO, 35–46.

21 R. Jean Cadigan, "Woman to Woman Marriage: Practices and Benefits in sub-Saharan Africa," *Journal of Comparative Family Studies,* vol. 29 (1998): 89–98.

22 Denise O'Brien, "Female Husbands in Southern Bantu Societies," in *Sexual Stratification: A Cross-cultural View,* ed. Alice Schlegel (New York: Columbia University Press, 1977), 109–121.

23 Chikas Ohadoma, "Power of the Nigerian Woman." *ThisDayOnline,* July 4, 2001.

24 Chioma Filomena Steady, "Women and Collective Action: Female Models in Transition," in *Theorizing Black Feminisms: The Visionary Pragmatism of Black Women,* eds. Stanlie M. James & Abena P. A. Busia (London: Routledge, 1993): 90–101.

25 For more information on the Aba riots, see Sylvia Leith-Ross, *African Women: A Study of the Ibo of Nigeria* (New York: Praeger Publishers, 1965).

26 Augustine Ikelegbe, "Engendering Civil Society: Oil, Women Groups and Resource Conflicts in the Niger Delta region of Nigeria," *The Journal of Modern African Studies* 43, no. 2 (June 2005): 241–270.

27 Makinde, "Motherhood."

28 Johnson-Odim, "Women and gender."

29 Ibid., 32.

30 The scramble probably began 300 years earlier and the act was the legitimacy Europe needed to quell its own infighting.

31 Laray Denzer, "Yoruba Women: A Historiographical Study." *The International Journal of African Historical Studies,* 27 (1994): 1–39.

32 Carol P. Christ, "Whose History Are We Writing? Reading Feminist Texts with a Hermeneutic of Suspicion." *Journal of Feminist Studies in Religion,* 20, no. 2 (2004): 77.

33 Mojubaolu Olufunke Okome, "Women, the State, and the Travails of Decentralizing the Nigerian Federation," *West Africa Review* 2, no. 1 (2000).www.africaknowledgeproject.org/index.php/war/issue/view/25 (accessed October 16, 2002), 1.

34 Koni Benson and Joyce Chadya, "*Ukubhinya:* Gender and Sexual Violence in Bulawayo, Colonial Zimbabwe, 1946–1956," *Zambezin,* 30 no 1 (2003), 111.

35 Ibid., 112.

36 Barbara J. Callaway, *Muslim Hausa Women in Nigeria: Tradition and Change* (Syracuse, NY: Syracuse University Press, 1987).

37 Women in Kano were secluded after King Muhammadu Rumfa introduced Islam from North Africa and Medina in the fifteenth century. He removed women from active governmental and societal positions, a situation the Fulani Empire maintained.

38 Callaway, *Muslim Hausa.*

39 Ayesha Imam, "Politics, Islam and Women in Kano, Northern Nigeria," in *Identity Politics and Women: Cultural Reassertions and Feminisms in International Perspective,* ed. Valentine M. Moghadam (Boulder, CO: Westview Press, 1993), 123–144.

40 Barbara Cooper, "Gender and Religion in Hausaland: Variations in Islamic Practice in Niger and Nigeria," in *Women in Muslim Societies: Diversity within Unity,* ed. Herbert L. Bodman and Nayereh Tohidi (Boulder, CO: Lynne Rienner Publishers, 1998), 21–37.

41 Niger kept the Bori and Karuwanci systems. This is credited to France's taking over the country from the British.

42 Although women did not have the right to vote in the region, they played a role in politics. Two political parties dominated the region, the Northern People's Congress and Northern Elements Progressive Union. While the NPC believed Islam and tradition forbade women's right to vote, the NEPU believed women should and had women's political wings. The NPC won the elections and disallowed women's suffrage. Northern women did not get that right until universal suffrage was granted in Nigeria in 1976 (some records say 1975). For more information, read Jonathan T. Reynolds "Islam, Politics and Women's Rights." *Comparative Studies of South Asia, Africa and the Middle East,* vol. Xviii no. 1 (1998), 64–72.

43 Johnson-Odim, "Women and Gender."

44 Margaret Strobel, "African Women," *Signs* 8, no. 1 (1982), 109–131.

45 Cheryl Johnson, "Female Leadership during the Colonial Period: Madam Pelewura and the Lagos Market Women," *Tarikh* 7, no. 1(1981), 1–10.

46 Benson and Chadya, "Gender,"112.

47 Jessica Horn, *Christian Fundamentalisms and Women's Rights in the African Context: Mapping the Terrain,* www.wluml.org/node/6563, 2010 (accessed March 1, 2011).

48 Coquery Vidrovitch, *African women,* 161.

49 Strobel, "African Women," 130.

50 Ifi Amadiume, *Male Daughters, Female Husbands: Gender and Sex in an African Society* (London: Zed Books, 1987).

51 Modupe Nimah Abdulraheem, *Rights of Women in the Pre-colonial and Post-colonial Era: Prospects and Challenges,* www.unilorin.edu.ng/publications/abdulraheemnm/ RIGHTS_OF_WOMEN_IN_THE_PRE_COLONIAL_AND_POST_COLONIAL_ERA.pdf (accessed January 14, 2011).

52 Cheryl Johnson, "Class and Gender: A Consideration of Yoruba Women during the Colonial Period," in *Women and Class in Africa*, eds. Claire C. Robertson and Iris Berger (New York, Africana Publishing, 1986), 237–254.

53 John Thornton, *The Kongolese Saint Anthony: Dona Beatriz Kimpa Vita and the Antonian Movement, 1684–1706*, (Cambridge, UK: Cambridge University Press, 1998).

54 John N. Orji, "Ibo Women from 1929–1960," *West Africa Review*, 2, no. 1 (2000), www.africaknowledgeproject.org/index.php/war/issue/view/25 (accessed October 16, 2002).

55 Coquery-Vidrovitch, *African Women*.

56 Abdulraheem, *Rights of Women*.

57 Johnson, "Female Leadership," 4.

58 Johnson-Odim, "Women and Gender."

59 Ibid., 55.

60 Ibid.

61 Aje-Ori Agbese, "Maintaining Power in the Face of Political, Economic and Social Discrimination: The Tale of Nigerian Women," *Women and Language*, XXVI, no. 1, 22 (2003): 18–25.

62 Oyeronke Oyewuni, "The White Woman's Burden; African Women in Western Feminist Discourse," in *African Women and Feminism: Reflecting on the Politics of Sisterhood*, ed. Oyeronke Oyewumi (Trenton, NJ: Africa World Press, 2003), 27.

63 Aili Mari Tripp, "Women in Movement: Transformations in African Political Landscapes," *International Feminist Journal of Politics*, 5, no. 2 (2003), 235.

64 Kathleen M. Fallon, "Transforming Women's Citizenship Rights within an Emerging Democratic State: The Case of Ghana," *Gender and Society*, 17, no. 4 (2003): 525–543.

65 Peter Schraeder, *African Politics and Society: A Mosaic in Transformation* (New York: Bedford/St. Martin's, 2000).

66 For more information, read George Ayittey, *Africa in Chaos* (New York: St. Martin's Griffin, 1999).

67 J. Craig Jenkins and Augustine J. Kposowa, "The Political Origins of African Military Coups: Ethnic Competition, Military Centrality and the Struggle over the Postcolonial State," *International Studies Quarterly*, 36 (1992): 271.

68 Frances E. White, "Women in West and West-Central Africa," in *Women in Sub-Saharan Africa: Restoring Women to History*, eds. Iris Berger and Frances E. White (Bloomington: Indiana University Press, 1999), 63–129.

69 Fallon, "Transforming women."

70 Ibid.

71 Virginia DeLancey, "The Economies of Africa," in *Understanding Contemporary Africa* eds. April A. Gordon and Donald L. Gordon (Boulder, CO: Lynne Rienner, 2001), 101–142.

72 Priscilla Jere-Mwiindilila, "The Effects of Structural Adjustment on Women in Zambia, 1994." http://warc.ch/pc/rw942/02.html (accessed March 11, 2011).

73 Jean M. Due and Christina H. Gladwin, "Impacts of Structural Adjustment Programs on African Women Farmers and Female-headed Households," *American Journal of Agricultural Economics*, 73, no. 5, Proceedings Issue (December 1991), 1431.

74 Amina Mama, *Women's Studies and Studies of Women in Africa during the 1990s*. Working paper series 5/96 (Dakar, Senegal: CODESRIA, 1996), 6.

75 Carole B. Davies, "Introduction: Feminist Consciousness and African Literary Criticism," in *Ngambika: Studies of Women in African Literature*, eds. Carole B. Davies and Anne A. Graves (Trenton, NJ: Africa World Press, 1986), 3.

76 Maryam Babangida, *Acceptance Address for the Africa Prize for Leadership*, www.thp.org/prize/91/mb991.htm (accessed July 17, 2002).

77 Frank Nwonwu, *The Role of Adult Education in Women Empowerment: An Assessment of the Better Life for Rural Women Program in Nigeria*. Paper presented at The Project Literacy International conference, South Africa, www.projectliteracy.org.za/tmpl/Frank%Nwonwu.htm (accessed December 15, 2002), 1.

78 Tripp, "Women in movement," 236.

79 Celestin Monga, "Eight Problems with African Politics," *Journal of Democracy*, 8 (1997): 156–170.

80 Tripp, "Women in movement."

81 Ibid., 240.

82 Ibid., 253.

83 Ibid.

84 Sarah Bosley, *Rwanda: A Revolution in Rights for Women,* www.guardian.co.uk/world/2010/may/28/womens-rights-rwanda (accessed March 1, 2011).

85 www.ladybrillemag.com/2009/09/genevieve-nnaji-on-oprahs-most-famous-people-in-the-world-show.html (accessed September 12, 2009). The Nigerian movie industry, Nollywood, is the second largest movie producer in the world. Women have been quite active in the industry in front of and behind the camera. Movies by Amaka Igwe, Vivian Ejike, Funke Akindele, and Emem Isong examine women's issues in a variety of ways. Watch Ego Boyo's 30 Days, Shirley Frimpong-Manso's *The Perfect Picture, Life and Living It,* Emem Isong's "Games Men Play," "Reloaded," to name a few.

86 AIDS/HIV is not an African disease, something every African has. By generalizing the disease to everyone, the specifics are ignored. For instance, in South Africa's population of more than 43 million, only 7 percent of the population is HIV-positive. Moreover, like in the United States where people have not been diagnosed or anonymity prevents inclusion, it is difficult to determine what the true numbers are. Since there is so much money in AIDS/HIV research, it is possible that the numbers are exaggerated for effect. Old stereotypes, namely that Africans are oversexed and promiscuous, have made the "Africa is HIV/AIDS-ridden" an easy pill to swallow. People have ignored or refused to critically examine the bigger issues of poverty, inequality between the West and the East, conditions for aid and availability of affordable retro-viral medications and their immense contributions to the problem globally, not just in Africa.

87 Asma'u Joda and Iheoma Obibi, *Grace Ushang's Death and the Indecent Dressing Bill,* October 5, 2009 http://fiyanda.blogspot.com/2009/10/grace-ushangs-death-and-indecent.html (accessed October 10, 2010).

88 *Nigeria: Grace Ushang's Death and the Indecent Dressing Bill,* www.wluml.org/node/5565 (accessed March 2, 2011).

REVIEW QUESTIONS

1. In light of the changes that have occurred in the lives of women in Africa, why does the negative stereotypical image of them still prevail in Western literature, movies, and rhetoric?
2. It is generally assumed that everyone from the African continent self-identifies as African. In what ways do you think this limits debate and examination of issues affecting women in Africa?
3. How can we improve women's rights both in Africa and around the world?
4. Identify and discuss the successes women have had in parts of Africa in politics, economy, and society. In what ways can more changes be created across the continent?

Writing Prompt

1. If you could contribute to the historiography of women in Africa, what would you like the world to know about them?
2. Check the Internet or an African store for a movie made by a woman in Africa. What made you choose that movie? What did you learn about the people? Did the movie challenge your impression of women and their issues in Africa? Did it teach you something new?

CHAPTER 8

Educational Development in Modern Africa: History, Politics, and Challenges

Ogechi E. Anyanwu and Chukwunenye C. Njoku

Education is the heartbeat of every society. It is crucial in preparing members of a society to participate fully and effectively not only in maintaining the social structure, but also in promoting social change. Precolonial indigenous education in Africa aimed at producing individuals equipped with the skills necessary to contribute to the development of their society. It inculcated knowledge largely through words and examples of parents, relatives, and members of the community, as well as lessons and rituals taking place both at home and outside. Educational instructions were lifelong, enduring from the womb to the tomb. Mostly practical, utilitarian, and informal, the precolonial system of education shaped Africa's socioeconomic and political developments until the introduction of Islamic and Western education. While Islamic education sought to spread Islamic and Arabic values, Western education, as introduced by Christian missionary bodies, aimed at spreading both Christianity and European civilization. Because the possession of Western education became the foremost path to social mobility in colonial Africa, cultural imperialism was easily entrenched.

For more than a century since the introduction of Western education in Africa, European powers in Africa emphasized only primary and secondary education. Access was highly limited. Missionary bodies lacked sufficient financial resources to expand educational facilities to meet local demand for education. Although colonial governments in Africa later played a decisive role in funding and regulating the spread of Western education, access to education remained inadequate while curriculum was narrow. Colonial regimes resisted calls to diversify the curriculum or expand access. Even toward the last decade of colonial rule in Africa, European powers still maintained a "conservative, cautious, [and] elitist" educational philosophy.[1] Moreover, for the greater part of colonial rule, European powers rejected the idea of establishing institutions of higher learning principally because they feared that African educated elite would seek to undermine colonialism. It was rather in the aftermath of World War II, following years of persistent agitations by nationalists, that colonial governments established universities in Africa. Yet, like primary and secondary education, university education was limited in both admission and curriculum. Due to their conservative colonial ideas, European powers established these institutions mainly to train future political elites, thus they were naturally alienated from the realities of the African environment and needs. Consequently, after independence, leaders in postcolonial African countries pushed to reconceptualize and reconfigure the role of education in order to facilitate nation building and economic development, resulting in an unprecedented reform and expansion of education at all levels.

This chapter is a historical analysis of educational development in Africa during the precolonial, colonial, and postcolonial periods. It argues that the dynamic sociopolitical and economic circumstances in Africa have determined the nature of educational practices since the precolonial era. The chapter presents a better understanding of modern Africa by showing the important role education played in precolonial indigenous Africa, the origins and shortcomings of Western education in colonial Africa, and efforts by postcolonial governments to reorganize the inherited European educational systems to meet their needs. By examining the origins, progress, shifts, and pitfalls of education in Africa, this chapter provides a priceless insight into the accomplishments, problems, and promise of Africa itself.

EDUCATION IN PRECOLONIAL AFRICA

Before the advent of Western and Islamic systems of education in Africa, a long and rich educational tradition had flourished on the continent. Africa's precolonial educational system was largely informal and lifelong, designed to prepare individuals to assume their dynamic place in the society. In its 1996 report, the United Nations Educational, Scientific and Cultural Organization (UNESCO) reaffirmed the importance of the following four pillars to education: "learning to know, learning to do, learning to be, and learning to live together."[2] It regrets, however, that the existing "education systems tend to emphasize the acquisition of knowledge to the detriment of other types of learning."[3] It therefore urged nations "to conceive education in a more encompassing fashion" and insisted that such an idea "should inform and guide future educational reforms and policy, in relation both to contents and to methods."[4] Undeniably, precolonial African education upheld the four pillars outlined by UNESCO. With the help of the family, kinship groups, and the larger community, systematic instructions were delivered through the medium of native language (mother tongue), and delivered orally by way of songs, examples, stories, legends, and dancing, all aimed at stimulating children's emotions and intellect to "explore, exploit and interpret their natural environment."[5] The educational system administered different contents based on age or gender, and as Walter Rodney stated, it hinged on a "progressive developments in conformity with the successive stages of physical, emotional and mental development of the child."[6]

UNECSO's educational principles evoke precolonial educational practices. First, in "learning to know," UNESCO believes that education "provides, so to speak, the passport to lifelong education, in so far as it gives people a taste—but also lays the foundations—for learning throughout life."[7] In precolonial Africa, education consciously aimed at providing individuals with relevant knowledge about the history, laws, customs, environment, and religions of their societies to enable them assume active and functional roles. Among other things, children learned the correct way of speaking and the proper way of behaving. According to R.M. Ruperti, educating the youth was a crucial part of the culture, as one was impossible without the other. He concludes that "When one talks of education, therefore, one is also inevitably talking of community, culture and cultural communities."[8] Above all, precolonial education helped in the transmission of cultural identity and values, through activities at home and outside, inculcating in children the behavior and knowledge needed to function effectively in the society.[9]

Second, another crucial component of precolonial education was acquiring knowledge and skills by observing and doing. UNESCO upholds this method of learning when it states that "competence and skills are more readily acquired if pupils and students have the opportunity to try out and develop their abilities by becoming involved in work experience schemes or social work while they are still in education."[10] As a matter of necessity, precolonial education provided broad range of skills required to survive in the society and cope with the environment. Precolonial education fit the needs of the society, and the environment determined the educational emphasizes within the society. Among the Bemba people of Zambia, as Rodney reveals, 6-year-old kids could easily name fifty to sixty species of trees, but they knew little about ornamental flowers. The reason, according Rodney, is "that knowledge of the trees was a necessity in an environment of 'cut and burn' agriculture and in a situation where numerous household needs were met by tree products. Flowers, however, were irrelevant to survival."[11]

Individuals acquired knowledge of the environment and the skills to exploit it through examples shown at home and outside, learning through "observation, imitation and participation . . . to farm, hunt, cook, fish, play, wrestle, deliver messages, run homes, and build houses."[12] The extent to which one mastered these skills largely determined one's productivity, success, and position in the society. It separated the rich from the poor, the powerful from the weak, and the knowledgeable from the less informed. As demonstrated by Chinua Achebe in *Things Fall Apart*, Okonkwo—unlike his poor, lazy father—worked hard to distinguish himself in his society as a rich farmer, great wrestler, and prominent political leader.[13]

Third, the survival of any society is based on shared ideals and understandings that are vital in promoting social solidarity. Therefore, learning to live together becomes imperative and thus constitutes an essential component of precolonial educational practices. This pillar of education, as UNESCO sees it, helps to develop "an understanding of others and their history, traditions and spiritual values and, on this basis, creating a new spirit which, guided by recognition of our growing interdependence and a common analysis of the risks and challenges of the future, would induce people to implement common projects or to manage the inevitable conflicts in an intelligent and peaceful way."[14]

Fourth, one of the crucial elements of precolonial education was learning to be. UNESCO report stresses that "none of the talents which are hidden like buried treasure in every person must be left untapped. These are, to name but a few: memory, reasoning power, imagination, physical ability, aesthetic sense, the aptitude to communicate with others and the natural charisma of the group leader."[15] Precolonial education was not an end in itself; it was a means to an end. In serving as a means to nurture members of the society from childhood to adulthood, it stressed personal and social responsibility and moral and spiritual values.[16]

Inculcating the four pillars of education to individuals in precolonial Africa involved some form of formal education and in some cases higher education. In *An African People in the Twentieth Century*, Lucy Mair reveals how Ganda parents formally taught their children correct etiquette and genealogical positions of different ethnic groups.[17] As Joma Kenyatta shows in *Facing Mount Kenya*, educational systems among the Kikuyu provided organized instructions to individuals at different social levels through succeeding stages of initiation.[18] In most African societies, series of initiation ceremonies (coming of age) existed to mark the transition from adolescence to adulthood. Only those who successfully passed various tests participated in those ceremonies. Before these ceremonies are held, teaching programs, like those of Poro brotherhood in Sierra Leone, are held.[19] These programs provided formal training in preparation for the test. Other specialized occupations required formal training outside the home. The fishing profession required knowledge of navigational techniques like seafaring and the behavior of fish. Professions such as blacksmithing, weaving, woodwork, and bronze work also required longer period of apprenticeship. To become a priest, village head, king, medicine man or woman, diviner, or rainmaker one underwent a longer period of meticulous and complex training and rituals to prepare them for these vital jobs.[20] Training of rulers, more than any other job, required some form of higher education, and as J. F. Ade Ajayi, Lameck K. H. Goma, and G. Ampah Johnson have shown,

> Selection of candidates was rather complex, including membership of particular families and some evidence of special vocation or calling by the divinities concerned. Essentially the training was through attachment and apprenticeship. Favored children accompanied their parents and grandparents to meetings where they learnt the art of public speaking and observed customary ways of dealing with issues.[21]

Precolonial indigenous education in Africa aimed at producing people who "possessed a combination of good manners, respect for elders, a sense of reciprocal obligation to others and to nature, and a willingness to conform to ancestral precedents. . . . It was intended to make learning a relevant and essential vehicle for coping with life."[22] For generations, indigenous education served the needs of African societies. Like other societies, it laid the foundation upon which Africa's future social-economic and political developments hinged. However, the spread of Islam in Africa since 700 CE, shortly after its birth in the Middle East, led to the introduction of a new, formal, and chiefly religious-based system of education. Islamic schools emerged in precolonial Africa. Most societies that converted to Islam, such as in Nigeria, Mali, Ghana, and Somalia, established Koranic schools. Since every Muslim ought to read and recite the Qu'ran, Qu'ranic schools provided needed religious instructions. Other schools, such as Madrassas (centers of learning), offered both religious and secular subjects such astronomy, mathematics, architecture, and philosophy. Fatimid caliphs in Egypt established the first known Madrassa in 1005 CE. It had a library, and teachers taught different subjects.[23] Some of these Madrassas were institutions of higher learning. There was the Al-Azhar University in Egypt, the University of Fez in Morocco, and the University of Timbuktu in Mali. Their emergence testifies "to the standard of education achieved in Africa before the colonial intrusion."[24]

Although Islamic education was affected by the Westernizing influence of Christian missionaries and colonial rule, it has competed well with Western education, especially in predominantly Islamic countries in Africa. For most of the non-Islamic areas, however, the coming of Christian missionaries and the introduction of Western education led to the decline of indigenous systems of education, hastened, of course, by the unprecedented social transformation that accompanied European encroachment on the continent.

MISSIONARIES, RELIGION, AND WESTERN EDUCATION

European encroachment in Africa and the subsequent introduction of new forms of education by Christian missionaries reshaped the direction of educational development in Africa. Before the late 1700s, Europeans were familiar with the coasts of Africa, but the interior of the continent remained a mystery to them. Although Prince Henry the Navigator, Bartholomew Diaz, and Vasco Dagama explored the continent in the fifteenth and sixteenth centuries, they did not venture into the interior. In many ways, Africa was still the "Dark Continent." However, a new generation of European explorers since 1768 tried to solve a mystery that had puzzled geographers for centuries by moving into the African hinterland. The activities of James Scot Bruce, Mungo Park, Richard and John Lander, Huge Clapperton, Rene Calle, Stanley and David Livingston were crucial in the navigation or "mapping out" of land, mountains, rivers, and lakes.

The sensational reports of European explorers about Africa and Africans understandably enhanced the curiosity of different groups in Europe, providing the groundwork for the subsequent increase in European interference in African affairs. As Philip Curtin shows, as early as 1788, the African Association emerged in Europe with a commitment to sending travelers into the heart of Africa to report on topography, ethnography and life of the people.[25] In *African Reactions to Missionary Education*, Edward Berman argues that these explorers gave objective accounts of Africans but stressed the sensational, which they often took out of context, thus confirming European suspicion that Africans were depraved creatures that needed salvaging.[26] For instance, Robert Moffat, a London Missionary society pioneer in South Africa, wrote that the peoples of Bechuana, Hottentots and Bushmen, were "without a single ray to guide them through the dark and dreary futurity or a single link to unite them with the skies."[27] Likewise, W.A Elmslie concluded that the Ngoni people "sadly lack God and are living in a dreadful degradation," stressing that they lived in an atmosphere "charged with vice which runs through songs and games and dances, whose every movement was awful in its shamelessness."[28] These ignorant reports and assessments of Africa informed the assumptions of African inferiority and partly encouraged missionaries to travel to Africa in order to bring the "blessings of European civilization" to the natives.

The opening of Africa by European explorers, which coincided with religious revival in Europe in the late 1700s, gave impetus to the growth of missionary enterprise in Africa. The *Great Awakening*, as the movement was known, witnessed the proliferation of missionary societies such as the Church Missionary Society (CMS), the Wesleyan Methodist Missionary Society (WMMS), the Presbyterian Church of Scotland, the (American) Southern Baptist Convention, the Catholic Church's Society of African Missions, the Jesuits, the Basel Missionaries, and the Lutherans.[29] These missionary bodies were primarily concerned with two issues: the abolition of slavery and extension of Christianity outside Europe. European public officials knew the importance of missionaries and education in the eventual control of Africa, which explains why Thomas Fowell Buxton, a prominent member of the British parliament and vice president of the CMS, urged the cooperation of the government and the missionary societies in the "deliverance" of Africa:

> Let missionaries and schoolmasters, the plough and the spade, go together and agriculture will flourish; the avenues to legitimate commerce will be opened; confidence between man and man will be inspired; whilst civilization will advance as the natural effect and Christianity operate as the proximate cause, of this happy change.[30]

Buxton's declaration gave momentum to European interest in opening Africa for capitalist exploitation, and missionaries became the pathfinders. Missionaries recognized that education was essential to converting Africans to Christianity. They built schools where they taught religious instructions side by side with reading, writing, and arithmetic. The school in a sense became "the nursery of the infant church" and it formed the foundation to future colonial rule.[31] The missionaries dominated education throughout the colonial period. Thus, the spread of Christianity and Western education became interwoven. As Murray brilliantly stated in *The School in the Bush*, "To all intents and purposes, the school is the Church. Right away in the bush or in the forest the two are one, and the village teacher is also the village evangelist. An appreciation of this fact is cardinal in all considerations of African education."[32] In underscoring the importance of education to Christian activities, Father Wauter, a Catholic missionary in Western Nigeria, stated that "We knew the best way to make conversion in 'pagan' countries was to open school. So, when the district of Ekiti-Ondo was opened . . . we started schools even before there was any church or mission house."[33] The establishment of schools was a priority for European missionaries largely because the natives could neither read nor write in English. As Elias Shrent, a missionary puts it, "I have a low opinion of Christians who are not able to read their bible."[34]

In 1827, the CMS built the Fourah Bay College in Sierra Leone to train African clergy. The school laid the foundation to the future University of Fourah Bay where many prominent Africans and Sierra Leoneans studied, such as Samuel Crowther. In 1857, Crowther was commissioned to establish an African mission for evangelizing Africans. He was involved in the establishment of schools and mission in eastern Nigeria and before 1935 the CMS had established schools and churches in virtually all parts of the present day Nigeria. In Kenya, Anglicans, Scottish Episcopalians, and Methodists cooperated in establishing churches and schools. One of such schools was the Alliance High School, which opened in Kikuyu in 1926, and a CMS missionary, Carey Francis, became the first headmaster. Education and religion also went hand in hand in Uganda where Alexander Mackay, a teacher, evangelist, builder and printer, played a central role in the country's educational development. Mackay was instrumental in the first translation of parts of the Bible, which his own press printed.[35]

Since the possession of Western education was crucial to social mobility in the new colonial economy, missionaries played a significant role in preparing Africans through the expansion of mission schools in Africa. In Nigeria, for instance, the CMS, which started with 6 schools in 1849, increased the number to 150 by 1909. The Wesleyan Mission went from 3 schools, 255 pupils, and nine teachers in 1861 to 138 schools, 5,361 pupils, and 285 teachers in 1921. The Roman Catholic Mission increased its number of schools from 2 in 1893 to about 127 in 1922.[36] The trend duplicated itself in other regions. In Uganda, the CMS had 72 schools with 7,683 students in 1900, but by 1913, they had 331 schools with 32,458 students. In Nyasaland, the Dutch Reformed Church reported 111 schools and 10,000 students in 1903, but in 1910, the figures went up to 865 schools and 25,796 students. Likewise, the Basel Mission Society in the Cameroon counted 100 students in 1904, but 2,520 in 1910 and 6,600 in 1914. The Moravian Mission in Tanganyika, now Tanzania, reported 329 students in its schools in 1900, but 7,931 in 1913. In the same way, the Lutheran Berlin Mission, also in Tanganyika, reported 63 students in their school in 1900, but 11,101 in 1913.[37]

Despite the expansion of schools, access remained limited for most Africans. In fact, in a letter in which he complained about the depressing nature of his work, a CMS mission secretary wrote: "My work is pathetic in the extreme low, in one aspect: almost every week I have to turn away deputations from both near and distant begging us to come teach them."[38] Elitist education was a common feature of Western education. Missionary bodies had insufficient resources to expand educational facilities to accommodate rising demand. Africans, who were already accustomed to mass access to education under the indigenous educational systems, were frustrated with the new elitist education. An African historian, Kenneth Dike, captured the problems thus:

> The overriding complaint was that there was not enough education—of any kind—for the masses of the people. The key to the understanding of the whole problem of education in Africa is the appreciation of the fact that the whole region thirsts for knowledge. The wealthy and the poor, the aristocrats and the lowest peasants, Christians, Moslems and the "pagans" cry for it.[39]

That thirst for education was not satisfied even as European powers established colonial rule in Africa and soon after dictated the direction of educational development. Notwithstanding the interference of colonial governments in education, Coleman reveals that missionaries controlled all education until 1898, and as late as 1942 they controlled 99 percent of schools.[40]

COLONIAL RULE, EDUCATION, AND WESTERNIZATION

The period between 1880 and 1900 was the high-water mark of European conquest and occupation of Africa. European countries such as Britain, France, Italy, Germany, Spain, Belgium, and Portugal launched an unprecedented and murderous campaign to seize and occupy African territories. They were essentially emboldened by the doctrines of "sphere of influence" and "effective occupation" adopted at the Berlin West African conference of 1884–1885 where European leaders met to partition Afric among themselves. In less than two decades after the conference, the entire continent, except Ethiopia and Liberia, came under European control. Following the successful establishment of colonial rule in Africa, European powers realized the importance of education in consolidating imperial rule. Although missionaries exclusively controlled education, colonial powers believed that direct government involvement would help align education to serve colonial needs. Britain, for instance, promulgated the 1882 Colonial Educational Ordinance for West Africa, later revised in 1887 and 1905. The highlight of the ordinance was the stipulation that "the subject of teaching shall be the reading and writing of the English language."[41] The government tied financial allocations to schools to the observance of this language policy. Europeanizing Africans was the ultimate goal of colonial education and the British were eager to produce young Africans who would despise of their own cultures but filled with admiration for Western culture.[42]

British educational policy undermined the use of native language (mother tongue or "vernacular"), which missionary schools upheld. Missionaries and natives unsuccessfully resisted the imposition of English language as a medium of instruction in schools. In rejecting the mother tongue campaign, Metcalf Sunter, the Nigerian government spokesperson, stated: "I regard these said languages as only interesting to the comparative philologist and never likely to become of any practical use to civilization."[43] Insisting on the significance of English language in the British empire, he further noted that "The native must and will know English in spite of all well-meaning but diseased notions; it is the language of commerce and the only education worth a moment's consideration."[44] Since English was the medium of communication and reporting to the imperial government as well as a powerful tool for cultural assimilation, it was no surprising that the British did not make many compromises. Other subjects such as geography and history were added to the curriculum in keeping with British colonial policy of creating a group of Nigerians sufficiently literate and skilled to integrate fully into the mainstream of the colonial economy and administration as clerks, messengers, and interpreters.

The colonial view of education, as articulated by H.S. Scott, a British educator, was to create "useful citizens," which means "literally citizens who would be of use to us. The conception was one of exploitation and development for the benefit of the people of Great Britain—it was to this purpose that such education as given was directed."[45] Thus colonial education merely trained a few Africans who would fill position in local administration at the lowest ranks and staff the private capitalist firms owned by Europeans. The colonial educational system, as Walter Rodney argues, "was not an educational system that grew out of the African environment or one that was designed to promote the most rational use of material and social resources. It was not an educational system designed to give young people confidence and pride as members of African societies, but one which sought to instill a sense of deference towards all that was European and capitalist."[46] Worse still was that access to education was highly limited. Britain, for instance, stubbornly insisted that mass education was not "necessarily the most urgent aim" of education.[47] Likewise, in Northern Rhodesia (present day Zimbabwe) the British Colonial Office declared in 1958 that "Until more money becomes available for the building of schools, no rapid progress can be expected and the practical prospects of providing full primary education for all children therefore remains fairly remote."[48] It is indisputable that the overriding goal of European rule was to maximize profits and minimize losses, and it was not surprising that they resisted demands to allocate adequate funds for educational expansion.

Following Nigeria's constitutional changes of 1951 (the Macpherson Constitution) and 1952 (the Lyttleton Constitution), the regional governments were granted power over primary and secondary education. Consciously rejecting the elitism that characterized colonial education, leadership in these regions embarked on universal free education. In the western region, primary school enrollment rose from 811,432 in 1955 to 1,080,303 in 1959, while enrollment in secondary grammar schools rose from 10,935 during the same period to 22,374.[49] In the eastern region, primary school enrollment rose from 742,542 during the same period to 1,378,403, and the number of secondary grammar school students rose from 10,584 to 15,789.[50] In the northern region, primary school enrollment increased from 168,521 to 205,912, and secondary grammar school enrollment from 2,671 to 4,683 during the same period.[51] Similarly, when the "national government" under Balewa enacted the Education (Lagos) Act of 1957 for the federal capital, Lagos, the number of primary school students grew from 37,038 to 66,320, and secondary grammar school admissions grew from 3,157 to 4,804 during the period between 1957 and 1959.[52] By 1959, about 2,775,938 students were registered in various primary schools all over the country, while 47,650 students were in secondary grammar schools.[53] According to Fafunwa, "more primary and secondary schools were built and more children enrolled at the two levels between 1951 and 1959 than during the one-hundred years of British rule."[54]

British educational practices paralleled those of other colonial powers. France's insistence on the use of French language as the medium of instruction in schools in its colonies was a crucial part of their assimilation and association policies. Assimilation policy sought to disseminate French culture among the indigenes and help them become black French people.[55] Education was central to that policy. Yet the gap between policy and practice was wide. Out of the 13 million Africans in the French colonies, fewer than 100,000 Africans achieved that status by 1945.[56] The Portuguese policy of paternalism perceived the African "as a primitive child and the purpose of the policy [was] to lead him to Portuguese adulthood."[57] The selective and discriminatory educational policy of the Portuguese, the absence of popular education, and the undue emphasis on primary education while neglecting higher education, quantitatively affected educational development in Portuguese colonies in Africa. Portugal during Salazar's regime envisaged "the formation of a devout, semi-literate, hardworking and conservative African population."[58] So for "a general mass, the policy of psychological assimilation" is okay, but for the "few an intensive cultural and political assimilation."[59] The result was that at independence the level of illiteracy was very high in Portuguese Africa.

Similarly, Belgian educational policy did not favor educational expansion in its African colonies.[60] Like other colonial powers, Belgian educational policy was limited to primary school education. As articulated by Professor George Kimble, this educational practice was based on the belief "that it is better to have 90 per cent of the population capable of understanding what the government is trying to do for them . . . than to have 10 per cent of the population so full of learning that it spends its time telling the government what to do."[61] It was this wisdom that largely shaped colonial anti-higher education stance. In the British colonies, the implementation of indirect rule, especially before World War II, meant that colonial administrators relied on "illiterate" indigenous African rulers for daily administration. There was no place for highly educated Africans. In fact, those few Africans who travelled abroad to obtain higher education were excluded from colonial administration. They were embittered. In response, they intensified their call for independence, which threatened colonial rule. According to James Coleman, "It was the educated who . . . provoked disturbances in the provinces, published vituperative articles in the local press, and made life miserable and insecure for British administrators. There was nothing a district officer, a resident, or a governor dreaded more than political disturbances and unrest during his tour of duty."[62]

In fact, even as early as 1854, Charles Wood, president of the Board of Control (1853–1855) and Secretary of State of India (1859–1866) set the tone for British colonial higher education policy when he declared: "I do not see the advantage of rearing up a number of highly educated gentlemen at the expense of the State, whom you cannot employ, and who will naturally become depositories of discontent. If they choose to train themselves, well and good, but I am against providing our own future detractors and opponents and grumblers."[63] Therefore, British colonial authorities frowned on the idea of establishing universities in African to either train or to expand the educated elite, as the nationalists demanded. Given the strong opposition to the colonial government emanating from the educated elite, "the expansion of the educated class remained an anathema."[64] No less importantly, since European powers did not imagine Africans playing important roles in colonial administration and economy, they had little interest in investing in educational expansion.

Modern universities in sub-Saharan Africa are a recent creation, emerging in the aftermath of World War II. Notable among these colonial universities were the University College at Ibadan, Nigeria; University College of East Africa at Makerere, Uganda; University College of the Gold Coast; and Fourah Bay College, Sierra Leone. These institutions were quite limited in number, offered limited access, limited curriculum, and limited academic freedom and autonomy. Indeed, these institutions, like those at the primary and secondary school levels, were colonial, elitist, and alienated from the realities of the African environment. By 1959, after eleven years of existence, the University College of Ibadan (UCI) in Nigeria was able to absorb only 939 students. Many qualified Nigerians who were denied admission at the UCI travelled overseas to study.[65] The total number of Nigerian students attending universities in the UK, Canada, and the United States rose from 542 in 1948 to 1686 in 1953.[66] Since only few Nigerians could afford the funds to study abroad, thousands of qualified Nigerians failed to obtain training in higher education. Independence from European colonial rule meant that radical changes were necessary to expand access as well as tie education to the needs and aspirations of Africans.

"DECOLONIZING" EDUCATION IN POSTCOLONIAL AFRICA

Limited access to higher education was a common feature of colonial higher education policy. Thus, when most countries achieved independence, foreigners, mostly Europeans, dominated high-level positions in the African civil service, trade, and industry.[67] There were, for instance, only 100 university graduates in Zambia. With a combined population of 23 million, Kenya, Tanzania, and Uganda had only 99 university graduates trained in the University of East Africa. The Democratic Republic of Congo fared worse. It had no African university graduate in engineering, law, or medicine. Further, less emphasis was placed on producing graduates of agriculture, given its relevance to the African economy largely based on farming during the colonial period. While French colonies in Africa produced only four graduates in the field, there were 150 in English-speaking colonies.[68] Because of the failure of colonial university education to train sufficient human resources to champion nation building in Africa, postcolonial governments sought to reconceptualize and reconfigure the role of education to facilitate overall national development and nation building. African leaders were driven by the human capital theory, which argues that a country's human resource is "the ultimate basis of wealth of nations. Capital and natural resources are passive factors of production, human beings are the active agencies who accumulate capital, exploit natural resources, build social, economic and political organization, and carry forward national development."[69] According to Harbison and Myers, "Education does contribute to growth but growth also makes it possible to expand and develop education. It is both the flower and the seed of economic development."[70]

The African elite perceived education, especially higher education, as "the key that will open the door to a better life."[71] The president of Tanzania, Julius Nyerere, called on universities to "join with the people of East Africa in the struggle to build a nation worthy of the opportunity we have won."[72] Félix Houphouët-Boigny, the president of Côte d'Ivoire, declared that the "problems of political, economic, and cultural development of our societies, and rising of the standard of living constitute immediate objectives [and] require us to enlist the help of all the institutions of our states."[73] Universities, Emperor Haile Selassie of Ethiopia stressed, "stand as the most promising hope for constructive solutions to the problems that beset the modern world . . . and the money spent in coordinating, strengthening, and expanding higher education in Ethiopia is well invested."[74] These sentiments correctly capture the mood of most countries in Africa after independence. True to their promises, leaders in postcolonial Africa expanded education rapidly and reached "more people of all ages than in any previous efforts in history. They mobilized entire populations to achieve universal literacy over a short period and invented new ways to expand and deliver all levels of schooling to their citizenry.[75]

One of the most significant steps taken by postcolonial African governments was to push for the massification of higher education.[76] This policy shift was articulated in 1962 at a conference on the *Development of Higher Education in Africa* held in Malagasy Republic between September 3rd and 12th. Endorsing the new vision for higher education, the conference declared that the "establishment and development of higher education facilities . . . is basic to social and economic reconstruction of Africa."[77] It further stressed that "in order to provide the high-level manpower that [Africa] will require in the process of social and economic development, [they] . . . will need, in the next twenty years, to increase many times the number of students in their universities."[78] Contrary to the elitist educational traditions of colonial powers, the conference encouraged all countries to throw "open the university to all students who show capacity to benefit from a university education of internationally acceptable academic standards."[79]

Driven by the goals of national building and economic development, leaders in postcolonial Africa invested financial resources to facilitate educational expansion. Universities increased. Demand rose. Enrollment surged.[80] The number of universities in Africa rose from 52 in 1960 to 143 by 1980, and then proliferated to 316 by 2000.[81] In 1960 the number of students in African universities was less 100 but in 2000 it rose to 3.5 million.[82] Egypt topped the list with an enrolment of 1.5 million students. Nigeria comes second, followed by South Africa with total enrollment of about 1 million and half a million, respectively.[83] According to the World Bank, this impressive growth "represents one of the highest regional growth rates in the world for tertiary enrollments, averaging 8.7 percent a year."[84] Growth rates, according to 2009 UNESCO report, reached 10 percent between 2000 and 2005.[85] The report further noted that in 2009 there were "20 times more students than in 1970, with an additional 3.9 million enrollments."[86]

African countries also made remarkable progress in expanding primary and secondary school education since independence. Their participation in many international conferences gave added impetus to their postcolonial vision of educational expansion. The World Conference on Education for All held in Jomitien, Thailand, in 1990 called for universal access to basic education and African countries participated. African countries were signatories to many educational declarations to commit to universal education, such as the 1992 Ouagadougou Pan-African declaration, the 1995 Amman Re-affirmation, the 1998 Durban Statement of Commitment, the OAU Decade of Education (1997–2006), and the 2000 Dakar World Education Forum.[87] In fact, between 1990 and 2002 student enrollment in primary school jumped from 81 million to 123 million, and enrollment in secondary school likewise rose from 24 million to 44 million.[88]

Although the number of students in schools increased dramatically in Africa, it has not improved the enrollment ratio, especially at higher institutions, largely due to population pressure and resource constraints. Since the 1970s, as a UNESCO report states, "the 'tertiary age group' population has grown by an average annual rate of 3%. Consequently, participation ratios only rose from 0.8% to 5.6% during this period."[89] Besides, the expansion of education strained financial resources to a breaking point. African governments have been the sole proprietors of education in Africa in their establishing, funding, and management. Over 90 percent of the funds for schools come from government, and many African governments lived up to expectation in the 1960s and 1970s. During this period, universities, for instance, did quantitatively and qualitatively well in training the high-level workforce required as evident in the resultant expansion in civil service. Investment in higher education for government, parents, and stakeholders yielded dividends. Demand for more access rose rapidly. Universities were now seen as amenities as most governments, especially in Nigeria "opted to mushrooming them," sometimes with no long-term planning of their future and sustainability.[90]

From the 1980s, however, crisis began to set in, and since the 1990s African education, especially universities entered the state of emergency. The global economic downturn and the consequent collapse of national economies in Africa severely affected universities. Grave economic and financial difficulties worsened by debilitating external debts and debt-servicing, a steep fall in the prices of commodity export in the international market, devaluation of national currencies, and, above all, the implementation of structural adjustment policies as prescribed by the IMF and World Bank became crippling to all state agencies and parastatals, which included the universities. From 1980 through 2002, the World Bank had advocated that the social rates of return on investment in basic education are higher than in higher education. African countries largely subscribed to this position as state support for higher education declined while the demands for higher education increased simultaneously. Although the World Bank reversed this policy in 2002, government apathy toward higher education was already entrenched with dire consequences for the universities. Expansion of facilities was halted while enrollment grew faster than the absorptive capacity of the universities. This resulted in overcrowding, infrastructural decay, and an unhealthy learning environment for both students and faculty. Irregular payment of faculty salaries created related problems, as faculty either engaged in part-time jobs or received bribes from students. In such a lawless and crowded environment, cultism thrived.

Lack of adequate funding eroded both the quality and relevance of higher education to societal needs. Constant, contentious, and justifiable government intrusion in the internal academic and administrative affairs of universities led to the erosion of academic freedom and university autonomy. In Nigeria, this has resulted in the continuous tension between the government and the academic staff of universities since the late 1970s. Under these conditions, privatization of higher education became a welcomed initiative. Notably, Kenya, Sudan, Democratic Republic of Congo, Ghana, Uganda, Togo, South Africa, Ethiopia, and Nigeria are now in the forefront of the privatization policy.[91] Whether privatization will reverse the rot or not remains to be seen. There is no easy solution to the problems and challenges facing African universities. Any rescue package will clearly require long-term strategic planning and a focus primarily on the reconceptualizations of the mission of higher education in order to respond proactively to the demands of the global age while maintaining their unique identities. Encouraging more private sector involvement in higher education while governments continue to fund public institutions adequately is a path to sustainable expansion of education in Africa. Cost-sharing and cost-recovery measures should be applied and strengthened in order to minimize waste of resources and ensure greater accountability.

CONCLUSION

Both formal and informal systems of education thrived in precolonial Africa before the introduction of Western education by Europeans missionaries and the subsequent imposition of colonial rule reshaped educational practices in Africa. This chapter has demonstrated that although Europeans did not introduce the idea of education in Africa, they did much to reshape Africa's socioeconomic and political development since the early nineteenth century. Since the precolonial period, sociopolitical and economic realities in Africa determined the nature, quality, and quantity of education provided. In precolonial Africa, education was available to all and was tailored to meeting the needs of the society. The societies were independent and were thus able to align education to fulfill the end they sought. As demonstrated in this chapter, precolonial education served the needs of various African societies and adequately provided the four educational competencies that UNECSCO later adopted as a model: learning to know, learning to do, learning to live together, and learning to be. Like Islamic education, European missionaries who introduced Western education used it as an effective tool in executing their proselytizing activities in Africa. No wonder they largely emphasized religious instruction in their curriculum. Following the imposition of European rule, colonial administrators reshaped education to serve colonial objectives. They insisted on the use of European languages as the only medium of instruction in schools, emphasized liberal arts subjects and pure sciences instead of applied sciences and vocational courses, and limited access to education at all levels. This chapter has revealed that the Westernization of African society following colonial rule caused Europeans to adjust education to meet colonial needs. Formal education in schools, particularly at the primary and secondary school levels, was emphasized because colonial administrators sought to train low-level skills vital in exploiting African resources. They shunned higher education, afraid that highly educated Africans would threaten European colonial domination.

In the aftermath of World War II—and conscious of formidable rise of nationalist movements in Africa—European powers, especially the British, established universities in Africa to facilitate the training of Africa's future political elites. Although access and curriculum in these universities were highly limited, the few Africans who received higher education in them joined forces with those who obtained theirs abroad to champion the course of African decolonization. As Eric Ashby aptly states, "from the graduates of the universities the currents of nationalism flowed."[92] Driven by the need to promote economic development and nation building, and facilitated by financial donations from abroad, most postcolonial African countries invested in educational expansion at all levels in the 1960s and 1970s. However, because of the economic depression of the 1980s and 1990s—and influenced by IMF and World Bank flawed advice—investment in education declined, leading to an educational crisis from which most countries have not fully recovered.

Educational expansion at all levels was the priority of postcolonial governments in Africa. Although they surpassed colonial records by making significant progress in providing qualitative and quantitative education to Africans, unmet demand and limited opportunities still typify the African educational scene, threatening to sabotage the continent's future. Education remains the engine of societal growth and development, and leaders in Africa should take investment in it as an overriding concern. In his recently serialized article entitled "Gone to the Dogs," Ray Ekpu of *Newswatch* magazine bemoaned the rot and degeneracy in Nigerian institutions. "If we don't rescue education," Ekpu cautioned, "we can't rescue anything, not the economy, not democracy, not development, not our values."[93] This warning applies to other African countries as well.

ENDNOTES

1 K.O. Dike, "The Ashby Commission and Its Report," in *Twenty Years of University Education in Nigeria,* ed. Amaka Chizea Chinelo (Lagos: National Universities Commission, 1983), 2.

2 *UNESCO,* "Learning: The Treasure within," *Report to UNESCO of the International Commission on Education for the Twenty-first Century* (Paris: UNESCO, 1996), 86.

3 Ibid., 37.

4 bid.

5 See T.A. Awoniyi, "Mother Tongue Education in West Africa: A Historical Background" in *Mother Tongue Education: The West African Experience,* ed. Ayo Bamgbose (Paris: The UNESCO Press, 1976).

6 Walter Rodney, *How Europe Underdeveloped Africa* (Washington, DC: Howard University Press, 1981), 239.

7 *UNESCO,* "Learning: The Treasure within," 21.

8 Cited in Tsehloane Keto, "Pre-Industrial Education Policies and Practices in South Africa," in *Pedagogy of Domination: Toward a Democratic Education in South Africa,* ed. Mokubung Nkomo (Trenton, NJ: Africa World Press, 1990), 19.

9 ADEA Working Group on Educational Statistics, *Assessment of Basic Education in Sub-Saharan Africa 1990–2000* (Harare: NESIS Regional Center, 2000), 10.

10 *UNESCO,* "Learning: The Treasure Within," 21.

11 Rodney, *How Europe Underdeveloped Africa,* 239:

12 Romanus Ogbonnaya Ohuche, "Ibu Anyi Ndanda: The Centrality of Education in Igbo Culture," in 1991 *Ahiajoku Lecture* (Owerri: Culture Division Ministry of Information, Culture, Youth & Sports Owerri, 1991), 4.

13 Chinua Achebe, *Things Fall Apart* (New York: First Anchor Books Edition, 1994).

14 *UNESCO,* "Learning: The Treasure within," 2.

15 Ibid., 21.

16 Romanus Ogbonnaya Ohuche, "Ibu Anyi Ndanda," 4.

17 L. P. Mair, *An African People in the Twentieth Century* (London: George Routledge & Sons, 1934).

18 Joma Kenyatta, *Facing Mount Kenya: The Tribal Life of the Kikuyu* (New York: Vintage Books, 1965).

19 Rodney, *How Europe Underdeveloped Africa,* 239.

20 Magnus O. Bassey, *Western Education and Political Domination: A Study in Critical and Dialogical Pedagogy* (Westport, CT: Bergin & Garvey, 1999).

21 J. F. Ade Ajayi, Lameck K. H. Goma, and G. Ampah Johnson, *The African Experience with Higher Education* (Athens, OH: Ohio University Press, 1996), 4.

22 H. A. Oluwasanmi, "The Preservation of Intellectual Freedom and Cultural Integrity" (paper presented at a symposium on *The Role of the University in a Post-Colonial World,* Duke University, Durham, North Carolina, 11–13 April 1975), 7.

23 Munir D. Ahmad, "Muslim Education Prior to the Establishment of Madrasah," *Islamic Studies* 26, no. 4 (1987), 321–348.

24 Rodney, *How Europe Underdeveloped Africa,* 240.

25 Philip D Curtin, *The Image of Africa: British Ideas and Action, 1780–1850* (Madison: University of Wisconsin Press, 1964).

26 Edward H Berman, *African Reactions to Missionary Education* (New York: Teachers College Press, Teachers College, Columbia University, 1975).

27 R. Moffat, *Missionary Labours and Scenes in South Africa* (New York: R. Carter, 1847).

28 Walter Angus Elmslie, *Among the Wild Ngoni; Being Some Chapters in the History of the Livingstonia Mission in British Central Africa* (London: Frank Cass, 1970).

29 Magnus O. Bassey, "Missionary Rivalry and Educational Expansion in Southern Nigeria, 1885–1932," *The Journal of Negro Education* 60, no. 1 (Winter, 1991), 36–46.

30 Thomas Fowell Buxton, *The African Slave Trade and Its Remedy* (London: Frank Cass, 1840), 282.

31 J. F. A. Ajayi, *Christian Missions in Nigeria, 1841–1891: The Making of a New Elite* (Evanston, IL: Northwestern University Press, 1965).

32 A.V. Murray, *The School in the Bush,* New Impression of the 2nd. ed (New York: Barnes and Noble, INC, 1967), 65.

33 Cited in David Abernethy, *The Political Dilemma of Popular Education: An African Case* (Stanford, CA: Stanford University Press, 1969), 39.

34 Cited in H. Debrunner, *A History of Christianity in Ghana* (Accra: Waterville Publishing, 1967), 145.

35 Magnus O. Bassey, "Missionary Rivalry and Educational Expansion."

36 Ibid.

37 Edward H. Berman, *African Reactions to Missionary Education* (New York: Teachers College Press, 1975).

38 See Emmanuel Ayandele, *Nigerian Historical Studies* (London: Frank Cass, 1979), 178.

39 Kenneth O. Dike, "Development of Modern Education in Nigeria," in *The One and the Many: Individual in the Modern World*, ed. J.N. Brookes (New York: Harper & Row, 1962), 233.

40 James Coleman, *Nigeria: Background to Nationalism* (Berkeley: University of California Press, 1958).

41 For the 1882 Education Ordinance, see National Archives Ibadan (NAI) CSO/26: "A Special List of Records on the Subject of Education."

42 See Maynard Smith, *Frank Bishop of Zanzibar: Life of Frank Weston, D.D. 1871–1924* (London: Society for Promoting Christian Knowledge, 1926).

43 Cited in A. Fajana, *Educational Policy in Nigeria: A Century of Experiment* (Ile-Ife, Nigeria: University of Ife Press, 1982).

44 Ibid.

45 H.S. Scott, "The Development of the Education of the Africans in Relation to Western Contact," *The Year Book of Education*, 1938 (London: Evans Brothers, 1938), 737.

46 Rodney, *How Europe Underdeveloped Africa*, 240–241.

47 *Annual Report of the Development of Education, 1/4/51-31/3/52* (Lagos: Government Printer, 1952), 30.

48 Cited in Rodney, *How Europe Underdeveloped Africa*, 240.

49 *Western Region of Nigeria: Triennial Report on Education 1/4/55–31/3/58, Sessional Paper No. 11 of 1959* (Ibadan: Government Printer, 1959), 10.

50 *Report on the Educational System in Eastern Nigeria, No. 19* (Enugu: Government Printer, 1962).

51 D. H. Williams, *A Short Survey of Education in Northern Nigeria* (Kaduna: Ministry of Education, 1960), 45–47.

52 Education Sector Analysis, *Historical Background on the Development of Education in Nigeria* (Abuja: Education Sector Analysis, 2003), 88.

53 Federal Ministry of Education, *Digest of Statistics 1959* (Lagos: Federal Ministry of Information, 1959).

54 Aliu Babatunde Fafunwa, "The Growth and Development of Nigerian Universities," Overseas Liaison Commission, *American Council on Education*, no. 4 (April 1974), 7–8.

55 Ralph J. Bunche, "French Educational Policy in Togo and Dahomey," *The Journal of Negro Education* 3, no 1 (January 1934), 88.

56 Basil Davidson, *Modern Africa: A Social and Political History*, 3rd ed. (London: Longman, 1994), 38.

57 James Duffy, "Portuguese Africa (Angola and Mozambique): Some Crucial Problems and the Role of Education in Their Resolution," *The Journal of Negro Education* 30, no.3 (Summer,1961), 295.

58 Ibid.

59 Ibid., 301.

60 See Bernard B. Fall, "Education in the Republic of the Congo," *The Journal of Negro Education 30*, no. 3 (Summer, 1961), 267.

61 George H.T. Kimble, *Tropical Africa*, Vol.11 (New York: The Twentieth Century Fund, 1960), 115.

62 Coleman, *Nigeria: Background to Nationalism*, 150.

63 Wood to Halliday, 24 July 1854, *Wood Papers, India Board: Letter Book*, vol. 4 (Wood Papers at the India Office Library, London), cited in Suresh Chandra Ghosh, "The Genesis of Curzon's University Reform: 1899–1905," *Minerva* 26, no.4 (December 1988), 463–492.

64 Apollos Nwauwa, *Imperialism, Academe and Nationalism: British and University Education for Africans, 1860–1960* (London: Frank Cass, 1996), 81.

65 J. T. Saunders, *University College Ibadan* (Cambridge: Cambridge University Press, 1960), 194.

66 A. B. Fafunwa, *A History of Nigerian Higher Education* (Yaba, Nigeria: Macmillan, 1971), 19–20.

67 World Bank, *The African Capacity Building Initiative: Towards Improved Policy Analysis and Development* (Washington, DC: World Bank, 1991).

68 T.O. Eisemon, *The Science Profession in the Third World: Studies from India and Kenya* (New York: Praeger, 1982).

69 G. Psacharopoulos and M. Woodhall, *Education for Development,* 102. For more information, see D.A Olaniyan and T. Okemakinde, "Human Capital Theory: Implications for Educational Development," *Pakistan Journal of Social Sciences* 5, no. 5 (2008), 479–483.

70 Frederick Harbison and C.A. Myers, *Education, Manpower and Economic Growth* (New York: McGraw-Hill, 1964); Frederick Harbison, "The African University and Human Resource Development," *Journal of Modern African Studies* 3, no. 1 (1965), 53.

71 Gray Cowan, James O'Connell, and David Scanlon Cowan, eds., *Education and Nation Building in Africa* (New York: Praeger, 1965), v.

72 *West African Journal of Education* (February 1964): 9.

73 *Fraternité* (Abidjan), 15 February 1963, 6.

74 *Voice of Ethiopia,* 18 December 1961, 1.

75 Martin Carnoy and Joel Samoff, *Education and Social Transition in the Third World (Princeton,* NJ: Princeton University Press, 1990), 7.

76 Massification is a term used to describe the expansion, democratization, and liberalization of education. It represents a departure from the colonial elitist system of education.

77 *The Development of Higher Education in Africa: Report of the Conference on Development of Higher Education in Africa,* Tananarive, 3–12 September 1962 (Paris: UNESCO, 1963), 11.

78 Ibid., 12.

79 Ibid.

80 For detailed information, see Damtew Teferra and Philip. G. Altbach, eds., *African Higher Education: An International Reference Handbook* (Bloomington: Indiana University Press, 2003).

81 UNESCO/IAU, *International Handbook of Universities,* 16th ed (New York: Palgrave Publishers, 2002).

82 Task Force on Higher Education and Society, *Higher Education in Developing Countries: Peril and Promise* (Washington, DC: World Bank, 2000).

83 See Teferra and Altbach, 4 and 492–499.

84 World Bank, *Accelerating Catch-up: Tertiary Education for Growth in Sub-Saharan Africa* (Washington, DC: World Bank, 2009), 46.

85 UNESCO, *Global Education Digests 2009: Comparing Education Statistics Across the World* (Paris: UNESCO Institute for Statistics, 2009), 10.

86 UNESCO, *Global Education Digests 2009.*

87 See Ogechi Anyanwu and Apollos Nwauwa, "The Concepts and Challenges of the Universal Basic Education (UBE) Policy in Nigeria," *International Journal of Social and Management Sciences* 1, no 2 (December 2007), 114–142.

88 Adriaan M. Verspoor, *At the Crossroads Choices for Secondary Education in Sub-Saharan Africa* (Washington DC: World Bank, 2008), 27.

89 UNESCO, *Global Education Digests 2009,* 15

90 Ray Ekpu, "Gone to the Dogs," *Newswatch,* 3 May 2004, 10.

91 N.V. Varghese, *Private Higher Education in Africa* (Paris: UNESCO, 2004).

92 Eric Ashby, *African Universities and Western Tradition* (Cambridge, MA: Harvard University Press, 1964), 3.

93 Ekpu, "Gone to the Dogs," 10.

REVIEW QUESTIONS

1. Discuss the four pillars of education in relation to precolonial education in Africa.
2. What essential roles did rituals and initiation ceremonies play in precolonial education in Africa?
3. What inspired Christian missionary work in Africa, and why was education crucial to that mission?
4. Compare and contrast precolonial education with Western educational systems.
5. What were the educational mission and problems of European colonial powers?
6. Critically analyze the progress and problems of educational experiments in postcolonial Africa.

Writing Prompt

Access to higher education was strictly restricted during the period of European colonial rule. Analyze the factors responsible for this mindset on the part of European colonizers. What role would you assign to Western education in the consolidation as well as the destruction of colonial rule in Africa? With Nigeria as your case study, account for the postcolonial shift in policy choices in favor of massification of education since 1960.

CHAPTER 9

Oral and Written Literatures of Africa

Salome C. Nnoromele

In the Fall of 2002, I had the opportunity to teach a course titled "Literatures of Africa" to a group of undergraduate students in an American university. During our first day of class, the students engaged in an ice-breaker activity that asked them to share with class members why they were taking the course and what they hoped to get out of the experience by the end of the semester. Several of the students offered the usual responses about the course being an elective that fulfilled a part of the university requirement for graduation. I was, however, surprised when one of the students shared that he was taking the class out of curiosity. He had been shocked to see a course titled "Literatures of Africa" on the university schedule of courses. Prior to this, he had never considered that Africa might have developed a collective body of literary works to warrant a course on its literatures. "How can a people constantly at war with each other, dying of hunger and many diseases have time to compose literature?" he asked.[1]

Admittedly, even though the student was very honest in his confession and quite obviously meant no harm, I was, nonetheless, shocked. Growing up in Nigeria, surrounded by the spoken and written words of generations of poets and storytellers, it had never occurred to me to doubt the presence or validity of African literature or even to ask the primary question of what constitutes or would constitute African literature. Native Africans take it for granted that African literature exists much at the same practical level as water, air, and food. Its essence surrounds us at the beginning of life and shrouds us with its rhythm, reflections, and assurance when we join our ancestors at the end of life. African literary elements, in their various poetic and prose forms, showcase who we are as a people and who we aim to become. This chapter approaches the subject and substance of African literature in response to the thousands of Western and non-Western audiences who want to know and understand the literary traditions of the African continent. It addresses the basic question of what constitutes African literature. What are the distinguishing features and genres of African literature? What roles have the various forms of African literary tradition played and continue to play in the historic and cultural development of Africa? What issues of culture, history, and aesthetics does African literature attempt to define, contain, or transform?

Some scholars argue that African literature consists of works, written or oral, composed and produced in Africa about life in Africa.[2] This rather simple definition contains some elements of truth, but raises more questions than it solves. For example, would all literary works produced in Africa be considered part of the African literary tradition, in spite of who may have composed them or their subject matter? Can work by Europeans and European descendants born and raised in Africa be included in the cannon of African literary tradition? How about writings by Africans who no longer live on the continent, but write from the perspectives of their experiences as Africans? Furthermore, how about the works of European, Asian, or American travelers or visitors who write about their interpretation of life on the continent and their experiences with the people and the land? These are no easy questions. But, they point to the diversity and richness of voices and peoples whose experiences inform, question, critique, and encapsulate life on the second largest continent in the world. In taking these questions and many others into account, some scholars concede, as O. R. Dathorne argues in his seminal work on African literature, that perhaps "African literature, oral and written, may be conceived as a cohesive whole . . . undertaken by group spokespeople for the group and on behalf of the group."[3] In other words, African literature represents the values, experiences and interests of Africa.

Africa is a giant continent, with more than a billion peoples, living in diverse environments, speaking more than one thousand different languages, and enjoying multifaceted cultures and ways of life within fifty-four politically and economically autonomous nations. Africans have used numerous means to document, question, and/or reflect upon their unique experiences in their environment, their relationship to each other and their relationship to people outside their world. They have developed varieties of literary forms, oral and written, that collectively reveal the intricacies of the lives and point of views of the cultures and the peoples who produced them. As Lindsfors aptly concludes, African literatures are woven out of the substance of their experiences from the very first group of people to inhabit the continent to the present day.[4] Therefore, any viable understanding or discussion of African literature must recognize the multifarious nature of the continent and the various peoples and cultures that call Africa home. Even though the Western media attempts to portray the continent as a place where nothing good happens, the literature of Africa is one visible testament to both the vibrancy, complexity, and richness of life on the continent.

TRADITIONAL AFRICAN LITERARY FORMS

At the most basic level, we can subdivide African literatures into two major categories, namely, traditional or oral literature and contemporary, modern, or written literature. Traditional literatures cover myths, legends, epic tales, historical poems, and other traditional oral literary forms in pre-colonial Africa. Prior to the nineteenth century, the dominant literary tradition in Africa was based on the spoken word. According to Harold Courlander, "The oral literature of Africa reflects ideas, themes, suppositions, and truths that are widely shared, at the same time that it reveals creations unique to particular groups or regions."[5] The range of African oral literary forms is seemingly endless, and as Courlander noted:

> It includes creation myths, myth-legends, half-legendary chronicles and historical narratives either in song or prose: tales that explain natural phenomena, cultural practices and taboos, and political institutions; stories and fables that reflect on human nature, strengths and weaknesses; tales of adventures, courage, disaster and love; epics of legendary heroes and fictitious heroes; tales of confrontation with the supernatural and unseen forces or nature; moralizing stories that define human place and role in the universe; riddles that amuse and teach, and proverbs that stress social values; and virtually inexhaustible reservoir of animals tales, many of which, at bottom, are morality plays, while others are pure humor.[6]

However, while there are a variety of literary forms within the oral tradition, scholars recognize three major categories: proverbs, storytelling (including folktales, folklore, parables, myths, and legends both for formal and informal occasions), and poetry (traditional praise poems and epics for formal occasions, such as coronations, naming ceremonies, and community festivals; dirges for funerals; lullabies for informal occasions; and everyday poetry describing peoples ways of life and values).

Proverbs

Proverbs form one of the most prominent aspects of traditional African literature. They consist of short poignant phrases used as parts of speech or dialogue. In their use of proverbs, Africans capture the leanings of centuries of the human character and the intricate balance between people and the world around them. Consider these proverbs from the Yoruba people and the Igbo people of Nigeria: "A proverb is like a horse; when the truth is missing, we use a proverb to find it"; "Proverbs are the palm-oil with which words are eaten." Both statements illustrate the practical value and significance of proverbs in African communal life. While the Igbo proverb expresses the aesthetic value of proverbs, the Yoruba proverb suggests the use of proverbs as a tool or instrument for finding truths. Throughout Africa, proverbs perform these and other important functions, as an expressive art. They are often used as linguistic ornamentation in formal discourse. During public occasions and events, speakers intersperse their speeches with proverbs, making it a requirement for every man or woman of substance to know how to use proverbs. It would be difficult to attend a meeting of elders and not be astounded by the number of proverbs used. Sometimes entire conversations are carried on in proverbs, as people greatly versed in the art of speaking show off their skills.

Furthermore, proverbs express ages of proven wisdom. While some proverbs are regional, many are universal in their meaning. For example, one does not have to know how to play a drum to understand the following proverb—"When the drumbeat changes, the dance changes." This means that the circumstances of each situation will determine how a person will respond. In a given community, the meaning of a proverb is often clear and stable, as affirmed by this proverb—"If you tell a fool a proverb, he will ask you for its meaning." Because the specific meanings of proverbs are clear and stable, they do not invite interpretations. People understand them within the context of what is going on at the moment the proverb is spoken. In other words, proverbs are moment specific. Being versatile also means knowing the appropriate time to use them.

Proverbs are diplomatic; they never make their points in a direct manner. This makes them an indispensable political tool. They are effective for adjudicating cases and resolving conflicts. They are also used to instruct or provide advice, without being overly aggressive. Their highly metaphorical nature also provides an intrinsic medium for introducing abstract thoughts as well as shared community values. Whereas stories are told on occasions for entertainment, proverbs are rarely told solely for their entertainment value. The social and political uses of proverbs mandate that children do not address proverbs to adults. Their instructive value, their association with eloquence, experience, and wisdom make them the prerogative of the older people and inappropriate for children to use, especially when relating to adults. Etiquette indicates that if a child must use proverbs in the presence of the elderly, he must first provide an apology. The standard politeness formula runs like this . . . "I do not claim to know any proverbs in the presence of the old people, but you elders have the saying . . . ."[7]

Folktales

Equally important to life in African communities is storytelling. The term "storytelling" is used here to include folktales, folklore, myth, and legends. In traditional African society, storytelling remained primarily oral, stored in the memory of each generation and passed on to the next generation through family members and community storytellers, often called the griots or mandigas. The griots were trained professionals; they were people who specialized in collecting and performing the oral histories and stories of their communities. One may consider them human archives or libraries for their communities. Because of their significant to the community, before a griot retired from public performance, he or she is required to train another person to take over the functions. In this way, the tradition was continued and the collective memories, histories, and values of a community were maintained.

Folktales are the most popular form of storytelling in Africa. Retaining their entertainment properties, folktales serve many important functions in the life of a community. They are used as a primary means of communicating communal values, morals, and etiquette; some are used to reflect and explain the hopes and fears of the community. They can also be used to explain a people's spiritual and religious beliefs and serve as tools used to explain our relationship with the natural world and/or why things are the way they are. The characters in folktales can be gods, spirits, animals, or even insects that take on human qualities, or humans that acquire godlike or animalistic qualities. Folktales can make you laugh and they can make you cry; they can make you think, and they can teach you about the world we live in, lending explanations that are sure to delight our imagination.

When Africans tell a tale, whether it be a myth, legend, or folktale, they do not simply recite it to their listeners. As Susan Feldman so aptly states in *African Myths and Tales*, "The oral tale lives in the telling."[8] The African tale is always a public occasion. Whether told within a family situation or as part of a community celebration, the telling of folktales creates occasions for public performances. The griots use many dramatic techniques to bring the story to life before their audiences, using different voice pitch or tempo, motions, dances, and elaborate costumes. This is necessary because "The telling of a story is often a dialogue between the narrator and his listeners; the former unfolds the events, and the latter responds vocally in affirmation."[9] Each griot who tells a story makes the story his or her own. Each listener molds the story to his or her ear. In some cases, the storyteller addresses direct questions to the audience, which they answer; and the storyteller may seek assurance from the audience that they are following the story. In addition, it is usual for the storyteller to place "helpers" in the audience, persons who aid in the storytelling by providing responses at appropriate moments in the storytelling. This is why one can find different versions of a story, even within the same community. Each storyteller modifies the story to suit individual occasions, skills, and talents. Thus, the same story, told repeatedly, is never quite the same. Because of the dramatic nature of storytelling and the role of the narrator, many African cultures sculpt images of their gods and spirits to aid them in the storytelling and passing down of religious and cultural beliefs. During formal occasions, such as festivals, the storytellers may also wear masks during their performances. The masks symbolize that the griots are no longer themselves but function mainly as mediums through which the histories and collective values of the people are communicated and maintained.

There are many varieties of folktales, some with animal characters, others with human characters. All folktales make commentary about relationships between humans, animals and animals, humans and animals, and the natural world. Most folktales celebrate the triumph of good over evil or the power of the human imagination, instincts, and intelligence. Folktales most often include elements of the magical or the supernatural world. As such, characters in folktales frequently have exaggerated traits or the ability to perform unusual deeds aimed at setting things right or changing the course of events. In addition, a large portion of African tales has been classified as "trickster tales" because they rely on tricksters as the central characters. A trickster is usually small in size and strength but highly clever. He is usually represented as the underdog who lacks scruples when planning his ruthless antics on others. As Feldmann notes, "He is by no means an exemplary moral figure; he displays cupidity, gross appetite, and ruthlessness and often gains the advantage over his dull-witted and earnest opponent by sheer lack of scruple. . . . Suave, urbane and calculating, the African trickster acts with premeditation, always in control of the situation; though self-seeking, his social sense is sufficiently developed to enable him to manipulate others to his advantage."[10] In many African tales, the trickster is Anansi (the spider) or tortoise; and there are many stories to illustrate his wit, trickery, and ruthlessness.

One of my favorites is the tale about "The Squirrel and the Spider." As the story is told: long time ago, the Squirrel planted corn in a piece of land in the middle of the forest, far away from all activities. Since the Squirrel was good at climbing trees, he saw no need to create a path to his farm. He tended his crop carefully and was looking forward to a rich harvest. One day, however, he noticed that someone else was harvesting his crops. He hid himself in the forest in order to discover who was harvesting his corn. When he found the Spider and his family at the farm, he confronted them. During the quarrel that ensued, Spider claimed that the farm was his because he had created a path to it. A Council of Elders was called to settle the dispute. The Spider argued that since he had created a path to the land that the farm belonged to him. Even though the Council knew that Spider was lying, they had to rule in favor of the Spider when Squirrel confirmed that he had created no path to the property. The Council "had to admit that all the fields it had seen had paths leading to them."[11] But the story does not ultimately end in Spider's favor as a greater force outmaneuvers him and his family. For after the Spider had claimed the field, a thunderstorm and a crow succeed in denying Spider the fruit of his deceit. As Katherine Arnott shows in her retelling of the story:

> Suddenly, a great storm came. The sky was black with clouds and the rain beat down so heavily that Spider and his family had to leave their bundles of corn at the road-side and dash to shelter in a near-by hut. . . . when the sky finally cleared and the sun shone again, they made their way back to where they had left the bundles of corn. Then they stood still and gazed in surprise at a gigantic black crow which was perched on the corn with outstretched wings. . . . Spider was very delighted. "Thank you, Crow. Thank you," he said happily. "You have kept my corn dry and now I shall not have to spread it all out in the sun again. "Your corn," object the Crow. "It is my corn now. Whoever heard of anyone leaving bundles of corn unattended by the side of the path? Go Away! This belongs to me." Then the Crow gathered up all the corn in his huge claws and flew away out of sight. So there was nothing left for Spider and his family to do, except to return home empty handed and very angry.[12]

Thus, the Spider's trick backfires and he and his family are taught a very important lesson. But, one should never count on the trickster learning his lesson, because he is always presented in tale after tale as an unrepentant and artful manipulator who is not deterred by failure.

While some tales have clear concluding messages as in the story of the Squirrel and the Spider, some have open-ended conclusions. These types of stories, called the dilemma tales, leave the audience with the task of finding a solution or conclusion to the tale. Such tales end with a question the audience is supposed to answer. An excellent example is the story: "A Test of Skills," also known as "Contest of the Baobab Tree," or "The Three Brothers."[13] A long time ago, there was a chief who had three sons. Even though he loved his sons greatly and equally, he always wondered which of them was the wisest. One day, he decided to test them in order to settle the question for himself. He called his sons and told them to show off their skills near a huge baobab tree a little distant from the chief's house. "My sons," said the chief, "I want each of you to mount your horse in turn and show your skill."[14] The sons agreed to the challenged, for each of them secretly believed that he was indeed the strongest and the wisest. The townspeople were called together to witness the event. As the contest began, the first son rode furiously toward the baobab tree, held his spear high in the air, and thrust it forcefully into the trunk of the baobab tree. The force created a large hole in the center of the tree through which the rider and his horse made their way effortlessly to the other side. Then, the second son came riding toward the tree. When he came near the tree, he pulled the bit and the horse and its rider rose in the air and sailed right over the baobab tree unharmed. The third son also galloped fiercely toward the three; when he came level with the tree, he grasped the tree with one hand and pulled it out of the ground by the roots, and waved it victoriously at the people. The question at the end of the story asks, "Which of the three sons would you have chosen as the winner, had you been the chief?"[15]

Like all dilemma tales, the story poses a challenge because each of the three sons displays incredible skills and dexterity in his performance. As my students remind me each time I introduce them to this tale, choosing one son over the other may indicate favoritism and a preferential treatment of one son over the other. This may be true if one looks at the tale from a Western perspective. Analyzed from a different perspective, one may realize that the question the chief is asking is not whether one son is stronger or better than the other. The real subtext to the challenge and the real question the chief poses to the community is to help him identify the son with the greatest understanding of his community and its values and, hence, the son who is best fitted to lead the community successfully. One can have immense physical strength and still be an ineffective leader.

Dilemma tales, therefore, cannot be solved satisfactorily without taking into account the cultural contexts and the values of the community from which the tale originates. In the preceding tale, if one truly understands the value of the baobab tree to the community in question, it would appear that the second son who performs his feat without damaging the tree is indeed the winner of the contest. In Southern Africa, from where the tale originates, the baobab tree is viewed as the "life-giving tree." It serves many functions within the community, providing food for both humans and animals, water, shelter, and other forms of sustenance. Anything that harms the tree in essence harms the community. However, as some scholars recognize, even when dilemma tales are solved, the story still haunts us. Feldmann reminds us that "in contrast to the moral tales where right and wrong are clearly defined, the dilemma tale specializes in ambiguous cases where the questions continue to haunt us even after a decision has been reached."[16]

Traditional African Poetry

Traditional African poetry, also known as oral poetry, includes epics that record the histories of Africa's past kings and kingdoms; praise poems used for such events as coronations, naming ceremonies, and community festivals; dirges for funerals; lullabies for informal occasions; and everyday poetry describing people's ways of life and values. African oral poetry is very lyrical because it is meant to be sung and performed, not to be read. This is especially noteworthy today because most of the African oral poetry has been preserved for modern audiences in books and in some written form. The most well-known epic that has survived to-date is the *Epic of Sundiata* detailing the narrative history of the great king of the Old Mali Empire, Mansa Sundiata, during the thirteenth century. Even though the epic comes to us today in the written form from scholars who have studied and recorded the poetry as it was recited by the griots, the epic still retains its orality as evidenced by the songs interspersed within the poetry, its call and response techniques and, the questions posed by the griots as they advanced the narrative. These elements collectively remind us that the poem was meant to be performed, and was indeed performed among the Mandigo people of Mali in celebration of their hero and history, and not read.

The purpose of praise poems is to remind the community of the special skills and contributions of recognized individuals to the community. The praise singers use voice and pitch manipulation, change in tempo, speech rhythm, and gestures in reciting and performing the poems. Ben Amos rightly notes that "The professional court singer accompanies his recitation of the chief's praises not only by walking but by leaping about with gesticulations as the excitement increases. He suits the actions to words, the words to actions; the performance is indeed dramatic."[17] Astute griots also use their composition and recitation of praise poems as occasions for social criticism, complaints, or comparison between two competing houses, individuals, and leaders within the community. An example is an excerpt from Akintude Akimyemi, *Yoruba Royal Poetry,* where the griot uses his poetic skill to compare life during the rule of two chiefs or kings, Abiodun and Arogangan. The griot obviously prefers the Abiodun to Arogangan. He recites: "During the days of Abiodun/. . .We measured money in calabash." Measuring "money in calabash" refers to the idea that the people had food and an enriched life as compared to the reign of chief Arogangan when "Frogs took over the whole place.[18] Using the metaphor "Frogs took over the place," does not mean that frogs literally took over the place; it merely uses the powerful visual to suggest the extent to which the people's lives were altered and destroyed by Arogangan. As in the above example, praise poems usually tell a story and they are very lyrical. Similar to praise poems, dirges also tell a story, but they are funeral or burial poems composed in honor of a deceased loved one. They highlight important events in the person's life and how the person should be remembered. The dirge is sung as a part of the funeral ceremony. Recently, however, modern African poets are co-opting the dirge format and using it to express dissatisfaction over some aspects of Africa's political and social problems. They seem to be mourning those things that have negatively affected the African continent and slowed its growth. Lullabies are poems that celebrate our lives as children. They are mostly composed for the entertainment of children. In the United States, there are so many lullabies, such as "Mary had a little Lamb" or "Itsy Bitsy Spider."[19]

CONTEMPORARY AFRICAN LITERATURE

Emmanuel Obiechinna writes that perhaps the single most important element responsible for the transformation of literature in Africa after the nineteenth century was the introduction and spread of literacy across Africa.[20] Literacy transformed African literature from its primary reliance on the spoken word to the written form. It meant that people not only learned to read and write their own languages, but they could read and write other people's languages as well. The immediate impact of literacy in widening the scope of experience for the African peoples is that it brought them in contact with other ways of seeing and thinking. These are reflected in the poetry, essays, short stories, novels, nonfiction about personal/community histories, and plays/drama/films that constitute modern literary history. The written word permits writers to enter literary spaces previously unavailable with the spoken word. For example, social decorum might require that certain things are easier communicated through writing than through speech. Modern African writers, thus, have utilized the freedom afforded through written spaces to enter complex topics that would have been difficult to maneuver with the spoken word, as well as to interface different genres in a way that would not have been possible with oral literature. Each of the fifty-four African countries has major and minor authors who have distinguished themselves in many literature genres. Some of these writers include Wole Sonyika (Nigeria), Nadine Gordimer (South Africa), Naguib Mahfouz (Egypt), and J. M. Coetzee (South Africa) who won the Nobel prize for literature in 1986, 1988, 1991, and 2003 respectively.

Because of Africa's colonial experience, modern African literature comes in a variety of different languages, including African indigenous languages, Arabic, Swahili (which is a blend of Arabic and some indigenous African languages), as well as European languages. Most African countries have tended to adopt the language of their former colonial masters as their lingua franca or official languages. Hence, writings from each country reflect whichever European language the country adopted as its official language after its independence. Literary scholars use different terms to reference African works written in European languages. Anglophone refers to works written in English; Francophone refers to works written in French; Luscophone refers to works written in Portuguese. While there is substantial work written in Portuguese, Anglophone and Francophone African literatures currently dominate the field, as many writers prefer to write in English or French in order to reach a wider audience in their home countries and abroad. South African and North African literature are also viewed as distinct categories when discussing African literatures. Literatures coming from the northern part of Africa tend to emphasize the Islamic nature of the region's cultural experiences more so than those coming from western or southern Africa. "In all these works, the Islamic experience is presented as a distinctive current of a modern awareness and sensibility, and Islamic religion and tradition an essential component of universal humanism."[21] Due to its mild, temperate climate, especially in the Cape Town region, South Africa attracted a large population of European immigrants who arrived during the colonial era, and subsequently made the land their home. The mixture of European settlers, the indigenous Black South African population, and the East Asian migrants who arrived later, gives South Africa and its literatures their own unique flavor that is different from any part of Africa. In addition to the diverse peoples that make up the population of South Africa, the South African experience is also complicated by its history of apartheid. In 1948, the ruling European South African population, even though they constituted only a minority, decided to introduce measures that would allow them to sustain political and economic power in South Africa. This initiated almost fifty years of political and economic disenfranchisement of the majority black South Africans as well as all other non-European South Africans (called "the colored peoples of South Africa"). Even though apartheid officially came to an end in 1994, with the election of Nelson Mandela as the first black President of South Africa, the effects of apartheid are still felt and will continue to be felt for the foreseeable future as the country attempts to create a society where all its peoples can co-exist peacefully and productively. The literatures of South Africa, hence, reflect the unique experiences of the country and the diversity of voices that make up its population.[22]

The African Novel

The novel, as is almost everywhere in the world, remains the dominant modern literary genre on the African continent.[23] Even though, historically, one can trace the development of the African novel to as early as 1908 with the composition of Mofolo's work, *Chaka,* written in the Sesotho language of South Africa, it was not until the 1950s that the international community developed an interest in the African novel. This makes the African novel relatively new when compared to novels from Europe and even the Americas. Nonetheless, the African novel has established its own unique identity as writers have found ways to adapt the structure of the novel to expressing African themes, thoughts, narrative traditions, and ways of life. Thus, O. R. Dathorne reminds us that the collective body of modern African literature reflects the synthesis in some degree of African traditional literary forms and values and Western literary influences.[24] In many ways, the novel serves as an extension of the forms and functions of folktales and myths in synthesis with other traditional forms of narrative. This "oral-literate interface," as it has been called, is explained as reflecting "either a conscious design or, as is often the case, the effect of a cultural retention determined by the African background."[25] This means that when African authors began writing about their unique experiences, they did not leave their own culture, modes of speech, and storytelling techniques behind. They both consciously and unconsciously carried traditional modes of storytelling and use of language into their writing. On the same hand, one also finds examples of Western influences in these writings. Since most of these writers are products of colonial missionary education and were exposed to writings by Western authors, it is not surprising that some aspects of the Western literature they had studied would find their way into their works. For example, Achebe borrowed the title of his novel, *Things Fall Apart,* from a line in Yeats' poem, *The Second Coming*; and even though the East African writer, Ngugi W' Thiong'o, is still yet to acknowledge his Western literary influences, one cannot read his early novels, such as *A Grain of Wheat* and *The River Between* without thinking of works by D. H. Lawrence and Joseph Conrad.

Most importantly, however, the development of the African novel is said to parallel the historical developments on the continent since the nineteenth century. The history of the African novel in many ways reflects the social, political, and intellectual changes taking place on the continent from colonial times to the present. This reality has led such critics as Emmanuel C. Eze to suggest that modern African writing is a form of experience in history writing; it is a form of historical understanding of a people, a culture, or a tradition, past and present.[26] Early writers of the later nineteenth through the mid-twentieth centuries used the novel form to explore the African encounter with the European world. The best known of these novels is Chinua Achebe's *Things Fall Apart* (1958). Others include Ngugi's *Weep Not Child* (1964) and *The River Between* (1965) and Camara Laye's *L'Enfant Noir (The African Child)* (1953), among many others. "These novels serve the major function of trying to recreate life in traditional Africa, the changing nature of the colonial experience, and the drastic reordering of African lives by Western cultural imposition," according to Abiola Irele.[27] One of the defining characteristics of the works from this period is a tendency to present pre-colonial African life and setting from a nostalgic viewpoint. They attempt to reconstruct the essence of African traditional society as idyllic; they present warm and celebrative pictures of traditional African village life and values. However, in spite of the criticism levied on these works as being overly nostalgic, they succeed in recapturing and recording precolonial African values and lives. During the independence movements, these novels, working together with other forms of modern African literatures, such as poetry, drama, essays, and short stories, became powerful tools for creating and maintaining strong nationalist sentiments aimed at political freedom and decolonization. They critiqued colonial regimes and served as tools to galvanize Africans as well as the international community to sustain the push for political and economic independence for Africans and their countries.

Subsequent works, even by already established writers, transitioned during the 1960s and 1970s to capture the expectations that preceded independence for most of the African nations. They reflect the hopes and aspirations for the newly independent nations and the challenges of forging self-reliant political and social institutions, in spite of the dividing experience of colonization. These novels include Achebe's *No Longer at Ease* and *A Man of the People* and Ngugi's *A Grain of Wheat*. A major theme of these novels is the conflict between the old and the emerging cultural attitudes and values that would define new Africa and the bewildering and unnerving experience of trying to come to terms with its meaning for Africa, its conscience and identity. A decade later, however, few of the expectations of independence had come close to being realized. For the majority of the African population, conditions of living did not improve after independence as had been promised. As a matter of fact, the standard of living deteriorated for the average African. As Derek Wright captured it, "Independence had not brought unity, social justice, peace, or prosperity to Africa; on the contrary, it had produced division and fragmentation, inequality and class elitism, political violence, and economic stagnation."[28] The novels of the 1980s and 1990s shifted themes to reflect the reality of the decade and the increasingly crumbling dreams of the African peoples as they watched the political, economic, and social structures of their countries collapse. Writers of the after-independence period have been critiqued for having an "inflated" view of the post-independence era and unrealistic expectations of the newly established countries and their fledgling leaders. The argument is that both the African peoples as well as the writers of the period unrealistically assumed that all political, social, and economic problems will be solved immediately after independence, and that the political leaders would somehow act as messiahs and magically solve all pre-independence problems.

During Africa's first round of independence, the 1950s to 1970s, as Lazarus argues, many writers and intellectuals of the period fell into the trap of mistaking political freedom for social struggle, failing to see that nationalism and revolution were incompatible agendas.[29] Analysts overlooked the conflicts and dissensions present between the nationalist leaders as well as internally within the individual countries. They also underestimated the effects of the flawed political structures that the nationalist governments inherited from the colonial regimes. Independence was never the staging arena for revolution that the writers took if for.[30] It was unrealistic to think that the effects of more than 400 years of European exploitation and oppression under the colonial regimes would be eradicated by a few years of independent rule.

As African countries have continued to construct and reconstruct their nations through the mangled structures of postcolonial existence and the demands of a consistently expanding and changing global community, the themes and structures of the novels of the 1980s and 1990s reflect the tenets of this phase of national building. Still decrying the failure of the African states to live up the expectations of the people, the works of this period began the all important work of self-reflection. Works like Achebe's *The Trouble with Nigeria* and *Anthill of the Savannah*, Ngugi's *Petals of Blood*, and Armah's *The Beautyful Ones Are Not Yet Born* attempt to look at Africa's problems from an inward viewpoint. While acknowledging the debilitating wounds of colonization, the novels, however, move forward to asking African natives to evaluate how they themselves may have contributed to stunting the economic and political growth of their individual countries. These novels initiated discussions on the necessary theme of self-assessment that is required for a people to move forward in ending sufferings and building healthy societies.

Life in Africa during the twenty-first century is quite different from life during the nineteenth and twentieth centuries. As such, the novels of the twenty-first century continue to expand on the themes of earlier novels and to complicate the themes by introducing the complex and globalized experiences of the twenty-first-century

Africa. Unlike writers of the previous generations, especially the pioneer writers of the 1950s and 1960s, who grew up reading Western literature and learning the tools of the trade by emulating Western authors and literary traditions, the writers of the twenty-first century are the first generation of African writers who can claim the privilege of having grown up reading African writers and having a clear sense of the African written tradition. As such, this new generation of African writers enjoys the special position of functioning as "the literary children" of accomplished writers who have labored to establish distinct African literary traditions upon which to continue the exploration of the story of Africa. Writers like Chris Ubani, Chimamanda Adichie, Yvonne Vera, and a host of others explore the new facets of the African experience on the solid foundation built by their literary predecessors. Central to the novels of these writers is an attempt to reflect experiences in contemporary African societies and to correct the distorted image of Africa in the Western world. In her essay, "The Danger of a Single Story," Adichie argues that telling only one story about Africa is a form of continued oppression of the continent.[31] There needs to be a presentation of multiple stories that highlight the different aspects of life on the continent. Only when we are able to see a balanced picture of Africa can a healthy relationship develop between Africa and the outside world. Literary critics posit that in reworking the themes of earlier works and introducing new ones, these writers tell a story of the ending of old nations and the making of new ones. "With these writers, the novel has entered a new phase and assumed a new complexion in Africa. The raffia skirt and the kola nut have been left behind as indices of African life, along with the village environment; the focus has shifted to the new social configuration of the urban milieu which provides the significant context of experience in the post-independence period."[32] In addition to novels that focus on contemporary life in Africa, the twenty-first century is also witnessing the emergence of new genre of literature classified as literature of the new African Diaspora, transnational literature, or African immigrant literature. These works explore the lives of African sons and daughters who live away from their homelands in Europe, United States, Canada, and other parts of the world. In this category, we have works by Dinaw Mengestu, Lawrence Hill, Olufemi Terry, Benjamin Kwakye, Simi Bedford, and many others.

War or trauma literature represents a new genre of African literature that has grown out of the wars and conflicts in contemporary Africa. Even though the average Westerner tends to think of Africa as a place of war or conflicts, not every part of Africa is at war. The majority of Africans live in relative peace and tranquility as they negotiate the daily challenges of life. However, we cannot deny the fact that a significant part of the history of postcolonial Africa consists of war and conflict that resulted mostly from the colonial experience and the desire of distinct groups to determine their own autonomous way of life. Most of the conflicts in Africa are internal; they are rarely between independent nations. They are often between different groups within a particular country attempting to work out and settle internal differences that were left to fester during and after the colonial era. The trauma literature reflects the reality of life for immediate survivors of these conflict as well as those who reflect on past conflicts as part of Africa's history. Thus, in *Half of a Yellow Sun*, Chimamanda Adichie writes about the Nigerian-Biafran war, even though she was born after the war. Ishmeal Beah's *A Long Way Gone* relives his personal experiences during the Sierra Leone civil war. Paul Rusesabagina's *An Ordinary Man* recounts the experience of the Rwandan civil war. Mashingaidze Gomo, in *A Fine Madness*, reflects on Zimbabwe's struggle for independence.

WOMEN WRITERS

It is true that African women had access to the literary tradition in precolonial Africa as both private and public performers, depending on locale. But, the written word in its many forms—poetry, drama, novel—provides African women writers greater avenues through which to cross cultural boundaries in order to highlight issues that particularly affect women. Even though women are present in male-authored texts, examination of their unique experiences as women has not always been given significant attention in these works. In fact, some critics concede that male-authored texts not only have continued to marginalize women experiences, but have insisted on stereotypical images of African women as passive and subordinate. African women writers, therefore, attempt to present a balanced exploration of the varying experiences, circumstances, and challenges faced by women in different African societies. They reposition women's issues and experiences as pivotal to understanding the totality of the African experience. They share a belief that neglecting, marginalizing or dismissing women experiences from any conversation on the future of the continent harms rather than promotes growth and development. Mariama Ba's *Une Si Longue Lettre* (*So Long a Letter*) published in 1979 is credited as the first "feminist" African novel in calling attention to how cultural and social institutions often serve as tools for the abuse and oppression of women in society. The forerunners of this novel, of course, include Flora Nwapa's *Efuru* (1966) and Grace Ogot's *The Promised Land* (1966), both of which discuss the experiences of African women in traditional Africa. *Une Si Longue Lettre* deviates from both novels in focusing on gender relations in a postcolonial society trying to come to terms with its identity. Since its publication and the conversation it introduced among literary critics on the reality of women lives in contemporary African society, many other women writers, including Buchi Emecheta, Tsitsi Dangaremba, Ama Ata Aidoo, Chimamanda Adichie, to name a few, have used their own works to probe and extend the discussion. Their works problematize issues of political and social disenfranchisement, discrimination, inequality, human rights, domestic violence, and many others as they affect men and women in society. As is often the case, works by African women writers, and their exploration of issues of gender and culture are not without controversy as most have been accused as favoring concepts that are Western. "Feminism" is viewed as a Western ideology that imposes foreign ideas of womanhood on Africa. It is also viewed as being anti-African values and traditions, and anti-men. However, very few of their critics, if any, would accept the premise that being African should be equated with marginalization, abuse, or disenfranchisement of women. As the writer Ama Ata Aidoo noted in her response to her critics, "To try to remind ourselves and our brothers and lovers and husbands and colleagues that we also exist should not be taken as something foreign, as something bad. African women struggling both on behalf of themselves and on behalf of the wider community are very much a part of our heritage. It is not really new and I really refuse to be told I am learning feminism from abroad."[33] There is a tacit understanding, as Gibreel Kamara notes, that rather than advancing the notion that "the African man is directly responsible for the problems of the African woman,"[34] it is more productive to realize that confronting the problems of African women in society requires the effort of both genders. The social, economic, and political health of any group of people can most certainly be measured by the health and progress of its women. As such, despite the controversial conversations on gender generated by the works of African women writers, their works continue to call attention to the woman question, illustrating the complex range and the narrative possibilities of African feminist themes, and suggesting the avenues through which to solve the problems.

THE ROLE OF THE LITERARY ARTIST

Any discourse on African literatures, oral or written, will be incomplete without touching on one of the issues that continues to engage African literary scholars—that of the role of the writer as an artist. This is especially important in contemporary African life as the concept of art for art sake is steadily explored by modern writers who see themselves as mediums solely for the transmission of the creative energy. Olufemi Terry, who won the 2010 Caine Prize for African writing states, "My life experiences undoubtedly inform my writing but in an inorganic and imprecise way that I neither direct nor understand, and which leaves no room for a conscious 'Africanness.' . . . I am free to pick and choose what and who I write about, from whose perspective to tell a story and in what voice. For me, this freedom is as indispensable an asset as curiosity and the reluctance to take sides."[35] But, many argue, just as they have argued throughout history, whether one is looking at British, American, French, or African literatures, that writers do not and cannot live in a vacuum. The writer speaks for the community through his or her art. According to Dathorne, "The creative art which is taking place is not that of the proselytizer but that of the spokesperson. . . . the artist is re-arranging traditional images of the group and in so doing becomes an affirmer. . . . The writer had to be a part of the group, he had to live with the group and use the tools of the group."[36] Serving as the spokesperson for the community places an enormous responsibility on the writer. One surely can understand why many would prefer not to assume such a duty, especially in modern society with differing views and perspectives. In a rapidly changing world with many social and political issues warring with each other, what position should the artist assume? What collective idea, assuming that one exists, should the writer give voice? Undeniably, African literatures, both traditional and modern, have played and continue to play pivotal roles in the survival of the African spirit, its values, identity and essence. However, while in traditional society, the griot understood the fact that he or she worked for and on behalf of the community, the modern writer does not necessarily share this vision or community goal. He or she may work on behalf of the community in telling its many stories, but the writer does not necessarily work for the community. As Binta Fatima Ibrahim states, "the literary artist goes beyond the creation of culture. He aims at actually redesigning society. Meaning that literature in Africa is not just a visual and auditory art but also a critical medium. The African writer attempts to criticize, communicate with his people and argues for a change in the order of things. He is in fact an auditor of the socio-cultural order."[37] The debate about the role of the artist highlights both the recognized importance of the literary artist and the changing nature of the African society. Even though African literatures remain functional, for literature will always be a product of the community from which they are composed, contemporary writers understand the wider context for their work, and the transformational spirit and identity of modern Africa. They know they must wrestle with the dual role of serving as the spokespeople and conscience of their communities while remaining true to essence of their art and creativity.

CONCLUSION

Literatures from the continent of Africa in its many forms reflect the diversity of African voices and the complexities of African life and experience since the precolonial. If someone were to select representative literatures from the different periods in the history of Africa, that person will be able to gain a comprehensive understanding of the African experience. This is because the literatures of Africa play a pivotal role in chronicling the history of Africa, past to the present. This is the gift that African literatures give and continue to give to the African continent, and why Africans cherish and will continue to cherish their writers and storytellers. Without them, Africans will lose an essential part of who they are as a people, their values, identities, and realities.

Traditional African literatures, consisting mostly of folktales, oral poetry, proverbs, myths, and legends help us to understand and to examine the values and perspectives of old Africa. In a way, they are mediums through which life before the African encounter with the western world is acknowledged and celebrated. Through precolonial literatures, we gain an appreciation of what precolonial life consisted of and how this way of life was irrevocably altered by the colonial encounter and the influence of the outside world. Contemporary literatures extend the conversation. They remind us how traumatic and culturally destabilizing colonialism was to Africa. They reinforce the fact that the colonial experience is still very much a significant part of the character and identity of the continent and will remain so for the foreseeable future. But, the new generation of writers also offers a new approach, a different way of looking at their roles as writers and as citizens of the African world. In taking stock of their Africanized identity in synthesis with their diverse global experiences, these writers interrogate the place of new Africa within the world community. They force us to begin the arduous, but important task of revaluating past and present African experience, to question preconceived assumptions, and to develop multiple stories about the continent that reflect its diversity of peoples, experiences, and perspectives.

ENDNOTES

1   For a fuller discussion of how the western media distorts Africa, see Michael Mahadeo and Joe McKinney, "Media Representations of AFRICA: Still the Same Old Story," *Policy and Practice: A Development of Education review,* issue 4 (Spring 2007):14–20.

2   George Joseph, "African Literature," in *Understanding Contemporary Africa,* ed. April A. Gordon and Donald L. Gordon (Boulder, CO: Lynne Rienner Publishers, 2001).

3   O. R. Dathorne, *African Literature in the 20th Century* (Minneapolis: University of Minnesota Press, 1975), x.

4   Bernth Lindfors, ed, *Forms of Folklore in Africa* (Austin: University of Texas Press, 1977), 2.

5   Harold Courlander, *A Treasury of African Folklore: The Oral Literature, Traditions, Myths, Legends, Epics, Tales, Recollections, Wisdom, Sayings, and Humor of Africa* (New York: Crown Publishers, 1975), 3.

6   Ibid.

7   Dan Ben-Amos, "Folklore in African Society," in *Forms of Folklore in Africa,* ed. Bernth Lindfors (Austin: University of Texas Press, 1977), 22.

8   Susan Feldmann, ed., *African Myths and Tales* (New York: Dell Publishing, Inc, 1970), 12.

9   Ibid.

10   Ibid., 15.

11   Kathleen Arnott, *Tales from Africa* (Oxford, UK: Oxford University Press, 2000), 67.

12   Ibid., 68.

13   Ibid., 41–43; Courlander, *A Treasury of African Folklore,* 67–68.

14   Arnott. *Tales from Africa,* 41.

15   Ibid., 43.

16   Feldmann, *African Myths and Tales,* 18

17   Ben-Amos, *"Folklore in African Society,"* 13

18   Akintude Akimyemi, *Yoruba Royal Poetry: A Socio-historical Exposition and Annotated Translation* (Bayreuth, Germany: Thielmann and Breitinger, 2004), 86–87.

19   See this youtube rendition of a favorite African lullaby—"Be Still my Child." www.youtube.com/watch?v=ElBmQXrqVdg&feature=related. One would usually sing this song to soothe a crying baby.

20   Emmanuel Obiechina, *Culture, Tradition and Society in the West African Novel* (Cambridge, UK: Cambridge University Press, 1975), 3.

21   F. Abiola Irele, "Introduction: Perspectives on the African novel," in *The Cambridge Companions to the African Novel,* ed. Abiola Irele (Cambridge, UK: Cambridge University Press, 2009), 5.

22   For an extensive discussion of South African literatures, see Gareth Cornwell, *The Columbian Guide to South African Literatures in English* (New York: Columbia University Press, 2010).

23   Irele, "Introduction: Perspectives on the African Novel," 1.

24   Dathorne, *African Literature in the 20th Century,* 1.

25   Derek Wright, *New Directions in African Fiction* (New York: Twayne Publishers, 1997), 3.

26   Emmanuel Chukwudi Eze, "Language and Time in Postcolonial Experience," *Research in African Literatures* 39, no. 1 (Winter 2008), 27.

27   Irele, "Introduction: Perspectives on the African Novel," 8.

28   Wright, New *Directions in African Fiction,* 3.

29   Neil Lazarus, *Resistance in Post Colonial African Fiction* (New Haven, CT: Yale University Press, 1990), 27.

30   Ibid., 11.

31   Ngozi Chimamanda Adichie, "The Danger of A Single Story," www.youtube.com/watch?v=D9Ihs241zeg (accessed 8/7/2011).

32   Irele, "Introduction: Perspectives on the African Novel," 11.

33 Ama Ata Aidoo, "To Be an African Woman Writer: An Overview and a Detail," *Criticism and Ideology,* ed. Kirsten Holst Peterson (Uppsala, Sweden: Scandinavian Institute of African Studies, 1988), 183.

34 Gibreel M. Kamara. "The Feminist Struggle in the Senegalese Novel: Mariama Ba and Semebe Ousmane. *Journal of Black Studies* 32, no. 2. (November 2001):213.

35 Olufemi Terry, "I Am Not an 'African'," *Focus on Africa* (October-December, 2010), 65.

36 Dathorne, *African Literature in the 20th Century,* x–xi.

37 Binta Fatima Ibrahim, "The Appropriation of Linguistic Forms for Better Cognitive Comprehension of the Nigerian Pragmatic Literature," *Babel* 56, no. 2 (2010):119.

REVIEW QUESTIONS

1. Discuss why it is difficult to come up with a comprehensive definition of what constitutes African literature. Discuss the strengths and weaknesses of defining African literature as "works that represent the values, experiences and interests of Africa."
2. Discuss the various genres of traditional African literature. What roles did the different genres play in the communal life of the community?
3. Identify and discuss the ways modern African literature can be said to trace or parallel the development of Africa's political history since the beginning of the twentieth century.
4. Discuss the roles women writers/performers play in African literary traditions.
5. Reflect on the question of the role of artist in the community. Do you think that the tendency to think of the African writer as the spokesperson for his or community is justified? Why or why not?

Writing Prompt

One criticism against the writers of the 1970s and 1980s is that they expected too much and too soon from the fledgling leadership of the newly independent African nations. These writers pointed to the political essays that some members of the leadership crafted both during and after independence movement. Acquire through your school library several of the political speeches by the "fathers" of African independence, such as Kwame Nkrumah of Ghana, Julius Nyerere of Tanzania, and Jomo Kenyatta of Kenya. Evaluate the speeches, indicating how the leaders saw their roles within independent Africa and their promises, if any, for their individual nations. Based on your evaluation, do you think that the writers of the period after independence were too optimistic in their expectations? Did they have any reasons to be frustrated by the inefficiencies of their leaders?

CHAPTER 10

Art in Africa

Ida Kumoji-Ankrah

The African continent has produced a great diversity of art forms. In many instances, art production has been related to ritual or ethnic ceremonies; art has also been used for decorative functions in corporate and residential spaces. The study of art in Africa has been plagued by the problems of cross-cultural interpretation. Until recently, the designation "African" was usually only bestowed on the arts of "Black Africa," people living in sub-Saharan Africa. The people of North Africa were not generally included under the genre of African art. However, there has been a movement among African art historians to include the arts of both sub–Saharan and North Africa since they are within the same geographic boundaries of the African continent.

African artists do not create or produce art in a vacuum, and the fact that different stylistic similarities can be recognized is evidence that they were influenced not only by other artists in their societies but also by their neighboring groups.[1] To the Western eye, "African art" equals "African sculpture"—masks, headdresses, and ritual figures. However, any contemporary African artists would point to textiles rather than sculpture as the tradition with the strongest impact on their work.[2] European observers have created a problem that sculpture (wood, metal, terracotta, or more rarely stone) is the pre-eminent African art. Sculpture is, however, only one aspect of the visual arts in Africa, alongside painting, pottery, architecture, textiles, jewelry, and various forms of body decoration and painting.[3]

This chapter will present the history of African art; explore the rock art of Africa, and highlight the pivotal ethnic art forms across the continent. Some of the ethnic groups to be examined are the Ndebele of Southern Africa; Benin, Ife, and Nok of Nigeria; Baoule of Ivory Coast; Bambara and Dogon of Mali; Akan of Ghana; Makonde of Tanzania and Mozambique; and the Berbers of Northern Africa. These are some of the areas where natural resources dictated the materials used, while ethnic power and wealth determined the type of art produced.

Furthermore, the chapter will discuss the formal aesthetic principles of African art and the moral and religious ideas they express. Aesthetics often establish the pattern that connects cultural functions in a society. Also, this chapter will explore the role of contemporary African art, highlighting some of the contemporary and traditional African artists. It will conclude by investigating the influences of African art on Western art and how, with the Westernization of African society, "traditional" art forms have become commercialized and have led a number of African artists to adopt Western art forms into their work.

HISTORY OF AFRICAN ART

Art is an integral part of the everyday life of Africans. It is used for dialogue and to communicate with the gods and ancestors. There are five regions in Africa and each region has produced its own different art form that reflects regional, historical, cultural, and religious values and beliefs. These regions are North Africa, East

Africa, West Africa, South Africa, and Central Africa. The art of the various geographical regions were largely dictated by the natural resources that flourish within their territories. The first known sculpture in Africa was by the Nok people of central Nigeria, dating from 500 BCE to 200 CE.[4] The sculptures were molded out of clay, which took the form of human figures and heads. These artworks were eventually damaged due to their everyday use in rituals and ceremonies. The majority of African artworks that we are familiar with today date from after 1850.[5] The first examples of African art to gain public attention were the bronzes and ivories made in Benin. The amazing technology of the Benin bronzes won the praise of experts like Felix von Luschan, who wrote in 1899, "Cellini himself could not have made better casts, nor anyone else before or since to the present day."[6] The Benin bronze had a realistic treatment of human features, which conformed to the prevailing European aesthetic standards of the time. Because of these features, it was first maintained that Europeans had produced them—a view that was still current when the more realistic bronze head was discovered at Ife in 1912.[7]

The arts of North Africa include pottery, embroidered and woven textiles, woodwork, leatherwork, metalwork, and silver and gold jewelry. The Egyptian form of art is highly symbolic, as illustrated by the artifacts still being discovered in monuments and tombs. They symbolize the ethnic culture that gives life to mythical gods and goddesses, emphasizes life after death, and upholds the knowledge of ancestors. Due to the Egyptians' resistance to internal change and foreign influence, their part in shaping the history has remained amazingly unvarying for a period of 3000 years.[8] East African art is a reflection of the various communities in the region. Stretching over the island nation of Madagascar through Uganda, Tanzania, Somalia, Kenya, Eritrea and Ethiopia, East African arts flourish. The ancient trade between the ethnic groups situated at the eastern African coast and the Arabs brought forth strong foreign influences that made East African art more distinct. The huge foreign influences on East African art are also highly evident in the different religions that some of the communities have adopted. The religions in these parts of Africa have also influenced many sacred art objects like masks and statues that are used in ritual initiations, sacred ceremonies, death, and marriage ceremonies.

In Kenya, for example, the ethnic group known as Mijikenda[9] carves and erects wooden poles to commemorate the dead. Many of the ethnic groups in eastern Africa, including Turkana of Tanzania and the Masai[10] of Kenya and Somalia, lead a partially nomadic existence, seasonally moving to be able to herd livestock to richer pastures. Their lifestyle made way for crafts that can easily be packed and transported from one place to another. Among these nomadic East Africans, arts consist of headrests carved from wood, finely patterned baskets, and wooden drinking vessels of different designs, shapes, and sizes. A common East African art that most groups in this region share is elaborate and beautifully patterned beadwork. Colorful beads are vital components in the body adornment of the Masai, Turkana, and other eastern ethnic groups. These vibrantly hued materials are created into jewelry or ornaments embroidered into clothing and incorporated into complex hairstyles. The different styles and designs of this East African art symbolizes differences in age, gender, and social status between group members, marital status, and the number of children for women.[11]

Artists in West Africa spend most of their lives perfecting skills that are passed down from one generation to another. Each society contributes its own interpretations and representations of art to create distinctive art forms. West African art includes ceramics and metalworking. Tools made from iron helped ancient people in the region to efficiently till the soil, harvest crops, and clear forests faster. Iron tools also simplified and furthered woodcarving and sculpture. Among the first themes or scenes that have been captured in this medium include the series of chiefs and powerful kingdoms of the grasslands in Cameroon, the lavishly diverse artistic traditions of the Yoruba of Nigeria, and the royal arts of the Akan people of Ghana. The practice of casting metal sculpture in different compositions of copper alloys started in the eastern area of Nigeria, known as Igbo-Ukwu. This innovation was soon introduced and flourished in Benin. Having a huge amount of gold and bronze readily accessible, the major ethnic group of the Ashanti in Ghana abounds with art forms from these materials. The Baoule people are famous for their figurines sculpted from dark wood from the Ivory Coast, with heads made from terracotta.[12]

South African art is an interesting mixture of both indigenous creations and European influences. South Africa's experience of colonialism followed by apartheid had a profound influence on its art. The traditional African art, which was rooted in African aesthetics, combined with European realism to form unique artworks admired around the world. South African art includes all forms and genres, ranging from traditional to the abstract. It represents the people's collective memory and includes paintings, sculptures, resistance art, European art, and many other forms.[13] Colonial artists, such as Thomas Baines and Jan Volschenk created paintings and sculptures that were clearly African based. Traditional art is a portrayal of ethnic people creating exceptional paintings and engravings, including painted ostrich eggshells and stone ruins. Terracotta heads were found in the sixth through the eighteenth centuries. The purpose of these heads remains a mystery, but they illustrate the ceremonial aspect of some African art. Unlike traditional sculptures, which can be destroyed by insects and decay, the terracotta heads survived because the termites in Africa only eat wood.

Central African art reflects the dominance of ancient powerful kingdoms and other forms of government that took over this part of the land. The reinforcement of ethnic leadership and execution of important ritual, ceremonial, and spiritual functions would not have been as vibrant without objects of Central African art. The countries that make up this region of Africa include the stretch from Chad, Cameroon, and the southern areas of Zambia and Angola to the Republic of Congo, Gabon, Burundi, Rwanda, and equatorial Guinea. The different ethnic groups contributed to the birth and development of the various types of art from this region. The densely vegetated rain forest basin that envelopes the Congo River in most parts provides a very rich source of wood. This makes the majority of art from this area mostly, but not limited to, wooden works.

THE ROCK ART OF AFRICA

Rock art painting and engraving are Africa's oldest and continuously practiced art form. They were discovered earlier than the European rock art. Paintings of animals were reported in Mozambique as early as 1721[14], and the first mention was made of Bushmen painting in South Africa in 1752[15], whereas the European ones were totally unknown until Sautuola's daughter looked up at the roof of the cave of Altamira in 1878[16]. The engraving of North Africa were first discovered by a group of French Army officers travelling in Southern Oran in 1847 where they reported engravings of elephants, lions, antelopes, ostriches, bovids, gazelles and human beings armed with bows and arrows.[17] Another discovery was made by the explorer, Heinrich Barth, when he crossed the Sahara from Tripoli to Timbuktu in 1850; he found similar engravings in Fezzan. With the accumulation of continued discoveries, half of these rock art are in Tassli.[18] The rock art of Africa depict elegant human figures, hued animals, and figures combining human and animal features called *therianthropes*[19] and associated with Shamanism[20]. African rock art can be divided into three broad geographical zones, namely the Central, Northern and Southern Zones.

The Rock Art of Central African Zone

The Rock Art of Central African Zone stretches from the Zambezi River to below the Sahara Desert. The art differs in that images of animals and human beings do not predominate; instead, the art is principally comprised of finger-painted and monochromatic geometric images. Because of these images, some scholars are investigating the link between the central zone and the Khoi art of the southern zone. However, the art of the Kondoa region in central Tanzania is fading with age. The art in this region unlike the Khoi art is not finger-painted but instead portray fine-line southern African images that are brush painted. The subject matter and style are more closely related to southern African San Painting, Zimbabwe in particular, than to any of the images in the central zone. It is believed that this body of art is closely related to the Hadza and Sandawe people who, until recently, were still involved in hunting and gathering.[21] The geometric art comprises of concentric circles, oblongs, nested 'U' shapes, parallel lines and rare handprints. The shapes initially defy recognition, but researchers have commented that a few of the designs resemble meteorological subjects like the sun, the moon, rainclouds, rain and rainbows. Others have seen sexual symbolism in the art, identifying some of the designs as vulva and phallic depictions. The art depicts a wide variety of animals and a few birds and reptiles. It is also painted in varied collection of manners from outline, through linear, dotted and gridded fills to partial and fully filled forms. Humans are depicted in these same manners in a range of standing, bending and 'floating' postures, sometimes with bows, and often with large and bizarre 'mop style' head forms. A few humans are painted with animal heads.[22]

The Rock Art of the Sahara (Northern Zone)

Saharan Rock Art indicates that there has been human habitation in the Sahara since 8,000 B.P. Tassili-n-Ajjer in Algeria is one of the most famous North African sites of rock painting. Engravings and paintings on rock surfaces found in the Tassili Plateau documents a verdant Sahara teeming with life that stands in stark contrast to the arid desert the region has since become. The rock engravings of the northern Zone are divided into four major periods that is based on the subject matter, content and the style of the art. The earliest of these is known as the *Bubaline Period*, which is comprised of engravings only, and there are many images of wild animals and *therianthropic* (part-human, part-animal) figures. The three later periods, *Bovidian*, *Caballine*, and *Camelline* include both paintings and engravings and are marked by the appearance of specific domestic animals in the art.[23] Engravings of animals such as the extinct giant buffalo are among the earliest works, followed later by paintings in which color is used to depict humans and animals with striking naturalism. In the last period, chariots, shields, and camels appear in the rock paintings. Although close to the Iberian Peninsula, it is currently believed that the rock art of Algeria and Tassili developed independently of that in Europe.

The *Bubaline Period–formerly the hunter Period (8000–7000 BP)*–reflect the hunting way of life where wild animals like buffalo, elephant, rhinoceros, hippopotamus, giraffe, large antelopes and ostriches were represented. Many of the animals represented are extinct. The animals are drawn in a naturalistic way, often with great detail and drawn on a large scale (an example is a rhinoceros in Wasi Djerat in the Tassli which is twenty six feet six inches long). The men are armed with clubs throwing sticks, axes and bows. This period was formerly called the *Hunter period* but due to the drawings of rams and cattle, this has caused the term to be abandoned.[24] The *Bovidian Period–Pastoral Period (6,000–2200 BP)*– is the Cattle (or Pastoral Period), which correspond to the arrival of cattle in North Africa between 4500 and 4000 B.C. This style is less naturalistic, less detailed and the poses are stiff; horns are represented in a twisted perspective frontally when the rest of the animals are drawn in profile. The engravings are smaller in size mostly between eighteen inches and four feet long. The men are armed with bows and are depicted with cattle. Smaller scale paintings are done with red ochre and white.[25]

The *Caballine Period–Horse Period (3200–1200 BP)* is divided into three periods namely the Chariot Period, Horseman Period and Horse and Camel Period. The Horse tradition corresponds to the appearance of horses in North African archaeological record from about 2000 B.C. onward. The Chariot Period is the earliest phase. Elephants are occasionally represented; cattle, mouffons and domesticated dogs are common. The style becomes more artificial where artistic conventions are used to create effects in the rock art. The earliest horse drawn chariots are well illustrated with a single shaft and a horse on the other side. The human figures are represented by two triangles. Later the wheels and shaft of the chariots are represented while the human figures are reduced. The engravings are smaller between ten and twenty inches. A few bows are found and spears and round shields have been added and later pictures show a dagger hanging from the forearm.[26] The Horseman Period reflects the change from horse driving to horse riding, although a few chariots are represented. Animals are drawn in a semi-naturalistic style, human are still represented by two triangles, and the size remains the same as the chariot period. The weapons used are spear, round shield, knife, and bows. These weapons reflect local preference in different areas. In all areas the warriors wear plumed headdresses and the phrase "Libyco", Berber written characters appear on the engravings of the central Sahara. The Horse and Camel Period reflects the introduction of camel in the art although the horse still remains. During this period cattle are less represented. The style has coarseness with a few semi-naturalistic drawings. The drawings are of smaller size, seven to sixteen inches. The weapons used are spear, round shield, knife, and bows and the warriors wear plumed headdresses.[27]

The *Camelline Period–The Camel Period [2700 BP]* is the current period of rock art that was painted by the present day inhabitants of the Sahara. The camel is the principal domestic animal in the Sahara and it is represented in both engravings and paintings. There are other animals shown and there are inhabitants in the area: antelopes, Oryx, gazelles, moufflons, and ostrich humped cattle and goats. The horse is still occasionally found in Mauritania fitted with an Arab saddle with stirrups. The style is very schematic. A double triangular form represents the human figure and the drawings are smaller than ever, six to eight inches. The weapons shown in the drawings are spear, sword and firearms.[28]

The Rock Art of the Southern Zone

The Rock Art of the Southern Zone stretches from the South African Cape to the border between Zimbabwe and Zambia formed by the Zambezi River. The rock painting of this region is characterized by exquisitely detailed and complex techniques of shading. The Engravings are generally on boulders and rocks in the interior plateau of southern Africa, while paintings are found in the mountainous regions that fringe the plateau. There are only a few places where paintings and engravings are found in the same shelter. Aboriginal San hunter-gatherers made most of these paintings and engravings named the San Rock art.

San rock art is perhaps the best known of all of Africa's rock arts. For decades, researchers believed that the art was simply a record of daily life. Those were the days of gaze and guess, when it seemed that the longer one gazed at the art, the better ones guess would be as to its meaning. By linking specific San beliefs to recurrent features in the art, researchers have been able to understand the meaning of San rock art. The symbolic art focuses on a particular part of San experience, the spirit world journeys and experiences of San shamans. These are features from San trance dance, the venue in which the shamans gained access to the spirit world. Dancers with antelope hooves show that they have taken on antelope power. Then, shamans climb up 'threads of light' that connect to the sky-world, then the trance flight. To show their experiences, the artists also used visual metaphors such as showing shamans 'underwater' and 'dead.' These capture aspects of how it feels to be in a trance. The artists also show their actions in the spirit world, such as their capturing of the rain animal, their activation of potency for use in healing or in fighting off enemies or dangerous forces. But, the art was far from just a record of spirit journeys. Powerful substances such as eland blood were put into the paints to make each image a reservoir of potency. As each generation of artists painted or engraved layer upon layer of art on the rock surfaces they were creating potent spiritual places.[29]

In addition to San rock art, there are also rock paintings and engravings made by closely related Khoi pastoralists. These people acquired domestic stock through close interaction with Bantu-speaking people some 2,000 years or more ago. Although there is some evidence that they also made engravings, Bantu-speakers' rock art is characterized by finger painting in a thick, white pigment. Often found superimposed over San or Khoi paintings, this art is implicated in initiation rituals and in political protest and is not a shamanistic art.[30]

The rock art of southern Africa is different from that of the central and northern zones. There is, for example, great diversity between the art of the Matopo Hills in Zimbabwe, the Brandberg in Namibia, and the Drakensberg Mountains in South Africa. Nevertheless, scholars have suggested that a great deal of San art throughout southern Africa may be explicitly and implicitly linked to San shamanic religion. A great deal of San art depicts their central most important ritual, the healing or trance dance, and the complex somatic experiences of dancers.[31] The Rock Art of Africa covers a period that shows the changing life of African art up to the present day.

PIVOTAL ETHNIC ART FORMS ACROSS AFRICA

African art is a utilitarian and an integral part of daily life. The most common objects have meaning and purpose, which turns them into art. The concepts underlying African art give them intrinsic and extrinsic values. Although art differs by region in its forms and materials, the characteristics of African art provide common ground for understanding the complexity of the art. In Africa, art is intended to portray ideas, beliefs, status, and workmanship. This section highlights the pivotal ethnic art forms across the continent.

Bambara of Mali

The Bambara people live on the upper Niger River in Mali, Guinea, and Senegal. Historically, they founded two separate empires, with capitals at Kaarta and Segue, which controlled large areas from the western Sudan from the seventeenth to the nineteenth centuries.[32] The art of Bambara was created both for religious use and for defining cultural and religious differences. Bambara artistic traditions include sculptures, masks, headdresses, and statuettes.[33] They are known for their carved antelope headdresses known as the *chiwara* (*tyiwara kun* or *sogoni kun*), which are fastened to a cap woven in a basket form and worn on top of the head. This type of art is made out of wood, crafted into an abstracted antelope form with its horns, and adorned with twine and metal. The figure symbolizes a legendary being who is half antelope and half human and who taught the Bambara people how to till the soil; thus, the *chiwara* introduced agriculture to the Bambara people. For example, when a new patch of soil is cleared, two members of the *tyiwara* association would appear wearing a pair of antelope headpieces, one male and one female. They bend over their sticks to imitate the play of young antelopes in order to appease the earth spirits and ensure a fertile soil.[34] The style of *tyiwara* headdresses is distinctive and recognizable by its typical flat face, arrow-shaped nose, all-over body triangular scarifications, and, on the figures, splayed hands.

Bambara sculptures are primarily used during the annual ceremonies of the Guan society. The main sculptures are fertility statues, meant to be kept with the wife at all times to ensure fertility. Women with fertility and childbearing problems in Bambara society affiliate with *gwan,* an association that is especially concerned with such problems. Women who avail themselves of its ministrations and who succeed in bearing children make extra sacrifices to *gwan,* dedicate their children to it, and name them after the sculptures associated with the association. *Gwan* sculptures occur in groups and are normally enshrined. An ensemble includes a mother-and-child figure, the father, and several other male and female figures. They are considered to be extremely beautiful. They illustrate ideals of physical beauty and ideals of character and action. The figures are brought out of the shrine to appear in annual public ceremonies.

Bambara masks are notably distinguished in four types. The first type is used by the *ntomo* society, a traditional association for uncircumcised boys. There are two main style groups of their masks. One is characterized by an oval face with four to ten horns in a row on top like a comb, often covered with cowry shells or dried red berries. The other has a ridged nose, a protruding mouth, a superstructure of vertical horns, in the middle of which or in front of which is a standing figure or an animal. The second type of mask is associated with the *Komo* society. The *Komo* is the custodian of tradition and is concerned with all aspects of community life—agriculture, judicial processes, and passage rites. Its masks are of elongated animal forms decorated with actual horns of antelope, quills of porcupine, bird skulls, and other objects. These headdresses, worn horizontally, consist of an animal, covered with mud, with open jaw; often horns and feathers are attached. The third type includes the masks of the *Kono,* which enforce civic morality; they are also elongated and encrusted with sacrificial material. The *Kono* masks were also used in agricultural rituals, mostly to petition for a good harvest. They usually represent an animal head with long open snout and long ears standing in a "V" shape from the head and often covered with mud. In contrast to the *komo* masks, which are covered with feathers, horns, and teeth, those of the *kono* society are elegant and simple. The fourth is from the *korè* society. They are perceived by the Bambara people as the "father of the rain and thunder." Every seven years a new age-set of teenagers experiences a symbolic death and rebirth into the *korè* society through initiation rituals whose symbols relate to fire and masculinity. Initiations take place in the sacred woods where the youths are harassed by elders and clown-like performers called *korédugaw.* In their general form and detail, a group of *korè* masks conveys concepts, such as knowledge, courage, and energy through the representation of hyenas, lions, monkeys, antelopes, and horses. In addition, there are masks of the *nama,* which protect against sorcerers. To the Bambara, masks transcend art; they are also the culture and the life of the tribe. As an agricultural people the art of Bambara features strong references to animals that are believed to promote farming and work ethics.

Dogon of Mali

The Dogon people are an ethnic group living in the central plateau region of Mali. They live south of Timbuktu on the cliffs of *Bandiagara.* The Dogons' social and religious organizations are closely interlinked, and out of this connection some principal cults arose, which accounts for the richness and diversity of Dogon culture and art. The ethnic group is subdivided into lineages, overseen by the patriarch, the guardian of the clan's ancestral shrine and officiant at the totemic animal cult.[35] Dogon art is mainly sculpture, which revolves around religious values, ideals, and freedoms.[36] Dogon sculptures are not made for the public; instead, they are kept within the houses of families, sanctuaries, or kept with the *Hogon.*[37] The importance of privacy is due to the symbolic meaning behind the pieces and the process by which they are made. The sculptures are also preserved in sites of worship, personal or family altars, altars for rain, altars to protect hunters, and in markets. Dogon sculpture consists of figures with raised arms, superimposed bearded figures, horsemen, stools with caryatids, women with children, figures covering their faces, women grinding pearl millet, women bearing vessels on their heads, donkeys bearing cups, musicians, dogs, quadruped-shaped troughs or benches, figures bending from the waist, mirror-images, broad figures, and standing figures.[38] These themes show that the Dogon people are an agrarian society.

The art of Dogon is versatile, and the style has evolved into geometric forms, like egg-shaped heads, squared shoulders, tapered extremities, pointed breasts, forearms, and thighs on a parallel plane; and hairdos stylized by three or four incised lines. The sculptures serve as a physical medium in initiations and as an explanation of the world. The Dogon have eighty styles of masks, with characteristics that show the use of geometric shapes, independent of the various animals they are supposed to represent. The structure of a large number of masks is based on the juxtaposition of vertical and horizontal lines and shapes; another has triangular, conic shapes. The masks are often polychrome, but many of the colors have been lost due to the fact that after the ceremonies they were left on the ground and quickly deteriorated because of termites and other conditions.

Ndebele of Southern Africa

The Ndebele are dispersed widely across Zimbabwe and South African's Transvaal province. They are all descendants of the same ethnic group as the Zulu and Xhosa people and divided into the northern and southern Ndebele. The northern group has been assimilated into neighboring ethnic groups, but the southern Ndebele have retained their unique cultural identity. Beadwork is a 150-year-old art among the Ndebele, and it plays an important role in their customs. To them, beadwork is more than just an art form; instead, it is an essential part of their cultural and ethnic identity and serves several functions in society. For instance, beads are used to adorn the body and decorate ceremonial objects and items of clothing.[39] Among the Ndebele, the women wear beadwork. To women of Ndebele, the different beadwork and beaded garments serve as an identification of status from childhood. For example, a bride may work for two to three years on a piece of beadwork to present to her future in-law family. The more intricate and impressive the piece, the more she will be favored by her husband's family and respected by the community. Likewise, a woman may spend many months or even years on intricate beadwork to adorn funeral garments because the Ndebele have a strong belief in the afterlife, so a great deal of care goes into the manufacture of burial garments.[40] The Ndebele are well known for their painted houses and colorful beadwork. For over a hundred years, the Ndebele have decorated the outside of their homes with designs.

Multicolored wall paintings are painted by using their fingers, the most frequent theme, as in wall painting, is the house (Figure 10.1). Gables, gateways, steps, roofline's and light fixtures may all be recognized on women's aprons and on walls. These reflect the domestic interests of women and may point to aspirations of idealized homes. The dresses and beautifully decorated homes of the Ndebele in South Africa are unique in Africa. Their beadwork and bead pattern-inspired mural paintings, in particular, have become an integral part of Ndebele culture. The motifs used in beadwork and in wall paintings show great vitality and dynamic response to the changing world around the artists. Stylized plant forms may express the hope for good harvests in a dry region. To begin a wall painting, the artists divide the wall into sections and then snap chalk lines diagonally across each section. Next, the artists begin painting the black outline of the design for each section. Painting is done freehand, without a scale design. Neither rulers nor squares are used, and yet, symmetry, proportion, and straight edges are exactly maintained. Then, the black outline is filled in with color, and white spaces offset

Figure 10.1. Designs of wall paintings by Ndebele women.
(Illustration by Ida Kumoji-Ankrah)

painted areas. After the color has been applied, the final step is to repaint or touch up the black outlines. The earliest paintings were done with earth pigments, whitewash, and laundry bluing. Although commercial paints have replaced the older pigments, the artists still use chicken feathers as paintbrushes. Ndebele painters distinguish styles and origins among different forms of mural decoration. Through their bold, geometric designs, the women artists of the Ndebele affirm the identity of the group and proclaim their uniqueness to all who see their art.[41]

Akan of Ghana

The Akan are hierarchical and matrilineal people who distinguish status through art.[42] The majority of the Akan-speaking people live in central and southern Ghana (called the Gold Coast in colonial times) and in the southeastern Ivory Coast. The Asante, the dominant nation of the Akan group, are centered in Kumasi, with the Fante in the coastal area, the Aowin, Adansi, and Akwamu, among others, in the central forest zone, and the Bron (also Brong or Bono) in the northwest. Until the nineteenth century, the Akan practiced their indigenous African religions, which include a belief in the supreme God and creator *Nyame*, as well as in spirits of rivers and the bush, witchcrafts. They also believed in the power of protective charms, and for chiefs; this often took the form of a golden or leather talisman worn as a pendant or sewn onto garments. While some art may be described as "spirit oriented," with roots in these ancient beliefs, most Akan art serves as a symbolic art form of the state, the court and chiefs, personal prestige, and trade or domestic requirements.[43]

Trade, based on the rich gold deposits of their society, accounted for the great development of the arts of the Akan people.[44] In 1750, the Asante Confederacy had developed a trading state centered on the inland city of Kumasi. By 1800, the Asante joined together other Akan and came under the leadership of a "divine" king and his wealthy court, who made lavish use of gold and gold-plated regalia and were supported by a standing army, royal spies, and diplomats, all nourished by military conquest and control of the lucrative gold and slave-trading routes to the north and south.

The Akan regalia of state and leadership stems through the power of the Asante kingdom, which lasted until the nineteenth century and was based on the unifying symbols of the Golden Stool. This stool represented the power and spirit of the entire nation of Gold Coast (now Ghana) who believe that their well-being depended on the safety of the stool.[45] It is believed that it contains the "Sunsum" that is the spirit or soul of the Asante people. The Golden Stool is not just sacred; it is a symbol of nationhood. The Golden Stool has a round base, and the seat, although curved, is made up of the three sections of a circle, instead of being rectangular in shape. It is supported by a circular openwork column and two tubular braces and hung with bells and golden effigies of slain enemies.[46] Ceremonial state swords are part of the Asante regalia, carried by sword bearers when the Golden Stool is paraded and on many other occasions.

Akan art is known for Akan gold weights, as well as cultural jewelry. The gold weights are made of copper, bronze, and brass. They are cast using a method of casting known as *cire perdue*.[47] The gold weights served a vast amount of roles in their culture and everyday life. The Akan people are known for their strong connection between visual and verbal expressions. Akan culture values gold above all other metals, so the artwork and jewelry made of gold reflects a great deal of worth and status, whether it is made for appearance, artistic expression, or more practical trading purposes. Akan gold weights are used as counterbalances in the gold trade, visual representations of oral tradition, representations of proverbs, as pictographic script in social and political systems, and in the knowledge system of the Akan people.[48] According to the Akan scholar Nitecki, Akan gold weights were "created and used like spoken language to commemorate social or historical events or entities, to express philosophical or religious views, aspirations, and dreams, or simply to ask questions, or to express displeasure." There are four major categories of gold weights. The first kind of gold weights depicts people. The second consists of the local flora and fauna. The third are likened to man-made objects. The final category is abstract and open to interpretation by the individual. Akan cultural jewelry has a variety of forms. The Akan people make neckwear, wristbands, elbow wear, knee wear, and ankle wear. Gender-specific jewelry includes hatpins and headbands for men, and earrings and hairpins for the women.[49]

Akan sculptors were best known for their wooden carvings. The most significant were the *akua ba dolls* (Figure 10.2), the style of which varies according to age and area of origin. An *akua ba* is wooden ritual fertility doll. The best-known type associated with the Asante has large, disc-like heads (oval heads) said to represent the people ideal of beauty. The torso is most often a cylinder, straight, or conical with breasts and navel

Figure 10.2. The akua ba dolls of Ashanti, Ghana.
Illustration by Ida Kumoji-Ankrah

indicated and with horizontal arms or sometimes with no arms.[50] The *akua ba* is a female because the Akan are matrilineal society.[51] They are used as fertility figures in shrines or worn by women either to induce conception, during pregnancy, or to ensure the beauty of the child being carried, preferably a daughter.[52]

Cloth was also a symbol of rank and status in the Akan kingdom. There were three types of fabrics produced by the Akan craftsmen. The first was made of strips with woven designs called the *Kente*, which was a very beautiful, multicolored cloth and made into splendid garments for kings and chiefs. Like most of Africa's visual art forms, *Kente* is a visual representation of history, philosophy, ethics, oral literature, religious beliefs, social values, and political thought. Originally, its use was reserved for royalty and limited to special social and sacred functions. When production increased, it became accessible to more people. However, its prestigious status was maintained, and it has continued to be associated with wealth, high social status, and cultural sophistication. The second was the *adinkra*[53] cloth, traditionally made of single dyed strips sewn together and hand stamped with a*dinkra* symbols.[54] *Adinkra* cloth is the most highly valued, hand-printed textile in African art. Its origin is traced to the Asante people of Ghana and the Gyaman people of Côte d'Ivoire (Ivory Coast). The *adinkra* symbols have been used by both royalty and the people as a system of writing with which the Akan tribe of Ghana communicate. These visual marks served to evoke and record certain things about the Akan.[55] The third consist of appliquéd or embroidered fabrics called *akunitan,* or "cloths of the great." It is a type of embroidered cloth worn only by senior chiefs and kings.[56]

Makonde of Tanzania and Mozambique

The Makonde are an ethnic group in southeastern Tanzania and northern Mozambique. They developed their culture on the Mueda Plateau in Mozambique.[57] Presently, the Makonde live throughout Tanzania and Mozambique and have a small presence in Kenya. They speak Makonde, a Bantu language, although many speak other languages, such as English in Tanzania, Portuguese in Mozambique, and Swahili and Makua in both countries. The Makonde are traditionally a matrilineal society where children and inheritances belong to women, and husbands move into the village of their wives.[58] The art of Makonde consists of traditionally carved household objects, figures, and masks. The Makonde are known as master carvers throughout East Africa. Makonde carvers are prolific producers of masks, statues, and decorative objects. The most famous Makonde masks are their helmet masks, which are used to mark a boy's initiation into adulthood; they are also used in girl's initiation ceremonies. These masks, called *Mapiko* or *Lipiko*, have realistic heads with strong facial features, real human hair applied in shaved patterns, and raised facial scarification. They represent an ancestral spirit in initiation ceremonies and served to express their moral code. These masks are carved from a single block of lightwood and may represent spirits, "shetani," ancestors, or living characters that are real or idealized. The dance shows men in a powerful role, often evoking fear in women and children. The dancer pretends to be the spirit. During the boy's initiation training, a *mapiko* dancer comes to the initiation house and takes off his mask, which shows the boy that he is a man and not an evil spirit. The dancer symbolically reveals the secrets of manhood, and thereafter, the initiated boy can participate in the ritual.[59] The Makonde also play an important part in the contemporary African art scene with internationally acknowledged artists, such as George Lilanga.

Yoruba, Ife, and Nok from Nigeria

The Yoruba people live on the west coast of Nigeria and can also be found in the eastern Republic of Benin and Togo. Their art traditions are of considerable antiquity, and they are one of the largest ethnic groups in West Africa. Their artistic traditions include woodcarving, sculpture, metalwork, textiles, and beadwork.[60]

Ife, on the other hand, is an ancient Yoruba city in southwestern Nigeria. Ife is known worldwide for its ancient and naturalistic bronze, stone, and terracotta sculptures, which reached their peak of artistic expression between 1200 and 1400 CE. Excavations at Ife, in the central land of Yoruba, have shown that naturalistic sculptures in brass and pottery were being produced sometime between the eleventh and fifteenth centuries. The sculptures may represent royal figures and their attendants, and life-sized portrait heads in brass were perhaps used as part of funerary effigies. During this time, Ife appears to have had widespread artistic importance, and the naturalism of its art forms may have influenced the basic development of the Yoruba sculptural style. Throughout the land of Yoruba, human figures are represented in a fundamentally naturalistic way, except for bulging eyes; flat, protruding, and usually parallel lips; and stylized ears. The evolution of these characteristics can be observed in a number of pottery sculptures at Ife, which, on stylistic grounds, are considered to be relatively late. Their native masterpieces include naturalistic stone, bronze, and terracotta sculptures. The sophisticated artistic culture of the Yoruba is best known for its discoveries of sensational life-sized bronze and terracotta figures between 1910 and 1942. The customs of art and artisans among the Yoruba are deeply rooted in the *Ifa* (religion of Yoruba people) literary corpus, indicating the *Orishas* (spirits or deities) *Ogun, Obatala, Oshun,* and *Obalufon* as central to creation mythology, including artistry that is the art of humanity. Yoruba are known for their *Adire* and *Oso Oke* textiles. *Adire* (Yoruba tie dye) textile is the indigo-dyed cloth made in southwestern Nigeria by Yoruba women using a variety of resists dye techniques. The earliest cloths were probably simple tied designs on locally woven, hand-spun cotton cloth much like that still produced in Mali. *Aso oke* is a hand-loomed cloth woven by Yoruba men. It is woven in narrow strips of machine spun cotton; this textile has sections of openwork, with the holes linked by decorative, carry over threads. Motifs laid in by weft patterns are usually symbolic of stylized plants.

The Nok culture was considered to be the earliest sub-Saharan producer of life-sized terracotta. Nok culture terracottas are heralded as the prime evidence of the refinement of African civilizations, and it is suggested that the society eventually evolved into the later Ife Yoruba community because later brass and terracotta sculptures of the Ife and Benin cultures show significant similarities with those of the Nok.[61] In 1928, in central Nigeria, tin miners uncovered clay shards that, when reconstructed, were found to be fragments of terracotta sculptures. The unique representations of human heads and other figures date from 500 and 200 BCE are attributed to a culture known today as Nok.[62] Stylistic characteristics of Nok art are an elaborate coiffure; cylindrical heads; pierced eyes, nose, mouth, and ears; semicircular/triangular eyes and lids; ears set back, often low and small; and flared nostrils. Nok figures were made for religious purposes as evidenced by subject and attitude, while their terracotta figures are cult objects representing deities, spirit figures, mythical beings, or deified ancestors.

Baoulé of Ivory Coast

The Baoulé are an Akan people and one of the largest groups in the Ivory Coast. The Baoulé are skilled at carving wood, and the culture produces wooden masks in wide variety. The Côte d'Ivorian peoples use masks to represent animals in caricature, to depict deities, or to represent the souls of the departed. Their masks can be divided into two groups: animal and human. Human masks are produced and worn by men only, although Baoulé carvers do not inherit the profession by the right of birth. The masks are used to make contacts with

Gu, the ruler of the world. Since the masks are held to be of great spiritual power, it is considered a taboo for anyone other than specially trained persons or chosen ones to wear or possess certain masks. These ceremonial masks each are thought to have a soul or life force, and wearing these masks is thought to transform the wearer into the entity the mask represents. Baoulé figures and masks are of serene beauty with an attractive dark metallic patina. Masks called "go" had a naturalistic, yet stylized, human face. The best-known type is *Guli* with a disk-shaped face, powerful and round eyes set into the heart-shaped sockets, and rectangular mouth; the mask is surmounted by horns. *Guli* masks are abstractions of the buffalo, said to represent the sun, and are in the service of the sky god *Nyame*. The Baoulé carved both standing and seated figures, and though they have an ancestor cult, they did not carve ancestor statues. The male and females made by them are either figures to accommodate dangerous spirits of nature or they are spirit lovers.[63] These are carved on the advice of a diviner to promise a home either for the nature spirit or for the prenatal lover.[64] The Côte d'Ivoire also has modern painters and illustrators. Gilbert G. Groud criticizes the ancient beliefs in black magic, as held with the spiritual masks mentioned above, in his illustrated book *Magie Noire*.

Berber of Northern Africa

Berbers are the indigenous peoples of North Africa west of the Nile Valley. Today, most Berber-speaking people live in Morocco, Algeria, Libya, and Tunisia. The history of Berbers in North Africa is extensive and diverse. Their ancient ancestors settled in the area just inland of the Mediterranean Sea to the east of Egypt. Over the last several hundred years many Berbers have converted to Islam. Berbers have lived in Africa since 3000 BCE. They tend to live in desert regions like the Sahara and in the Atlas Mountains.[65]

Berber art are form of jewelry, leather, and finely woven carpets. Women are generally involved with weaving and pottery. The origin of Berber carpets dates back to the Paleolithic era and made by Berbers in North Africa. The handspun cloth they created was named for the tribe, and they used natural fibers to create cloaks, rugs, and other fabrics. Many Berber families gain their daily bread from manufacturing carpets manually and selling them in local markets or even to art merchants and tourists. Traditional Berber carpet is totally different from the modern mass produced Berber carpets usually known in the West. They are much more sophisticated and are made of natural materials. Today, there are several types of modern Berber carpets made from a range of materials. Nylon, olefin, and wool are the most common materials, and the size of loops and cut pile varies for each manufacturer. Olefin is the most commonly used and the most affordable material, and carpets with blends of the different materials are also available. Their pottery is handmade with no pottery wheel. Berber pottery is the fruit of an astounding art. The objects (plates, vases, soup tureens, and animal figurines) are molded from clay paste and dried in the open air before being baked in the oven. Thereafter, they are decorated with black and brown geometrical design shades reminiscent of the color of Tunisia's earth. Berber jewelry is well known for its craftsmanship. Created out of pure silver or a silver mix, pendants with the hand of Fatima or other traditional motifs are inlaid with semiprecious stones and are very fetching. The bracelets are usually heavy and broad with engravings and stone inlays. The necklaces are either in pure silver strewn with coins, oval-like pieces, and other patterns, or in coral and amber, embellished with silver pieces in between.[66]

AESTHETIC PRINCIPLES AND CHARACTERISTICS OF AFRICAN ART

African art constitutes one of the most diverse legacies on earth. Although many casual observers tend to generalize "traditional" African art, the continent is full of peoples, societies, and civilizations, each with a unique visual culture. Despite this diversity, there are some unifying artistic themes, aesthetic principles, and characteristics when considering the totality of the art from the continent of Africa.[67]

While the African continent is vast and its peoples diverse, certain standards of beauty and correctness in artistic expression and physical appearance are held in common among various African societies.[68] These values and standards have been characterized as comprising accepted African aesthetic.[69] Susan Vogel from the New York Center for African Art described "African aesthetic" in African artwork as having the following five aesthetics principles: (1) the resemblance to a human being, (2) luminosity, (3) self-composure, (4) youthfulness, and (5) clarity of form and detail, complexity of composition, balance and symmetry, smoothness of finish, and material choices.

With the principle of the *resemblance to a human being*, African artists praise a carved figure by saying that it "looks like a human being." Artists seldom portray particular people, actual animals, or the actual form of invisible spirits. Rather, they aim to portray ideas about reality, spiritual or human, and express these ideas through human or animal images. Furthermore, *luminosity* applies to the lustrously smooth surface of most African figural sculpture, often embellished with decorative scarification, indicating beautifully shining, healthy skin. Figures with rough surfaces and deformities are intended to appear ugly and morally flawed. *Self-composure*, on the other hand, applies to the reserved demeanor representing a person in control. A composed person behaves in a measured and rational way. *Youthfulness* represents vigor, productiveness, and fertility. Finally, with *clarity of form and detail, complexity of composition, balance and symmetry, smoothness of finish, and material choices*, African artists place a high value on workmanship and mastery of the medium.[70] The last element coincides with Western art elements. The other four elements are used to describe the art's intuitive, religious, and aesthetic values to the peoples of the varying African regions. The five aesthetic principles of African art define five thematic characteristics that Africans imbued in their artworks in an effort to relate to the seen and unseen world in which they live.

The first characteristic is the emphasis on the human figure. The human figure has always been the primary subject matter for most African art, and this emphasis even influenced certain European traditions. The human figure symbolizes the living or the dead; it may reference chiefs, dancers, or various trades, such as drummers or hunters; or it even may be a representation of a god.

The second characteristic is comprised of visual abstraction and stylization, the reduction of an image to a set of lines, colors, and patterns that results in a stylized representation of the object. African artworks tend to favor visual abstraction over naturalistic representation. This is because many African artworks generalize stylistic norms.[71] Ancient Egyptian art also usually thought of as naturalistically depictive and makes use of highly abstracted and regimented visual canons, especially in painting, as well as the use of different colors to represent the qualities and characteristics of the individual being depicted.[72] African art is characterized by its pronounced stylization. We can recognize, for example, in African sculpture, a hairdo by the Senufo women, Yoruba facial marks, or the headdress of a Kuba king figure. These are used to indicate status and are only minor details on stylized figures. African artists usually depart from realism that one sees in nature and often portray mythical beings, which may combine human and animal forms in an abstract manner or may make parts of the body longer or shorter, thicker or thinner, larger or smaller or flatter, and barely suggested or simply omitted. In a number of societies, the size of the head is exaggerated in relation to the rest of the body.[73]

The third element is consistency. African artists had limitations within their own art traditions. They were working within these stylistic limitations, creating artworks that their customers found acceptable and that they found aesthetically satisfying. African artists, therefore, were trying to achieve these standards in their own work.[74]

The fourth element is diversity. What may seem to people to be the result of freedom from tradition was, in fact, due to the differences in stylistic standards from one society to the other. Because of the large number of distinct art styles, both between and within the many art producing societies, diversity may seem to be overwhelming looking at African art the first time. For example, the Ashanti of Ghana used gold and bronze, whereas the Baluba, a tribal people in the Congo, specialized in carved images of women holding bowls. The Bambara, on the other hand, were known for elaborate headdresses, which were used during ceremonies, in contrast to the simple wooden masks of the Dogon people of West Africa. The dark wood of the Ivory Coast was the basis for sculptural figurines of the Baoulé people, who produced classically naturalistic masks, and terracotta was the material used for heads produced by the Nok peoples of central and north Nigeria.[75]

The last characteristic is emphasis on sculpture. African artists tend to favor three-dimensional artworks over two-dimensional works. Even many African paintings or cloth works were meant to be experienced three-dimensionally. House paintings are often seen as a continuous design wrapped around a house, forcing the viewer to walk around the work to experience it fully, while decorated cloths are worn as decorative or ceremonial garments, transforming the wearer into a living sculpture.[76]

INFLUENCES OF AFRICAN ART ON WESTERN ART

African art has played an important role in the culture and history of the world. The continent's rich and dynamic history, dating back to prehistoric times, played a major role in the artwork that is seen today. For example, the Hamar people of southwestern Ethiopia are a living example of the rich history of the African people. The Hamar still live an existence barely touched by Western civilization, still practicing one of the original forms of African art: the art of body scarification. The Dogon people of Mali made African masks and carvings out of wood, since wood was readily available locally. The lifestyle of the indigenous society played a role in defining the artistic expression of the African artist. These artistic expressions and stylization of most African art attracted the artists of France and Germany when they made their own discovery of it in museums and curio shops in the first decade of the twentieth century. The bodily distortions and bizarre combinations of human and animal features were beyond what the average European could appreciate; however, they were characteristics that appealed to the painters. They saw in African sculpture a freedom from the stereotyped standards of naturalism against which they were themselves revolting.[77]

At the start of the twentieth century, the aesthetics of traditional African sculpture became a powerful influence among European artists who formed an avant-garde movement in the development of modern art. In France, Henri Matisse, Pablo Picasso, and their School of Paris friends blended the highly stylized treatment of the human figure in African sculptures with painting styles derived from the post-Impressionist works of Cézanne and Gauguin. The resulting pictorial flatness, vivid color palette, and fragmented Cubist shapes helped to define early modernism. While these artists knew nothing of the original meaning and function of the West and Central African sculptures they encountered, they instantly recognized the spiritual aspect of the composition and adapted these qualities to their own efforts to move beyond the naturalism that had defined Western art since the Renaissance. The study of and response to African art by artists at the beginning of the twentieth century facilitated an explosion of interest in the abstraction, organization, and reorganization of forms and the exploration of emotional and psychological areas hitherto unseen in Western art. By these means, the status of visual art was changed. Art ceased to be merely and primarily aesthetic; it also became a true medium for philosophic and intellectual discourse and, hence, more truly and profoundly aesthetic than ever before.[78]

Furthermore, Picasso, Braque, and others saw the particular formal solutions to the representation of the human face and figure in certain African masks and sculptures as corresponding to their own desire to break away from the constraints of European classicism. Their interest in form did not extend to any corresponding interest in the local meanings of the art and the artists who created them. The fashion for collecting and displaying African art alongside contemporary Western art was set in this period. The tastes of early collectors and few of the powerful dealers who supplied them established a canon of major African art and that has only recently been challenged. The values and associations formed then still exert a powerful influence on collectors, museums, and scholars today. For example, a sculpture owned by the artist Man Ray was sold in 1990 for nearly $3.5 million, a record for a piece of African art.[79]

By the early twentieth century, African American modernists had joined other American artists in exploring the formal qualities of African art. In 1925, at the height of the Harlem Renaissance, black philosopher Alain Locke argued that African American artists should look to African art as a source of inspiration. A variety of influences informs the work of artists such as Elizabeth Catlett and Romare Bearden, who came of age in the aftermath of this important period in black cultural history. In the contemporary postcolonial era, the influence of traditional African aesthetics and processes is profoundly embedded in artistic practice.

CONTEMPORARY AFRICAN ART

Contemporary art in Africa has been created through a combination of allusions from the traditional African values with contemporary content and imagery. But the artists, although rooted in tradition, use materials, methods, and images foreign to traditional art, and their art forms are usually based on a personal aesthetic, reflecting the changing social, political, and cultural environment they live in. Unfortunately, this area has been understudied until recently, due to scholars' and art collectors' emphasis on traditional African art.[80] Contemporary African art was pioneered in the 1950s and 1960s. Some of the artists are Stephen Kappata (Zambia), Marlene Dumas (South Africa), Olu Oguibe (Nigeria), Henry Tayali (Zambia), Cheri Samba (Democratic Republic of Congo), Belkahia Farid (Morocco), Mahmud Mukhutar (Egypt), Ben Enwonwu (Nigeria), Akwete Kofi (Ghana), George Kakooza (Uganda), Ahamed Shibrain (Sudan), Boghosssian Skunder (Ethiopia), Afwerk Tekle (Ethiopia), and Julian Motau (South Africa). Recently, a number of African artists have produced works exploring new methods and ideas, such as Kane Kwei (Ghana) and Willie Bester (South Africa).[81]

The most important African art has always been considered to be antique and traditional art. However, over the last forty years, modern African artists have sought to bring the qualities of tradition to present-day art while seeking a forum in the world's art community. Contemporary art within the continent can be traced to the sub-Saharan region where artists began to combine ancient art forms with creative media. Whereas a person might not be able to visually recognize the meaning in traditional African art, the contemporary versions include allusions and references to the past. There is also greater use of personal preferences and a creative freedom that does not exist in ancient art. While ancient African art was often limited by regional material availability, modern African art can use new materials at will.

Contemporary artists have studied at schools around the world over the last fifty years in an attempt to define and develop modern African art. Contemporary African art has not been widely recognized in the traditional art world for many reasons. One of the main reasons is the generalized belief among western culture that African art is primitive and undeveloped. Yet, when African artists display unique creativity and stunning art, they are criticized for abandoning their traditional roots. Much of this attitude is changing with the recognition of the African Artist in Diaspora. The use of the word "primitive" and the anonymity accorded indigenous art by foreign institutions have worked in subtle ways to the artists' detriment, denying them respect and recognition. Contemporary artists have expanded beyond painting and sculpture and now include videos and other modern inventions in their work. Some people have had a difficult time seeing this modern art as being true African art. Contemporary African art blends the past with the present. Realizing that the African continent is the human story, past values and regional cultures become the groundwork beneath the modernist styles. The result is a fascinating art form that speaks to the viewer of the present turmoil while evoking a rich cultural past.

There are new genres of art that owe their existences to the social processes that accompanied European colonialism of Africa. These are urbanization, the introduction of Western technology and material culture, and the expansion of literacy through Western education.[82] These genres could be seen through the works of Cheri Samba, a Congolese who has emerged as a highly successful painter following his inclusion in the *Magiciens de la Terre* exhibition in Paris held in 1989. Prior to his discovery, he created flour sack paintings for a Kinshasa audience. Samba's developing reputation among collectors since the late 1980 allowed him to begin painting in acrylic on canvas.[83]

Also, the development of the art market through European patronages arose during these times. The most publicized early patronage was by Frank McEwen who started the Shona art movement in 1957 that first gained international exposure in the 1950s. Much of Shona was inspired by the artists' spiritual beliefs. Instigator of the movement and curator of the National Gallery in Harare, Zimbabwe, McEwen encouraged a creative atmosphere of individual "drawing out" rather than didactic art school process. In response, the artists' instincts were to draw on their belief systems and represent the spirit world through their art. Some of the artists believe they are possessed by a shave, a wandering spirit who confers artistic ability, or by ancestor spirits with traditional talents, such as carving. Some of the sculptors are Munyaradzi, Nicholas Mukomberanwa, Sylvester Mubayi, Joseph Ndandarika, Colleen Madamombe (the best-known female sculptor), Bernard Matemera John, Bernard Takawira, and Brighton Sango (a leading light of the second generation until his untimely suicide in the 1990s). The sculptures created in the 1950s and 1960s by early sculptors, such as Thomas Mukarobgwa and Joram Mariga, were primarily inspired by Shona mythology where various spirit guises, animal metamorphoses, and spirit mediums were represented. Traditional beliefs in spirits and witchcraft are modern beliefs for both urban and rural Shona. While they may be inspired by new influences, young artists retain and express the belief systems of their elders. Young artists' work continues to be "culturally authentic," in that they represent the same set of beliefs, although the sculpture has evolved over the last fifty years.[84]

Furthermore, another genre of art called "transitional" was based on the ideas already socially embedded in local communities.[85] These arts were not made for the art market but for the community. For example, the late

Kane Kwei (and now his son Samuel Kane Kwei) in Ghana and Sundhay Jack Akpan in Nigeria make funerary art for their own communities. Kane Kwei coffins, which are made like vehicles, fruits, animals, objects, and so on, represented the innovation and monument to his client's world prestige. His first coffins were made for local burials. For example, if you were a fisherman, your coffin was made like a fish. A California gallery owner discovered the development of the funerary coffins as an art form. In contrary, Akpan's cement funerary portraits have remained largely local.[86]

Advertising art (painted vehicles and signage) is another genre. Due to the influx of various print media and the impact of literary text, messages are often combined with visual images on vehicles, as well as other mural work and smaller scale paintings. Language is powerful, whether spoken or written. In Africa, trucks and buses display slogan and messages. Some of the slogans read: "No condition is permanent" (Ghana and Nigeria), "Fear woman" (Ghana), and "No hurry in Africa" (Kenya). These slogans on vehicles reflect everyday life, frustrations of travel, and diseases, like AIDS. Also, advertisements also appear on roadsides, bars, and hotels that emulate their Western counterparts. The work of Nigerian sign painter Augustine Okoye, called "Middle Art," was promoted by Ulli Beier, and Okoye emerged as an internationally recognized artist. While the content of signage texts is usually as advertisement for goods and services, it is usually an explanatory device to heighten their visual and verbal messages in an effort to attract an audience that is newly literate.[87]

Africa's artists today demonstrate their openness to their subject matter. Like other artists, they respond in their work to political and social change and to momentous processes or events, such as the inroads made by Christianity and Islam, the Nigerian Civil War, the altered political system in Ethiopia, and apartheid in South Africa. In spite of this subject matter, they need more local patronage. Governments' support, in the form of commissions, purchases, or exhibitions, is gaining ground, especially when they recognize that artists' work can be used to express the country's identity. Foreign businesses have commissioned works as a way of cementing relationships with host countries. Nevertheless, because much of the work of modern African artists exists outside religious contexts, they are denied the traditional constituency of the community. Now, however, their accomplishments have commanded attention around the world, and more of their compatriots are becoming their clients.

The contemporary culture facilitated the commercialization of African art and its artists. The Western colonization in the nineteenth and twentieth centuries has brought forth the commercialization and the trade of traditional African art. This also led to the development of colleges that have exposed African artists to the designs of the West, which they are slowly incorporating in their works. However, even with the influences of the European colonizers, this type of art still thrives, and various ethnic groups in Africa have retained and continue to live the rich tradition and culture they have inherited from their ancestors.

CONCLUSION

The history of art in Africa is very rich with a large collection of artworks across the continent. There are many styles of art in Africa, but they are continually evolving each day, and the influence of African art can be seen and felt across the globe. African art, like art in other non-African traditions, is connected to political and religious subjects. As demonstrated in this chapter, African art was an integral part of its societies' rituals, dances, and ceremonies. It was used for dialogue, personal therapy, and to communicate with the gods and ancestors.

African art has always been representative of African customs, the environment, their traditions, and their culture. It serves a more important role in the African society than merely to beautify the human environment, as art is usually employed in contemporary Western societies. The beauty of African art is simply an element of its function, for these objects would not be effective if they were not aesthetically pleasing. Its beauty and its content thus combine to make art the vehicle that ensures the survival of traditions, protects the community and the individual, and tells much about the person or persons who use it.

The history of African art has had a huge influence on Western artists. As a source of inspiration, many Western artists during the twentieth century recognized the intrinsic and aesthetic value of the various art forms across the continent. African cultural traditions remain strong, and they are still capable of absorbing external influences and transforming them into their own. The beauty of African art can convey various feelings and messages to the casual observer. However, true appreciation can only arrive through an understanding of the culture and environment that influenced the art.

ENDNOTES

1 William Bascom, *African Art in Cultural Perspective: An Introduction* (New York: W.W. Norton & Company Inc., 1973), 16.

2 Karen Rosenberg, "African Art, Modern and Traditional: Seductive Patterns from a Rich Palette," in Art Review, "The Essential Art of African Textiles," *The New York Times,* October 10, 2008 (New York edition), C32.

3 Duncan Clarke, *African Art* (London: PRC Publishing Ltd., 1998), 6.

4 Visonà Monica Blackmun, Robin Poyner, Herbert M. Cole, Michael D. Harris, Rowland Abiodun, and Suzanne Preston Blier, *A History of Art in Africa* (Upper Saddle River, NJ: Prentice Hall/Harry N. Abrams, 2000), 79–80.

5 Clarke, *African Art,* 12.

6 Felix Ritter von Luschan was a doctor, anthropologist, explorer, archaeologist, and ethnographer. In 1885 he was the assistant director at the Royal Anthropological Museum (now the Ethnological Museum) in Berlin, where from 1904 to 1911 he was Director of the Africa and Oceania Department. In this capacity, he acquired one of the most beautiful and important collections of Benin antiquities, ivory carvings and bronze figures, that he published in his multi-volume magnum opus. See, for example, *Furtwängler, Andreas E.:Luschan, Felix von. In NDB, vol 15.* (*Historische Kommission bei der Bayerischen Akademie der Wissenschaften,* 1987, ISBN 3-428-00196). Benvenuto Cellini was an Italian goldsmith, sculptor, painter, soldier, and musician who was one of the most important artists of Mannerism. See, for example, Cellini, *Vita,* Book 1, Ch III, *Encyclopedia Britannica,* Eleventh Edition (1910–1911).

7 William Bascom, *African Art in Cultural Perspective: An Introduction* (New York: W.W. & Company Inc., 1973), 4.

8 "African Art and Culture Cannot Be Separated," *All-About-African-Art.com* www.all-about-african-art.com /african-art-and-culture.html (accessed May 2, 2010).

9 The Mijikenda are the nine ethnic groups along the coast of Kenya from the border of Somalia in the north to the border of Tanzania in the south. Gilbert, Erik, and Jonathan T. Reynolds. *Africa in World History: From Prehistory to Present* (New Jersey: Pearson Education, 2008), 229.

10 The Masai are from Kenya and northern Tanzania. Due to their distinctive customs, dress, and residence near the many game parks of East Africa, they are among the most well known of African ethnic groups. See, for example, Jens Fincke, "Maasai: Introduction," from *Traditional Music and Cultures from Kenya,* 2000–2003, www.bluegecko. org/kenya/tribes/maasai (accessed May 2, 2010).

11 "African Art and Culture Cannot Be Separated."

12 Clarke, *African Art,* 34–36.

13 "African Art and Culture Cannot Be Separated."

14 Willet, Frank. African Art An Introduction (New York: Thames and Hudson, 1985) 43.

15 Willcox, Alex R *The rock art of South Africa.* Nelson, (Johannesburg, 1963)1.

16 Willet, *African Art An Intrdouction,* 75.

17 Ibid., 45.

18 Henri Lohte, "The rock art of the Maghreb and the Sahara in Bandi et al, 1961 pp.99–152, and JD Lajoux 1963) [Willet, 45].

19 *Therianthropes* is a term used to describe the representations of people with animal features often illustrated in African Rock art who are experiencing the spirit power of trance dancers in action.

   These features include hoofs, antelope heads, and tusks and so on. Moreover, human beings are also depicted combined with a range of creatures such as elephants, baboons, antelopes and birds. [Le Quellec, Jean-Loïc. *Rock Art in Africa: Mythology and Legend.* (Paris: Flammarion) 2004.]

20 Shamanism is a practice that involves a practitioner reaching altered states of consciousness in order to encounter and interact with the spirit world and channel these transcendental energies into this world (Hoppál, Mihály. *Shamanism: An Archaic and/or Recent System of Belief,* Nicholson, Shirley, "Shamanism", Quest Books, (1987) 76.

21 Blundell, Geoffrey, ed. Origins: The Story of the Emergence of Humans and Humanity in Africa (Cape Town: Double Storey) 2006.

22 The African Rock Art Digital Archive, 2014. http://www.sarada.co.za/traditions/african_hunter-gatherers/pygmy/ (Accessed April 10, 2014).

23 [Blundell, Geoffrey. "African Rock Art of the Northern Zone". In Heilbrunn Timeline of Art History. New York: The Metropolitan Museum of Art, 2000–. http://www.metmuseum.org/toah/hd/nroc/hd_nroc.htm (Accessed, April 10, 2014)]

24 Willet, *African Art An Intrdouction*, 48.

25 Ibid., 48

26 Ibid., 49

27 Ibid., 49

28 Ibid., 50

29 Lewis-Williams, J. David, and David G. Pearce *San Spirituality: Roots, Expression, and Social Consequences.* Walnut Creek (California: AltaMira Press) 2004.

30 Blundell, Geoffrey. *Nqabayo's Nomansland: San Rock Art and the Somatic Past.* (Uppsala: Uppsala University; Johannesburg: University of the Witwatersrand) 2004.

31 Blundell, Geoffrey, ed. *Origins: The Story of the Emergence of Humans and Humanity in Africa*, 2006 | Lewis-Williams, J. David *Images of Mystery: Rock Art of the Drakensberg.*, 2003.

32 Ibid., 32.

33 Stephen R. Wooten, "Antelope Headdresses and Champion Farmers: Negotiating Meaning and Identity through the Bamana Ciwara Complex," *African Arts* 33, no. 2 (2000): 18–33 and 89–90.

34 Bascom, *African Art in Cultural Perspective*, 33.

35 Ibid., 37.S

36 Jean Lade, *African Art of the Dogon: The Myths of the Cliff Dwellers* (New York: The Brooklyn Museum, 1973), 19.

37 The *Hogon* is both priest and political chief of the village. He is also in charge of the cult of *lebe*, the mythical serpent. Assisted by the blacksmith, he presides over agrarian ceremonies. The smiths and woodcarvers, who form a separate caste, transmit their profession by heredity. They may only marry within their own caste. Women are in charge of pottery making. See, for example, Jean Laude, *African Art of the Dogon: The Myths of the Cliff Dwellers* (New York: The Brooklyn Museum, 1973), 20.

38 Ibid., 46–52.

39 Mark Lewis, Ivor Powell, and Mark Hurwitz, *Ndebele: A People and Their Art* (Cross River, NY: Cross River Press, 1995).

40 Aubrey Elliot, *The Ndebele: Art and Culture* (Cape Town, SA: Struik Publishers, 1993).

41 Margaret Courtney-Clarke, *Ndebele: The Art of an African Tribe* (New York: Thames & Hudson, 2002).

42 Susan Peirce, Akan *Art of Ghana.* (2005). www.canyonlights.com/akanartofghana.html (accessed May 19, 2011); Arthur, G. F. Kojo. *Akan Gold Weight Symbols.* (2001). www.marshall.edu/akanart/abramo.html (accessed May 19, 2011).

43 Gillon Werner, *A Short History of African Art* (London: Penguin Books, 1984), 137.

44 Ibid., 138.

45 Ibid., 139.

46 Ibid., 146–147.

47 This represents the lost-wax casting method in which a bronze or brass form is cast from an artist's sculpture. See, for example, Bunker E. C. and R. Maddin R., *Lost Wax and Lost Textile: An Unusual Ancient Technique for Casting Gold Belt Plaques* (Cambridge, MA: The MIT Press, 1988).

48 Werner, *A Short History of African Art,* 139.

49 Susan Peirce, *Akan Art of Ghana.* G. F. Kojo Arthur, *Akan Gold Weight Symbols.*

50 Werner, *A Short History of African Art,* 139.

51 This is a system in which one belongs to one's mother's lineage, which involves inheritance of mother's property. See, for example, Alice Schlegel, *Male Dominance and Female Autonomy: Domestic Authority in Matrilineal Societies* (New Haven, CT: HRAF Press, 1972).

52 Werner, *A Short History of African Art,* 140.

53 The word *adinkra* is made up of three words. The *di* means, "to make use of," *nkra* means "message," and *a* is the Akan prefix for an abstract noun. Together, *a* with *di* and *nkra* means "to part," "to be separated," or "to say goodbye." In the word *adinkra*, *nkra* means the message that each individual soul takes with him from god on departing from the earth (*kra* is a Twi word for the soul. Twi is a language spoken by the Akan tribe of Ghana.) Thus, *adinkra* implies the message that a soul takes along when leaving the earth, hence, the expression "saying goodbye to one another when parting." See, for example, Kwaku Ofori-Ansah, *Meanings of Symbols in Adinkra Cloth* (Hyattsville, MD: Sankofa Edu-Cultural Publishing, 1999), pamphlet.

54 Ibid. The *adinkra* symbols are visual markers to express their worldview, beliefs, attitudes, and thoughts of the Akan. They are based on various observations and associations between humans and objects.

55 Ibid.

56 Werner, *A Short History of African Arts,* 153–154.

57 Mueda is the largest town of the Makonde Plateau in northeastern Mozambique. It is the capital of the Mueda District in Cabo Delgado Province. It is also the center of the culture of the Makondes, and the production of their ebony sculptures. See for example, Mary Fitzpatrick, *Lonely Planet: Mozambique* (Footscray, Vic., Australia: Lonely Planet Publications Pty., Ltd., 2007), 162.

58 John Stoner and Okeke-Ezigbo, "Makonde," in *Heritage Library of African Peoples Southern Africa* (New York: Rosen Publishing Group, 1997), 21.

59 Ibid., 26.

60 "African Art and Culture Cannot Be Separated."

61 Gert Chesi and Gerhard Merzeder (eds.), *The Nok Culture: Art in Nigeria 2500 Years Ago* (New York: Prestel Publishing, 2006).

62 Fred S. Kleiner and Christin J. Mamiya, *Gardner's Art through the Ages: Non-Western Perspectives,* 13th edition (Beverly, MD Wadsworth Publishing, 2009), 193.

63 Susan M. Vogel, "People of Wood: Baoulé Figure Sculpture," *The Art Journal* 33 (1973): 23–26.

64 Werner Gillon, *A Short History of African Art* (Harmondsworth, England: Pelican Publishing Co., 1986), 140–141.

65 Michael Brett and Elizabeth Fentress, *The Berbers: The Peoples of Africa* (Hoboken, NJ: Wiley-Blackwell, 1997).

66 Fergus Millar, "Local Cultures in the Roman Empire: Libyan, Punic and Latin in Roman Africa," *The Journal of Roman Studies, The Society for the Promotion of Roman Studies* (1968); Anne M. Spencer, "Berber, Moor and Bedouin: The Cultures of North Africa," *African Arts,* UCLA James S. Coleman African Studies Centre, Regents of the University of California (1978).

67 Suzanne Blier, *A History of Art in Africa* (Upper Saddle River, NJ: Prentice Hall/Harry N. Abrams, 2000), 15–19.

68 M. Adams, "African Visual Arts from an Art Historical Perspective," African Studies *Review* 32, no. 2 (1989): 55–103.

69 Kariamu Welsh-Asante, *The African Aesthetic: Keeper of the Traditions (Contributions in Afro- and African-American Studies)* (San Francisco, CA: Greenwood Press, 1993), 280.

70 Ibid.

71 Monica Blackmun Visona, et al., *A History of Art in Africa* (Upper Saddle River, NJ: Prentice Hall, 2001), 16.

72 Visona, *A History of Art in Africa,* 49.

73 Bascom, *African Art in Cultural Perspective,* 5.

74 Ibid, 6.

75 Ibid.

76 Ibid.

77 Ibid., 5–6.

78 Denise Murrell, "African Influences in Modern Art," in *Heilbrunn Timeline of Art History* (New York: The Metropolitan Museum of Art, 2000). www.metmuseum.org/toah/hd/aima/hd_aima.htm (accessed April 2008)

79 Clarke, *African Art,* 8.

80 Sidney Littlefield Kasfir, *Contemporary African Art* (World of Art) (New York: Thames & Hudson, 2000), 9.

81 Fred S. Kleiner and Christin J. Mamiya. *Gardner's Art through the Ages: Non-Western Perspectives,* 12th ed. (Stanford, CT: Cengage Learning, 2006), 212–214.

82 Sidney Littlefield Kasfir, *Contemporary African Art* (World of Art), 8.

83 Kasfir, *Contemporary African Art,* 24–25.

84 Ibid., 68–75.

85 Ibid., 44.

86 Ibid., 45.

87 Ibid., 38.

REVIEW QUESTIONS

1. Discuss the attitudes and preconceptions that kept Europeans from appreciating African art in the nineteenth century. How was African art treated then?
2. What influences did African art have on the avant-garde movement? Describe the three distinctive styles of sculpture of the Dogon in Mali.
3. Twentieth-century artists developed a true appreciation for African art. Name three of these artists and discuss the various effects of African art on their work.
4. Discuss the geographic differences between the western and the eastern parts of Africa, identifying the important features and reasons for these differences.
5. The author suggests that art is an integral part of the everyday life of Africans. How do some of the African artifacts discussed in this chapter illustrate this statement?

Writing Prompt

1. Certain standards of beauty and correctness in artistic expression and physical appearance are held in common among various African societies. These values and standards have been characterized as comprising an accepted African aesthetic. Identify and discuss these values and standards in African art.
2. The history of African art is complex. Historians, archaeologists, and researchers all have their own opinions on influences and the origins of the various types of arts in Africa. Select two ethnic art forms across Africa and explain the similarities and differences between them.

CHAPTER 11

African Musical Traditions and Practices: Past and Current Trends

E. Kwadwo O. Beeko

This chapter discusses broadly the entire musical practices that can be found on the African continent, ranging from traditional to modern or contemporary music. There has been much interest generally in "African musical practices," which has led many scholars, research fellows, travelers, and amateurs to advance their understanding and appreciation of the musical practices in Africa. What they all fundamentally embrace as obvious is the view that most of what is unique about African musical cultures is credited to the persistence of an African heritage; one that has given rise to the expansion of African music cultures or traditions. Such a distinction of African "music culture," according to Eileen Southern, was noticed from the time of the earliest contacts between the European and African, when people became aware that African music was distinct in many ways. According to her, "One of the first Europeans to attempt to describe some of the special features of (African) music, Richard Jobson, wrote in 1623, 'There is without doubt, no people on the earth more naturally affected to the *sound* of music than these people.'"[1]

Present-day Africa impresses the first-time visitor as an intense, fascinating, and sometimes confusing combination of old and new, often beyond categorization. According to Carol A. Muller, all those who know Africa and its music as cultural outsiders come to African music with a particular set of ideas, imaginings, and stereotypes. And many people can tell some kind of personal story of their first encounter with Africa and its music, regardless of where they live or what their cultural or ancestral heritage is. Thus, their typical understanding of Africa is shaped as much by what they see or hear as it is by where they come from.[2]

As visitors find themselves in an isolated village, like Adaso in southeastern Ghana, Benda in southeastern Nigeria, or Kapimbi in western Congo, they begin to sense the various musical styles that are expressed, ranging from songs to instrumental music. Likewise, they may hear songs sung for the birth of a child in one area, then songs sung at a puberty rite initiation for young girls and boys in another area in the village; they may also hear songs sung at marriage ceremonies and festivals in one area, while at another, they may hear songs sung for a funeral ceremony. By moving further into particular townships, they may hear songs that go with several working situations, such as hoeing, pounding millet, chopping a tree, drawing water, hauling fishing nets, or paddling a canoe. As they head toward various houses, where people living around the area gather and play music after dark, they may hear from some distance powerful verbal utterances expressed in a dramatic performance. By entering the dimly lit corners around some houses, they may also see a complete involvement of these inhabitants, singing, clapping, dancing, and playing various kinds of instruments.

Later, as the visitors find themselves in one of the major urban cities or towns, like Dakar in Senegal, Accra in Ghana, Lagos in Nigeria, Kinshasa in the Congo, or Johannesburg in South Africa, they may feel a bit different in such an environment. They may sense from the urban streets several aspects of musical life performances, ranging from traditional to neo-African art and modern popular music, an intriguing mix of the traditional and the foreign elements or idioms. The visitors, looking for entertainment, would find all kinds of live musical performances in concert halls, theaters, clubs, and bars, which range from traditional to popular to neo-art music. They would see how concerts have become the center of the modern social life of the urban communities, as a large proportion of the neo-African traditional music concerts continue to be held, with television, radio, tapes, and compact discs providing recorded music of every kind drawn from all neo-African musical forms.

As Ruth M. Stone claims, much evidence will show that African music has always changed, even if some forms have changed more rapidly than others. With increasing travel and mass media, the pace of change has quickened, and context of performance are shifting. And it comes to prove that music in Africa today accompanies a wide variety of events, involving dazzling arrays of instruments, customs, movements, and forms and, sometimes, juxtaposing the old and the new; a carved drum may be played alongside a synthesizer or an electric guitar. The international world, in which performers oscillate between the global and local forms, is very much in evidence; the Internet, MTV, and international popular music flavor and color local performances as people incorporate may influences, shaping them in ingenious ways and presenting results that surprise and delight audiences.[3]

According to Ewen, the continuous flow of people between village and town and country is a significant characteristic of the continent–a trait that remains basic to emerging expressive forms. This shows that modern-day national boundaries do not necessarily reflect differences between people, nor do they always carry meaning in relation to cultural and musical development. The movement and interchange between artists from different countries, with different ethnic background, who play similar kinds of music tend rather to reflect related languages, religions, and cultural practices. For instant, Manding *griot* music is played across West Africa; Congolese rumba is prevalent throughout the Central and Eastern regions; *taarab* is performed by most coastal Swahili peoples; and elements of South African township music can be identified in the popular music of most Southern African countries.[4]

The visitors would therefore notice that the fundamental aesthetics in such process of creativity, discovered in all these environments, are governed by the nature of the sounds that are produced and the concepts or conceptual approaches, attitudes, and behaviors that are brought into the process of musical performance, which they all share in common. Thus, although there are apparent differences existing between the villages and the urbanized, there are strong similarities that the people in these two seemingly different sectors share in common. As Olly Wilson emphasizes, "the sub-Saharan African peoples' conceptual approach to the process of music making is a reflection of their collective cultural experiences. It includes many dimensions, and among these is the affective power of music, that is, the belief that music is a force capable of making something happen."[5] The totality of such music tradition, as Portia K. Maultsby emphasizes, can thus be viewed as "an expression of cultural values which is dictated by the aesthetics defined and recognized by the people of that culture."[6] According to Ruth M. Stone:

> Music permeates the daily life of people in Africa. An ivory-horn ensemble precedes a chief as he travels with his entourage. Highlife singers promote candidates for political office. Professional praise singers convey messages to and for their patrons. For ordinary citizens on the streets of Monrovia, Liberia, the sounds of Bob Marley and reggae come from the "money bus": to the rhythm of the music, the driver's assistant jogs alongside the vehicle, supervising its passengers. At local market, cassette sellers promote recordings by local bands and international music artists. . . . In all these settings, music tightly interweaves with dance, words, drama, and visual art to create complex events.[7]

"African music" then, as Kofi Agawu claims, "is best understood not as a finite repertoire but as a potentiality. In terms of what now exists and has existed in the past, African music, designating those numerous repertoires of song and instrumental music that originate in specific African communities, are performed regularly as part of play, ritual, and worship, and are circulated mostly orally/aurally, within and across language, ethnic, and cultural boundaries."[8] Thus, it is this "potential infinite set" of repertoire, as he stresses, which covers all aspects of musical performances, ranging from the old traditional types to the current, prevailing neo-traditional categories (neo-art, neo-popular, modern-popular, etc.).[9]

In the study of African music, the line between what is music and what is not music often blurs, especially as "musical" elements in everyday life of the societies are heard and experienced. As such, "music" in Africa is usually conceptualized within a wide set of parameters.[10] The study of African music, therefore, cannot be limited to a discussion of its formal structure. It is necessary to consider the place of music in the life of the people and to examine the value judgments by which it is sustained.[11] All these illustrations point to the fact that although by examining the whole continent of Africa one finds more variation among the assorted cultures and nations, African music shares common cultural characteristics that can be identified.[12] It shows how people in these areas—both rural and urban—make use of traditional musical performance as a way of fostering social cohesion in the community. As Gregory Barz stresses, documenting, understanding, and representing African musical culture, from the past centuries to the present, becomes increasingly important to students, historians, ethnomusicologists, and the recording industry.[13]

SOCIAL AND CULTURAL BACKGROUND OF AFRICAN TRADITIONAL MUSIC

A close look at the musical tradition among sub-Saharan African societies reveals a series of features and aesthetic preferences that are common to many of them. It is a tradition that evolved gradually during precolonial times with the growth of societies and became part of the process of enculturation. According to Ruth M. Stone, scholars have noticed that it is difficult to find a word in any African language that is equivalent to the Western concept of "music." Instead, there are terms for more specific action, like singing, drumming, or dancing, as well as broader terms such as performance, which encompasses song as well as dance, and oration as well as instrumental playing.[14]

In Africa, the art of music and dance, like religion, penetrates every level of human existence and serves as reinforcement not only of religious beliefs but of societal attitudes and values as well. Music and dance are interwoven throughout the culture to provide unity among its members. They permeate every social activity from youth to old age; thus, no one is excluded from performance, because everyone is expected to sing and dance.[15] Music and dance are deliberately cultivated in the communities for their social benefits and for their impact on daily and occasional events. They are so pervasive and so much a part of the environment that they are seldom viewed as separate entities. Thus, while African cultures have words to express distinctive forms and genres of music, few have separate words for the art of music.[16]

Music in the traditional African societies is practiced mainly as a function of social activity, where the stylistic features of given types of music are often defined by the particular nature of the social event in which the music is used. As Patricia S. Campbell stresses, "That music is life and that music learning occurs through life experiences seems to be a perspective shared by Africans. For instance, a mother's lullaby, children's game songs, songs of passage through life stages, and occupational songs are examples of the integral part music plays in African life."[17] The various social events that constitute the overall life stages or lifecycle are naming ceremonies, puberty rite initiations, marriage ceremonies, and funerals, which are marked by musical performances, and occasions during which specific musical items relative to the occasions are performed.[18] There are also various kinds of musical types used for specific ceremonies, and occasions such as music for religious ceremonies, music for masquerade theatre, and kingship music. Below (Figure 11.1) is a photograph of a marriage ceremony among the Fantis, (in the Akan community), which began with the bridegroom's family carrying drinks, clothes, and money, while singing, to the bride's family.

Music making in Africa is a communal activity in which the acquisition of musical sounds and genres occurs through social experience.[19] It is generally organized as a social event or activity that brings people together to share their creative experience and participate in the process as an avenue for the expression of their sentiments.[20] It is fundamentally created to fulfill both practice and aesthetic functions; it is always linked to some aspects of social activities or social occasions in which performances are judged by their social relevance. And it often happens in social situations where people's primary goals are not artistic but to contribute to an event's success by focusing attention, communicating information, encouraging social solidarity, and transforming consciousness.[21]

Music making in such a setting or tradition is integrated into every aspect of African life, for music is communicated in conjunction with non-musical elements and is not perceived in isolation from the other elements.[22] It becomes essentially a community experience and as part of the institutional life of the people in the societies.[23] Because it is employed as a means of social interactions, there is always a strong social cohesion

Figure 11.1. Sewurada group, marching through the town from one end to the other—that is, the bride's house—where the marriage ceremony is supposed to take place. The picture shows the women carrying drinks, clothes, and money meant for the bride's family and being followed with singing, drumming, and dancing. (Picture taken by E. Kwadwo Beeko during his research on January 19, 2004)

in such communities where members are bound by a network of social relations.[24] For example, in addressing social aspects of music making in Africa, as Barz stresses, sometimes the opportunity arises to explore how rivalries can serve to solidify friendships while simultaneously expressing attitudes of community and difference.[25]

The association of music with social events implies that when music is performed it is one of several other things going on at the same time, some of which are not artistic. And of all the various elements that constitute a social event in which music is used, music may not necessarily be the most important and may even be the least important. Thus, a person observing a musical event has much to occupy his or her attention, and he or she can concentrate solely on the musical aspect only at the risk of missing other elements that may be equally important as the music.[26] This phenomenon demonstrates the multivalent nature and functions of traditional way of "music making" as rooted within musical and social systems that in many ways unify much of Africa.[27]

THE ART OF SINGING AND DANCING

Singing

Generally, singing is the most common and universal characteristic of all the music languages of the world. In terms of singing during performance, as we all know about every culture, the voice, as compared to any other instrument, is the most natural, artistic, and spontaneous way of making music by means of the human body. However, the songs, their characteristics, and the way they should be sung vary from culture to culture in their content, purpose, structure, form, text, aesthetic, performance, and many other defined social traits.[28] In Africa, the utilization of voice—its timbres and the different nuances obtained by means of artifices unknown to the rest of the world (stopping the ears, pinching the nose, vibrating the tongue in the mouth producing echoes by directing the voice into a receptacle, etc.)—largely accounts for the confusion, or rather the incomprehension that almost inevitable confronts the non-African listener when he or she at first hears black African music.[29]

Nonetheless, the art of singing among African societies remains purely functional and retains a simplicity of form that makes it readily accessible to all. Singing is not a specialized affair, as everybody *can* sing and, in practice, everyone *does* sing;[30] however, particular individuals are still singled out in their respective communities for the beauty of their voices and their performing abilities.[31] During a performance, the voices adapt themselves to the musical context; for example, there is a mellow tone to welcome a new bride, a husky voice to recount an indiscreet adventure, a satirical inflection for a teasing tone with laughter bubbling up to compensate for the mockery; voices may be soft or harsh as circumstances demand.

The various sound qualities, therefore, that can be heard often include *open-throated quality* (typical of the non-Islamic cultures), *nasalized quality* (usually found among the Islamized peoples), *ululation* (a shrill high-pitched intermittent vocal expression used by women), *yodeling* (used to show appreciation for an on-going performance and encouraging the performers), *falsetto* (one voice chording or screaming), *glissando* (wide vibrato and wavering of pitch, such as vocal sighs, sobs, melismas, spoken or chanted interpolations), *shouty delivery*, and *raspy tone* production. The various performance styles that are also incorporated, in most cases, include improvisation; spontaneous interjection of words into the main original lyrics; immediacy of communication; emotional delivery of text by the leaders or sub-leaders; and oral transmission of the idiom. In addition to these sound qualities and styles are also the dramatic variations of dynamic, tempo, and intensity throughout the performance and the shifts between softer and louder sections, indicating the importance of timbre as a compositional element in the traditional music of the various regions.[32]

Dancing

Generally in Africa, according to J. H. Kwabena Nketia, there are various types of basic movements used in traditional dances, which range from simple to somehow complex and "intricate in conception."[33] Every society has its own set of movement sequences used in a particular dance, and the differences among them lie in the traditional norms that each society has to follow in the dances. And in many of these dances, *rhythm* and *movement* are more closely tight, involving a series of prearranged movement sequences or figures, and each is identified with distinctive rhythmic patterns so that changes in rhythm are automatically accompanied by changes in dance movements. And as Nketia emphasizes, "the range of diversity extends even to quality, timing, and flow of movement." Simply put, "each ethnic group has the tendency to specialize and stress some movements and progression more than the other."[34]

Figure 11.2. "Owu Mpɛ Sika" group performing at the residence of the leader, Okyeame Ofosu, who is seen standing, at Abrew in the Eastern Region of Ghana. In the front row, and from left to right, are the accompanists with the *apentema, tamalin,* and *petia* drums, respectively. (Picture taken by E. Kwadwo Beeko during his research on January 13, 2004)

Figure 11.3. Two dancers of the Tanokrom Agorōmma, dancing the *adowa* dance. Note the performance arrangement: dancers in front, drummers sit behind them with singers standing behind the drummers. (Picture taken by E. Kwadwo Beeko during his research on January 13, 2004)

One of the underlying features governing these dances is the *dramatization*. And in Africa, because there is a "structural relationship" between dance and music, such relationship, as Nketia emphasizes, " . . . facilitates their integrated use of dramatic communication." This communication may concern itself with enactment of episodes from history on ritual and ceremonial occasions or during festivals. It may also be used either at story-telling sessions or during the performance of traditional plays, designed for entertainment." Such dramatic use of music and dance, as Nketia claims, always "finds its highest expression in the dance drama, which may be based on one or many themes."[35] In all these arenas of performance, music becomes central to the flow of life of the people in these communities. During performance, some groups may sit down and sing with handclapping and drumming, while others may have some dancing to the music. An example of those in the first category is the "Owu Mpɛ Sika" group performing at Abrew in the Eastern Region of Ghana.

An example of the second category—those who perform with dancers—is the Tanokrom Agorōmma in the Ashanti Region of Ghana.

In addition, the art of dancing or even displaying any kind of movement of gestures, like singing, penetrates every level of an African existence and serves as reinforcement not only of his or her religious beliefs but of societal attitudes and values as well. Dancing is interwoven within every performance, and it is a higher level of expression; thus, no one in the communities is excluded from dancing, as everyone may be expected to dance. J. H. Kwabena Nketia stresses that dance can also be used as a social and artistic medium of communication. In this respect, it may be used to convey thoughts or matters of personal or social importance through the choice of movements, postures, and facial expressions. And it is through the dance that individuals and social groups in the communities show their reactions to occurring events. Furthermore, because in Africa, the dance is an avenue of expression, it may be closely related to the themes and purpose of social occasions through the guiding principle.[36] However, as he points out, "one can also dance without attempting to convey anything apart from one's personal feeling of exhilaration, restlessness, or even sorrow, with nothing more specific to express."[37] Dance in Africa, therefore, becomes deliberately cultivated in the communities for its social benefit and for its impact on daily and occasional events.

ORGANIZATION OF VOCAL AND INSTRUMENTAL MUSIC

Vocal Music

In Africa, the bond between language and music is particularly intimate; it is a place where the music loosely follows both melodic and rhythmic contours of speech, and where instrumental melodies and percussion at different pitches frequently act as speech surrogates.[38] Vocal music, which is truly the essence of African musical art, occupies a predominant place in all African societies. According to Bebey, unlike instrumental music, vocal music is truly popular, as it draws its inspiration from the people and graciously endows the most banal event with philosophic wisdom. It is, therefore, hardly necessary to add that it is vocal music alone that can adequately express the meaning of a rite, offer up a prayer to the gods, pronounce sentence and order execution, or preach love and unity within the community.[39]

The vocal forms used among African societies for performance include accompanied and unaccompanied solos, songs performed by two people in unison or in harmony, and songs performed by the chorus. However, there are a great many unaccompanied or recitative songs in addition to the accompanied songs that may be in free rhythm as well as in strict time; declamatory style as well as sustained style, and combinations of the above.[40] Songs are usually built from short phrases, which are reiterated, and varied continually and cumulatively. Songs that are sung as solos may be organized in a way where, in addition to the normal strophic form, a single verse is repeated, often with slight variations, for the desired number of stanzas—in the form of a series of declamations or cumulative non-stanzaic utterances, which is possibly rounded off by closing refrains or pauses.[41]

Works for group singing, found in at least three standard forms, may be organized in pairs: The first is the call-and-response form or a similar form in which the second singer echoes every musical phrase sung by the first. The "response" normally repeats the melodic contour of the "call;" it may repeat the call, more or less exactly, or it may vary it substantially. Alternatively, the call may be in a stanzaic form of verse, in which case, the response will take the form of a refrain;[42] sometimes the call will overlap, or incorporate the response. Most frequently, however, the call is varied or elaborated according to the requirements of the text, while the response remains largely unaltered. Most songs are performed antiphonally, in which a call from a leader is answered by a response from the group.[43]

The second standard form is that in which the first singer begins with a brief lead of a few notes, and then the second singer joins in as soon as possible to sing along to the end of the section. The third standard form is that in which singers begin simultaneously in duets (or sometimes in trios) and sing each stanza together. The group singing is arranged either as a simple call-and-response or a leader beginning, followed by a second singer or more singers. Pieces intended to be sung by the chorus are, in most cases, designed so that a leader or a cantor, as well as a chorus will sing.[44] Typically in Africa, the relationship between call and response often reflects the social function of the music. For example, in storytelling songs, the call may predominate, whereas in songs used on ceremonial occasions, the response may predominate as an affirmation of group solidarity.[45] Songs truly come to life when a professional poet-singer varies the works in accordance with the particular social occasion and the melodic patterns to enhance the new meaning.[46]

Instrumental Music

Africans generally make use of a vast array of musical instruments and they frequently employ other ways of grouping instruments. Thus, their ways of categorizing these instruments differ somewhat from other cultures; for example, the Western orchestral categories of strings, woodwind, brass, and percussion sections. And also the ways of groupin their instruments may even differ from the ethnomusicological classification of *idiophone, aerophone, chordophone,* and *membranophone.*[47] However, in helping outsiders to understand these instruments, there will be the need to place them under such ethnomusicological categories.

Idiophones are "instruments upon which a sound may be produced without the addition of stretched membrane, a vibrating string or reed."[48] There are two types of idiophones used in Africa, which are the rhythmic idiophones and melodic/tuned idiophones. There are four categories under the rhythmic idiophones, which are the *shaken idiophones*, such as rattles of all kinds, containing bread network on the outside or inside; *struck idiophones*, such as the clapperless iron bells, struck with sticks; *scraped idiophones*, which include the rasp, a piece of notched bamboo or palm stem scraped with another stick; and *stamped idiophone*, an instrument with either a stamping sticks used for hitting the ground to produce the sound, or a stamping tubes made out of an elongated gourd with long narrow neck. There are two categories under the melodic idiophones, which are the *mbira* (sansa, hand piano); and Xylophones, which have several categories such as *pit xylophone* with a box, trough, or clay pot; *xylophone* with banana stems; and *xylophones* with number of suspended gourd resonators under them.[49] There are also hollowed-out logs which are played alone or in ensemble and often reproduced the relative pitches of speech in tonal languages to communicate specific messages. The variety of struck, plucked and shaken instruments is broad.[50]

Aerophones are "instruments upon which a sound may be produced with a vibrating reed, or with a column of air."[51] The three broad groups used in Africa are the *flutes*, which may be open-ended or stopped and may be designed in playing in vertical or transverse position; the *reed pipes*, which are more of a single-reed type that can be found more in the savannah belt of West Africa; and *horns* and *trumpets*, with the horns made of animal horns and the trumpets made out of gourd or bamboo or both.[52]

Chordophones are "instruments upon which a sound may be produced with vibrating strings."[53]. The main types used in Africa are the *musical bows*, such as earth bows (consisting of a flexible stick stuck in the ground or buried in the earth), mouth bows, held across the mouth by one finger and played with the other, and *bows* with calabash resonators, placed in the middle of the bow or towards the tip; *zithers*, whose distinguishing characteristic is the horizontal position of its strings; *lutes*, an instrument whose strings run parallel to its neck—an example is the one-string fiddle; *bow lutes* and *harp lutes*, with the strings running parallel to the necks to which they are secured; *harps*, which although are closely related to the harp lute and the bow lute, are ached (or bow) harps, with strings running from the nick to the sound box at an angle; and *lyres*, whose strings run from a yoke to a resonator.[54]

Membranophones are "instruments upon which a sound may be produced on stretched membranes."[55] These instruments range from small hand-held instruments or simple makeshift types to special constructed instruments with elaborate decorations and those that need large stands to support them or several people to carry them in procession. These drums are usually carved out of solid logs or wood or may be made out of strips of wood bound together by iron hoops. Examples of these membranophones are the drum instruments found in many shapes, ranging from goblet, hourglass, conical, barrel, cylindrical, and frame (tambourine). These drums produce a broad spectrum of "voices" or timbre.

Sometimes there could be a combination of these instruments with the aim of producing specific communication. From instance, certain instruments sport attached idiophones in the form of rattles which enrich the sound. Chordophones, or string instruments, are sometimes 'hidden' instruments of Africa, no less remarkable than the percussion instruments but often unheard outside individual cultures.[56]

In respect to the use of instruments, Africa is a place where these instruments are selected in relation to their effectiveness in performing certain established musical roles or for fulfilling specific musical performance. Thus, while some of these instruments are designed for use as solo instruments, others are used purely in ensembles. Furthermore, there are differences in those that are designed for use in ensembles: while certain instruments are used as leading instruments, others are used as subordinate or supportive instruments that only accompany. The combinations of these instruments always tend to follow definite patterns. In most cases, the voice is combined with these instruments; however, the actual role of the vocal part or its importance in the design of the music is variable. It may be subordinate to the instrumental part or it may be of equal or greater importance.[57]

Also apart from instrumental music played with these instruments, various categories of these instruments are used to also accompany the singing. Furthermore, while many types of music are a combination of singing with instrumental accompaniment, the vocal-instrumental music is almost invariably accompanied with dancing. Although it is not uncommon to find that singing, the playing of instruments, and dancing are done by people considered as expert performers, non-experts—in other words, all other people present on an occasion—are not discouraged from joining in at least the singing and dancing.[58] According to Nketia, the general pattern of musical organization in Africa is one that emphasizes the integration of music with other activities, and the attitudes required of performers and their audiences are generally not those of restrained contemplation behavior.[59]

As Ruth M Stone claims, musical instruments used in Africa are more than material objects, as they frequently take on human feature and qualities. For example, certain solo instruments may have personal names, be kept in special houses, receive special sacrificial food or other offerings, and be regarded as quasi-human. Also these musical instruments are believed to carry human attributes and can become more or less human, depending on their roles within the music they produce. For example, carved humoid features adorn many instruments. These instruments, to the musicians, provide power and sometimes special aid. And a close humanlike partnership sometimes develops between musicians and instruments. These musicians may designate parts of their instruments by the names of human parts, such as the waist, the foot, and the ear. For many musicians, these material objects possess human and spiritual attributes. They serve to connect the various worlds that people inhabit as well as to denote objects that are not simply material culture in nature.[60]

PERFORMANCE OF TRADITIONAL MUSIC

Musical performance in Africa, according to Ruth M. Stone, "is a tightly wrapped bundle of arts that are sometimes difficult to separate, even for analysis; singing, playing instruments, dancing, masquerading, and dramatizing are part of a conceptual package that many Africans think of as one of the same."[61] The processes of music and dance are so closely bound together that they cannot be separated from each other; for example, song from movement or playing the drum from speech. Even drama becomes part of this tightly bound complex of the arts.[62] Furthermore, just as music is set in a social context, it is also associated with other expressive media, such as drama, dance poetry, costuming, and sculpture.[63] Musical performances are likened to some aspect of social activities, and they are judged not so much by their entertainment values—although entertainment may be one by-product of it—as by their social relevance.[64]

The performances of traditional music actually function in different ways within different communities. And what constitutes this function, as Barz describes, are (a) *events*, for which the performances are planned, rehearsed, and celebrated, and through which the important aspects of the culture are transmitted from one generation to the next; (b) *principle*, which constitutes the community's formation, reflecting the varying ways traditional music performance is understood, used and embraced to express both interdependence and integration within communities; and (c) *institutions*, which are particular ways in which traditional music performances aid in establishing and solidifying social institutions that not only define communities by also distinguish internal differences within communities.[65] From this perspective, the traditional musical performance in the societies may, in some cases, often occur within highly competitive events constituting an important form of and contribution to popular entertainment, which includes song duets, choir competitions, drumming and dance contests, sporting events, religious rituals, and games. Furthermore, because in Africa aesthetic values are held in respect to musical performance, there is, to quote Gregory Barz, "a multivalent nature and function of traditional music performance as rooted within musical social systems that in many ways unify much if not all of Africa."[66] Below is an example of a performance of Central Folkloric Group of the Center For National Culture (CNC) in Ghana, whose performances are always linked to some aspect of social activities; that is, performing something that must have its social relevance to the community. The first is the drummers and the singers, while the second is the dancers.

During musical performance, audience participation can also occur in a variety of ways. Because "performing" is considered as normal in Africa, most people in the communities are expected to perform music and dance at a basic level. Everyone is expected to be able to sing and dance to a certain level of competence.[67] The people who really constitute the "audience" in a musical performance, and who do not actually participate on the artistic side of the event but are rather involved in the non-artistic aspects, include, for example, those who guide the masquerade, those who display physical endurance by whipping one another, and those who just typically follow the masquerade. With the exception of the limitations on performance imposed by custom, in Africa, no one is barred from active participation as a singer, a dancer, or an instrumentalist. Even in a very serious or formal occasion, such as a religious ceremony, some of the participants may still be involved in the act of worshipping while others assist the priest as bearers of sacrificial offerings.[68]

Beyond that, talented young men and women are selected for special training, and there are also some people who because of their knowledge of the repertoire or their superior performing ability are regarded as leaders; however, this does not even stop the audience from giving the performers practical support, by

Figure 11.4. Central Folkloric Group of the Center for National Culture (CNC) in one of their performances in Cape Coast in the Central Region of Ghana (Picture taken by E. Kwadwo Beeko during his research on January 23, 2004)

clapping their hands, stamping their feet, or making rhythmic sound with their voices to outline the pulsation of the music. Every individual who has the urge to make his or her voice heard is given the liberty to do so.[69] This simply points out that although it is often possible to distinguish between musical and non-musical roles and between artistic and non-artistic roles of participants in all these performances, it is more difficult to make a rigid separation of the people attending the event into an "audience group" and "performing group." Even when the people are in theory onlookers, most of them would be involved in varying degrees and forms of active participation.[70] Music making among African societies should therefore be seen as a reflection of the peoples' collective cultural experiences that permeates the daily life of the entire communities as a whole.

Figure 11.5. Central Folkloric Group, performing the *asafo* dance. This section shows the female dance movements and gestures. They dance with scarfs in the hand. (All pictures taken by E. Kwadwo Beeko during his research in January 2004)

NEO-AFRICAN OR MODERN AFRICAN MUSIC

European contact with Africa dates back to the fifteenth century; however, the impact of Western culture and music on Africa was not apparent until the nineteenth century, which began with the arrival of the Christian missionaries and the colonial powers at least in Africa south of the Sahara; a time when Western art music was first introduced to Africans.[71] Prior to the arrival of European missionaries in Africa in the middle of the nineteenth century and the intervention of Christianity and other outside forces on the continent, African music was predominantly a religious or social event. And the concept of music as a purely contemplative tradition was not widespread, as the traditional societies were strongly tied to their own religious, social, and political activities. Although there were examples of traditional music performances that took place outside specific social or religious contexts, music was purely regarded as an integral part of social or ritual events. The introduction of Christianity and European (or Western) culture to Africa was definitely bound to have a significant impact on its musical culture.[72]

Also, some of the notable changes that came as a result of such impact include the major global changes, which first began with colonization in most part of the continent and were followed by other external forces of change that affected political, economic, and religious institutions in many societies in Africa. Furthermore, these major political changes were accompanied by the emergence of cosmopolitan towns and cities, the emergence of modern means of communication—the cinema, radio and television, and of Western-trained Africans.[73] These developments in turn resulted in several innovations, such as the democratic and governmental systems, the banking and economic systems, and the Christian and Islamic religious systems, among others.[74] Western musical instruments that were introduced into Africa by Christian missionaries and other European traders include organ, piano, accordion, concertina, string instruments (e.g. violin), wind instruments (e.g. flute), and brass instruments (e.g. trumpet). However, although these instruments were adopted, they were reinvented to suit indigenous systems of tuning and styles of performance. The spread of acoustic guitars, and later electric guitar, was one of the most important developments in African popular music, both as topical acoustic music performed solo, or in small groups, and as amplified music for dancing.[75] It was this impact that provided the socioeconomic and cultural basis for the development of modern musical idioms, which resulted not only in adoption of Western musical idioms by Africans but also in new ways of using and practicing African traditional music.[76]

As a result of this process of acculturation, various neo-art and popular musical types and styles, both sacred and secular, emerged and developed in most African countries. Some of them arose out of traditional music, with most of them containing the imprints of Western musical culture. The rise of these new types or idioms thus became a major departure from the precolonial tradition in which music and social activity are so integrated that the meaning of a musical type is dependent upon its role within its customary social activity. They began to develop alongside the precolonial idioms of African traditional music, representing both a fusion of Western and African characteristics as well as reorganization of African traditional styles. In the following sections, we will discuss (1) the neo-African choral and gospel music and (2) the modern African popular music.

Neo-African Choral And Gospel Music

Various types of neo-African choral or vocal music that emerged and developed in Africa in the course of the twentieth century have become authentic traditional idioms that really testify to the African genius for creativity.[77] The neo-African choral tradition has become particularly prominent in various areas in Africa, especially in places such as Ghana, Nigeria, Kenya, and South Africa. The tradition has become strong and a large number of choirs have blossomed. Thus, apart from church choirs, it is very common to come across several choirs or choral groups formed in schools—primary, elementary/middle, and secondary/high schools—and even in the workplaces—business centers, hospitals, etc. These choirs mostly sing compositions by African composers, typically in four-part harmony (a legacy of the church), and they are often performed *a cappella* (i.e., unaccompanied) or sometimes accompanied by African instruments and/or Western instruments. Actually, the formal structures of these compositions vary greatly. There are relatively short choral pieces, especially those with highlife-styles, and there are also long pieces like an anthem in character. Moreover, they typically use local languages, with performers (especially in certain countries) often moving in rhythm while singing.[78]

In addition to the neo-African choral music, there also arose neo-African or African contemporary gospel music, which was different from the neo-African choral music. The difference is that, while the neo-African choral music emerged as a result of European encounter (and interaction of European church music), the emergence and development of neo-African gospel music was rather influenced by Pentecostal church musical traditions in the United States, especially the African American tradition. It was performed by choirs and singing groups in several African countries, such as Ghana, Nigeria, Congo, Kenya, Uganda, Tanzania, and South Africa. Although these contemporary gospel musical groups draw on diverse traditions, the African influences still render this kind of gospel music unique. The formal structures of these songs, like the choral music, vary greatly. There are relatively short choral pieces especially those with highlife-styles.[79] In addition, they typically use local languages, with performers often moving in rhythm while singing. There also emerged the neo-African instrumental art music that became particularly prominent in areas like Ghana, Nigeria, and South Africa. The number of musical instruments that Africans adopted, especially from the West, also includes the guitar, keyboard/piano, and organ, as well as wind and string instruments.

Most of these choral and gospel songs are sung in local language, with few sung in English, especially in some urban cities. This type of music has, as a result, gone down to reach the grassroots of the Christian community and to even become a popular music to the non-Christians. Although most of the songs were based on religious topics, sometimes certain songs, depending on the nature of the occasions, often take up contemporary topics—politics, health, famine, good crop culture, and advice about AIDS.[80]

As a response to all these development, every township and rural area in Africa has countless choirs, groups, and soloists, many of which are powerful and thriving. Live performances, whether in a church, night vigil, or simply in someone's backyard, are a rich and unforgettable part of the people's cultural life, providing important clues about the sources of its people's legendary resilience and forbearance.[81] Some of the musicians and singers, especially those in Ghana, Tanzania, and South Africa are active around the churches, writing religious songs, training musicians and singers, and turning out cassettes in the lucrative choir business.[82] Despite the current lack of infrastructure in some of these countries, there seems to be an enduring strength to many of them, especially Tanzanian music.[83]

Modern African Popular Music

Several modern African popular musical genres emerged and developed throughout the twentieth century and the early part of the twenty-first century in the urban centers of many countries in sub-Saharan Africa; they have developed alongside the indigenous musical traditions. Thus, as Angela Impey claims, Africa can be said to host an immeasurable range of popular music, with a comprehensive overview of the range of styles, with each one's own blend of local and external influences and fascinating social histories, regional permutations, and influences on diasporic music. They are styles that can be said to embody creative interaction between foreign values and local styles. Popular music is therefore, a site for adaptation, assimilation, eclecticism, appropriation, and experimentation. In light of the intensity of global communication (which have accelerated during the past century), stimulated by capital, conquest, migration and technology, African pop has become a global phenomenon, consumed internationally under the marketing tag of world music.[84] Some of the various categories of these modern popular musical genres that have therefore developed and struck a nerve throughout Africa, by bringing together dances of all ages and social classes, include Senegalese *mbalax*, Ghanaian *highlife*, Nigerian *juju*, Cameroonian *makossa*, Congolese *soukous*, Zimbabwean *chimurenga*, and South African *marabi* and *mbaqanga*. They came as a major response to the new urban social life of the communities, and to the challenge of urban ballroom dancing, which has been firmly embedded in the clubs and dance halls of these cities.[85] Few examples of these can be outlined as follows:

Mbalax is a Senegalese popular music. The term is a Wolof word referring to percussion-based music with much mystical oratory and vocal styles. The genre is a combination of *kora*-based traditional melodies and Cuba rhythms, sung in high-pitched style. It is a style that probably emerged and developed after the country's independence from French colonial rule, but it was primarily more in a Cuban musical style, until later, local musicians began to substitute traditional melodies and lyrics, introduce the *kora* and gourd-resonated xylophone in the lineup, and then the drums, such as the tama talking drum and the *sabar*, a conga-like upright drum.[86]

Highlife, affectionately termed "palm wine" music, first started relatively slowly in contrast to a ballroom dance orchestral style influenced by various European musical forms, drawn from church music, military brass bands, and sea chanties. During the 1930s and 1940s, some of the Ghanaian *highlife* style began to spread throughout the continent. For instance, the musical style began to spread along the African coastal areas, such as Sierra Leone and Nigeria, and even the Belgian Congo. It finally established its strength in the entire West Africa and continued to flourish in some major cities of the United Kingdom by the end of World War II. Later, it moved to North America, as typifying virtually all modern African dance music.[87]

Juju is a syncretic popular music performed and patronized by the Yoruba of Southwestern Nigeria. The development of juju music can be divided into two periods: first, the early juju, which dominated from 1932 through World War II, and second, the modern juju, which began to emerge in 1948 and attained domination by the early 1950s. The early *juju* originated in Lagos, Nigeria, during the early 1930s as a localized variation of the pan-anglophone West Africa urban palm-wine music style. It happened at what is characterized as "the Lagos melting pot," where indigenous Yoruba people mixed with the descendants of freed slaves from Sierra Leone and Brazil, which brought in new styles and aesthetics that led to the emergence of palm-wine music. The strong changes in juju came with a mixture of several elements, thus leading to the emergence of what came to be known as modern *juju*, which emerged with exciting blues guitar work and lyrics that were steeped in Yoruba tradition and at the same time addressed issues affecting the new urban elite.[88]

Makossa is a Cameroonian popular music with a *Doula*-based style that developed and reached an international audience. *Makossa*, in its earliest form, emerged as a folk dance and music played on guitars and accordions at the mission school of Doulala in Cameroon. Although it had been dominating the country's pop scene since the 1960s, in the early 1970s it actually became an increasingly urban electric style with a dance rhythm precisely cut for the night clubs (and the funky hybrid "Soul Makossa" in 1972). In the 1980s, it was transformed into "pop-makossa" and produced largely from Paris.[89]

Soukous is a Congolese popular music that originated as a musical genre in the neighboring countries of the Democratic Republic of Congo (formerly, the Belgian Congo) and the French Congo during the 1930s and early 1940s. The music has become renowned for the stylistic intricacies of electric guitars, which combine melody and rhythm in a way that is both mellow and highly charged. It came as a blend of the French-style *variéte* or *cabaret* music with other ingredients, such as vocal harmonic skills learned at church, and combined with religious fanfares played on brass-band instruments to form the classic Congolese sounds. Congolese *soukous* also had a strong impact on musicians in many cities in East Africa, especially Kenya.[90] With its spiraling guitar and hip-swinging rhythms, the *soukous* is able to have a major effect even on Western dance floors.[91]

Marabi-Jive music (often referred to as *Jive*—as in "violin jive" or "Ndebele jive") originated in Johannesburg, South Africa, and began to develop with elements of styles from Johannesburg's black slumyards called *marabi*. Its melodic framework is a highly syncretic form that provides enough space for improvisation to incorporate snatches of anything from traditional melodies to hymns with the same underlying structure.[92]

ENTERTAINMENT INSTITUTIONS, MASS MEDIA, MUSIC PRODUCTION AND MARKETING

The development of modern popular music in Africa has also led to the development of various kinds of entertainment, which normally take place at several concert and dance halls. Concert programs and organizations have developed in several African countries, and they continue to receive vigorous support in the mass media. They conquered a vast public by completely crossing the entire sociocultural spectrum, filling the theaters, clubs, and traditional centers in major cities and giving rise to arenas for performances, such as the open-air festivals, with massive audiences. They have thus become the most important centers for the production and dissemination of pop music. These large-stage performances at concert halls have further enhanced stage performances and encouraged the development of professional choreographing of movements and dances by professional dancers. The development of these concerts has given rise to new forms of professionalism, as many of these musicians and their bands continue to perform their music to urban audiences in theaters, concerts halls, and other places of entertainment.[93]

A complex corporate network involving companies that record, manage, advertise, publish, and broadcast mass-produced popular music first reached Africa around 1900. It was the time when entrepreneurs in the

West began to recognize the potential for marketing musical instruments, gramophones, and records in Africa. And since then, musical styles and peoples have circulated extremely between African centers and countries abroad. This circulation has included African influences on the music of the diaspora extending back through the slave trade, a circulation that is as much about commonalities of style as it is about ideologies of blackness. The introduction of gramophone record, especially from 1907, presented African musicians with a new spectrum of imported styles. Among these were African-American jazz, Dominican *merengue*, Cuban *salsa* and *son*, Anglo-American soul, and Jamaican *reggae*.[94]

The mass media has thus become very effective in promoting popular culture worldwide. Such development provides opportunities for musicians to travel and record their compositions, leading to the development of recording studio techniques that support modern commercial systems and the promotion of trade in musical products, such as recordings, playback equipment, musical instruments, amplifiers, speakers, and microphones. Thus, since such commercial music recording has been happening in many urban centers, the method of composing and performing, and the appreciation of music, have also changed dramatically. Songs that are recorded specifically for commercial release to the mass audience exhibit several characteristics: For example, music in such context is performed within a set time limit; the performances are focused on themes that appeal to a broad public; and performers' interest in live performance is to reproduce the recorded version of the music so as to fulfill audience expectations.[95]

Furthermore, the establishment of broadcasting institutes became critical to the development of popular music, with competition between multinational companies and emerging local ones being a recurrent theme. And as Angela Impey points out, by 1930s, many artists had started distributing their products across Africa. Most foreign companies established subsidiaries in Africa, and the most advanced infrastructures were developed in countries like Nigeria, Côte d'Ivoire, South Africa, Tanzania, Kenya and Zimbabwe. Local production of popular music formerly took the form of 45- and 78-rpm records. Albums were often released as compilations of national hits and were produced in small numbers so as to be affordable to local buyers. The 1980s marked more or less the end of vinyl. Most local companies invested in the high-speed C-60 cassette market, and cassettes now outsell records five to one. Although recording on CD emerged, there is little evidence that such CD market would succeed on the continent apart from South Africa, as it is expensive.[96]

What can be found today in this popular setting in Africa is how various images of tradition have been partly created by the market to appeal to local tastes. For instant, As Impey illustrates, some pop styles have been consciously *traditionalized* or *Africanized* within African markets to reflect nationalist movements and to symbolize cultural unity. African pop styles have deliberately maintained an indigenous sound through the use of traditional instruments to appeal to the Western audiences whose need for roots appeal to their own sense of communal loss. The growing demand for "authentic" African music by the world-music market place has profoundly affected the nature of the production of music, whose construction involves a complex trade in opportunity and exploitation, fantasy and imagination, style and recollection, appropriation, assimilation, and dispossession.[97]

In terms of distribution or dissemination of musical products, one can say that much has been well-done. Since the last decades of the twentieth century, for instance, Zaire (formerly the Belgian Congo and now the Democratic Republic of the Congo) has become a major dissemination center for modern African popular music; even long before that time, Radio Brazzaville (located in the former French Congo, which is now the Republic of the Congo) started becoming a favorite of West African listeners because of its coverage of modern popular music. There is no doubt that Radio Brazzaville has become influential in the spread of Congolese idioms within Africa. It was all these interactions that have brought members of distinct ethnic or linguistic groups together, as they find themselves interacting with and living alongside one another.[98]

Also in East Africa the manufacture and distribution of music has a long history. Nairobi has always been the hub of the East African music industry.[99] The first recordings in Kenya, as Angela claims, were made in 1902, shortly after the establishment of British colonial rule. Much trade in East Africa was conducted by Asian merchants, and by the 1920s, 78-rpm recordings served to attract consumers into their shops. The market potential for African music was soon recognized, and by 1928, musicians were being sent to Bombay to record for the Indian branch of the British HMV label. According to Impey, in East Africa, the market potential for African music was soon recognized, and by 1928, musicians were sent to Bombay to record for the Indian branch of the British HMV label. The first genre of music recorded was *taarab*, the music of Zanziba, and records of performance of *taarab* were distributed throughout Kenya, Tanzania, the Democratic Republic of Congo and Uganda. By the 1940s, non-Islamic popular music began to flourish, and styles generally called *dansi* began to be performed in all dialects. One of the first interethnic styles to emerge was *beni*, associated with British marching bands from WWI (1914–1918). This genre spread to Tanzania, and became known as *mganda*, then in Malawi as *malipenga*, in Zambia as *kalela*.[100] Today *beni* continues to be performed in modified forms in Malawi, northern Mozambique, and Zimbabwe.[101]

Furthermore, new African urban styles have also begun to appear at the height of the popularity of these commercial recordings. The music scene began to improve considerably at a time when migration slowly began to evolve in many African countries. For example, since the end of the (original) Kerekon regimes in Benin's capital Cotonou, many cities have begun to get more media exposure through a new private TV channel, and the private music radio stations have begun to spring up.[102] Cameroon, which was one of the last African countries to get a TV station, began broadcasting in 1985.[103] *Soukous* pop music began to take hold in international markets during the mid-1980s, when musicians began to record in Europe. *Highlife* music also began to flourish in some major cities of Europe and North America where recordings were made of resident and visiting bands.[104] There has been much greater development recently in concert performances, studio recordings, and mass media productions in most African countries, an environment that has given several musicians the opportunity to travel and perform both inside and outside the continent.

CONCLUSION

Much has been discussed in this essay, which covers all aspects of African musical performance practices, ranging from the traditional music, through neo-African art music and modern popular music. Under the section of the *African musical tradition*, we learned about African traditional music; how they are performed regularly as part of social events; how the music permeates the daily life of people in Africa; and how Africans' conceptual approach to the process of music making is a reflection of their collective cultural experiences.

We acknowledge that music in African tradition is fundamentally created to fulfill both practice and aesthetic functions, as it is always linked to some aspects of social activities or social occasions in which performances are judged by their social relevance. Thus, the totality of tradition, as emphasized, is an expression of cultural values dictated by the aesthetics defined and recognized by the people and their culture. We have also learned that a close look at the musical tradition always reveals a series of features and aesthetic preferences that are common to many Sub-Saharan African traditions. Therefore, by examining the whole continent of Africa, one finds more variation among the assorted cultures and nations; however, African music share identifiable common cultural characteristics.

The sections on *neo-African art music* and *modern-African popular music* examine the impact of the intervention of Western (European) cultures and music on Africa; the factors that facilitated the assimilation of foreign idioms in Africa; and the notable changes that brought in a significant impact on its musical culture. We have learned how such an impact provided the socio-economic and cultural basis for the growth and development of modern musical idioms, thus leading to the development of other new musical types, such as neo-African choral or vocal art and instrumental art music, and the new popular musical genres that emerged and developed alongside the indigenous musical traditions in Africa in the course of the twentieth century. These sections further discuss how these contemporary genres were built on the integration and blending of African musical idioms and foreign musical styles; how these elements emerged and struck a nerve throughout Africa, by bringing together concerts and dances of all ages and social classes; and how some of these styles began to spread throughout the continent, and continue to flourish in some major cities outside Africa.

There are, of course, various factors that led to the growth of neo-African music, such as inter-ethnicity (the product of de-ethnicized societies); urbanization (the development of modern urban centers); intercultural (the product of cultural-mix); Afro-Diaspora-Interaction; modernization (modern systems of commerce, communications and technology); and globalization (the development in increasingly integrated economy marked especially by trade, free flow of capital, etc.). However, these factors did not destroy African music traditions even though they had a strong impact on many societies. What can be embraced as obvious is the view that most of what is *unique* about African musical cultures is credited to the persistence of an African heritage.

ENDNOTES

1   Eileen Southern, "African Retentions in Afro-American Music (U.S.A.) in the Nineteenth Century," *Jamaica Journal* 43 (March 1979), 88.

2   Carol A. Muller, *South African Music: A Century of Traditions in Transformation*, (Santa Barbara, California: ABC-CLIO's, 2004).

3   Ruth M. Stone, 2008:20

4   Ewens 1991:24; cited in Angela Impey, "Popular Music in Africa," in *The Garland Handbooks of African Music*, 2nd edition, edited by Ruth M. Stone, New York: Routledge, 2008:124–2.

5   Olly Wilson, "The Association of Movement and Music as a Manifestation of a Black Conceptual Approach to Music Making," *Jamaica Journal* 43 (March 1979), 98.

6   Portia K. Maultsby, "Africanisms Retained in the Spiritual Tradition," *Jamaica Journal* 43, (Marck 1979):75–82.

7   Ruth M. Stone, "African Music in a Constellation of Arts," in *The Garland Handbook of African Music* (New York: Garland Publishing, 2000), 3.

8   Kofi Agawu, *Representing African Music: Post-Colonial Notes, Queries, Positions* (New York: Routledge, 2003), xiv.

9   Ibid.

10 Gregory Barz, *Music in East Africa: Experiencing Music, Expressing Culture* (New York: Oxford University Press, 2004).

11 Edna Marilyn Smith, *Music in West Africa: A Report of a Type C Project* (New York: Columbia University Press, 1961).

12 Ruth M. Stone, *Music in West Africa: Experiencing Music, Expressing Culture* (New York: Oxford University Press, 2005).

13 Barz, *Music in East Africa*.

14 Stone, *Music in West Africa*.

15 John Blacking, *Venda Children's Songs* (Johannesburg: Witwatersrand University, 1967).

16 Patricia Shehen Campbell, *Lessons from the World: A Cross-Cultural Guide to Music Teaching and Learning* (New York: Shirmer Books, 1991).

17 Ibid., 159.

18 J. H. Kwabena Nketia, *The Music of Africa* (New York: W.W. Norton, 1974); Francis Bebey, *African Music: A People's Art* (New York: L. Hill, 1975).

19 Campbell, *Lessons from the World*, 1991.

20 Nketia, *The Music of Africa*.

21 David Locke, "Africa/Ewe, Mande, Dagbamba, Shona, BaAka," in *World of Music: An Introduction to the Music of the World's Peoples*, 4th edition, ed. Jeff Todd Titon, et al (Stamford, United States: Schirmer Thomson Learning, 2002).

22 Akin Euba, "African Traditional Music as a Contemplative Art," in *Notes on Education and Research in African Music*, No. 2, (Legon, Accra: Institute of African Studies, 1975), 61–68.

23 Nketia, The Music of Africa; E. Kwadwo O. Beeko, *Creative Processes in Akan Musical Cultures: Innovations within Tradition* (Saarbrücken, Germany: VDM-Verlag Dr. Muller Aktiengesell Schaft & Co., 2009).

24 Smith, *Music in West Africa*; Nketia, *The Music of Africa*.

25 Barz, *Music in East Africa*.

26 Euba, "African Traditional Music as a Contemplative Art."

27 Barz, *Music of East Africa*.

28 Ashenafi Kebede, *Roots of Black Music: the Vocal, Instrumental and Dance Heritage of Africa and Black America*. (Englewood Cliffs, NJ: Prentice-Hall, 1982).

29 Bebey, Francis, *African Music: A People's Art* (New York: L. Hill Press, 1975).

30 Ibid.

31 Smith, *Music in West Africa*; Nketia, *The Music of Africa*.

32 Barz, *Music of East Africa*.

33 Nketia, *The Music of Africa*, 1974.

34 Ibid., 210.

35 Ibid., 218.

36 Ibid., *1974*.

37 Ibid., 208.

38 Peter Fletcher, *World Music in Context: A Comprehensive Survey of the World's Major Musical Cultures* (Oxford, UK: Oxford University Press, 2001).

39 Bebey, *African Music: A People's Art.*

40 Smith, *Music in West Africa.*

41 Nketia, *The Music of Africa.*

42 Ibid.

43 Fletcher, *World Music in Context.*

44 Nketia, *The Music of Africa.*

45 Robert A. Kauffman, "African Rhythm: A Reassessment," Ethnomusicology (September 1980), 403–404.

46 Fletcher, *World Music in Context.*

47 Stone, 2008.

48 Nketia, 1974:69.

49 Ibid., 69–84.

50 Stone, 2008.

51 Nketia, 1974:69.

52 Ibid., 92–97.

53 Ibid., 69.

54 Ibid., 98–107.

55 Ibid., 69.

56 Stone, 2008.

57 Nketia, *The Music of Africa.*

58 Euba, "African Traditional Music as a Contemplative Art."

59 Nketia, *The Music of Africa.*

60 Stone, 2008:18–19.

61 Stone, *Music in West Africa.*

62 Ibid.

63 Locke, "Africa/Ewe, Mande, Dagbamba, Shona, BaAka."

64 Fletcher, *World Music in Context.*

65 Barz, *Music of East Africa.*

66 Ibid., 16.

67 Stone, *Music in West Africa.*

68 Euba, "African Traditional Music as a Contemplative Art."

69 Stone, *Music in West Africa.*

70 Euba, "African Traditional Music as a Contemplative Art."

71 Ibid. See Beeko, *Creative Processes in Akan Musical Cultures*; E. Kwadwo O. Beeko, "Historical and Intellectual Determination of Identity: The Case of Kwabena Nketia's Akan Solo Pieces," in *The Life and Works of Emeritus Professor J. H. Kwabena Nketia: Festschrift Presented to J. H. Kwabena Nketia* (yet to be published).

72 Bode Omojola, *Nigerian Art Music, with an Introductory Study of Ghanaian Art Music*, (Ibadan: IFRA, 1995); Beeko, Creative Processes in Akan Musical Cultures.

73 Omojola, *Nigerian Art Music, with an Introductory Study of Ghanaian Art Music.*

74 Akin Euba, *Essays on Music in Africa 2* (Bayreuth: Iwalewa-Haus, 1989).

75 Angela Impey, 2008.

76 Beeko, *Creative Processes in Akan Musical Cultures.*

77 Euba, *Essays on Music in Africa 2.*

78 E. Kwadwo O. Beeko, "Toward a New Stylistic Identity: An Analytical Overview of Ghanaian Contemporary Choral Music," in *Composition in Africa and the Diaspora Series*, Vol. 2, (Richmond, CA: MRI Press, 2010).

79 Ibid.

80 Sten Sandahl, "Uganda: Exiles and Traditions," in *World Music: Africa, Europe and the Middle East* (The Rough Guide) Volume 1, Simon Broughton, Mark Ellingham, and Richard Trillo, eds. (New York: Penguin Books USA, 1999), 698–701.

81 Gregory Mthembu-Salter, "South Africa: Gospel Music: Spirit of Africa," in *World Music: Africa, Europe and the Middle East* (The Rough Guide) Volume 1, Simon Broughton, Mark Ellingham, and Richard Trillo, eds. (New York: Penguin Books USA, 1999), 658–659.

82 Beeko, "Toward a New Stylistic Identity"; Werner Graebner, "Tanzania Popular Music: Mtindo-Dance with Styles," in *World Music: Africa, Europe and the Middle East* (The Rough Guide), Volume 1, Simon Broughton, Mark Ellingham and Richard Trillo, eds. (New York: Penguin Books USA, 1999), 681–689; Rob Allingham, "South Africa: Popular Music—the Nation of Voice," in *World Music: Africa, Europe and the Middle East* (The Rough Guide), Volume 1, Simon Broughton, Mark Ellingham, and Richard Trillo, eds. (New York: Penguin Books USA, 1999), 638–657.

83 Graebner, "Tanzania Popular Music."

84 Impey, 2008:127.

85 Simon Broughton, Mark Ellingham, and Richard Trillo, eds. *World Music: Africa, Europe and the Middle East* (The Rough Guide) Volume 1 (New York: Penguin Books USA, 1999).

86 Impey, 2008.

87 Ronnie Graham and John Collins, "Ghana: Gold Coast—Highlife and Roots," in *World Music: Africa, Europe and the Middle East* (The Rough Guide) Volume 1, Simon Broughton, Mark Ellingham, and Richard Trillo, eds. (New York: Penguin Books USA, 1999), 488–498; Ronnie Graham, "Nigeria: From Hausa Music to Highlife," in *World Music: Africa, Europe and the Middle East* (The Rough Guide) Volume 1, Simon Broughton, Mark Ellingham and Richard Trillo, eds. (New York: Penguin Books USA, 1999), 588–600; Richard Trillo and Ed Ashcroft, "Sierra Leone: Palm-Wine Sounds," in *World Music: Africa, Europe and the Middle East* (The Rough Guide) Volume 1, Simon Broughton, Mark Ellingham, and Richard Trillo, eds. (New York: Penguin Books USA, 1999), 634–637.

88 Christopher Waterman, "Juju History: Toward a Theory of Sociomusical Practice," in *Ethnomusicology and Modern Music History*, Stephen Blum, Philip V. Bohlman, and Daniel M. Neuman, eds. (Chicago: University of Illinois Press, 1993); Ronnie Graham, "Nigeria: From Hausa Music to Highlife."

89 Jean-Victor Nkolo and Graeme Ewens, "Cameroon: Music of a Small Continent," in *World Music: Africa, Europe and the Middle East* (The Rough Guide) Volume 1, Simon Broughton, Mark Ellingham, and Richard Trillo, eds. (New York: Penguin Books USA, 1999), 444–447.

90 Doug Paterson, "Kenya: The Life and Times of Kenya Pop," in *World Music: Africa, Europe and the Middle East* (The Rough Guide) Volume 1, Simon Broughton, Mark Ellingham, and Richard Trillo, eds. (New York: Penguin Books USA, 1999), 509–522.

91 Graeme Ewens, "Congo: Heart of Danceness," in *World Music: Africa, Europe and the Middle East* (The Rough Guide) Volume 1, Simon Broughton, Mark Ellingham, and Richard Trillo, eds. (New York: Penguin Books USA, 1999), 458–471.

92 Rob Allingham, "South Africa: Popular Music," in *World Music: Africa, Europe and the Middle East* (The Rough Guide) Volume 1, Simon Broughton, Mark Ellingham, and Richard Trillo, eds. (New York: Penguin Books USA, 1999), 638–657.

93 J. H. K. Kwabena Nketia, The Arts in Contemporary Contexts: An Overview (Paper presented at An International Conference on the Performing Arts of Africa, 1979); Allingham, "South Africa: Popular Music,"; Beeko, *Creative Processes in Akan Musical Cultures.*

94 Impey 2008:126.

95 Barz, *Music in East Africa;* Beeko, *Creative Processes in Akan Musical Cultures.*

96 Impey, 2008:126–27.

97 Ibid., 127–28.

98 Ewens, "Congo: Heart of Danceness."

99 Paterson, 1994:337; cited in Impey, 2008.

100 Ranger, 1975:x; cited in Impey, 2008:135.

101 Impey, 2008:135.

102 Richard Trillo and Erica Audra, "Benin and Togo: Afro-Funksters," in *World Music: Africa, Europe and the Middle East* (The Rough Guide) Volume 1, Simon Broughton, Mark Ellingham, and Richard Trillo, eds. (New York: Penguin Books USA, 1999), 432–436.

103 Nkolo and Ewens, "Cameroon: Music of a Small Continent."

104 Graham and Collins, "Ghana: Gold Coast—Highlife and Roots."

REVIEW QUESTIONS

1. Identify and discuss the various social events that constitute the overall life stages or lifecycle of the individual in African societies.
2. What are the social events or the occasions that are marked by musical performance, and what specific musical items are used for the occasion?
3. What are the different sound qualities that the singers use during singing? Give examples of the various performance styles that are incorporated into the music-making events.
4. Explain how African dances are used as a social and artistic medium of communication.
5. In addition to setting music in a social context, music in Africa is also associated with other expressive media. What are these media?
6. What are the differences in the developments of neo-African choral music and neo-African gospel music?
7. What features do neo-African choral music and neo-African gospel music share in common?
8. Give examples of the neo-African popular musical types that originated or started relatively as *palm-wine* music.
9. From which neighboring countries in Africa did *soukous* music originated as a musical genre during the 1930s and early 1940s?

Writing Prompt

1. That music is life and that music learning occurs through life experiences—such as a mother's lullaby, children's game songs, songs of passages through life stages, and occupational songs—seems to be a perspective shared generally by Africans. Choose *one* country in Africa as a case study and discuss *one* of these life experiences during which certain types of music are used.
2. In Africa, there are various social events that constitute the overall life stages or lifecycle, such as naming ceremonies, puberty rite initiations, marriage ceremonies, and funerals that are marked by musical performances, and occasions during which specific musical items are performed. Choose *one* country in Africa as a case study and discuss *one* of these life stages during which specific music is always performed.
3. Several modern African popular musical genres emerged and developed throughout the twentieth century and the early twenty-first century, alongside the indigenous traditional music in the urban centers of many countries in the sub-Saharan region of African. Choose *one* of the modern popular musical types performed in a particular country (or countries) in Africa and discuss it by looking at (a) its origin and development; (b) its characteristic features (African and Western elements); (c) the musical instruments used; (d) its performance; and (e) examples of bands that perform that type of popular music.

CHAPTER 12

European Expansion and the Scramble for Africa

Michael Kasongo

European colonization of Africa was a monumental milestone in the history of the continent. The "Scramble for Africa," as African colonial rule was dubbed, is a striking example of attempt by historians to recapitulate the historical process by means of metaphor. "Scramble" suggests rapid and confused activity. The popular conclusion has long been that the opening up of Africa in the nineteenth century was done with great haste and reckless abandon. Within the incredibly short period between 1880 and 1900, all of Africa except Liberia and Ethiopia capitulated to the European imperial powers of Britain, France, Germany, Belgium, Portugal, Spain, and Italy. Africans were then converted from sovereign and royal citizens of their own continent into colonial and dependent subjects.[1] The impact of colonization on Africa is perhaps the most important factor in understanding the present condition of the African continent and the African people. Therefore, a scrutiny of the phenomenon of colonialism is necessary to appreciate the degree to which it influenced not only the economic and political development of Africa, but also the African people's perception of themselves. The Scramble was carried on in three stages. The first was the conclusion of treaties between African rulers and European imperial powers. The second was the signing of bilateral treaties between the imperial powers. The third and final stage was the European conquest and occupation of their spheres. First, however, it is important to understand the factors that set the stage for the imposition of European rule in Africa.

The circumstances surrounding colonialism have been a matter of contention among historians, both African and European, and have been discussed at length. The main focus of this chapter is to examine some contributing factors common to most explanations. Although the chronological order of the events may be listed differently by some historians, they all agree that economic, political, and social factors, as well as the unofficial mind, led to the European imperialism. The factors mentioned above are not mutually exclusive; indeed, they are very much interrelated. For example, the expansion of capitalism and the desire for profits led the European patriots to contribute to their country's grandeur by laying claim to other countries overseas. They believed that colonial possessions conferred prestige and status. Evidence of cultural arrogance can be found in the statements of the European explorers, missionaries, and humanitarians.

THEORIES OF COLONIALISM

Many theories have been used to explain European colonialism of Africa. Economic factor is the most crucial. The source of European scramble for Africa was the unprecedented development of forces and relations of production that is usually referred to as the Industrial Revolution but could more properly be called the breakthrough of Industrial Capitalism. It led to a tremendous increase in production and productivity. Having started in the latter half of the eighteenth century in the British cotton industry, industrial capitalism spread at the turn of the century to Belgium and France and then to Germany and the United States.

These developments created in the industrialized and industrializing countries an urgent need for colonies whose markets could become their exclusive monopoly. It became equally urgent to obtain raw materials to feed the new European factories; and again, these materials—cotton, palm, phosphates, oil, rubber, ivory, rubber, peanuts, minerals, among other things—could be obtained or developed in the tropical areas of Africa. Outside of the mining and petroleum industries, very few of these economic activities required great capital investment in order to be realized.[2]

As the European economics expanded, captive markets in the developing world were needed for disposing of surplus goods. The desire for wealth, trade, resources, and cheap labor did certainly motivate European expansion into Africa. According to the economic theory of imperialism, colonization had everything to do with greed and very little, if at all, to do with race or religion.[3]

Besides the economic forces, there were also political forces precipitating the European Imperialism. The most important of these political factors was an exaggerated spirit of nationalism in Europe, following the unification of both Germany and Italy and especially after Germany's defeat of France in 1871. With the emergence of a strong national consciousness, nations began to think not only of their power and progress, but also of their prestige, greatness, and security.

It was during the latter part of the nineteenth century that nationalism became a major force in European politics. One manifestation of this was that people began to think in terms of national statistics and interests. Nationalism in itself plainly was nothing new, but its appeal as a political force increased greatly while its political content was transformed. European ruling elites found it increasingly expedient to harness national sentiments, based on shared language and popularized through the spread of primary education and literacy, to the purposed of political mobilization.

Political mobilization through the device of the nation-state, defined as a political unit consisting of an autonomous state inhabited predominantly by a people sharing a common culture, history, and language. Leaders in states that had long claimed a national character, such as Britain and France, put ever more emphasis on prestige and status, while others, such as Germany and Italy, created quite "new" nation-states. The rise of this militant nationalism led not only to a heightened rivalry among the European states but also a shift in their internal power relations. The men who made the ultimate historical decision on the participation of Africa were neither industrial or other capitalists, nor lobbyists, but holders of state power, including sovereigns, top ministers and a handful of high officials in the major European countries. The partition of Africa was essentially a state action, not a private venture.[4]

In Europe, the number of overseas colonies a nation possessed became a measure or symbol of its prestige and greatness. Portugal, then regarded as "the sick man of Europe," Germany, and later Italy all rushed for colonies overseas to prove that they had acquired a place in the sun. France did so to prove that she was still a great power despite her humiliating defeat by Germany in 1871.

For the individual, claiming land overseas in the name of country became the highest mark of patriotism. There were several examples of European patriots who contributed to their country's grandeur by laying claims to other countries in distant lands. Karl Peters' adventures in East Africa secured Tanganyika for his Kaiser, German emperor. Cecil John Rhodes' exploits in Central Africa yielded a huge chunk of territory for his British king. Henry Morton Stanley's expeditions to Africa paved the way for the Belgian King Leopold II to acquire the Congo.[5]

The main social condition contributing to the rise of the European expansion and the Scramble for Africa was the need to acquire colonies where the surplus labor produced by the industrial system as well as the large number of the unemployed could be settled. The late nineteenth century was a period of unprecedented and unrepeated population growth in Europe. The total population of Europe rose from 144 million in 1750 to 423 million in 1900.

One of the implications was that people were now pushed to move over the seas to other continents. European rulers advocated the "opening up" of African markets or the linking of a part of European emigration to Africa as a means of relieving the distressed condition of working classes in Europe and, by implication, keeping them from falling victim to socialist agitation. The European powers, such as France, Portugal, Germany, and Belgium, that applied direct rule, brought thousands of men and women from Europe to work in administrative, educational, church, medical, military and business institutions.

Even David Livingstone, who is usually considered the explorer most concerned with African welfare, understood his vision of flourishing agricultural communities to be set up in Central Africa as a measure to improve the condition of the poor in Britain. However, the social reason for colonization was deeply rooted in the ethnocentrism and cultural arrogance of the European people, who regarded anyone different as being culturally inferior. Because Africans were not technologically advanced or the rest of the world did not know their achievements, the Europeans felt that it was their duty to "civilize" and "uplift" the African people.[6] Europe justified its colonization of Africa on grounds that it was its moral duty to take the light to the "Dark Continent."

It has been established that the Scramble was an endeavor of European imperialist rulers, or the Official Mind. The Unofficial Mind, however, also played a role. It is made up of non-governmental individuals and institutions whose voices were attracting attention to Africa before the Age of Imperialism. These individuals came from quarters and motives that can be called *religious, humanitarian, scientific,* and *personal*. However, it has to be acknowledged that such categories are loose and often overlapping with varying social content.

The religious aspect of the Unofficial Mind was the spread of Christianity in Africa, which was part of a larger global movement. The writings and reports of David Livingston, a Scottish missionary, doctor, and explorer, who helped open the heart of Africa to missions, and Henry M. Stanley, a naturalized American, born in Wales, who was a journalist and explorer famous for his exploration of Africa, stimulated missionary fervor to a high water mark during the 1880s and 1890s.

The revivals set in motion by Dwight L. Moody, an American evangelist, also contributed to a great expansion of missionary work in the latter part of the nineteenth century. This missionary spirit was the religious aspect of a broader socioeconomic and political movement that looked beyond the limits of national boundaries. The French missionaries, for example, believed that their native country had been commissioned by God to preach the gospel and to extend the Kingdom of Christ overseas while enlarging the frontiers of their own territorial empire.[7]

The missionaries' attitude toward expansionism and colonization was generally positive. They had much to gain from the peaceful conditions and protection provided by the colonial government, and in fact most missionaries favored territorial acquisitions and some worked actively to bring them about. *Pour Dieu! Pour la France!* was a recognizable Catholic approach, while English Anglican missionaries put constant pressure on the British Foreign Office to incorporate new territories into the empire.[8]

The missionaries believed that they should offer to other peoples the elements in Western civilization that they valued for themselves. Speaking at an interdenominational Conference of Foreign Missionary Boards and Societies in 1893, a Presbyterian clergyman said:

> The great work of Foreign Missions is God-ordered. This must be the end of all controversy. At no other period in the world's history has the Church of God had such resources as she has today in money to carry the Gospel to all lands. No other generation has ever had, all things considered, such power to grapple with the needs of the heathen world. No other generation has witnessed such God-given mastery of physical forces and useful inventions, so that all lands can be easily reached. The great birthday in the Kingdom of God is at hand. . .[9]

Major British missionary societies, which had sprung from the religious revival in the late eighteenth century, went to work first in South and West Africa and in the 1840s in East Africa, to be followed by the French, the Germans, and the others.

Sometimes intermingled with Christian missionary concerns was the humanitarian strand of the Unofficial Mind: the British anti-slavery campaign. The abolitionist argument was extended to include a concern not only for the African slaves, but also for Africa: the slave trade and slavery were to be attacked at their roots, inside the "Dark Continent."

Scientific interest was at first primarily geographical: filling in the white spaces on the "Africa maps." The Association for Promoting the Discovery of the Interior Parts of Africa was founded in London in 1788 and merged in 1830 with the newly founded Royal Geographical Society; the Societe de Geographie was established in Paris in 1821 and the Gesellschaft fur Erdkunde in Berlin in 1828. These societies and many later ones dispatched expeditions to the interior of Africa that were sometimes financially supported by their respective governments. Those who were successful brought back material for the maps to be drawn by home-based geographers. Later also representatives of other sciences, especially anthropology, were furnished with materials from "exotic" lands by African explorers.

Travelers themselves were a mixed collection. Some subscribed to humanitarian ideals and harbored scientific ambitions; many were drawn to Africa by a hope of gain, a love of adventure, and just plain curiosity.[10]

STAGES OF THE SCRAMBLE FOR AFRICA

Again, the term "Scramble" refers to the frantic pace that characterizes the partition and colonization of Africa by European powers between 1880 and 1900. However, the first of the three stages of the Scramble really began slightly earlier and maintained a more leisurely pace until the growing number of European powers gone imperialist and the magnitude of their aspirations created a new sense of urgency.

Four major events that took place before 1800 provided the foundation for the eventual scramble for Africa in the 1880s and 1990s. The first was Britain's occupation of Egypt and the Cape Colony, which contributed to a preoccupation over securing the source of the Nile River. Egypt was occupied by British forces in 1882 (although not formally declared a protectorate until 1914 and never a colony proper). The Cape Colony, which was acquired by the British in 1795, provided a base for the subjugation of neighboring African states and the Dutch African settlers. The second event was the dispatch of three French missions to explore routes for the trans-Saharan railway. The third was the appointment of Major Gustave Borgnis-Desbordes as the commander of the Upper Senegal to push French imperial interests inland. The fourth was the dispatch of Stanley by the Belgian king and de Brazza by the French king to conclude treaties with the rulers of the Congo basin.

Pierre de Brazza raised the French flag over the newly founded Brazzaville in 1881, thus occupying the French Congo. Stanley also explored the Congo Kingdom in the early 1880s on behalf of King Leopold II of Belgium, who made the Congo territory his personal property. While pretending to advocate humanitarianism and denounce slavery, Leopold II used the most inhumane tactics to exploit his newly acquired lands.

The Congo Free State was seventy-five times larger than Belgium. It imposed such a terror regime on the colonized people, including mass killings of victims and slave labor, that Belgium, under pressure from the international community, ended Leopold's rule and annexed the Congo Free State in 1908 as a colony of Belgium, known as the Belgian Congo. According to the official records, up to 8 million of the estimated 16 million native inhabitants died between 1885 and 1908 in the King Leopold's personal property called, ironically, Congo Free State.[11]

The sudden intrusion of Stanley and de Brazza greatly alarmed Portugal and Britain, which had hitherto regarded that area as their exclusive preserve, and they therefore began their counter-moves. To checkmate both the French and Leopold, Britain backed Portugal on the Congo issue, while her interests in the Bight of Benin and Biafra, now threatened by the French who sent Hewett to declare a protectorate over the Oil Rivers and the Cameroons in May 1884.

With the entry of Germany, the scramble was well and truly on. It was with a view of formulating rules for the conduct of the ongoing race in order, particularly, to avoid any armed confrontations among the imperial powers that an international conference was held in Berlin from November 15, 1884, to January 31, 1885, under the chairmanship of Bismarck, the Chancellor of Germany. Although fourteen countries, including the United States, attended the Berlin Conference, no African state was invited to attend.[12]

Bismarck had not been a notable friend of imperialism up to this point. He believed that colonies were expensive to acquire and almost never paid off. Besides, rivalry over colonies added unnecessarily to international tension. But Bismarck knew that the intensely nationalistic German public was wild about empire.

German people were saying and writing that "because all Great Powers have empires, Germany should have one."[13] Always an astute politician, Bismarck realized he would have to make some concessions to the public enthusiasm for colonies. This would require immediate action, before the British and French had managed to seize everything in Africa.[14]

Bismarck wanted not only to expand German spheres of influence in Africa, but also to play off Germany's colonial rivals against one another to Germany's advantage. Of these fourteen nations, France, Germany, Great Britain, and Portugal were the major players in the Conference, controlling most of colonial Africa at the time. The measures agreed by the Berlin Conference included the following:

(a) Leopold II was given the green light to establish a commercial monopoly over the Congo region; eventually, the area would be known as the Congo Free State. In return, the king promised to make the Congo a free trade zone, to open its rivers to all comers, to fight the slave trade, and to save the indigenous populations from the evils of drink.

    (b) The French and British positions in West Africa were frozen; no new coastal areas were to be acquired and no deals to exchange territories were to be struck.

    (c) Germany received title to Togo and Cameroon in West Africa, and South West Africa in southern Africa.

    (d) The participants in the conference agreed that henceforth claims for control over territories could not be accepted unless they were effectively occupied. It would have to be shown, for example, that officials of the European claimant were resident in the interior and that indigenous peoples of the region recognized their authority.[15]

All these rules were embodied in the Berlin Act, ratified on February 26, 1885. This act, then, cleared the last main hurdle in the way of the Scramble of Partition—that of a possible military conflict between the imperialists—and European occupation continued with renewed vim and vigor from then on. It should be emphasized that the Berlin Conference did not start the scramble for Africa but merely accelerated a race that was already in progress. Italy belatedly entered this race with her occupation of the Eritrean coast in 1889.

The Scramble was carried on in three stages. The first stage of the Scramble for Africa was the conclusion of treaties between African rulers and European imperial powers. According to these treaties, African rulers were usually accorded protection and undertook not to enter into any treaty relation with another European power. European countries were granted certain exclusive trading and other rights.

Between 1880 and 1895, the British concluded treaties with many rulers in northern Ghana and Yorubaland and Benin in Nigeria and offered protection to the king of Asante. During the same period, the French signed treaties with Ahmadu of the Tukulor Empire, with Samori Ture and the king of Dahomey, and with some of the rulers of the Congo basin. Some of these treaties were in fact forced on the Africans, a typical example being the treaties between the British East Africa Company and Buganda in 1890 and 1892. In other cases, the treaties were fraudulently obtained by European colonists with the help of missionaries who misinterpreted the real contents of those papers that non-literate African leaders signed. In some cases, the African rulers were deceived or misled into signing treaties that contained clauses whose full meaning and implications were not explained or even made known to them. That such tricks were played was admitted even by Lord Lugard, the leading British imperialist agent, himself.[16]

The second stage was the signing of bilateral treaties between the imperial powers usually based on the earlier treaties of protection that defined their spheres of interest and delimited their boundaries. European states were laying claim to coastal regions and navigable rivers and were defining on paper the boundaries running inland from these first footholds. The bilateral treaties were accomplished with surprisingly little bloodshed and conflict. The reason for this was that the first occupying groups consisted of small, mobile expeditions of European officers or chartered-company officials accompanied by a few dozen lightly armed porters, scarcely distinguishable from the expeditions of the first explorers.

Africa itself was so immense that these first little groups of Europeans seldom came into contact with each other. Their attitude to the African peoples had necessarily to be that of negotiators rather than conquerors. They entered into the local politics of every region that they came to, supporting the groups and factions that had some reason to be friendly and avoiding those which were hostile.

Toward the close of the nineteenth century, when forces were somewhat larger and when the final, interior frontiers were being claimed, meetings between rival European expeditions became more frequent. By the Anglo-German Treaty of 1890, Germany recognized British claims to Zanzibar, Kenya, Uganda, Northern Rhodesia, Buchuanaland, and eastern Nigeria; the Anglo-French Treaty of the same year laid down the western boundary of Nigeria while Britain recognized French claims to Madagascar.

The Franco-Portuguese Treaty of 1886 and the German-Portuguese Treaty of 1891 accepted Portugal's supremacy in Angola and Mozambique and delimited Britain's sphere in Central Africa. It should be emphasized that these European bilateral treaties were concluded without any consultations whatsoever with the African states.[17]

The third and final stage was that of the European conquest and occupation of their spheres. This phase has been described in typical Eurocentric terms as the phase of pacification. It was, however, the bloodiest and the most brutal of all the stages of the scramble from the Afrocentric standpoint.

Collisions occurred between the occupying forces and those of the larger and more organized African states, which often fought desperately for their survival. Numerically, the armies of these states often outnumbered the European expeditions by many hundreds to one, but the technological advancement of European weapons was overwhelming. A single machine gun could put to flight a whole army of undisciplined men armed only with less sophisticated weapons.

According to historical records, Africans reacted differently to the creeping European imperialism and that the initiatives and responses of each state or group were very much influenced by several factors. These included political and social structure of each state, its level of contact with Europeans and Islamic influences, the prevailing political and environmental conditions at the time, and the methods adopted by the European imperialists to establish their control over the group.

Also, as has been seen already, the Scramble was accomplished in three different phases, and each stage generated its own type of reactions. The available evidence indicates that Africans devised three main strategies during the period under review. These were submission, alliance, and confrontation.[18]

While some African rulers and leaders stuck to one strategy throughout, several others used a combination of these strategies. Some African rulers used the first strategy of submission. Aware of the futility and cost of confronting the imperialists and because they themselves urgently needed European protection, some rulers readily submitted to European invaders. In French West Africa, M'backe of Sine and Guedal M'bedj of Salum in the region of Senegambia submitted. So did nearly all the Yoruba states of Nigeria, including Abeokuta, Ibadan, Oyo, Ekiti, and Ijesa. In southern Africa, the rulers of the Ngwato, Lozi, Sotho, Tswana, and Swazi also surrendered readily. The second strategy was that of alliance. Some African rulers formed alliances with the European powers. They did it not to further the interests of the European imperialists or even to gain their own selfish ends, but to preserve the sovereignty and independence of their states. King Mbandzeni of the Swaza, for instance, asked for British protection against the Boers and the European concessionaries; the emir of Nupe similarly invited the French to form an alliance with him against the British Royal Niger Company. The King of Daboya in northern Ghana also sought the British alliance.[19]

The third and final strategy Africans resorted to in the face of European colonial imperialist aggression and occupation was confrontation. As already indicated, there were two variants of this strategy, the armed or military form and the peaceful or diplomatic form. Relatively few African rulers decided to stick to diplomacy alone as a means of maintaining their independence. Many African rulers, however, adopted the militant option. In southern Africa, the major African nations of the area, such as the Zulu, Ndebele in Zimbabwe; Bemba in Zambia; Yao in Malawi; Ovimbudu, Lunda, and Chokwe in Angola; and Manyike and Makua in Mozambique fought the British and the Portuguese in defense of their lands. In Central Africa, the Yeke, Chikunda, Bakongo, Chewa, and Dinka forcefully opposed the Belgians and British. In East Africa, the Nandi, Masai, Akamba in Kenya and Mbunga, Makonde, Hehe in Tanzania also forcefully resisted the British and the Germans. In West Africa, Ijebu, one of the Yoruba states, and the northern Nigerian states, namely Nupe, Iliorin, and Sokoto Empire opted for militant confrontation with Britain.[20]

Although the Europeans enjoyed triumphant technology in gun designs, they had to rely on local warriors. European officials were able to recruit large armies of African troops. The nineteenth-century European armies, faced with pressing commitments elsewhere and still fearful of tropical diseases and hostile African climate, turned to indigenous soldiers to wage war on their behalf in Africa.

The availability of these African soldiers was largely the result of the internal African politics in the nineteenth century, as empires expanded and retracted and smaller states rose and fell. The decline of African states (and sometimes also their growth, as in the case of Samori's empire in Guinea) gave the European invaders the opportunity to insert themselves into local political disputes and, ultimately, to divide and conquer. Taking advantage of the internal conflicts between African states and the civil wars, European invaders were able to draw the workers they needed to build their armies.[21]

Before the Berlin Conference, France occupied Tunisia in May 1881 and entered Bamako, the capital of Mali, in 1883. These actions convinced Italy to adhere in 1882 to the German-Austrian Dual Alliance, thus forming the Triple Alliance. After the Berlin Conference, the French took steps to consolidate their possessions on West African coast. From 1885 the French began their invasions and occupations in the western Sudan and conquered Cayor in 1886 and Soninke Empire of Samori in 1898. The British also moved troops and occupied Ijebu in 1892, Asante in 1896, Benin in 1897, the Sudan in 1899, and the Sokoto Empire between 1900 and 1904. The Germans conquered and occupied what became known as German East Africa between 1888 and 1907.

By 1893, the colonies of the Ivory Coast and French Guinea had been officially established. In the same year, French troops entered Dahomey, which became a French colony in 1900. The French moved into the central Sudan from three directions: from the Niger Valley, from Gabon, and from Algeria.

By 1900, expeditions from all three were converging on Lake Chad. In 1894, the French troops took Timbuktu, and they took Say in 1896. In 1895, the French General Gallieni came from his campaigns in West Africa to conquer (or "pacify," as this action used to be called) Madagascar, which was declared to be a French colony.

Federation of the French West African Colonies (AOF) was founded in 1895, and the Federation of the French Equatorial African Colonies (AEF) was founded in 1910. As to the northern part of Africa, the last two territories were seized by the European powers. France and Spain partitioned Morocco, Spain taking the smaller portion. Italy entered the scramble in order to gain its "place in the sun."[22]

Following the defeat of the First Italo-Ethiopian War (1895–1896), it acquired Italian Somaliland in 1889–1890 and the whole of Eritrea in 1899. In 1911, Italy acquired Tripolitania and Cyrenaica (modern Libya) from the Ottoman Empire. The Second Italo-Abyssinian War (1935–1936) ordered by Mussolini, was one of the last colonial wars. Italy occupied Ethiopia for five years, which had remained the last African independent territory apart from Liberia.[23]

In 1900, the British government took over the control of northern Nigeria. The British expansion continued in the direction of Bornu and Lake Chad. Kano was occupied in 1902. However, in Central Africa, the British government had left the task of occupation to Cecil Rhodes and his British South Africa Company.

The company was incorporated by Royal Charter in 1889 and was empowered to develop the region between Bechuanaland and the Zambezi, which became Northern Rhodesia. South of the Zambezi, Rhodes's agents founded the Southern Rhodesian capital at Fort Salisbury. Nyasaland became a protectorate under the direct control of the British government in 1891.

Rhodes was the prime minister of the Cape Colony from 1890 to 1896. In addition, he directed the activities of the British South Africa Company in the territories to the north. Rhodes had visions of uniting the whole of southern Africa, including the Boer republics, as a self-governing dominion under the British flag.

Following the Anglo-Boer War (1899–1902), the Boer republics were conquered by the British troops, which created the British colonies. These colonies later formed part of the Union of South Africa. The whole of South Africa was in British hands. By 1910, the European occupation of Africa had been completed and the colonial system had been imposed.[24]

CONCLUSION

By as late as 1880, with very few exceptions, Africans were enjoying their sovereignty and were very much in control of their own affairs and destinies. However, within a short period between 1880 and 1900, all of Africa except Liberia and Ethiopia was seized and occupied by the European imperial powers of Britain, France, Germany, Portugal, Belgium, Italy, and Spain. By the 1900s, in place of the numerous African independent states and polities, a completely new set of some only forty artificially created colonies had emerged. Governors and officials were appointed by their metropolitan governments and were in no way responsible to their African "subjects" administered these colonies.

By 1910, the colonial system had been firmly imposed on virtually the whole of Africa. The circumstances that led to the Scramble or the Partition of Africa that were examined in this chapter include economic, political, social, religious, humanitarian, scientific, and personal. The Industrial Revolution created in the industrialized and industrializing countries an urgent need for colonies whose markets could become their exclusive monopoly.

Besides the strong economic factors, there were also political forces, the most important of which was the exaggerated spirit of nationalism in Europe. The main social condition contributing to the rise of the European expansion and the Scramble for Africa was the need to acquire colonies where surplus labor and the large number of unemployed Europeans could settle.

The fourth and the last cause of imperialism was labeled as the Unofficial Mind. While the Official Mind represents the European governmental officials who participated in the Scramble for Africa, the Unofficial Mind was made up of non-governmental individuals and institutions whose voices drew European attention to Africa before the Age of Imperialism. These individuals came from quarters and motives that can be called religious, humanitarian, scientific, and personal.

Regardless of the fact that the Europeans had a foot in Africa, they still felt the need to set some ground rules for the Scramble. This was achieved through the international Berlin Conference during 1884–1885. Four main rules were agreed upon at the conference.

As discussed in this chapter, the Scramble was accomplished in three different stages. Each stage generated its own type of reactions. These were submission, alliance, and confrontation. One can also point out that the era of European dominance in Africa was rather brief—in most cases it was clear by 1955 that independence was just a matter of time in most colonies. German rule in Africa was the briefest of all colonial regimes, having begun in the late 1880s and having terminated with the signing of the Treaty of Versailles in 1919, following their defeat in World War I. Germany was deprived of all her colonial possessions, which were parceled out to the victorious allies as trust territories under the League of Nations Mandate system. Tanganyika (which is the mainland portion of Tanzania) went to Britain. Rwanda and Burundi, which together with Tanganyika formed what was called German East Africa, went to Belgium. Cameroon was split into two, a small western portion going to Britain and the remainder to France. Namibia, then known as South West Africa, was assigned to South Africa as a sort of trophy for South Africa having fought in the war on the side of the allied powers. Togo, then called Togoland, became a French trust territory, but a small sliver along its western border to Britain, which governed it together with Ghana.

Table 12.1: Table 12.1 shows how Africa was divided among European powers

Belgium

Congo Free State and Belgian Congo (today: Democratic Republic of Congo)
Ruanda and Urundi (comprising modern Rwanda and Burundi, 1922–1962)

France

French West Africa	French Equatorial Africa	French Algeria
Mauritania	Gabon	(now Algeria)
Senegal	Middle Congo	Tunisia
French Sudan	(now Republic of Congo)	French Morocco
(now Mali)	Oubangi-Chari	French Togoland
French Guinea	(now the Central African	(now Togo)
(now Guinea)	Republic)	
Cote d'Ivoire	Chad	French Somaliland
Niger	Madagascar	(now Djibouti)
French Upper Volta		Comoros
(now Burkina Faso)		
French Dahomey (now Benin)		

Germany

German Kamerun, 1884–1916 (now Cameroon)
German East Africa, 1885–1919 (now Rwanda, Burundi and most of Tanzania)
German South-West Africa, 1884–1915 (now Namibia)
German Togoland, 1884–1914 (now Togo)

Italy

Italian North Africa (now Libya)
Italian Eritrea (now Eritrea)
Italian Somaliland (now part of Somalia)

Table 12.1: (Continued)

Portugal	
Portuguese West Africa (now Angola)	Cape Verde Islands
Portuguese Congo (now Cabinda Province of Angola)	Sao Tome Island
Portuguese East Africa (now Mozambique)	Principe Island
Portuguese Guinea (now Guinea-Bissau)	Fort of Sao Joao Baptista de Ajuda (now Ouidan)

Spain	
Spanish Sahara (now Western Sahara)	Spanish Morocco
Rio de Oro	Saguia el-Hamra
Tarfaya Strip	Spanish Guinea (now Equatorial Guinea)
Ifni	Fernado Po
Rio Muni	Annobon

ENDNOTES

1 Raymond F. Betts, *The Scramble for Africa: Causes and Dimensions of Empire* (D.C. Health and Company, 1972), 7.

2 Raymond F. Betts, *Europe Overseas: Phases of Imperialism* (Basic Books, 1968), 58–60.

3 Juhani Koponen, "The Partition of Africa: A Scramble for a Mirage?" *Nordic Journal of African Studies* 2 (1993), 128.

4 A. Adu Boahen, *African Perspectives on Colonialism* (Baltimore, MD: The Johns Hopkins University Press, 1989), 31.

5 Vincent B. Khapoya, *The African Experience: An Introduction* (New York: Longman, 2010), 110.

6 Toyin Falola, *Key Events in African History: A Reference Guide* (London: Greenwood Press, 2002), 178.

7 Robert Delavignette, *Christianisme et Colonialisme* (Paris: Fayard, 1960), 49–51.

8 Ibid., 71.

9 *Report of the Interdenominational Conference of Foreign Missionary Boards and Societies in the United States and Canada, held in the Presbyterian Mission House*, New York, January 12, 1893, Union Theological Seminary Library, Richmond, Virginia, Archival material.

10 Juhani Koponen, "The Partition of Africa: A Scramble for a Mirage?" *Nordic Journal of African Studies*, Vol. 2 (1993), 128.

11 Adam Hochschild, *King Leopold's Ghost: A Study of Greed, Terror, and Heroism in Colonial Africa* (New York: Mariner Books, 1999), especially ch. 8. "Where There Aren't No Ten Commandments," 115–139.

12 A. Adu Boahen, *African Perspectives on Colonialism*, 33.

13 Bruce Vandervort, *Wars of Imperial Conquest in Africa, 1830–1914* (Bloomington: Indiana University Press, 1998), 35–37.

14 Ibid.

15 Ibid.

16 A. Adu Boahen, *African Perspectives on Colonialism*, 38.

17 Ibid., 34.

18 Ibid., 39.

19 Ibid., 37.

20 Ibid., 45–50.

21 Bruce Vandervort, *Wars of Imperial Conquest in Africa, 1830–1914*, 29–30.

22 Roland Oliver and Anthony Atmore, *Africa Since 1800* (New York: Cambridge University Press, 2004), 131.

23 Ibid., 143.

24 Ibid., 145.

REVIEW QUESTIONS

1. Why was European colonialism of Africa inevitable? Discuss the causes of the Scramble for Africa?
2. What is the Berlin Conference? Why was it convened? How did it impact the scramble for Africa?
3. Discuss the various initiatives and reactions of the Africans in the face of the European imperialist activities.
4. Discuss the impact of the Unofficial Mind on the Official Mind during the Age of Imperialism.

Writing Prompt

Select one country in Africa and discuss its experience with colonialism and colonial polices, the peoples' responses to social transformation of their societies, and the ways they engaged with the process of colonial rule.

CHAPTER 13

The Economic, Political, and Social Impact of the Atlantic Slave Trade on Africa

Babacar M'Baye

The Transatlantic slave trade radically impaired Africa's potential to develop economically and maintain its social and political stability. The arrival of Europeans on the West African Coast and their establishment of slave ports in various parts of the continent triggered a continuous process of exploitation of Africa's human resources, labor, and commodities. This exploitative commerce influenced the African political and religious aristocracies, the warrior classes and the biracial elite, who made small gains from the slave trade, to participate in the oppression of their own people. The Europeans, on the other hand, greatly benefited from the Atlantic trade, since it allowed them to amass the raw materials that fed the Industrial Revolution to the detriment of African societies whose capacity to transform their modes of production into a viable entrepreneurial economy was severely halted.

Between the sixteenth and the nineteenth centuries, millions of Africans were forcefully sold and transported to Europe and the Americas as slaves. Known as the Atlantic slave trade (hereafter the Atlantic trade or the Atlantic commerce), the forced auction and relocation of Africans into Europe and the Americas was part of a global economic enterprise that lasted from the 1440s to the 1860s. This commerce spread from the Western coast of Africa to the rest of the continent, winding its course from the islands of Gorée and Saint-Louis, in current Senegal, to Quelimane, in present Mozambique.[1]

The Atlantic trade affected the lives of millions of Africans who came from such diverse regions such as Senegambia, Sierra Leone, West-Central Africa, South-East Africa, the Bight of Benin, the Gold Coast, and the Bight of Biafra. While the effects of the Atlantic trade on the enslaved Africans have been partly documented, those on the non-enslaved Africans remain largely unknown.[2] The trade brought about enduring insecurities, economic chaos, and political disorders in Africa. It arrested its development by exploiting its technological, agricultural, and cultural skills for the development of the West only. It hampered Africa's mercantilist economy by halting its capacity to be transformed into a capitalist economy. Moreover, it started the systemic and continuous process of economic exploitation and social and political fragmentation that Europeans later institutionalized through colonization and neocolonization.

Furthermore, the Atlantic trade led to the formation of semi-feudal classes in Africa that collaborated with Europeans to sanction the oppression of their own people. These classes came from the African aristocracy and middlemen who facilitated the capture and sale of Africans and made substantial gains from the trade. Yet, despite these gains, Europeans, not Africans, benefited from the trade the most. Europeans received from the trade unprecedented human labor and economic capital that allowed them to develop their societies at the expense of Africa.

HISTORICAL BACKGROUND

The Atlantic slave trade was initially a small commercial system based on the exchange of African material or human capital, such as gold or slaves, with few European material goods, such as guns and silk. By the end of the sixteenth century, this trade became a large market that promoted the barbaric capture and transportation of millions of Africans to the Americas. The commerce started in 1441 when ten Africans were taken from the Mauritanian coast and shipped to Lisbon. Three years later, 240 Africans from the same coast were brought to Lisbon.[3]

It is often said that Europeans did not begin the Atlantic trade and that they simply tapped into a human trade that already existed in Africa. While domestic forms of slavery and the trans-Saharan slave trade existed in Africa prior to the arrival of Europeans in the 1400s, these had a lesser impact on the continent than did the Atlantic trade. The latter surpassed the earlier trade in terms of the immeasurable loss of lives and resources it brought about in Africa and the Black Diaspora.[4] The three forms of slavery relegated Africans to an inferior social status and deprived them, partly or wholly, of their freedom. They legitimized the removal of Africans from their homeland and their relocation in foreign territories. Yet, the Atlantic trade differed from African slavery and Arab slavery because it was founded on a unique and rigid concept of bondage.[5] Unlike the Arabs and Africans, Europeans had a theory of slavery in which conversion to the religion of the master or marriage with the master did not prevent a person and his/her descendants from inheriting the status of a slave.[6]

Despite this fundamental difference, these forms of slavery complemented each other, because the slave markets that Europeans established in Africa developed out of the earlier Arab and African trades. The Portuguese, whose navigation system was better than those of any European empire of the 1400s, traded in African gold, ivory, gum, hide, wax, and slaves, which the Arabs had dominated for centuries. By the end of the fifteenth century, the Portuguese had total control over this commerce. As Basil Davidson documents: "By about 1506, Duarte Pacheco Pereira is writing that the goods exchanged at Arguim and elsewhere consist of gold, black slaves, oryx leather for shields, and other items, against Portuguese red and blue stuffs and various textiles, both poor and good quality, as well as horses."[7] This anticipates Philip D. Curtin's argument that the Africans received from European traders more than "worthless goods such as cheap gewgaws, beads, rums and firearms." According to Curtin, African importation of European textile increased from 28.2% in 1730 to 58.9% in 1830 before plummeting to 4% in 1860, casting doubt on the role Africa played in the development of European export products before the nineteenth century.[8] Joseph Inikori, however, questions the credibility of the Inspector General's Ledgers of Imports and Exports of Great Britain, on which Curtin based his study of the yearly value of commodity exports from Britain to the African coast from 1797 to 1808:

> Any calculations of British slave exports based on these figures of commodity exports will, of necessity, understate, the quantity of slaves exported because, in the first place, a large proportion of the goods employed in the purchase of slaves on the African coast by British citizens were taken from ports outside Britain and were therefore not included in the Inspector General's accounts; in the second place, the latter accounts have been found seriously to understate both the volume and value of goods exported from Britain to Africa and elsewhere.[9]

Inikori suggests that Britain's economy made substantial profit from the Atlantic trade and, specifically, from the importation of African slaves. Anticipating Inikori's thesis, Eric Williams pointed out that England was devastated when the 13 American colonies announced in 1783 their withdrawal from its control, fearing that independence would lead to the collapse of its economy by removing its manufactures from American markets. Therefore, in July 1783, the British Order in Council decreed a Treaty with the colonies that allowed England to import slaves from its former US colonies. The effect was a catastrophic 50% increase in British imports from North America between 1784 and 1790.[10] Meanwhile, the English had secured their ongoing importation of slaves from Africa at unbeatable prices. Between 1680 and the 1730s, the price of a slave on the African Slave Coast rose from £3 to £10, and between 1700 and 1790, England imported 10 billion cowry shells for use on the Coast and spent only £1 for 2,000 shells.[11] Consequently, the African population taken to the British colonies in the West Indies grew drastically, as Williams notes:

> With free trade and the increasing demands of the sugar plantations, the volume of the British slave trade rose enormously. The Royal African Company, between 1680 and 1686, transported an annual

average of 5,000 slaves. In the first nine years of free trade Bristol alone shipped 160,950 Negroes to the sugar plantations. In 1760, 146 ships sailed from British ports for Africa, with a capacity for 36,000 slaves; in 1771, the number of ships had increased to 190 and the number of slaves to 47,000. The importation into Jamaica from 1700 to 1786 was 610,000, and it has been estimated that the total import of slaves into all the British colonies between 1680 and 1786 was over two million.[12]

These statistics are among the most quoted estimates of the number of slaves that were brought to the United States and to the Caribbean from the sixteenth to the nineteenth century. The disparity between the number of slaves who embarked from Africa and of those who disembarked in the Caribbean, the United States, and Brazil between 1580 and 1840 is shown in the following:

Caribbean
Slaves embarked from Africa: 4,084,565
Slaves disembarked in the Caribbean: 3,446,600

United States
Slaves embarked from Africa: 317,748
Slaves disembarked in the United States: 270,976

Brazil
Slaves embarked from Africa: 1,308,479
Slaves disembarked in Brazil: 1,165,366.[13]

These numbers derive from Curtin, who argues that nearly 9.4 million Africans were enslaved in the Americas while about 175,000 were brought to Europe and the African Atlantic islands.[14] Corroborating Curtin's assessment, Postma adds that, "allowing for an estimated 12 to 15 percent mortality rate during the Atlantic crossing, approximately eleven million must have been shipped from Africa. Some scholars believed that Curtin's figures were too low, but more and more data were collected, new estimations deviated only slightly."[15] Inikori, one of Curtin's critics, argues "that they resulted from some unspecified bias on Curtin's part and that a more accurate count would be just over 15 million."[16] While he recognizes that scholars have contested the global figure of 15.4 million, Inikori admits that "the ultimate figure is unlikely to be less than 12 million or more than 20 million captives exported from Africa in the transatlantic slave trade."[17]

The divergence between Curtin's and Inikori's estimations epitomizes the differences in the interpretation of the history of the Atlantic trade. For example, according to David Henige, Louise-Marie Diop-Maës argues that the population of Africa, on the eve of the slave trade, was as great as 270 million and that "such a dense population must have been predicated on agrotechnological capabilities on a par with those of Europe at the time." Diop believes that "the slave trade involved a loss on the order of 100,000,000 persons," double Inikori's estimate. She rejects the theory that disease and famine took the lives of more Africans than the slave trade did.[18] Disproving this theory, Diop argues that:

1. The evidence of the exported number of slaves and that of the multiple kidnappings, raids, contradict the notion that there were 4 or 5 inhabitants in Africa in every km^2.

2. The population density of Africa during the fifteenth and sixteenth centuries was at least 15–20 inhabitants per km^2 for a total population of 300–400 million people.

3. The idea of under-population must be abandoned, because even the population density of Europe was about 10 inhabitants per km^2 from the fifteenth to the seventeenth centuries.

4. In the late fifteenth and early sixteenth centuries, better climate and sophisticated pre-industrial economy supported the lives of 600–800 million Africans with an average population density of 30–40 inhabitants per km^2.[19]

Diop's thesis suggests that Africa was not undeveloped at the beginning of the Atlantic trade; its populations had demographical, climatological, and agricultural conditions that allowed them to develop in their own contexts. Recognizing this fact requires us to remove the notion of development from the capitalist framework in which it is commonly understood. Walter Rodney describes this capitalistic framework as the correlation of "economic development" with "factors of production" such as "land, population, capital, technology, specialization, and large-scale production." For Rodney, these factors are limited, because they do not mention "the exploitation of the majority which underlay all development prior to socialism," "the way that factors and relations of production combine to form a distinctive system or mode of production, varying from one historical epoch to another," and the manner in which imperialism is "a logical phase of capitalism."[20] Thus, assessing the level of Africa's development at the time of the trade requires us to subtract the inestimable consequences of slavery, imperialism, and colonization on its economic, social, and political development.

ECONOMIC IMPACTS

Africa did not play a secondary role in the Atlantic trade system. Africans dominated the local commerce of resin, orchil, gold, spices, cattle and people before the Europeans arrived, proving that Europe's political and commercial powers on the Atlantic coast were far less important than historians assume. Thornton comments on the high purchasing power of West Africans in 1650 when, in search of fancy and variety, 1.5 million Senegambians imported 1,200 tons of iron for 300,000 households, and, in 1680, needed 300 tons of iron a year just for their households. Since the Portuguese brought little iron to Africa, where else but in Africa could they get it? In other words, Africans were economically self-sufficient and socially stable when Europeans came to trade with them. Thornton points out that "the Atlantic trade of Africa was not simply motivated by the filling of basic needs, and the propensity to import on the part of Africans was not simply a measure of their need or inefficiency, but instead, it was a measure of the extent of their domestic market."[21] Yet, within less than a century of commerce with the Western world, Africa lost both its economic autonomy and social peace, becoming a land where local states, chiefs, and warlords allied with insatiable European traders to oppress the vulnerable populations they captured, as Inikori argues:

> The European demand for more and more captives soon gave rise to the formation of groups of bandits all over western Africa. In places where the foundations already laid had not yet given rise to firmly established large political organization, the process was hijacked by these bandits. . . . Overall, the conditions created by the large-scale European demand for captives over a period of more than three hundred years severely retarded the long term process of socio-economic development in western Africa.[22]

The disruption of Africa's political structures and socio-economic potentials was part of the stagnation of Africa's technological progress caused by the slave trade. As Rodney has shown, the trade affected Africa's economy by bringing about a loss of industry, skills, technological invention and production of Africans. On the one hand, Rodney argues that "what Africa experienced in the early centuries of the trade was precisely a loss of development *opportunity*," that is, the ability to achieve the self-sustaining growth and progress that its enslaved young population could have secured. On the other hand, he contends that the trade took away *opportunity* by disorienting the purpose of African traders: "In Africa, the trading groups could make no contribution to technological improvement because their role and preoccupation took their minds and energies away from production."[23] By contrast, the trade benefited the West by developing its technology with the importation of skilled Africans of all ages. This importation marked the beginning of Africa's brain drain that continues to hamper development in the continent.

The economic impact of the Atlantic slave trade on Africa varied according to time and geographic context. The Senegambia (including the Senegal and the Gambia rivers) was the first sub-Saharan region the Portuguese encountered in the 1460s. Here, the Portuguese settled in the Cabo Verde Island and the James Island and intermarried with neighboring Africans who later became invaluable suppliers of local goods. For most of the fifteenth century, the Portuguese traded in gold from the Banbuk goldfields of the Gambia–Senegal hinterlands, hides from the savanna cattle herders, and other local products along with slaves who came both from the coast and from the savannas of the Upper Niger interior. Africans from the interior traded in European products such as iron, cotton, mats, and textiles. In return, the Africans received products such as guns, liquor, beads, mirrors and some slaves. In the seventeenth and eighteenth centuries, the Atlantic commerce started to have profound effects on the size of the African population that was rapidly decreasing. Between 1450 and

1850, in rough terms, over 11.5 million people were exported from the Atlantic coast of Africa, nearly 10 million of whom arrived in the New World.[24] The trade, according to Inikori, had substantial economic impact on the local African economies:

> It is generally accepted that the export centers on the African coast benefited economically and demographically from the trade. Where they succeeded in insulating themselves from the socio-political upheavals provoked by the trade in their hinterlands, these port towns (or city states) realized short-term benefits that have been equated with private gains. Market production of agricultural commodities to meet the limited needs of the slave ships for foodstuffs was stimulated, their populations expanded as the coastal traders retained some of the captives for their business needs and for the production of their subsistence products, and so on. These port towns or city-states typically grew as enclave economies.[25]

In the eighteenth and nineteenth centuries, the Europeans brought retail goods to local African markets such as those in the Gorée Island (in Senegal), El Mina (in Ghana), and Alladah and Whydah (in the former Kingdom of Dahomey, today called Benin) and further inland. The Dutch created the Gorée slave house in 1776, many years after the English first built the James Fort in James Island in The Gambia in 1661. The El Mina Castle was a major commercial base established by the Portuguese in El Mina, Ghana, in 1482. The Dutch constructed the slave fort in Alladah early in the seventeenth century, while the French built the fort in Whydah in 1671. European goods—silks, linen handkerchiefs, Indian cloths, and china—became available not only to African dignitaries but also to the population at large, as long as they could afford the price. These goods became more abundant as the trade progressed and became cheaper.[26] In this respect, Africa was not a passive participant in the Atlantic slave trade. Thornton criticizes French annalistes, such as Fernand Braudel and Pierre and Hugette Chaunu, who claimed that Africa did not make substantial contributions to the development of the Atlantic World. Refuting this Eurocentric assumption, Thornton shows that Africa's long-held maritime and international commercial culture along the Egyptian Nile, the Nile of Sudan, the Niger, and the Senegal River had given the continent autonomy, experience, and economic power that predated the Atlantic commerce and which later dictated its rules and regulations.[27] Klein confirms Thornton's argument:

> Long-term contact with the Islamic states in North Africa and the Near East, and even long-distance trade between Asia and East Africa prior to the arrival of the Europeans, meant that Africans could negotiate from a reasonable knowledge of international markets what items of European or even Asian production most appealed to them.

While it shows the sophisticated level of the African commercial system at the beginning of the trade, Klein's statement, like Thornton's, conjures up the troubling, yet inevitable, notion that some Africans used their genius to profit from a trade in human beings. The controversial idea that the African economy profited from the slave trade often centers on Klein's logical question: "If Africans were definitely not passive economic actors, what about the price they received for their slaves?"[28] Klein's query introduces the economic dimensions of the trade, which, when considered, show how the trade was ultimately detrimental to Africa no matter what pittance local African merchants received from it. It was Europeans, not Africans, who eventually benefited from the trade. Donald Wright provides astounding statistics on the financial gains made from African slaves in the pound sterling currency:

> In the 1680s one healthy adult slave cost an English buyer on average 5.47 [£], but that price rose gradually to 9.43 [£] in the 1720s, 10.05 [£] in the 1740s, 14.10 [£] in the 1760s, and 20.95 [£] in the 1780s. Profit is evident in prices for slaves in the American market. A healthy adult slave in Virginia in 1690 brought 15 [£], in 1760, 45 [£].[29]

Another factor that suggests that the Atlantic trade had negative impacts on Africa's economy was the prevalence of European and African raiding, capture, and torture of Africans from the coasts and the hinterlands. These disruptions prevented Africans who were not involved in the trade from doing business in peace and security without the threat of being kidnapped and sold to Europeans, as Inikori indicates: "It is difficult for many studying the slave trade to imagine any kind of economic growth under the conditions of violence and insecurity that the trade promoted."[30] It is equally impossible to presume that Africa's economy could have remained developed during a brutal period when it was increasingly based solely on the sale of slaves, as Davidson explains:

> After about 1650, with diminishing exceptions, African production-for-export became a monoculture in human beings. This can be seen to have suffocated economic growth in coastal and near-coastal Africa as surely as the extension of European production-for-export of consumer goods gave the maritime nations of Europe, at the same time, their long lead in economic development.[31]

The metaphor of "suffocation" is appropriate: the trade stifled the continent's technological and commercial potentials, preventing Africans from being on the same economic level—the playing field—where they would have been had the Europeans not exploited them so viciously and for so long. Had history unfolded differently, Africans would have realized that the trade was going to benefit Europeans only; they would have collectively and radically opposed the trade in all its forms.

POLITICAL IMPACTS

The political impact of the Atlantic trade is visible in the changes it wrought in African societies. It subverted the existing political balance in traditional African societies. Since slavery became a dominant source of revenue in the continent, personal wealth was thought to derive from one's ability to help capture and sell one's neighbors or criminals to strangers. As a consequence, the scenario Europeans created became a Darwinian universe in which the African turned into a wolf preying on other Africans. James Searing argues that in the 1770s, the King of the Geej Dynasty organized several grand pillages in the Kajoor and Bawol Kingdoms in north-western and central Senegal, kidnapping slaves who were later sold to the Europeans on the Gorée Island.[32] Likewise, the territories of the Coniagui and the Bassari, in eastern Senegal, were "preserves for slave-hunt" before they became the main suppliers of slaves for Europeans to the detriment of the Dioula, Mandjaque and other populations who settled by the rivers of the South.[33] These raids resulted from clashes among Africans, spurred by growing European competition in the continent. Martin Klein sees the increase in raids in Senegambia as the effect of the newly introduced cultivation of peanuts in the 1830s, and cites an Englishman's account: "As soon as each [Senegambian] has been able to purchase a horse and a gun, he considers himself a warrior, lives by plunder and works his field by the slaves he captures in his expeditions, and thinks it beneath his dignity to perform any work whatsoever, which is left to women and slaves."[34] This suggests the violence, chauvinism and classism that resulted from the new forms of social and economic relationships, centered on the combination of slave ownership and peanut production. Unlike slave ownership, peanut production was new to the continent. The Portuguese had introduced groundnuts to Africa in the sixteenth century in the Upper Guinea Coast. They probably learned to cultivate the vegetable from the South American Indians, since, as George Brooks argues, the plant existed there before Columbus traveled to this hemisphere. Yet it was from Africa that peanuts were later introduced into North America, by way of the West Indies, during the Atlantic trade.[35]

Before 1830, the cultivation of peanuts in Africa was minimal and mainly served to feed horses. Yet, as Brook suggests, "peanuts came to be grown in the drier areas of the Senegambia as a safeguard against failure of the millet harvest, and along the coast to the southwards as a subsidiary food crop of marginal, though increasing, consequence." Between 1830 and 1840, the production of peanuts increased dramatically as the British, French, Portuguese and African chiefs competed in a lucrative market in which slaves and peasants paid the highest price for its cultivation and sale: "Spurred by European and Eurafrican coastal traders, African agriculturalists opportunistically responded to the new market opportunities with remarkable swiftness. Wherever peanut production spread, it occasioned far-reaching economic and social changes for the African societies concerned."[36] A major impact of the introduction of this crop was the drop in millet production, formerly a staple food and commercial product. Focusing on the upper basin of the Senegal River, where the Galam Kingdom used to be, the Senegalese historian and political leader Abdoulaye Bathily argues that millet was a primary foodstuff for the inhabitants of the empire and a major part of the economic history of the region during the eighteenth century. In 1720, 1731, 1737, 1744, 1753, and 1754, both the inhabitants of Galam and those of the French ports in the territory suffered from millet shortages due to a series of raids from the Moors and from the Xaaso and the Bambuxu kingdoms that were rivaling Galam.[37] Part of this crisis derived from a climate change that resulted in poor agricultural yields and famine. While Bathily believes that it would be vain and false to claim that "natural calamities" such as drought, inundations, locust invasions, and epidemics are the determining factors that led to famine and food shortage in Senegambia during the seventeenth and eighteenth centuries, Charles Becker argues that some natural factors affected the living conditions in that region. Yet, as Becker suggests, raids, wars, and migrations created more food crises and death in Senegambia than did climate factors,[38] arising primarily from the raids that the peanut rush encouraged among the Wolof states, which was so detrimental for the more reliable and nourishing cultivation of millet. As a result, the Wolof states became dependent on a staple that was mainly designed for western consumption. According to Brooks, Allan McPhee described the trade in peanuts and palm oil before the mid-nineteenth century as "a reflex action of the Industrial Revolution" and "a consequence of the growing demand in industrializing countries for oils and fats of all kinds."[39]

Another predicament arising from peanut cultivation in Senegambia was the formation of a feudal class that depended on a lower class that produced or collected peanuts and Arabic gums. The French, who had promoted this systemic oppression in Senegambia, later sought to fight it by giving slaves who had escaped from the African empires the opportunity to declare their freedom once they reached their forts. The irony was that the planter–slave relationship that the French had promoted among the African chiefs was so solid that it became integrated even in societies that were fighting for the spread of Islam. Klein gives the example of Ma Ba Jaxoo (or Maba Diakhou Ba), the King of Saloum, in West-Central Senegal, who tried to convert the Serer people of Sine and encouraged the enslavement and execution of "pagans" or their exploitation as peanut farmers. When Maba died in 1867, his lieutenants "were primarily slave-raiders."[40] The continuous raids in Africa, after the abolition of slavery in the West, were due to the feudal and anarchic class relationships that the Atlantic trade had promoted. In this sense, as Searing points out, slavery among Wolof states was "linked to the rise of aristocratic power, but also contributed to a process of peasantization and thereby reinforced the social groups who came to oppose the aristocracy. The attempt of the aristocracy to create a regime based on slavery was never entirely successful, and slavery was only one form of dependency in a regime that also exhibited seigniorial features."[41]

In Senegambia too slave ownership had a political function that added to the African kings' dominance of the peasantry. It allowed kings to impose their hegemony on surrounding kings and provided them with ways to procure individuals to sell to Europeans. Discussing slave raiding in Kajoor, Senegal, in the 1770s, Searing writes:

> State violence served the interests of the monarchy in several ways. Slave sales paid for military expeditions by providing revenues to purchase guns and horses, which were needed to defend dynastic interests, to intimidate villagers enough to ensure tribute payments, and to keep foreign military predators at bay. If slave raids eliminated or weakened independent populations who refused to pay tribute, they also contributed to the state's broader effort to tax the population. . . . In spite of its brutality, the state was weak and used naked force to support its authority.[42]

This suggests that slave raiding did not evolve out of the Kajoor chiefs' reckless use of force, but from their calculated strategy to resist domination and strengthen their position in a highly unstable and economically competitive region. Thus, it resulted from new traumatic human and economic relations imposed by the slave trade as much as from differentiations between Africans on grounds of caste, class, or creed.

Another negative impact the Atlantic trade had on the political life of Africans was the formation of a pseudo-feudal class which Europeans created in major slave islands after their intermarriage with some Africans. In the four Senegalese regions, then called "les quatres communes," including Gorée, Dakar, Rufisque and Saint-Louis, a new Afro–French class, the "métisses" or "mulâtres" emerged at the top of a local political hierarchy that included local mayors, subordinates and slave soldiers. This hierarchy of corrupt individuals facilitated the slave and economic policy of the French in the country.[43] The stratum was maintained by an Afro–French upper class that organized the capture, stockage and sale of slaves. According to Inikori, historians such as

Claude Meillassoux, Martin Klein, and Paul Lovejoy have argued that such small-sized geographic areas, dominated by corrupt political and military aristocracies, led to the creations of African societies that were inimical to capitalist development. Inikori also notes the emergence, during the nineteenth century, of a slave warrior class in Senegal, the "Ceddo," which brought about such widespread insecurity and exploitation that even the Muslim leadership in West and East Africa could not subdue: "This Islamic alternative, intended to contain the disruptive effects of the Atlantic trade, was soon caught up in the vicious circle of the forces it sought to control and ended up depending on slaving for survival."[44] This allows us to introduce Lovejoy's transformation thesis, which holds that warfare, political fragmentation, and dependency became endemic in Africa as a result of the massive scale of the slave trade, forced upon Africans by commercial and military pressures:

> The external demand for slaves and the rivalry between African states directly affected the spread of slavery, for both caused tensions that led to the enslavement of people. The economy became dependent upon exports to satisfy the personal desires of merchants and rulers and to provide many parts of Africa with a money supply, textiles, firearms, and other goods that were essential to the economy and political rule. The fragmented political structure, reinforced by military purchases and the need to acquire slaves to finance imports, was related to a general state of insecurity that facilitated enslavement. These two conditions, the slave market and institutionalized enslavement, set the stage for the extension of slavery in Africa.[45]

Lovejoy illustrates this process with the examples of the Songhay, Borno and Kongo empires in which increasing interest in slave raids and trade and continuous political fragmentation led to collapse. Before the nineteenth century, Songhay was the largest state in Africa, yet in 1591, a Moroccan army crossed the Sahara and invaded it. The empire was so decentralized that it was unable to consolidate political power to resist the invasion. As a result of its vulnerability, the Songhay empire fell into a state of confusion and political instability. A similar downfall occurred in the state of Borno, in the sub-Saharan region, which was actively engaged in slave raiding to finance its trade with the Ottoman Empire in North Africa. Borno hoped that this alliance would grant it legitimate hegemony south of the Sahara. Borno's policy produced adverse effects such as increasing slave raiding and limiting conversion to Islam. Along the West Coast, rivalries between the Kongo, Oyo, the Gold Coast, and Guinea Shores brought about increasing political disintegration and small-scale states: "Between 1650 and 1750, two larger states emerged in the coastal zone: Oyo after 1650 and Asante after 1700, but they were never very large."[46] The root cause of the downfall of these states was the expansion of empire through war and slavery, instigated by the European Atlantic trade.

SOCIAL IMPACTS

The question of the social impact of the Atlantic trade on Africa is difficult to tackle because it is here that intense emotions and the weight of collective memory press most heavily. Contemporary Africans are constantly told that the present state of their societies derives from their "ugly" and "savage" participation in the slave trade. While some historians have approached the matter objectively, others have merely reiterated the myth of African savagery. Curtin explains the historical misconceptions that underlie the denigration of Africa:

> Some historians have been too willing to accept, and to interweave into their own specific research, some of the assumptions earlier Europeans had made about Africa—usually without research. Among these was the belief that African economies must have been static. It follows from the myth of a savage, and it led to the assumption of African weakness and perhaps inherent inferiority.[47]

These misconceptions are reinforced by stereotypes that go so far as to question the very humanity of Africans. Oliver Ransford develops the eugenicist theory that "the trade deprived the continent of its most valuable genes. As a result for generations Negro Africa lay dazed, helpless, and exhausted." He continues: "As a legacy to their descendants they [Africans] left no benefits or improvements but merely a traditional belief that it was cleverer to get rich quickly than to work hard; today easy money is still regarded with approval on the coast." But the greatest insult is in the following:

> The man-hunt which raged through Africa bred and sustained inter-tribal hostility, and so contributed to the present-day instability of the continent's internal relationships. The wars fomented by slavers also unmasked the demon of brutality which lurks in the background of the Negro soul no less than it haunts the white men's; for centuries it knew no moral censor and burst out of control. The Africans' dark obsession with death and evil spirits, their grotesque and awful superstitions, the macabre humour and relish with which they explore the depths of other people's fears and torments, were all now released and given full rein. Even today, one sometimes senses among Africans a feeling that they regard such evil passions as meritorious and healing, and in this context we may recall the screaming theme of the modern black militants whose flavours was so clearly projected by Franz Fanon when he preached that Violence is a cleansing force.[48]

Clearly, Ransford is misinformed; the present political and social problems that confront Africa have nothing to do with any biological, psychological, behavioral, or spiritual characteristics or values of Africans. The roots of the predicament facing Africa are in the structural, economic, and political disruptions that the continent inherited from the European slavers and colonizers. African societies have difficulty in advancing their economic development because the constitutions that they inherited from European powers do not reflect the structural realities of their societies. Instead of understanding Africa's problems in the context of its history, Ransford makes the fatal mistake of confusing colonization with precolonization. The militant theme of violence that Fanon preached was an intellectual commitment that sought to rid Africa of colonial exploitation, not to subject her to it. Fanon never celebrated violence of Africans against Africans.

However, there is no doubt that the slave trade created tremendous social problems in Africa, and that these problems have drastic effects on its current realities. Surely, the demography of Africa was greatly affected by the unprecedented transportation of African populations to foreign lands. As Klein points out:

> It is argued that the population of western Africa actually declined by 2 million between 1700 and 1850. The estimate is that the western African population declined from a projected 25 million to 23 million in this 150-year period. Had the population grown at a conservative 0.3 percent per annum in the same period, it would have reached 39.3 million in 1850.[49]

In addition, as shown earlier, a dominant factor in the enslavement of Africans was the participation of some Africans in the trade. In their response to European demands, some Africans created social systems of production that proved to be beneficial to Whites and detrimental to Blacks. Claude Meillassoux shows that these systems were founded on a constant and permanent transfer of human beings within a four-dimensional organic and economic space:

- the societies within which slaves were captured, which represent the milieu in which they were produced, demographically and economically;
- the aristocratic slave-owning societies which made use of a military apparatus to tear these human beings from the milieu in which they were produced and reproduced;
- the merchant societies which controlled the commercial apparatus necessary for the sale of captives;
- the merchant societies which were consumers of slaves.[50]

The irony is that these social networks, traditionally based on legality and respect toward the individual domestic slave, later became tyrannical systems of kidnapping vulnerable individuals during the eighteenth and nineteenth centuries. By abducting and selling Africans to Europeans, the African social networks, supported by African political leaders, became agents of tyranny and social insecurity against Africans. This sense of insecurity finds expression in Olaudah Equiano's memory from his childhood in Benin (Nigeria):

One day, when all our people were gone out to their works as usual, and only I and my dear sister were left to mind the house, two men and a woman got over our walls, and in a moment seized us both, and, without giving us time to cry out, or make resistance, they stopped our mouths, and ran off with us into the nearest wood.[51]

Another social effect of the trade was the widening gap between social classes. Inikori has argued that the trade produced islands of growth and prosperity that contrasted sharply with the misery and poverty of the raided populations.[52] Once slave ownership became the basis of economic success, it became quite impossible for poor Africans to achieve success. Only the brave and corrupted individuals such as "the slave warriors" could profit from it. For example, "the dynastic factions in the principal African states of the agricultural regions south of the Senegal River—Kajoor, Bawol, Waalo—became dependent on slave warriors for the power they exercised."[53]

The sexual demography of the continent also changed as a result of the trade. By comparing the percentage of male and female slaves landed in the West Indies between 1781 and 1798, Inikori found that "the number of females annually exported was of a magnitude that must have drastically reduced the region's capacity."[54] Strong evidence supports Inikori's thesis. Claire C. Robertson and Martin A. Klein have shown that in Mombassa and in the Upper Zaire, female slaves used to do as much work as free women. They grew indigo, made dye and helped their mistresses with dyeing cloth.[55] When the trade took most of the men away, women slaves were asked to take their jobs. Thornton cites Lemos Coelho, a Portuguese traveler, on the roles of slave women on the Bissago Islands in the late seventeenth century: "They are the ones who work the fields, and plant the crops, and the houses in which they live, even though small, are clean and bright, and despite all this work they still go down to the sea each day to catch shellfish."[56] Thornton explains that, "because of the established institution of polygamy, the almost undiminished numbers of women were able to counterbalance some of the losses to the slave trade by continued reproduction."[57] Thornton points to the important role of keepers of their communities that African women played not just in the continent but also in the Western world, where many of them had been enslaved with African men and children whose full stories remain to be told.

CONCLUSION

The Atlantic slave trade had drastic impacts on African societies. Initially conceived by both Europeans and Africans as a small-scale enterprise for the exchange of goods and a few slaves, it later became a ruthless and demonic machine that drained Africa's human and economic resources. By massively responding to Europe's growing demand for slaves, African societies started up a commercial process that progressively hampered their economic, political and social developments. The trade inflated Africa's economy by reducing it to a monoculture based on the sale of human beings. As a result, the once strong and developed African states lost their stability and became fragmented by internal and external conflicts that still affect the continent today. Surely, the current economic and social problems that plague contemporary Africa have their roots in the Atlantic trade. The unprecedented violence among African societies, ethnic groups and states, and the subversion of social and gender roles which resulted from such anarchy would never have taken place had the Atlantic trade, followed by imperialism and colonialism, not taken root in Africa. What therefore needs to be taken into account in the study of the Atlantic slave trade is the force of these historical circumstances and not the so-called "evil" nature of the African.

ENDNOTES

1 Samir Amin, "Underdevelopment and Dependence in Black Africa: Origins and Contemporary Forms," *The Journal of Modern African Studies* 10.4 (December 1972): 505.

2 Ivan Van Sertima, "Black History: African Civilization is a Shattered Diamond," *USA Today*, 23 February 1989, 09A.

3 Johannes Postma, *The Atlantic Slave Trade: Greenwood Guides to Historic Events, 1500–1900* (Westport, CT: Greenwood Press, 2003), 5.

4 Stephen Behrendt, "The Transatlantic Slave Trade," *Microsoft® Encarta® Africana* CD ROM (Microsoft Corporation, 1999).

5 For a discussion of the differences between European and African concepts of slavery, see Suzanne Miers and Igor Kopytoff, "African 'Slavery' as an Institution of Marginality," in *Slavery in Africa: Historical and Anthropological Perspectives*, ed. Suzanne Miers and Igor Kopytoff (Madison, WI: University of Wisconsin Press, 1977), 3–81; and Wyatt MacGaffey, "Economic and Social Dimensions of Kongo Slavery," in *Slavery in Africa*, ed. Miers and Kopytoff, 235–57.

6 For a discussion of instances of flexibility within Arab forms of slavery, see J. O. Hunwick, "African Slaves in the Mediterranean World: A Neglected Aspect of the African Diaspora," in *Global Dimensions of the African Diaspora* (Washington, DC: Harvard University Press, 1993), 289–323; Pekka Masonen, "Trans-Saharan Trade and the West African Discovery of the Mediterranean," in *Ethnic Encounter and Culture Change*, ed. M'hammed Sabour and Knut S. Vikør (London: C. Hurst & Co., 1997), 116–42.

7 Basil Davidson, *The African Slave Trade: Pre-colonial History, 1450–1850* (Boston: Brown and Company, 1961), 39.

8 Philip D. Curtin, *Economic Change in Precolonial Africa: Senegambia in the Era of the Slave Trade* (Madison, WI: University of Wisconsin Press, 1975), 309. See also J. Suret-Canale, "La Sénégambie a l'ère de la traite," *Canadian Journal of African Studies* 11.1 (1977): 126.

9 Joseph E. Inikori, "Measuring the Atlantic Slave Trade: An Assessment of Curtin and Ansey," *Journal of African History* 17.2 (1976): 205–6.

10 Eric Eustace Williams, *Capitalism and Slavery* (1944; New York: Capricorn Books, 1966), 124.

11 In addition to these figures, Herbert Klein argues that between 1680 and 1760, the price of a slave in Africa increased from 1,000 shells to 8,000 shells. See Herbert S. Klein, *The Atlantic Slave Trade* (Cambridge: Cambridge University Press, 1999), 110, 113, 114.

12 Williams, *Capitalism and Slavery*, 32–33.

13 *The Trans-Atlantic Slave Trade: A Database on CD-ROM* (1999).

14 Philip D. Curtin, *The Atlantic Slave Trade: A Census* (Madison: University of Wisconsin Press, 1969), 268.

15 Postma, *The Atlantic Slave Trade*, 35.

16 Inikori, "Measuring the Atlantic Slave Trade," 197–223; Joseph E. Inikori and Stanley Engerman, "Introduction: Gainers and Loosers," in *The Atlantic Slave Trade: Effects on Economies, Societies, and Peoples in Africa, the Americas, and Europe*, ed. Joseph E. Inikori and Stanley Engerman (Durham, NC: Duke University Press, 1992), 5–6; Postma, *The Atlantic Slave Trade*, 35–36; Mohamed Mbodj and Charles Becker, "A Propos de l'histoire et des populations de l'Afrique Noire: Propositions Pour de Nouvelles Approches," *Canadian Journal of African Studies* 23.1 (1989): 42–43.

17 Inikori and Engerman, *The Atlantic Slave Trade*, 6.

18 David Henige criticizes both Diop and Inikori for their estimates: "Conversely, taking advantage of the opportunity to base himself on actual evidence, [Joseph] Miller argues that, for West Central Africa at least, drought, famine, and disease were, in aggregate, more effective constraints on population growth than the slave trade. It does appear that from the sixteenth century West Africa became more humid, which should have (and maybe did) reduce the probability of frequent and severe droughts and famines. But any such blessing was not likely to have been unmixed since higher levels of humidity frequently bring with them a higher incidence of such diseases as malaria and plague." See David Henige, "Measuring the Immeasurable: The Atlantic Slave Trade, West African Population and the Pyrrhonian Critic," *The Journal of African History* 27.2 (1986): 307–8.

19 Louise Marie Diop-Maes, *Afrique noire démographie, sol et histoire* (Paris: Présence Africaine, 1996), 290–99, my translation.

20 Walter Rodney, *How Europe Underdeveloped Africa* (Washington, DC: Howard University Press, 1982), 13.

21 John Thornton, *Africa and Africans in the Making of the Atlantic World, 1400–1680* (Cambridge: Cambridge University Press, 1992), 47, 45.

22 Joseph E. Inikori, "Africa and the Transatlantic Slave Trade," in *Volume I: African History before 1885*, ed. Toyin Falola (Durham, NC: North Carolina Academic Press, 2000), 393–94.

23 Rodney, *How Europe Underdeveloped Africa,* 105–6.

24 Klein, *The Atlantic Slave Trade,* 58, 59.

25 Inikori and Engerman, *The Atlantic Slave Trade,* 2.

26 Robin Law, *The Slave Coast of West Africa, 1550–1750: The Impact of the Atlantic Slave Trade on an African Society* (Oxford: Clarendon Press, 1991), 220.

27 Thornton, *Africa and Africans,* 7.

28 Klein, *The Atlantic Slave Trade,* 107.

29 Donald R. Wright, *African Americans in the Colonial Era: From African Origins through the American Revolution* (Wheeling, IL: Harlan Davidson, 1990), 36–37.

30 Inikori and Engerman, *The Atlantic Slave Trade,* 39.

31 Davidson, *The African Slave Trade,* 278.

32 James F. Searing, *West African Slavery and Atlantic Commerce: The Senegal River Valley, 1700–1860* (New York: Cambridge University Press, 1993), 35.

33 Boubacar Barry, *Senegambia and the Atlantic Slave Trade* (Cambridge: Cambridge University Press, 1997), 436.

34 Martin A. Klein, *Slavery and Colonial Rule in French West Africa* (New York, NY: Cambridge University Press, 1998), 68-69.

35 Mary Tolford Wilson, "Peaceful Integration: The Owner's Adoption of His Slaves' Food," *The Journal of Negro History* 49.2 (April 1964): 121–22.

36 George E. Brooks, "Peanuts and Colonialism: Consequences of the Commercialization of Peanuts in West Africa, 1830–70," *The Journal of African History* 16.1 (1975): 30, 32.

37 Abdoulaye Bathily, "La Traite Atlantique des Esclaves et ses Effets Economiques et Sociaux en Afrique: La Cas du Galam, Royaume de l'Hinterland Sénégambien au Dix-huitie`me Siècle," Special Issue in Honour of J. D. Fage, *The Journal of African History* 27.2 (1986): 285.

38 Charles Becker, "Conditions écologiques, crises de subsistance et histoire de la population à l'époque de la traite des esclaves en Sénégambie (17 e–18 e siècle)," *Canadian Journal of African Studies* 20.3 (1986): 359–60, 368.

39 Brooks, "Peanuts and Colonialism," 29.

40 Klein, *Slavery and Colonial Rule,* 68–69.

41 James F. Searing, "Aristocrats, Slaves, and Peasants: Power and Dependency in the Wolof States, 1700–1850," *The International Journal of African Historical Studies* 21.3 (1988): 475.

42 Searing, *West African Slavery,* 35.

43 Curtin, *Economic Change in Precolonial Africa,* 115–16.

44 Inikori and Engerman, *The Atlantic Slave Trade,* 3, 4.

45 Paul E. Lovejoy, *Transformations in Slavery: A History of Slavery in Africa* (New York: Cambridge University Press, 1983), 108–9, 66–67.

46 *Ibid.,* 67.

47 Curtin, *Economic Change in Precolonial Africa,* 310.

48 Oliver Ransford, *The Slave Trade: The Story of the Transatlantic Slavery* (London: Fakenham and Reading, 1971), 73, 74.

49 Klein, *The Atlantic Slave Trade,* 127.

50 Claude Meillassoux, *The Anthropology of Slavery: The Womb of Iron and Gold* (Chicago, IL: University of Chicago Press, 1991), 72.

51 Olaudah Equiano, *The Interesting Narrative of the Life of Olaudah Equiano,* ed. Robert J. Allison (New York: Bedford Press, 1995), 47.

52 Joseph Inikori, "Africa in World History: The Export Slave Trade from Africa and the Emergence of the Atlantic Economic Order," in *General History of Africa. V: Africa from the Sixteenth to the Eighteenth Century,* ed. B. A. Ogot (California: Heinemann, 1992), 40.

53 Joseph C. Miller, "Review of *West African Slavery and Atlantic Commerce: The Senegal River Valley, 1700–1860,* by James Searing," *The American Historical Review* 100.1 (February 1995): 1.

54 Inikori, "Africa in World History," 104.

55 Claire C. Robertson and Martin A. Klein, "Women's Importance in African Slave Systems," in *Women and Slavery in Africa,* ed. Claire C. Robertson and Martin A. Klein (Portsmouth, NH: Heinemann, 1997), 15–16.

56 John Thornton, "Sexual Demography: The Impact of the Slave Trade on Family Structure," in *Women and Slavery in Africa,* ed. Robertson and Klein, 44.

57 *Ibid.,* 39–40.

CHAPTER 14

European Colonialism and Holocaust: A Study of the Colonial Experiences of Namibia, Kenya, Democratic Republic of Congo, and Algeria

Kenneth R. White

No greater evil in modern African history—besides the transatlantic and Arab slavery—has befallen Africa and its people, with longer lasting consequences, than the Berlin Conference of 1884/1885.[1] The partition of Africa decided at the conference was a continuation of previous policies of European exploitation from the 400 years of transatlantic slavery.[2] In order to prevent further loss of European lives and destruction of economic resources from the conflicts over the slave territories in Africa, Chancellor Otto von Bismarck convened the Berlin Conference. The conference was attended by Austria-Hungary, Belgium, France, Germany, Great Britain, Italy, Netherlands, Portugal, Russia, Spain, Sweden-Norway (unified from 1814–1905), Turkey, and the United States. Its purpose was to set the rules of engagement among the European nations for the "Scramble for Africa."[3] The Scramble for Africa unleashed a maelstrom of genocide on the African continent for decades. For example, Cecil Rhodes and his British South African Company killed thousands of Mashona and Ndebele men, women, and children to crush opposition against the imposition of British rule in Southern Rhodesia, present-day Zimbabwe.[4] Italians also killed 750,000 Ethiopians between 1935 and 1939.[5]

European colonialism driven, by racism and greed, led to the enslavement and massacre of millions of Africans. Crimes against Africans are often minimized, ignored, disbelieved, trivialized, ridiculed, and/or disputed. Some commentators maintain that genocidal wars waged by European colonial governments and colonial administrations against indigenous peoples or nations before 1948 did not violate international law. Rachel Anderson, however, contends that some forms of genocide, such as wars of annihilation or extermination, were illegal under customary international and multilateral treaties, as stipulated in documents from the 1884 Berlin Conference, the 1890 Anti-slavery Conference in Brussels, and the 1899 Hague Conference on the Laws of War.[6] Parshall, likewise, argues that British colonial government [and other colonial governments] violated the precepts of international law as codified in the Fourth Hague Convention of 1907.[7] Nevertheless, the West's denial of responsibility reflects the development of a culture and conspiracy of silence to avoid responsibility for genocide, war crimes, crimes against humanity, human rights violations, and reparations to individual victims, ethnic groups, and former colonized countries in Africa.

Whereas Europeans believed that they brought civilization to Africa, Africans viewed them as those who came from "the land of the dead."[8] Thus, the predatory mad scramble to consume some of the magnificent African cake caused the entire continent to experience European colonialism's Orwellian governments and Crusoe-esque outcomes, including "the making of civil war among and between African ethnic groups."[9] Since Africans were perceived as sub-humans and Europeans as the superior race, John Stuart Mill wrote, "despotism is a legitimate mode of government in dealing with barbarians, provided the end be their betterment."[10] Instead, this betterment included rape of men, women, and children, murder, and cannibalism. Africans were beaten or whipped to death, worked to death, forced to work in slave-like conditions, and starved to death due to increasingly frequent famines.[11] In an article, "Michael Scott and the Hereros," Michael Scott reports that

Germans in Southwest Africa killed babies of various African indigenous nations with bare hands and sick old women were burned alive in their huts.[12] Other atrocities included babies tossed into the bushes to die or to be eaten alive by wild animals, women held as hostages, mass rapes, and severed right hands of the Congolese by the colonizers.[13] Mark Twain reported acts of cannibalism by other African ethnic groups in the employ of the Belgians.[14]

This chapter illustrates how Europeans committed genocidal acts against selected African countries during colonial rule. These countries are Namibia, Democratic Republic of the Congo (DRC), Kenya, and Algeria. This chapter shows that many of the present-day problems of Africa, such as interethnic wars, burgeoning international debt, ethnic cleansing, hunger, inequitable distribution resources, and structural violence have their roots in European colonialism. European colonialism represents a strategic, wholesale underdevelopment of Africa for the express purpose of developing Europe.[15] Also, it was a crime against humanity.[16] Thus, an African Recovery Program (ARP), similar to the Marshall Plan of Europe in the aftermath of World War II, is needed to promote sustained human and environmental development on the continent. A major element of the ARP should consists of reparations to former colonized African countries, ethnic groups, organizations, and individuals.

CONCEPTUAL ANALYSIS OF GENOCIDE

The term genocide was first used by Raphael Lemkin to describe Nazi policies of systematic, political repression, including the mass murders of European Jews and other social groups, such as people of African descent, Sinti and Roma, Jehovah Witnesses, and people with different sexual orientation in concentration camps. The Convention on the Prevention and Punishment of the Crime of Genocide of the United Nations on December 9, 1948, defined genocide as any of the following acts committed with intent to destroy, in whole or in part, a national, ethnical, racial, or religious group: (a) killing members of the group; (b) causing serious bodily or mental harm to members of the group; (c) deliberately inflicting on the group conditions of life calculated to bring about its physical destruction in whole or in part; (d) imposing measures intended to prevent births within the group; and, (e) forcibly transferring children of the group to another group.[17]

Genocide is one aspect of political repression. Other features involve discriminatory policies, human rights violation, surveillance abuse, police brutality, imprisonment, involuntary settlement, stripping of citizen's rights, stripping of citizenship, starvation, torture, mass arrests, domestic spying, extrajudicial execution, and death squads, all of which are features of first-generation political repression.[18] Second-generation rights (e.g., economic, social, and cultural) and third-generation rights (e.g., the right to peace and a clean environment) are included in this understanding of political repression, too. In addition, the deleterious after effects of structural violence (e.g., poverty or the inequitable distribution of resources) experienced over long periods of time are forms of political repression, all of which lead to genocide, crimes against humanity, and state and settler-colonists sponsored violence.[19]

The total way of life of the oppressed is destroyed and/or dismantled, which includes their culture, various institutions, the environment, and political economy. They are replaced with those of the oppressor. The entire group and country are remade into the image of the colonizer-oppressor. Lemkin, thus, understood genocide as a "total social practice," that is, a series of processes that affect all aspects of group life and differ between several techniques of group destruction:

a) political (cessation of self-government and destruction of political institutions),
b) social (annihilation of national leadership, attack on legal system),
c) cultural (ban on the use of language),
d) economic (destruction of the foundation of the economic existence),
e) biological (decreasing the birth rate),
f) physical (mass murder, endangering health, starvation, scorched earth policy),
g) religious (disruption of religious influence, destruction of religious leadership), and
h) moral (creation of an atmosphere of moral debasement.[20]

Furthermore, he viewed genocide as a process that occurs in two phases: (1) destruction of the national pattern of the oppressed group, and (2) the imposition of the national pattern of the oppressor.[21]

European colonial governments and settler-colonists in collusion with various corporations and religious organizations in Africa systematically implemented all forms of political repression. Europeans established the legitimacy of their regimes through institutionalization. Verdeja states that one of the means of legitimacy involves the regime ruling through the use of formal and bureaucratic mechanisms, so that different aspects of governance are managed and coordinated by various departments. The second means of legitimacy entails the penetration of civil and political society systematically and deeply. The third observation on establishing legitimacy is that it must be seen as permanent and strong.[22] Miller and Garran concur that institutional oppression manifests itself through laws, policies, and formal and informal practices.[23] They maintain that there are five aspects of institutional oppression. First, it is systematic and comprehensive. Second, it is on many levels. Third, it combines formal and informal practices—some overt and others covert. Fourth, it is cumulative, that is, built on attitudes and practices that have lasted for hundreds of years and have resulted in disinvestment and disempowerment, thus limiting opportunities to generate and maximize social, economic, and natural resources. Thus, institutional oppression is historical and contemporaneous. The fifth aspect is that it represents power, that is, power to make laws and policies, to enforce them, to fund them, to define and present them, and to create a public narrative and discourse that normalizes them. Lacking empathy for the oppressed, for example, the normalization of these laws include physical violence and armed violence, as well as mental abuse, land dispossession, exploitative labor, a variety of other exactions through legal means, and mistreatments often legitimated the colonial regimes in Africa.[24]

Thus, Verdeja contends that institutionalization is normally accompanied by an increase in legal justifications for crimes through the emergence of a large body of state security laws, which is a perverted "rule of law." This perverted rule of law is shaped by errors of criminal thinking, which include a lack of empathy, a distorted self-image, and a lack of time perspective.[25] For example, Danielson maintains that a lack of time perspective is a failure or refusal to consider the long-term benefits of providing all people with equal opportunities and equal access to opportunities.

HOLOCAUST IN NAMIBIA: WAR OF EXTERMINATION

The German-Herero War was one of the world's bloodiest conflicts, and the twentieth century's first genocide.[26] The war of annihilation against the Hereros was initiated in retaliation for the Hereros' resistance against the German colonial administrative oppressive treatment.[27] For example, in giving testimony in court, seven Hereros were needed to equal one German.[28] The oppressive treatment also included broken treaties with the Herero nation and the paternal right of correction that permitted German colonists to beat Herero people with whips and fists.[29] In addition, Germany's colonizing of land owned by the indigenous people was based on the assumption that "superior cultures" would destroy "inferior" peoples in battles for "living space."[30] To acquire more space for German people, a conscious, deliberate policy of genocide was authorized by Kaiser Wilhelm II who ordered German soldiers and settlers under the leadership of Lt. General Lothar von Trotha (who often referred to himself as the great general to the Herero), to seek, shoot, hang, starve, beat, and rape Herero men, women, and children.[31] In an environment of judicial and governmental dysfunction that created a climate of impunity, African children over the age of eight were ordered to wear metal passes. African men, women, and children were summarily slaughtered in battle, poisoned, hanged, and summarily executed by firing squads of German soldiers, burned to death with their families, and driven into the Kalahari Desert to die of hunger and thirst.

The Herero attempted negotiations with the great general. However, in the documentary film, *Genocide and the Second Reich 4*, von Lothar viewed "negotiations as a shame to German honor and a sign of weakness."[32] The Herero attempted to avoid war by moving to Waterberg (the Great Plateau). Instead of pursuing peace and being honorable, the German army relentlessly pursued the Herero into the Kalahari Desert, where thousands died from thirst and starvation. Through trickery and deceit, often with the assistance of missionaries, 13,000 Herero were rounded up by the German army. Johanna Kah, a Herero historian, stated that dog tags were placed on the Herero for identification purposes in the concentration camps.[33]

On October 2, 1904, the Annihilation Order by General von Trotha laid out his genocide policy of destruction of the Herero people.[34] The war of annihilation was intended to wipe out the Herero people. Tens of thousands died in the Kalahari Desert from starvation, dehydration, and poisoned water locations. Many more were bayoneted, shot, and burned alive en masse by the German army. Women and children who surrendered were burned alive in their huts.[35] It is estimated that the German army massacred 60,000 Herero people out of 80,000. Those who surrendered were placed in slave labor and concentration camps, which resulted in more deaths. However, Jeremy Sarkin claims a higher figure. He states that by machine-gun massacres, starvation, poisoning, and forced labor in Germany's first concentration camps, the German Schutztruppe (protection troops) systematically exterminated as many as 105,000 Herero women and children.[36] Also, the Germans massacred almost half of the 20,000 Nama population.[37]

The Nama also fought the Germans. After their defeat, they were detained at the Shark Island Death Camp and slave labor camps with installations in Lüderitz, Okahandja, and Swakopmund in German South West Africa. Also, there were smaller installations of labor camps throughout the country. These were usually under the auspices of private companies. Benjamin Madley of Yale University in the documentary film, *Germany's First Holocaust: 1904–1908*, stated, "Shark Island was the blueprint for death annihilation camps from which the Nazis learn the art of killing people quickly."[38] Still further, the Herero and Nama prisoners of war, including noncombatants, were worked, raped, starved, and beaten to death. The focus on death in these camps was so strong and certain that preprinted death certificates with "death from exhaustion" as the cause of the death were produced in the thousands.[39] A researcher at the United States Holocaust Memorial Museum states, "the policy of the German government was to deport and destroy the Nama, . . . the Witboois and Bethanie people held in concentration camps at Windhoek and Karibib."[40]

In addition, Herero and Nama were subjected to medical experiments, that is, selective genocide, specifically using the science of eugenics, to confirm their racial inferiority to the German race.[41] The documentary film, *Hitler's Forgotten Victims*, shows that Germany's most senior Nazi geneticist, Dr. Eugen Fischer, developed racial theories (e.g., master race) in German South West Africa long before World War I. He purportedly identified genetic dangers arising from race mixing between German colonists and African women. German leaders, scientists, and people were obsessed with maintaining German racial purity.

HELL-O-CAUST IN KENYA: LIFE BEHIND THE WIRE

Seven years after the defeat of Nazi Germany by the Allied powers, Britain through its Colonial Office and the willing participation of the settler-colonists committed war crimes, crimes against humanity, and genocide in Kenya against the Kikuyu and other ethnic groups in Kenya. Colonialism everywhere in Africa depended upon the threat and use of coercive power to sustain its authority.[42] In Kenya, physical violence was an integral and characteristic part of European domination and race relations. For the British, Kenya was the "White man's/woman's country" or "the jewel of the British empire"—after the loss of India—with its privileged lifestyle along with a sense of entitlement, decadence, ex: Heroin) economic prosperity, and racial hierarchy that, according to Anderson, "placed the European on top of Asians, and relegated the African majority very firmly to the bottom of the pile." The British, like other Europeans, brought their racist ideologies, such as the Great Chain of Being and master race, to Africa and used them as a means of exclusion. Racial hierarchies were institutionalized through laws and policies to subjugate the African population in an unprecedented manner in the twentieth century.[43]

Kikuyu and other indigenous groups lived under colonial repression and tyranny. Every law, policy, and regulation was aimed at controlling every aspect of the people's lives. For example, many of the Kikuyu were forced off their land to live on African reservations. The political, economic, and social oppression endured by the Kikuyu caused a grassroots movement to develop among them. Kikuyu men, women, and children made the oath of unity. As the mass movement of oathing became popular, it became known as the Mau Mau. The movement called for armed resistance against the British. It also demanded land and freedom from British oppression. The initial support for the movement was largely limited to the Kikuyu population and was supported by the Kikuyu independent schools and churches.[44]

The minority settler-colonists, colonial administration, and the British government mistakenly criminalized the Kikuyu of Kenya. They viewed every Kikuyu as a Mau Mau. Elkins states that they were portrayed as a barbaric, anti-European, and anti-Christian sect that reverted to tactics of primitive terror to interrupt the British civilizing mission in Kenya.[45] In addition, they were portrayed as gangsters and criminals who terrorized and murdered Europeans in the country. The Mau Mau were diagnosed to be an infectious mental illness that threatened the civilization of the British. As a result, nearly all of the Kikuyu population was arrested, detained, and charged as being Mau Mau. The British in Kenya developed a vast system of detention and concentration camps throughout the countryside.[46] They turned villages into detention camps for the entire Kikuyu population.

Another example of British oppression is the Highlands of Kenya. The Kikuyu were the original owners of this area. The land was stolen from the Kenyans. The chief reason was to prevent the Kikuyu from competing economically with British settler-colonist farmers. Just as in their other colonies in Africa, the British abrogated Kenyan laws and customs, such as the rights of land use given to the indigenous people and the rights of ownership to tenant farmers and their families.[47] Many were forced to live in the urban areas to eke out their survival in the informal economy of selling merchandise on the street, brewing beer, and prostitution. Thus, many were made landless by the British in colonial Kenya. This had dreadful social consequences for the Kikuyu man and woman. Elkins states that to be a man or woman—to move from childhood to adulthood—a Kikuyu had to have access to land.[48] According to Elkins, a Kikuyu man needed land to accumulate the necessary resources to pay bridewealth for a wife or wives, who would, in turn, bear him children. Land and family entitled him to certain privileges within the Kikuyu patriarchy. Without land, a Kikuyu man remains socially a boy. Likewise, a woman needed land to grow crops to nurture and sustain her family. She further says that for a Kikuyu woman without land is still considered as a girl, and not an adult in the eyes of her people. A Kikuyu could not be a Kikuyu without land.

The various laws implemented by the British forced many of the Kenyans into abject poverty. Furthermore, like all colonial governments, Kenya's derived its power from a host of repressive laws, imprisonment, legal floggings, and terror.[49] For example, four laws by the colonial government sowed the seeds of revolutionary war waged by the Kikuyu: the establishment of African reservations; the hut and poll taxes—taxation without equitable political representation in "a land of 5 million Africans and 125,000 Asians, and both ruled by 30,000 Europeans."[50] The *kipande* or pass was required by law, and it recorded a person's name, fingerprint, ethnic group, past employment history, and current employer's signature.[51] It also forced Africans to become wage earners by limiting their agricultural production for the marketplace in favor of the settler-colonist farmers. Consequently, these unjustly harsh measures, along with other laws, created the Mau Mau movement by the Olenguruone peasants, which eventually spread to the urban areas of Nairobi that eventuated into a war for land and freedom.

Life Behind the Wire

The acts of war by the Mau Mau provoked the colonial government headed by Governor Sir Evelyn Baring to declare a state of emergency on 20 October 1952. At the conclusion of the war for liberation and the continued state of emergency, the total population of 1,500,000 Kikuyu was thrown into 854 village concentration camps.[52] In addition, between 20,000 and 30,000 Africans were killed in combat.[53] Caroline Elkins, however, puts the figure from 240,000 to 320,000 killed in the war with the British.[54] Also, Jeremy Sarkin contends that 100,000 Mau Mau died in those concentration camps.[55] Moreover, the state of emergency systematically subjected 150,000 Kenyans to years on end without trial in concentration camps, where they became victims of arbitrary killings, severe physical assaults, homosexual assaults during interrogation, sexual violence, forced labor, constant beatings even while working, screenings, forced removal, and extreme acts of inhumane and degrading treatment.[56]

Life behind the wire, whether in the detention or village concentration camps, was a matter of survival. Some of the prisoners of war and civilian noncombatants did not care about the constant rapes, beatings, sodomy, forced labor, forced starvation, and so forth; it was all about surviving. According to Caroline Elkins, "some detainees served the sexual needs of the camp officers and by becoming the wives of the camp commandants. . . . Others traded sex with the guards to ensure their protection, . . . Some became the junior wives of fellow detainees."[57]

Regarding constant beatings, Kikuyu and other ethnic groups were beaten with various objects. Demanding confessions and intelligence from the Mau Mau, the interrogations and torture teams made up from settlers, British district officers, Kenya police force, the Special Branch (colony Gestapo), African loyalists, and soldiers from British military forces used torture. Examples of torturous means included electric shock, cigarette burns and fire, gun barrels, knives, snakes, vermin, hot bottles, and hot eggs thrust up men's rectums and women's private parts, and carrying buckets on their heads filled with overflowing urine and feces while being beaten.[58] Zarina Patel reports that another form of torture was cattle dip full of pesticide thrown into their eyes.[59]

Women endured the worst of the atrocities, which included mothers and daughters raped together in the same hut, meted out by the British soldiers, settler-colonists, and Home Guard allies.[60] In addition, many of the Kikuyu experienced forced marriages, rape-induced pregnancies, and the crushing of their customary controls over fertility and burdened with the additional stigma of carrying the enemy's child.[61] One survivor, Jane Marhoni Mata states that, "her interrogator filled a bottle with hot water and pushed it into my private parts with his foot."[62] Any infraction and/or the capricious whims of those in charge were reasons to be shot dead, beaten all day, raped all day and night in front of fathers, mothers, and children, and still shot dead in the morning.

Some of the perpetrators of crimes against humanity and war crimes became experts at interrogating Mau Mau prisoners of war. The infamous Dr. Bunny in the Rift Valley was known as the Joseph Mengele of Kenya.[63] It is reported that his exploits for extracting intelligence and confessions included burning the skin off live Mau Mau suspects and forcing them to eat their own testicles. State judicial executions, the highest form of institutional violence under European rule of law, accounted for 1,090 hanged Mau Mau Freedom Fighters.[64] Also, during Operation Anvil on April 24, 1954, each Kikuyu male resident was required to carry five separate documents: an employment registration; a card setting out his employment, including salary history; an identity card; a poll-tax receipt; and a Kikuyu Special Tax receipt, too.[65] Regarding the Kikuyu Special Tax, Kikuyu paid higher taxes than the other African ethnic groups.

The Kenyans were living in an Orwellian state that was clearly Britain's Nazi Kenya and Soviet Gulag. The Final Solution policy of Britain included violations of international laws, such as "the derogation of the European Convention on Human Rights and the International Labor Organization Forced Labor Conventions,"[66] all of which were committed in the name of national security, that is, to enforce the implementation of its exterminationist policy regarding the Kikuyu civilian population.[67] Also, the British nurtured a loyalist movement by recruiting Kikuyu, Christians, and non-Christians to become members of the Home Guards; thereby, laying the groundwork for a civil war that carried over into present day Kenya.[68]

DEMOCRATIC REPUBLIC OF THE CONGO: KING LEOPOLD'S KILLING FIELD

Under the guise of humanitarian efforts, free trade, scientific enterprises, Christian missions, bringing civilization, and stopping the Arab slave trade, King Leopold II, through his various companies, such as the International Congo Society, established control over the present DRC. Commenting on Leopold's activities in DRC, Joseph Conrad states, "the vilest scramble for loot that ever disfigured the history of human conscience and geographical location eventuated into one of the bloodiest episodes of genocide in the history of humankind."[69]

Contrary to the promises made through his intermediaries at the Berlin Conference, King Leopold II established a private army of 19,000 called the Force Publique (FP), whose "primary role was to enforce Leopold's exploitive economic policies in the Congo Free State."[70] The FP served as an army of occupation, counterinsurgency troops, and as a corporate labor police force. Schimmer notes that the Force Publique's officer corps was comprised entirely of whites—Belgian regular soldiers, mercenaries from other countries, and neighboring non-Congolese ethnic groups. To meet the demands for inflatable bicycle tires and the automobile mass produced in the United States by Henry Ford, the Force Publique killed over half the population during Leopold's twenty-three years of holocaustic reign of terror.[71]

On the death toll of the Congolese, Adam Hochschild suggests the figure of 10 million[72], while Hanna Arendt puts the figure at 12 million.[73] These deaths came through Leopold's policy of forced labor, that is, slave labor system, euphemistically called "liberated men." Isidore Ndaywel e Nziem places the figure at 13 million.[74] So many people were killed and entire regions of the country were depopulated that Mark Twain referred to the DRC as the "Land of Graves or the Congo Free Graveyard."[75] It could also be called the Land of Death.

As "liberated men," the Congolese endured some of the worst brutalities and heinous acts of mass killings ever recorded by researchers and writers. For example, Joseph Conrad's *The Heart of Darkness* details the savagery and atrocities committed in the name of empire building, civilization, and the racial theories of Social Darwinism and Western progress. Mark Twain's *King Leopold's Soliloquy: A Defense of His Congo Rule* reports acts of cannibalism, mutilations, mass executions, rapes of men and women, beatings, castrations, genitals and other body parts being hung to dry, starvation, worked to death, children left in the bush to die and/or eaten alive by wild animals, and the encouragement of interethnic slave trafficking. Also, while the women and wives of the Congolese men were held as prisoners, many were raped and/or eaten by some of the king's soldiers.

Adam Hochschild's *King Leopold's Ghost* provides detailed information of specific massacres regarding the king's regime of terror. People were outright murdered. As proof of their kill, FP had to show the right severed hands of their victims. If the Congolese were not killed by the soldiers, whipped to death, worked to death, starved to death, burned villages, children beaten to death with rifle butts, or taxed to death, there were the diseases brought by the Europeans. Hochschild states that disease killed more Congolese than did bullets.[76] He further contends that population losses in the millions were due to four closely connected sources: murder; starvation, exhaustion, and exposure; disease; and a plummeting birth rate.[77] As Hochschild states, "Once under way, mass killing is hard to stop; it becomes a kind of sport, like hunting." Decades before the Holocaust in Nazi Europe, Hell-O-Caust in the Congo Free State occurred under the tyrannical rule of King Leopold II of Belgium.

ALGERIA: THE QUESTION—TORTURE

Algeria was the venue for one of the most ruthless and "cruelest wars of French decolonization in the 20th century."[78] The Algerian War was a continuation of the systematic genocide begun by French settler-colonial rulers in 1830 that resulted in the decimation of the Algerian population from over four million to less than 2.5 million by 1890.[79] France committed acts of genocide against Algerians and established a Gestapo-state that rivals the atrocities of Nazi Germany. The war resulted in transforming the entire country into a vast concentration camp, in which more than two million Algerians were forcefully removed by the French army and the Special Administrative Section (SAS) into internment camps from the countryside.[80] A contested but definitive figure is three million by the Front de Libération Nationale (FLN; National Liberation Front).[81] However, Blake states that "since 1900 between 12 to 15 million people were displaced, most of them permanently."[82] Also, the war in Algeria resulted in more than one million Algerian deaths, 300,000 war orphans, 400,000 refugees, and 700,000 migrants from the rural areas into the cities.[83] Marianne Arens and Françoise Thull reported that French army casualties were more than 25,000 and 60,000 wounded.[84]

The advent of the French into Algeria created a culture of violence that reached a paroxysm of genocidal proportion with human rights violations committed by all involved combatants, military, paramilitary, loyalists, and civilians. Robert Aldrich states that violence was a fact of life in the empire.[85] Thus, in Algiers, torture had been institutionalized, "with the agreement of the highest governmental authorities," according to General Massu.[86]

Most acts of violence perpetrated by the French army targeted civilians.[87] Branche further states that the Algerian population became the chosen field of battle, and torture was widespread throughout the army, the Special Administrative Section, and the Organization de l'Armée Secrete (Secret Army Organization)—a far right terrorist group. In an interview with Lucy Garnier, Branche reported that torture always began with systematic stripping of the victim under the supervision of a superior and included beating combined with any number of the following acts by the French army: hanging by the feet or hands, water torture, torture by electric shock, and rape.[88] She further stated that objects, such as a rope, a jerry can of water, and funnel, were objects used for sexual violation of men and women. Branche further reported that rapes were most often committed in a collective manner with other soldiers watching the despicable crime.

The heinous, depraved acts of sexual crimes against Muslim women as well as other war crimes committed by soldiers and members of the Secret Army Organization and the Special Administrative Section went unpunished by the French government. Instead, the government instigated coverups as well awarded medals of honor and commendations to military personnel for bravery. In addition, amnesty laws were passed in order to prevent prosecution of war crimes. There are plenty of documents detailing the use of torture to inflict not only physical pain but also psychological pain and destruction of the civilian population during the Algerian War.[89] In addition, there is information provided by "some 350,000 French ex-combatants seeking psychiatric treatment for Post Traumatic Stress Disorder (PTSD), depression, suicidal impulses, and other psychiatric disorders, who participated or witnessed acts of torture, illegal executions, and generalized and horrific violence on the Algerians."[90] Their narratives are a treasure trove of information. Perhaps, the state secrets about sensitive documents have more to do with the atrocities of the elites—past and present leaders of France.

CONCLUSION

European colonialism was genocide unleashed on Africa. The Berlin Conference was Africa's undoing in many ways with long lasting consequences discussed in this chapter. Many of the conditions of contemporary African countries were shaped by their colonial origins. Maintaining state secrets, continued denial of responsibility by the West, blaming the victim (Africa), minimizing the crimes against humanity and European colonial genocides, and outright dismissal only hamper, and perhaps prevent, healing on the continent. The healing process in all of its various components, such as reconciliation (truth commissions), justice (tribunals), structural (systemic reformation), land reformation, and economic adjustments must be holistic and multifaceted in its approach to promote long-lasting peace on the African continent. Furthermore, as Dr. Leila Gupta states, "buildings can be repaired and damage can be cleared but the psychological suffering and scars are harder to see and are much longer lasting."[91] There must be a fundamental connection between the well-being of individuals and the well-being of communities in the healing process.[92]

The psychological and spiritual dimensions of justice, rehabilitation, reconstruction, and reconciliation must not be neglected in the healing of the continent. If reparations are to promote justice and a lasting peace, they must incorporate social reparations that address the vast social problems rooted in the inequalities constructed during the colonial era.[93] Brownhill maintains that reparations can help rebuild community relations—between women and men, between people and nature, and between ethnic groups. Furthermore, social reparations could be delivered in-kind, in form of water systems, micro-power generations, housing, environment rehabilitation, land for small-scale and cooperative farming, free schools, clinics, sports facilities, and other shared common amenities. In addition, social reparations must include Africans creating a culture of respect for women, and, as well, improving their status throughout Africa. Reparations involve the concept of repairing. As Professor Chinweizu states, "reparation is mostly about making repairs, organizational repairs, social repairs, institutional repairs, technological repairs, economic repairs, political repairs, educational repairs, repair of every type . . ."[94]

The subject of reparations is a much-debated topic. There are many arguments against reparations. First, colonial genocide and other atrocities must not be judged by the laws of today, but by laws of the time.[95] Second, historical violations of human rights happened a long time ago. Third, the word "genocide" was not in use in the early part of the twentieth century. Fourth, monetary reparations may not be the best solution to assist victims to heal. Brandon Hamber and Richard Wilson state that monetary reparations to individuals along with commemorations, monuments, and reburials are symbolic acts that acknowledge and recognize suffering.[96] They maintain that the psychological and emotional pain of individuals is not adequately addressed in this manner. Peter Stoett maintains that this "backward looking" tends to cultivate awareness of the victims' suffering, explicitly involving the mobilization of ethno cultural consciousness.[97]

Fifth, the limited goals of poverty alleviation programs and courts, such as the Highly Indebted Poor Countries Initiative and the South African Truth and Reconciliation Commission failed to take into account the systemic nature of global apartheid.[98] For example, globalization maintains unequal access to healthcare and life-saving medications in many African countries. Sixth, Nesbitt reports that atrocities committed during the era of European colonialism were legal, and that accepting responsibility would open the door to lawsuits. Seventh, Michael Dynes and Richard Beeston state some African nations (Nigeria and South Africa) insist that increased Western assistance for economic recovery programs would be more appropriate forms of reparations than to individuals and groups.[99] Eighth, it is argued that the amount of aid being given by former colonizing nations is so significant that they are reparations for past wrongs.[100] Ninth, Sarkin and Fowler point out the argument regarding whether today's international human rights and international humanitarian laws can be applied to crimes of the past during the colonial era. All in all, many in the reparations movement, including the judiciary and scholars, argue over the forms of reparations, such as direct payment of cash settlements to individuals and groups, land and legal autonomy. Nevertheless, as Albert Einstein stated, "we cannot solve the problems of today with the same level of thinking [individual and group behaviors, values, belief systems, structural, systemic] that created them."

Regarding the subject of reparations, the recent settlement and apology from the British Government is a big milestone toward justice for the Mau Mau Freedom Fighters of Kenya. Britain agreed to pay about $30 million dollars to thousands of Kenyans who were tortured in the most despicable and shameful of ways. [101] This successful litigation against the British Government was made possible by a confluence of events: 1) The

Mau Mau were still outlawed in Kenya until 2003, so the plaintiffs [members of the Mau Mau War Veterans Association] were not able to freely discuss legal actions; 2) The British military kept extensive records of their activities; and, 3) That archival material surfaced in two books in 2005[102] Ian Cobain, Owen Bowcott, and Richard Norton-Taylor reported that "8,800 files from 37 former colonies are held at the highly secured government communications center at Hanslope Park in Buckinghamshire.[103] These records are often referred to as "the migrated files."[104] Many of the most damaging ones were destroyed to prevent embarrassment to Her Majesty Government (HMG).

Gituwa Kahengeri stated that, "there is no amount of compensation that can cover for those who suffered"[105] from legal sanctions of genocide, crimes committed by Britain on Kenya and its other colonies. Atsango Chesoni (executive director of the Kenyan Human Rights Commission) states, "Many of the Mau Mau Veterans have long standing issues around land rights."[106] She further contends that many continue to in object poverty and squalor.

The foreign ruling could set a precedent for other cases of atrocities with implications for France, Germany, Belgium, other European countries, and the United States. This era of history will remain controversial for several reasons: 1) many of the most damaging documents were destroyed; 2) despite the payout and apology the British government does not accept liability for the actions of previous colonial governments; 3) the foreign ruling may have an impact in the United States regarding reparations for slavery; 4) the brutal war for liberation in Kenya involved atrocities committed by the Mau Mau Freedom Fighters; and, 5) the role of the Christian church, its missionaries, and Christianized Africans in the genocidal onslaught, war crimes and crimes against humanity need to be investigated. The British High Commissioner Christian Turner says, "History teaches us you can't have lasting peace with [out] justice, [accountability], and reconciliation.

ENDNOTES

1 Osei Boateng, "Licence to Colonise," *New African* (February 2010), 14–20.

2 Ibid., 14.

3 Ibid., 16.

4 Robert Blake, *A History of Rhodesia* (New York: Alfred A. Knopf, 1978), 115. See also Philip Mason, *The Birth of a Dilemma: The Conquest and Settlement of Rhodesia* (London: Oxford University Press, 1958), 188.

5 Global Alliance "Vatican Apology for Complicities in the Ethiopian Genocide 1935–1941," www.gopetition.com/petitions/vatican-apologyforethiopian-holocaust.html (accessed February 5, 2011).

6 Rachel Anderson, "Redressing Colonial Genocide under International Law: The Hereros' Cause of Action Against Germany" *California Law Review* 93 (2005): 1155–1189.

7 Nicole K. Parshall, "Mau Mau: A Test Case for Justice," *New African* (August/September, 2009), 30–31.

8 Adam Hochschild, *King Leopold's Ghost: A Story of Greed, Terror, and Heroism in Colonial Africa* (Boston: Houghton Mifflin Company, 1998), 16.

9 David Anderson, *Histories of the Hanged: The Dirty War in Kenya and the End of Empire* (New York: W.W. Norton & Company, 2005), 240.

10 John Stuart Mill, "On Liberty," in *On Liberty and Other Writings*, ed. Stefan Collinie (Cambridge, UK: Cambridge University Press, 1859/1989), 13.

11 Michiko Kakutani, "King Leopold's Ghost: Genocide with Spin Control." www.nytimes.com/books/98/08/30/daily/leopold-book-rev (accessed May 6, 2010). See also Adam Hochschild, *King Leopold's Ghost: A Story of Greed, Terror, and Heroism in Colonial Africa*.

12 Jan-Bart Gewald, "Imperial Germany and the Herero of Southern Africa: Genocide and the Quest for Recompense," in *Genocide, War Crimes, and the West: History and Complicity*, ed. Adam Jones (London: Zed Books, 2004), 68.

13 Adam Hochschild, "Leopold's Congo: A Holocaust We Have Yet to Comprehend" *Chronicle of Higher Education* 46, no. 36, EBSCOhost (accessed September 12, 2010).

14 Mark Twain, *King Leopold's Soliloquy: A Defense of His Congo Rule* (Boston: P. R. Warren, 1905).

15 Carina Ray, "The Empire's Ghost Returns" *New African* (August/September, 2009), 18–22. See Eric Williams, *Capitalism and Slavery* (Richmond, VA: University of North Carolina Press, 1944/1994); Walter Rodney, *How Europe Underdeveloped Africa* (Washington, DC: Howard University Press, 1982).

16 Mukoma Wa Ngugi, "Mau Mau Ever-present Past" *New African* (August/September, 2009), 24–27.

17 United States Holocaust Memorial Museum, *What Is Genocide?* www.ushmm.org (accessed April 23, 2009), 1. See also Raphael Lemkin, *Axis Rule in Occupied Europe: Laws of Occupation, Analysis of Government, and Proposals for Redress* (Washington, DC: Carnegie Endowment for International Peace, 1944).

18 Christian Davenport, "State Repression and Political Order," *Annual Review of Political Science* 10 (2007), 1–23.

19 "Johan Galtung, a Norwegian academic, is universally hailed as one of the most influential thinkers in the field of peace research and conflict resolution. . . . In 1981, he advanced a new theory on violence and its various manifestations in modern society. This theory articulated the difference between direct and structural violence." See also Johan Galtung, "Violence, Peace, and Peace Research," *Journal of Peace Research* 6 (1969), 167–191.

20 A. Dirk Moses, "Empire, Colony, Genocide: Keywords and the Philosophy of History," in *Empire, Colony Genocide: Conquest, Occupation, and Subaltern Resistance in World History*, ed. A. Dirk Moses (New York: Berghahn Books, 2008), 3–54. See also Dominik J. Schaller, "From Conquest to Genocide: Colonial Rule in German Southwest Africa and German East Africa," in *Empire, Colony, Genocide: Conquest, Occupation, and Subaltern Resistance in World History*, ed. A. Dirk Moses (New York: Berghahn Books, 2008), 296–324.

21 A. Dirk Moses, "Raphael Lemkin's View of European Colonial Rule in Africa: Between Condemnation and Admiration," *Journal of Genocide Research* 7, no. 4 (2005): 531–538.

22 Ernesto Verdeja, "Institutional Response to Genocide and Mass Atrocity," in *Genocide, War Crimes, and the West: History and Complicity*, ed. Adam Jones (London: Zed Books, 2004), 327–345.

23 Joshua Miller and Ann M. Garran, "The Web of Institutional Racism," *Smith College Studies in Social Work* 77, no. 1 (2007), 38.

24 Robert Aldrich, "Colonial Violence and Post-Colonial France" (2007), 1–24, http://conferences.arts.usyd.edu.au/viewpaper.php?id=745&cf=18 (accessed August 20, 2010), 1.

25 Patricia Danielson, "Is Racial Discrimination Based on Criminal Thinking?" in *Understanding Human Behavior and the Social Environment*, 8th ed., eds. Charles Zastrow and Karen K. Kirst-Ashman (Belmont, CA: Brooks/Cole, 2007), 229–230.

26 Henning Melber, "Genocide and the History of Violent Expansionism", *Pambazuka News* http://africa.peacelink.org (accessed May 23, 2009).

27 Rachel Anderson, "Redressing Colonial Genocide under International Law: The Hereros' Cause of Action Against Germany," 1160.

28 Jeremy Sarkin and Carly Fowler, "Reparations for Historical Human Rights Violations: The International and Historical Dimensions of the Alien Torts Claim Act Genocide Case of the Herero of Namibia," *Human Rights Review* 9 (2008), 346.

29 Benjamin Madley, "From Africa to Auschwitz: How German South West Africa Incubated Ideas and Methods Adopted and Developed by the Nazis in Eastern Europe," 438.

30 Ibid., 433.

31 Jan-Bart Gewald, "Imperial Germany and the Herero of Southern Africa: Genocide and the Quest for Recompense," 60.

32 Hamara TV, "Genocide and the Second Reich 4: Vernichtungsbefehl (accessed May 25, 2009).

33 Ibid.

34 Benjamin Madley, "From Africa to Auschwitz: How German South West Africa Incubated Ideas and Methods Adopted and Developed by the Nazis in Eastern Europe," *European Quarterly History* 35 (2005), 429–464. See also Anderson, "Redressing Colonial Genocide Under International Law: The Hereros' Cause of Action Against Germany," 1161.

35 Benjamin Madley, "From Africa to Auschwitz," 445.

36 Jeremy Sarkin, *Colonial Genocide and Reparations Claims in the 21st Century*, (London: Praeger, 2008).

37 Delroy Constantine-Simms, review of the film, *Hitler's Forgotten Victims* by David Okuefuna and Moise Shewa, www.amonhotep.com (1997). This documentary film is known in the United States as "Black Survivors of the Holocaust." It provides disturbing photographic evidence of German genocidal tendencies in Africa . . . suggests links between German colonialism and Nazi policy, and examines the treatment of Black prisoners-of-war.

38 Hannah Lickert, "Germany's First Holocaust: 1904–1908," http://apscuhuru.org/analysis/germany-first-holocaust/index.xhtml (accessed May 25, 2009), 1–2. See also Anderson, "Redressing Colonial Genocide under International Law: The Hereros' Cause of Action Against Germany," op. cit. Joachim Zeller states, "in Windhoek, the capital of the territory, a separate camp was created in which Herero women were kept specifically for the sexual gratification of German troops," 1165.

39 Madley, "From Africa to Auschwitz," 449.

40 United States Holocaust Memorial Museum, *What Is Genocide?* www.ushmm.org (accessed April 23, 2009). See Patricia Mazon and Reinhild Steingrover, eds., *Not so Plain as Black and White: Afro-German Culture and History, 1890–2000* (Rochester, NY: University of Rochester Press, 2005). Part I provides a historical perspective and investigates racist and racializing policies [laws] and practices introduced and carried out in the colonies and in Germany.

41 Hamara TV, www.you tube.com/watch, November 22, 2007 (accessed April 19, 2009); See also Hamara TV, *Genocide and the Second Reich 5: Concentration Camps in Namibia*, which contains graphic photographs of Herero tribes people being herded like cattle in cattle cars to concentration camps, mass starvation, and medical experiments by German scientists; See also *Genocide and the Second Reich, I, II, V, & VI* aired on BBC, Channel Four, and you tube. Very graphic and shows thirty years before Hitler came to power, the first genocide of Germany, which has never come to grips with this aspect of its history, e.g., the mass rapes of African women, starvation, mass murders, killing of children, and mass graves.

42 David Anderson, *Histories of the Hanged: The Dirty War in Kenya and the End of Empire*, 78. Anderson further states that the poorest, most ill-educated [W]hite person in Kenya enjoyed a higher social and political status than any person of African or Asian origin.

43 Ivan Hannaford, *Race: The History of an Idea in the West* (Baltimore: Johns Hopkins University Press, 1996). See also George L. Moss, *Toward the Final Solution: A History of European Racism* (Madison, WI: University of Minnesota Press, 2000).

44 Caroline Elkins, *Imperial Reckoning: The Untold Story of Britain's Gulag in Kenya* (New York: Henry Holt & Company, 2005), 25.

45 Ibid., xi.

46 Ibid., xii.

47 Peter A. Dewees, "Trees and Farm Boundaries: Farm Forestry, Land Tenure, and Reform in Kenya," *Africa* 65, no. 2 (1995).

48 Elkins, *Imperial Reckoning*, 14.

49 Ibid., 55.

50 Derwent Whittlesey, "Kenya, the Land, and Mau Mau," *Foreign Affairs* (2004), 86.

51 Elkins, *Imperial Reckoning*, 16.

52 David Anderson, *Histories of the Hanged: The Dirty War in Kenya and the End of Empire* (New York: W.W. Norton & Company, 2005), 294.

53 David Anderson, "Atrocity Factor," *New Statesman* 17 (July 2006), 18.

54 Caroline Elkins, "The Struggle for Mau Mau Rehabilitation in Late Colonial Kenya," *International Journal of African Historical Studies* 33, no. 1 (accessed June 8, 2010), 21, World History Collection Database.

55 Jeremy Sarkin, *Colonial Genocide and Reparations Claims in the 21st Century* (London: Praeger, 2008).

56 Ray, "The Empire's Ghost Returns," 21.

57 Elkins, *Imperial Reckoning*, 181.

58 Ibid., 66.

59 Zarina Patel, "Mau Mau: Raw British Brutality," *New African* (August/September, 2009), 18–22.

60 Elkins, *Imperial Reckoning*, 244.

61 Leigh Brownhill, "Mau Mau Demand Reparations from Britain for Colonial Crimes," *Capitalism Nature Socialism* 20 (June 2009), 103.

62 Zarina Patel, "Mau Mau: Raw British Brutality," *New African*, 487 (August/September 2009), 281.

63 Elkins, *Imperial Reckoning*, 67.

64 Anderson, *Histories of the Hanged: The Dirty War in Kenya and the End of Empire*, 291.

65 Ibid., 201.

66 Elkins, *Imperial Reckoning*, 129.

67 Joanna Lewis, "Nasty, Brutish and in Shorts? British Colonial Rule, Violence and the Historians of Mau Mau," *Round Table* (April 2007), 204.

68 David Anderson, "Burying the Bones of the Past," *History Today* 56, no. 2 (February, 2005) (accessed May 27, 2010), World History Database.

69 Joseph Conrad, *Last Essays* (London: Ayer Company, 1926), 17.

70 Russell Schimmer, "Belgian Congo," *Genocide Studies Program* (New Haven, CT: Yale Univesity, n.d.), 1.

71 Michiko Kakutani, "King Leopold's Ghost: Genocide with Spin Control," 1.

72 Adam Hochschild, "Leopold's Congo: A Holocaust We Have Yet to Comprehend," *Chronicle of Higher Education* 46, no. 36 (May 2000), 2.

73 Hanna Arendt, *The Origins of Totalitarianism*, rev. ed. (New York: Schocken, 2004).

74 Isidore Ndaywel e Nziem, *General History of the Congo: The Ancient Heritage of the Democratic Republic of the Congo* (Paris: Duculot, 1998).

75 Mark Twain, *King Leopold's Soliloquy: A Defense of His Congo Rule*, 2nd ed. (Boston: P.R. Warren Company, 1905).

76 Adam Hochschild, "Leopold's Congo, 230.

77 Ibid., 226.

78 Algerian War Reading, "The Algerian Civil War, 1954–1962: Why Such a Bitter Conflict? (n.d.). http://usf.usfca.edu/fac_staff/webberm/algeria.htm, p. 1 (accessed May 30, 2010). See also Anthony Clayton, *The Wars of French Decolonization* (London: Longman, 1994); John Talbott, *The War Without a Name: France in Algeria, 1954–1962* (London: Faber & Faber, 1981).

79 Al-Ahram Weekly On-line, "Ahmed Ben Bella: The More It Changes" (10–16 May 2001), 533, BBC NEWS (20 April 2006).

80 Michel Cornaton, *The Regroupings of Decolonization in Algeria* (Paris: Library Publishing, 1967), 63–66. See also K. Sutton and R. I. Lawless, "Population Regrouping in Algeria: Traumatic Change and the Rural Settlement Pattern," *Transactions of the Institute of British Geographers*, NS 3 (1978), 331–350; Mohammed Harbi, *The National Liberation Front: Illusion and Reality* (Paris: J. A. Publishing, 1980), 208.

81 Algerian War Reading, "The War's Toll," 46.

82 G. H. Blake, "Settlement and Conflict in the Mediterranean World," *Transactions of the Institute of British Geographers,* NS 3 (1978), 256.

83 Algerian War Reading, "The War's Toll," 46.

84 Marianne Arens and Françoise Thull, "Torture in the Algerian War (1954–1962): The Role of the French Army – Then and Now", http://www.wsws.org/articles/2001/apr2001 (accessed May 30, 2010).

85 Robert Aldrich, "Colonial Violence and Post-Colonial France" (2007), 16. http://conferences.arts.syyd.edu.au/viewpaper.php?id=745&cf=18 (accessed June 3, 2010).

86 Neil MacMaster, "The Torture Controversy (1998–2002): Towards a 'New History' of the Algerian War?", *Modern & Contemporary France* 10, no. 4 (2002), 452. See also Alistair Horne, "Shades of Abu Ghraib," *National Interest* 104 (Nov/Dec 2009), 3.

87 Raphaelle Branch, "Torture and Other Violations of the Law by the French Army during the Algerian War," *Genocide, War Crimes, and the West* (London: Zed Books, 2004), 138.

88 Lucy Garnier interview with Raphael Branche, "The French Army and Torture During the Algerian War (1954– 1962)," *Oxford French House of Minutes* (2004), 2.

89 Henri Alleg, *The Question* (Winnipeg, Canada: Bison Books, 2006). At the time of his arrest by French paratroopers during the Battle of Algiers in June of 1957, Henri Alleg was a French journalist who supported Algerian independence. He was interrogated for one month. During his imprisonment, Alleg was questioned under torture, with unbelievable brutality and sadism. Jean-Paul Sartre's preface remains a relevant commentary on the moral and political effects of torture on both the victim and perpetrator.

90 Neil MacMaster, "The Torture Controversy (1998–2002)," 451.

91 B. Sehene, "Rwanda's Collective Amnesia" *UNESCO Courier* (1999, December), 33–34.

92 V. M. Mays, M. Bullock, M. R. Rosenzweig, and M. Wessells, "Ethnic Conflict: Global Challenges and Psychological Perspectives," *American Psychologist* 53, no. 7 (1998): 737–742.

93 Leigh Brownhill, "Mau Mau Demand Reparations from Britain for Colonial Crimes," *Capitalism Nature Socialism* 20, no. 2 (June 2009), 103.

94 Brandon Hamber, "Repairing the Irreparable: Dealing with the Double-binds of Making Reparations for Crimes of the Past," *Ethnicity & Health,* 5 (August/November 2000), 2.

95 Jeremy Sarkin and Carly Fowler, "Reparations for Historical Human Rights Violations: The International and Historical Dimensions of the Alien Torts Claim Act Genocide Case of the Herero of Namibia," *Human Rights Review* 9, no. 3 (2008), 331–360.

96 Brandon Hamber and Richard A. Wilson, "Symbolic Closure through Memory, Reparation and Revenge in Post-conflict Societies," *Journal of Human Rights* 1, no. 1 (March 2002): 35–53.

97 Peter Stoett, "Shades of Complicity: Towards a Typology of Transnational Crimes against Humanity," in *Genocide, War Crimes, and the West: History and Complicity,* ed. Adam Jones (London: Zed Books, 2004).

98 Francis N. Nesbitt, "Coming to Terms with the Past: The Case for a Truth and Reparations Commission on Slavery, Segregation and Colonialism," 375.

99 Michael Dynes and Richard Beeson, "African Nations Row over Slavery Compensation," *Times* (September 5, 2001), Overseas News, 12.

100 Jeremy Sarkin and Carly Fowler, "Reparations for Historical Human Rights Violations," 332.

101 Lee Stranahan, "After a Long Legal battle, The British Government has apologized and agreed to pay € 19.9 Million (about $30 million) to thousands of Kenyans who were tortured between 1951 and 1962 in the Mau Mau uprising. Daily Mail (June 6, 2013).

102 Ibid.

103 The Guardian (Tuesday 17, April 2012).

104 Anthony Cary, "Migrated Archives" The Telegraph (24 February 2011).

105 Ibid.

106 Jason Straziuso and Gregory Katz, "UK to Compensate Kenyans," Denver Post (6 June 2013).

107 Ibid.

108 Jason Straziuso and Gregory Katz, 6 June 2013.

REVIEW QUESTIONS

1. Define genocide and critically discuss Raphael Lemkin's understanding of genocide and its applicability to colonial Africa.
2. What is reparation? Do you think economic and social reparations are needed in rebuilding Africa? Do you think an African Recovery Program is needed in Africa?
3. Do you agree with John Stuart Mill's statement that "despotism is a legitimate mode of government in dealing with barbarians, provided the end be their betterment"? Discuss this as it relates to the holocaust in colonial Africa.
4. Discuss torture. Is it ever justified to use it? Are there justifiable uses of certain methods of torture?

Writing Prompts

Write a brief essay identifying some of the ways in which colonial rule in Africa still affects the continent's current social, political, and economic realities.

CHAPTER 15

Apartheid in South Africa

Michael Mwenda Kithinji

Defined in Afrikaans as "separateness," *apartheid* was a systematic and legalized policy by the white minority government of South Africa to enforce racial and ethnic discrimination against the majority non-whites. Apartheid was based on unfounded racial notions that justified white superiority. The proponents of apartheid demanded for separation of races through enforcement of racial categorization in social, economic, and political affairs. In practice, the implementation of apartheid involved state enforced program of white supremacy, racial and ethnic segregation, and outlawing of interracial marriages. Although officially introduced in 1948 by the descendants of Dutch settlers known as Afrikaners or Boers, the origin of apartheid is deeply rooted in South African history as European settlers applied various means to subjugate the native Africans and other immigrants of non-European descent. The policy was a product of the long conflict between the British and the Afrikaners in South Africa. The supremacist ideology came to full realization in 1948 following the rise to power of the National Party (NP), which professed apartheid ideology and lasted until 1994 when the first multiracial elections were held. This chapter examines the historical origins and imposition of apartheid, the anti-apartheid liberation campaign, the decline of apartheid rule, and its impact on South Africa. It argues that apartheid is central in understanding modern South Africa.

THE COMING OF THE EUROPEANS AND THE DUTCH EAST INDIA COMPANY RULE

Racial discrimination and segregationist policies in South Africa began after the arrival of the first Europeans at the Cape in 1652. The pioneer Europeans were the representatives of the Dutch East India Company, a chartered Dutch company that was granted monopoly control by the government of Netherlands to exploit its colonial enterprises in Asia. The company established a supply outpost at the Cape in South Africa to service its ships on the journey to and from East Asia. Decades afterwards, new European immigrants arrived. They were mostly from Netherlands. Migrating to South Africa were also French and German puritans who were escaping from religious persecutions in Europe. An oppressive system of subjugating the indigenous KhoiKhoi people became a common practice as immigrant Europeans annexed their land, subjected them into slavery, and forcefully seized their livestock.[1] The KhoiKhoi population of South Africa declined tremendously as they succumbed to the hostile conditions created by the immigrant Europeans, a development that in turn affected the cheap labor supply for the settlers who opted to importing slaves from other parts of Africa and indentured servants from Asia.[2] In about a century and half of European presence at the Cape, the area underwent a demographic transformation as the increased cohabitation of slaves and masters produced a new social class of mixed race who were later classified as a distinct racial group known as the coloureds.[3] Also during that period, the European settlers at the Cape underwent a process of acculturation, shedding their original

European identities and instead forging a new European-African identity, which they referred to as Afrikaner. The process of cultivating a new identity by the Afrikaners, who initially spoke a variety of European languages such as Dutch, French and German involved forging of a new language, the Afrikaans, which although mostly intelligible with Dutch borrowed heavily from African languages.

BRITISH IMPERIAL RULE

The Afrikaner dominance at the Cape ended in 1806 when the British, who were engaged in the Napoleonic wars, annexed the area to preempt French control. The British control changed the political, economic, and sociocultural dynamics of the Cape and by extension the entire South Africa. Afrikaners resented British imperial control and the Anglicization policies that they pursued. In the 1830s, many of them fled the Cape, migrating to the hinterland regions of South Africa, away from the reach of the British in what came to be referred to as the Great Trek.[4]

As the Afrikaners spread inland, they encountered different African ethnic groups whom they sought to conquer and control, leading to vicious warfare. A number of factors favored the Afrikaners in their encounter with the Africans. First, the Mfekane, a period of natural disasters and ethnic rivalries that saw the emergence of a ruthless empire builder, Shaka Zulu, weakened the African groups in South Africa. The Mfekane and Shaka wars of attrition created a demographic crisis due to the wiping out of many African groups with many others fleeing to escape the ongoing chaos. Second, the Afrikaners had more effective artillery weapons that allowed them to subdue the weakened Africans, dispossessing them of their land. Ultimately, the Afrikaners created two states named Transvaal and Orange Free State in the northern interiors of South Africa. The Great Trek would later become a mythologized symbol of the Afrikaner "divinely inspired" struggle to survive in a hostile environment and inspired a later Afrikaner cultural and political renaissance that sought to stir a nationalist uprising against the British imperial administration in South Africa and install an Afrikaner supremacist rule.[5]

Eager to avert further confrontation, the British recognized the Afrikaner states of Transvaal and Orange Free State. By the mid-1850s, the two European groups were in firm control of South Africa, the British administering the coastal regions of Natal and Cape provinces and the Afrikaners in the hinterland regions of Transvaal and Orange Free State. However, the discovery of diamonds and gold in the second half of the nineteenth century in the Afrikaner states of Orange Free State and Transvaal would soon disrupt the relative tranquility between the Afrikaners and the British. The mineral discovery created two main trends that had a defining role in South Africa's racial history. First, many mineral prospectors from Britain, North America, Australia, and other parts of Europe flocked to South Africa. These mineral prospectors increased the population of Anglicized Europeans in the Afrikaner provinces, thereby threatening the economic and political power of the Afrikaners. The threat to the Afrikaners posed by the Anglo-Europeans revived their latent animosity toward the British. Second, the mineral revolution produced a racialized labor pattern of control and discrimination. The mine owners, seeking partly to check against mineral theft from their mines and aiming at having a greater labor control, instituted a system of housing their workers in closed barracks known as compounds. The housed workers would have little contact with the outside world and would dedicate all their time and energies to their employers. The workers would also have little chance of deserting to other higher-paying jobs and therefore help keep mine wages depressed. The intolerable working conditions that evolved in the mines did not attract white workers who had more career opportunities. Africans, however, many of whom had been displaced from their land by the expanding European colonialists, did not have much choice other than to work in the mines. The rising sense of racial supremacy by the Europeans also contributed to the evolving industrial relations at the mines and the emerging cities nearby. While the privileged positions and higher wages became a preserve for the whites, only non-skilled lower wage positions were available for Africans. The discriminatory and segregationist policies in industrial and residential relations became one of the key elements of apartheid South Africa.[6]

The discovery of minerals in South Africa triggered the British ambitions to extend its imperial control over the entire South Africa by annexing the Afrikaner states of Transvaal and Orange Free State. In the subsequent period, the British got into serious conflicts with the Afrikaners and some African groups such as the Zulu and Pedi that had retained some measure of sovereignty in the face of immense imperial onslaught. In order to fulfill their imperial ambitions, the British first sought to conquer the combative Zulu and Pedi. The two African groups however were determined to retain their freedom and fiercely resisted the British. The British only subdued the Zulu and Pedi after receiving military reinforcements from Britain and India, setting stage for a final offensive against the Afrikaners in the form of the decisive Anglo-Boer war that broke out in 1899. While the British expected a quick and easy outcome, the Anglo-Boer war dragged on for three years with heavy casualties on both sides. The British victory eventually came in 1902 with the signing of the Peace of Vereeniging, which ended the war.[7]

Although victorious in the Anglo-Boer war, the experience convinced the British that their continued control of South Africa would prolong the conflict with the Afrikaners, with whom they sought to mend fences after the signing of the peace treaty. Subsequently, the two groups embarked on a process of constitutional reform that resulted in the creation of the Union of South Africa. Through the Union Constitution, Britain agreed to cede power to the Afrikaners with the understanding that British interests in the Union would be safeguarded and that South Africa would become a member of the Commonwealth, a community of former British colonies. The Union was inaugurated on May 31, 1910, with Louis Botha, an Afrikaner veteran of the Anglo-Boer war and leader of the moderate South African Party (SAP), as its Prime Minister. By creating the Union of South Africa, the British government was much more concerned about reconciling with the Afrikaners than creating an inclusive multiracial nation. The new political dispensation spelled doom to the country's African majority because it only provided enfranchisement for white males, although plans were in place to facilitate the enfranchisement of white women. Failure by the union constitution to grant the majority non-whites full citizenship rights within the Union laid the basis for their future subjugation by the Afrikaners.[8]

UNION OF SOUTH AFRICA AND THE RISE OF AFRIKANER NATIONALISM

The period between 1910 and 1948 witnessed intense radicalization of nationalist politics as Afrikaners sought greater control and monopolization of power and to avenge what they considered historical injustices perpetrated on them by the English speakers. It is, however, the Africans who bore the brunt of Afrikaner parochialism. During this period, the Afrikaner government enacted laws and policies that further dehumanized and dispossessed the majority Africans. Some of the racist laws that were passed included the 1911 Mines and Work Acts, which reserved all skilled and most semi-skilled jobs exclusively for whites, and the 1913 Native Land Act, which reserved one-eighth of South African land for the African majority and the remaining seven-eighths for the exclusive use of the white minority. In 1918, the Afrikaner government passed the Natives in Urban Areas Bill, which forced Africans into their restricted locations in urban areas. The 1923 enactment of the Native (Urban Areas) Act attempted to control the African migrations into and within the towns, while the 1936 Natives Act disenfranchised Africans in the Cape Province where propertied Africans had enjoyed voting rights.[9]

The enactment of segregationist laws mirrored the radicalization of Afrikaner politics. The period between 1910 and 1948 witnessed the declining fortunes of the moderate ruling South African Party (SAP) and the rise of the extremist National Party (NP) formed in 1914 by J.B.M. Herzog, a radical Afrikaner politician. The NP exploited the Afrikaner antipathy for the British in its quest for power. The NP popularized itself by advocating for the interests of ordinary Afrikaners and demanding that South Africa sever all ties with Britain who it claimed was responsible for the economic dispossession of most Afrikaners. Although an extremist, Herzog was a pragmatist seeking to shore up his support and attain power. In 1934, he led his NP into a merger with the moderate SAP to form the United Party (UP), a development that infuriated the hardcore Afrikaner nationalists led by D. F. Malan, a clergy of the Dutch Reformed Church. Malan and his followers refused to join the UP but instead formed a splinter Purified National Party. Malan's fortunes would rise tremendously as his party gained more support from Afrikaners who opposed South Africa's support of the Allies in World War II. Herzog joined other Afrikaner nationalists in protesting the South African entry into the war on the side of the Allies by quitting the UP in 1940 and reuniting with the Purified National Party to form the Reunited National Party.[10]

Thereafter, the reinvigorated National Party embarked on refining its nationalist ideology by embracing the policy of apartheid, which became its campaign blueprint as the 1948 elections approached. The NP waged a spirited grassroots campaign among the Afrikaners, promising to ensure their supremacy over other races and delivering them from Anglo domination. The message of apartheid resonated especially with the poor

Afrikaners whose vote helped the NP to manage a slim victory of 79 seats as opposed to 65 for the United Party and six for the Labour Party. Malan expressed the meaning of this victory when he arrived in Pretoria to take the reins of power. In his address to supporters, Malan noted that in the past, Afrikaners "felt like strangers in our own country but today South Africa belongs to us once more. For the first time since Union, South Africa is our own. May God grant that it always remains our own."[11]

APARTHEID IN PRACTICE

Upon coming to power, Malan and the National Party (NP) embarked on a process of consolidating its superior position in parliament by engaging in electoral manipulation in South Africa's colony of Namibia where it created six electoral constituencies for white settler population. The NP won the additional seats, giving it a superior position in parliament. One of the key pillars of apartheid policy was the idea of separation of different races and ethnic groups residing in South Africa. Thus, the apartheid government initiated its rule, by creating and assigning to everyone residing in South Africa solid racial and ethnic categories. Henceforth, access to opportunities or enjoyment of civil liberties depended upon one's social group designation. Implementation of apartheid involved the enactment of a series of legislations starting with the 1949 Prohibition of Mixed Marriage Act that banned interracial marriages followed by Immorality Act that forbid any sexual relations between whites and non-whites. The formal separation of races started in 1950 with the enactment of the Population Registration Act of 1950 that categorized, classified, and registered everyone according to racial characteristics. In the same year, parliament enacted the Group Areas Act that provided for gradual introduction of residential segregation of all races and gave the urban authorities powers to demarcate racial areas. This law paved the way for the ethnic balkanization of Africans, a goal enumerated by Hendrik Verwoerd, one of the architects of apartheid and minister for Native Affairs. According to Verwoerd, "as the nations of the world, each in its own territory, accomplishes its own development, so also the opportunity will be given here to the various native groups each to accomplish its own development each in its own territory."[12] Verwoerd's goal was accomplished through the enactment of the 1952 Bantu Authorities Act and the 1959 Promotion of Bantu Self-government Act that classified Africans according to their ethnic identities, created tribal administrative units called Bantustans, and provided a form of self-government to these units. The creation of Bantustans was a way to distract the attention of Africans from national politics by keeping them preoccupied with local issues. In addition, Bantustans were an active propagation of tribalism to keep Africans divided and incapable of forming a united front against the apartheid regime.

Apartheid theory of separate development was extended to education with the 1953 enactment of the Bantu Education Act that aimed at bringing African education under state control. It is important at this point to clarify that in apartheid jargon, the term *Bantu* was not a simple anthropological designation of a cultural group that migrated from west to southern, eastern, and central parts of Africa over thousands of years. Rather, it was a racially offensive term used by the apartheid regime to refer to all black people in South Africa. Verwoerd justified Bantu education claiming that until the coming of apartheid, Africans had been subjected to a school system that drew them away from their community. Accordingly, it has misled him (African) "by showing him the green pastures of the European life but still does not allow him to graze there."[13] According to Verwoerd, this unplanned education "creates many problems, disrupts the communal life of the Bantu, and endangers the communal life of the European."[14] Bantu education was therefore an antidote to the problems enumerated by Verwoerd because it would limit the intellectual horizons of the Africans and make them acceptant of their "inferior" position in South Africa's society.

The first guiding principle for the Bantu education as provided by the act was that African education was to be different from that of Europeans because it was based on different kinds of knowledge. Second, education was supposed to prepare people for their opportunities in life, which for Africans was to be in the reserves or as migrant workers in cities. Last, education had to instill within Africans the belief that they had no equal rights with whites and that their development was confined within their own sphere. As Verwoerd stated, "education had to stand with both feet in the reserves and have its root in the spirit and being of Bantu society."[15] The content of African education as mandated by the Bantu act was supposed to be explicitly both Christian and Afrikaner in character. African teachers were charged with instilling in their pupils a worldview that would make them acceptant of all inequalities of apartheid as well as the white supremacist contentions that justified them.

The Bantu education was extended to universities with the passing of University Education Acts of 1955 and 1959. These legislations established Bantu colleges in areas designated as African reserves or tribal homelands. In addition, the University of Fort Hare, the oldest black college, was turned into a Bantu institution after it was forced to abandon its open admission policy. Henceforth, it could only admit African students. The Universities of Cape Town, Witwatersrand, and Natal, which had also maintained an open enrollment policy, were prohibited from admitting African students.[16] While it disenfranchised Africans educationally, the apartheid government on the other hand, took steps to improve white education, especially that of the Afrikaners. The National Party made Afrikaner education compulsory and free and expanded it by building Afrikaans-language schools, colleges, and universities.[17]

Like in education, the Afrikaner nationalists saw apartheid as a means to achieve economic superiority for the whites at the expense of other races. In particular, the apartheid regime aimed to bolster the existing racial policies that protected the poor Afrikaners from economic competition with Africans, especially in the job market. The minority regime dealt with this challenge by passing a number of laws, such as the Prevention of Illegal Squatting Act in 1951 and instituting a Labour Preference Policy (LPP) that prohibited black immigration to urban areas until those who were already there had been absorbed by the white labor market. In 1952, the apartheid regime passed the cynically entitled Abolition of Passes and Documents Act, which replaced the earlier passbook with a 96-page reference book. The passbook had a person's photograph and noted his or her personal history, such as place of origin, employment record, police encounters, tax payment, and residence rights. All black people over the age of 16 were legally mandated to carry the passbook at all time; failing to do this, they risked severe punishment. The Native Laws Amendment Act of the same year controlled African movement in all urban areas and included a vagrancy clause that gave powers to local officials to remove "idle or undesirable natives." Africans were prohibited from remaining in any urban area longer than seventy-two hours without appropriate permission stamped in their passbook. The only Africans recognized as legal residents in urban areas were those who had lived there for fifteen years continuously or had served the same employer for ten years. Apartheid regime continued to drive deeper racial wedge in South African society with the 1953 passing of the Reservation of Separate Amenities Act that forced segregation in all public places. The act was explicit that the facilities provided for different races need not be equal, as "Europeans Only" and "Non-Europeans Only" signs appeared all over the country.

The enactment of segregationist laws presented the apartheid government with an opportunity to clear several commercially attractive African neighborhoods in cities, turning them into either white suburbs or commercial centers. An example of such cruel eviction of Africans from their homes happened in 1956 when Sophiatown, a black suburb of Johannesburg was cleared and replaced by a white suburb, cynically named Triomf (Triumph). The African residents of Sophiatown were relocated to Soweto Township.[18]

Although the apartheid government prided itself as a preserver and promoter of Christian values, and South Africa, a bastion of western civilization away from Europe, its policies deviated sharply from the anti-racist, pro-human rights trends that were gaining current in the West and around the world. The apartheid regime interpreted Western civilization in terms of exclusion and tried to reproduce the Jim Crow era racial segregationist laws of the southern states of the United States of America. The implementation of the segregationist policies, however, was happening at a time when the reverse was the norm in the United States where in 1954 the Supreme Court in *Brown v. Board of Education of Topeka, Kansas* ruled against school segregation and, subsequently, segregation in general. Similarly, the rise of anachronistic apartheid regime with its ideology of racism and white domination was contrary to the prevailing trends in Africa where European colonialism was under intense pressure. The "wind of change" prominently referenced by Harold Macdonald, the British Prime Minister in his tour of South Africa in 1960, was blowing across Africa in the form of intensified nationalistic activities and decolonization. Although African nationalism in South Africa was on the rise like in the rest of the continent, apartheid regime violently resisted calls for change.

RESISTANCE TO APARTHEID

The various segments of South African society had a long history of resisting racial oppression and disregard of human dignity. The Indians, for instance, organized by Mohandas Gandhi under the Natal Indian Congress (NIC), engaged in a campaign of peaceful protest against discrimination in the late 1890s and early 1900s.[19]

Following the enactment of the Union constitution and with the civil liberties of non-whites under intense assault, the African leaders in 1912 formed the South African Native National Congress (SANNC) to articulate the rights and freedoms of all races and ethnic groups in South Africa.[20] The SANNC in 1923 changed its name to the African National Congress (ANC). In its early days, the ANC was a moderate, reformist organization dominated by a few educated Africans who were influenced by the ideas of African American leaders such as Booker T. Washington and W.E.B. Dubois. The events of World War II characterized by the rise of Pan-Africanist Movements, the declaration of the Atlantic Charter in 1941 that stressed the right to self-determination, the establishment of the United Nations, and the war experience by African troops prompted a revival of the ANC. In 1943, Nelson Mandela, Walter Sisulu, and Oliver Tambo, three young African professionals, founded a Youth League within the ANC. In the same year, the ANC adopted a manifesto, "Africans' Claim in South Africa," which demanded the full implementation of the principles of the Atlantic Charter in Africa and the recognition of the aspirations of black people once the War concluded. While the Youth League shared the traditional ANC goal of a democratic, nonracial society, it also endorsed more militant tactics, such as street protests and mass action to attain them. The ANC led by the members of the Youth League vigorously resisted the rise of apartheid and in 1949 adopted a Program of Action that included active resistance such as strikes, boycotts, and civil disobedience.[21]

In June 1952, the ANC teamed up with several other anti-apartheid organizations and launched a Defiance Campaign of active resistance against discriminatory legislations. The apartheid regime reacted to the campaigns violently by invoking the Suppression of Communism Act of 1950, which outlawed communism, and the Communist Party in South Africa. The apartheid government defined communism broadly and used it to outlaw any dissent groups, and in the process, arrested thousands of people involved in the Defiance Campaign. While the Campaign of Defiance served to boast the popularity of the ANC among Africans, Asians, and coloureds, on the other hand, it frightened the white population, helping the National Party to gain more votes in the 1953 elections and giving the government an excuse to pass new repressive measures.[22] To enforce the draconian measures, the apartheid regime created a highly equipped and trained police force, military, and intelligence service, which served as instruments of terror and were notorious for brutal treatment of political opponents.

The suppression of dissenting political activities only served to reinvigorate the opposition forces. In a defining moment in 1955, the anti-apartheid movements, including the ANC, the South African Indian Congress, the South African Coloured Peoples' Organization, the predominantly white Congress of Democrats, and the multiracial South African Congress of Trade Unions came together to form the Congress Alliance. The Alliance convened a Congress of the People on June 26, 1955, in Johannesburg where the delegates approved the Freedom Charter, a document boldly declaring that South Africa belonged to all who lived in it regardless of their race and that no government could claim authority unless it was based on the will of the people. The Freedom Charter attracted swift reaction from the government, which labeled the document a communist manifesto, arrested the top leaders of the Congress Alliance including luminaries like Nelson Mandela, Walter Sisulu, Helen Joseph, and Lillian Ngoyi and charged them with treason. The Supreme Court finally acquitted the arrested leaders in 1961. Despite the state repression, the anti-apartheid activists continued with peaceful protests throughout the 1950s.[23]

The intensification of state repression, however, rendered the peaceful protest methods ineffective but more importantly served to create fissures among the anti-apartheid forces as the 1950s ended. In 1959, the ANC experienced a major split when the more radical members who opposed multiracial cooperation of the Congress Alliance broke away to form the Pan African Congress (PAC). The militant PAC played a critical role in reviving anti-apartheid activities in the early 1960s when it called anti-pass laws demonstrations throughout the country. Although the campaign was nonviolent, the state security organs reacted violently by arresting, beating, and detaining the participants. Undeterred by state suppression, on March 21, 1960, Africans in Sharpeville, a black township near Vereeniging, 50 miles south of Johannesburg, converged outside the city's police station in a defiant expression of their disgust with oppressive laws. The large crowd of more than 5,000 people overwhelmed the police who in the scuffles that ensued opened fire on the demonstrators, killing 69 and wounding hundreds more.

The news of the killings at Sharpeville and violence visited on demonstrators in other parts of South Africa horrified and outraged the world. The international condemnations that followed precipitated the increased isolation of the apartheid regime. International investor confidence also suffered a blow as exports declined, gold and foreign currency reserves dropped by more than half within a year, and capital flow out of the country accelerated. In South Africa, Sharpeville became a rallying cry for anti-apartheid movement as the ANC joined the protest in support of the PAC. On March 27, the ANC president, Albert Luthuli, burned his own pass and called for people nationwide to stay at home mourning the dead. Thousands attended the funerals for the fallen and the stay-at-home protests extended beyond the mourning day. Ultimately, the police and soldiers had to force people from their homes and back to work.[24]

REACTION TO DISSENT

Verwoerd, who became Prime Minister in 1958, reacted to the rising opposition in 1960 by passing the Unlawful Organizations Act, which outlawed the ANC and PAC, mobilized the Active Citizens Force (the white military reserves), declared a state of emergency throughout the country, banned public meetings and detained more than 18,000 dissidents. Among those arrested included Robert Sobukwe, the president of the PAC, who was sentenced to a nine-year prison sentence for his role in the uprising. Alfred Luthuli, who in the same year won the Nobel Peace Prize, received a one-year jail term for destroying his reference book.

The intensification of state repression reflected the expansion of the police and the military. The government spending on defense rose from US $63 million in 1960 to over $1 billion by 1975, gobbling nearly 20 percent of the national budget. With international isolation increasing, the government established the Armaments Corporation of South Africa (ARMSCOR) in 1964 to manufacture military artillery. South Africa also imported enormous amounts of military arsenal from the western nations of the United States, Britain, France, and Israel. Sadly, the atrocities perpetrated by the apartheid regime upon non-whites of South Africa did not offend the moral sensibilities of the western powers that supplied it with deadly arsenal. In fact, its western allies went a step further to help the apartheid regime develop a nuclear capability. By 1993, South Africa had an arsenal of seven nuclear bombs.[25] The state repression against anti-apartheid forces extended to suppression of all avenues of producing and transmitting divergent ideas or information. In 1963, the government formed the Publications Control Board, which closely controlled and monitored books, periodicals, music, and films. The state also closely controlled the media to limit the propagation of opposing views.[26]

MILITARIZATION OF RESISTANCE

The clampdown on all political activities by the apartheid regime compelled the anti-apartheid forces to reassess their strategies. While the main strategy of expressing opposition to apartheid had involved nonviolent protests, the government had activated and enhanced its coercive agencies that visited untold terror on those who dared articulate change. Frustrated by the obstinacy of the apartheid regime, in 1962, the members of the ANC's Youth League led by Mandela and Sisulu founded an underground guerilla army known as Umkhonto we Sizwe (Spear of the Nation). The PAC also founded its military wing named Poqo (Xhosa for "pure," or standing alone), while a group of mainly white radical liberals and communists formed the African Resistance Movement (ARM). The formation of guerilla units in the early 1960s transformed the resistance efforts against apartheid from the earlier Gandhian peaceful protests to more combative militant form. The militant movements staged guerilla attacks on important government installations such as railroads, bridges, power-generating centers, and so on while trying to minimize the number of human casualties.

The apartheid regime responded to the establishment of militant units and increased acts of sabotage by passing the Sabotage Act in 1962 that gave immense powers to the Justice ministry, allowing it to restrict political activism and to place "communist agitators" under house arrest. The newly appointed Minister for Justice, John Voster, a former member of Ossewabrandwag, an extreme rightwing paramilitary group, undertook with gusto the powers conferred to him by the sabotage act, demanding the judiciary to hand severe punishment to those suspected of engaging in activities deemed a danger to national security. The General Law Amendment Act of 1963 allowed the police to arrest those suspected of engaging in subversive political activities for questioning without charging or allowing them access to family or lawyers for up to twelve days. Subsequent amendment to the law allowed for indefinite periods of detention.

THE PURGE OF ANC LEADERSHIP

The vast powers given to the security agencies and the emasculation of the judiciary by the executive allowed for ruthless crackdown on the opposition. Nelson Mandela, who had gone into hiding fearing arrest for his dissident activities, was among those who faced the immediate wrath of the new laws. Mandela was captured in his hideout near Pietermaritzburg on August 5, 1962, and received a swift sentence of five years prison term for incitement and leaving the country without passport. A few months later, on July 11, 1963, the other senior members of the Umkhonto we Sizwe, including Walter Sizulu and Govan Mbeki, were arrested at their secret command center of Lilliesleaf, a farm near Rivonia north of Johannesburg. The apartheid government took Mandela out of prison and back to court where he was charged alongside other Umkhonto leaders of sabotage and belonging to a communist organization. During the trial, the prosecution relied heavily on documents seized during the raid that detailed the plans and the operations of the Umkhonto movement. At the trial, Mandela argued that the guerilla activities were an option of the last resort after the "government met our peaceful demands with force."[27] On June 12, 1964, the court found the following guilty of sabotage and sentenced them to life in prison: Nelson Mandela, Walter Sizulu, Govan Mbeki, Raymond Mhlaba, Elias Motsoaledi, Andrew Mlangeni, Ahmed Kathrada, and Dennis Goldberg. All but Dennis Goldberg were sent to Robben Island, the prison for black male prisoners located five miles off the coast from Cape Town.

The imprisonment of the ANC leaders reflected the ruthless suppression of all nationalists. In addition to the crackdown of the top brass of the ANC, the security agencies rounded up and jailed many leaders and activists associated with other anti-apartheid organizations. Those who avoided arrest went into hiding or fled to exile. Through enforcement of its harsh laws, torture, and intimidation, the government had succeeded in crushing the anti-apartheid movement. It would take several years for the anti-apartheid movement to rebound.

BANTUSTANS

The successful crackdown on opposition in the early 1960s further entrenched apartheid rule. The government wanted to prevent future recurrence of anti-apartheid activities by directing African political energies to their homelands. Parliament had passed the Promotion of Bantu Self-Government Bill in 1959 that allowed the homelands to become fully independent states. Transkei, a Xhosa homeland, became the first "independent" Bantustan in 1963. In the subsequent period, the apartheid government designated several other homelands as either independent or partially independent. By granting "independence" to Bantustans, the apartheid regime intended to nurture a sense of national consciousness among the various groups it created. Bantustans would, therefore, affirm the ideology of separateness by portraying Africans as citizens of separate countries within the boundaries of South Africa and thus subject to deportation if found in "foreign" homeland.[28] The Africans who became the leaders of the Bantustans such as Kaiser Mantanzima, the first prime minister of Transkei, were opportunists only interested in achieving their individual political ambitions even if it meant oppressing their own people. The Bantustans as political units were devoid of any real sovereignty as their defense, immigration, internal security, and foreign policy remained under the control of apartheid government. Further, they relied on South Africa for provision of postal, railway, banking, and air transportation services. A majority of the Africans, Asians, and coloureds resented the Bantustan policy because it advanced their continued disenfranchisement and oppression. Consequently, the Bantustan governments lacked international recognition and domestically suffered a crisis of legitimacy.

THE BLACK CONSCIOUSNESS MOVEMENT

A casual glance at the late 1960s can mislead one to conclude that it was the golden age of apartheid rule due to its success in derailing opposition. In reality, however, the anti-apartheid movement was in hibernation, undergoing a transformation whose effect was felt in the coming decades. Several forces were at play during this period, most importantly, the emergence of the Black Consciousness Movement (BCM), which was a product of the reaction by young people to segregationist education policies. Inspiring the movement also were the social and political transformations taking place around the world in the 1960s in the form of "winds of change" that led to freedom and independence from colonial rule of most countries in Africa, and the American Civil Rights and Black Power movements. Leading the BCM in South Africa was Steve Biko, a medical student at Natal University. Biko had helped found the South African Students Organization, which broke off from the white-dominated National Union of South African Students in 1968. In 1972, he brought together the organizations that were advocating Black Consciousness principles in a convention and, thereafter, transformed the union of represented organizations into the Black People's Convention (BPC). Through the BPC, the BCM challenged Africans to overcome attitudes of inferiority and subservience as a first step toward overcoming oppression.[29]

The BCM became very popular in black universities before spreading to secondary and primary schools. These young people would form a rebellious generation that confronted and shook the apartheid system to its core. While the government maintained a watchful eye on the activities of Biko and other leaders of the BCM, an ill-fated decision by the Ministry of Education to make Afrikaans the medium of teaching in African schools ignited a pent-up rage and frustration that seethed among the youth. Already, the young people abhorred the underfunded Bantu education system, viewing it as a means to keep them as a permanent subordinate class. The declaration by the Ministry of Education in 1975 for the adoption of Afrikaans in black schools only served to ignite the suppressed range. On June 16, 1976, 15,000 unarmed students in Soweto matched in protest against the declaration but were met by the police who tried to disperse them using tear gas, water cannons, rubber and live bullets. In the process, two students were killed, provoking an even bigger revolt by African youths. Within days, the revolt spread throughout the country. The apartheid government clamped down on the uprising in its usual abrasive manner, leading to many deaths and arrests. The brutal suppression of the revolt compelled many youths to flee the country where they joined the ANC guerilla brigades that were based in the neighboring countries. The revolt triggered by the 1976 Soweto uprising revitalized the ANC and to a lesser extent the PAC, infusing them with new blood of discontented youths. The uprising also turned Steve Biko into a martyr after the police arrested and tortured him to death in 1977.[30]

INTERNATIONAL ISOLATION AND CRISIS

The death of Biko and the changing political situation in neighboring Mozambique and Angola, which had achieved their independence from Portugal in 1975, served to expose the soft underbelly of the apartheid system. The independence of Mozambique and Angola and later that of Zimbabwe in 1980 saw the rise of ANC allies to power greatly boosting the ongoing rebellion against apartheid. Moreover, in the cold war politics of the day, the ANC and its ally, the Communist Party, received material and moral support from the USSR. The violent response to Soweto uprising and the killing of Biko managed to weaken the apartheid regime, which found itself increasingly isolated in the global arena. In 1977, the United Nations passed a mandatory arms embargo while the United States under President Jimmy Carter approved a tightened economic embargo on South Africa and demanded the institution of full democracy. The events of the second half of the 1970s greatly worried the Afrikaner leaders, who now agreed that compromises would have to be made if white dominance in South Africa were to survive. Their fears had basis since the western multinationals responded to the crisis and economic sanctions by either reducing their level of investments or pulling out all together from the country. Soon, the economy went on a recession, and living standards especially for whites who had everything to lose started to decline as businesses failed and the housing market collapsed.

The economic problems were aggravated by a 1977 declaration that all young white men had to perform two years of compulsory military service with periodic service in the military reserve until they were 60 years old. The military conscription, coupled by increased white emigration out of the country and the falling white birth rate, meant that there were fewer whites available for jobs in business and industry. In 1977, for instance, over 3,000 mostly highly skilled and educated white professionals left the country. At the same time, the proportion of white population to the total population declined from a high of 21 percent to 16 percent.[31] The declining white population was a boon for blacks, whose numbers in the work force and thus in cities increased tremendously, negating the apartheid's principle of separate development. More importantly, the increasing black population in the workplace gave black people an opportunity to demand for the reform of some disenfranchising apartheid laws.

MANAGING THE CRISIS

The apartheid government attempted to halt the economic decline by appointing the Riekert and Wiehahn commissions in 1977 that would study ways of stemming the crisis. The Riekert Commission proposed the recognition of skilled and employed Africans in urban centers as permanent residents, enjoying the rights of suitable housing and other amenities. Although Africans would not enjoy any political rights, the "total strategy" advanced by the Commission envisaged the creation of a black middle class that owed its privileged positions to the system. The Wiehahn Commission on its part recommended reforms in industrial labor that would lead to the recognition of black trade unions, the abolition of the statutory job color bar and the opening of apprenticeships to Africans. Parliament enacted some of the recommendations of both Riekert and Wiehahn commissions with the reforms consequently leading to the formation of several black labor unions in the early 1980s, including the Federation of South African Trade Unions (FOSATO), the Council of Unions of South Africa (CUSA), and the National Union of Mineworkers (NUM). In 1985, the major trade unions combined to form the Congress of South African Trade Unions (COSATU). The new labor organizations formed an important platform for political expression in an environment that suppressed non-white political organizations. These organizations would soon play an even greater role in undermining apartheid rule.[32]

Meanwhile, P. W. Botha, a former Defense Minister who succeeded John Voster as Prime Minister in 1978, accelerated the pace of reform with the hopes of maintaining a modified form of white domination. In 1983, Botha inaugurated a new constitution that created a three-chamber parliament and a powerful presidency with himself occupying the position. The tricameral parliament gave representation to coloureds and Indians but denied the same to Africans. The apartheid government still argued that Africans could exercise their rights through the Bantustans. Botha's reforms were, however, unacceptable to the increasingly assertive Africans who formed the United Democratic Front (UDF), a nonracial coalition of trade unions and other community-based organizations including churches, civic organizations, and student unions. The UDF filled the void of the banned anti-apartheid political organizations and derived its strength from the local issues around which the various affiliates were able to mobilize. The UDF and its affiliates were successful in undermining the new apartheid constitution when they organized a successful boycott of the 1985 elections by coloureds and Indians. Thereafter, the UDF encouraged civil disobedience characterized by students and worker strikes. A protest mood engulfed the entire country as diverse grievances against the apartheid regime triggered violent responses from the aggrieved. For instance, opposition to the rent collected by black local authorities in the Vall townships of Sebokeng and Sharpeville in 1984 led to a prolonged and bloody confrontation between black youths and the authorities.[33]

The protests also took the form of economic sabotage with Africans boycotting white businesses. By 1986, the UDF controlled several townships in areas such as Pretoria, Witwatersrand, Johannesburg, Cape Town, and the Bantustans of the Transvaal. The civil disobedience helped to increase the profile of the ANC, as many UDF leaders were clandestine members of the organization and based their activities on the Freedom Charter.[34]

APARTHEID IN CRISIS

The UDF protests put a halt on President Botha's reform process as the state attempted to stamp out the sources of the revolt. The government proclaimed a State of Emergency in June 1986 followed by a campaign of repression with the security forces given greater powers to suppress the uprising. The government banned the UDF and several of its allies in 1987. It also recruited some African traditional leaders, local warlords, and vigilante squads who tried to suppress the revolt by harassing and in some cases assassinating those organizing the protests. The cooptation of Mongesuthu Buthelezi, a Zulu chief and the leader of the Inkatha Freedom Party, by the government led to a full-scale civil war between his supporters and those of the UDF in Kwazulu Natal. The use of deadly force, however, did not achieve its intended goal but rather inflamed the revolt as funerals for those killed turned into political rallies.

The prolonged social and political instability inflicted further damage on the economy, creating structural weaknesses that became apparent in the South Africa's military involvement in Angola where it supported the rebel National Union for the Total Independence of Angola (UNITA) of Jonas Savimbi that was fighting to overthrow the leftist government of Popular Movement for the Liberation of Angola (MPLA). The military adventure in Angola brought the South African army in direct conflict with the Cuban troops supporting the government. After suffering some early defeats, the Cuban and Angolan forces soon recovered and inflicted severe defeat on South African and UNITA forces in 1988. Facing a real threat of annihilation, South Africa acceded to Cuba's demands that it should accept the United Nations Resolution calling for the independence of Namibia. At the same time, the declining health of President Botha allowed the reform-minded F.W. De Klerk to rise to power in 1989. De Klerk instituted far-reaching restructuring of the political system that saw the dismantling of apartheid.[35]

DISMANTLING APARTHEID

De Klerk commenced his term in office by releasing from prison many of the leading ANC figures, notably Walter Sisulu and Ahmed Kathrada. In February 2, 1990, he lifted the ban on the ANC, the South African Communist Party, the Pan-African Congress, and all other proscribed organizations and announced his readiness to start national negotiations on a new political order. Nine days later, he released Nelson Mandela from prison after serving for twenty-seven years. In the same year, the seventy-five-year South African rule of Namibia ended with the South West Africa Peoples' Organization (SWAPO), an ally of the ANC, winning the first democratic elections.

Subsequently, De Klerk inaugurated talks to usher in a new constitutional order. The negotiations brought together various groups organized under the forum known as the Conventions for Democratic South Africa (CODESA). This period also witnessed the return of thousands of exiles who had formed the core of the ANC membership and had kept its campaign alive internationally. Despite the unfolding progress, danger loomed in the form of civil breakdown due to the use of criminal and opportunistic elements within the black community by security forces to suppress the anti-apartheid mass action. Consequently, a low-intensity civil war convulsed several areas such as Kwazulu Natal, where the Inkatha Freedom Party sought to fend off opposition from the ANC and consolidate its control. The situation worsened due to the acts of sabotage and random attacks on blacks by secret forces and Afrikaner extremists who were attempting to stop the ongoing dialogue and the overzealous ANC members who were inpatient with the slow pace of progress. The long and acrimonious CODESA talks further aggravated matters threatening to scuttle the reform process. Ultimately, however, an interim constitution was agreed upon in November 1993 and the first elections date was set for April 26 to 29, 1994.

The main provisions of the new constitution provided for a government of national unity after the elections, in which parties with over five percent of the vote would have ministerial office. In addition, two-thirds majority would be needed to write the constitution. The new constitution divided South Africa into nine provinces, which were charged with responsibilities in matters such as education and healthcare. Despite some initial challenges from the right-wing Afrikaner nationalists and some leaders of the Bantustans who resented their looming loss of power, the elections were conducted successfully. As expected, the ANC received a substantial majority of 62.65 percent of the vote and won control of seven out of the nine provinces. Coming a distant second was the NP, which received 20.4 percent of the vote across the country and won control of the province of the Western Cape. Buthelezi's Inkatha Party came out the third with 10.54 percent of the total national votes, taking control of the KwaZulu-Natal province. The new democratically elected government of national unity was inaugurated on May 10, 1994, with Nelson Mandela as president and F.W. De Klerk and Thabo Mbeki as the two vice-presidents of a united South Africa.

CONCLUSION

The end of apartheid paved the way for a new era marked by serious attempts to build free, democratic, and multiracial society. This undertaking was difficult due to the brutal legacies of foreign domination and apartheid rule. One of the main challenges that threatened post-apartheid reconstruction was the deep-rooted social divisions and suspicions among the various racial and ethnic groups in South Africa. The first democratically elected president, Nelson Mandela, handled this challenge tactfully by leading the way in promoting reconciliation and reaching out to the Afrikaner community, which had wielded power at the exclusion of everyone else for many decades. The new South Africa Mandela sought to build came to terms with the brutalities of the apartheid period by establishing the Truth Justice and Reconciliation Commission (TJRC) under Archbishop Desmond Tutu in 1995. The TJRC listened to testimonies from the perpetrators and victims of apartheid atrocities. The Commission granted amnesty to the perpetrators who gave a truthful account of their activities and proved that their actions were due to political pressure. Those who refused to appear or lied in their testimony faced prosecution. While South Africa has succeeded in achieving unity, the lingering challenge remains mostly economic, caused by the effects of apartheid policies and the poor quality of Bantu education system imposed on Africans during the regime. Moreover, many blacks boycotted schools in the 1970s and 1980s when a generation of children spent its youth challenging apartheid rule under the slogan of "Liberation Now! Education Later!" Consequently, the effects of unemployment and crime, due to missed educational opportunities, continue to ravage the black community more than any other racial group. Millions more suffer from homelessness and what former president de Klerk described as "conditions of unacceptable poverty and deprivation."[36] While a small class of black elite has scaled the commanding heights of the economy, the gap between the poor and the rich is one of the widest in the world, with less than 10 percent of the population controlling more than 90 percent of the wealth. Nonetheless, there is a cause for optimism due to relatively well-managed political transitions, a culture of negotiation and compromise, an accomplished civil society, and sophisticated industries and economic infrastructure.

ENDNOTES

1 The Khoikhoi are an indigenous nomadic pastoral people of Southern Africa, linguistically and culturally related to the hunter-gatherer San people of the same region.

2 Leonard M. Thompson, *A history of South Africa* (New Haven: Yale University Press, 2001), 45.

3 John Western, *Outcast Cape Town* (Minneapolis: University of Minnesota Press, 1981), 12.

4 Dunbar T. Moodie, *The Rise of Afrikanerdom: Power, Apartheid, and the Afrikaner Civil Religion* (Los Angeles: University of California Press, 1975), 4–6.

5 Ibid., 73–95.

6 Robert Ross, *A Concise History of South Africa* (Cambridge, UK: Cambridge University Press, 1999), 56.

7 For more on the Anglo-Boer War see Peter Warwick, *The War for South Africa: The Anglo-Boer War 1899–1902* (Harlow, Essex: Longman, 1980).

8 Robert Ross, *A Concise History of South Africa*, 81–82.

9 Roger B. Beck, *The History of South Africa* (Westport CT: Greenwood Press, 2000), 101–124.

10 Eric Louw, *The Rise, Fall, and Legacy of Apartheid* (London: Praeger 2004), 33.

11 *Rand Daily Mail*, June 2, 1948.

12 Cited in Davis Hunt, *Bantu Education and the Education of Africans in South Africa* (Athens: Ohio University Center for International Studies, 1972), 4.

13 Cited in Zandile Nkabide, *An Analysis of Educational Challenges in the New South Africa* (Lanham, NY: University Press of America, 1997), 8.

14 Zandile Nkabide, *An Analysis of Educational Challenges in the New South Africa*, 8.

15 Davis Hunt, *Bantu Education and the Education of Africans in South Africa*, 14.

16 Roger Beck, *The History of South Africa*, 132.

17 Eric Louw, *The Rise, Fall, and Legacy of Apartheid*, 45.

18 Robert Ross, *A Concise History of South Africa*, 119.

19 Francis Meli, *A History of the ANC: South Africa Belongs to Us* (Bloomington: Indiana University Press, 1989), 30–31.

20 Ibid., 36–40.

21 Ibid., 117–118.

22 Roger Beck, *The History of South Africa*, 139.

23 Brian Lapping, *Apartheid: A History* (New York: George Braziller, 1987), 123–127.

24 Roger Beck, *The History of South Africa*, 142.

25 Ibid., 131.

26 Robert Ross, *A Concise History of South Africa*, 134.

27 Nelson Mandela, *I Am Prepared to Die* (London: International Defense and Aid Fund for Southern Africa, 1979), 32–33.

28 Francis Meli, *A History of the ANC: South Africa Belongs to Us*, 137.

29 Thomas Karis, "Black Politics: the Road to Revolution" in *Apartheid in Crisis*, ed. Mark A Uhlig (New York: Vintage Books, 1986), 118.

30 Robert Ross, *A Concise History of South Africa*, 141.

31 Roger Beck, *The History of South Africa*, 164.

32 Steve Friedman, "The Black Trade Union Movement" in *Apartheid in Crisis*, 176–179.

33 Robert Ross, *A Concise History of South Africa*, 170–171.

34 See Cyril Ramaphosa address at the inaugural session of COSATU on November 19, 1985, reproduced in Mark A Uhlig (ed) *Apartheid in Crisis* (New York: Vintage Books, 1986), 212–215.

35 For more on the end of apartheid, see Lindsay Eades, *The End of Apartheid in South Africa* (Westport, CT: Greenwood Press, 1999).

36 F. W. de Klerk, *The Last Trek—A New Beginning: The Autobiography* (New York: St. Martin's Press, 1999), 398.

REVIEW QUESTIONS

1. Define apartheid and discuss how it shaped modern South Africa.
2. How did the National Party transform the theory of apartheid into practice?
3. Account for the rise and evolution of the protest movement in South Africa, noting its various transformational phases. What were the main features, major stages, and constraints characterizing the African nationalist movement in South Africa?
4. What were the major social and economic consequences of the policy and practice of apartheid in South Africa?
5. Why did the apartheid regime manage to defy the global trend toward majority rule, surviving for almost half a century? Explain the reasons for the eventual collapse of apartheid regime.

Writing Prompt

While international factors were responsible for perpetuating apartheid in South Africa, they also contributed to its demise. Analyze the justifications for Western support for apartheid until the late 1980s. How did international factors ultimately coincide with internal forces to bring about the collapse of the apartheid rule? In your opinion, which countries take most credit for sabotaging the apartheid regime and facilitating its collapse?

CHAPTER 16

Towards an African Renaissance: Pan-Africanism and Africans in the Diaspora

Timothy G. Kiogora

One of the most significant developments of the last twenty years has been the growing presence of African professionals in many Western institutions. This phenomenon, touted by some as "brain drain" and more recently hailed by others as "brain gain," or a reversal of fortunes for African countries, is worth investigating. Many see Africa as entering a new era in which they are likely to make credible advances towards a continental renaissance or renewal. In this era of rapid global transformations, Africa has been belatedly going through rapid, inevitable transformations that require an intensive, sustained infusion of both material and human resources. This chapter is an attempt to assess the impact of this group of Africans who we shall hereafter refer to as the New African diaspora on the future of Africa in the next few years. Historically, the term *diaspora* has been used to refer to people living outside their country of birth. The chapter examines the role the African diaspora played in the Post-World War II period in shaping Africa's political destiny even as European powers were at their inevitable decline. It also examines in brief the systemic displacement or dispersal of many African professionals to the West in post-colonial Africa and the reasons behind this mass emigration. We argue that the African diaspora has had a historic continuum in African affairs by briefly outlining the contributions of the African diaspora in the past.

This chapter also assesses the rise of globalization and hence the rise of the second wave of the African diaspora's presence in African affairs and the rebirth of a new vision for Africa. With the independence of South Africa, colonialism was dealt a final blow on the continent even as the global templates of global cultural, economic, and political arrangements were shifting, defying previous historical modes of international relations. Clearly, in this epoch, a new image of Africa emerged with global connectivity as its sole rationality, releasing unprecedented energies in the continent the effects that have not been fully addressed. This chapter examines the shifting paradigms at the global level and the impact on Africa. It looks at the way Africa has recently engaged her diasporas, from the Pan-African movement in the early 1900s through the African Union (AU)-an umbrella continental body formed to oversee Africa's political, economic, and social affairs in the post-colonial era-in an attempt to reconfigure an African renaissance. It argues that the viability of a sustainable African renaissance in the twenty-first century will be consolidated with the involvement of African diaspora.

AFRICA, THE DIASPORA, AND PAN-AFRICANISM

Popular discourse on the origins of Pan-Africanism tends to view it as an exilic movement from outside Africa rather than a historic movement born on the shores of Africa at the very onset of the European slave trade. Thus, as a concept, Pan-Africanism is often touted as the effort of those outside Africa to link with the realities of Africa throughout history. In retrospect, however, the process of remembering Africa must surely have begun on the shores of Africa with those Africans who lost their family or members of their communities to slavery as they grieved and hoped for their return some day. Equally, those who were enslaved responded to their plight in the foreign lands by contemplating their eventual return to Africa. In an illuminating essay on Pan-Africanism, Michael Williams has aptly observed:

> Perhaps the most balanced approach to this question, for now, is to argue that the origin of Pan-Africanism was characterized by a form of mutual duality, thus recognizing the genuine sentiments and concrete efforts of the struggle for Pan-Africanism in Africa and in the African diaspora.[1]

It is important to emphasize this mutual duality especially at this historic conjuncture as persons of African descent have been forced to revamp their memory of Africa and redefine their significance in the new global environment. Through Pan-Africanism, peoples of African descent were historically united in their efforts to liberate Africa and its peoples as well as the scattered descendants of Africa around the world. European hegemony and the expansion of capitalism internationally formed the springboard for radical political, cultural, and even religious resistance. To counter Western domination over Africa and to champion the cause of persons of African descent in the historic diaspora, Henry Highland Garnet founded the African Civilization Society in North America in 1858 whose aim, among others, was "to establish a grand centre of negro nationality, from which shall flow the streams of commercial, intellectual, and political power which shall make colored people respected everywhere."[2] Although Garnet's movement was initially based on Christian Eurocentric notions of a "backward" Africa needing to be "civilized," this radical statement betrayed his belief in an African renaissance. Later, towards the end of the nineteenth century, Garnet's compatriot Bishop Henry McNeal Turner believed[3] that African descendants in the United States and elsewhere should return to Africa to free her.[3] He travelled to Africa himself severally, while encouraging emigration to Africa. These initiatives lacked a serious understanding of the complexities of the situation on the ground in Africa and tended to be more emotive than realistic. Nevertheless, emigration to Africa remained a Pan-Africanist ideal. It is to be noted here that earlier efforts in the nineteenth century to transport freed slaves to Liberia and Sierra Leone lay outside the lofty ideals of Pan-Africanism properly understood. Under European tutelage, Liberia and Sierra Leone were extensions of Western colonies by their sheer capitalist infrastructure: land was acquired from indigenous Africans and class differentials were exaggerated. Latent conflict between the privileged, the new "arrivals," and indigenous Africans loomed just below the surface. Moreover, the motives of the American colonization society smacked of racism in what appeared to be an effort to rid North America of the black race through deportation. Before the nineteenth-century emigration efforts, however, it is instructive to note, as Prof. Ohaegbulam states:

> Interest in emigration to Africa, collectively or individually, continued in varying degrees from the eighteenth century to the last years of the twentieth century and, to some degree, to the early years of the current millennium.[4]

Broadly speaking, the fuel that kept the Pan-Africanist spirit burning was largely provided by European colonization of Africa. The decision to partition the continent into enclaves of European physical presence during the Berlin Conference (1884–1885) added insult to injury in the minds of the African diaspora: Slavery had taken them from their ancestral lands, and now those very ancestral lands had been "named and claimed" by imperial powers.[5] Thus, while emigration to Africa was not embraced enthusiastically by all Africans in the diaspora, this single event functioned as a catalyst in the flowering and development of the Pan-Africanist movement as a global forum for the struggle for self-determination of the African diaspora. It set the stage for a wider conflict between European powers and people of African descent everywhere. Any hopes of emigrating to a tranquil, vast land of their ancestors, if at least to "civilize" it, were dashed.

European economic interests, just like in North America, had once again triumphed over any other considerations, and *race* was at the center of this new hegemony. Although slavery had ended in the nineteenth century and emancipation after the civil war in the 1860s, political, social, and economic barriers created through discriminatory racial laws kept black people at the lowest levels of social existence in North America. Before the colonization of Africa, radical emigration advocates like Edward Wilmot Blyden had pleaded with African Americans in the 1850s to emigrate to Africa because Africa needed them for her regeneration as much as they needed her for the restoration of their dignity and respectability. He held that "outside Africa, the fatherland, dignity and respectability were beyond the reach of blacks."[6] The answer lay in establishing a distinct nationality for themselves.

RESPONSES OF THE AFRICAN DIASPORA TO COLONIZATION

The racist worldview upon which the entire colonization project in Africa was based resonated well with Africans in the Diaspora. It is no wonder then that the responses to the colonization of Africa among the African diaspora had race as a mediating factor that helped "to bridge (the) gaps in the objective realities among disparate groups."[7] Pan-African theory as a product of the African diaspora especially in the early years of the twentieth century was politically militant as exemplified by Marcus Garvey's back-to-Africa movement.

In 1921, Marcus Garvey, himself an immigrant from Jamaica to North America, proclaimed himself president of an empire he said existed in Africa, and encouraged black people to emigrate to Africa. Emotionally, he envisioned a united Africa ruled and controlled by black people. This was clearly unrealistic on several fronts. Garvey had never been to Africa himself; Africa was already under various European colonial powers, so freedom was not guaranteed in Africa after all; the cost and sheer logistics of such an effort called for a more sober calculation; and in any case many blacks would have found it difficult to leave North America to take citizenship in a land they had been cut off from for such a long time. He nevertheless organized a mass emigration scheme, the Universal Negro Improvement Association in Harlem, New York, where he resided. He asked his followers to exude racial pride and embrace their history. He asked them, through a propaganda publication, *The Negro World*, to rise up and redeem Africa as a homeland for black people everywhere.[8]

Garvey's activism, although fraught with many failures, some due to his egocentric, eccentric nature, shook the colonial setup in Africa and helped to water the seeds of anti-colonial rebellion among those who came into contact with his teachings. He was, in many ways, an influential figure in shaping the consciousness of black people in regard to their African origins. Masses of poor black people in the United States formed the base of his movement, while the more elite blacks hated him for his attempt to link them to an Africa they had come to hold in disdain as backward and primitive. They also regarded him as a suspect "foreigner" who lacked a sufficient understanding of black issues in the United States. Strategically, his movement, with all its other flaws, lacked a serious political foundation in Africa and in North America, and when Garvey was deported from the United States in 1927, it collapsed. In spite of his many critics, Garvey placed Africa at the center of a radical pan-Africanist discourse. The question was not if there was a strong case for Africanity as an ideology, but on what this Africanity was to be founded. His fiercest critic in North America, W.E.B. Du Bois, could not shake himself off from the larger dream Garvey held of a free Africa ruled by and controlled by Africans. With Du Bois the debate shifted more to means than ends: how does one become a "freed African" wherever one may be?

Dubois held that African dignity could be regained through both political agitation and intellectual self-determination. Ironically, bending over to what he regarded as incorrigible American racism, he moved to Africa in 1961 and became a citizen of independent Ghana at the age of 95 after living there for two years and having been denied a new U.S. passport. He died on August 27, 1963, and was buried in Ghana. His role in the founding of the Pan-African Congress places him at the pinnacle of the historic diasporas' contribution to the self-image of Africa and persons of African descent.

THE PAN-AFRICAN CONGRESS AND THE LIBERATION OF AFRICA

W.E.B. Du Bois had founded the Pan-African Congress in February 1919 in Paris, France, as a general response to World War I and a search for lasting peace.[9] It was through this Congress that Africans in diaspora addressed the world in regard to the plight of black Africans and decolonization in particular in its subsequent gatherings. Operating parallel to Garveyism, the Pan-African Congress held racial discrimination and imperialism to be inconsistent with the claims of a civilized world, challenging the British empire directly. Five of its meetings in 1919, 1921, 1923, 1927, and 1945 were devoted to liberating Africa from European colonialism. The 1921 London Manifesto of the Second Pan-African Congress declared:

> England, with all her Pax Britannic, her courts of justice, established commerce, and a certain apparent recognition of native laws and customs, has nevertheless systematically fostered ignorance among the natives, has enslaved them, and is still enslaving them, has usually declined even to try to train black and brown men in real self-government, to recognize civilized black folk as civilized, or to grant to coloured colonies those rights of self-government which are freely given to white men.[10]

In 1923, the third Pan-African Congress met in Paris, London, and Lisbon, Spain, and made explicit demands for the creation of African governments in West Africa, West Indies, Kenya, Rhodesia, and South Africa. It also condemned the lynching and mob law in the United States targeted on black Americans. Asserting that the development of Africa should be for the benefit of Africans and not European economic interests, the Pan-African Congress had become the only movement of its kind among the peoples of African descent abroad and a fertile ground for the growth of early African nationalism. The fifth Pan-African Congress held in October 1945 in Manchester, England, at the end of World War II rallied together all the various constituencies of the African diaspora and representatives of the African masses behind the cause of decolonization. It included thirty-three delegates from the West Indies, thirty-five from various organizations based in Britain, and at least several future African heads of state such as Kwame Nkrumah of Ghana, Jomo Kenyatta of Kenya, Nmandi Azikiwe and Obafemi Owolowo of Nigeria, and Hastings Banda of Malawi. Towering intellectual and political elder statesmen like W.E.B. DuBois and George Padmore of Trinidad gave intellectual and strategic guidance to the deliberations of this watershed congress, with W.E.B. DuBois as chairman. The success of this congress lay in its ability to make the case for African emancipation and unity. Kwame Nkrumah, who became the first African head of state in Ghana in 1957, was the secretary-general of the congress. The resulting resolutions called for the urgent independence and liberation of Africa. Thus, African liberation movements were intensified and radicalized, marking a departure from passive protest to active mass demands.[11]

Without the political clout of the historic African diaspora in the mid-twentieth century, the independence of African countries would have been delayed by decades. Change would have come because the aftermath of the World War II had brought the issue of human rights to the attention of the world through a renewed League of Nations, which adopted a new name, United Nations, on October 24, 1945. The former, founded in 1919 after World War I, had not met its full mandate to stop the onset of another war, and its declarations were couched in general terms. By seizing the moment in 1945 through a radical and politically astute Pan-African movement, the historic African Diaspora ushered Africa onto the global stage.

INDEPENDENT AFRICA, THE DECLINE OF PAN-AFRICANISM, AND THE RISE OF THE NEW AFRICAN DIASPORA

By the time W.E.B. Du Bois died in Ghana in 1963, many of Africa's European colonies had gained political independence. The most radical and ambitious of Africa's new leaders was Kwame Nkrumah of Ghana. He had single-handedly organized the All Africa Peoples' Conference in 1958 with the hope of pulling together African intellectuals and other resources for the benefit of the transformation of Africa, as well as freeing remaining colonies on the continent. Concerning this new era, Mazrui writes:

This was the golden age of high Pan-African ambitions and towering intellectual aspirations in Africa. Great minds articulated Africa's great dreams. Both Pan-Africanism and African intellectualism were flying high.[12]

The onset of political independence in Africa vindicated the combined struggles of both the colonial and historic diasporas. African students who had left their countries to study in the West had been radicalized by their encounter with Africans in diaspora. All the ironies and contradictions of the philosophies of Garvey and Du Bois were, in a sense, reconciled in this post-colonial period. According to Gomez, Nkrumah's ascendancy to political power was a major symbolic event in reconciling the two camps, which in any case seemed to have moved closer during the 1945 congress in Manchester. Tensions between Du Bois and the Garvey camp lessened when the two personalities collaborated in organizing the 1945 Manchester Pan-African Congress. The tempestuous relationship between these two pan-Africanist pioneers was settled on African soil under Kwame Nkrumah, independent Ghana's first president.[13]

In May 1963, thirty-two independent African States converged in Addis Ababa, Ethiopia, to form the Organization of African Unity (OAU). The goal of the OAU was to strengthen Africa and to enable her to fend off outside influences. Nkrumah's all Africa Peoples' Conference had been overtaken by events, especially by the OAU's reluctance, after vigorous debates, to embrace his vision of the immediate unification of Africa. So much else was at stake: The link between post-colonial African leadership and the historic diaspora of North America seemed to have been weakened as Africa entered a period of introspection and, as fate would have it, the ghosts of the colonial past proved hard to exorcise and remained to haunt Africa for a long time.

Beyond the euphoria of political independence and a possible continental unity, the task of rebuilding postcolonial societies proved almost insurmountable due to a combination of leadership lacking in experience and a thin resource base in most of the states. Very often, the dictatorial rule that discouraged external contacts was the norm rather than the exception. Externally, the historic diaspora, especially in North America, was caught up in civil rights campaigns, often invoking emotive cultural affinity with Africa but lacking in political strategy to rescue Africa often from her own civil unrest. For nearly thirty years, this regrettable historic disconnect only contributed to the delay of a truly African renaissance. During those years, the standoff between the West and the Soviet Union during the Cold War meant that African states were "strategic vantage points" for either the Soviet Union or the United States. Any African leader or dictator who supported either side would receive financial and military backing to keep him in power as "an ally". As economic fortunes of African states declined with misrule, the majority of African states resorted to massive repression to quell the growing voices of dissent from students, priests, and professionals at all levels in many academic institutions of learning. As a result, between 1960 and 1975, 24,000 Africans left the continent for industrialized countries of the West to escape murder or imprisonment, or simply to look for better living conditions for themselves and their families. From 1975 to 1984, the figures rose to 40,000, and since 1990, about 20,000 Africans leave the continent annually. There are many reasons for this apparent "brain drain" such as failed or failing economies, high unemployment, human rights abuses, armed conflict, and inadequate social services. Obviously, there is a critical interrelationship between these factors, and, in the final analysis, poor leadership factor looms large.

The prevailing attitude of the ruling elite toward those who had left the continent was mostly negative. Castigating the exiles as opportunists and traitors on the payroll of "foreign masters," these groups of Africans were stigmatized as unpatriotic and ridiculed and generally regarded as "good riddance." On their part, the exiles became ever more impatient about the declining fortunes of their homeland and the continuing erosion of Africa's self-image through corruption, ineptitude and blatant abuse of human rights by cliques in power. Africa's future seemed uncertain, and the 1980s and 1990s were touted as Africa's lost decades. However, the most significant event at the beginning of the 1990s was the end of the Cold War between the United States and the Soviet Union, symbolized by the Malta Summit in December 1989, between U.S. President George W. Bush and USSR's Mikhail Gorbachev. After the summit's deliberations, Gorbachev declared during a joint press conference that "The world is leaving one epoch and entering another. We are at the beginning of a long road to a lasting, peaceful era. The threat of force, mistrust, and psychological and ideological struggle should all be things of the past."[14]

Prior to the summit, a whirlwind of change had blown throughout much of Eastern Europe, sweeping aside authoritarian regimes in Poland, Romania, East Germany, Bulgaria, Hungary, and Czechoslovakia. In Africa, the dawn of the "Second Liberation" of the continent had finally appeared. African dictatorial regimes would receive no more aid from the West unless they subscribed to a superimposed, verifiable doctrine of human rights and democracy. Emboldened by this move, opposition groups in Africa began agitating for what was to become the "Second Liberation" of Africa and gained considerable ground as several repressive one-party regimes conceded, under pressure, to multiparty systems of electoral politics. In 1994, South Africa gained independence from the repressive minority Afrikaner regime, and Nelson Mandela became the first president of a free South Africa with a new constitution based on majority rule. Mandela, an icon of African political militancy, dignity, and self-determination, cast a regal presence in African affairs and represents the single most important figure in African and pan-Africanist politics since the 1945 Pan-African Congress. His inauguration as president of the last African colony stoked all the latent political fires of both the historic diaspora and the new African diaspora of postcolonial Africa. In North America, his presidency meant the triumph of the civil rights era because his stature matched that of Martin Luther King, Jr. and Malcolm X, among Africa's diasporic figures. It meant there was still hope of overthrowing some of the most repressive regimes in Africa and beyond. He seemed to restore a sense of purpose and the eroded African self-image. Africa as both a geographic entity and a psychological "motherland" had entered a new liberative space. By the end of his first term in 1999, Africa and the whole world was entering another phase in human social relations on a global scale. Thus, the onset of the twenty-first century unleashed forces that were to usher in radical energies within the continent of Africa and among the entire spectrum of the African diaspora, presenting new paradigms for redefining Africa's self-image.

GLOBALIZATION, AFRICAN RENAISSANCE, AND EMERGING PARADIGM SHIFTS

Writing in 1999 in regard to the significance of Nelson Mandela's presidency and the era that was to follow, Elliot B. Skinner stated:

> With the presidency of Nelson Mandela, the ancestral continent has finally thrown off the yoke of alien rule, and African peoples in the diaspora are anxious to achieve full equality. Today, the twin desires of a cultural renaissance and economic development are necessary if African peoples (are to) attain equality with human beings everywhere.[15]

In the same year, Mandela was succeeded by Thabo Mbeki, a young, cosmopolitan intellectual of the new African diaspora. Having spent twenty-eight years in exile and at least a decade in England both as a student and political activist, Mbeki had experienced first-hand the sad vicissitudes of life in exile and Africa's plight both in the postcolonial days in much of Africa and particularly the apartheid era in his native South Africa. His rise to power as president of South Africa in 1999, at the very turn of the twenty-first century, coincided with the emergence, at the conceptual and other levels, of what many scholars and observers of the global scene have dubbed as globalization. While not agreed as to its precise meanings, the scholarly analysts and commentators, perhaps informed by their particular disciplinary interests and other subtexts, nevertheless are agreed on its pervasive, omnipresent manifestations. In a formal, disciplined definition of this phenomenon, James H. Mittelman writes:

> A world-wide phenomenon, globalization is a coalescence of varied transnational processes and domestic structures, allowing the economy, politics, culture, and ideology of one country to penetrate another. Driven by changing modes of competition, globalization compresses the time and space aspects of social relations. In short, globalization is a market-induced, not policy-led, process.[16]

Driven by technological revolutions especially in communications, globalization as a process radicalized the power of the market and free-wheeling capital well beyond the borders of single states. Those who oppose it argue thus:

> The primary emphasis of globalization has been economic liberalization, with very little attention paid to the importance of international equality and solidarity. As the remote forces of globalization hobble governments and weaken the bonds of social solidarity, anger is growing among those whose social existence is being threatened.[17]

According to Fantu Cheru, in popular media and corporate boardrooms, "the rapid integration of national markets with one another is presented as the only means to bring unprecedented world prosperity and freedom in the post-Cold War era."[18] Conceding the ubiquitous nature of globalization, Fantu Cheru takes a middle of the road position: Globalization is indeed a contradictory process, with perils as well as promises for Africa. He argues that in the past, Africa was drawn into capitalist, Western-induced forms of globalization through the slave trade in 1650 and the colonial mandate of the Berlin Conference of 1884. He likens the present global initiatives to the latter and warns that "unless African governments redirect their efforts to manage it successfully to their own advantage, Africans would go through 'a repeat of the degrading and inhumane treatment (they) received from the colonial and capitalist forces."[19]

The debate on the role and nature of the requisite African state for the new millennium is ongoing, but it is outside our focus here.[20] Instead, it is important to examine briefly some of the paradigm shifts ushered in by globalization in Africa and the role of the New African diaspora. Our argument is that globalization in its twenty-first century manifestation does present us with the second diasporic movement with promising signs of an African renaissance. That is to say, the opportunities presented by globalization for engaging African's problems and renegotiating her place in global affairs are unprecedented. This second diasporic moment is characterized by radical connectivities between persons of African descent everywhere. Unlike the days of the Manchester Pan-African Congress in 1945 when Africa's political liberation was the main issue linking the historic diaspora with Africa, today the struggle for economic and cultural renewal is driven by an impatient, creative new generation of Africans both on the continent and in the diaspora.

The idea of a paradigm shift originated with Thomas Kuhn's writing in 1962 to explain that scientific advancement is not evolutionary but rather is a "series of peaceful revolutions." In those revolutions, he argued, "one conceptual world view is replaced by another."[21] For this to occur, there are numerous agents for change. Although his theory was focused on the physical sciences, his idea of paradigm shift is relevant in exploring the dynamics of globalization. In the African context, the new diasporic moment is occasioned by certain tangible paradigm shifts within the continent and in the diaspora. For the sake of brevity, we list a few of these shifts. In the twenty-first century, Africans entered the "New World" or so-called "New World order" not in slave chains but as a relatively free people, with South Africa as the last colony to be freed after 300 years of colonization. Although the political and economic hegemony of the West remains, it is being challenged from the East, giving Africa new options and models for economic and social self-determination.

The notion of "space" replaces "place" as Africans who had left the African continent begin to relate to Africa through instant telecommunications networks: They remit enormous amounts of money to support their kin in Africa, invest in real estate, and keep up with daily events in their countries through the Internet and mobile phones. The political and economic impact of this group of "cyberspace" Africans on the future of the African continent is unprecedented and remains to be fully accounted for. George Ayittey, describing the advent of a new breed of youthful Africans driving change from within Africa and beyond has this to say:

> They may be classified as the cheetah generation- Africa's new hope. They do not relate to the old colonial paradigm. . . . They brook (sic) no nonsense about corruption, inefficiency, ineptitude, incompetence, or buffoonery. . . . They do not have the stomach for colonial-era politics. . . . they do not make excuses for or seek to explain away government failures in terms of colonialism and the slave trade.[22]

According to Ayittey, Africa's future is in the hands of this new generation, as opposed to the "hippo generation" who he describes as "intellectually astigmatized and stuck in their colonialist pedagogical patch."[23] These are the members of the older generation of African politicians who, having liberated their countries from colonial yokes, were incapable of seeing atrocities committed in Africa by fellow African leaders. Ayittey's metaphors as he contrasts the older generation with the new are intriguing: the African hippo is a short-sighted animal that enjoys wallowing in muddy, dirty waters, and is too heavy to be bothered to engage in any kind of racing, whereas the cheetah is defined by speed, alertness and agility, traversing varied landscapes as need dictates!

African leadership in global institutions has elevated the African profile in a global era: Boutros Boutros-Ghali of Egypt headed the United Nations (1991–1996) as did Kofi Annan of Ghana (1996–2006). The United Nations is the only major authoritative entity in the modern world in mediating social, political, economic and cultural affairs on a global scale. Thus, paradoxically, African leadership, often challenged at state levels, has been recognized at the global level. Few examples include Nobel Prize winners Prof. Wangari Maathai, Bishop Desmond Tutu, Nelson Mandela, Prof. Wole Soyinka, and Kofi Annan. The recent election of Barack Obama, an African-American with recent roots in Africa, as the president of the United States is perhaps the most significant event for the entire spectrum of Africa's diasporas. Not only does it constitute a major paradigm shift in regard to race, empire and power, it situates Africanity at center-stage in global affairs, as well as changing once and for all ways in which Africans and African Americans redefine and relate to both an inclusive Pan-Africanism and global reaches of power. As Africans are bound to claim president Obama as one of their own through his paternal link (in most African societies a child ultimately belongs to the father), we predict this event alone will be a major catalyst for change in the African psyche and beyond. As a matter of practical necessity for example, Africans are going to have to reject the negative roles that ethnicity and tribal consciousness often play in national politics as the continent struggles with the transition to a mature and orderly democratic space.

Furthermore, the establishment of the African Union on July 9, 2002 to preside over the affairs of the African states is a significant event in the review of Africa's place in the new millennium, and this body is gradually moving toward a realistic, viable United States of Africa. Dissatisfied with the ineptness of the previous Organization of African Unity (OAU) established in 1963, the African Union describes itself as "an efficient and effective African Union for a new Africa" in its official logo. Remarkably, it explicitly describes the role of the diaspora in its constitutive act in the following words: "The AU shall invite and encourage the full participation of the African diaspora as an important part of our continent in the building of the African Union."[24] It defines the African diaspora as "consisting of people of African origin living outside the continent, *irrespective of their citizenship and nationality* and who are willing to contribute to the development of the continent and the building of the African Union (italics ours)."[25]

The growing power of the market revolutionizing the economic fortunes of both China and India, all former members of the so-called Third World is exerting positive, creative revolutionary pressures on Africa. In a recently published well-researched text by economist Vijay Mahajan, himself a member of the Indian diaspora in the United States, an unassailable case has been made in regard to Africa's emerging significance as a diverse, energized market-place with local and international linkages. Backing his writing with statistics, he writes:

> Across the continent, Africa is richer than India on the basis of gross national income (GNI) and is per capita richer than China. Rising investments from private enterprise and an active diaspora are expanding investments and opportunities. Communications, banking, and other drivers are creating the infrastructure for further development.[26]

As a former dean of the Indian School of Business, Mahajan cautions against conventional scholarship that always sees Africa as a basket case: "It is particularly surprising to me that I failed to recognize the story in Africa because I remember when India was discussed in the same way."[27] Vijay questions the rigid descriptions of Africa as a lost cause, very much like descriptions of India in the 1960s, as a laboratory of failed experiments in democracy and nation-building:

> In 2002, I had the opportunity to return to India as dean of the Indian School of Business in Hyderabad. I saw how a country that had been written off as a charity case was now seen as a powerful emerging market. Now I (hold) the same view of Africa.[28]

If indeed the perceptions of Africa are changing, in the next few years there will be a growing interest in the real wealth of Africa driven by more than 900 million consumers, a vibrant middle-class, a growing number of creative entrepreneurs, and small-scale as well as medium-scale business leaders. Business affects politics, as in the case of China, rather than the other way around.

CONCLUSION

Those who live in Africa are often puzzled and appalled by negative coverage of the continent in the Western media at the expense of the larger story of Africa's resilience and latent, untapped wealth of both her human resource base and natural resources. Perhaps what is so dark after all about the "dark continent" is our shared ignorance of Africa. Nevertheless, in the annals of human history, it is often the coalescing of events at certain rare momentous periods that, given just the right kind of wind behind the sails, thrusts human beings into the high seas of unparalleled achievement. It is an understatement to say that in the twenty-first century, fixed notions of reality couched in presumed "unassailable theories" can be relied upon as timeless dogma. Thus, in this new epoch, the Chinese Taoist adage holds true: "*...those who know do not speak; those who speak do not know.*"

When Thabo Mbeki took up leadership of South Africa after Nelson Mandela, he envisioned a continent that had at last began a walk toward daybreak. Addressing a conference on September 28 1998, he declared in an elaborate address that a new era was upon Africa, an *African renaissance*.[29] Although his vision was more about hope than immediate reality or an elaborate program of action, the signs of the times seem to indicate he has been vindicated. An African Renaissance may indeed be emotive and not necessarily characterized by grandiose political and economic programs of action, essential as these may be. History constantly attests to the fact that dreams do indeed find wheels to propel them forward. Africa today stands at a unique historic juncture, at daybreak, with her dreams still intact.

In the current environment, it is not autarky that wins the day. Rather, the world community is rehearsing what appears to be her own *dance of new life,* inviting the many to take part in it, and in short order too. The drums beating are loud and clear, and the rhythm is quite inviting.

Clearly, there now exist, in this apparent drama, new players on stage. In this global drama, how will Africa and the New African diaspora feature? It just may be that the role of the New African diaspora in the shaping of the African renaissance in the foreseeable future is going to be that of a dynamic catalyst in all spheres of African life in Africa and on the global stage simultaneously. It is through this group of Africans with their ongoing transfer of skills and capital to Africa in an environment of knowledge–based global economies that significant dents will be made on endemic African problems. There will be the added advantage of untapped wealth of the African continent (material and otherwise), as Africa looks East and West for meaningful partnerships. In this regard, the ongoing global moment is in fact Africa's new moment, and not necessarily a rehearsal of the old conspiracies and theories that have for centuries made Africa a periphery, a disfigured and a severed arm of the rest of civilization. This moment is a gift to Africa willed upon her by the shifting templates of history.

The task of African scholars in particular, apart from purposefully engaging selected, crucial historic themes in diasporic history, lies in the critical, creative social construction of this emerging reality in Africa and beyond. To "name and claim" certain historic moments, as Prof. Ngugi has put it, is not to engage in esoteric constructions of reality but to define and shape new visions to serve Africa's common good. According to him, Europeans "named and claimed" Africa and Africans at will on the eve of colonization, at the very start of modernity. The New African diaspora must now "name and claim" Africa's future.[30] Here, the "witchcraft" at the heart of the construction of modernity in the twentieth century has now been reversed in the twenty-first century. This time around, it is in the interests of the entire global community, that Africa blossoms. One factor overrides all others in this regard. Africa is the third continent in the current world with over one billion people today after China and India, with a growing middle class of over 300 hundred million persons.[31] In the ongoing environment, Africa's potential to influence and impact upon the rest of the world is clearly enormous.

ENDNOTES

1 Michael Williams, "The Pan-African Movement," in *Africana Studies: A Survey of Africa and the African Diaspora*, ed. Mario Azevedo (Durham, NC: Carolina Academic Press, 2005), 175.

2 Ibid.

3 Ibid. 176.

4 F. Ugboaja Ohaegbulam, "Continental Africans and Africans in America: The Progression of a Relationship" in *Africana Studies: A Survey of Africa And the African Diaspora*, ed. Mario Azevedo (Durham, NC: Carolina Academic Press, 2005), 228.

5 Professor Ngugi Wa Thiongo offers a most lucid, anecdotal, and revealing account of this colonial *modus operandi* in his essay, "Europhone or African Memory: The Challenge of the Pan-Africanist Intellectual in the Era of Globalization," in *African Intellectuals*, ed. T. Mkandawire (Dakar: CODESTRIA Books, 2005).

6 F. Ugboaja Ohaegbulam, "Continental Africans and Africans in America," 231.

7 See Alvin B. Tillery, Jr, "Black Americans and the Creation of America's Africa Policies: The De-Racialization of Pan-African Politics," in *The African Diaspora: African Origins and New World Identities*, ed. Isidore Okpewho, Carole Boyce Davies, and Ali A. Mazrui (Bloomington and Indianapolis: Indiana University Press, 1999), 512.

8 F. Ugboaja Ohaegbulam, "Continental Africans and Africans in America," 232.

9 Michael L. Conniff and Thomas J. Davis, ed., *Africans in the Americas: A History of the Black Diaspora* (New York: St. Martin's Press, 1994), 295.

10 "The Pan-African Vision, The Story of Africa: Between World Wars (1914–1945)," BBC News, April 15, 2008.

11 Mursi Saad El-Din, "Pan African Odyssey," *Al-Ahram Weekly Online*, July 19-25, 2001.

12 Mazrui's perspective is that this was a short-lived phenomenon as African leaders soon became less idealistic in favor of cautious pragmatism and lost the anti-colonial radicalism of the previous era. See his "Pan-Africanism and the Intellectuals: Rise, Decline and Revival," in *African Intellectuals: Rethinking Politics, Language, Gender and Development*, ed. Thandika Mkandawire (London: Zed Books, 2005), 56.

13 Michael A. Gomez, *Reversing Sail: A History of the African Diaspora* (New York: Cambridge University Press, 2005), 179.

14 BBC News, "1989: Malta Summit Ends Cold War."

15 Elliot P. Skinner, "The Restoration of African Identity for a New Millennium" in *The African Diaspora: African Origins and New World Identities*, ed. Isidore Okpewho, Carole Boyce Davies, and Ali A. Mazrui (Bloomington and Indianapolis: Indiana University Press, 1999), 29.

16 James H. Miltelman, ed., *Globalizations: Critical Reflections* (Boulder, CO: Lynne Rienner Publishers, 1996), 3.

17 Fantu Cheru, *African Renaissance: Roadmaps to the Challenge of Globalization* (New York: Zed Books, 2002), 1.

18 Ibid.

19 Ibid. 2.

20 For a lucid, thorough treatment of the salient features of this debate, see, for example, Abdi I. Samatar and Ahmed I. Samatar, ed., *The African State: Reconsiderations* (Portsmouth, NH: Heinemann Press, 2002).

21 Thomas S. Kuhn, *The Structure of Scientific Revolutions* (Chicago: The University of Chicago Press, 1965), 10.

22 George Ayittey, *Africa Unchained: The Blueprint for Africa's Future* (New York: Palgrave MacMillan, 2005), xx.

23 Ibid.

24 Dallas L. Browne, *Pan-Africanism and the African Union* (unpublished essay).

25 Ibid.

26 Vijay Mahajan, *Africa Rising: How 900 Million African Consumers Offer More Than You Think* (Upper Saddle River, NJ: Pearson Education, 2009), 29.

27 Ibid.

28 Ibid.

29 Malagapuru William, ed., *African Renaissance* (Cape Town: Mafube & Tafwelberg, 1999).

30 Ngugi Wa Thiongo, "Europhone or African Memory: The Challenge Of The Pan-Africanist Intellectual In The Era of Globalization", keynote address to the CODESRIA Conference held in Dakar, Senegal, December 10, 2003.

31 The African Development Bank Group, *Quarterly Report*, March 2011.

REVIEW QUESTIONS

1. What role did Africans in diaspora play in the decolonization of the continent? Highlight the contributions of some of the main figures involved.
2. Why did the involvement of the African diaspora in African affairs decline in postcolonial Africa?
3. Discuss the "the second liberation of Africa," why this was necessary, and how this gave rise to the possibility, yet to be fully realized, of an African renaissance. Be specific in your discussion, mentioning events that appeared to make this possible.
4. According to what is discussed in this chapter, discuss the significance of the election of Barack Obama in 2008 as the first black U.S. president in regard to the diaspora consciousness in Africa and around the world.

Writing Prompt

Taking into account the changes that swept through Africa over the last four decades, what do you see as the strategies for the future socioeconomic and political transformation of the continent? Analyze the paradigm shifts brought about by the rise of globalization, showing the problems and promise it holds for Africa.

CHAPTER 17

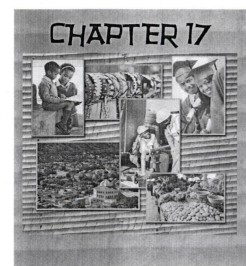

African Immigration to the United States: Trends, Ramifications, and Challenges

Emmanuel N. Ngwang

Immigration is the movement of a people from their original land to another habitat. This movement is often created by internal or externals factors such as plagues, illnesses, hunger, or catastrophes, and it has been part of human history. Immigration has always resulted in demographic, political, and economic changes. Today, immigration has become important because it has had a very profound and significant cataclysmic effect on global politics, resulting in changing relations among nations. The use terms such "globalization" and "pluralistic society" has its origins in the national and cultural hybridity occasioned by the continuous movement of peoples over national boundaries and the creation and re-creation of societies and ethnicities beyond national boundaries. Immigration has been an integral part of American history. Political campaigns dwell on its problems and promise. However, no concrete efforts have been made to address the issue.

The legal and illegal immigrants that flock daily into the United States from all continents have become forerunners of the trend toward transnationalism. The United States now has the burden of meeting the pressing economic and demographic challenges and demands while at the same time struggling to cope with the internal problem of cultural diversity that continues to challenge national hegemony and rights. Indeed, the statistical distribution of legal visas and Green Cards through the Diversity Visa Lottery (commonly and thereafter referred to as the DV Lottery) have called attention to the various nationalities admitted into the United States, thereby revealing the United States as one of the leading absorbers of immigrants. The Office of the Homeland Security's *April 2010 Annual Flow Report on Naturalizations in the United State* reveals in detail the region by region and country by country distribution of immigrants in the United States. The DV Lottery yearly results again indicate the significant number of immigrants granted entry visas. Incidentally, each wave of immigration comes with its own challenges, characteristics, and ramifications both for the receiving country, which in our case is the United States of America, and the regions/nations losing these immigrants. These figures create a real need to verify and analyze these regional, if not continental, migrations to the United States. Hence, it is the intention of this chapter to focus on the African perspective of this immigration. This paper focuses on the trends, ramifications, and challenges of recent African immigration to the United States. In fact, this immigration is gathering momentum as researchers are increasingly awakened to the continuous difficulties these new immigrants confront. Moreover, the cultural shock and reversal of family roles and responsibilities have produced profound effects on most African families, often leading to and resulting in changing the traditional family structure and the waning of African cultural hegemony.

TYPES AND WAVES OF AFRICAN IMMIGRATION

African immigrations to the United States, like all other regional types of movements of people from their original land to another habitat created by internal or externals factors such as plagues, illnesses, hunger, or catastrophes, have been part of history and have always resulted in very significant demographic, political, and economic changes. In particular, the immigration of Africans to the United States has left indelible scars on the continent and significant repercussions on the American psyche. The first wave of significant migration of Africans to the United States was inextricably aligned to slavery, whose stigma has continued to plague American society. The other waves of movement or immigration were caused by extenuating circumstances such as wars, natural disasters, unemployment, political persecution, and hunger. While the former was a timed event that ended with the abolition of the Trans-Atlantic Slave Trade, the latter has continued to exist in different forms.

The twenty-first century has seen a significant movement of African populations from Africa to the Americas, especially to the United States and Canada. This immigration has been unique in the fact that the immigrants have most of the time been adults who made personal decisions to relocate for various reasons. One of the significant reasons for this relocation has been the American Diversity Visa usually called the Lottery,[1] which has opened up America to millions of legal immigrants who otherwise might not have come. The second reason is education whereby the immigrant students relocated temporarily to the United States to pursue higher education. Furthermore, still another significant group of immigrants is made up of those who are fleeing political persecution and are on some sort of self-exile. But whatever the reasons each immigrant group gave, the constant movement of Africans to America has caused a significant shift in race relations, demographics, and economic impacts on the African continent and the United States. It is ironic, if not coincidental, that this Africa-to-America migration is in the direction of the west and could geographically be termed the "Third Westward Movement," coming after the historic American Pioneer's Westward Movement of the 1630s to acquire land from the Indians and settle, and the Gold Rush Movement to California in 1848 respectively. However, this third Westward Movement differs from the other two because it is external to the United States, i.e., coming from the outside, while the others were orchestrated by internal forces of settlement and economics, respectively.

Each group of immigrants arrived from the African continent in the so-called "Promised Land" with all types of pent-up ideas about the whole concept of the "American Dream." The initial reaction has always been one of frustration, since the period of adjustment has never been easy, for the students, workers, or the winners of the lottery. History books have dealt extensively with the first wave of Africa-to-America immigration (forced immigration through trans-Atlantic slavery) of over 300 years ago.[2] While this trans-Atlantic slave trade continues to attract researchers and historians, it is important for us to see how the modern forms of immigration are built on the earliest form, which was and is typically economic, and how these new forms have changed the whole concept of immigration. At this point, it is germane to begin first with the deliberate and celebrated form of immigration, which I call literacy immigration, or the spontaneous and well-deserved movement of young scholars from African countries to the United States for academic reasons. Many of them had American scholarships, were sponsored by their home countries or religious groups, or were funded by their individual families who could afford that much money.

Literacy immigration, which Vernon Briggs, Jr. refers to as the "Fourth Great Immigration," started in the latter part of the twentieth century,[3] after the decolonization or independence of African countries in the late 1950s and early 1960s, when many Africans came to the United States to pursue or to further their education. Initially, those who came were sponsored by their various governments for training to replace the colonial masters who were abdicating their positions and returning home or to assume new positions created for them in their home countries in Africa. Most of the immigrants who came under this caveat were eager to return to Africa because there were lucrative positions and ministerial posts waiting for them. As these positions became filled, other African students who thought they were late decided to remain and pursue their economic and educational dreams in the United States. This was the group that started the voluntary immigration and eventually settled in the United States. According to Briggs, Corwin, and USCIS, there has been an increase in this group of African immigrants interested in gaining permanent residency in the United States.[4]

Another wave of voluntary immigration has been encouraged by the DV Lottery, which was instituted in 1990 to give foreign nationals legal immigration to and residency in the United States. The 2000 census conducted by the U.S. Bureau of the Census, the *Department of Homeland Security* and *African Immigration into the USA* revealed that the Green Card Lottery has resulted in the immigration of over 881,000 Africans to the United States, with the most immigrants coming from Nigeria, Ghana, Ethiopia, Eritrea, Egypt, Somalia, and South Africa. Of the over 881,000 African immigrants in the USA, 55 percent are males, while 45 percent are females, many of whom live in major cities. It is estimated that the highest concentrations of these immigrants are found in the East and North-eastern United States (Washington, DC, Maryland, Virginia, West Virginia, New York, and Boston, MA), Midwest (Chicago, IL, Minneapolis/St. Paul, Detroit, and Cincinnati, OH), South (Atlanta, GA, Houston and Dallas, TX), and West in Greater California.[5] These African immigrants settled in urban areas first and gradually moved to suburban areas over time where they eventually engaged in gainful employment such as marketing and minimum wage jobs to acquire money to live on and to send some back to their home countries. The Ethiopians and Somalians are indeed noted for airport and urban auto parking, rental facilities, and taxi driving businesses. As these immigrants acquire jobs and get settled, they organize themselves into meaningful units and communities in subdivisions and invite their country folk to congregate in clusters for security reasons and to help each other by retaining their cultural identity and customs. This arrangement was and is gainfully deployed in northern Cincinnati where the Ghanaians have formed trading units, African churches, and even schools to take care of their children and protect cultural hegemony.[6]

According to researchers, one major factor that has continued to fuel African immigration to the United States is the inadequate job creation in most African countries. For instance, in the early 1990s, Cameroon universities produced students who could not be absorbed by the government, which was the primary and, in most cases, the sole employer. There was virtually no private sector employment for degree holders, and the government positions were virtually all filled. The graduates, over 80 percent of them, roamed the streets unemployed, and many of them found ways to immigrate to other countries. In such cases, the United States tended and continues to be the country of irresistible attraction. The situation in Cameroon was not unique; it was shared by many African countries where the governments in power became increasingly incapable of supporting all these qualified yet unemployed graduates. Some of them wanted to pursue education, and their best options were foreign countries out of Africa that have well-structured educational systems and work ethics to support those who are capable of working and going to school. Unfortunately, some of these Africans scholars acquired training in areas that could not be used back home in their African countries. Consequently, they ended up staying in the United States where they could use their expertise to earn substantial salaries to sustain their families both in the United States and back home in Africa. The population of the educated who decided to stay in the United States initiated the process of labor drain, where the most intellectually and academically trained remained in the United States instead of returning to their home countries to use that knowledge to foster development and progress.[7]

Moreover, there is a political dimension to this immigration even when the intellectually and academically trained returned to their home countries to work. In "Contemporary African Immigrants to the United States," Joseph Takougan maintains that the "severe economic difficulties, increased poverty, and the political instability that have plagued many African countries in the last two decades have resulted in the large scale migration of Africans to Europe and the United States."[8] He further reveals that the numbers of "immigrants from the continent to the USA have been fueled by a majority of recently educated Africans who refuse to return home after their education; they are more interested in establishing permanent residency in the United States." In most cases, like in Cameroon, those who return home meet a country that is radically different from the country they left years ago. They are no longer at ease with the political setup, constructed on a system and practice of tribalism, nepotism, favoritism, and the aggression that is aimed at them by those citizens who could not go to the United States or other foreign countries. Those who stayed behind claim a special responsibility for holding the fort, and they accuse those who have gone out of the country to study of abandoning the homeland only to return to usurp power from those who stayed behind. In some instances, those who return home are expected to toe the line of the ruling political party, a party often out of synch with global political realities, such as equality, freedom of expression, and the unfettered exercise and enjoyment of human rights. If they resist or propose any other formula or new ideas contrary to the government's position, they are persecuted or considered subversive or classified as *personae non grata*. Many of those intellectuals who fall within this category end up migrating to the country where they studied, which in most cases is the United States. They undertake this second immigration in order to avoid political persecution, and many such individuals end up applying either for asylum or work authorization under the caveat of the H-1B visa status, which later becomes converted to permanent residency. These permanent residents form a special class of immigrants who are forced out of their countries and who avail themselves of the American welcoming spirit and freedom to migrate to the country.

Whether it is economic, political, and educational or Green Card–type of migration, many African families who arrive to the United States encounter serious, if not insurmountable problems. The greatest challenges African immigrant families face is manifested in the new values these couples and families or families who have never been to the United States face here. The newfound culture that they must adapt to in order to survive is radically different from the African cultures they left behind. They attempt to adjust to the new American culture while still holding tenaciously to the African culture, which has all along defined them and at the same time set them outside the mainstream American culture. While the African culture has always been a culture of identity, the American society introduces a new culture: one of survival. Ultimately, the survival culture takes precedence over the identity, which is negotiable, and leads to what Ngwang calls double identity[9]. Their survival and success depends on how well they balance this double identity and how much they tilt toward the American cultural values.

The qualification for entering the Green Card competition is a minimum of high school diploma, which opens the competition mainly to high school and college graduates, many of whom are working. In some countries, whether by design or accident, many of those who win these competitions are workers, who would prefer the American Dream as projected in Hollywood pictures to the quandary of home life. So they leave their lucrative jobs at home to suddenly face new choices in the United States: They must look for jobs again, especially jobs that are sometimes not even there. In most cases, those jobs that are readily available are the minimum wage jobs that in real value are demeaning when compared to the prestigious jobs they held in their home countries. While the husband, who was probably a university professor at home earning a reasonable salary, finds it incredible to start off life at McDonald's, it is the wife, the stay–home wife in Africa, who suddenly rolls up her gown and embraces the job. The family has to survive, and they have to do anything possible to earn an income for food, rent, and utilities. Fortunately, the wife suddenly finds herself now competing with the husband in the bread-winning field, which was previously "reserved" for the husband. More often than not, such minimum wage jobs suit the wives very much since these jobs require the type of labor that they (the housewives) were used to at home: Their motherly instincts readily accept nursing-home care jobs, cooking in restaurants, hotel and motel cleaning, janitorial work, and babysitting, while the husbands find it demeaning to "stoop" that low.

This reversal of roles creates an uncomfortable arrangement at home: The woman becomes the breadwinner, while the husband now stays at home to take care of the children (if any) or continues to look for the caliber of job that will enhance his "manliness." Such reversal of roles is the starting point of most of the problems such couples face. There is the problem of the allocation of funds. In some cases, the husbands still strongly believe that their wives should hand over their earnings to them to control and to decide how the money should be used. The wife, who actually works for the money, soon stands up to challenge the husband's unilateral decision to spend her money without her consent or without consulting her. The fear of the husband's misuse of money forces some of these wives to be unwilling to surrender their earnings to their husbands. Consequently, some husbands find themselves in the position of begging for the pocket money or walking out of the marriage. Those who cannot stand it find themselves vacillating between returning to the continent and striking it out on their own or staying in the United States under the tutelage of the wife who is now the de facto head of family.

Most families cannot stand the new arrangement where the woman now competes with the husband or changes roles with the husband. For the time being, the husbands stay at home while their wives go to work, make the money, and return home tired from working the back-breaking jobs, and still cook and serve the husband food on the table. Any resistance from the woman to any of the enumerated roles and chores is considered subversive and punishable by those men who fail to adjust to this new reality. There have been many cases of spousal abuse when the husband physically assaulted the wife for neglecting or complaining about performing any of the supposed traditional roles and chores of the wife. In some cases, the wives have had to take recourse in the law or social work where the husband was chastised or repatriated or the woman put in protective custody. Such cases have increased the incidence of divorce in African marriages.

It should be noted that divorce, as a single word or lexical item, does not exist in most African languages because these ethnic groups did not and still do not believe or practice divorce. In the Mbum group of the North West Province of Cameroon, divorce exists as a descriptive phrase that approximates "a marriage that is dead." These "dead marriages" are one of the most significant consequences or fallouts of the African immigration to the United States. The pressure on each family to survive is so much that it takes a strong will power to survive the onslaught of bills, poverty, food, clothing, medicines, and all the demands of the "civilized' world. It is becoming more and more common now to talk about divorce and single-parent homes among African immigrants in the United States. The fiber that used to hold the family together—the respect for traditions and family, parental status, and respect—weakens as the African families become increasingly assimilated into the mainstream American culture and values and things fall apart.

The trauma of facing these new challenges has pushed some men into trafficking in illegal substances and currency counterfeiting. We have read instances of families or individuals apprehended for belonging to a gang of traffickers or "money doublers" or dabbling in modern slavery.[10] Recently, there have also been cases of family abuses and slavery that came as a result of this immigration. In short, while this concept of immigration brought with it several advantages and excellent benefits, it nevertheless came with a baggage of ill fortunes. On the one hand, there are the obvious advantages of providing sustenance for the family, providing better job opportunities through enhanced technical and professional education, an opportunity to progress academically and economically, and the opportunity to see children grow up in a country where there is relative peace and a prosperous future for those who are hard working. On the other hand, there are those African immigrants who have been heavily hit now by the economic crisis that has undermined global economies, especially the United States. This has affected mainly those who immigrate to the United States for economic reasons, those commonly referred to as "economic immigrants." Fortunately, the standard of life and living conditions here in the United States are relatively better than those in the original homelands, which still makes living here much easier and better. To use a common expression from the movie *Rambo: First Blood*, what we call hell here is heaven to some of the immigrants, who compare the squalor of their homeland with the facilities that the United States provides. Many of these immigrants are condemned to remain in the United States because returning home is not so much an option.

The lack of jobs has definitely obligated some of the immigrants to go back to school to increase their power to get better jobs in future. Unfortunately, this is happening at a time when the cost of going to these schools has increased as a result of reduced and curtailed government subsidies that have forced schools to raise fees in order to survive. Still, most of the permanent residents have availed themselves of the scholarships, grants, and other resources available to them as permanent residents or citizens to pursue higher education. Statistics revealed by the United States Citizenship and Naturalization Fact Sheets of 2000 reveal that 80 percent of the blacks who earned terminal degrees (Ph.D. Ed. D, D. Pharm, M.D. etc.) are Africans. This fact is also validated by the statistics provided by the United States Citizenship and Immigration Services through the Office of Homeland Security's Office of Immigration Statistics, which ascertained that "Africans have the highest educational attainment rates of any immigrant group in the United States.[11] Estimates indicate that a significant percentage of black students at elite universities are Africans or children of African immigrants, a notable example of this being Barack Obama". These statistics confirm the fact that the African immigrants take education seriously as a means by which they can rise up in the corporate world or even the economic world. Furthermore, they see education as the weapon they can use to break through the barrier of discrimination and non-acceptance. Many of these African graduates hold very lucrative jobs because they are the best and the most trained in those areas, especially where the Americans cannot provide the same quality of service that is required for such positions.

Indeed, Okome, in his write-up entitled "African Immigration to the United States: Dimensions of Migration, Immigration, and Exile," has made a distinction between immigration and exile, which to me is a matter of semantics.[12] Although one is voluntary and the other is forced or self-imposed, both of them presuppose the physical movement of persons from Africa to the United States, irrespective of the reason. However, Okome goes on to discuss the ramification of this immigration both on America and the immigrant's homeland. The impact on both countries is profound. While the homeland country loses trained manpower and brain drain in whom they have invested a lot of money, the receiving country benefits from this influx of trained cadre.[13] Very often, the United States gains at no cost the expertise and training of those immigrants who seek sustenance and basic survival. It has been clearly noted that such immigrants earn by far less than their American counterparts and colleagues of the same rank, status, and qualification. This unfortunate design is typical in many universities and colleges where salary ranges are set arbitrarily and privately negotiated between the employee and employer. Most libraries in public universities have on reserve salary scales of professor revealing these gross irregularities.

AFRICAN IMMIGRANTS AND THE AFRICAN AMERICAN DREAM

Most Africans who immigrate to the United States are attracted to the major cities where their friends and relatives provide them with temporary shelter and sustenance until they can find their own living facilities and jobs. These major cities provide these immigrants opportunities to obtain advice and guidance from friends and relatives who have lived in the United States for a while. Some other immigrants, especially those escaping wars and persecution in Africa, sometimes search for quieter and suburban areas where they can raise their children in peace and tranquility. They are very sensitive to racial relationships and the prevailing political climate, which may look hostile to foreigners and blacks. Others search for places where they can easily get jobs and employment opportunities without the loss of their personal pride and sense of being. This may explain why there are so many African immigrants in locations where there is a greater degree of racial mixing and racial tolerance like New York, Minnesota, Chicago, Atlanta, Washington, DC, and California, to name a few.[14]

Many of these African immigrants are willing to accept any type of job just to earn a living. It is common to see highly educated immigrant Africans taking up jobs that are not commensurate with their level of education. In order to survive, many of the immigrants quickly realize that working one job will not be enough for them to sustain their families. Hence, many of them end up doubling as taxi drivers, parking and gas station attendants, waiters and waitresses, fast-food restaurant workers, and security guards at night and white collar workers in the day. The most popular profession for the newcomers is in the healthcare business such as nursing, nursing homes, and live-in facilities especially in larger cities like New York, Washington, DC, Boston, Chicago, Cincinnati, Ohio and other fast-growing cities where the relatively wealthy prefer to have trustworthy live-in workers than entrust their parents and grandparents to the sometimes abusive conditions that exist in group nursing homes or retirement residences. Such immigrant workers complement the hardship of the daytime work with the sometimes laid-back, though sleepless jobs of the night, just to enable them earn a little more money to sustain their families here in the United States and the extended families back on the continent.

It is equally common to find African immigrant populations engaged in African food restaurant business in cities like Washington, DC, Baltimore, Atlanta, Cincinnati, OH, and Columbia, SC, and where there is a significant population of Africans who will readily consume those African foods. However, some Americans have become increasingly attracted to the spicy African foods and the delicacies of the stock fish and goat meat and tend to patronize these African food restaurants. In addition, we find African women engaged in the exotic and enchanting hairstyling business where they plait hair. Many of these women have opened salons or are engaged in some form of joint venture with regular American hair salon operators to offer their services in areas of braiding. Another group of women, especially the elderly who cannot withstand the rigor of the American work ethos, find themselves babysitting at home. Although this is done at a very low level, it is picking up momentum and becoming increasingly popular in bigger cities where this cheap labor tends to offset the traditional expense of officially operated babysitting and daycare facilities.

Unfortunately, most of these immigrants find the American Dream a bit elusive because of the extraneous demands and responsibilities they face daily.[15] These immigrants are excited about the minimum pay they are promised at the end of the month or on payday. When they convert the amount into the currency of their African country, such amounts look fabulous. However, when the pay comes and much of it is taken for all sorts of taxes and insurances, they end up disappointed with what is left. From that meager sum, they have to pay their utilities (light and water), phone bills that run into hundreds of dollars, food, rent, and more importantly, money to send back home to take care of their extended families and, in some cases, their spouses and children. At the end of each month, they find themselves farther away from the American Dream than they had anticipated. Apraku noted that 37 percent of those African immigrants surveyed maintained that they sent between $1,500 and $3,000 annually, while 20 percent sent between $3000 and more than $10,000 annually to support friends and families back in their home country.[16] Most of these Africans fall within what is popularly called the "sandwich generation," a generation that takes care of the children who come after them and looks forward to taking care of their parents who came before them. They are sandwiched between the children and the parents. The typical African immigrant believes that he or she is not wealthy until the entire family shares in this wealth or are equally better off. However, present-day hardship is affecting this attitude as individuals think more now of themselves and their immediate families. Such sums of money sent home have saved lives, sent and sustained children in colleges and universities, built houses, and provided livelihood, all projects that would not have been realized without this immigration.

The African immigrants are not just interested in making money and capturing the American dream; they are interested in building stronger communities and organizing their people in order to become a powerful political and economic force in their respective communities.[17] Takougang identifies some of those very powerful African immigrant communities in the United States and how they work tirelessly to establish meaningful units of self-support and cooperatives: All African Peoples Organization in Omaha, Nebraska; the Nigerian-American Chamber of Commerce in Miami, Florida; the Tri-State (Ohio, Indiana, and Kentucky) Cameroon Family; the Nigerian Women Eagles Club in Cincinnati, Ohio; and the African Heritage Inc., in Wisconsin. These communities were created to cater to the local interest of the immigrants, especially those arriving newly from the continent by providing immediate financial loans and relief to them. However, many of these groups, like the Wimbum Cultural and Development Association–USA (WICUDA-USA), have identified and initiated development projects back home in Cameroon. Some of these groups have organized scholarship competitions back in their home countries and sponsored the deserving students in home and foreign universities, particularly in the United States, Greet Britain, and France.

The biggest winners in this game of immigration are the children. Nearly every elderly immigrant or aspiring African immigrant has contended that he or she immigrated to the United States because of and for their children. Many of these immigrants are of an age where education is not one of their priorities, and they will want to see their children acquire that American Dream in their stead; many of these children have not disappointed them. It is remarkable to perceive how fast these children, especially those born in Africa, have overcome the language and cultural barriers and are doing well in school. They win academic scholarships and many go to professional schools of medicine, law, pharmacy, engineering, and business. The children, like their parents, have come to realize that they can only survive in this rat-race existence through education. The parents have no other inheritance for them except their exposure to the education that will open up avenues to greater life. The children are computer savvy and know that liberal education or "education just for the sake of an education" is not an option; education should be tailored toward a better-paying job, immediate employment, and the opportunity for a better life. After all, education in the African context is investment, and those who have invested (parents, brothers, relatives) are patiently waiting for the dividends. So children grow up embracing and internalizing this concept and know that they cannot disappoint their parents.

Although this attitude sometimes puts unnecessary pressure on these immigrant children to select professions that are high paying and some of them may not be good in those areas, they nevertheless realize the importance of accountability. The family invests the money in them and they cannot idle or laze around because they have to prove to the parents that they (the parents) did not err in investing in them. Even if the parents do not look forward to having direct benefit from those children, the dream is to make their children financially viable and independent to release the parents from continuous financial responsibility for them. For no African parent will fold his or her arms and do nothing if the child is in financial difficulties simply because the child has attained maturity after the age of 18. Manhood, in most African cultures, is a measure of material and emotional independence, not biological age. It is when a child can stand on his or her own financially that a parent can breathe a sigh of relief and satisfaction, knowing that he or she has made a woman or a man out of his or her child.

CHALLENGES OF AFRICA-TO-UNITED STATES IMMIGRATION

Although African immigration to the United States seems like a win-win situation, it has come at a very high cost for both continents. From the African perspective, the immigration has had profound and far-reaching ramifications, some of them which are negative. As already discussed, the most evident loss is in the domain of trained manpower.[18] Many African universities have trained experts who eventually immigrate either willingly or not, through the now very popular DV Lottery or for further education. Many of those who came for further education are reluctant to return to often poor and politically corrupt countries ruled by tyrannical leaders poised to silence or eliminate opposing voices. Even many Africans who studied in the United States and voluntarily returned to the African countries confronted a different and difficult country where they were no longer at ease. Many of them ended up coming back to the United States either as refugees, asylees, on H-IB or Exchange Visas. If the greatest investment a country can engage in is in its people, then these African countries are facing human investment crises.[19]

A major fall out of the African immigration has been the rising number of broken families through divorce. Some families had difficulties adjusting to the new familial rearrangement the American society imposes on them. There is the reversal of roles where the wife becomes the breadwinner and the husband remains at home or becomes the "Mr. Mom." Many of the men have found it unacceptable to succumb to low or minimum wage jobs and have preferred to stay at home. However, they would dictate how the meager pay the wife brings back from daycares, residential cares, and nursing homes should be used. Moreover, the husband continues his nasty habit of drinking and waiting at home for his wife, who has been out at work all day, to return and go to the kitchen, cook and serve him food on the table. Most of these women are exhausted and feel exploited by husbands who cannot help them clean the house or prepare meals for them to eat on their return. They become stubborn and the husbands accuse them of infidelity and stubbornness. These are cases of women who, because of lack of adequate education back on the continent could not acquire any office or white-collar jobs. The little money some of them brought in from the sale of their farm produce is incomparable with the thousands of dollars they bring home at the end of the month here in the United States. Some frustrated husbands start abusing them. The women call the social welfare and the police and the next we hear is that the husbands are repatriated or they are divorced.[20]

On the other hand, some of the wives respond differently to this new reversal of roles. They suddenly find themselves empowered through earning money, which they never did back in the continent. They now have the power to settle scores with the husbands who were either abusive or never gave them adequate money for their daily needs and allowances. So these women find themselves now in the seat of control and can decide to do whatever they want with their money. It has been reported that some have even used their power of earning to sponsor the younger and more energetic boyfriends and relatives against the advice of their husbands. Such attitudes foment disagreements and inevitably divorce, for no husband will stand the thought of his wife using money as leverage against him and to abuse his manhood. Although such cases in which the husbands suffer in silence constitute a microscopic minority, they nevertheless exist.

There is also the loss of status for the immigrants who came to the United States with certain traditional ranks. The one card that America deals to each of the immigrants is the card of equalitarianism and a fresh start. Everybody comes in equal and starts to differentiate his or her role and personality through personal achievement. That explains why many professors and government elites who immigrate to the United States find it difficult to start "a new life" on the same level with those who were illiterate or of a lower rank than them in their home country. Except for those with American degrees and professions that are in high demand, many of those immigrants who arrive here start with minimum pay while waiting for that opportunity to slide to their actual functional level or status. An exception to this rule comes from immigrants who have relatives who are already well-established in the United States and allow them to stay without working until they get the requisite job. Even when this is the case, the immigrant soon gets bored staying at home without doing anything. Folks do not have the time and luxury to visit and chat with others daily like they do back in the home country. The immigrants start complaining of boredom and wanting to return to their home country. Others stay and soon gain weight from lack of exercise and work and many of them have ended up with strokes, heart attack and diabetes.

Furthermore, those immigrants who want to wait until "things get better" and they get a job soon encounter social stigmatization. They soon become profiled as lazy, drug dealers, criminals, and all kinds of things. They find themselves sometimes doubting their own true identities since they have never before been relegated to these stereotypes, strip searched and tailed in shops because they are black. This is particularly hard on those immigrants who are running away from ethnic cleansing or political discrimination on the basis of ethnic or regional origins. These incidents accentuate their continuous fear of humanity; they see history repeating itself, as well as the tentacles of oppression extending across the ocean. Although this situation may be bearable because the immigrant is in a foreign country as opposed to being persecuted and called a foreigner in his or her own country, it nevertheless does not diminish the psychological impact of distrust such an attitude produces in the immigrant.

Some other African immigrants bring with them their regional conflicts and disagreements from the continent to the United States. So whenever they meet, they tend to see themselves as an extension of their African localities. This was particularly evident in the 1970s and 1980s among the Nigerian Ibos and Hausas in response to the political tension that existed between them following the Nigerian Civil War. In 1980, I watched with dismay some of these tensions that were sometimes violent and disrupted our African Student meetings at the University of Wisconsin, Madison and Oklahoma State University. Similar situations arise when Cameroonian Francophones attended the Anglophone gatherings and tended to impose their agenda and the French language on the meetings. Instances like these, some of which have been national in nature, have been counterproductive and unhealthy to immigrants who thought they were running away from persecution in the home country. The problem resurfaces in the United States, reminding them of the common fact that we are all the same, irrespective of where we are.

The other very embarrassing and frustrating problem faced by African immigrants continues to be the lack of acceptance and cooperation from some of their African American counterparts. In an interview with my African American colleague Dr. Donald Pardlow, he admitted and also revealed that this aggression toward foreigners is buried deep in the African American distrust for foreigners. To him, "the typical African American culture is conservative, suspicious of foreigners and xenophobic. Consequently, the typical African American looks at these foreign blacks as rockers of the boats in the calm seas, as individuals who would rather meet the white man half way than lay back and do nothing."[21] The African Americans find themselves being challenged to wake up and meet the moving society or be left behind. On the other hand, the Africans who are eager to identify themselves with the African American are easily rebuffed by some African Americans who perceive Africans as responsible for the fact that their African ancestors sold them into slavery. So, they hold the Africans responsible for the slave status that has remained permanently seared into their brains. Moreover, some of the African Americans complain that the Africans who pass for African Americans have appropriated their share of the national cake, thereby taking away the portions that were supposed to be given to the real/true African American. This outcry has been heard very loudly in the application of Affirmative Action for professional schools and white-collar employment.

Many African American students confess that the African Americans are turned off by the hard work of the African, who is used to working hard for what he or she gets. Vis-à-vis the African, the African American student sometimes therefore appears lazy, always complaining and wanting things the easy way.[22] The African student who pays almost twice as much as his American counterpart for tuition and fees (as evidenced in most university catalogs where there are the international fees and out-of-state tuition rates, restriction of scholarships for first-year international scholarships), works harder to get his or her money's worth, and ends up performing very well in classes. Soon the African American accuses the African of hubris and of seeing themselves as better, if not superior to the African American counterparts. This has not only led to uneasy relationships between the African and the African American, but has continued to make the African immigrant feel unwelcomed.

From the American perspective, there is the continuous fear of the "other," where this "other" may be a terrorist, supporter of some gangs, or an agent for drug trafficking and crime. Although the crime rate among African immigrants has been small as compared to those from Central and South America, there is always the disadvantage of receiving an influx of needy people who will cost the government significant amounts of money to maintain.[23] For instance, all immigrants who are admitted into the United States as refugees, DV Lottery winners, or aylees are entitled to food and money until they are gainfully employed. This is taxpayer's money to which these refugees and asylees have not contributed. Thus, the government has to look for money or redistribute its income in order to accommodate those immigrants coming in legally. Moreover, there is the temptation for those who are unable to find good jobs to easily join gangs or drug traffickers as a quick fix for cash. According to Tony Waters in *Crime and Youth*, new immigrants are susceptible to gang influences and activities because of language barriers, employment difficulties, support, protection, and fear.[24] Unfortunately, this study did not focus much attention on African immigrants. However, I remember isolated cases of drug trafficking among African immigrants in the early 1980s, which were few and spaced out over long periods of time. Recently, there have been money-doubling and counterfeiting activities among Cameroonians in Washington, DC, Chicago, and other major cities that was quickly apprehended and dismantled. It goes without saying that African immigrants are not immune to crimes, but they do not figure significantly on the scene of heinous crimes to be documented.

CONCLUSION

The story of the African immigrant to the United States of America is still unfolding, and it is becoming much more exciting, complex, and complicated. In this age of globalization and hybridity, this story seems only to be gathering momentum as the American society has a double-edged responsibility in this movement. There is the DV Lottery inviting more Africans to immigrate to the United States, and at the same time, the Department of Homeland Security has stepped up the process of repatriating illegal immigrants, even those without criminal records back to their respective homelands. The continuous proliferation of civil wars, ethnic cleansing, poverty, corruption, and tyranny that have consumed most of Africa will continue to give Africans more reasons to immigrate legally and even illegally to the United States. Many of these illegal immigrants know the danger entailed in these missions, but they would rather die trying to accomplish these "missions impossible" that promise them the American Dream than continue to wallow in abject poverty, underemployment, diseases, and hunger.

Moreover, the achievement of Barack Obama, the son of a Kenyan immigrant, has galvanized and solidified the reality of this Africa-to-America immigration and given the immigrants real hope for a better future in a country where anything is possible. Indeed, the African children are the greatest beneficiaries of this westward movement. The proof is seen in the increasing number of Africans filing for entry visas in American embassies all over the word. Again, the number of Africans filing for Green Cards and those winning the DV Lottery continues to rise. As long job opportunities exist in the United States, the United States remains a world superpower, the Hollywood continues to glamorize the American Dream, and the DV Lottery remains open to Africans, African immigration will continue to increase in numbers while the challenges to immigration will continue to mutate in form, content, and complexity.

ENDNOTES

1 The Diversity Immigration Visa Program is a U.S. congressionally mandated lottery program for receiving U.S. permanent resident cards. Administered by the Department of State and conducted under the terms of Section 203(c) of the Immigration and Nationality Act (INA) of 1990, it has given many Africans direct access to American citizenship. See Department of State and USCI Services and http://dvlotter.state.gov (accessed October 11, 2010).

2 For more recent research on trans-Atlantic slavery, see Alexander Ives Bortolot's "The Transatlantic Slave Trade" in *Heilbrunn Timeline of Art History* (New York: The Metropolitan Museum of Art, 2000); Allstair Boddy-Evans, *The Trans-Atlantic Slave Trade: A Review of the triangular trade and reference to maps and statistics.* http://africanhistory. about.com/trans-atlanticslavetrade and Herbert S. Klein, *The Atlantic Slave Trade* (Cambridge, UK: Cambridge University Press, 1999).

3 Vernon M. Briggs, Jr., *Mass Immigration and the National Interest* (New York: M.E. Sharpe, 1992), 143; See also Arthur Corwin, "The Fourth Wave of Mass Immigration," in *The Social Contract* 3, no. 2 (Winter 1992–1993), which discusses the role of the churches in population growth, immigration, and environment.

4 Briggs, *Mass Immigration and the National Interest;* Corwin, "The Fourth Wave of Mass Immigration"; and U.S. Citizenship and Immigration Services, Citizenship & Naturalization Based Resources, www.uscis.gov.poryalsite/uscis (accessed October 11, 2010).

5 Homeland Security, Office of Immigration Statistics, *Annual Flow Report. Naturalization in the United States.* April 2010. www.dhs.gov/immigrationstatistic; Also see *African Immigration to the USA.* Other sources include www. africaresource.com/index.php?option=com_content&view=article&id=3 77:the-impact-of-africa-on-the-world& catid=135:immigration&Itemid=348. (accessed October 11, 2010).

6 Ian Yeboah, "Identity Politics of Ghanaian Immigrants in the Greater Cincinnati Area: Emerging Geography and Sociology of Immigrant Experiences." This is an ongoing research paper on the growing Ghanaian community in S.W. Ohio that was delivered at a Miami University Regional Campus Symposium on the title "Out of Africa: New African Diasporas in the US" on March 31, 2011. This paper complements Joseph Takougang's research and paper "Recent Immigrants to the United States: An Historical Perspective" published in *The Western Journal of Black Studies* 19 (2002), where both of them tackle the regional distribution of African immigrants in the United States with particular references to the East, Midwest, and Western United States.

7 Soumana Sako, "Brain Drain and Africa's Development: A Reflection," African *Issues* 30, no. 1 (2002): 28.

8 Joseph Takougang, "Recent Immigrants to the United States: A Historical Perspective," *The Western Journal of Black Studies* 19, no. 1 (2002).

9 Emmanuel N. Ngwang, "Survival and Personal Identity in Arthur Miller's Plays," (Dissertation, Oklahoma State University, 1986). Chapter three of this dissertation discusses issues relevant to multiple identities where the individual puts on several identities in order to survive.

10 Carl F. Horowitz, "Immigration Policy Importing Slavery" (December 27, 2002), www.vdare.com/horwitz/021227_ immigration.htm (accessed May 24, 2011); Also see http://msnbc.msn.com/id/28415693: "Child 'slavery' now being imported to the US. One Child's Story speaks for the thousands locked in silent servitude." (accessed October 11, 2010).

11 Also see DHS, *Profiles on Legal Permanent Residents.* http://www.dhs.gov/files/statistics/data/dslpr.shtm (accessed September 23, 2010); and "African Immigrants in the United States Are the Nation's Most Highly Educated Group." *The Journal of Blacks in Higher Education* 26 (Winter 1999–2000), 60–61.

12 Mojubaolu Olunfunke Okome, "African Immigration to the United States: Dimensions of Migration, Immigration, and Exile." www.africaresource.com/index.php?view=article&catid=135%3Aimmigration&id (accessed October 11, 2010).

13 Ibid.; Sako, "Brain Drain and Africa's Development," 28; and Claire Mencke, "Immigration: Who Suffers? An Interview with Vernon M. Briggs, Jr." *The Social Contract Journal Issues* 10, no. 1 (Fall 1999).

14 Emmanuel Yewah and Dimeji Togunde, eds., *Across the Atlantic: African Immigrants in the United States Diaspora* (Champaign, IL: Common Ground, 2010). Also see Professor Ian Yeboah, "Identity Politics of Ghanaian Immigrants," and Joseph Tarkougang, "Recent Immigrants to the United States," and *Contemporary African Immigration to the United States* (2010).www.africanmigration.com/archive_02/j_takougang.htm (accessed October 11, 2010).

15 James Butty, "Dream or Drain?" *West Africa* (March 4–10, 1991), 295.

16 Kofi K. Apraku, *African Émigrés in the United States: A Missing Link in Africa's Social and Economic Development* (New York: Praeger Publishers, 1991).

17 Joseph Takougang, *Contemporary African Immigration to the United States.* www.africanmigration.com/ archive_02/j_takougang.htm. (accessed October 11, 2010).

18 Ikubolajeh Bernard Logan, "The Brain Drain of Professional, Technical and Kindred Workers from Developing Countries: Some Lessons from the Africa-United States flow of Professional, 1980-1989," in *Immigrants in Two Democracies*, ed. Donald L. Horowitz and Gerard Noiriel (New York: New York University Press, 1992).

19 I am in the group that returned to Africa in the 1980s and had to migrate back to the United States after ten years because of the problems of insecurity, political persecution, and the difficulties of readjusting to an environment that was totally different from my expectation in terms of sociopolitical progress, efficiency, freedoms, and peace.

20 I have personally intervened in marital disagreements where money and the spending of it have been at the center of these conflicts. Some of these problems resulted in the breakup of traditional marriages and meetings in Atlanta, Cincinnati, Dallas, Washington, DC, and other cities where Cameroonians of a significant group have constituted cultural groups to meet frequently and raise money for businesses. The stigma of the situation has caused many victims to be silent about it rather than ask for help. And it is our hope that some researcher will come up with a study to identify and attempt to resolve the frequency of these issues.

21 Donald Pardlow. Interview by author, January 20, 2011.

22 The author was initially attracted to this conflict as a professor teaching at Kentucky State University in 1997, an HBCU where the conflict between the African and African American students was very prominent in classrooms. The professor came up with a set of questionnaires that were distributed to several classes soliciting answers to the continuous problems between Africans and African Americans. These responses were put together and written up in another paper and presented in the SIRAS Conference.

23 Mencke in Briggs. *The Social Contract Journal Issues* 10, no. 1 (Fall 1999). www.thesocialcontract.com/artman2/ publish/tsc/article-838 (accessed October 11, 2010).

24 Tony Waters, *Crime and Youth* (San Francisco: Sage Publishers, 1999).

REVIEW QUESTIONS

1. Name three types of immigrants and write briefly about each type. Analyze the uniqueness of the different types and phases of African immigration to the United States.

2. What were the political and economic circumstances in Africa that encourage Africans to immigrate to the United States and what solutions could be found for this dilemma?

3. Discuss the concept of brain drain how it has positively or negatively affected both the United States and the African continent.

4. Discuss the concept of the reversal of roles and how it has affected the African communities, especially families in the diaspora.

6. Discuss some of the major problems African immigrants face on arrival in America and how they resolve each of them. Why do African immigrants tend to perform so well in school?

Writing Prompt

1. Discuss the American Dream and how it has defined the lives of many African families. You may want to discuss how the African interpretation of this dream differs from the American interpretation leading to complete misunderstanding of the concept.

CHAPTER 18

Human Rights in Africa: Commitments, Realities, and Prospects

Lovetta A. Thompson

In the history of all societies, people acquired rights and responsibilities through their membership in a group—a family, indigenous nation, religion, class, community, or state. Some early texts that address questions of people's duties, rights, and responsibilities include the Judeo-Christian Bible and the Islamic Qu'ran. Most societies, whether in oral or written tradition, have had systems of propriety and justice as well as ways of tending to the health and welfare of their members.[1] The African continent, for instance, has dominated many discussions pertaining to human rights, be it implementation or violations. The state of human rights in Africa continues to be a fertile subject for historical and social science analysis and commentary in academic circles.

Academic preoccupation with the subject of human rights derives from both its absorbing intellectual interest and its all-encompassing practical dimensions, touching and concerning the basic human values of life, liberty, and property – the normative underpinnings of modern civilization. On a practical level, it is irrefutable that the neglect of human rights at national and international levels does have grave political, social, and economic repercussions for the population. For example, empirical studies reveal that in the Africa region, the food crisis in 2008 had a disproportionate impact on vulnerable population groups, especially those already living in poverty. Across the region, people demonstrated against the desperate social and economic situation and the sharp rise in living costs.[2] The most recent example surrounding the discussion of human rights would be the subject of child marriage, an issue that is said to 'plague' developing nations mainly in Africa. A glimmer of hope, however, is the new two-year campaign launched by the African Union (AU), governments, and civil society organizations to end child marriage across Africa.[3]

Nonetheless, more often than not, discussions of human rights in developing nations, especially those in Africa are, as Nhlapo puts it, "attended by a sinking feeling that such attempts are a pointless exercise, and merely lawyers' games fated to achieve nothing of significance to the ordinary person."[4] Skepticism about human rights protection in Africa originated from the perception of the human rights' philosophy as an intellectual conceptual contrivance of Western thought designed to perpetuate foreign domination of Africa and reflecting the liberal, individualistic tradition of Western Europe and America.[5]

Ake poses what in my view is a very important and thought-provoking question: "If I am not in a position to realize this right, then what is the point of saying I have it?"[6] According to Ake, "The Western notion of human rights stresses rights which are not very interesting in the African context of realities."[7] He argues that rights such as freedom of speech and assembly "appeal to people with a full stomach who can afford to pursue the more esoteric aspects of self-fulfillment," a position in which the vast majority of Africans do not occupy.[8] Scholars leaning on this school of thought often look to the precolonial era and the communitarian ideal as a model of how to address the "Africa problem" within a context of its cultural realities. Ake, along with other scholars, believes that it is necessary to "extend the idea of human rights to include collective human rights for corporate social groups such as the family, the lineage, the ethnic group."[9]

Baah also contends that the Universal Declaration of Human Rights is a Western concept, and that there is a disagreement between the stance of Akan culture of Ghana and the Western-style human-rights ideology. He argues that the Akan recognize the concept of human dignity, and he views human dignity as a precursor to human rights. Thus, the interpretation and implementation of "human rights" in any society must be linked to the people's concept of human dignity and how best to protect it for:

> If the purpose of human rights is to protect human dignity, and as has been shown in this research, human dignity is relative to the particular society under consideration, why do we have a uniform standard of human rights, when in fact certain human rights principles may undermine or conflict with certain human dignity orientations that human rights are supposed to protect?[10]

Baah gives credence to the view that an African government may be too preoccupied with helping its citizens gain supposedly more important things—like food, shelter, and healthcare—to pursue a 'blanket solution' of human-rights implementation.[11] The development of Africa, much like the concept and practice of human rights, should not be achieved by proxy, but by the domestication and re-creation in light of African conditions.[12]

On the other end of the spectrum, scholars see the communitarian ideal as something that would take away from the inherent rights of the individual. Mahmud views the argument of incorporating the African cultural emphasis on community as problematic when addressing human rights issues because the communitarian ideal is "privilege," not rights; and while focused on interdependency, is not one of equality. For example, privileges are not available to every member of the societies on an equal basis, nor are resources centrally controlled; land may be communally owned but not distributed equally because some families may own more.[13] Deprived individuals cannot lay claim to these freedoms as something owed them by their communities. Some individuals can be denied basic rights sanctioned by the community, such as the right to a decent life or even the right to life.[14] Collective rights cannot be realized if the people do not have equal individual rights under the law. Mahmud makes a very compelling argument as regards the fallacy of the communitarian ideal in these terms:

> Compounding the problem of equating cultural privileges to human rights is the fact that even if these privileges could form the basis of an African concept of human rights, one must still explain the change in the historical context of these privileges and the contemporary forms of social organization which now characterize African countries.[15]

While Ake argues that the whole concept of human rights emerged as a tool for opposing democracy, other authors view human rights and democracy as two points along a continuum.[16] Mahmud's key assumption is that democratization provides the best means to create and uphold individual rights on the continent.[17] Aidoo also views human rights and democracy as inextricably linked, and the possibilities of the realization of human rights in undemocratic societies as slim to none; yet democracy does not automatically bring about conditions favorable for human rights.[18] And indeed, a real need arises, namely, to put more emphasis on the realization of human rights. Another school of thought, posed by Alison Dundes Renteln, combines the ideal of human rights as universal (based on the Universal Declaration of Human Rights) and cultural relativism as the way to approach human rights implementation across the globe. Renteln argues that conducting empirical research in non-western countries could lead the discovery of shared values across all cultures – a point of reference that could possibly lay avoid the argument of cultural imperialism.[19]

Regardless of the merits or demerits of these arguments based on skepticism for the human rights' ideal, the contemporary reality is that African states have come to embrace the idea of the internationalization and regionalization of human rights as a normative yardstick for measuring progress in democratic governance and political, social, and economic development in Africa. This is due in part to the pressures of globalization. Predicated upon this recognition of the human rights ideal, it becomes imperative to examine commitments, realities, and prospects for the protection and preservation of human rights in Africa. This chapter explores the correlation, if any, between principles and practice or between rhetoric and reality in the realm of human rights protection and the enhancement of human dignity in Africa.

AFRICAN STATES AND CONSTITUTIONAL BILLS OF RIGHTS

The process of incorporation of fundamental human rights and freedoms in the constitutions of African nations initially took the form of Bills of Rights. In a scholarly analysis of Sierra Leone's constitutional development from 1961–1995, Bankole Thompson, a noted constitutional law scholar, traces the incorporation process back to 1960 when certain specific rights and freedoms were incorporated in the Federal Constitution of Nigeria, a large African country with a vast majority of ethnic groups within it. The guaranteed rights and freedoms included, mainly, the right to life, freedom from torture or inhuman treatment, freedom from slavery or forced labor, personal liberty, right of privacy and of enjoyment of family life, freedom of thought, conscience, religion, and freedom of speech and expression.[20] The idea of incorporation was essentially a constitutional paradigm designed to secure the effective and adequate protection of human rights and freedoms in the newly independent African countries. Based on the notion that the former British colonial African territories had acquired sufficient instruction in British constitutionalism, it was claimed that these so-called export models of British constitutionalism "were aimed at capturing the spirit and practice of the British Constitution." Thompson views this claim with some skepticism.[21] He contends that a close analysis of the British Constitution and the independence constitutions of Commonwealth African states reveals a critical difference for modern constitutionalism, namely, that the latter constitutions do embody written Bills of Rights, the British Constitution does not.[22]

The Nigerian precedent was then extended to other Commonwealth African states, notably, Sierra Leone, Malawi, Uganda, Kenya, Zambia, and Zimbabwe, with the notable exception of Ghana for the reason that the Ghanaian delegation to the drafting conference on the independence constitution vigorously repudiated the idea of a written Bill of Rights as inefficacious and a serious limitation on executive and legislative authority.[23] Today, Bills of Rights providing for the protection and enforcement of fundamental human rights and freedoms are embodied in several African constitutions. Hence, it is the case that the process of incorporating human rights provisions in Africa preceded the voluntary acceptance, recognition, and adoption, at the regional level, of international human rights instruments by many African states.

GENESIS OF AFRICAN COMMITMENT TO INTERNATIONAL HUMAN RIGHTS PHILOSOPHY

While modern human rights, as codified in international and domestic laws, are strictly a post–World War II phenomenon drawing their impetus from the violations of human rights during Third Reich Nazi Germany, human rights as a concept and as a movement in the Africa region and international community dates back centuries. Arguments surrounding the human rights debate have held that it is inextricably linked to democracy, thus solidifying its Western underpinnings. Aidoo quotes Franklin D. Roosevelt as saying:

> There is nothing mysterious about the foundations of a healthy and strong democracy. The basic things expected by our people of their political and economic systems are simple. They are: equality of opportunity for youth and for others; jobs for those who can work; security for those who need it; the ending of special privilege of the few; the preservation civil liberties.[24]

He furthers his argument by including Africanist scholars that hold similar views that democracy should be on the agenda for African countries because of its "recognition of the legitimate rights of the African people."[25] The argument is that human rights is the basis of democracy. One could argue, however, that the two did not develop in tandem. The earliest historical and philosophical foundations of democracy are generally traced to Greco-Roman times. Democratic heritage did not necessarily mean respect for human rights. Human rights philosophy, as we know it today, can be traced only to the seventeenth to eighteenth centuries.

The basis of this philosophy and its Western underpinnings often find its genesis in the philosophical writings of the likes of Thomas Hobbes and John Locke. It is argued that their writings were among the first to emphasize the abstraction from the holistic totality of medieval society to human rights as a state of human nature.[26] According to Hinchman, the "liberty each man has to use his own power as he will himself, for the preservation of his own nature—that is to say, his own life."[27] Hobbes and Locke's theory of natural rights is credited for forming the basis for the mainstream human rights scholarship because of the emphasis of equality in nature, and especially because of its contention on individualism. As Cobbah puts it, "From the revolutionary ideas of Hobbes and Locke a new Western world evolved."[28] Thus, they are said to have set the groundwork for our modern day understanding and conceptualizing of human rights as a theory and movement.

The Western concept of individual rights and law found its place in many non-Western parts of the world through colonialism. In the late nineteenth century, for instance, Africa would unknowingly be catapulted into the human rights movement when news spread of King Leopold II's dark reign in the Belgian Congo. According to Adam Hochschild, individuals such as black American journalist George Washington Williams, William Shepphard, an African American reverend, and Edmund Dene Morel, an employee of a Liverpool shipping line, uncovered and shed light on the brutal treatment of the African people under Belgium's colonial rule. These men, among others, exposed the slavery-like conditions of the African people in the Congo, and thus ignited "the first great international human rights movement of the twentieth century."[29]

The genesis of Africa's commitment to the human rights' ideal is conceptually linked with Western legal and political philosophy, emanating principally from the Universal Declaration of Human Rights, the International Covenant on Civil and Political Rights, the International Covenant on Economic, Social, and Cultural Rights, and other regional treaties such as the European Convention on Human Rights and the American Convention on Human Rights. In effect, it is true that African regional instruments on human rights do patently bear the imprint of their Western and international prototypes. The irresistible inference, therefore, is that the Western-led human rights' movement has not only become relevant to African communities but has also had a significant impact on the African continent.[30]

AFRICAN IMPLEMENTATION OF HUMAN RIGHTS INSTRUMENTS

The regional implementation of international human rights standards and norms in Africa began with the adoption of the African Charter on Human and People's Rights at the Eighteenth Assembly of Heads of State and Government of the Organization of African Unity in Nairobi, Kenya, in 1981.[31] It entered into force on October 21, 1986. The germ of the idea can be traced back to the 1960s with calls for an African Human Rights Charter being made by African jurists meeting under the auspices of the International Commission of Jurists in Lagos, Nigeria, in 1961 and Dakar, Senegal, in 1967, and in sessions by the UN Commission on Human Rights.[32] The African Charter sought to depart from regional models such as the European and American Conventions by emphasizing issues of a social, economic, and cultural nature in language found in some of the preambles to the Charter. One such emphasis is that "civil and political rights cannot be dissociated from economic, social, and cultural rights" and that the satisfaction of these latter rights "is a guarantee for the enjoyment of civil and political rights."[33]

Another focus that gives the Charter a uniquely African character is the pledge "to eradicate all forms of colonialism from Africa" and a reaffirmation of the duty of African states to achieve "the total liberation of Africa . . . . and . . . . to eliminate colonialism, apartheid, Zionism, and to dismantle oppressive foreign military bases" from Africa.[34] Unquestionably, the African Charter on Human and Peoples' Rights is the main source of African international or regional human rights law. To understand fully the normative significance of the Charter, it is instinctive to outline the specific rights and freedoms guaranteed under the Charter.

First, Articles 1–18 enumerate individual rights of the kind provided for in prior international and regional instruments, notably the United Nations Universal Declaration of Human Rights, the European Convention on Human Rights, and the American Convention on Human Rights. These are civil and political rights as well as economic, social, and cultural rights.[35] Articles 19–24 specify the rights of peoples, and the entire Chapter II (articles 27–29) provides not only for rights and freedoms but also for so-called duties and obligations owed by the individual to the African family, community, the State, and the international community, insisting that "Every individual shall have the duty to respect and consider his fellow beings without discrimination, and to maintain relations aimed at promoting, safeguarding and reinforcing mutual respect and tolerance."[36]

Part II of the charter provides measures of safeguard by establishing the African Commission on Human and Peoples' Rights. According to the charter, the commission "shall be established within the Organization of African Unity to promote human and peoples' rights and ensure their protection in Africa."[37] At the time of the Charter's adoption, the Commission was the only body responsible for the promotion and protection of human rights.

Article 2 of the Charter stipulates that the rights and freedoms provided for in the Charter shall be enjoyed "without distinction of any kind such as race, ethnic group, colour, sex, language, religion, political or any other opinion, national and social origin, fortune, birth or other status."

The next major regional instrument on human rights adopted by the African states is the African Charter on the Rights and Welfare of the Child.[38] Like the African Charter on Human and Peoples' Rights, the context of the African Charter on the Rights and Welfare of the Child exhibits, in tenor, a uniquely African flavor, despite the fact that the Charter was modeled on the United Nations Convention on the Rights of the Child. This is evident from the preambles to the Charter. For example:

> Noting with concern that the situation of most African children remains critical due to the unique factors of their socio-economic, cultural, traditional and developmental circumstances, natural disasters, armed conflicts, exploitation and hunger, and on account of the child's physical and mental immaturity he/she needs special safeguards and care.[39]

The specific rights provided for in the Charter included, mainly, freedom from discrimination (Article 3), the right to life (Article 5), the right to a name from birth (Article 6), the right to nationality (Article 6), freedom of expression (Article 7), freedom of association (Article 8), freedom of thought, conscience, and religion (Article 9), the right to education (Article 11), the right to rest and leisure (Article 12), the right to special measures, if handicapped (Article 13), protection against harmful social and cultural practices (Article 21), and protection from direct participation in hostilities (Article 22).

The Charter also imposes, in several provisions, a wide range of parental, family, and state responsibilities in respect to the welfare of the child. These include, mainly, the obligation to ensure, in respect to the child, "the best attainable state of physical, mental, and spiritual health" (Article 14), freedom "from all forms of economic exploitation and from performing any work that is likely to be hazardous or to interfere with the child's physical, mental, spiritual, moral, or social development" (Article 15), and protection against child abuse and torture (Article 16). There are also some key provisions securing safeguards for the child in the context of judicial settlement of disputes involving children. One such safeguard is the very important principle of the "best interests of the child." In this regard, the Charter provides that "In all actions concerning the child undertaken by any person or authority the best interests of the child shall be the primary consideration."[40]

Another provision is that "every child accused or found guilty of having infringed penal law shall have the right to special treatment in a manner consistent with the child's sense of dignity and worth and which reinforces the child's respect for human rights and fundamental freedoms of others," ensuring (i) "that no child who is detained or imprisoned or otherwise deprived of his/her liberty is subjected to torture, inhuman or degrading treatment or punishment", and (ii) "that children are separated from adults in their place of detention or imprisonment."[41]

Evidently, both these principal regional instruments on human rights, the African Charter on Human and Peoples' Rights and the African Charter on the Rights and Welfare of the Child, do constitute a major progressive development of international human rights norms in Africa. The critical question now is: To what extent, if any, was there a commitment to human rights' in both theory and praxis?

The answer to the question of how committed the African nations are to the human rights' ideal does not depend merely upon the adoption of the two Charters or their commitment to them. It depends mainly upon the extent to which each country has, since the adoption of the Charters, taken the necessary measures to implement the secured rights and freedoms and put into effect governmental measures and policies to ensure the promotion, protection, enforcement, and preservation of those rights at every level of their respective societies and communities.

It was noted earlier that the human rights' philosophy had been a key feature of the Constitutions of the Commonwealth African states, in the form of Bills of Rights, as far back as 1960. In determining whether the relevant governmental agencies and institutions, assigned with the task of protecting human rights, have indeed performed effectively or otherwise in discharging their mandates, some key questions seem relevant. One such is: What is the record of the courts in African countries in providing adequate and effective protection of human rights and freedoms within their territorial jurisdictions? The answer is fraught with difficulties. In this regard, Amnesty International reports that "in many African countries the judicial system lacks independence.

In addition, the justice system is often under-resourced, poorly equipped, and understaffed, leading to excessive delays in hearing criminal issues."[42] It is observed that "in Nigeria, for example, those who are poor face numerous obstacles to obtaining a fair trial within an acceptable period of time. Although some efforts have been made to provide legal aid, it is not nearly enough to grant legal representation for all who need it but cannot afford to pay for a lawyer—even in cases carrying the death penalty. The more than 700 people living on death row in Nigeria in 2008 all had one thing in common—they were poor."[43] Similarly, the United States is the world's leader in regards to prison population, at more than 2 million at the end of 2009.[44] Moreover, those that represent the prison demographic (the majority of whom are incarcerated for nonviolent offenses) are largely from historically oppressed groups, be it the poor or racial minorities. For example, blacks and Hispanics together make up 59 percent of the prison population in the United States.[45] Scholars have termed the rapid expansion of the U.S. inmate population as the "prison industrial complex."[46]

Likewise, in Sierra Leone, during the early years of independence, public expectation was very high that the courts would adequately and effectively protect the fundamental rights and freedoms contained in the country's Bill of Rights. There was a widely voiced allegiance to the human rights' ideal enshrined in the 1961 Constitution. It is observed that "the courts interpreted literally and restrictively the relevant constitutional provisions regarding the circumstances which could justify derogation from the rights and freedoms of the individual."[47] In addition, it has been contended that "experiences in majority of the new states in the Commonwealth have shown that the problem of adequate and effective protection of fundamental rights and freedoms remains intractable."[48]

Furthermore, on Sierra Leone, Thompson observed that two key features were at play in the thirteen years during which the one-party Constitution was in force. They were:

> the rise of monolithism and the extensive use of public emergency powers as a technique of statecraft . . . In specific terms, the introduction of the one-party system of government (i) effectively precluded citizens from presenting their candidature for elections if they were not of the same political persuasion as the ruling party . . . ; (ii) banned freedom of assembly and associations . . . ; (iii) seriously undermined the independence of the judiciary; (iv) subverted the rule of law in favor of the rule of thuggery (largely reflected in widespread electoral violence whenever election were forthcoming); and (v) severely restricted press freedom.[49]

In Tanzania, the trend during the early years of that country's Bill of Rights was equally unimpressive. Addressing the issue, one scholar commented that, "initially it was expected that, given the active part taken by the senior members of the judiciary in the debates for the amendment of the Constitution in 1983/84, the judiciary would have taken an active role in enforcement of the provisions on the Basic Rights. However, to the disappointment of everybody, the judiciary, which has been attacked for its conservative attitude has decided to take a safe and "wait and see" attitude.[50]

REALITIES ABOUT HUMAN RIGHTS PROTECTION IN AFRICA: EXISTING PROFILE

A report of Amnesty International provides valuable insights into the realities of human rights protection in Africa. First, in so far as deprivation of basic needs is concerned, the profile is that millions across Africa continue to be deprived of their basic needs in spite of the sustained economic growth in many countries in Africa during past years. People face enormous challenges in securing daily livelihood, often aggravated by marginalization or political repression and attempts to muffle their voices and render them powerless.[51]

Second, with regard to security, the true position is that armed conflict and insecurity in several African countries force hundreds of thousands of people to flee from their homes, trying to find protection across borders or some form of security within their own country. In some of the worst armed conflicts still affecting the region, government forces and armed groups completely disregard the dignity and physical integrity of the population. This is not unique to Africa. Civilians are often treated badly in war-torn countries whether in Africa, Asia, Latin-America, or Europe. The civilian population is routinely the object of attacks by parties to the conflict; rape and other forms of sexual violence remain widespread; children are often recruited to take part in hostilities; and humanitarian workers are targeted.[52]

Third, with respect to exclusion, the current profile is that many groups in African societies continue to face discrimination and exclusion from protection or the means to get redress for the abuses they suffered. In Uganda, for example, victims of numerous human rights abuses during the armed conflict in the north of the country remain destitute and traumatized, often excluded from any means of redress.[53]

Fourth, as regards freedom of expression, association, and peaceful assembly, there is compelling evidence that African governments continue to restrict these rights, without justification. Despite the emergence of vibrant civil society organizations asserting the right to freedom of expression, association, and peaceful assembly, legislation or other forms of regulation are frequently used to restrict the work of such societies. In Ethiopia, a draft bill criminalizing human rights activities has been in preparation. In Swaziland, the Suppression of Terrorism Act has had a chilling effect on the activities of civil society organizations. In numerous countries, including Angola, Cameroon, Chad, Equatorial Guinea, Gambia, Niger, Nigeria, Senegal, Sudan, Tanzania, and Togo, media outlets are suspended because the authorities disapprove of their stories. Journalists are routinely arrested and sometimes charged with criminal offenses, purely for carrying out their work.[54] Furthermore, political opponents of the government have been arbitrarily arrested and detained in Burkina Faso, Burundi, Cameroon, Chad, Equatorial Guinea, Ethiopia, Gambia, Mauritania, Democratic Republic of Congo, Swaziland, and Zimbabwe.[55]

Fifth, as to harmful sociocultural practices, it is common knowledge that in many African countries, Sierra Leone not excluded, female circumcision (or female genital mutilation/cutting) continues to be a widespread sociocultural practice despite legislative reform efforts to abolish it. It is practiced on very young girls, who cannot be said to have voluntarily consented to the act, particularly given parental and societal pressures. This practice constitutes a violation of the African child's right to personal liberty, which includes the right to protection from inhuman treatment. In a cross-disciplinary article on the medico-legal aspects of this custom in Sierra Leone, Thompson et al. reasoned that "from the standpoint of modern medicine, female circumcision is a health hazard, and from a Western legal perspective, it is a harmful social practice that may, in certain circumstances, be characterized as wrongful or criminal."[56] However, from an African perspective, it is true that under the customary law systems and traditions that regulate family rights and obligations of the majority of the African population, there is no prohibition against female circumcision. It is perceived as a sociocultural prerequisite for marriages in certain communities.[57]

Sixth, as to the issue of accountability, it cannot be denied that unless African governments address the phenomenon of impunity in the sphere of human rights violations in a serious manner, the widespread human rights violations across the African region will continue. Occasionally, after large-scale human rights violations, commissions of inquiry or other types of investigation panels are set up, but they are often more to appease public opinion than to establish the truth and identify those responsible.[58] It is noteworthy that the International Criminal Court has assumed responsibility for holding some of those in positions of political responsibility in Africa, their agents as well as other leading violators of human rights in the region accountable. For example, the court's prosecutor issued an arrest warrant against President Omar Al Bashir of Sudan for war crimes, crimes against humanity, and genocide—making him the first sitting head of state indicted by the ICC.[59]

CONCLUSION

Unquestionably, there is still a gap between the rhetoric found in the commitment of African governments to the protection and preservation of human rights and freedoms in the respective African countries and also at the regional level, and the grim reality depicting human rights' violations as the norm rather than the exception. Hence, the realities of human rights' protection in Africa can only leave one with a feeling of much skepticism, if not pessimism, as to the future of human rights protection and enforcement in the region.

The recent kidnapping of nearly 300 school aged girls by Boko Haram in Nigeria unleashed a major discussion surrounding how well African governments who espouse democracy are in fact keeping the rights and will of the masses at the fore. While this was an act committed by a major terror network, questions abound as to how well African governments are protecting the citizens of their respective nations.

A few questions have yet to be answered concerning human rights protection and enforcement in Africa, in both theory and practice. One in particular is whether the Universal Declaration of Human Rights and the two

African Charters were set up as a solution. If violations are occurring more than implementation, then there may be a serious problem with said "solutions." As Mahmud contends, violations occur more often than implementation and with dire consequences for the victims.[60] There are many explanations regarding gross human rights violations on the African continent. One such reasoning, similar to many, dates back to the early days of independence. The masses' preference for collective rights and not demanding the creation of structures for implementing human rights is considered to be a culprit. Another explanation for mass human rights abuses or violations in the Africa region relates to the majority of people living beneath the poverty line. This view comes from the basic tenets of many certain rights instruments as promoting basic human needs. For example, the legacy of racism from the apartheid regime is to blame for human rights violations in the South African healthcare system. In Sierra Leone, the human rights abuses that occurred as a result of the decade-long civil war is attributed to youth marginalization and unemployment, exacerbated by successive government regimes.

It must be noted, however, that there are also several positive examples of human rights implementation on the African continent. For example, in April 2010, the Sierra Leone government launched the Free Health Care Policy for pregnant women, lactating mothers, and children under 5 years of age.[61] This move illustrated the importance of adequate healthcare as a basic human need and right, especially for pregnant women and young children. Another example of the push for positive implementation of human rights in Africa occurred in January 2009 in Nigeria. For nearly a decade, Muslim women endured gender-based discrimination under the newly reinstated Shari'ah law. Women were marginalized in many ways, especially in the justice system. Female judges were banned from serving in Shari'ah courts, rape cases were rarely investigated, and women's testimonies during trials were rated as "half that of a man."[62] Fed up, women finally displayed their opposition to the injustice of the system that was supposed to protect them by planning a public demonstration in the Kano region.[63] This act illustrated the growing trend of African people pulling together to hold their governments and leaders accountable. Additionally, a point referenced earlier, is the End Child Marriage campaign recently launched by the AU and several civil society organizations. This demonstrates, if anything, that Africa and Africans are fully capable of addressing and leading the charge against issues that plague them.

In articulating the prospects or the enforcement of human dignity in Africa, the critical question is: How do the ordinary Africans, adults and children alike, whose rights have been enshrined in the two regional Charters, realize them in practice? It seems that the future development of human rights protection and enforcement in Africa does revolve around several complex, unresolved issues. These include mainly: (i) whether, as a region, Africa will in the future be guided in the conduct of its affairs by the precept that history teaches us to learn from the mistakes of the past and not to repeat them; (ii) whether African governments will accept the human rights' philosophy as the normative yardstick for a viable, stable, democratic, and an economically prosperous Africa; (iii) whether the existing regional institutional mechanisms for the enhancement of human dignity will be adequately and effectively utilized for the protection and enforcement of human rights in the region; (iv) whether Africans have now developed a mindset that perceives national and regional unity as an important force that assist in combating human rights abuses, more so than ethnicity; (v) whether future constitutional governments in Africa will ensure that the democratic bond between them and the citizenry, never gets eroded leaving open the possibility of military rule with adverse consequences for the protection and preservation of human rights; (vi) whether those who govern are prepared to adhere to the principle of legality in the protection of human rights; (vii) whether Africa, regionally, comes to a full realization that social justice for the African people is a moral imperative to be pursued earnestly by every African government; and (ix) whether the current humanitarian issues in Africa should justify the argument that "the Western notion of human rights stresses rights which are not very interesting in the African context of realities." Perhaps when African governments have become more sensitized to the need for democratic governance and have become more aware of their collective responsibility to uphold the principles of human dignity, equality, and equity in their respective countries will they be able to bring to realization most of the values, rights, and freedoms enshrined in the various charters. Specifically this means, among others, that there should be a governmental consciousness on the part of African leaders that African men and women have the right to live their lives and raise their children in dignity, free from hunger and from the fear of violence, oppression, and injustice, and that democratic and participatory governance based on the will of the people best assures these rights. Without this realization, human rights protection in Africa would be meaningless.

ENDNOTES

1 Nancy Flowers, *Human Rights Here and Now: Celebrating the Universal Declaration of Human Rights* (London: Amnesty International, Human Rights Educators' Network, 1998), 1.

2 *Amnesty International Report 2009: The State of the World's Human Rights* (London: Amnesty International Publications, 2009), 1.

3 Marthe van der Wolf, African Union Starts Campaign to Curb Child Marriage, *Voice of America* (May 28th, 2014).

4 Ronald Thandabanta Nhlapo, "International Protection of Human Rights and the Family: African Variations on a Common Theme," *International Journal of Law and the Family* 3, no. 1 (April 1989), 1–20.

5 Nhlapo, "International Protection of Human Rights," 2. See also A. Pollis and E. Schwab, "Human Rights: A Western Construct with Limited Applicability" in *Human Rights: Cultural and Ideological Perspectives*, ed. Pollis and Schwab (New York: Praeger Publishers, 1979).

6 Claude Ake, "The African Context of Human Rights," *Africa Today* 34, no. 142 (1987), 88.

7 Ibid., 84.

8 Ibid.

9 Ibid., 87.

10 Richard Amoako Baah, *Human Rights in Africa: The Conflict of Implementation* (Lanham, MD: University Press of America, 2000), 86.

11 Nonso Okereafoezeke, "Human Rights in Africa: The Conflict of Implementation," *Africa Today* 50, no. 1 (Spring 2003): 122.

12 Ake, "The African Context of Human Rights," 86.

13 Sakah S. Mahmud "The State and Human Rights in Africa in the 1990s: Perspectives and Prospects," *Human Rights Quarterly* 15, no. 3 (1993), 489.

14 Ibid., 490.

15 Ibid., 491.

16 Ake, "The African Context of Human Rights, 84.

17 Mahmud, "The State and Human Rights in Africa in the 1990s, 486.

18 Akwasi Aidoo, "Africa: Democracy Without Human Rights?" *Human Rights Quarterly* 15, no. 4 (1993), 705.

19 Alison Dundes Renteln, *International Human Rights: Universalism Versus Relativism*, (Quid Pro, LLC, 2013), 3.

20 Bankole Thompson, *The Constitutional History and Law of Sierra Leone, 1961–1995* (Lanham, MD: University Press of America Inc., 1997), 49.

21 Thompson, *The Constitutional History*, 15; For this viewpoint, see also S. A. de Smith, *The New Commonwealth and Its Constitutions* (London: Stevens, 1964); See also, generally, T.O. Elias, *The British Commonwealth: The Development of its Laws and Constitutions*, vol. 14 (London: Stevens, 1962); and O.C. Eze, *Human Rights in Africa: Some Selected Problems* (Nigeria: Macmillan, 1984).

22 Bankole Thompson, *The Constitutional History*, 15–16.

23 Thompson, *The Constitutional History*, 49; See also F.A.R. Bennion, *The Constitutional Law of Ghana* (London: Butterworthss, 1962).

24 For more information on the link between democracy and human rights conceptualization, See Akwasi Aidoo, *Africa: Democracy Without Human Rights?* 703; and Zehra F. Arat, *Democracy and Human Rights in Developing Countries* (London: Lynne Reiner Publishers, 1991), 1.

25 Thandika Mkandawire, "Comments on Democracy and Political Instability," *Africa Development*, XIII, no. 3 (1988), 78.

26 Josiah A. M. Cobbah, "African Values and the Human Rights Debate: An African Perspective," *Human Rights Quarterly* 9, no. 3 (1987), 312.

27 From Lewis P. Hinchman, "The Origin of Human Rights: A Hegelian Perspective," *Western Political Quarterly* 37, no. 1 (1984), 8.

28 Cobbah, "African Values and the Human Rights Debate," 314.

29 Adam Hochschild, *King Leopold's Ghost: A Story of Greed, Terror, and Heroism in Colonial Africa* (Boston: Mariner Books, 1998), 2.

30 Nhlapo, "International Protection of Human Rights," 6.

31 African Charter on Human and People's Rights, Organization of African Unity Documents CAB/LEG/67/3/Rev. 5 (1981) reprinted in 21 I. L. M. 58 (1982).

32 Nhlapo, "International Protection of Human Rights," 7.

33 Ibid.

34 African Charter, paragraphs 3 and 4.

35 African (Banjul) Charter on Human and Peoples' Rights, Part I: Rights and Duties, Chapter I: Human and Peoples' Rights (Articles 1–18), adopted 27 June 1981, OAU Doc. CAB/LEG/67/3 rev. 5, 21, I.L.M. 58 (1982), entered into force 21 October 1986. *See pages 28–31 for listing of said articles of the Charter.*

36 Ibid.

37 Ibid., Part II.

38 See under "African Legal Materials" the document entitled *African Charter on the Rights and Welfare of the Child* in the *African Journal of International and Comparative Law* 3, no. 1 (March 1991), 173–209 for both the English and French texts of the Charter.

39 African Charter on the Rights and Welfare of the Child, Preamble, Organization of African Unity Doc. CAB/LEG/24.9/49 (1990), *entered into force* Nov. 29, 1999.

40 Ibid.

41 Ibid.

42 Amnesty International Report 2009: *The State of the World's Human Rights* (London: Amnesty International Publications, 2009), 26.

43 Ibid.

44 Lauren E. Glaze, *Correctional Populations in the United States 2009*, (Washington, DC: U.S. Bureau of Justice Statistics, 2010), 2.

45 Heather C. West, *Prison Inmates at Midyear 2009—Statistical Tables* (Washington, DC: U.S. Bureau of Justice Statistics, 2010), 2, 19–22. See tables 16–19.

46 Angela Y. Davis, "Masked Racism: Reflections on the Prison Industrial Complex," *ColorLines* (1998).

47 Thompson, *Constitutional History*, 48.

48 Ibid., 50.

49 Ibid.

50 Chris Marina Peter, "Five Years of the Bill of Rights in Tanzania: Drawing a Balance-Street," *African Journal of International and Comparative Law* 4, no. 1 (March 1992),139.

51 Amnesty International Report, 2009, 1.

52 Ibid., 2.

53 Ibid., 5.

54 Ibid., 7.

55 Ibid.

56 Bankole Thompson and Adiatu Thompson, "Female Circumcision in Sierra Leone: Medico-Legal Perspective," *Journal of the World Medical Association* 4, no. 3 (May/August 1993), 36.

57 Ibid., 40.

58 Amnesty International Report 2009, 8.

59 Ibid.

60 Mahmud, "The State and Human Rights in Africa in the 1990s," 485.

61 Patricia Ndanema, "Health: Is It a Human Rights Issue?" *Human Rights Commission Sierra Leone Newsletter* 1, no. 1 (2011), 5.

62 Ogechi Anyanwu, "Enforcing Shari'ah in Nigeria: Women, Justice, and Muslim's Collective Conscience," *American Journal of Islamic Studies* 26, no. 3 (Summer 2009), 29.

63 Ibid., 36.

REVIEW QUESTIONS

1. Some scholars have maintained that the human rights philosophy is nothing but a conceptual contrivance by the Western powers to continue to perpetuate their domination of Africa. Give your opinion with reasons for your answer.
2. How valid is the view that the doctrine of human rights is universal?
3. What factors account for human rights violations on the African continent? What six points are referenced as to the existing profile of human rights in Africa?

Writing Prompt

Critically analyze the state of human rights in one country in Africa? How does the observance or violation of human rights in that country compare and contracts with selected Western countries? Is Africa's problem unique?

CHAPTER 19

The Causes of Wars and Conflicts in Africa

Ogechi Emmanuel Anyanwu
and Raphael Chijioke Njoku

Although scholars agree that conflicts of interests, whether social, political, economic, or ideological, have been the main cause of wars in Africa, this chapter argues that the driving force behind African wars is rooted in the human fear of, and response to domination and deprivations. These two forces are the omnipresent cancer that runs through virtually all wars and conflicts. From the ancient civilization of Egypt to the forest kingdoms of the Oyo and Dahomey, the intent of the strong states to dominate the weak states has led empire builders and fortune hunters to make wars against both their neighbors and opponents. European acts of domination on socio-economic and political interests inspired the violent colonization of Africa from the late nineteenth century. The wars of liberations that characterized the post-1945 decolonization movements in Africa, as well as almost all of the continent's postcolonial conflicts were brought about by interplays of domination, deprivations, and reactions. Driven by the determination to avert real or imagined injustices of domination and dispossession, both the marginalized and privileged individuals and ethnic, religious, ideological, and political groups in Africa have fought relentlessly for positions of power in wars often complicated by shifting external politics and economic interests, Thus, no understanding of wars and conflicts in Africa or elsewhere would be complete without examining how the fear of, and response to domination and deprivations commingles with internal and external variables to shape the character of warfare in modern Africa.

INTRODUCTION

Modern Africa has had more than its share of bloody crises. However, wars and conflicts (terms used interchangeably in this chapter) are a part of human history and politics. They are not peculiar to Africa. Most scholars agree that the last century was the most violent and destructive in all human history, with armed conflicts affecting virtually all countries and claiming over 100 million lives.[1] Particularly in the past five decades, many conflicts and wars have beleaguered virtually all African countries fundamentally defining the image of the continent in world politics. Wars in Africa have continued to occupy the attention of policymakers, scholars, students, and stakeholders, and there is seemingly no end in sight—thus reminding scholars of the words of Plato, "Only the dead have seen the end of war."[2] This chapter is an attempt to formulate a paradigm for historical analysis of the dynamic but complex causes of conflicts and wars in Africa. It examines the socioeconomic, religious, political, and ideological underpinnings of these wars, highlighting their different nature and dimensions. As the ancient Greek historian Thucydides stated in the *History of the Peloponnesian War*, "Identity of interest is the surest bonds, whether between states or individuals."[3] In other words divergence of interest is the surest disunity.

Conflict, therefore, can be defined as a hostile and unilateral expression of incompatible differences within and among states. According to Michael Lund, conflict arises when two or more parties recognize that their interests are incompatible, and thus express aggressive attitudes, or even pursue their interests through acts that may incapacitate or completely eliminate the opponents.[4] Conflict is also a struggle "in which the aims of the groups or individuals involved are to neutralize, injure or eliminate rivals."[5] In conflict, parties pursue seemingly irreconcilable interests and employ aggressive means to meet a targeted end. Such a bellicose attitude makes large-scale warfare unavoidable.

War is closely related to conflict and it is—rightly or wrongly—considered a means to settle differences among antagonistic parties. War is a violent expression of disagreement between and among nations. "War," according to Clausewitz, "is only a mere continuation of policy by other means."[6] It is also, "an act of violence intended to compel our opponent to fulfill our will."[7] Dennen sees it as a "collective, direct, manifest, personal, intentional, organized, instrumental, institutionalized, sanctioned and sometimes ritualized and regulated violence."[8] Perhaps war could be considered certain because the pursuit of man's key concern—self-preservation—makes it so. According to a seventeenth century British philosopher, Thomas Hobbes, self-preservation leads man to be either aggressive or defensive, and it is rooted in man's fear of death, which drives him not in passivity but towards aggressive and violent behavior. Self-preservation underlines man's awareness of the consequences of domination and deprivations. This consciousness has resulted in wars caused by competition, which makes humans invade or resort to diffidence. Self-preservation compels humans to seek safety, sometimes through a preemptive attack aimed to destroy or minimize the perceived threat or danger.[9]

It is possible that this tendency towards self-preservation is more prominent in Africa where domination and deprivations have made the lives of the average citizen cheap. According to the 1999 report of the Stockholm International Peace Research Institute (SIPRI), "Africa is the most conflict ridden region of the world and the only region in which the number of armed conflict is on the increase."[10] Although inter-state wars have occurred in Africa, most of the wars have been intra-state or civil wars. Civil war occurs when "(a) military action was involved, (b) the national government at the time was actively involved, (c) effective resistance (as measured by the ratio of fatalities of the weaker to the stronger forces) occurred on both sides, and (d) at least 1,000 battle deaths resulted."[11] Between 1960 and 2000, Africa witnessed 56 wars out of a total of 141 wars fought world-wide.[12] The disastrous impact of these wars on all aspects of life is well known and has been well documented.[13]

Despite the efforts by international organizations such as the United Nations (UN) and Organization of African Unity (OAU), now African Union (AU), at regulating armed conflicts, "war remains the form of the test whereby the claims of states [and groups] are decided. And of all the sins of the state, the most unpardonable is weakness, a sin against the Holy Ghosts of politics."[14] Obsessed with keeping, increasing, and demonstrating power, most postcolonial governments in Africa's pluralistic societies have alienated groups, forcing them to engage in a mode of conduct that is still predominant in international relations: self-help. As Fisher once said about the United States, "One way for us to achieve an objective is to do it ourselves. If we cannot persuade an adversary to give us something, perhaps we can take it."[15] Conflicts and wars have always been the logical consequence of this dictum.

CAUSES OF WAR: THEORETICAL FRAMEWORK OF ANALYSIS

While there are several theories on the causes of war in Africa, one of the often-cited paradigms remains Collier and Hoeffler's theory of "Greed and Grievance in Civil War."[16] This model of analysis holds that African wars are driven by the desire to take more than one deserves (greed) and/or to take out vengeance on the unjust system or for past injustices suffered. In essence, fear of, and response to domination and deprivation are the driving forces for practically all major conflicts propelling the spiral of crisis in Africa and this helps explain Collier and Hoeffler's theory of "Greed and Grievance." For a concise and better understanding of the dynamic causes of conflicts and wars in Africa, it is imperative to analyze causation under three theoretical themes—namely (a) the Theory of Human Nature; (b) the Theory of Societal Conditions; and (c) the Theory of Natural Conditions. From one historical era to another, the causes of war have differed, but every war represents merely another "outbreak of the same old disease" and through the ages only the actors and severity of the malady have changed.[17]

THEORY OF HUMAN NATURE

The theory of human nature identifies humans as fundamentally flawed since creation—a natural stain that makes war inevitable. This viewpoint is prominent in the classical works of St. Augustine of Hippo, Plato, Sigmund Freud, Thomas Hobbes, and Hans Morgenthau. St. Augustine, one of the most influential early Christian theologians, perceived war as the "burden" that humanity must bear because of the corruption inherent in human nature. Like most early Christian political thinkers, St. Augustine believed that the human race was irreparably flawed by original sin—that is by Adam and Eve's violation of God's Commandments in the Garden of Eden.[18] This inherent evil nature has led man to transform "churches into political organization . . . revolutions into dictatorships . . . love for country into imperialism."[19] In his book, *The Republic*, Plato attributed the cause of war to the humankind's feverish passion for worldly possessions and creature comfort.[20]

Plato's idiom of "feverish passion for worldly possession" is crucial to explaining the wars of colonial conquest and African resistance to colonial rule. Beginning from the late nineteenth century to the early twentieth century, European powers like Britain, France, Italy, Germany, Spain, Belgium, and Portugal launched unparalleled and vicious campaigns to seize and occupy African territories. That was the period of the scramble for, and partition of, Africa. Motivated by economic interests that underline the principles of "sphere of influence" and "effective occupation," as adopted at the Berlin Conference (1884–1885), the seven European countries pushed forward and forcefully annexed and colonized the continent. At this point, African states and kingdoms were left with two hard choices: either adjust to the new reality or fight it. Initially the colonized peoples chose the latter and thus engaged in one form of war or the other with European powers. Except for the Ethiopians who successfully defeated the Italians at the battle of Adowa in 1896—and as a result retained the country's sovereignty—the rest of Africans fell to superior arms of the invaders.

The Maji Maji Rebellion against the Germans in Tanganyika (Tanzania) between 1905 and 1907 was directed at regaining freedom from German domination and exploitation. The rebellion caused about 70,000 casualties on the African side.[21] The Anglo-Ashanti wars, particularly the third war (1873–1874) and the fourth war (1894–1921), highlight the people's resentment for British colonial intrusion in their domestic affairs.[22] Further, resolute to safeguard the independence of Somalia, Sayyid Muhammad Abdille Hasan, a young Somali Muslim, raised 5,000 men and put up stiff resistance against Britain in fierce wars that lasted two decades from 1899 to 1920.[23] Likewise, Abd al-Krim al Khattabi of Morocco led a long-term revolt against a Spanish-French alliance in the North African kingdom, winning many battles until 1926 when a combined team of Spanish and French army crushed the resistance with advanced weapons, supported with aerial bombardments.[24]

In explaining the causes of war from a psychological standpoint, Sigmund Freud, the founder of psychoanalysis, stated that human beings are born with a "death wish," an innate self-destructive tendency that they somehow manage to redirect into other activities most of the time. Freud argued that war serves the important psychotherapeutic function of providing an outlet for the self-destructive impulse in man.[25] Early on, Thomas Hobbes had postulated that this defect in man manifests in aggressive wars caused by competition, defensive wars caused by fear, and agonistic wars caused by pride and vanity. He noted that human beings would constantly be at each other's throats save for the civilizing effect of government.[26] In *Politics Among Nations*, Hans Morgenthau, a pioneer in the field of international relations, agreed with other writers on the flaws in human nature. According to Morgenthau, objective laws that have their roots in human nature have been governed by politics since the classical period, and he accepted the realist view "that the world imperfect as it is from the national point of view, is the result of forces inherent in human nature."[27]

THEORY OF SOCIETAL CONDITIONS

Removing the blame on human nature, the theory of societal conditions associates the cause of war with the bad nature of the society that men live in. The works of Rousseau, Frederick Hartmann, Kant, and Lenin have provided deeper insights into the theory of societal conditions. In his classic work, *The Social Contract or Principles of Political Right*, originally published in 1762, Jean-Jacques Rousseau, a French philosopher of the eighteenth century, argued that humankind is in chains even when born free.[28] Challenging the assertion that human beings are naturally bad, Rousseau stated that human beings are naturally peaceful and all the bad traits emanate from the society not human nature.[29] Nationalism, an "idolatrous religion" and a patriotic feeling felt by the members of a nation towards their homeland, is another societal condition responsible for wars. Defending a nation becomes a duty of citizens, a duty that can be fulfilled via war. According to Frederick Hartmann, "Each nation has its own rose colored mirror. It is the particular quality of such mirrors to reflect images flatteringly . . . . Each nation considers to itself or proclaims aloud, depending upon its temperament and indignation, that it is God's chosen and dwells in God's country."[30]

Immanuel Kant squarely placed the societal conditions of tyranny and dictatorship at the center of forces responsible for war. He argued that absence of democratic government usually resulted in conflict and violent confrontation. Kant believed that democracies were inherently peace loving compared to dictatorship.[31] This claim is controversial given that while some dictatorial regimes in Saudi Arabia and Cuba, to mention just two examples, have remained relatively at peace with their neighbors, others like the United States and its European allies have fought Saddam Hussein's Iraq on flimsy excuses. Nobel Laureate, Wole Soyinka, however, has explored the Kant dictum, in a studious analysis of the "National Question in Africa."[32] Soyinka argues that because dictatorial regimes are shadowed by crisis of legitimacy, their repressive method of state control tends to strengthen "ethnic identity and encourages separatism."[33] Citing the Ogoni case in his home country Nigeria, Soyinka contends that the tragic genocidal onslaught perpetrated by the vicious military dictatorship of Gen. Sani Abacha on the Ogoni provoked resentment (even from unexpected quarters) "increasingly [tested] the assumptions of nation-being—whether as an ideal, a national bonding, a provider, a haven of security and order, or as an enterprise of productive co-existence."[34]

Soyinka underlines that a nation should share a perception of a community whose fundamental existence is rooted in ideas shared by all human beings. Under a dictatorship, contends Soyinka, there is no nation. All that remains is "a fiefdom, a planet of slaves, regimented by aliens. This marks the period of retreat into cultural identities"—a process he sees as logical, because then "the essence of nationhood has gone underground."[35] Thus, the longer the dictatorship lasts, the more tenacious the hold of that cultural nationalism becomes, attracting to itself all the allegiances, social relevance, and visceral identification that should belong to the larger nation.[36] For Soyinka, a society can speak in terms of nationhood only when the cause of democracy and legitimacy has been espoused, alongside the eradication of military governments. Only when there is a freedom of thought, association, and belief without threat of death and without discrimination in social rights would legitimacy and national unity be fostered.[37]

In his work entitled *Imperialism: The Highest Stage of Capitalism*, originally published in 1916, Lenin advanced the Marxist interpretation of conflict and war, blaming capitalism as a mode of societal organization prone to anarchy. Imperialism, Lenin reasoned, was a logical outgrowth of the cutthroat competition characteristic of monopoly capitalism. Lenin theorized that capitalists eventually had to seek foreign markets for investments and sell off their industrial surpluses. The capitalists, through their control of the machinery of the state, push their societies into war for their own selfish interest.[38] Writing in the second decade after the European colonization of Africa and Asia, Lenin was obviously making a case for communism as a better alternative to capitalist system of state organization. Yet, Lenin's thesis retrospectively calls for closer attention to the capitalist culture of the endless quest for wealth, market, and power that brought the Europeans to Africa with all the attendant backlashes.

African resistance against European domination continued throughout the colonial era even after the Africans had been defeated and the mechanisms for colonial rule effectively established. Now and then, the colonized people found new reasons to rebel. Increasingly worried over labor conscription; unfair taxation; labor conscription; land expropriation; and ill treatment of workers and women, many resistance movements emerged in the 1920s. These uprisings sought for reform within the colonial system or total independence and they posed a great threat to the established colonial order. Colonial response was predictable, and as Davidson notes, "To all these protests, whether violent or not, the colonial powers replied with some form of 'pacification' . . . designed to repress, or to frighten."[39] Tens of thousands of Africans lost their lives.

Africans who participated in these early resistance movements wanted to preserve the independence of their lands against the invading powers. The dominant force that drove these wars was the people's realization that European political domination equaled economic exploitation. Exploitation, of course, entails humiliating the indigenous people and depriving them the power, freedom, and privileges they previously enjoyed. Whatever dimensions these early wars of resistance took, they were driven by new societal conditions brought about by colonial domination that threatened Africa's well being. Therefore, African responses to European colonial aggression were, in fact, rooted not only in the human need for self-preservation but also in the obvious frustration with the new social order. The Africans understood the political, social, and economic ramifications of colonial control and put up spirited campaigns against it. Although the early resistance movements failed, they sowed the seeds for the more successful postwar wave of liberation movements that ultimately ended colonialism in many African countries.

All the anti-colonial liberation movements in Africa were inspired by the intent to overcome the depravities of colonial rule. Liberation movements took the forms of either small-scale or large-scale armed struggles. In each case, Africans were responding to the fear of continued deprivation under the oppressive colonial system. While independence in many non-settler colonies came through relatively peaceful, constitutional talks, prolonged bloody wars marked the quest for independence in the settler colonies as well as in the Portuguese colonies.[40]

Tunisians and Algerians waged a prolonged war of independence against the French from 1952–1956 and 1954–1962 respectively; however, the Algerian war of independence was more famous and bloody. When France imposed colonial rule on Algeria—and on Marshal Bugeaud's advice, the French Parliament approved the rule that "Wherever good water and land are found settlers must be installed without questioning whose land it may be"—they unmistakably sowed the seed for an enduring resistance and war.[41] The French settlers followed their words by appropriating about 5,940,000 acres of land—one-third of all Algerian fertile land. Instead of using the land for food production, the settlers used it for wine production. The post-1945 widespread food shortages and hunger radicalized Algerians and, under the umbrella of the Font of National Liberation (FLN), notable Algerian nationalists such as Ahmed Ben Bella embarked on an eight-year formidable, violent resistance against France until independence was won in 1956. More than one million Algerians lost their lives in the struggle.[42]

Similar armed struggles occurred in the British colonies of Kenya and Rhodesia (now Zimbabwe). Stripped of their land by the British settlers, the Kikuyu ethnic group organized an armed, bloody guerrilla revolt called the Mau Mau Uprising between 1952 and 1960. The insurgency shattered the official complacency of the British, forcing them to grant independence to Kenya in 1963.[43] In Rhodesia, Africans fought in the famous Bush War (1966–1979) to unseat the white minority government of Ian Smith with great human and material loss. Portugal, one of the poorest countries in Europe, saw its colonies in Africa as an extension of the mother country. As such, the Portuguese did not want to contemplate granting independence to their colonies in Africa. The fascist government in Portugal resisted any form of negotiation with African nationalists. Resorting to violence, therefore, became the only choice for Africans in those colonies. Across the Portuguese African colonies, fierce anti-colonial wars beginning in 1961 resulted in the independence of Guinea Bissau in 1974, followed by Angola and Mozambique in 1975.[44]

Furthermore, liberation movements have been waged against African governments. Resisting the Moroccan invasion, the Polisario Front waged a war against Morocco in 1973 in order to regain the independence of Western Sahara. Eritrea, under the platform of the Eritrea Liberation Front (later Eritrean People's Liberation Front) fought a long, bitter war with its neighbor Ethiopia until 1991 when it achieved independence. The South West Africa People's Organization, SWAPO (1960–1990), of Namibia, as well as the African National Congress (ANC) of South Africa, employed violence during their march to free their countries from entrenched white settler colonialism. These armed struggles resulted from a combination of human, societal, and natural conditions. In each case, the dominant power was driven by greed and the desire to maintain the status quo while the marginalized groups fought to overcome the system for a better life.

Africa inherited the artificial boundaries carved by the European colonial powers. Within each country are multi-ethnic, lingual, and religious societies held together previously by European superior military power. Postcolonial nation building in pluralistic societies has been painful, often provoking bloody combats. Worse still, the arbitrary creation of Africa meant that one ethnic group would be scattered in more than one country. Thus, separatism and irredentism, often motivated by fear of domination or deprivation, led to wars. The experience of Somalis illustrates this.

The European arbitrary partition of Africa resulted in the dismemberment of the Somali ethnic group in East Africa. While two-thirds of the Somali population lives in the Somalia Republic, the remaining Somalis are spread in Djibouti, Ethiopia, and Kenya. As minorities in these countries, the Somalis are marginalized in their host countries. The historical experiences of Kenyan Somalis further illustrate the problem. The Kenyan

Somalis, who inhabit the Northeastern Province of Kenya, have a distinct language, culture, religion, and lifestyle from other Kenyans. Their subjugation, administrative isolation, and political disenfranchisement began during the period of British colonization of Kenya. Although the British encouraged the Somalis to believe that their right to self-determination would be granted through peaceful and legal means, the Somalis were denied self-autonomy at Kenya's independence in 1963. Their attempt to express their disappointment with the postcolonial state through secession in 1963 resulted in a struggle known as the Shifta war. Although the Shifta war ended in 1968 with the defeat of the Somalis, the Northeastern region of Kenya became a site for small-scale skirmishes between the Somali fighters—supported by the Somali government—and the Kenyan army. Prominent among the tactics used by Kenyan Somalis since the 1970s to express their dissatisfaction with the status quo is banditry, later worsened by the post-Barre exodus of Somali refugees into Kenya.[45] Several wars, such as the Nigerian civil war, the Congolese civil wars, and the Sudanese civil wars, among others, were sparked by fears of internal domination and deprivations by rival ethnic groups. At the center of these wars is the fear that the interests of the marginalized groups would not be served as well as the desire of the dominant groups to hold on to power at all cost.

The postcolonial order was ushered in with high expectations on the part of Africans. African leaders seeking votes in elections conducted by departing European powers promised rapid socio-political transformation of their countries. Their people anxiously awaited a fulfillment of electoral promises, but they were let down. Corruption, poor resource mobilization, nepotism, mismanagement of resources, and anti-rural biases characterized the administration of many new governments in Africa. Frustrated and disappointed citizens who challenged their governments were often brutally suppressed, leading to unrests and in most cases outbreak of wars. Weary of failed promises of elected leaders, military officers have overthrown elected governments in military coups that time and again enjoyed public support. Instead of serving the interests of all, many Africans were soon disappointed to realize that the new military leaders were not different from the civilian regimes they unseated. The military dictatorships of Emperor Bokassa I of Central Africa, Mobutu Sese Seko of Zaire, Mohammed Siad Barre of Somalia, Samuel Doe of Liberia, Idi Amin Dada of Uganda, and Yakubu Gowon of Nigeria, among others, caused bloody national unrests that made counter-coups unavoidable. Between 1956 and 2001, there were 80 successful coups, 108 failed coup attempts, and 139 reported coup plots.[46] The death toll that resulted from these coups and the brutality and human rights abuses that followed was anything short of war.

Some of these political crisis and unrests degenerated into full-scale civil wars. The Nigeria civil war (1967–1970) was one of the bloodiest in Africa and was fought between the predominantly Muslim North and predominantly Christian East. The easterners felt unsafe and attempted to secede when a northern president, Yakubu Gowon, failed to prevent mass killings of Igbos resident in the north. Other wars include the Ethiopian civil war (1974–1991) and the Ogaden war (between Somalia and Ethiopia from 1977 to 1978). The war in Sudan is the longest war in Africa, occurring since the country gained independence in 1956 with few years of truce. Many other African countries have not been spared, with further examples being the Burundi civil war (1993–2005); the Eritrea-Ethiopian war (1998–2000); the Somali civil war (1988–present); the Sierra Leone civil war (1991–2002); the Battle of Mogadishu (1993); the Liberian civil war (1989–1996); the Guinea-Bissau civil war (1998–1999); and the civil war in Cote d'Ivoire (2002–2004).[47]

Altogether, these wars have provided non-African powers the opportunity to intervene in Africa's internal conflicts. Especially during the Cold War, Western and Eastern powers took sides in the internal wars either to further their interests or to prove opposing ideological positions. Some excellent examples include the wars in Angola and Mozambique, Ethiopia, Somalia, Egypt, Namibia, and Zaire.

THEORY OF NATURAL CONDITIONS

The theory of natural conditions suggests that circumstances beyond human control cause wars. Insufficient, inaccessible, and uneven distributions of resources are some of the reasons that propel nations to wage wars against one another. In *The Second Treatise on Civil Government,* John Locke, an Enlightenment thinker, posited that in the state of nature, humanity lived in poverty and hardship and that the major threat to life lies not in the murderous inclination of men but in the poverty and hardship of their natural condition.[48] Locke believed that the desire for more land and resources or property is one of the most common objectives of war.

On the whole, Locke advanced the theory that wars are fought because of poverty and the need to end it and usher in the conditions that would promote wellbeing.[49] Likewise, Richard Falk had implicitly recognized that inequalities of resources and power create incentives to acquire what a neighboring state possesses, compelling nation-states to regard their own security as being directly proportionate to the security or insecurity of their neighbors.[50]

The uneven spread of resources and the struggle to control abundant or scarce resources has been responsible for many wars in Africa. Given the ethnic divisions that characterized postcolonial African politics, control of the available resources of the land has been a major source of tension between both dominant and minority groups within countries. Sierra Leoneans suffered years of anguish and horror as the Revolutionary United Front (RUF) competed for economic power with the national government. Beneath the earth in the eastern town of Sefadu lie precious high grade diamonds that are worth millions of dollars in the international market. The control of these diamonds determines the control of power in Freetown. For about six years, Foday Sankoh and the RUF controlled the diamond regions of Sierra Leone, thereby holding the nation to ransom and forcing the government to engage the rebels in a protracted confrontation. The resources that came through the illegal sale of diamonds enabled Sankoh and his rebel force to prosecute the war—looting properties, raping women, mutilating children and adults alike, burning houses, and committing all manner of atrocities.[51]

The power struggle between the Tutsi and the Hutu ethnic groups in Rwanda and Burundi led to genocidal consequence. What divides these two groups has its roots in fear of domination and deprivations that shaped their relations since the colonial period. The Tutsi, a minority group in Rwanda, had emerged over the years until the 1950s as the elite. The German (and later Belgian) authorities entrenched Tutsi domination, using them as tools in colonial administration. At independence, a Hutu government came to power at the discomfort of the more educated Tutsi. In both Rwanda and Burundi, the Tutsi and Hutu have increasingly seen the exclusive control of the state as an essential precondition to their survival as a people. This has piled the mountain of grievances leading to unending conflicts. Thus, when Ndadaye, the Hutu President of Rwanda, was assassinated in 1993, the Hutus accused the Tutsis, who have been fighting a guerrilla war against the government. The rumored assassination of the Rwandan president by the Rwandan Patriotic Front in 1994 resulted in the genocide that took the lives of nearly a million Tutsis and moderate Hutus.[52]

The unrest in Rwanda and Burundi has affected the geopolitical balance of the entire Central African region where resources are plenty but their use has become a curse to the people. In 1998, Rwanda, Uganda, and Burundi sent troops to fight on the side of a rebel group attempting to overthrow President Laurent Kabila of the Democratic Republic of the Congo. The coalition accused Kabila of failing to stop attacks on the Rwandan government by the Hutu rebel group operating out of eastern Congo. As a countermeasure, neighboring countries such as Zimbabwe, Namibia, Chad, and Angola sent troops into the Congo to support Kabila, invariably throwing the region into a lake of fire. The mediatory efforts of Nelson Mandela, the visit of Bill Clinton in 2000, and the signing of a framework agreement—together have not resulted in an enduring peace. Many lives have been lost, facilities destroyed, and genuine economic development hampered as a result of the wars.

The three theories of war have their individual merit and validity, but they do not in-dividually explain the causes of all wars in Africa. There is a danger in a mono-causal explanation of the causes of conflicts and wars because the reasons why nations fight lie in some mixture of human psychology, societal problems, and natural conditions. However, beneath the cause of these wars lie the fear of, and response to existing or imagined domination and deprivations. Additionally, African wars, especially since the 1990s, share some basic features as outlined by Tom Porteous:

> First, one of the main underlying causes of these wars was the weakness, the corruption, the high level of militarization, and in some cases the complete collapse, of the states involved. Secondly, they all involved multiple belligerents fighting for a multiplicity of often shifting economic and political motivations. Thirdly, they all had serious regional dimensions and regional implications. And fourthly they were all remarkable for the brutality of the tactics (ranging from mass murder and ethnic cleansing, to amputation, starvation, forced labour, rape and cannibalism) used by belligerents to secure their strategic objectives.[53]

CONCLUSION

As Collier states, "the big brute fact is that civil war is heavily concentrated in countries with low income, in economic decline, and dependent upon natural resources."[54]Our conclusion here is that these issues are, however, the dependent variable causes of wars and conflicts. The independent and dominant factors are practices of domination—including political, economic, and ideological. The tendency of individuals and groups to dominate others also implicates leadership failures, which has largely helped to fuel conflicts and wars. Problems of leadership, mismanagement of natural and human resources, corruption, and excessive intervention in domestic policies have worsened poverty, inequality, unemployment, and escalated conflicts. Faced with uncertain futures, deprived or greedy groups resort to violence to advance or protect their interests, thereby promoting a climate of insecurity in which foreign power came to play a prominent but, arguably, negative role. Had the leaders of African countries recognized the need to share power and enthrone social justice; had they managed their resources well; had there been rapid improvement in the living standards of Africans after independence; had there been high prospects of comfort and optimism for the future; had the leaders harnessed ethno-religious diversity into potential sources of greatness; had they allocated resources equitably, thus erasing fear of domination, then perhaps the bitter and destructive wars that have continued to threaten the future of Africa would have been avoided.

Wars have clearly widened the divisions in African societies—thus creating conditions for more conflicts. As Clausewitz puts it, "in war the result is never final . . . . Even the ultimate outcome of war is not to be regarded as final [for] the defeated state often considers the outcome merely as a transitory evil for which remedy may still be found in political conditions at some later date."[55] Africa has lost the twentieth century and in order to recapture its destiny in the twenty-first century, the new wave of leadership in Africa has to manage internal differences such that the choice of war to settle them will become an unacceptable option. They should recognize and embrace, as well, the wise words of John F. Kennedy:

> So, let us not be blind to our differences—but let us also direct attention to our common interests and to the means by which those differences can be re-solved. And if we cannot end now our differences, at least we can help make the world safe for diversity. For, in the final analysis, our most basic common link is that we all inhabit this small planet. We all breathe the same air. We all cherish our children's future. And we are all mortal.[56]

ENDNOTES

1 See UN1CEF, *The State of the World's Children 1996* (New York: Oxford University Press, 1996).

2 Cited in Edward Teller, "The Laboratory of the Atomic Age," *Los Alamos Science* 21 (1993): 34.

3 Cited in Hans J. Morgenthau, *Politics Among Nations: The Struggle for Power and Pence* (New York: Knopf, 1967), 36.

4 Michael Lund, *Preventing and Militating Violent Conflict: A Revised Guide for Practitioners* (Washington, D.C.: Creative Associates International, 1997).

5 Lewis Coser, *The Function of Social Conflict* (New York: New York Free Press, 1956), 8.

6 Von C. Clausewitz, *On War,* trans. J. J. Graham (London; N. Trübner, 1873), 17.

7 Clausewitz, *On War,* 1.

8 J. M. G. Dennen, "On Peace," *P100M Newsletter & Progress Report* 7, no. 1 (Winter 1995): 4.

9 Thomas Hobbes, *The Leviathan,* ed. by A. R. Waller (Cambridge: Cambridge University Press, 1904), 63–5.

10 Stockholm International Peace Research Institute (SIPR1), *Yearbook of World Armaments and Disarmaments* (Oxford: Oxford University Press, 1999), 20.

11 Cited in John Anyanwu, "Economic and Political Causes of Civil Wars in Africa: Some Econometric Results," *Peace, Conflict and Development* 4 (April 2004): 5.

12 Harvard Strand, Lars Wilhelmsen and Nils Petter Gleditsch, "Armed Conflict Dataset, Version 2.1." [Computer File] (Oslo: International Peace Research Institute, 2003).

13 See Ali M. Taisier and Robert O. Matthews (eds.), *Civil Wars in Africa; Roots and Resolution* (Montreal & Kingston: McGill-Queen's University Press, 1999); P. Anyang Nyong'o (ed.), *Anns and Daggers in the Heart of Africa: Studies on Internal Conflicts* (Nairobi: African Academy of Sciences, 1993); Ricardo Rene Laremont (ed.), *The Causes of War and the Consequences of Peacekeeping in Africa* (Portsmouth, NH: Heinemann, 2002); and John W. Harbeson and Donald S. Rothchild (eds.), *Africa in World Politics: Post-Cold War Challenges* (Boulder, CO: Westview Press, 1995).

14 George A. Obiozor, "Power, Principle and Pragmatism in International Politics," paper delivered at the Pre-Convocation Lecture of Imo State University (Owerri, Imo State, March 6, 1998), 10.

15 Cited in Obiozor, "Power, Principle and Pragmatism," 20.

16 See Paul Collier and Anke Hoeffler, "Greed and Grievance in Civil War," *World Bank Working Paper No. 2355* (May 2000); and Paul Collier and Anke Hoeffler, "On the Incidence of Civil War in Africa," *Journal of Conflict Resolution* 46, no. 1 (2002): 13–28.

17 Thomas M. Magstadt and Peter M. Schotten, *Understanding Politics: Ideas, Institutions, and Issues* (New York: St. Martin's Press, 1984), 440.

18 St. Augustine quoted in Magstadt and Schotten, *Understanding Politics,* 440.

19 Kenneth Neal Waltz, *Man, the State and War: A Theoretical Analysis* (New York: St. Martin's Press, 1984), 24.

20 Plato G. R. F. Ferrari and Tom Griffith, *The Republic* (Cambridge and New York: Cambridge University Press, 2000).

21 National Archives Kew (NAK), FO 881/8402X, Africa: Military Report. German East Africa (WO), 1905; FO 704, Consulate, Dar-es-Salaam, German East Africa: General Correspondence, 1899–1914.

22 See NAK, CO 879/5/3 Gold Coast: Ashanti invasion: further correspondence, 1873; CO 843 Colonial Office: Ashanti Acts, 1920–1934; and CO879/18/8 Affairs of Gold Coast; and threatened Ashanti invasion Jan–July, 1881.

23 Basil Davidson, *Modern Africa,* 3rd ed. (London: Longman, 1994), 24.

24 Davidson, *Modern Africa,* 24.

25 Sigmund Freud and A. A. Brill, *The Basic Writings of Sigmund Freud* (New York: Modern Library, 1938).

26 Hobbes, *The Leviathan,* 63–5.

27 Morgenthau, *Politics Among Nations,* 36.

28 Jean-Jacques Rousseau, The *Social Contract and Discourses* (New York Dutton, 1950).

29 Rousseau, *Social Contract.*

30 Frederick H. Hartmann, *The Relations of Nations* (New York: Macmillan, 1978), 32.

31 ImmanueJ Kant and Carl J. Friedrich, *The Philosophy of Kant: Immanuel Kant's Moral and Political Writings* (New York: Modern Library, 1949).

32 Wole Soyinka, "The National Question in Africa: Internal Imperatives," *Development and Change* 27 (1996): 279–300.

33 Soyinka, "National Question in Africa," 279.

34 Soyinka, "National Question in Africa," 280.

35 Soyinka, "National Question in Africa," 280.

36 Soyinka, "National Question in Africa" 297–8.

37 Soyinka, "National Question in Africa," 298–9.

38 Vladimir Lenin, *Imperialism: The Highest Stage of Capitalism* (Moscow: Progress Publishers, 1982).

39 Davidson, *Modern Africa*, 23.

40 Non-settler colonies in Africa were those colonies that attracted few European settlements (who considered themselves visitors), while settler-colonies were those that attracted large numbers of Europeans (who considered themselves indigenes) and seized African lands and appropriated privileges that were denied the indigenes.

41 Cited in Basil Davidson, *Modem Africa*, 119.

42 See Martin Alexander and J. F. V. Keiger, "France and the Algerian War: strategy, operations and diplomacy," *Journal of Strategic Studies* 25, no. 2 (June 2002): 1–32.

43 Ian Henderson and Phillip Goodhart, *Man Hunt in Kenya* (New York: Doubleday, 1958).

44 Norrie MacQueen, *The Decolonization of Portuguese Africa: Metropolitan Revolution and the Dissolution of Empire* (London: Longman, 1997).

45 See John Drysdale, *The Somali Dispute* (London: Pall Mall Press, 1964); and Nene Mburu, "Contemporary Banditry in the Horn of Africa: Causes, History and Political Implications," *Nordic Journal of African Studies* 8, no. 2 (1999): 89–107.

46 See Samuel Decalo, *Coups and Army Rule in Africa: Studies in Military Style* (New Haven: Yale University Press, 1976); and Nicole Itano, "Africa takes Tough Stand on Coups," http://www.csmonitor.com/2004/0831/p06s01-woaf .html (accessed April 8, 2008).

47 Collier and Hoeffler "On the Incidence of Civil War in Africa," 13–28.

48 John Locke, *The Second Treatise on Civil Government* (Amherst, N.Y.: Prometheus Books, 1986), 6–8.

49 Locke, *Second Treatise*, 6–8.

50 Richard A Falk, *This Endangered Planet* (New York: Vintage Books 1973).

51 See *Telegraph* (London), Wednesday July 30, 2003; *Cocorioko Newspaper* (Freetown), Wednesday August 27, 2008; and *Cry Freetown*, produced by Sorious Samura, I hour, 2000, DVD.

52 See Raphael Chijioke Njoku, "Deadly Ethnic Violence and the Imperatives of Federalism and Power-sharing: Could a Consociation Hold in Rwanda?" *Journal of Commonwealth and Comparative Politics* 43, no. l (March 2005): 82–101.

53 Tom Porteous, "Resolving African Conflicts," *Crime of War Project*, October 2004. http://www.crimesofwar.org/ africa-mag/afr_01_porteos.html (accessed January 25, 2009).

54 Paul Collier, "Natural Resources and Conflict in Africa," *Crime of War Project*, October 2004. http://www. crimesofwar.org/africa-mag/afr_04_collier.html (accessed January 25, 2009). See also E. Wayne Nafziger, "Development, Inequality, and War in Africa," *The Economics of Peace and Security Journal* 1, no. 1 (2006): 14–19.

55 Clausewitz, On *War*, 80.

56 John F. Kennedy, Commencement Address at American University in Washington, June 10, 1963. http://www.ratical. org/co-globalize/JFK061063.html (accessed December 6, 2008).

REVIEW QUESTIONS

1. Discuss the theory of human nature and how it explains the causes of conflicts and wars in Africa.
2. Discuss the theory of natural conditions and how it explains the causes of conflicts and wars in Africa.
3. Discuss the theory of societal conditions and how it explains the causes of conflicts and wars in Africa.

Writing Prompt

Do you agree with Plato's statement that "Only the dead have seen the end of war"?

Discuss the strategies of preventing wars in Africa. How could preventive diplomacy, peacemaking, peace-keeping, peace enforcement, and peace building help address the root causes and after effects of conflicts and wars in Africa?

CHAPTER 20

Understanding Leadership in Postcolonial Africa

U. D. Anyanwu

Leadership in postcolonial Africa has been a subject of intense discussion among scholars and other stakeholders in and outside the continent. The main reason for this is that the problems in Africa since independence have been linked with poor leadership. In fact, the development crisis in the continent is usually explained in terms of the failure of the successive leaders in respective African countries. This chapter, therefore, seeks to examine the leadership question in Africa by focusing on the surrounding issues, trends, attainments, failures, problems, and prospects. In this way, the ambiguities surrounding leadership in postcolonial Africa will be understood. Largely due to individual or ethnic selfish considerations, leadership in postcolonial Africa was marked by violence stirred by desperate struggle for power among groups and individuals. As a result, leaders were too attached to their respective narrow, primordial interests while neglecting to emphasize national cohesion, stability, and development. Leadership crisis in the years following independence in many African countries led to many civil wars and conflicts. However, since the 1990s there have been significant changes in leadership as many African countries, long ruled by military dictatorships, have established effective democratic institutions. Gradual but sustained economic growth and political stability have characterized those states where democratization has become a norm.

CONCEPT OF LEADERSHIP

Perceptions of leadership among scholars, theorists, and related groups or persons have manifested varying categories of emphasis. Consequently, the study of leadership over time has been highly involved and complicated.[1] Historically, the concept of leadership reveals a shifting focus in the theoretical orientations that can be summarized as follows in terms of what we identify as the dominant emphasis in the orientations. The first dominant concept or idea of leadership is based on the individual attributes or characteristics of a leader. This is referred as the Trait Theory of Leadership. The claim is that leaders possess certain talents, skills, physical characteristics, intelligence, dominance, adaptability, persistence, integrity, socioeconomic status, and self-confidence absent in non-leaders.

Thomas Carlyle,[2] Francis Galton,[3] and S.J. Zaccaro[4] are notable exponents of the Trait Theory of Leadership. The ultimate view of the Trait Theory is that leaders are born, not made. But this is largely false. It is obvious that leaders do not possess common characteristics, traits, or consistent patterns. Furthermore, it is not possible to predict potential for leadership based on personality, intelligence, stature, or scholarship.[5]

The second dominant idea or concept of leadership is the Situationist Theory or Times Make the Man Approach. This emphasis emerged in the late 1940s and early 1950s and asserted that leaders emerged from circumstances, not necessarily from endowed traits. The main proponents of this are Bird (1940),[6] Stogdill (1948),[7] and Mann (1959).[8] For instance, Stogdill and Mann show that persons who are leaders in one situation may not necessarily be leaders in other situations. Situational approaches posited that individuals could be effective in certain situations but not others.

Finally, there is the Follower-oriented or Interactional Approach, which stresses that followers are the most crucial factor in any leadership since they determine the leaders' power by accepting or rejecting it. Thus, leadership cannot be fully studied in isolation, since it does not exist separately from a group just as an effective group does not exist without leadership.

These views of leadership are universal and although they apply to Africa, they do not seem to explain fully the African perspectives. Generally, African communities at all levels of government believe in the Trait Theory of leadership. They accept the impact of variables due to circumstances, yet they put much premium on features such as parentage, nurturing, character, personality, physical and emotional stability, accessibility, and availability. Leadership found deficit in any of these elements was ideally unacceptable. This has been the case among the Igbo of Nigeria, for instance both during and since after colonial rule.[9] Various Nigerian ethnic groups identify with this perception of leadership as well. And like other African groups in central, eastern, northern, and sub-Saharan Africa, the perception has been sustained in the leadership ideology. This means that a complete appreciation of the leadership question in postcolonial Africa ought to consider this feature.

THE HISTORICAL BACKGROUND OF STUDY

There were two sides to the historical background of leadership in Africa since the 1960s when most African countries became independent, although the settler territories like Rhodesia and Mozambique followed much later. One side is that despite the overwhelming impact of the colonial experience, ideals, values, and principles traceable to the indigenous or precolonial Africa world continued in varying degrees to challenge and impact on leadership. The second side is that in fundamental ways, colonialism subverted, supplanted, and distorted the leadership ideals, principles, and systems so much that at independence most African states were in a kind of confusion on the options for effective leadership in their respective countries.

On the surface, the granting of independence to the African colonies suggested that the new nations had full or unrestricted freedom to choose their leaders, their political institutions, and ideas, and to exercise their sovereignty, as they deemed proper to their national interests. In reality, the erstwhile colonial powers did not see political power in independent Africa in that way. Instead, their continuing economic and other interests in the continent made them enter into some form of alliance with groups or individuals in respective African countries to either formally or tacitly ensure that the leadership in each country would cherish the same Western political ideals and practices held by former colonial powers. Such leadership had to be friendly to the same power and embraced patterns of administration that would protect the interests of the power in question. This attitude was very common in countries like the Congo Republic with precious minerals, Sudan, and Nigeria.

If the leadership of an independent state proved unwilling to cooperate in these regards, the power and its associates promptly confronted it. Notable cases of this phenomenon were the conflicts between France and Guinea under Sekou Toure and Britain and Ghana under Kwame Nkrumah, a point aptly noted at the third-world level by Frantz Fanon and elucidated in the challenge of the Congo by Kwame Nkrumah.[10]

Political control also took the form of constitutional control that was achieved by the independent constitutions. Europeans often shaped many independent constitutions without paying attention to nation building. In the case of Nigeria, for instance, the 1960 constitution maintained the unequal division of Nigeria into three competing, conflicting, and autonomous regions. The inability to create a constitution that would foster unity ultimately led to the Nigerian civil war for which former colonial masters got involved one way or the other to assert their influence and further their economic interest.

A third type of political control is the projection of conservative or anti-patriotic leaders into government. Such leaders would not try new experiments while in office as presidents, prime ministers, and political party leaders to the disadvantage of the past colonial powers. Training links and other strategies were put in place (including the infiltration of the public services and trade unions) to control key personnel and policymakers as well as the intellectual elite.

Political control was also exercised through regional groupings like the Commonwealth in the case of Britain and the French Community for France. African involvement in these groups represented another form of colonialism, often termed neo-colonialism. The advantages that France or Britain conferred on African member-states came with economic and political strings that undermined the independence of African states. Sanctions have been used as a tool to punish African states whose actions threatened the interest of the former colonial power, as in the case of the Commonwealth sanction imposed on former Nigerian military leader, General Abacha.

Unstable structures and institutions and contradictory ambitions characterized the heritage of leadership in postcolonial Africa. Internally, cohesion among the African successors of the colonial regimes never existed. Severe fissures and unhealthy platforms for intense rivalry existed. Externally, the interest of new African states was not the priority of the former colonial powers that started a new scramble for Africa as the Cold War intensified. Their main purpose at the dawn of independence was to prevent communist takeover of the continent in order to protect and entrench Western economic investments and interests.[11]

Another aspect of the heritage had to do with the fact that the new political leaders in the continent had no genuine tutelage in democracy. At all levels of government, the successor indigenous African leaders were nurtured by authoritarian and repressive mechanisms practiced during the colonial administrations that were themselves for all practical purposes military regimes. It is ironic that at independence the newly elected African leaders who were nurtured during the colonial period were being expected to practice free and fair elections and other principles, values, and institutions of the open society that they never experienced throughout the colonial period. The emphasis here is that the heritage of colonialism did not endow future African leaders with the necessary tools for carrying out the expected exercise. At independence, individuals and groups within the politically ambitious classes at the local, regional, and national government levels promptly rationalized the inherited platforms in selfish terms expressed in individual, group, ethnic, religious, and other primordial points of loyalty. The ideology of narrow-minded interests and concerns triumphed over those of the nation-state.

In all spheres of the respective national life, narrow nationalism overtook the broader nationalism of the whole country. Many African countries were now divided along ethnic and religious lines as was the case with Nigeria, Kenya, Sudan, among others countries. Ethnicity, religion, and in some cases ideology, became instruments for promoting social solidarity among a group. Consequently, the emergent political actors in the structures and institutions put in place for national development took off as competing and often antagonistic rivals.[12] Since the rivalry was largely based on the principle of the survival of the fittest and winner takes all, it is easy to understand why the new leaders were ill-prepared to serve as first rate nationalists with few exceptions, of which Nkrumah of Ghana was an one.[13]

The way the heritage evolved meant that the successor leadership to colonial regimes in Africa lacked the necessary foresight required of individuals entrusted with defining and nurturing Africa's political leadership tradition at independence.

LEADERSHIP TYPES

The confusion generated by ill-prepared leadership largely explains the varieties of styles or types in the African leadership at the dawn of independence and since then. Ali A. Mazrui appreciates this feature by stating that the history of leadership in Africa has stood on eight principles or pillars. At the same time he enquires whether those pillars were merely eight styles of command or eight categories of commanders.[14] Whichever way the inquiry is answered, it seems that styles of command and categories are inextricably interlinked and could be interchanged without harm to our comprehension.

Kwameh Nkrumah of Ghana in leadership style was clearly both a style of command and in a category of commanders. Izu Marcel Onyeocha (1997)[15] is correct in his assessment that Nkrumah believed that African society was in a crisis of identity due to the impact of Christianity and Islam. Nkrumah, therefore, advocated the idea of consciencism to address the problem. The main features of his consciencism ideal include the principles of egalitarianism and the consideration of the human being as an end rather than a means to an end. He was thus of the view that ethical rules are not permanent but would depend on the stage reached in the historical evolution of a society. He also advocated the unity of African states and fought hard for Ghanaian true independence. He became very hostile to opponents whom he perceived as imperialist agents. He thus used brutal tactics similar to those the British used against him in 1950s. He faced the challenges of religion and ethnicity.

Nkrumah was a charismatic African leader who had a lot of personal magnetism. However, in his attempt to overcome internal and external sources of threats, Nkrumah attempted to create a monarchical tradition in independent Ghana by proclaiming himself a life president, by claiming divine affirmation for his authority with the title of Osagyefo or Redeemer. He also surrounded himself with a class of ostentatious consumers passing themselves off as Ghana's new aristocracy. Ultimately, over time Nkrumah increasingly regarded opposition to his government as treasonable.[16] Overall, Nkrumah desired to establish socialism in Ghana, which would result in common ownership of the means of production, distribution, and exchange, political power in the hands of the people and the application of scientific methods in all spheres of thought and production. Yet Nkrumah's materialist ideology and lack of enthusiasm for religion did not receive the approval of significant members of Ghana's population. Perhaps Nkrumah's main goal was to attain in practice his acclaimed view that one should seek the political kingdom for all other things to follow. This was not quite fully attained before his exit from office, largely because his politics created stiff opposition groups both within his party, the Convention People's Party (CPP), and among the ethnic groups—hence the coup d'état of February 1966 that ended his government.

Muammar Qaddafi of Libya was another African charismatic leader; he was also a great mobilizer. He worked relentlessly to rid his country of foreign (Western) domination and exploitation. For years, he "hated" the West, the United States in particular. The West understandably saw him as a terrorist of some sort. Largely, he retained the loyalty and support of his country people largely because of his strength of character and relative social and economic progress in Libya. Thus, despite the controversies generated by his domestic and foreign measures, Muammar Qaddafi has emerged a success story in African leadership since independence, representing both a style of command and a category of commanders. Indeed, Libya is ranked number one in Africa in human development index, an index that measures life expectancy, literacy, education and standards of living, well-being, especially child welfare. However, Qaddafi's human rights record has been less admirable. Following the uprising in the Middle East, dubbed, "Arab Spring," Qaddafi came under pressure from opposition forces seeking democratic change. His threat of violence against his own people was used as an excuse by NATO-led forces to seek his overthrow by supporting rebels fighting to remove him from power. Libyan rebels eventually murdered Qaddafi in 2011.

Qaddafi's condemnation by the West even in the face of the economic success Libya experienced under his leadership highlights Western determination to entrench economic tentacles in Libya. For years, inspired by his love for Libya, Qaddafi had greatly limited Western exploitative intervention in Libya, and the country prospered. The West never liked him. However, following Libya's gradual opening up to the West in 2004, foreign investment, and relationship have gradually grown, although the state still controls greater proportion of economy, to the discomfort of Western investors. According to Benjamin and Davis,

> In 2009 alone, European governments—including Britain and France—sold Libya more than $470 million worth of weapons, including fighter jets, guns and bombs. And before it started calling for regime change, the Obama administration was working to provide the Libyan dictator another $77 million in weapons, on top of the $17 million it provided in 2009 and the $46 million the Bush administration provided in 2008.[17]

Condemning the Western invasion of Libya, Benjamin and Davis declared,

> And so, after years of providing Libya's dictator with the weapons he's been using against his people, all the international community—France, Britain and the United States—has to offer the people of Libya is more bombs, this time dropped from the sky rather than delivered in a box to Muammar Qaddafi's palace.[18]

Other African leaders who made great success in their countries and brought glory to renascent Africa include Julius K. Nyerere of Tanzania, Gamal Abdel Nasser of Egypt, Jomo Kenyatta of Kenya, Nelson Mandela of South Africa, Kenneth Kaunda of Zambia, and Milton Obote of Uganda. Others include leaders of liberation movements like Mugabe of Zimbabwe, Sekou Toure of Guinea, and Samore Machel of Mozambique. In Nigeria, there was the Sir Tafawa Balewa among others. Nyerere's philosophy of Ujamaa in Tanzania pointed to uplifting the social and economic life of the villages. Although the Ujamaa could not be fully realized, by raising it, Nyerere made an important contribution to African political and development theory. Although, he died in 1999, his ideas continue to inspire modern Africa because many African countries such as Nigeria, Ghana, Senegal, and others have embraced the people-centered and socialist programs at the center of Nyerere's political philosophy.

Dr. Nnamdi Azikiwe of Nigeria, popularly known as Zik of Africa, was tall in the African leadership. Dr. Azikiwe represents an ideal for lessons in leadership for national integration: highly cosmopolitan, tolerant, inspirational, and an advocate and champion of rule of law, free and fair elections, politics without bitterness, and great crusader for peace and the use of dialogue in the resolution of human and political conflicts. Zik was a complete Nigerian, often identified with Africa at large, not just Igboland.[19] He was a consistent advocate of unity in Nigeria and Africa.

As a pre-eminent nationalist, Zik in the 1959 elections did not engage in do-or-die politics. Although he complained of the rigging that took place and that indeed worked against his victory, he accepted the result and pleaded with the nation to cooperate with the winner, Sir Abubakar Tafawa Balewa. He stressed that he did so in the national interest and that he was already happy because his life's greatest goal, namely, the independence of the country, had been achieved. It is perhaps important to note that in Africa of that time, Azikiwe was about the only nationalist leader of his status who did not become his country's prime minister or chief executive. He accepted to be Governor General, a position that was largely ceremonial. In this way, he saved Nigeria from the type of situation that bedeviled the Congo Republic in the aftermath of the elections manipulated against Patrice Lumumba.

BEYOND NATIONAL LEADERSHIP

One aspect of leadership in postcolonial Africa that is often given less attention is leadership below the national tier. This includes regional or state governors, local government leaders, and community leaders, including traditional rulers. Nigeria boasts of many leaders at these levels. A notable one was the late charismatic and development-oriented leader of old Imo State in southeastern Nigeria, who was known as Chief Samuel Onunaka Mbakwe. He is well remembered by his people as a successful governor who fought doggedly for his people during and after the Nigerian-Biafran war. In a lecture in his memory on March 10, 2004, B.E.B. Nwoke appropriately captured the peoples' view of the man they fondly call Dee Sam "who ruled well, governed justly, piloted the ship of the State with the fear of God and provided excellent administration to a war battered economy and people."[20] He is well remembered for giant strides in the development of education, repairing the schools and colleges destroyed during the civil war. He also made highly fundamental contributions to the electrification and industrialization of the state, locating at least a cottage industry in every local government. In fact, he built and sustained twenty-one such industries in the state. In the health sector, he built and commissioned twenty-two new health clinics, and three new hospitals and carried out a network of road construction connecting all parts of the state to the state capital, Owerri. The success story of Samuel Onunaka Mbakwe is a good example of the kind of useful leadership from below in the national leadership in Nigeria and other African countries. Another example was that of Alhaji Abubakar Rimi of Kano state, whose administration was hailed for its people-oriented and result-oriented nature.

Another aspect of this leadership from below, yet to be focused adequately on, is the role of women. African women both singly and corporately have made transformational contributions to their societies and communities. Many hospitals, orphanages, and charity institutions have been initiated and completed by women in Africa. A study of his aspect of leadership in post-colonial Africa is a project worth executing. In Nigeria, this would include women leaders such as Mrs. Kuti, Mrs. Margaret Ekpo, Professor Dora Akunyili, Wangari Muta Maathai, and Ellen Johnson Sirleaf, among other women.

THE UGLY IN POSTCOLONIAL LEADERSHIP

A good number of African civilian and military leaders have been notorious examples of bad leadership. Bribery and corruption, political savagery and vandalism, abuse of office, and other indices of bad governance have been reported and proven in several African states. This has led to a situation in which the affected countries have been described as "failed states." Cases of this are best illustrated in the Congo under Mobutu Sesse Seko, who was reported to be richer than his country, as well as in Jean-Bedel Bokassa of Central African Republic, who even tried to create a new monarchical and imperial dynasty, himself being the pioneer emperor. He renamed the country as "the Central African Empire" and held a lavish coronation modeled after Napoleon, even when the majority of masses were poor.[21]

However, nothing can be compared to the evil Idi Amin of Uganda represents in the history of leadership in postcolonial Africa. The litany of crimes he perpetrated cannot be exhausted here. He established the notorious State Research Bureau that on his orders killed thousands of innocent Ugandans in a program of ethnic cleansing. He executed his enemies live on television. He also mutilated his wife and murdered his ministers. In fact, he kept the head of one of his victims in his refrigerator as a warning to others. Over 30,000 people were murdered by the end of his reign. In every sense, Idi Amin engaged in a reign of terror, killed most of the officers and men of the Ugandan army within five months of his presidency. He replaced them with fresh recruits from his fellow Kakwa ethnic group who were only cooks, drivers, mess orderlies, and wireless operators. These were placed in officer cadre as majors, colonels, and so on.[22]

From all these, we can deduce the basic issues that determined the trends in leadership in postcolonial Africa. One is the issue of political struggle for influence and power by the emerging political groups in respective African states. Second, groups and persons who sought to get into political leadership often sought to do so with desperation and associated violence. Third, the desire to solidify political positions led African leaders to engage in programs that increased the need for reliance on coercive means in running the affairs of their states. Closely related to this was the high rivalry among the different persons and groups who sought to gain political ascendancy. Also, leaders became too attached to the selfish and primordial interests of their respective ethnic, religious, and cultural affiliations to the detriment of national cohesion. The new nation states did not evolve into structures for nurturing nationalism and patriotism. The instability that all these issues caused in the African states drastically affected the capacity of respective African leaders to engage in the effective mobilization of their countries for political, social, and economic transformation.

CONCLUSION

Political leadership in postcolonial Africa has been a mixed blessing due to internal and external pressures. Only a few leaders, notably in the first decade of independence, were able to mediate the pressures with reasonable degree of success. What worsened the situation was the self-serving disposition of most of the leaders, resulting in the enthronement of the values and patterns of undemocratic society in the nation states. However, it would be inaccurate to write as if political leadership in postcolonial Africa had been only one marked by failure, without positive results. The pace of attainments was no doubt slow, yet some progress was made. For instance, most African leaders seem to be very conscious of the fact that democracy through free and fair elections is the accepted means of installing leadership in Africa. It is now a dogma of leadership in postcolonial Africa that military and autocratic processes are an unwelcome aberration that will be resisted by the stakeholders, including the international community. Therefore, a major prospect for the triumph of democratic leadership in Africa is the fact that no serious-minded stakeholders question the value of democracy.

Democratization has become a striking and welcome theme in the post–cold war African politics. Led by the United States, Western powers have encouraged political reforms in countries ruled by either military dictators or sit-tight civilian regimes. Evidence of establishing functioning democracies has increasingly become a vital requirement for receiving monetary assistance from international financial institutions such as the IMF, the World Bank, among others. Supposedly driven by the noble desire to spread the principles of freedom, the United States, for instance, through its embassies and state department officials, has been deeply involved in the affairs of African countries preparing to conduct elections or experiencing post-election crises. While external pressure to democratize should be applauded, great care should be taken to resist excessive external meddling in the affairs of Africa, which carries the risk of reestablishing exploitative neo-colonial control. Insisting on democratic system of government while at the same time holding their leaders accountable is the sustainable route African people must take to create a class of leaders worthy of public trust.

ENDNOTES

1   Edwin P. Hollander and James W. Julius, "Contemporary Trends in the Analysis of Leadership Process." *Psychology Bulletin* 71 (1969), 387–397.

2   Thomas Carlyle, *On Hero Worship, and the Heroic History* (Boston: Houghton Mifflin,1907).

3   Fillmore H. Selznick, Authoritarianism and Leadership (Philadelphia: Institute for Research on Human Relations, 1950).

4   S.J. Zaccaro, "Trait-based Perspectives of Leadership," *American Psychologist* 62 (2007), 6–16.

5   General Pr. Firth, "Theories of Leadership: Where do we stand?" *Educational Leadership* 38 (1976), 327–331.

6   C. Bird, *Social Psychology* (New York: Appleton Century, 1940).

7   R.M. Stogdill, "Personal Factors Associated with Leadership: A Survey of the Literature," *Journal of Psychology* 25 (1948), 35–71.

8   R.D. Mann, "A Review of the Relationship between Personality and Performance in Small Groups," *Psychological Bulletin* 56 (1959), 241–270.

9   Ukachukwu D. Anyanwu, *Themes on Igbo Culture, History and Development Lagos*, Oke–Afa (Isolo: UBAOND and ASSOCIATES, 2010), 29–46; and Jack Woddis, *Introduction to Neocolonialism* (New York: International Publishers, 1967).

10 Frantz Fanon, *The Wretched of the Earth* (Harmondsworth: Penguin Books, 1976), 76.

11 B.J. Dudley, *Instability and Political Order Politics and Crisis in Nigeria* (Ibadan: Ibadan University Press, 1973), parts I and II.

12 Dennis Austin, "Opposition in Ghana, 1947–1967" *GOVERNMENT AND OPPOSITION A quarterly of Comparative Politics* 2 (London: Weidenfeld and Nicolson, 1967): 539–555.

13 A.B. Assensoh, *African Political Leadership: Jomo Kenyatta, Kwameh Nkrumah and Julius Nyerere* (Malabar, FL: Krieger, 1998).

14 Ali A. Mazrui, *Pan-Africanism, Democracy and Leadership in Africa: The Continuing Legacy for the New Millennium.* Institute of Global Cultural Studies, http:igcs.binghamton.edu/igcs_site/directon6.html (accessed September 12, 2010), 1.

15 Izu Marcel Onyeocha, *Africa: The Question of Identity* (Washington: Council for Research in Values and Philosophy, 1997), 89.

16 Mazrui, *Pan-Africanism, Democracy*, 3.

17 Medea Benjamin and Charles Davis, "Instead of Bombing Dictators, Stop Selling Them Bombs," Wednesday 23 March 2011, www.truth-out.org (accessed July 2011).

18 Ibid.

19 Dare Babarinsa, *From Zik to Babangida* (Nigeria: Newswatch Special Independence Edition, 1985), 47.

20 B.E.B. Nwoke, *Samuel Onunaka Mbakwe in History* (Owerri: First Lecture in Honour of Chief Samuel Onunaka Mbakwe, 2004), 1–26.

21 Izu Marcel Onyeocha, *Africa: The Question of Identity* (Washington: Council for Research in Values and Philosophy, 1997).

22 Miranda Twiss, *Evil Men* (New York: Michael D. Mara Books Ltd, 2003), 146–159.

REVIEW QUESTIONS

1. Is the trait theory of leadership relevant in contemporary leadership discourse in Africa? Discuss with examples from African countries.
2. The legacy of European colonial rule still shapes the nature and conduct of African leaders. Do you agree? Discuss.
3. How correct is the assumption that African leadership has been described as a mixed blessing? Discuss strategies to improve leadership in Africa.

Writing Prompt

Examine the contributions of any three African leaders to their countries development since independence stressing what they accomplished while in power and the problems they faced.

CHAPTER 21

From OAU to AU: The Search for African Unity

Lekan Badru

When people use the acronyms OAU and AU interchangeably, they are usually referring to the same institutional body that promotes the interests of Africa. These acronyms show the extent of the evolution of the African continent since decolonization through intergovernmental conferences and treaties to foster cooperation among African countries. Although conflicts have dominated the history of postcolonial Africa, many visions and promises have emerged in the continent. These deadly and grim experiences have been the primary focus of some Western researchers. The purpose of this chapter is to show the cooperation that exists among African states and to identify the growing depth and diversity in understanding African affairs and the issues that have shaped the continent on its path to postcolonial integration.

OAU stands for Organization of African Unity. It was an international organization mainly concerned with the promotion of the welfare and prestige of the African people. It made policies that directly affected all aspects of African lives. Recently, the organization transformed into a new relationship to bring about a closer and a more integrated African unity. This move, in a way, is a remake of the international image of the continent. As the world becomes globalized and more intertwined, Africa must design an appropriate instrument to enable it to achieve its objectives and goals in the international environment.

First, the birth of the Organization of African Unity (OAU) was the beginning of African integration as envisaged by its founding fathers. Thirty-two African countries gathered in Addis Ababa on May 25, 1963, to sign a Charter establishing the OAU with the goal of cooperating in economic, social, and political areas. The shared experience of colonization and independence was a major factor in the desire of the African leaders to have a common identity, "an African personality," and some kind of "African community."[1] Despite this background, there were disagreements among African leaders on how to go about the process of forging a continental unity or to what extent this integration must attain.[2] Nonetheless, the emergence of OAU represents a step forward for Africa in seeking total liberation from colonialism and external influence by the Western world in general and the Europeans in particular.

Second, the evolution of the OAU into the AU in 2002 represents the reassertion of independence by African states. Unlike the OAU, the African Union (AU) assumes a greater measure of capabilities to develop and produce a more stable framework for African integration. It has redefined the security conception and the prospect for a peaceful continent. In view of these and other challenges, it is important to look at the evolution of the integration process through the ratification of treaties and creation of structures that carry out the day-to-day activities of the organization. Hence, the most obvious question that has risen in the transformation of the African institution is, what impact would it have on the continent? To answer this question, it is important to explore the journey and challenges from OAU to AU.

ORIGIN OF THE OAU

The historical literature on the origin of OAU points to the Pan-African Movement, which was the struggle against racial discrimination and inhumane treatment of blacks in Diaspora. Blacks in North America started this movement in the early 1900s, with prominent personalities such as H. Sylvester Williams, Dr. W.E.B. Dubois, and Marcus Garvey. During its many meetings in the early 1900s, the concepts of "African personality" and "negritude" were formulated. Although no native African attended any of the meetings of the movement at its evolutionary stage, it was from this that Africans drew their inspiration for self-determination and political independence from the European colonial governments. From the 1940s to the 1950s, African leaders like Kwame Nkrumah of Ghana, Jomo Kenyatta of Kenya, Leopold Senghor of Senegal, Sekou Toure of Guinea, and even George Padmore of Trinidad, became prominent in the Pan-African movement. Soon, they used the movement as a platform to launch the idea of nationalism and African Independence. The end of World War II created a climate in which the Europeans began to give sovereignty to their African colonies and those elsewhere. Consequently, Ghana became the first country in sub-Saharan Africa to gain independence in March 1957. In April 1958, a conference of Independent African States was hosted in Ghana, where independence for all African states was the focus.[3]

Only eight independent African countries were at the meeting in Ghana in 1958. Concerned about the colonized countries that were absent, Ghana's president, Kwame Nkrumah, called another conference in December of the same year. The conference was named the "All African People's Conference," and its purpose was to find a way to encourage African nationalist leaders who were at least willing to implement a strategy to diminish European control in their countries. This time, attendees were nationalist members of still-colonized African countries; at this conference, the clamor for African unity was reiterated.[4] Based on this (the recognition that Pan-Africanism could be used for African unity), Nkrumah is often referred to as the father of African unity.[5] These conferences are regarded as the most significant in the path to the creation of African unity because they provided the framework for the integration process of the continent and brought the idea of "Africa for the Africans"[6] to the fore at these meetings. Many of the attendees at the conferences would later become the leaders of their countries.

As the wave of independence began to sweep across Africa in the late 1950s, many groups began to emerge to promote Africa integration and foster unity among African states. At the core of the founding of the OAU were three regional groupings of African countries that had attained independence, but remained committed to the struggle for African freedom and the protection of African interest. These groups such as the Casablanca Group, the Monrovia Group, and the Brazzaville Group assumed the responsibility of forging a continental unity.

The Casablanca Group

The Casablanca Group consisted of Ghana, Guinea, Mali, Morocco, Algeria, and the United Arab Republic (UAR). This group became chartered on January 7, 1961. Its name was derived from the largest city in Morocco, Casablanca.

The Monrovia Group

The Monrovia Group name came from Monrovia, Liberia, where this group held its conference in May 1961. This group was made up of Senegal, Malagasy Republic, Ivory Coast, Togo, Chad, Dahomey (Benin), Niger, Upper Volta (Burkina Faso), Congo Brazzaville, Central African Republic (CAR), Libya, Ethiopia, Gabon, Nigeria, Sierra-Leone, and Liberia.

The Brazzaville Group

The Brazzaville Group consisted of mainly all the French-speaking African countries within the Monrovia group: Cameroon, Chad, Gabon, Dahomey (Benin), Central Africa Republic (CAR), Senegal, Congo Brazzaville, Mauritania, Upper Volta, Madagascar, Niger, and Ivory Coast, and it came into force on September 12, 1961.

FORMATIVE CHALLENGES

Although these regional groupings came into being to build a closer union among African states, they had little agreement on how quickly the integration should be accomplished. For instance, the Monrovia Group was in favor of a gradual process, especially in the area of political unification. However, they were more inclined to move faster in other aspects such as economics and social unification.[7] The Brazzaville Group, which was mainly comprised of French-speaking countries, preferred a rather slow integration in all aspects of unification because they still wanted to keep their ties with France. But the leaders of Ghana and Guinea (sometimes called the radical group) within the Casablanca Group wanted an absolute integration with a centralized type of government, legislative assembly and ministries, and Armed Forces.[8]

Another challenge faced at the founding of the OAU was the religious and cultural divide that runs across the continent. Consequently, these dyadic factors put doubt to the establishment and cooperation of a unified institution in Africa because of the religious division between Christians, Muslims, and those that believe in indigenous African religions. The language barrier was also thought to be a challenge, as over 800 languages are spoken within the continent apart from the colonial languages of English, French, Spanish, and Portuguese. In addition, none of the countries involved in this quest for African unity was comparably industrialized, except for South Africa, which was not included because of its apartheid regime.[9] Despite these multifaceted problems that faced African leaders in their path to unity, they were able to rise above their competing differences, interests, and egos through compromises to achieve their goal of African unity.[10] The competing groups were able to reach an agreement on the May 22, 1963, in Addis Ababa, the capital of Ethiopia.[11] According to Nweke, it was "the mutual agreement among the contending groups to harmonize their positions into a unified document on African integration" that prevailed over ego and personal interest of leaders.[12]

Following the compromise between the groups, thirty-two African countries signed a Charter that established an organization that would be known as Organization of African Unity, in Addis Ababa, Ethiopia. The signing laid the foundation for the beginning of African integration. The momentum of the occasion made the Ethiopian Emperor, Haile Selassie, declare:

> [A] single African organization through which Africa's single voice may be heard, within which Africa's problems may be studied and resolved . . . which will facilitate acceptable solutions to disputes among Africans and promote the study and adoption of measures for common defense and programs for cooperation in the economic and social fields . . . to which we will all belong, based on principles to which we all subscribe . . . [and whose decisions] will take full account of all vital African considerations.[13]

However, the various conflicting groups reiterated their positions in their addresses at the conference. Nigerian Prime Minister Abubakar Tafawa Balewa delivered what is called the moderate position:

> Some of us have suggested that African unity should be achieved by political fusion of the different states in Africa; some of us feel that African unity could be achieved by taking practical steps in economic, educational, scientific, and cultural cooperation and by trying first to get the Africans to understand themselves before embarking on the more complicated and more difficult arrangement of political union. My country stands for the practical approach to the unity of the continent.[14]

President Nkrumah of Ghana criticized the moderate perspective when he gave his speech at the august event. He stated:

> African unity is, above all, a political kingdom which can only be gained by political means. The social and economic development of Africa will come only within the political Kingdom, not the other way round.[15]

Without doubt, both sides had a genuine and sincere vision for African integration, unity, and prosperity. What emerged from the conference was a cooperation based on intense negotiations that combined ideals from different political groupings, and the aims and principles of the OAU reflect such sentiment.

Finally, the OAU Charter was signed in Addis Ababa, Ethiopia on May 25, 1963.[16] At its core is the inalienable right of all people to control their own destiny; enjoyment of freedom, equality, justice, and dignity are essential objectives for the achievement of the legitimate aspirations of the African peoples. Furthermore, it called for the enhancement of unity, promotion of understanding, and cooperation among African states and their peoples in order to transcend all the differences that existed. It also maintained that Africa must fight against neo-colonization to safeguard its territories and sovereignty, which are paramount to the development of a unique African identity.

The official languages of the organization were French, English, and Arabic, which shows the diversity of the African continent.

AIMS, PRINCIPLES, AND ORGANS OF THE OAU

The aims and purposes of the organization were found in its Charter, and it specified in detail the goals of the organization, which reflected the motivation that led to its founding. It aimed at achieving the promotion of unity, solidarity, and cooperation among African states in order to achieve a better life for Africans as well as to defend their sovereignty, territorial integrity, and independence by eradicating all forms of colonialism from Africa, and at the same time respect the United Nations Charter. The Charter promoted African freedom, self-determination, equality, and political independence that advanced cooperation and respect amongst member states. Another important aspect of the OAU Charter was the awareness and operation of its principles.

The OAU principles embodied standard understandings for preserving the unity among members. Thus, it acknowledged the sovereign equality of all member states by non-interference in the internal affairs and peaceful settlement of disputes by arbitration among members.

The aims and principles of the organization Charter were the fulfilment of the compromise that shaped the formation of the OAU. On one hand, the aims were the embodiment of the beliefs that some founding fathers had—namely, that Africa should be safe from any external influence and the desire to be left alone to determine and choose what was better for its own community. It also underlies the ambitions of those founding fathers who wanted a closer and more integrated union. On the other hand, the principles of the Charter proved to be the antithesis of the aims because it clearly advocated for a non-inclusive union by pointing out that states should respect the domestic politics of each other. Hence, both the aims and principles of the organization were a logical conclusion to the disagreement and problems that confronted the founding fathers at the onset of creating a path for African unity. For this reason the OAU "seeks to be the basic law for all Africa."[17]

Like the United Nations, the OAU was made up of many structures that carried out its day-to-day activities, and these were its organs. They performed roles and range of functions that were significant to the development and welfare of African states. There were four principal organs of OAU, and they had all contributed to the shaping of the organization and its agenda: (1) The Assembly of Heads of States and Government, (2) Council of Ministers, (3) General Secretariat, and (4) the Commission of Mediation, Conciliation and Arbitration.[18]

The Assembly of Heads of States and Government was the highest body of the organization, charged with the main responsibility of maintaining, coordinating, and harmonizing functions and activities of all other organs and special agencies of the organization. It was the final decision maker of the institution, although some of its decisions were not always implemented when it came to domestic matters of member states. The functions of the Assembly, according to its Charter, were to decide on adherence or accessions to the Charter and to discuss matters of common concern to Africans with a view to coordinating and establishing special Commissions when necessary. It is also charged with the review of structures, functions, and acts of all the organs and any specialized agencies that may be created in accordance with the OAU Charter and to approve amendments to the Charter in conformity with the procedure by provision that a member state makes a written request to the Secretary-General and notifies all member states.

The Council of Ministers was the body that was given the responsibility of carrying out the decisions of the Assembly of Heads of State and Government. It supervised policies as the Assembly of Heads of States and Government formulated them. It was made up of foreign ministers[19] from member countries, and its functions were to implement the decisions of the Assembly of Heads of State and Government and to prepare the conference of the Assembly. It must also give its consent to the budget and the receipt of gifts, bequests, and other donations made to the organization and were equipped with the power to decide on the privilege and immunities to be accorded the personnel of the Secretariat in the respective territories of members.

Based on the Charter guidelines, the Council must meet twice per year to discuss important issues affecting the continent and to report to the Assembly of Heads of State. Each member state minister was entitled to a vote. A simple majority of the Council members' vote was needed for a decision in the council. A chair, two Vice-Chairmen, and a Rapporteur were elected for each time the council met and the elections were conducted in secret.[20]

The **General Secretariat** was located in Addis Ababa, Ethiopia, and a Secretary-General, who was given the administrative responsibility of running the activities of the organization, headed it. For instance, the Secretariat arranged meeting and schedule for the Heads of Government Assembly. The Secretary-General was responsible and reported to the Council of Ministers and also acted as the accounting officer of the OAU. Under the Charter, the Secretary-General and the staff were to maintain impartiality in the disposal of their duties and functions. Like other organs of the OAU, the Secretariat had functions that it performed in overseeing such a large organization. Besides the preparation of an annual report on the activities of the organization, its functions included the receipt of communications, documents, and files, the ratification of instruments of agreements entered into between member states, and the preparation of the programs and budget of the organization for each fiscal year, to be submitted to the Council of Ministers for its consideration and approval.

PROBLEMS WITH THE OAU

The OAU was formed to promote and preserve peace in Africa. It was understood that this would be achieved by promoting unity, tolerance, and solidarity among member states. In a number of ways, these promises were not kept, and Africa became engulfed in many crises that did not reflect the provisions of the Charter establishing the OAU. The various civil wars (Nigeria, 1967–1970; Sudan, 1955–1972, 2003–present; Somalia, 1991–present) that sprang up across the continent at the organization's infancy made it evident that the OAU's aims and objectives were inadequate. The non-interference in members' internal affair actually became an impediment to human security on the continent as the human rights of its citizens were constantly violated. It became common for member states to watch while another member state engaged in repugnant acts of violence against its own citizens to the extent that the social commonality of the African states was lost. Often, the Assembly of Heads of State and Government became a bulwark for the protection of African leaders in power. For instance, no member of the Assembly condemned Presidents Samuel Doe of Liberia, Mengistu of Ethiopia, and Idi Amin of Uganda for human rights violations.[21]

In the 1990s, Africa suffered one of the most human security catastrophic experiences as attacks and atrocities against unarmed civilians were used as strategies in waging wars. For instance, the OAU stood idle and watched as neighbors killed each other in Rwanda and Burundi in the late 1990s. The genocide that took place in this conflict highlighted the problems concerning OAU. The failure of the organization to stop this extraordinary human tragedy was a huge blot on its image because it reaffirmed the precedent in its history of failure to end the vicious circle of hostility and war and its inability to maintain stability throughout Africa since the 1960s.

Limited or lack of resources and commitment from members were other problems that the OAU had to confront. Members were not meeting their financial commitments to the organization, and as such the organization found it difficult to perform to full capacity. Although at the founding, financial obligations of member states were voluntary until in 1964 when the Assembly of Heads of State and Government made it compulsory just like the United Nations fee, still many African states failed to make payments and the organization continued to operate below its financial capacity.[22] For example, in 1965, twenty-four member states failed to make their financial contributions.[23]

THE AFRICAN UNION

Many principles enacted by the OAU prior to the 2000s did not help Africa to consolidate the basic aspiration of the organization's founding fathers such as better lives for Africans and solidarity among African states. In other words, the African member states did not take advantage of the structure of continental cohesion the OAU founding fathers had created. It was very different from what the founders had wanted. Although it was able "to eradicate all forms of colonialism from Africa," little was achieved in the area of social, economic, and human rights. Hence, "the creation of the African Union is at the very least an acknowledgement that the situation with regards to the OAU was untenable,"[24] and it "would have continued to perpetuate the conditions that undermine the prospects for peace building on the continent."[25]

Acknowledging that the OAU had not been successful with its core values and principles, Libyan president, Col. Muammar Gaddafi, signaled his desire to move OAU forward into the new century when he called for a new form of African continental unity at the 35th summit of Assembly of Heads of State and Government, held in Algeria in July 1999. This idea by the Libyan president was adopted into a resolution, and members agreed to meet for an extraordinary session in Sirte, Libya, in 1999, where a declaration was made that established the African Union.[26] This was a drastic attempt at revamping and reorienting what African continental unity means. For instance, the Libyan president Gaddafi has called this new partnership "United States of Africa."[27] Kwame Nkrumah had advocated for a similar partnership at the onset of OAU.[28] The fact that OAU has transformed into AU means that "the African Union is in effect the third incarnation of the process to institutionalize the idea of African unity through Pan-Africanism paradigm. It is a pragmatic transition which seeks to regenerate African solidarity and unity to confront the adverse consequences of economic and predatory globalization."[29]

The African Union was inaugurated in Durban, South Africa, on July 9, 2002. It succeeded the OAU in its mission to rid the continent of colonialism and its influence. More fundamentally, the AU pays greater attention to the issues of human rights and democratic structures through the creation of new institutional bodies. Thus, a vibrant civil continent with less conflict is the message the leaders are sending to rest of the world. The new or revitalized organization would seek to minimize destabilization that has made most of the countries in the continent fragile and incapable of promoting development beyond the rudimentary stage. For these reasons, states within the union have to change their political attitude along the reconstruction of new principles, structures, and organs of the organization.

The AU is an effort to reconstruct some of the principles of the old organization such as the one that prevents members' interference in each other's internal affairs. Under the umbrella of human right issues, this principle no longer holds weight. Apart from human rights issues, democratic and judicial issues become paramount in the AU. As a result of all these developments, more principal organs are envisioned to be added to the old ones. First is the African Court of Justice. It took four decades since the creation of OAU for Africa to establish a court that mirrors the International Court of Justice. The court acts as the principal judicial body of the Union and it has eleven Justices who are chosen from member states. No more than one Justice can be chosen from a country. The Court is headed by a president and vice-president, and the role of the Court is to interpret treaties and acts signed within the Union and how they are applied. Justices' terms can only be ended by death, resignation, or removal through the Assembly and Commission.

The Pan-African Parliament is another organ of the AU. According to its website, this parliament traced its origin back to 1991 and its inauguration to 2004. It is located in Midrand, South Africa. It hopes to "evolve into an institution with full legislative powers, whose members are elected by universal adult suffrage."[30] It is obvious that this body is still in its early stage. It consists of legislators from all African countries. Its roles are to serve as a consultative and advisory body to the organization in the areas of cooperation and development. The Permanent Representatives Committee, which is another organ of the AU, prepares the groundwork for the Executive Council and takes directives from it. This body is similar to its European Union counterpart. It mainly operates as a forum to discuss and make suggestion to the Council. The Peace and Security Council is an organ charged with overseeing the security and peace on the continent as its name denotes. According to AU, almost ten million African lives have been lost in conflicts, and close to $300 billion has been spent within forty-five years.[31] Thus, the organ will help promote peace and rule of law and to recommend to the Assembly of Heads of State and Government when to intervene in situations where crimes are being committed against humanity, such as genocide and other war crimes. It would have the power to use African Union military force for peacekeeping missions and to intervene in internal conflict of members. Additionally, parts of its responsibilities also require it to deal with the issues of democratization and human rights and freedom.[32] This body is essential to the success of the reorganization of the continental integration as it represents an improvement in the pursuit of peace and the willingness to correctly prevent conflicts before they result in death and misplacement of millions of Africans.

The Financial Institutions consist of African Central Bank (ACB), African Monetary Fund (AMF), and African Investment Bank (AIB).[33] The Union has an ultimate goal of using one monetary currency for the whole of Africa. AU plans to establish this body. The Commission is the old General Secretariat with the same functions and duties. In design, the AU is guided and ordered in the form of European Union, but the aspiration and motivation of AU is based on transforming Pan-African vision into reality. Unfortunately, these organs might face the same problem of underfunding that plagued the old ones. Until the Arab Spring, a mass revolt across the Arab world that started in early 2011, it seemed safe to assume that funding would not be an issue with the new transformed organization because of the tremendous commitment that a leader like Gaddafi had accorded it in the process of revitalization. In other words, the former Libyan president could mobilize African leaders to meet their obligations because of his own regional interest.[34] Sadly, Gaddafi's government and life was brought to a tragic end by the revolution in October 2011.

The argument is that OAU's transformation to AU clearly symbolizes a positive image for Africa and its complete unification ambition, but the commitment to the functionalism of the organization by member states and leaders may not have evolved beyond what it used to be in the old OAU. This chapter takes a cautionary view of the transition from OAU to AU in light of what has happened in the OAU era.

CONCLUSION

It is inevitable that the AU will face some difficulties in post OAU period—more especially since it has inherited the old problems from the OAU era. The history of the AU is that of overcoming developmental and political crises: the crisis of human rights, the crisis of underfunding, the crisis of democracy, and the crisis of war tragedies such as the 1994 genocide in Rwanda and the ongoing genocide in Darfur. The main challenges ahead lie in the way member states allow integrative implementation. In terms of identity and solidarity, there is a potential to build more interest in an understandable framework. In some respects, the members are moving closer; peace building is evident in the deployment of AU military force to some parts of the continent (Sudan and Somalia). For that reason, the AU has kept up with its responsibility to secure peace on the continent. Although the effort might be small, the principle behind it suggests the organization is clearly making the move to be the tool to bring peace to the region.

Meanwhile, as the AU moves forward with its efforts to securing the prosperity and safety of Africa, the process of integration and the effectiveness of the structures erected would be put to test in the coming years. Whether the transition of AU from OAU will increase the levels of living conditions on the continent, thus creating a more stable Africa, will heavily depend on the responsibility and the commitment of African leaders to act in reducing conflicts and acting quickly enough in the peace-building effort. As Murithi points out, "The African Union will need to seriously orient the political leadership of the continent and take decisive and necessary action, without which the challenges of peace building and development will not be resolved."[35] In other words, leadership in individual African state is pivotal to the success of the born-again organization. The AU needs leaders who are willing to truly promote the cohesion of a great continental Africa and harmonize the interest of African states with that of Africa's development.

Nevertheless, the future of AU will be decided by the effectiveness of its management, in the sense that if it is underfunded just like OAU, it will lack the capacities to perform its role in African integration. The members should find a way to remove this barrier that could cause delay or inadequacy in enforcing and enacting some of the organization's acts and functions. To achieve the perfect harmony, these challenges should not be allowed to be a deterrent to complete integration by all member states.

ENDNOTES

1 Tom Mboya, *Freedom and After* (Boston: Little Brown & Co., 1963), 4.

2 Alex Quaison-Sackey, *Africa Un-bound: Reflections of an African Statesman* (New York: Frederick A. Praeger, Publisher, 1963), 91–97.

3 Godfrey L. Binaisa, "Organization of African Unity and Decolonization: Present and Future Trends," *Annals of the American Academy of Political and Social Science* 432 (July 1977), 52–69.

4 Godfrey L. Binaisa, "Organization of African Unity and Decolonization."

5 Colin Legum, *Pan-Africanism: A Short Political Guide*, rev. ed. (New York: Praeger, 1965), 57.

6 Ibid., 22.

7 "Pan-African First Steps," *The Economist* 199, no. 6140 (April 29, 1961), 454–456

8 Virginia M. Thompson and Richard Aloff, *The Emerging States of French Equatorial Africa* (Stanford, CA: Stanford University Press, 1960); Ruth C. Lawson (ed.), *International Regional Organization; Constitutional Foundations* (New York: Frederick A. Praeger, Publisher, 1962), 301–302.

9 Norman J. Padelford, "The Organization of African Unity," International Organization. 8, no. 3 (Summer 1964), 525.

10 Aforka G. Nweke "The Organization of African Unity and Intra-African Functionalism," *Annals of the American Academy of Political and Social Science, International Affairs in Africa* 489 (January 1987), 133–147.

11 Gino Naldi, *The Organization of African Unity: An Analysis of Its Roles* (New York: Mansell, 1999), 2.

12 Aforka G. Nweke "The Organization of African Unity and Intra-African Functionalism," 138.

13 Emperor Haile Selassie I at *OAU Founding Conference*, Addis Ababa, May 1963.

14 *Proceedings of the Summit Conference of Independent African States, vol. 1, sec. 2* (Addis Ababa, May 1963), 104–105.

15 Ibid.

16 Ibid., Vol. 1, Sec.1, 1–7.

17 Boutros Boutros-Ghali, *L'Organisation de l'Unité Africaine* (Paris: Colin, 1969), 5.

18 Although there were more than four organs, the Specialized Commissions and the Liberation Committee hardly played a significant role as they were often replaced and were not a permanent organ of the institution, therefore, there is not much to tell. Based on this, I have chosen not to provide much detail on them. It is just that the chapter would not be complete if they were not mentioned briefly.

19 A Minister is an equivalent of a Secretary in the United States. For example, the Foreign Minister of Nigeria polity is the same as Secretary of State in the United States.

20 This is usually someone that is given a special assignment to work on issues concerning international institution.

21 Samuel Decalo, *Coups and Army Rule in Africa: Studies in Military Style* (New Haven, CT: Yale University Press, 1976).

22 Zdenek Cervenka, *The Unfinished Quest For Unity: Africa and OAU* (New York: Africana Publishing, 1977), 59.

23 Paul Saenz, "The Organization of African Unity in the Subordinate African Regional System," *African Studies Review* 13, no. 2 (September 1970), 217–218.

24 Timothy Murithi, *The African Union: Pan-Africanism, Peace Building and Development.* (Burlington, VT: Ashgate Publishing Company, 2005), 85.

25 Ibid.

26 *The 35th Summit of the OAU Heads of State and Government, Algeria, July 1999; Sirte Declaration, Fourth Extraordinary Session of the Assembly of Heads of State and Government*, EAHG/Draft/Dec I. (IV) Rev. 1. 8–9 (September 1999).

27 Ray Takeyh, "Has Ghaddafi Reformed?" *The Washington Post* (August 19, 2003).

28 Kwame Nkrumah, *Towards Colonial Freedom* (London: Panaf Books Limited), 1962.

29 Ibid., 23.

30 See www.pan-africanparliament.org/ ; www.pan-african-parliament.org/AboutPAP_History.aspx(accessed January 18, 2011).

31 Timothy Murithi, *The African Union: Pan-Africanism, Peace Building and Development, 82.*

32 *Protocol Relating to the Establishment of the Peace and Security Council of the African Union* (adopted Assembly of the African Union, First Ordinary Session, 9 July 2002).

33 The Financial Institutions. www.au.int/en/organs/fi(accessed January 18, 2011).

34 See www.nigeriavillagesquare.com/articles/chinweizu/arab-quest-for-lebensraum-134.html (accessed January 18, 2011).

35 Timothy Murithi, *The African Union: Pan-Africanism, Peace Building and Development*, 36.

REVIEW QUESTIONS

1. What do you understand by the term Pan-Africanism? Based on the information obtained in this chapter, what role did the Pan-African movement play in the creation of the Organization of African Unity?

2. Why did the founding fathers of the OAU long for African integration? Compare and contrast the functions of three of OAU principal organs with that of AU.

3. Explain the differences between the major groupings leading to the founding of OAU. What do you think were the main problems of OAU?

4. Which element of AU do you think is the most vital to the success of the organization? What criteria would you use to compare the success of AU?

Writing Prompt

What are the merits and demerits of African countries uniting into one nation-state as envisioned by Kwame Nkrumah in the 1950s? What are the likely challenges African politicians will face in realizing this dream?

CHAPTER 22

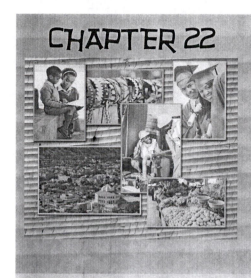

Economic Growth and Development in Africa: Challenges and Prospects

Aloysius Mom Njong

During the latter part of the twentieth century, sub-Saharan Africa (SSA) appeared to be a very promising continent with high potentials for economic transformation and development.[1] Based on its population, productivity, and vast natural resources, Africa was rated with higher possibility of catching up with the Western World than Asia and Latin America. In the 1960s, for instance, Myrdal projected in his celebrated volumes on Asian drama that Asia was doomed for stagnation, while Africa was poised for rapid economic prosperity.[2] This was certainly premised on SSA's strong natural resources and the potentials for high-level productivity, which are good ingredients for growth and development. As the 2008 UNCTAD *Economic Development in Africa* points out, SSA's growth performance was, on the average, quite strong for over a decade—from the mid-1960s until the first oil price shock in 1973.[3] During that period, the countries of SSA were potential giants among developing countries.

From the mid-1980s, the continent plunged into economic crisis. All predictions about its economic recovery have been proven wrong. Today, Africa remains the poorest continent in the world, while Asia is one of the highest emerging market economies. At the end of the twentieth century, Africa's per capita income was far less than what it was in the 1960s. In 1998, for instance, Africa's income per head was one-third less than East Asia and about one-quarter of Latin America. Today, all economic and social indicators show that Africa is caught in a development trap, thereby posing a vicious circle of low growth high poverty. The continent has failed to recover from economic chaos because of a combination of economic vulnerability and wrong application of domestic development policies. The misapplication and abuse of such domestic policies have resulted in lost opportunities, and what appeared to be an opportunity for rapid growth and development has unfortunately turned to be perpetual dependence on primary commodities and foreign support.

The major challenge, therefore, is how SSA can achieve high economic growth and translate it into sustainable poverty reduction and equitable social development, benefiting the population at large. This is a daunting challenge, but it can be achieved. This chapter highlights SSA's economic development pattern and trends. It discusses the obstacles that hinder growth and development and policies that can promote growth and sustain development in Africa.

ECONOMIC DEVELOPMENT IN SUB-SAHARAN AFRICA: PATTERN AND TRENDS

In the 1960s, the aspiration of most African leaders was to build a vibrant, self-reliant economy full of opportunities. With this determination, African economic growth was robust and faster than the growth rate of many other developing countries. For instance, between 1960 and 1973, the region recorded an appreciable

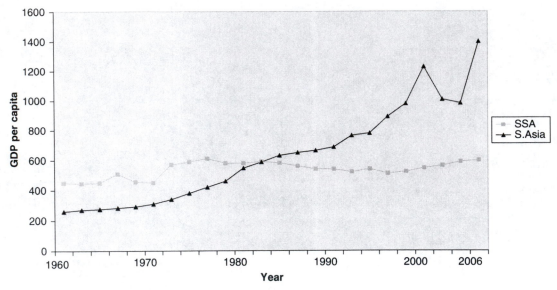

Figure 22.1. GDP per capita (constant USD) 1960–2006

Source: Summarized from World Development Indicators (WDI) of the World Bank. 1970–2006

real growth rate of 5.9 percent, an outcome relatively better than some regions of the world. In per capita terms the contrast in economic performance between SSA and other developing regions was even greater. Observe in Figure 22.1 that between 1960 and 1984, SSA enjoyed a higher per capita GDP than Southeast Asians. Infrastructure, education, and health were improving across much of the SSA region. Expectations during these years were high.

Then, it would appear something went wrong and the economic progress made in the 1960s gave way to a recession thereafter. Economic growth dropped from its annual average of 5.9 percent between 1965 and 1973 to 2.5 percent between 1974 and 1980, before it further declined to 0.5 percent in the late 1980s.[4]

Figure 22.1 reveals that in SSA per capita income stagnated in the 1970s, declined in the 1980s, grew weakly in the 1990s, and in 2006 was still lower than it had been in 1975. In Southeast Asia the whole forty-five-year period was, apart from a brief recession at the turn of the century caused by the Asian financial crisis, one of almost continuous economic growth and development. High per capita growth in Southeast Asia has been accompanied by substantial reductions in monetary poverty. In SSA, by contrast, poverty levels have remained high and rising, even after the return to growth in average per capita income during the late 1990s.

While the growth of gross domestic product (GDP) is a popular measure of economic growth, it is not a sufficient yardstick for development. Development is about many different things, including command over resources, choice of livelihood, human capabilities, living in a healthy and safe environment, adequate housing and food, political freedom, and many others. In other words, economic growth is important to, but not the only driver of, development. Sen points out, "Ultimately, the focus has to be on what we can or cannot do, can or cannot be."[5] Thus, development must be defined by an individual's achievements and by the means that the individual possesses.

While there are many ways to measure development, we focus on some key indicators; namely, $1.25-a-day poverty, $2-a-day poverty, per capita GDP at 2005 PPP, life expectancy at birth, net primary enrollment, adult literacy, under-5 survival, and births attended by skilled health personnel. From these indicators, one can gauge people's command over resources, nutritional levels, use of health and education services, access to clean water and sanitation, and others. As shown in Table 22.1, there is considerable disparity in the level of development across regions, and the disparity in per capita income is far greater than in non-monetary indicators.

Table 22.1: Key Development Indicators, 2007

Indicator		SSA	Southeast Asia	Latin America
Headcount Index (%)	$1.25-a- day poverty	50.9	27.0	8.2
	$2-a- day poverty	72.9	53.9	17.1
GDP per capita at 2005 PPP (US$)		1,698.1	3.060.9	7,719.3
Incremental output-capital ratio (%)		9.2	24.6	31.8
Exports per capita (US$)		98	79.8	565.4
Saving/GDP (%)		14.5	34.8	42
Life expectancy at birth (year)		50.8	68.1	72.1
Adult literacy (%)		61.2	79.1	90.1
Net primary enrollment		67.1	89.2	94.2
Under-5 survival (per 1000)		851.9	948.4	973.7
Births attended by skilled personnel (%)		46.5	69.2	89.2

Notes: Poverty rates are based on 2005 PPP; where PPP = purchasing power parity

Sources: Summarized from World Development Indicators Online Database (World Bank, 2010)

The evidence from Table 22.1 equally shows a disappointing performance in the selected key development indicators. For instance, in 2007, more than half of SSA's population lived in extreme poverty, that is, below the $1.25-a-day poverty line, while about 73% of the population fell below the $2-a-day poverty threshold. Among the non-income indicators, SSA's life expectancy at birth was 50.8 years, compared to 68.1 for Southeast Asia and 72.1 years for Latin America; its proportion of births attended by skilled health personnel was 46.5%, compared to Southeast Asia's 69.2%; and its adult literacy was 61.2%, compared to Southeast Asia's 79.1% and 90.1% for Latin America. There is also evidence of low capital productivity in SSA relative to the other regions. Observe in Table 22.1 that, during the 2007 period, SSA recorded an average productivity of 9.2 percent; in Southeast Asia the figure was 24.6 percent and 31.8 percent in Latin America.

While other regions were recording a decline in the prevalence of undernourishment, the situation became worse in SSA. Large numbers of children are undernourished or stunted, and many children die before their fifth birthday. For example, the under-5 mortality rate for SSA stood at 14.9 per thousand as compared to only 2.7 per thousand for Latin America (see Table 22.1). In education, SSA also recorded the lowest primary school enrollment among the developing countries of the world. Millions more do not attend schools, and many girls face limited opportunities simply because of their gender. In many ways the youth, who are the future of Africa, are already being mortgaged. Currently, the international community's attention has been seized by the United Nations Millennium Development Goals (MDGs), laid out in 2000 as development targets to be met within the first fifteen years of the twenty-first century.[6] Unfortunately, as the above statistics illustrate, many countries in Africa will not come even close to meeting most of these goals.

In many ways, the picture that emerges from the information presented above can easily lead to Afro-pessimism. But Africa is a continent, not a country, and within these often disturbing statistics, there are other more encouraging trends, particularly since the 1990s. There are countries that are growing economically, that are well governed, that are successfully fighting corruption, and whose leadership is serious about development and poverty reduction. These countries have a good chance to meet some, if not all, of the key Millennium

Development Goals. There are islands of real progress in improved economic policies, export growth, and governance and democratization. Africa is a diverse continent whose countries span a wide continuum—from fragile states such as Somalia and the Central African Republic to successful post-conflict countries such as Rwanda and Mozambique, and stable and growing countries such as Botswana and Mauritius. Painting the whole continent with a broad black brush is wrong.

OBSTACLES TO THE DEVELOPMENT OF SUB-SAHARAN AFRICAN ECONOMIES

Given the dismal economic performance of some SSA countries, it becomes difficult to break the vicious circle of low growth high poverty scenario; an issue that further weakens the development potentials. The major challenge is to design a policy package capable of pulling SSA out of this doldrums. To do this warrants a better understanding of the obstacles that inhibit growth and development in Less Developed Countries (LDCs) and SSA in particular. Even though the factors we discuss below are not common to all the countries, a broad answer to the question of "why the poor development outcome in SSA" is implicit in these factors.

VICIOUS CYCLES OF POVERTY

There are circular relationships of factors that tend to perpetuate the low level of development in LDCs. Nurkse Ragnar explains these relationships in these words: "It implies the circular constellation of forces tending to act and react upon one another in such a way as to keep a poor country in a state of poverty."[7] For example, a vicious cycle stems from the fact that in LDCs, total productivity is low due to deficiency of capital. There are two basic vicious cycles, one from the demand side and the other from the supply side. The demand side of the vicious cycle is that the low level of real incomes in LDCs leads to a low level of demand, which, in turn, leads to a low rate of investment and hence back to deficiency of capital. This is reflected in Figure 22.2.

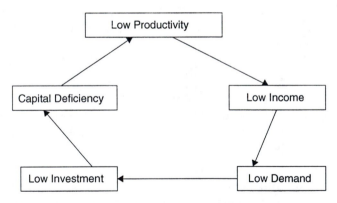

Figure 22.2: Demand side of vicious cycle

Low productivity is reflected in low real income. The low level of real income means low saving. The low level of saving leads to a low investment and to deficiency of capital. The deficiency of capital, in turn, leads to a low level of productivity and back to low income. Thus the vicious cycle is complete from the supply side. This is depicted in Figure 22.3.

The low level of income, reflecting low investment and capital deficiency, is a common feature of both cycles. We may sum up these cycles by observing that low incomes in poor countries lead to low consumption, which then leads to poor health and low labor productivity and eventually to the persistence of poverty. Poverty is both a cause and a consequence of a country's low rate of capital formation.

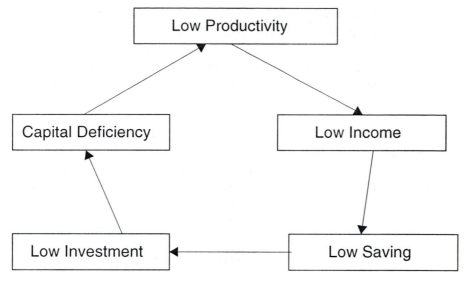

Figure 22.3: Supply side of vicious cycle

INAPPROPRIATE DOMESTIC POLICES

Inappropriate domestic economic policies have been advanced as a major obstacle to the development of some African countries. Notable among the policy mistakes has been an overreliance on the public sector and inadequate attention to private-sector development. Reasons for the creation of state-owned enterprises (SOEs) or para-public enterprises have been well documented in the literature.[8] One such reason is the persistence of monopoly power in many African countries. Direct government control may be required to ensure that prices are not set above the costs of producing the output. Moreover, certain goods that have a high social benefit are usually provided at a price below their costs or even for free; hence, the private sector has no incentive to provide such goods, and the government must be responsible for their provision. Despite the many valid reasons for the existence of SOEs, in recent years, the latter have come under increasing attacks for wasting resources and operating at large deficits. For example, Cameroonian SOEs averaged net losses equivalent to 3 percent of its GDP during 1979–1986.[9] Moreover, a World Bank study of four African countries (Ghana, Senegal, Tanzania, and Zambia) revealed a general poor performance of these enterprises.[10] Most of the para-public enterprises failed to show a profit. Operating on a deficit, they proved to be a massive drain on government resources. A major factor affecting the performance of SOEs is the over centralization of their decision making and bureaucratization of management. As a consequence, administrators and managers are not accountable for their performance. More often, such persons do not have the best talents and thus they stand in the way of efficient management of the enterprises. Such practices lead to nepotism, bribery, favoritism, and inefficient administration. These vices make economic development all the more difficult.

Another policy mistake is the neglect of the agricultural sector. African economies are predominantly agricultural. Agricultural production constitutes a large share of their GDP and agricultural commodities form a considerable part of the value of their total exports. For instance, in Cameroon about 60 percent of the population is engaged in agriculture, while it contributes roughly 50 percent to the national income. Despite this, agriculture remains in a state of stagnation and overall neglect. For example, agriculture lost out both in periods of economic contraction and expansion. During period of economic recession with hard budget constraint, agriculture was often the major victim of budgetary cuts. Almost all sub-Saharan African countries have suffered from the "Dutch Disease" paradox.[11] Essentially, the "Dutch Disease paradox" describes the idea that natural resources might be more of a curse rather than an advantage. The term usually refers to the inverse association between development and natural resource abundance. It describes a situation whereby an export-oriented natural resources sector in a country generates large revenues for government but leads paradoxically to economic stagnation and political instability. SSA is blessed with vast natural resource-rich environments. These resources constitute a principal source of public revenue and national wealth. Under the right circumstances a natural resource boom can be an important catalyst for growth and development. Unfortunately, in many SSA countries, natural resource booms have failed to lead to the expected economic growth and development. For example, the period of primary commodity expansion did not translate into equitable and sustainable growth in many resource-rich SSA countries, but instead caused highly overvalued exchange rates to the extent of making goods less competitive. Consequently, the added income accrued to a few, while the appreciation of the currency adversely affected the entire population.

The "Dutch Disease" phenomenon has occurred in countries such as Cameroon and Nigeria (during the oil booms in the mid and late 1970s, and early 1980), in Ghana and Ivory Coast (during the cocoa booms in the 1970s and 1980s, respectively), and in Zambia and Zaire (during the mineral booms in the 1990s). Such booms were not turned into sustained growth and development. In most of these countries, the abundance of petroleum and natural gas has brought trouble—waste, corruption, conflicts, and rent seeking by elites who could otherwise put their energies into profit-making activities.

LACK OF ACCOUNTABILITY AND TRANSPARENCY

SSA's dismal economic performance has been linked to lack of selfless and dedicated leadership. The preponderance of African countries in the list of corrupt nations as computed by the *Transparency International* has shown this to be a major weak link of growth and development. It has been alleged that most African leaders have been involved with serious embezzlement, mismanagement, and misappropriation of their country's scarce resources, such as Robert Mugabe in Zimbawe, Abacha in Nigeria, Arap Moi in Kenya, and Mobutu in Zaire. Apart from the fact that national resources found their ways into private accounts in overseas banks, successive governments in Africa have been wasteful and inefficient in the use of economic resources. The conclusion of Adjibolosoo provides an illuminating illustration. According to him,

> The scope of corruption, favouritism, negligence, inefficiency, deceit and cronyism is horrendous in countries such as Gambia, Nigeria, Ghana, Sierra Leone, Benin, Ethiopia, Sudan, Kenya and Zaire. It is lamentable that even though Congo and Nigeria are oil rich countries, their economies are still in severe economic difficulties, many of which are traceable to gross mismanagement and corruption. This is a trend across Africa.[12]

The pervasive lack of accountability and transparency has not only damaged African economies but has also destroyed the socioeconomic institutions (as infrastructures were left to decay without adequate maintenance), as well as the value system in these countries, consequently causing severe deterioration of living standards. For instance, in 1995, Nigerian military ruler General Sani Abacha was accused of embezzling US$150 million. In a like manner, former Malawi President Bakili Muluzi, who ruled Malawi from 1994 to 2004, was arrested and charged with 42 counts of theft, fraud, corruption, and breach of trust.[13] A 2004 Transparency International report listed Mobutu Sese Seko as one of the best known kleptocracies—regimes where rulers use political power to steal public money for private use. Mobutu is reported to have given members of his ruling *Mouvement Populaire de la Revolution* a brief tutorial on theft by public servant during a party congress in 1984: "If you steal, do not steal too much at a time. You may be arrested. Steal cleverly, little by little"[14] Yet another example of mismanagement of public funds is the case of Felix Houphouet-Boigny in Côte d'Ivoire. He built one of the world's largest cathedrals, Our Lady of Peace, in his village in Yamassoukrou at a cost of US$260 million in 1989. When criticized by opposition groups and donor agencies about the immorality of his extravagance, he said that the US$260 million he spent on the basilica came from his own pocket, not from the public treasury.[15] How did he get such a huge sum of money in the first place? That is the question.

CONFLICTS AND CIVIL WARS

A peculiar feature of SSA development challenge is the preponderance of conflicts and civil wars.[16] Although conflicts tend to manifest between ethnicities, fundamentally, however, conflicts in many African countries are driven by the exploitation of natural resources that have impeded capital accumulation and left these countries in a self-reinforcing mechanism of dependence on the export of raw materials, resulting in poverty traps.[17] This raises the question as to whether natural resources are not the very root of the misery that African populations continue to experience. Across the African continent, cases of dire poverty and misery attributable to the presence of natural resources are innumerable. The conflicts in Rwanda, Burundi, Sudan, Congo Democratic Republic, Liberia, Sierra Leone, Côte d'Ivoire, and Nigeria have been linked to economic mismanagement of the country's natural resources. Instead of benefiting the population, natural resources in these countries have been the major source of their misery. Indeed, the huge deposits of natural resources in these countries have attracted various foreign powers, as well as internal forces that have sought to gain an easy advantage by tapping into and using mineral revenues to acquire power and finance armed conflicts. Widespread conflicts impose serious economic cost on the economy through the destruction of human and material resources, diversion from development-oriented projects to rehabilitation and reconstruction. Meaningful development can only be achieved during peaceful sociopolitical conditions.

DEMOGRAPHIC, RELIGIOUS, AND SOCIOCULTURAL FEATURES

SSA countries differ greatly in demographic position and trends. Diversity exits in the size, density, age-structure, and the rate of growth of the population. However, there appears to be one common feature, a rapidly increasing population that adds a substantial number to the total population each year. With their low per capita incomes and low rates of capital formation, it becomes difficult for SSA countries to support these additional numbers. And when output increases due to improved technology, it is swallowed up by increased population. Almost all SSA countries possess high population growth potentials characterized by high birth rates. The advancement made by medical science has resulted in better methods of public health and sanitation that have reduced mortality and increased fertility. The increasing birth rates often result in high natural growth rate of population. For instance, the average annual growth rate in SSA is about 3 percent as compared to only 0.7 percent in developed countries. An important consequence of the high birth rate is that a larger proportion of the total population is in the younger age groups. The percentage of the population under 15 years of age is about 45 percent in SSA compared with only 20 to 25 percent in developed countries.[18] A large percentage of children in the population entail a heavy burden on the economy, which implies a large number of dependents who do not produce at all, but who do consume. With many dependents to support, it becomes difficult for the workers to save for purposes of investment in capital equipment. It is also a problem for them to provide their children with the education and bare necessities of life.

Economic development also has a lot to do with social and cultural attitudes. According to Ragnar Nurkse, "there are elements of social resistance to economic change in African countries which include institutional factors reinforced by traditional beliefs and values."[19] The family is the primary economic and social unit in African countries. Family attitudes are responsible for population pressures and attachment to land. They also limit the range of freedom in making economic decisions, which in turn influence the motives to save and invest. Social attitude toward education is inimical to economic growth. For instance, in Cameroon and most African countries, purely academic education that trains people for government and other clerical jobs is preferred to technical and professional education. There is prejudice against manual work, which is despised and ill rewarded. Consequently, there develops a natural distaste for practical work and training that leads to technological backwardness.

There are also traditional religions and cultural dogmas that inhibit progress because they prevent social, economic, and political institutions from changing in a way that is conducive to economic development. All traditional religions in SSA involve the veneration of ancestors and the belief that people, animals, and natural objects are invested with spiritual power. For example, among the rural Wolof in Senegal, household water jars are seldom cleaned because the spirit of an ancestor could come to drink at that moment and find no water. In Cameroon, some cultures, including the Bamiléké in the west and the Maka in the east, practice divination and/or perform public autopsies to determine the cause of death. These practices are contrary to good sanitation and could serve as vectors that spread disease and impair labor productivity. It has been argued in the literature that even Western religious practices do have possible negative effects on economic growth. These negative effects include religious restrictions on capital accumulation, profit making, credit markets, and interest. Beed and Beed support this view by arguing that several fundamental Christian beliefs contradict the values and morals of modern capitalism and secular economics.[20] Religion may also increase resource allocation toward church activities, such as cathedral building, thereby removing resources from more profitable free market activities. McCleary, who argues that the negative effect of religion reflects the time and resources used by the religion sector as well as adverse effects from organized religion, supports this view.[21] Religious people are found to be more intolerant, and often-violent behavior or civil unrest may erupt because of clashes among believers and non-believers and different religious faith groups. Empirically, Daniels and Ruhr have used individual survey data of U.S. residents to test the impact of religious affiliation on attitudes toward trade and immigration policies.[22] The results show that, in general, religious affiliation is a significant determinant of individual international policy preferences. Specifically, members of the three largest U.S. denominations—Catholics, Baptists, and Methodists—are more likely to favor policies that restrict imports into the United States. The authors, hence, suggest that religion is an important form of identity and may represent an important source of resistance to a greater economic integration.

TOPOGRAPHY AND GEOGRAPHICAL LOCATION

A basic and fundamental tenet of geography is that location matters. Location is the "where" element of geography. Knowing what is found in particular places and the human and physical characteristics of these places enables us to build an understanding of the ways in which space and place connect. SSA lies in the tropical and subtropical zones, and her developmental problems have been linked to geographical location. Throughout the region rainfall is rarely gentle and even. It usually comes as torrential downpours, which are destructive to soils and harmful to plants.

SSA is primarily an uplifted plateau. Its escarpment lies in close proximity to the coast and contributes to rapids on rivers and hampers transportation routes. Its coastal plains provide the settlement location for much of its population. Africa has a difficult shore characterized by a narrow continental shelf that makes transportation costly and ineffective. Land degradation is widespread and serious in SSA. Although degradation is largely fabricated, and hence its pace is governed primarily by the speed at which population pressure mounts, irregular natural events such as droughts exacerbate the situation. The 1982/85 drought, for example, had a dramatic effect on the speed of land degradation and desertification. It is a well-known fact that soil degradation not only results in decreased food production but also in droughts, ecological imbalance, and consequent degradation of the quality of life.

The problem of geographical location and disadvantaged topography has not only constrained meaningful agricultural transformation but has also limited the synergy between agriculture and industrial development. When agricultural production increases, expansion of the industrial sector is stimulated. First, expansion of farm output requires improved farm machinery and other inputs manufactured by the industrial sector. Second, increasing agricultural productivity and incomes expand the demand for consumer goods and services available in the industrial and tertiary sectors. With economic growth in the agricultural and industrial sectors, the demand for services such as transport, retail and wholesale distribution, credit and financial institutions are required.

EXTERNAL INDEBTEDNESS

Countries in SSA have low saving and investment rates; consequently, they lack in social overhead capital and basic key industries. Thus, to accelerate the rate of economic development, they borrow from foreign governments and international financial institutions such as the IMF and World Bank in order to import capital goods, intermediate goods, spare parts, and technical expertise. Besides, they also borrow to finance consumer goods to meet the demand of the growing population. Their exports being limited to a few primary products, they borrow to supplement and increase their domestic resources. These lead to huge deficits in the balance of payments, which means that the country is borrowing from abroad and thus accumulating external debts. The total debt burden of countries in SSA increased from $1,460 billion in 1990 to $2,350 billion in 2000. Their total debt service as percentage of GDP was 4.3 percent in 1990 and rose to 6.3 percent in 2000.[23]

The principal cause of the international debt crises has been attributed to the 1970s and 1980s oil-price shocks. The first oil shock to the international economy was an increase in oil prices by more than fourfold in 1970 and doubled in 1980.[24] This caused a large increase in the import bills of non-oil-producing less developed countries (LDCs). Simultaneously, their export earnings fell due to the recession in the developed countries. Consequently, the balance of payments deficits of oil-importing LDCs increased much.

The policies adopted by the developed countries and their banks were instrumental in reinforcing the debt crisis. The rise in oil prices had increased the revenues of oil-exporting countries. But they were unable to absorb them within their economies. They deposited huge volumes of petro-dollars in the commercial banks of the developed countries (DCs), which thus accumulated huge funds that could not be used in the developed countries, as the latter were faced with a recession. But the LDCs needed funds for their economic development programs that these banks recycled in the form of loans to LDCs. After 1979, many SSA countries and LDCs in general had accumulated huge external debts that they found difficult to repay, both the interest and principal. The situation was further aggravated in SSA with the fall in the prices of their primary commodities. The heavy burden of external debt has posed a constraint on the growth potentials of African countries thus limiting their ability to address persistent structural weaknesses.

DEPENDENCE ON PRIMARY PRODUCTS AND UNEQUAL EXCHANGE

Dependency economists contend that the Developed Countries (DCs) at the center exploit LDCs at the periphery by forcing them to specialize in the export of primary products with inelastic demand to both price and income.[25] Further, trade between the center and the periphery is characterized by unequal exchange. Dependency economists attach different meanings to "unequal exchange." Neo-Marxists mean by it deterioration in the terms of trade of African countries. According to UNCTAD,[26] unequal exchange means "exporters in industrialized countries possess more monopoly power than the exporters of underdeveloped countries," thereby leading to unfavorable terms of trade for the latter. To Jhingan,[27] it is the differences in techniques of production and differences in wages that lead to unequal exchange in trade for the latter. Since wages are low for SSA countries the cost of production of the commodity is also low and so is its price. On the other hand, because wages are high in the center, the cost of production of the commodity is high and so is its price. Thus, because the commodity of an LDC is cheaper than that of the DC, there is unequal exchange between the two. This is because an LDC exports more of its commodity in order to get a given unit of imports from the DC. For instance, the 1980s recorded dismal performance in terms of trade with an annual average growth rate of −1.0 before improving to 1.4 percent in the 1990s. For African countries that are not oil exporters, excluding South Africa, cumulative terms of trade losses in 1970 to 1997 represented almost 120 percent of GDP.[28] This represents a massive and persistent drain of purchasing power from the continent with harmful impacts on the economy.

Dependency theorists hold that the present economic and sociopolitical conditions prevailing in SSA may have originated during the colonial period. During that period, the complementarity between African natural resources and the human capital of the colonial powers defined the economic system. Unfortunately, the political independence of most African countries in the 1960s has not changed the underlying economic dependency principle. Instead of emancipating themselves from it, African countries continue to rely on the export of primary resources to their former colonial rulers and other developed countries. The percentage share of agricultural commodities, fuels, minerals, metals, and other primary products in the merchandise exports of the SSA countries, as revealed by the World Bank data, is on the average about 80 percent. For instance, the share of Ethiopia is 99 percent, of Uganda 99 percent, of Cameroon 89 percent, of Algeria 100 percent, and of Kenya about 86 percent.[29]

Too much dependence on exports of primary product has serious repercussions on their economies. First, such economies concentrate mainly on the production of primary exports and tend to neglect the other sectors of the economy. Second, their economies become particularly susceptible to fluctuations in the international prices of the export commodities. A depression abroad brings down their demand and prices, the terms of trade become adverse, and foreign exchange earnings fall steeply. As a result, the entire economy is adversely affected. Last, too much dependence on a few export commodities to the utter neglect of other consumption goods has made these economies highly dependent on imports. Imports generally consist of fuel, manufactured articles, machinery, transport equipment, and even food. Coupled with this is the operation of the demonstration effect, which tends to raise the propensity to import still further. In recent years, the slumping of exports and commodity prices has worsened the economic problems of countries in SSA countries.

STRATEGIC POLICY OPTIONS

An important lesson from development literature is that there is no unique model for economic development. The rapid transformation of the Asian economies provides good evidence on this. The diversity varies from such resources-poor countries as Japan and Korea to resource-rich ones like Malaysia and Indonesia; while some followed laissez-faire policies (e.g., Hong Kong), many adopted extensive state intervention. In spite of this diversity, some important commonalities served as essential ingredients for transforming their economies—commitment to long-term view of development as against the ad-hoc attributes of African leaders.

Strengthening the Human Capacity

An important policy option for countries in SSA is effective capacity building and utilization. An educated labor force, well-trained policymakers, and ethnically inclined professionals are ineluctable. This presupposes allocating substantial resources into education and enforcement of standards. To achieve this goal, there is need to focus more attention on science and technology. The current situation, where emphasis is placed on humanities and social sciences, and the diminution of science-inclined professionals into service and financial sectors (sectoral brain drain) makes development very elusive in Africa. To increase labor productivity, there should be a change in the outlook of the people toward work. The existence of educated and trained labor force leads to rapid economic development. Thus, the most important requirement of growth is people, people who are ready to welcome the challenge of economic change and the opportunities in it, as well as people who are dedicated to the development of their country.

Strengthening Growth by Diversifying the Economy

The need to diversify Africa's export base by revitalizing the private sector as the main engine of growth is vital.[30] Some lessons can be learnt from Asian countries. While Singapore and Hong Kong used manufactured export as the springboard for their incredulous growth, Malaysia and Thailand first developed their agricultural exports because of their landmass advantage. Taiwan developed her domestic food production before embarking on manufactured exports, while Indonesia developed both the oil and agriculture exports. This is a very good lesson for Africa. Maintaining competitive exports requires an efficient infrastructural system, effective policing, and an effective judicial system.

A key issue emanating from the current pattern of Africa's trade is the fact that exports are concentrated in primary commodities while imports tend to be manufactures, thereby reinforcing commodity dependence.[31] The increasing concentration of Africa's exports on primary commodities is and should be of concern to the region. Another concern for many African countries is that the large-scale imports of manufactures are increasingly competing with domestic production, with dire consequences for local manufacturing production. This is especially the case when the manufactured products imported are consumer rather than capital goods. These imports do not contribute to improving productive capacities of African countries. Rather, they tend to compete with products that were either imported from other sources or might previously have been produced in the region. Indeed, it has been reported in many African countries that the influx of cheap manufactured products, mostly from China, presents challenges for local manufacturing firms. So what should be done? An effective response to the challenges facing Africa's manufacturing sector requires lifting the constraints on international competitiveness of manufacturing firms in the region. In particular, it requires improving access to credit and addressing the problem of poor infrastructure.

Effective Exploitation of Natural Resources

In SSA, natural resources are abundant but are often unutilized, underutilized, or poorly utilized. This is one of the reasons for their slow economic progress. The presence of natural resources is not enough to trigger economic growth. What is required is their proper exploitation through improved techniques. There is little reason to expect natural resource development if people are indifferent to the products or services such resources can contribute. In reality, as pointed out by Lewis, "the value of a resource depends upon its usefulness, and its usefulness is changing all the time through changes in tastes, changes in technique or new discovery."[32] When such changes are taking place, any nation can develop itself economically through the fuller utilization of its natural resources. For example, Britain underwent agricultural revolution by adopting the method of rotation of crops between 1740 and 1760. France was able to revolutionize its agriculture despite shortage of land.

Thus, a necessary condition for development in SSA is to tap on the region's hidden growth reserve—agriculture. An agricultural region that is unable to feed itself is not likely to survive in the long run. Agriculture, apart from remaining a major source of income employs over 60 percent of the continent's labor force. Between 1980 and 1996, for instance, it accounted for 66 percent of the labor force in Africa.[33] In spite of its high employment capacity, its potentials are largely unexploited. Agricultural value added was very low in Africa between 1979 and 2000, as against appreciable levels recorded in developed and most Asian countries. Agricultural productivity, especially smallholder agricultural production, serves to establish the basis for lower food costs and exports. This shows that if the sector blossoms, many unemployed people will be employed. This, therefore, underscores the need to increase smallholder agricultural productivity through support for rural infrastructure, research and extension services, fertilizer subsidies supported with an effective implementation mechanism, and price support systems. Each country should identify the commodities in which it has comparative advantage, and such efforts should be supported with proactive campaigns among the farming population and effective supportive systems to intensify production processing and storage. On the other hand, the countries of Africa have not been able to develop their agriculture because they lack technological knowledge.

Economic growth is possible even when an economy is deficient in natural resources. As pointed out by Lewis, "a country which is considered poor in resources today may be considered rich in resources at some later time, not merely because some unknown resources are discovered, but equally because new uses are discovered for the known resources."[34] Japan is one of such country that is deficient in natural resources, but it is one of the advanced countries of the world because it has been able to discover new uses for its limited resources. Moreover, by importing certain raw materials from other countries, it has been successful in overcoming the deficiency of its natural resources through superior technology, new research, and higher knowledge. This can also be possible for resource-poor African economies.

Improving the Coordination of Foreign Loans and Aid

For the linkage between SSA's debt and long-term development to be positively related, the need for effective coordination from the points of the donors and recipients are essential. The management and use of such resources also deserve serious consideration. Aid should be spent on development-oriented projects as against recurrent expenditures and conspicuous consumption, while mismanagement should be guarded against. The donor partners should decentralize the delivery system, empower the local communities, and support strong ownership. The new donor-recipient partnership should be the one that strengthens institutions and empowers citizens to hold government accountable.

The effectiveness of aid in alleviating the development problems of SSA has been questioned. Moyo[35] believes that dependency on aid has undermined the ability of SSA countries to determine their own best economic and political policies. Moyo has plenty of examples to show how aid and haphazard loans have led to extreme corruption in SSA. For instance, after President Reagan met Mobutu Sese Seko of Zaire and agreed to his request to reschedule a $5 billion debt in the late 1980s, Mobutu leased the Concorde a few days later to fly his daughter to her wedding party. Moyo recommends indigenous economic activity as the only real engine of growth and development and offers a variety of solutions—all of them market-based. Moyo also notes, for instance, that most of Africa still lacks micro-financing schemes (where small amounts of money are lent to individuals and to communities), which have an excellent track record of actually working. Externally, there are still numerous obstructions on trade: The OECD should radically slash agricultural subsidies, which have the effect of blocking SSA farmers from being able to export their goods. Foreign investment is another area that may bring new benefits. In Moyo's opinion, Chinese direct investment and the resultant building of infrastructure such as roads and railways to extract minerals and foodstuffs have had a mainly beneficial effect. China remains popular in much of SSA, and "many Africans scoff at the notion that westerners should be outraged by Chinese implicit support for Africa's corrupt and rogue leaders. It is, after all, under the auspices of Western aid, goodwill, and transparency that Africa's most notorious plunderers and despots have risen and thrived."[36]

Improving the Institutional Framework, Administrative Management, and Governance

A corollary to the foregoing is the institutional dimension of rapid growth and development. The weak political and administrative structure has been a big hindrance to the economic development of SSA countries. A strong, efficient, and corrupt free administration is essential for economic development. As Lewis rightly observes, "the behaviour of government plays an important role in stimulating or discouraging economic activity."[37] Peace, stability, and legal protection encourage entrepreneurship. The greater the freedom, the more the entrepreneurship will prosper. Technical progress, factor mobility, and the large size of the market help stimulate enterprise and initiative.

Today all SSA countries have emerged as independent nations from colonial rule. But independence has not necessarily led to national consolidation. Myrdal regards national consolidation as "a pre-condition both for the preservation of the states as a growing concern and for its efficient functioning as a matrix for the effective formation and execution of national policies."[38] By national consolidation he means "a system of government, courts and administration that is effective, cohesive, and internally united in purpose and action, with unchallenged authority over all regions and groups within the boundaries of the state." Africa's current situation is characterized by untold politicization of the civil service. Nepotism has become the order of the day in most African countries, thereby relegating meritocracy to the background. There is, therefore, the need to embark on technocratic insulation and high-quality civil service. Their expertise is needed not only for policy advice but for effective policy formulation, implementation, and monitoring.

Developing indigenous institutions for mediating conflicts without undermining economic stability is equally essential. This is in addition to the economic empowerment of the civil society with a view to creating a virile public watchdog for governments' recklessness in most African countries. Gross mismanagement, misappropriation, and embezzlement are indications of lack of selfless and dedicated leadership. This has negatively affected the continent's scale of priorities, quality of investment decision, particularly in the public sector, proper management of resources, and financial discipline and integrity. Such poor leadership cannot take Africa to the path of sustainable growth and development. There is therefore, a need to break away from this trend. Effective leadership will generate public enthusiasm and support economic and social development; it will mobilize the citizenry for economic, social, political, and cultural transformation. A good leadership system promotes sociocultural institutional structures that condition people's behaviors and discourage destructive tendencies.

CONCLUSION

The development outlook in SSA is very daunting. The region plays host to the largest segment of the world's poor, experiencing the worst macroeconomic instability, grappling with the severe debt burdens, and lowest school enrollments rates and life expectancy at birth, among other development outcomes. Several factors have been linked to this dismal performance. Critical among these are rapid population growth, leadership crisis, pervasive conflicts, and unfair terms of trade, policy mistakes, and neglect of the agricultural sector as the driving force of the economy.

The way forward to SSA development problems lies in creating the right policy framework and incentives for a rapid growth in agriculture. Successful examples of economic growth—whether in Europe in past centuries or in the rapidly growing economies of Asia today—have all shown that agricultural growth is fundamental to economic growth and social development. Africa cannot be an exception. It cannot leapfrog this essential foundation. In SSA, efforts to develop agriculture must necessarily focus on smallholder agriculture, as it is the major sector in almost all the countries of the region. In light of today's challenges, resuming economic growth, resolving the food crisis, and tackling the challenge of poverty must necessarily be based on creating a dynamic smallholder agriculture sector. Investing in smallholder agriculture is the most sustainable safety net for these societies. Fortunately, Africa has the potential—both in terms of its human and in terms of natural resources—to lay the ground for a vibrant agricultural sector, which can meet its own food and raw material needs as well as the needs of other regions of the world.

Immense potential will remain unrealized unless countries in SSA themselves become organized and create the right conditions for growth. Growth and development are intrinsic and endogenous processes. No nation or people have developed by relying solely on external support. It is therefore essential that African countries continue to deepen the foundations for democracy to help ensure political stability—so critical for economic growth. In addition, it is essential that they continue to improve their systems of governance to unleash fully the entrepreneurship of their people.

ENDNOTES

1 The term *sub-Saharan Africa* is used to exclude South Africa and the Muslim northern African countries such as Egypt, Morocco, Tunisia, and Libya (which are relatively more developed than the other countries in the continent).

2 Gunnar Myrdal, *Asian Drama: An Inquiry into the Poverty of Nations (Harmondsworth-Middlesex:* Penguin, 1968), cited in M.L. Jhingan, *The Economics of Development and Planning* (Delhi; India: Vrinda Publications Ltd, 2007), 69.

3 United Nation Conference on Trade and Development (UNCTAD), *Economic Development in Africa*, Geneva, Switzerland, (2008), 113.

4 World Bank, *World Development Indicators of the World Bank* (New York: Oxford University Press, 2002), 8.

5 Amartya Sen, *Commodities and Capabilities* (Oxford University Press, UK, 1985), 28.

6 United Nations, *The Millennium Development Goals Report, 2009*; see also United Nations, *Africa and the Millennium Development Goals: 2007 Update*, United Nations, New York, USA.

7 Ragnar Nurkse; *Problems of Capital Formation in Underdeveloped Countries* (New York: Oxford University Press, 1952), 4.

8 IMF, *Social Dimension of Adjustment in Cameroon*, Washington DC, 1989; See also Erik Thorbecke "The institutional foundations of macroeconomic stability: Indonesia versus Nigeria" New World Press, Ibadan, 1998.

9 IMF, *Social Dimension of Adjustment in Cameroon*, Washington DC, 45.

10 World Bank, *World Development Report of World Bank* (New York: Oxford University Press, 1983).

11 The "Dutch Disease paradox" describes the idea that natural resources might be more of an economic liability rather than an advantage. The term describes how resource-rich countries are unable to use their wealth to boost their economies and how, counter intuitively, they have lower economic growth rates than resource-scarce countries. Resource booms in SSA have limited structural diversification and technology accumulation by creating opportunities for mismanagement, rent-seeking, and corruption that undermine effective spending of windfall gains. For a better understanding of the "Dutch Disease" syndrome, see Alexis Habiyaremye "Dependence on Primary Commodities and Poverty traps in sub-Saharan Africa" UNU-INTECH Discussion Paper No. 2005–09. Institute for New Technologies, The Netherlands.

12 Senyo, Adjibolosoo; *Perspectives on Economic Development in Africa*, Praeger, London, 1994 p. 32.

13 Edem Djokotoe and Pamela K. Chamma, *Show Me the Money*, Transparency International, Germany, 2007).

14 Michael Wrong worked for Reuters, the BBC, and Financial Times and spent many years covering political events across the African Continent. BBC Focus on Africa, April to June 2006.

15 Fuabeh P. Fonge, *Modernization without Development in Africa* (Asmara: Africa World Press, 1997), 286.

16 William Easterly and Levine Ross, "Troubles with the Neighbors: Africa's Problem, Africa's Opportunity," *Journal of African Economies*, 7, no. 1 (1998), 120–142.

17 Jeffrey Sachs, D and Andrew M. Warner, "Natural Resource Abundance and Economic Growth," *NBER Working Paper No. 5398*, Harvard University, Cambridge MA. (1995), 78. See also, Paul Collier and Anke Hoeffler, "On the Incidence of Civil War in Africa," *Journal of Conflict Resolution* 46, no. 1 (2002), 13–28.

18 IMF, *Regional Economic Outlook Sub-Saharan Africa*, Washington DC, (April 2008), 53.

19 Ragnar Nurkse; *Problems of Capital Formation in Underdeveloped Countries*, 75.

20 Clive Breed and Cara Breed, "A Christian Perspective on Neoclassical Rational Choice Theory," *International Journal of Social Economics* 26, no. 4 (1999), 501–520.

21 Rachel M. McCleary, "Religion and Economic Development," *Policy Review* (April & May 2008) Hoover Institution, Stanford University.

22 Joseph Patrick Daniels and Marc von Ruhr, "God and the Global Economy: Religion and Attitudes towards Trade and Immigration in the United States," *Socio-Economic Review* 3, no. 3, (2005), 467–489.

23 World Bank, *World Development Report* (New York: Oxford University Press, 2002), 45.

24 Wayne E. Nafziger, *The Debt Crisis in Africa* (Baltimore, MD: John Hopkins University Press, 1993). See also Gary Gardner, "Third World Debt Is Still Growing," *World Watch* (1995).

25 Michael P. Todaro and Stephen, C. Smith, *Economic Development*, Pearson Education Ltd, Delhi-India, 2005.

26 United Nations Conference on Trade and Development (UNCTAD), *Economic Development in Africa: Export Performance following Trade Liberalization—Some Patterns and Policy Perspectives*, Geneva, Switzerland, (2008), 69.

27 M. L. Jhingan, *The Economics of Development and Planning*, Vrinda Publications Ltd, Delhi; India, 2007), 35.

28 World Bank, *World Development Report*, 2002, 91.

29 UNCTAD, *Economic Development in Africa: Export Performance following Trade Liberalization*, 56.

30 Fahim Al-Marhubi, "Export Diversification and Growth: An Empirical Investigation," *Applied Economics Letters 7*, no. 9 (2000).

31 Paul Collier, "Primary Commodity Dependence and Africa's Future," in *Annual World Bank Conference on Development Economics: The New Reform Agenda* (2003), 139–162. See also Alexis Habiyaremye, "Dependence on Primary Commodities and Poverty traps . . ." UNU-INTECH Discussion Paper No. 2005–09, Institute for New Technologies, The Netherlands. (2005).

32 Arthur W. Lewis; *The Theory of Economic Growth*, Homewood Illinois, Richard D. Irwin. (1955) 79.

33 *African Development Bank; African Development Report, Abidjan; Ivory coast, 2003, 38.*

34 Arthur W. Lewis, *The Theory of Economic Growth*, 72.

35 Dambisa Moyo, *Dead Aid: Why Aid Is Not Working and How There Is Another Way for Africa*, New York: Farrar, Straus and Giroux, (2009).

36 Ibid., 89.

37 Arthur W. Lewis; *The Theory of Economic Growth*, 27.

38 Gunnar Myrdal, *Asian Drama: An Inquiry into the Poverty of Nations.*

REVIEW QUESTIONS

1. What are the benefits and costs of sub-Saharan African countries concentrating their exports on the export on raw materials?
2. There are two conceptual views of the vicious cycle of poverty in developing countries. Discuss these views.
3. Is natural resource abundance (especially crude petroleum and minerals) in sub-Saharan African economies a blessing or a curse? Use specific examples of countries that are more endowed to support your position.
4. Identify and discuss the major obstacles to the growth and development of sub-Saharan African economies.

Writing Prompt

Critically analyze the strategic policy options that sub-Saharan African countries have in promoting sustainable economic and social development.

CHAPTER 23

The Growth and Ramifications of Foreign Direct Investment in Africa: Problems and Prospects in the Age of Globalization

Samuel Ezeanyika

The important role Foreign Direct Investment (FDI) plays in transforming economies around the world cannot be overemphasized. For years, the amount of FDI flowing into Africa has been comparatively low. This chapter explores the obstacles and possibilities of increasing Africa's share of FDI. It analyzes the determinants of receiving FDI, Africa's current share of global FDI, and the potentials of FDI to help Africa maximize its chances of socio-economic development in the age of globalization. This chapter argues that for FDI to aid Africa's development, greater participation of the masses in governance as well as functional regional integration is crucial.

The International Monetary Fund (IMF) defined FDI as an investment involving a long term relationship and reflecting a lasting interest and control of a resident entity in one economy.[1] According to Rutherford, FDI is an investment in the businesses of another nation that often takes the form of setting up of local production facilities or the purchase of existing businesses. Rutherford contrasts FDI with portfolio investment that is the acquisition of securities.[2] The United Nations Conference on Trade and Development (UNCTAD) defines FDI as an investment involving management control of a resident entity in one economy by an enterprise resident in another economy. This implies that the investor exerts a considerable amount of influence on the management of the enterprise resident in another economy. FDI involves both initial transactions between two entities and all subsequent transactions between them and among foreign affiliates.[3] FDI definitions differ greatly across nations, but the differences are merely variations that are based on the criterion of the percentage of ownership of shares/control between foreigners and citizens in a nation's enterprises.

Foreign direct investments have been flowing to different countries in different proportions. The United States, the European Union (EU), and Japan have been the main FDI sources and destinations over time. The African continent has been receiving the lowest share of global FDI inflows. According to Bjorvatn, Africa's share of global FDI is less than that of Singapore.[4] This is in spite of the fact that African nations actively seek for FDI. The expected surge of FDI into the continent has not occurred, in spite of commendable efforts by some African nations like South Africa, Nigeria, and Egypt that have been highly desirous of repositioning their economies. The continent did not benefit from the FDI boom that began in the mid–1980s. Since 1970, FDI inflows into Africa have increased only modestly, from an annual average of almost $1.9 billion in 1983–1987 to $3.1 billion in 1988–1992, and $6 billion in 1993–1997. For comparing figures, the global FDI flows in 1998 reached a record $644 billion.[5] In the 1980s and 1990s, Africa's share was a paltry $6 billion. The inflow to Western Europe in 1997 was $114,857 million and to North America, the figure for the same year was $98,994 million.

According to UNCTAD and IMF sources, FDI inflows into developing countries as a group almost quadrupled from less than $20 billion in 1981–1991 to $75 billion in 1991–1995. Inflows to Africa in that period merely doubled. It is not an exaggeration to say that Africa's share in total inflows of FDI to developing countries dropped significantly from more than 11 percent in 1976–1980 to 9 percent in 1981–1985, to 5 percent in

1991–1995, and to 4 percent in 1996–1997. Its share of total outflows from the United States, the EU, and Japan, the most important source regions for FDI, was even lower during 1987–1997 periods as other developing regions such as Asia, Latin America, and the former communist states of Eastern and Central Europe became more attractive as FDI receptacles. The African share never exceeded 2 percent until 1996. It increased to 2.4 percent in 1997.[6]

Africa's global FDI share is also reflected in the ratio of FDI to Gross Domestic Product (GDP). In 1970, the region attracted more FDI per $1000 of GDP than Asia, Latin America and the Caribbean. The FDI in dollars per $1000 of GDP in 1970 was 7.9, 6.7, and 2.7 for Africa; Latin America and the Caribbean; and South, East, and South-East Asia, respectively. The corresponding figures for 1996 are 13.6, 24.8, and 25.7. For 1997, the figures are 14.7, 33.8, and 28.3, respectively. By 1990, Africa had fallen behind other developing areas in terms of its value of FDI inflows and the FDI/GDP ratio, and it has stayed behind since then. The flow of FDI dropped in West Africa, particularly in Nigeria, but in Southern Africa, South Africa experienced increases. In the 1990s, the gap increased widely when the worldwide surge in FDI flows into the developing world largely bypassed the region.[7] This downward trend has continued in the first decade of the new millennium.[8]

In Tanzania, the privatization policy encouraged the inflow of FDI. Most of the privatized enterprises were sold to foreign investors whose capital revitalized the economy. In this connection, it needs to be pointed out that Africa has the highest rates of return for capital investments in some cases.[9] When looking at these relatively very attractive rates of return and profitability in Africa, it becomes a paradox that the continent has not witnessed a proportional FDI inflow. Ordinarily, one would expect that investments would flow to Africa in great numbers so as to benefit from these high rates of return. But the opposite is the case. It seems that the logic of capital is pre-empted in Africa. Capital does not seem to flow to Africa despite the continent's promise of relatively high rates of return. Among the possible explanations of this paradox may be the assumption that these rates of return for capital investment are not widely known among the investor community abroad. Where the rates are known, they may reflect the risks of investing in the continent due to the absence of FDI determinants. It is possible that the high rates of return, from the point of view of potential investors, do not sufficiently offset the risks of investing in the continent. This may make investors look away from Africa as a profitable investment destination. If the high rates of return for capital investment in Africa are made widely known among the investor community and other risks of investing in the continent are substantially reduced, one can expect to see an increased FDI flow to Africa.

The share of FDI flowing into Africa has not been even in all nations. South Africa, Egypt and Nigeria have received a lion's share of FDIs flowing into the region in terms of absolute size. However, their share has declined from more than 67 percent in 1983–1987 to 54 percent in 1988–1992, to 38 percent in 1993–1997 and to below 20 percent in 2003–2007.[10] The low FDI share for African needs to be increased given the potential positive roles that FDI can play in the continent's development. FDI can also have some negative impacts to the host economies. This chapter highlights the positive impacts because overall, they more than compensate for the negative ones. FDI is desirable for Africa. However, Africa's ability to increase its share of FDI is doubtful since the continent has struggled to demonstrate the capacity in terms of enough of the FDI determinants required to attract substantial global FDI outflows.

FDI AND DEVELOPMENT IN AFRICA

Many people assume that FDI, if deliberately targeted, could be good and very significant for the development of Africa. FDI continues to be a driving force in the globalization process that characterizes the contemporary international economy. Globalization has diminished the importance of territorial boundaries and every part of the world is in one way or another involved in the process. Africa's largest economies (South Africa, Egypt and Nigeria) are not oblivious to this international trend. This explains why these African states have particularly made recent efforts targeted at boosting intra-continental FDI. Not only have these three major players been investing in each others' nations, they are also, in partnership with other international investors, deploying FDI in the oil and gas, telecommunications, manufacturing and agricultural sectors of other African nations such as Benin Republic, Togo, Ghana, Democratic Republic of Congo, Equatorial Guinea, Tanzania, Zambia and Algeria, among others. Their investments are based on the assumption that there is a potentially positive role that FDI can play in the development of the continent.[11] The author are not oblivious to the negative impacts associated with unregulated Western investments, particularly in small and weak African economies and corrupt nations, which usually results in neo-colonization with its multifarious ramifications. This justifies the concern about the need for the continent to acquire the capacity to adequately administer its states and, at the same time, increase its global share of FDI inflows. This chapter will discuss some of the potential roles that FDI can play in host economies. It is a fact that Africa, like many other underdeveloped and developing regions of the world, needs a substantial inflow of external resources in order to fill the savings and foreign exchange gaps associated with a rapid rate of capital accumulation and growth needed to alleviate absolute, acute and disproportionate poverty and to improve living standards to acceptable levels.[12] The need for external financing is nowhere more pressing than in Africa, where income levels are too low to generate adequate domestic resources for the attainment of even modest rates of investment and growth. In resource- viable and rich African states, these low savings rates are compounded by capital flight resulting from the corruption of African leaders and their business acolytes who deposit millions of dollars in Western banks and/or financial institutions. It is arguable that FDI is currently one of the best alternative sources of external capital for the development of Africa.

Through the 1960s and 1970s, nations were enticed by Western countries to borrow from the international markets to finance their own investments. Among the alternative means of financing these investments was FDI. It was erroneously argued that this alternative was one of the most expensive ways to finance capital accumulation. Many nations borrowed instead and, as a result, many developing nations, including those in Africa, accumulated huge debts. Because of these huge debts, they now have less accessibility to international capital. Private inflows of capital into the region have mainly consisted of FDI and short-term bank lending[13]

It is now widely recognized that FDI can play a useful role in development. With its creation of development opportunities and its subsequent increase in wealth of the host nation, benefiting African nations have considerably reduced their debt burden. This has been manifested either by a dramatic reduction in individual nation's debt portfolio or through partial or total cancellation of some existing debts. The usefulness of FDI is not only due to its financial contribution; rather, it is important because of other characteristics of FDI when it forms part of a package of investment options.[14] This position is substantiated by the fact that FDIs can (but do not always) attain the following goals:

1. Create and increase employment and wages in host economies;
2. Be a vehicle of 'transfer' of technology;
3. Provide advanced skills and management techniques to host economies;
4. Help in the capital formation process;
5. Facilitate local enterprises' access to international markets;
6. Use local resources more efficiently and productively;
7. Increase product diversity and output;
8. Use environmentally sustainable technology;
9. Observe human and labor rights;
10. Create both forward and backward linkages in the economy;
11. Increase exports and tax revenues.

The above goals could be achieved if host economies in Africa established the requisite institutions and engaged in an adequate learning process enabling the creation of a sustainable environment for the emergence, growth, and development of industrial sectors attracting the inflows of FDI. Such a progressive institutionalization process, also involving policymaking machinery (PMM), should be backed with a suitable and compliable legal framework, to monitor the activities of multinational corporations (MNCs).

It can therefore be said that in an African nation with well-articulated development policies, FDI can be an engine of economic growth. Such investments can sustain and improve economic development in a nation or a region. Given the economic conditions in Africa and the continent's comparatively low level of development, the need for FDI in the region cannot be overemphasized as shown in various *World Development Reports* by the World Bank and IMF, where this issue is extensively discussed. The continent needs to improve its share of global FDI inflows as one of the most likely ways to increase the needed external capital for its development.

DETERMINANTS OF FDI INFLOWS

FDI determinants are the factors that determine FDI inflows into a given geographical location. They give investors the confidence needed to invest in foreign markets. The list of these determinants may be very long, but not all determinants are equally important to every investor in every location at all times. Some determinants may be more important to a given investor in a given location at a given time than to another investor. A given determinant may be a necessary and satisfactory factor by itself for FDI inflow in one location but not in another. It is difficult to determine the exact quantity and quality of FDI determinants that should be present in a location for it to attract a given level of FDI inflows. What is clear is that every location must possess a certain critical minimum of these determinants before FDI inflows can take place. UNCTAD presents some host nations' determinants of FDI. The policies that engender FDI include the creation of economic, political, and social stability; the introduction of rules regulating entry and operations (of FDIs) and their international agreement; the introduction of downside privatization policy; and trade policies comprising tariffs and non-tariff barriers, and tax policy.[15]

While the policies of commercialization and privatization tend to open weak African economies up to questionable foreign control, the very control measures introduced in those applicable in Nigeria, Egypt and South Africa are progressively creating a sustainable environment for the emergence of South-South multinational corporations (SSMNCs) with commendable African shareholding and control. The newly created jobs and human capital development opportunities have been beneficial to Africans, thus improving their industrial and corporate productivity and competitiveness.[16]

UNCTAD lists the principal economic determinants in host nations. It matches types of FDI by motives of the firms with those principal economic determinants. Where there is a market-seeking type of FDI, it looks for criteria concerning market size and per capita income, market growth, access to regional and global markets, nation-specific consumer preferences, and structure of markets. In the case of FDI of a resource/asset seeking type, the focus would turn on raw materials, low-cost unskilled labor as well as skilled labor, technological, innovative and other created assets (such as brand names) and physical infrastructure (ports, roads, power, telecommunications). There is another type of FDI: one that is directed at ensuring efficiency.[17] This type looks for favorable balances in the costs of resources and assets listed above, adjusted for labor productivity as well as in other input costs, such as transport and communications costs within the host economy. Finally, it is interested in whether the host economy is part of a regional integration agreement that may be conducive to the establishment of regional corporate networks.[18]

Given that FDI is increasingly geared to technologically intensive activities, technological assets are becoming more and more important for MNCs to maintain and enhance their competitiveness. A destination's possession of a strong indigenous technology base expressed in well-articulated national technological capabilities (NTCs) is vital in attracting high-technology FDI and for research and development (R&D) investments by MNCs.[19] In order to attract scarce FDI, a potential host nation must be able to provide the requisite inputs for modern production systems. For example, efficiency-seeking FDI will tend to be located in those destinations that are able to supply a skilled and disciplined workforce and good technical and physical infrastructure. According to Bjorvatn, firms will locate their industrial activities in countries with superior quality of national infrastructure.[20] A good quantity and quality of infrastructure in a location is among the factors that facilitate business operations. Physical infrastructure includes roads, railways, ports, and telecommunication facilities. The latter include traditional postal services and modern communication facilities such as the Internet.

Regional Trading Blocks (RTBs) are essential determinants of FDI. These represent various forms of economic integration among nations. They are designed to promote cross-or international trade and mobility of factor services from within member nations by fostering a more market-oriented pattern of intra-regional resource allocation. They have the potential to increase the size of a unified market. Common external tariffs imposed by RTBs are likely to force non-members to enter the market through FDI rather than through trade. The importance of regional groupings as a factor in attracting FDI has also been advocated by the UNCTAD. This advice has not been heeded.

African nations' regional and sub-regional economic integration and cooperation has been recognized and accepted as a pre-condition for their long-term development. There are several tangible reasons to support this position. The single most important one is the fragmentation of the continent with the result that very few single African nations have adequate resources and viable markets capable of sustaining industrialization and the growth of large markets for manufactured goods. Those nations, such as South Africa, Nigeria, Ghana, Gabon and Egypt, capable of participating alone in the growing international technological and information revolutions are even fewer, because their potentialities have been dramatically reduced by the competition created by major Western MNCs very active in the ongoing waves of the globalizing process. Following this reasoning, African nations and the international community, in various convergent policy declarations, statements, and programs of action, have overtly emphasized the indispensability of intra-African economic integration and cooperation. Emphases on intra-African economic integration and cooperation have been expressed in the following declarations and programs in Africa: the Monrovia Declaration, 1979; the Lagos Plan of Action, 1980–2000; the Final Act of Lagos, 2000; Africa's Priority Program for Economic Recovery [APPER], 1986–1990; the African Alternative Framework to the Structural Adjustment Programs [AAF-SAPs] to the Compact for African Recovery, 2001; and the New Partnership For Africa's Development [NEPAD], 2001.[21]

UNCTAD argues that nations stand to gain some economies of scale in regional groupings and that it develops complimentarity of interests between land-locked and coastal countries. In the African context, such economic groupings as the Economic Community of West African States (ECOWAS) and the Southern African Development Corporation (SADC), among others, are RTBs. Their existence may have considerably helped to increased FDI flows to their respective sub-regions.[22]

Language and business culture are also determinants of FDI inflows. In a destination where the majority of the population commonly speaks a language such as English, one would expect more FDI inflows than otherwise.[23] Of course, there are cases where there have been more FDI inflows to destinations where language is on the surface a barrier, for example, South Korea, Indonesia, Taiwan ROC and China, than to where language seems to be an advantage as in most African countries like Nigeria, Liberia, Sierra-Leone and Ghana where English is the language of official communication. It may be difficult to account for such contradictions without further research. For instance, in the case of Africa, in spite of the two dominant languages (English and French) inherited from past colonial authorities, the large number of African ethnic nationalities still speak different languages. This situation is compounded by the predominantly very low educational level, particularly for the rural populations that constitute the majority. This situation contributes to the investment problem in Africa. Generally, it can be assumed that the former group of countries (South Korea, Indonesia, Taiwan ROC and China) possesses more of the other FDI determinants than the latter (Nigeria, Liberia, Sierra-Leone and Ghana). For example, the huge market that China represents is likely to overshadow the language problem there. In that case language, like many other determinants, seems to be an important but not a necessary and satisfactory factor by itself.

Tax exemptions, tax holidays or tax reduction for foreign investors and similar incentives would play a positive role in attracting FDIs into a given destination. Some other types of incentives that may play similar roles include guarantees against arbitrary treatment in case of nationalization; government provision of such utilities as water, power and communication at subsidized prices or free of cost; tariffs or quotas set for competing imports; reductions/elimination of import duties on inputs; interest rate subsidies; guarantees for loans and coverage for exchange rate risks; wage subsidies; training grants and relaxation of legal obligation toward employees. But the costs of these incentives to the host economy must be compared to the potential benefits that FDI may bring. Only when the benefits of the FDI projects more than offset the costs should host economies offer any incentives.[24]

Investors may also be attracted by other factors such as low-cost but high-quality inputs and minimal transaction costs in their interaction with the government and other bureaucracies. The extent to which unnecessary, distorting, and wasteful business costs are reduced will most likely contribute positively to FDI inflow into a given destination. The strength of a currency also may determine FDI inflow. A relatively weak currency would be more likely to attract FDI than a relatively strong one. Realizing potential losses inherent in converting weak currency to hard ones, many foreign investors may simply plough back into the host economy their profits and other remittances. Currency devaluation may lead to cheap assets. Cheap assets, on the other hand, are expected to attract more FDI, especially through mergers and acquisitions (M & As). Economic and structural adjustment programs (SAPs) in a nation are very important in winning foreign investors' confidence to take their investment funds there. The reforms derivable from these programs can be very wide and far-reaching. The various reform measures may overlap with each other. Reforms, whether social, political or economic, should aim at creating, maintaining and/or improving a sustainable environment for business, both local and foreign. Some of the important reforms can involve the relaxation of entry restrictions in various sectors, deregulation in various industries, and abolition of price controls, easing of controls over trade practices, removal of government monopoly, privatization, and independence of the Central Bank, elimination of import licensing, removal of foreign exchange, exchange rate, and interest rate controls. Such reforms are likely to create a business-friendly environment capable of attracting more FDI. But the reforms may be expensive to a nation and its people. For these reforms to be justified, they must take into consideration the impact on the populace of the nation concerned.

It has been argued that the attractiveness of underdeveloped and developing nations for foreign capital depends on their capabilities to apply existing technologies and not on their role in producing new ones. That is, FDI inflow to such nations in the first place will depend on, among other things, the existence of this capability. The ability to use the existing technology is yet another factor that can determine FDI inflow into a specific destination.[25] In addition, to be considered as one of the primary reasons for the low capability of African states is the brain drain, the consistent pooling of well-trained, young professional Africans to Western nations. Attracting this well-qualified pool of experts back home might go a long way toward increasing technological and professional capability of the workforce in African nations.

Non-discriminatory treatment of investors, consistency, and predictability in government policies are also among the FDI determinants. Investors need to be in a position where they can plan their activities efficiently within the policy environment of the government. Those government policies that directly or indirectly affect investments should be reliable, accessible, up to date and widely publicized. Government's credibility is essential if more FDI is to flow to a destination. Briefly, stability, as defined by the Western world, is the main concern of capitalist investors. After all, in spite of the fact that the democratization of African political systems has emerged as a *leitmotiv* for development and cooperation for nations mainly in North America and Western Europe, these developed economies still invest heavily in countries that are led by corrupt tyrants that have no credibility.[26] In this connection, the system of processing and approving new investments may be a crucial determinant for further FDI inflow into the same destination. A long, bureaucratic, non-transparent and corrupt process is likely to scare away potential investors. What is needed is a relatively short, transparent and non-corrupt process undertaken in, if possible, a one-stop-shop. Some other FDI determinants include a positive economic growth in a given destination.

Economic growth in turn determines market prospects. It is more likely that FDI will flow more to destinations with promising economic growth in both the short and long run. Other FDI determinants mentioned in the literature include low indirect social costs like bribery and corruption or their absence; the availability of risk capital; synergy between public and private research and development programs; low rate or absence of criminality, alcohol and narcotic abuse as these affect the security of personnel and the quality of the labor force as a whole. The values, norms, and culture of the population in the host economy must be ready to support the principle of free competition. Authorities must be able to adjust policy to reflect new economic, social, and political realities of the time. Prevailing views on environmental issues and the occurrence of activism, while important, must not be fanatical and detrimental to business operation. They must be reasonable. National health services, recreation possibilities and overall quality of life, too, influence FDI inflow.[27]

A nation's membership in a binding multinational investment agreement and institutions concerning FDI can reduce the perceived risk of investing there. When the risk of investing in a location is reduced, we expect to see an increase in investments there. Such agreements include several bilateral investment treaties and double taxation treaties. Among the organizations that have an impact on the flow of FDI are the World Intellectual Property Organization (WIPO), the convention establishing the Multinational Investment Guarantee Agency (MIGA), the Convention on the recognition and enforcement of foreign arbitral awards, and the Convention on the settlement of investment disputes between nations and nationals of other nations. These bodies are influential because they participate in the smoothening of transactions between partnering nations and the creation of a sustainable environment for the implantation of FDI.

The presence of investment opportunities in a nation is another important FDI determinant. The opportunities should be made known to potential investors through effective promotion that includes marketing a nation and coordinating the supply of a nation's immobile assets with the specific needs of targeted investors. One cannot always expect that investors will take the trouble of finding out the available opportunities in every nation. African nations must reach out to investors through a comprehensive national and international lobbying strategy, utilizing the services of their diplomatic missions, multilateral agencies, and specialized corporate organizations.

Where the world's largest MNCs invest is sometimes determined by access to technology and innovative capacity in particular nations. These factors, in contrast to natural resources, are called "created assets." They include communication infrastructure, marketing networks, knowledge that can be used as a proxy for skills, attitudes to wealth creation and business culture, technological, managerial, and innovative capabilities, competence at organizing income-generating assets productively, as well as relationships (such as between enterprises and contracts with governments) and the stock of information and, finally, trademarks or goodwill. Possessing the assets just enumerated is critical for competitiveness in a liberalizing and globalizing world economy. However, the traditional factors such as access to markets, natural and other resources like low-cost labor are still key FDI determinants, especially for many enterprises that have not yet developed large-scale international operations. The absence, in most African nations, of a combination of the discussed requisite developmental conditions and FDI determinants has been responsible for the low inflows of FDIs in the African region.

AFRICA'S DILEMMA IN THE GLOBAL SHARE OF FDI

One of the features that negatively affect the flow of FDI into Africa is the continent's negative image. In most instances, the industrialized nations' media present a negative image of the beautiful African continent. War, hunger, diseases, disasters, and so on dominate press coverage. This negative perception of the continent has become a recurrent theme in the Western-controlled media. And, since perceptions create impressions in the minds of people, including shareholders of potential corporations likely to invest, Africa is considerably disadvantaged because of its poor image and negative publicity in these media outlets.

The image of the continent as a location for FDI has not been favorable. Too often, potential investors discount the continent as a location for investment because a negative image of the region as a whole conceals the complex diversity and dynamism of economic performance and the existence of investment opportunities in individual nations. In the foreword for the UNCTAD, the former Secretary-General of the United Nations (UN), Kofi Annan, puts it this way: "For many people in other parts of the world, the mention of Africa evokes images of civil unrest, war, poverty, disease and mounting social problems. Unfortunately, these images are not just fiction. They reflect the dire reality in some African countries, though certainly not in all."[28]

When investors perceive the continent as a home for wars, poverty, diseases, and a generally unfriendly investment destination, the result is the diversion of these investments to other regions. Due to the current trends of globalization, almost every nation potentially and/or actually is competing with each other as a destination for the limited FDI outflows. It may then become very difficult for the continent to increase its global share of FDI if its current negative image continues to prevail. The central question to be posed is: What can African nations do about the negative media images? What is needed is for both the African continent and the international community, through a concerted effort, to engage in the elimination of those negative factors that give the continent its poor image. For instance, the Western-controlled media should not exaggerate the reality. Instead, it should give a more balanced and accurate picture of the continent. War in the Congo or Chad should be reported as war in the Congo and Chad and not as war in Africa, the way war in Yugoslavia is reported as war in Yugoslavia and not war in Europe. Most journalists in the Western media are simply ignorant about Africa and thus spread the myths and stereotypes about Africa they imbibed from childhood. Proper education of journalists about non-Western societies, devoid of racial prejudice (which is still prevalent in many Western societies today), is the key to a more thoughtful and accurate reporting about Africa.

The promotion of peace, economic prosperity, and sustainable development for Africa's people is still a big challenge. War and conflicts have sacred many countries. Examples of those countries include Sierra Leone, Liberia, Somalia, Rwanda, Algeria, Angola, Mozambique, and Sudan. The investment climate in such locations is not likely to attract a substantial quantity and quality of investments. However, some MNCs seem to be so much attracted by mineral deposits in some of these war-ravaged nations that they look the other way when there is unrest. This may be the case in Angola and Mozambique. The observation strengthens this chapter's position that different investors may give different emphasis to the same determinants in different time and location.[29] The peculiarities of the aforementioned locations do not suggest that the listed determinants might not be as important as valuable natural resources when it comes to FDI.

To the extent that conflict and war persists in some African countries, it can be very difficult for the continent to increase its global share of FDI inflow. The situation in Sierra Leone and other war-torn areas in Africa unfortunately has negative effects on the prospects of FDI inflow into other nations. As pointed out earlier, unrest in Sierra Leone is reported as unrest in Africa. Alongside Sierra-Leone, one can mention the seven-year civil war in Burundi that claimed at least 100,000 lives. One can also point to the "curtain of fire" stretching from Eritrea, through Ethiopia, Sudan, and Congo to Angola. A Norwegian newspaper, *VartLand*, reports that every fifth African is living in a conflict-prone zone.[30] It is a fact that few investors, if any, would like to operate in conflict-prone zones. This is clearly not good news if the region is to increase its global share of FDI.

Conflicts are a barrier to efforts at increasing a location's share of global FDI. They may be good for the armament industry as markets for weapons are increased, but the industry never locates near its consumers because, among other things, conflict in the production location increases uncertainty in the market. In 2000 the World Bank outlined some costs of conflict in Africa, including social and economic costs, where it occurs and in neighboring nations by generating flows of refugees, increasing military spending, impeding key communication routes and reducing trade and investment (domestic and foreign).[31] For example, Sudan's military spending is more than three times the African average. This may have caused investment to fall by 16 percent of GDP. Its civil war may have reduced growth by up to 8 percent, according to the *Trade and Development Report 1999*.[32]

It is a truism that conflicts divert resources from development uses, so do extractive FDI, and corrupt leadership. It is estimated that a total of $1 billion is used on conflict yearly in Central Africa. The figure amounts to more than $8 million in West Africa. On top of this comes the cost of refugee assistance, estimated at more than $500 million for Central Africa alone.[33] Crime and violence have many direct economic and human costs that may hinder FDI inflow directly or indirectly. They also inhibit development in many ways. For example, some factories may not operate more than one shift because employees cannot commute safely to work. FDI projects depending on operating several shifts may therefore not be able to invest under these circumstances. This may mean that they lose their profitability and competitiveness. They are therefore likely to be scared away from investing in Africa.

The availability of a healthy labor force is a very important FDI determinant. FDI will likely be scared away from Africa if the continent's already scarce human capital is further depleted by the acquired immune deficiency syndrome (AIDS). Besides reducing the badly needed labor force in Africa, the AIDS epidemic makes it necessary for authorities and individuals to divert scarce and very valuable pecuniary and non-pecuniary resources like time and personnel to AIDS and AIDS-related issues. These resources could have been used to create a more enabling environment for business in the continent. They could be invested in infrastructure and education. The latter steps would in turn facilitate the efforts to increase FDI inflow. The global share of FDI inflow to Africa would most likely increase by a substantial amount if it were not for the impact of the AIDS epidemic. AIDS therefore threatens future economic development of the continent.

From CNN "In-Depth Specials" of July 19, 2000, we learn that of the 33.6 million people infected with the human immunodeficiency virus (HIV) worldwide, 23.5 million (about 70 percent) are Africans.[34] The UN estimates that the number of AIDS orphans will reach 23 million by 2012. The continent has already lost 13.8 million people to AIDS, and nearly 10,500 new cases are diagnosed daily. AIDS may hinder FDI inflow in that it decimates the already scarce human capital.[35] According to *VartLand*, the International Labor Organization (ILO) estimates that the labor force in Africa will fall by 20 percent in the near future due to the AIDS epidemic.[36]

There are numerous other factors that mitigate against the inflow of FDI into Africa. These will include malaria and other tropical diseases, forces of nature such as floods and drought, and, on occasion, government-sponsored thuggery, and pervasive public and private corruption. The refugee problem adds to the bad image of Africa. The continent is home to more than half of the world's refugee population, about 12 million, including those internally displaced. But not all the countries in Africa are affected by this problem; however, many investors are ignorant of this fact. They use events in one country to generalize about the continent.

Life as a refugee is not the best one can wish for. Refugees can suffer psychological and emotional torture that makes them unable to work productively. That is to say, it can be difficult for most refugees to supply their labor force for productive work. The problem of refugees contributes to the shortage of the needed labor force in Africa. However, it is important to note that perhaps it is the way refugees are managed that constrains their inclusion in the workforce. Refugees are a cost to host governments and organizations, for example, the UN that finances them. Resources expended on refugees could have been used in creating a more competitive environment for investments.[37]

Africa's very low gross domestic product (GDP) is a handicap for the influx of FDI. According to World Bank, the GDP for the region is smaller than that of Belgium and is divided among 48 nations with a median gross domestic product of just over $2 billion, which is the output of a town of 60,000 in a rich nation. Africa accounts for barely 1 percent of global GDP and only 2 percent of world trade. Its share of global manufactured exports is almost zero.[38] The 2000 World Bank indicated that Africa is regressing because many nations are worse off in 2000 than they were at independence in the 1960s. Although the continent's present population of about one billion could potentially represent a huge market, low levels of income in the region erode this potential. Mozambique, Democratic Republic of Congo, Ethiopia and Malawi, for example, had a per head income of $286, $118, $107, and $144, respectively, in 2004. The region as a whole had an annual GDP per capita of $1200 in the same year. The low-income level in Africa, which translates to limited purchasing power, is a barrier to market-seeking FDI.[39]

Beside factors that are internal to Africa, there are other external factors equally playing a part in making it difficult for the continent to increase its global share of FDI. Those factors include the legacy of colonial rule, the Cold War rivalry, the debt crisis, exploitative trading relations, and strict and insensitive demands for economic reform from the IMF and the World Bank. Some of these factors are elaborated below. Africa's colonization by Europe led to the current artificial division of the continent. The division has been one of the major sources of war in Africa. Nations fight with each other mainly for the purpose of controlling resources found on the other side of boundaries. The consequences of war on the prospect of FDI in the continent have already been established. The economic foundations laid by the colonial authorities in Africa were directed at serving European interests. Africa was made to be a supplier of raw materials, primarily from the primary sector producing agricultural outputs and minerals. The continent was made to be a market for finished products. Such economic bases are among the factors that contribute to the current poverty level in Africa. This poverty makes it difficult for the continent to create an investment-friendly environment.[40]

The North-South exploitative trading relations partially account for problems in Africa. In the current trading relations, the North dictates the price of commodities in its favor and against the South. Most African nations find themselves on the losing side. They mostly experience deficits in their import-export performance. This leads to, among other things, the difficulty in using domestic sources to finance their development projects. As a result, most development projects, for example, infrastructure development, are likely to be abandoned. Poor infrastructure, in turn, becomes a barrier to FDI inflow.[41]

External borrowing may offer an alternative to financing development projects by using domestic sources. This alternative is not without potential problems for borrowing nations. When debts are accumulated, the payment of accruing interests may oblige the borrowing nations to divert local/national resources to the service of debt repayment instead of investing in the local/national economy in order to create a sustainable business environment for investments. Meanwhile, when African nations fail to repay (and this happens very often as a result of mismanagement, misappropriation of resources and pervasive corruption, among many other reasons), they fall into a debt crisis making it even harder for them to borrow more. In this way, the debt crisis in Africa is a barrier in the continent's drive at increasing its global share of FDI.

The presence and emergence of other developing regions of the world (Asia, Latin America, Caribbean and the former socialist states of Eastern and Central Europe) as more attractive investment locations adds to the challenges that Africa must face before it can increase its global share of FDI. Several regions of the world are competing for limited investments. Only those locations with adequate FDI determinants are likely witness appreciable increases in their global share of FDI.

Physical infrastructure is among the very important FDI determinants, particularly in Africa's underdeveloped and developing nations. Its value lies in its consumption, not its production. It is an input that is crucial to all other production. Its poor quality results in low competitiveness because cost, quality and access are important determinants of competitiveness. Poor infrastructure leads to weak market integration and slower growth. From the above, it should be clear that Africa's prospects of increasing its global share of FDI inflow are not bright.

Modern communication and information technology infrastructures such as the Internet are not common in the region. The gap created by the digital divide between Africa and the industrialized world is extremely huge. This is negative in terms of the ability to increase FDI in the region, especially in this e-commerce age. Ample resources will be required if this infrastructure is to be provided at acceptable standards. There must be exponential increases in access to electricity for more Africans, for instance. UNCTAD correctly points out that the African continent has many challenges to overcome before it can more fully exploit the advantages of e-commerce. They include the low level of economic development and small per capita incomes, the limited skill base with which to build the e-commerce services, the number of Internet users needed to build a critical mass of online consumers, and the lack of familiarity with even the traditional forms of electronic commerce such as telephone sales and use of credit cards.[42] Remedying the above depends on the provision of adequate telecommunication facilities in most nations of the continent.[43]

PROSPECTS FOR FDI IN AFRICA

In spite the problems that make it difficult for Africa to increase its global share of FDI, the region still has many opportunities and potentials to increase its share if policy makers take more decisive actions. An encouraging picture is slowly emerging in Africa in the form of some factors, such as greater political, economic, and social reforms in the continent; opportunities created by the end of the Cold War; and globalization and new technology, give rise to optimism that Africa may be on the right track to create an FDI-friendly environment. The presence of these factors alone does not automatically guarantee an increased FDI inflow. The factors must be optimally balanced. Additional actions geared toward proper promotion of investment opportunities in the region should be taken. Those encouraging factors that create an enabling environment for FDI should be made known to potential investors. This is because investors have been mainly hearing about the negative factors about the continent and may not be aware of these new realities. African nations such as Nigeria, Ghana, Togo and Gabon have embarked on SAPs intended to regain macroeconomic balance, improve resource allocation and restore growth. Privatization is opening a window to foreign investments and a door to domestic business, thus creating joint ventures and improving services. It is also very important to be critical of privatization as advocated by the IMF and the World Bank. These bodies are agents of neo-colonialism and therefore we should be wary of their suggestions. Besides, once public companies are privatized, few Africans could buy shares in them. The result is that rich foreign investors and corrupt African leaders in countries like Nigeria, Sierra Leone and their cohorts dominate ownership of companies and keep ordinary masses in perpetual financial slavery. Yes, privatization creates job opportunities, but they pay slave wages while huge profits made by these companies are not reinvested leading to capital flight.

The first window is the current greater political reform in the continent. There is a progressive rise in popular political participation in the continent today. This opens up spaces for the possibility of a greater transparency, responsiveness, and public accountability, resulting from the pressure created by the civil society insisting on a better management of public resources. Also, there is more focus on proper management of the economy today among African leaders than in the past. The second window is the end of the Cold War. After World War II, Africa became a strategic and ideological battlefield where external powers sought reliable allies rather than effective development partners. Many of the developmental problems Africa is facing today are traceable to Western policies on the continent during the Cold War era. By creating, propping, and nurturing undemocratic governments in many African countries, the West and the Soviet Union played a significant role in destroying African economies. Huge financial support provided for these dictators without seeking to hold them accountable were largely spent in buying weapons and other expenses unrelated to development. As a result, Africa was saddled with a debt burden from which it has never fully recovered. However, the end of the cold war signaled a reduction in external support for peacekeeping and aid flows due to waning geopolitical competition. But it also opened a window for donors and recipients to attend to issues pertaining to the effectiveness of different development strategies.

The third window is globalization and new technology. This seems to be offering, in some instances, greater opportunities for Africa. World markets are far more open now than ever before. The pool of capital seeking diversified international investment is growing rapidly, partly due to the demographic transition in industrial nations. Advances in the area of information technology offer huge potentials for Africa. The region has several economic groupings or integration that may represent different continuum of RTBs. These include the Economic Community of West African States (ECOWAS), Common Market for Eastern and Southern Africa (COMESA), and Southern African Development Community (SADC).[44] If these groupings are properly organized and the potentials that they represent are properly exploited, they can attract more market-seeking FDI.

Some African nations have signed several international agreements on investments. Thirty-seven African nations were members of the convention establishing the MIGA, and seven fulfilled their membership obligations. Forty-two African nations are signatories to the Convention on Investment Disputes between nations and nationals of other nations, and twenty-six to the Convention on Recognition and Enforcement of Foreign Arbitral Awards. Forty-one African nations have signed double taxation treaties with sundry other nations.[45] In concrete terms, these international agreements on investments have facilitated the process of establishing MNCs in Africa, made the continent more investment-friendly, and in the process increased the flow of FDI into the continent.

By January 1, 1999, fifty African nations had concluded Bilateral Investment Treaties (BITs) with other nations that aim at protecting and promoting FDI. They also clarify the terms to guide FDI between partner nations. They also concluded 335 BITs, the majority of which had been signed since the beginning of the 1990s. UNCTAD figures show that Africa had concluded the following number of BITs with the following nations and regions as of January 1, 1999: France (18), Germany (39), United Kingdom (18), United States (7), Japan (1), developed nations total (198), developing nations total (136), Africa (56), world total (369).[46] It is also worth mentioning that over forty African nations are now members of the World Trade Organization (WTO), and more are in the process of joining. Membership in the WTO is expected to have similar effects as BITs on the security of FDI.

Membership in these organizations increases investors' confidence in the nations concerned. This increased confidence is likely to enhance FDI inflow into the region. The fact that at least seventeen nations—including Africa's biggest economies of South Africa, Egypt and Nigeria—had broad-based privatization programs in place by the end of 1999 adds to the possibility of Africa's increasing its global share of FDI. The privatization of state-owned enterprises signals increased investment opportunities. In most cases outside Africa's biggest economies, the privatized enterprises are sold to foreign investors due to lack of capital on the part of the local population. Since very few Africans could buy shares in privatized African companies, only rich foreign investors and corrupt African leaders and their cohorts dominate ownership of these companies, thus marginalizing the poor majority.

Profitability is of prime interest to foreign investors. What may be the least known fact about FDI in Africa is the high rate of profitability for investments there and that in recent years, it has been higher than in most other regions. UNCTAD reports that "from the viewpoint of foreign companies, investments in Africa seem highly profitable, more than in most other regions."[47] For example, Japanese MNCs had the following percentage of profitability in the following regions in 1995: West Asia (12.6 percent), Latin America and the Caribbean (7.7 percent), Africa (5.6 percent), South-East Asia (2.9 percent), Pacific Rim (1.9 percent), North America (1.1 percent) and Europe (0.8 percent).[48] This profitability has been sustained by Africa's progressive openness.[49] A similar trend exists when one looks at the rates of return on U.S. FDI in Africa, except South Africa. For example, for 2005, the rate was 45.3 percent compared to 25.2 percent for Asia and the Pacific Rim. The figure for Latin America and the Caribbean for the same year was 12.5 percent. For the underdeveloped nations and all others, the rate of return was 14 and 12.3 percent respectively. In fact, between 1983 and 1997, it was only in 1996 that the rate of return in Africa for U.S. FDI was below 10 percent. Since 1990, the rate of return in Africa has averaged 29 percent. Since 1991, it has been higher than in any other region, in many years by a factor of two or more. The net income from British FDI in Africa (not including Nigeria) increased by 60 percent between 1989 and 1995.[50]

It is an acceptable truism that Africa has enormous untapped potential and hidden growth reserves. For example, the continent is home to the world's largest reserves of a number of strategic minerals, including gold, diamond, platinum, cobalt and chromium. The mining and petroleum sectors have, for this reason, great potential for attracting more FDI into the region if appropriate steps are taken. It is worth noting that contrary to common perception, FDI in Africa is no longer concentrated in natural resources. Services and manufacturing are key sectors for FDI. In Nigeria, manufacturing attracted almost 50 percent and services close to 20 percent of the total FDI stock in the nation at the beginning of the 1990s. Mauritius has been attractive as a location for manufacturing plants, including plants for electronic equipment, since the 1980s. All these give cause for optimism about Africa's ability to increase its global share of FDI.[51]

There are reasons to believe that the perception of Africa among investors may be changing for the better. On the one hand, corporate giants and MNCs such as Barclays Africa, Citibank and Coca-Cola Africa, Nestlé, Novartis Agro AG, Shell, Standard Chartered Bank, Unilever, Vodafone Group International and Mobile Telecommunication Network (MTN) acknowledge the impressive rates of economic growth in some key African economies. They also acknowledge growing political stability and financial prudence, great opportunities to market products to over 600 million consumers, long-term perspective and sustained efforts by MNCs and great confidence in the underlying potential of Africa.[52] On the other hand, the growing popularity of the emerging African companies, mainly from South Africa and Nigeria, listed on the London Stock Exchange (LSE) is increasing foreign investors' confidence in the prospect of Africa's development. To the extent that such positive corporate views of Africa will be widely shared by the investment community, it can be a good sign for more FDI inflow to Africa.[53]

The international community has made some efforts to promote FDI in Africa. Such efforts include measures to accelerate foreign debt relief as a means to support economic growth in the region. Official Development Assistance (ODA) has a significant role in helping the building of infrastructure and support domestic development generally. UNCTAD undertakes investment policy reviews in Africa and in collaboration with the International Chamber of Commerce (ICC); it has launched a project on investment guides and capacity building. The MIGA carries out assessments of institutional capacity for a large number of Investment Promotion Agencies (IPAs) and assists them to formulate effective strategies for attracting FDI, primarily through its *Promote Africa* field functions. All these seem to be opportunities that, if well exploited, can help the continent to increase its global share of FDI inflow substantially.

CONCLUSION

This chapter attempted to establish the need for Africa to increase its global share of FDI inflows. It showed that, for the most part, FDI could be a good omen for Africa. Among other things, such investments create employment, increase government revenue, and increase efficiency and competitiveness in the economy. However, once public companies are privatized, few Africans could buy shares in them; the result is that rich foreign investors and corrupt African leaders in countries like Nigeria, Sierra Leone, and their cohorts dominate ownership of companies and keep ordinary masses in perpetual financial slavery. Yes, privatization creates job opportunities, but these jobs pay slave wages while huge profits are made by these companies—profits that are not reinvested, thus leading to capital flight. Africa's share of global FDI inflows is insignificant.[54] Compared with the rest of the world, the continent does not receive an adequate level of FDI. Given the potential roles that FDI can play in the social and economic development of the continent, the need for it to increase its global share of FDI inflows is crucial and cannot be neglected by policymakers.

But given the fact that Africa lacks most of the FDI determinants that would attract more FDI into the region, the continent has a long way to go before it can increase FDI in any substantial manner. Some of the fundamental issues that make Africa less attractive for FDI compared to other regions of the world are the negative image of the continent in the external world, its poor and costly physical infrastructure and a low level of economic development reinforced by corruption. Despite the problems that hinder substantial inflow of FDI into the continent, however, Africa possesses the potential to increase its global share of FDI. The potential is traceable to increasing political participation and major economic reforms in the continent, the existence of some regional integration efforts, relatively high rates of return for capital investment in Africa, and positive views about investing in Africa from some corporate leaders. While these represent welcome developments, they are not enough.

As this chapter has shown, the Southern African Development Community (SADC) represents a model of internal development in Africa. The Southern African Development Coordination Conference (SADCC) was the forerunner of the socioeconomic cooperation leg of today's SADC. The adoption by nine majority-ruled southern African countries of the Lusaka Declaration on April 1, 1980 paved the way for the formal establishment of SADCC in July 1981. The SADCC was transformed into SADC on August 17, 1992, with the adoption by the founding members of SADCC and newly independent Namibia of the Windhoek Declaration and treaty establishing SADC. SADC provides for both socioeconomic cooperation and political and security cooperation. Its aims are set out in different sources such as the treaty establishing the organization (SADC Treaty), various protocols, development, and cooperation plans such as the Regional Indicative Strategic Development Plan (RISDP) and the Strategic Indicative Plan of the Organ (SIPO) and declarations such as those on HIV and AIDS and food security. Not all of the pre-2001 treaties and plans have been harmonized with the more detailed and recent plans such as the RISDP and SIPO. In some areas, mere coordination of national activities and policies is the aim of cooperation. In others, the member states aim at more far-reaching forms of cooperation. For example, the members largely aim to coordinate their foreign policies, but they aim to harmonize their trade and economic policies with a view to one day establishing a common market with common regulatory institutions.[55] SADC countries face many social, development, economic, trade, education, health, diplomatic, defense, security and political challenges. Individual members cannot tackle some of these challenges effectively. Cattle diseases and organized-crime gangs know no boundaries. War in one country can suck in its neighbors and damage their economies. The sustainable development that trade could bring is threatened by the existence of different product standards and tariff regimes, weak customs infrastructure and bad roads. The socioeconomic, political and security cooperation aims of SADC are equally wide-ranging, and intended to address the various common challenges.[56]

Finally, those responsible for decision-making in enterprise investment, advisers of MNCs, and others must be made to see the changing social, political, and economic realities in Africa. They must adopt a more balanced, not biased, view of the continent. It should be treated like any other continent or region in the world. It should not be written off as an unprofitable investment location. The tendency to lump all African nations together has not helped the continent. The continent should be looked at closely, nation by nation, industry by industry and opportunity by opportunity. The image of Africa should be changed. Decisive actions are needed in many areas. Those areas include resolving conflicts and increasing good governance to guide political and economic development, greater equity, more responsibility and responsiveness, and more investment in human capital, increasing competitiveness and economic diversification.

ENDNOTES

1 IMF, *Direction of Trade Statistics Yearbook 1998* (Washington, DC: IMF, 1998).

2 D. R. Rutherford, *Dictionary of Economics* (London: Longman, 1992, 1995).

3 E. S. Ezeanyika and A. A. Oruebor, *International Economic Relations in a Globalizing World* (Owerri: DESREG, in collaboration with Creative Educational Management and Consultancy Ltd., 2001).

4 K. Bjorvatn, "FDI in LDCs: Facts, Theory and Empirical Evidence," Manuscript, Norwegian School of Economics and Business Administration (2000).

5 UNCTAD, *Handbook of International Trade and Development Statistics* (New York and Geneva: United Nations, 1999a).

6 UNCTAD, *World Development Report 1997, 1999* and *Trade and Development Report 1999* (New York and Geneva: United Nations, 1997, 1998, 1999b).

7 UNCTAD, *Handbook of International Trade and Development Statistics*.

8 UNCTAD, *Capital Flows and Growth in Africa* (New York and Geneva: United Nations, 2007); IMF, *World Economic Outlook* (Washington, DC: IMF, 2005); and World Bank, *World Development Indicators* (Washington, DC: The World Bank, 2007a).

9 UNCTAD, *Capital Flows and Growth in Africa*.

10 UNCTAD, *Capital Flows and Growth in Africa*; and World Bank, *Global Economic Prospects and the Developing Countries* (Washington, DC: The World Bank, 2007b).

11 K. Ogundare, "More Money for Africa?" *The Business Eye* 2, no. 3 (January–February, 2008), 10–12; D. Abimboye, "The Story of Aliko Dangote," *Newswatch Magazine* 47, no. 16 (April 2008), 14–19.

12 E.S. Ezeanyika, *The Politics of Development Economy in the South: Problems and Prospects* (Owerri: DESREG, in collaboration with Gabtony Publishing Ltd, 2006), 123–125.

13 UNCTAD, *Trade and Development Report 2006* (New York and Geneva: United Nations, 2006); and IMF, *World Economic Outlook* (Washington, DC: IMF, 2007).

14 UNCTAD, *Trade and Development Report 2000* (New York and Geneva: United Nations, 2000a); UNCTAD, *Trade and Development Report 2003* (New York and Geneva: United Nations, 2003); UNCTAD, *Trade and Development Report*; IMF, *World Economic Outlook* (Washington, DC: IMF, 2001); *World Economic Outlook* (Washington, DC: IMF, 2004); and IMF, *World Economic Outlook*.

15 UNCTAD, *World Development Report 1998* (New York and Geneva: United Nations, 1998).

16 E.S. Ezeanyika, *International Political Economy: Themes and Perspectives* (Owerri: DESREG, in collaboration with Creative Educational Management and Consultancy Ltd., 2002); E.S. Ezeanyika, *The Politics of Development Economy in the South: Problems and Prospects*.

17 UNCTAD, *World Development Report 1998*.

18 K. Afriyie, "Foreign Direct Investment in Ghana's Emerging Market," in *Globalization, Trade and Foreign Direct Investment*, ed. J.H. Dunning (Amsterdam: Elsevier, 1988).

19 UNCTAD, *World Development Report 1998*; E.S. Ezeanyika, *Assessing Nigeria's National Technological Capabilities for Economic Development* (Owerri: Imo State University, Nigeria, DESREG Monograph Series no. 6, 2000).

20 K. Bjorvatn, "Infrastructure and Industrial Location in LDCs," *Journal of International Economics* 64 (1999), 89–112.

21 Ezeanyika, *The Politics of Development Economy in the South: Problems and Prospects*.

22 UNCTAD, *Capital Flows and Growth in Africa* (New York and Geneva: United Nations, 1999c).

23 Ibid.

24 R.T. Markus and J.L. Venables, *Foreign Direct Investment as a Catalyst for Industrial Development* (New York: United Nations, 1998).

25 J.D. Sachs and A.M. Warner, "Sources of Slow Growth in Africa," *Journal of African Economies* 6 (1997), 335–376.

26 A. Adedeji, "The African Challenges in the 1990s: New Perspectives for Development," *Indian Journal of Social Sciences* 3 (1990), 255–269; A. Diop, "Democracy for its Own Sake," 2 *Courier* no. 147 (September–October, 1994), 12–13; Ezeanyika, *International Political Economy*.

27 P. Collier and T.W. Gunning, "Explaining African Economic Performance," Center for the Study of African Economies, WPS/97-2.1 (Oxford, UK: University of Oxford, May 1997).

28 UNCTAD, *Trade and Development Report 1999*.

29 W. Easterly and R. Levine, "Troubles with Neighbors, Africa's Problem, Africa's Opportunity," *Journal of African Economies* 7 (1998), 120–142.

30 *VartLand,* "Africa and the Stigma of Conflict," S. Leonif, (June 17, 2000), 12.

31 World Bank, *Global Economic Prospects and the Developing Countries.*

32 Ibid. S.E. Ezeanyika, "The Social and Economic Impacts of Armed Conflicts on Women's Empowerment: A Critical Overview," *Journal of Conflict Studies* 2, no. 1 (2004), 40–45.

33 World Bank, *Global Economic Prospects and the Developing Countries.*

34 CNN "In-Depth Specials" (July 19, 2000).

35 UNCTAD, *Trade and Development Report 2003* (New York and Geneva: United Nations, 2003).

36 *VartLand* "Africa and the Stigma of Conflict," S. Leonif, (June 17, 2000), 12.

37 Ezeanyika, "The Social and Economic Impacts of Armed Conflicts on Women's Empowerment: A Critical Overview," 43.

38 World Bank, *Global Economic Prospects and the Developing Countries.*

39 Ibid.

40 E.S. Ezeanyika, *Introduction to African Politics* (Owerri: DESREG, in collaboration with Gabtony Publishing Ltd., 2007).

41 Ezeanyika, *International Political Economy.*

42 UNCTAD, *Capital Flows and Growth in Africa* (2000b).

43 World Bank, *Global Economic Prospects and the Developing Countries.*

44 Ezeanyika, *The Politics of Development Economy in the South.*

45 UNCTAD, *Trade and Development Report 1999* (1999b); Ezeanyika and Oruebor *Economic Relations in a Globalizing World.*

46 UNCTAD, *Trade and Development Report 1999* (1999b).

47 Ibid.

48 Ibid.

49 UNCTAD, *Trade and Development Report 2006* (2006); World Bank, *World Development Indicators* (2007a).

50 UNCTAD, *Trade and Development Report 1999* (1999b); *Trade and Development Report 1999* (2006).

51 Ezeanyika, *International Political Economy.*

52 *M. Ayhan* Kose, et al., "Financial Globalization: A Reappraisal" (IMF Working Paper 06/189, 2006); Luara Alfaro et al., "FDI and Economic Growth: The Role of the Local Financial Markets," *Journal of International Economics* 64, no. 1 (2004), 89–112; IMF, *World Economic Outlook* (2007); UNCTAD, *Capital Flows and Growth in Africa*; World Bank, *Global Economic Prospects and the Developing* Countries (2007b).

53 M. Ojelede, "The Race for Foreign Listing," *The Business Eye* 2, no. 3 (January–February 2008), 38.

54 Bjorvatn, "FDI in LDCs: Facts, Theory and Empirical Evidence" "Africa and the Stigma of Conflict," S. Leonif, (June 17, 2000), 12.

Ezeanyika, *The Politics of Development Economy in the South*; UNCTAD, *Capital Flows and Growth in Africa.*

55 R. Prega, "Global Partnership in Africa," Presentation at the Human Rights Conference on Global Partnerships for Africa's Development (Gaborone: SADC, 2003).

56 G. Oosthuizen, *The Southern African Development Community: The Organization, Its History, Policies and Prospects* (Midrand: Institute for Global Dialogue, 2006).

REVIEW QUESTIONS

1. What is foreign direct investment (FDI) and what impact has it had on postcolonial African economic development?
2. Analyze the considerations that determine FDI inflows in a given geographical location. Do you agree with those considerations?
3. What do you consider the problems and prospects of FDI flows to Africa? Will such inflows make meaningful impact on the continent?

Writing Prompt

Critically analyze the benefits of foreign direct investment and its applicability in aiding economic development in a selected African country. Make sure you identify the criteria used in providing FDI to your country of choice, analyzing the social, economic, and political transformation or lack of it in the country.

SOURCES FOR FURTHER READING

The sources below will be useful for instructors teaching *The African Experience* or other introductory courses on African studies as well as students and general readers eager to acquire comprehensive understanding of diverse African societies, issues, and peoples since the precolonial period.

BOOKS

1. Abegunrin, O. *Africa in Global Politics in the Twenty-First Century: A Pan-African Perspective*. Palgrave Macmillan, 2013.

2. Ahlers, T., Kato, H., Kohli, H. S., Madavo, C., and Sood, A. *Africa 2050: Realizing the Continent's Full Potential*. Oxford University Press, 2013

3. Binns, T., Dixon, A., and Nel, E. *Africa Diversity and Development*. Routledge, 2012.

4. Boone, Catherine. *Property and Political Order in Africa: Land Rights and the Structure of Politics*. Cambridge: Cambridge University Press, 2014.

5. Collins, Robert O. *Problems in African History*. New York: Markus Wiener Press, 1993.

6. Connah, Graham. *African Civilizations*. Cambridge: Cambridge University Press, 1981.

7. Davidson, Basil. Africa in History. New York: Collier Books, 1991.

8. Eko, A., and Iyam, D. U. *Matriarchy and Power in Africa*. Palgrave Macmillan, 2013.

9. Falola, Toyin and Nana Akua Amponsah, eds. *Women, Gender, and Sexualities in Africa*. Durham, NC: Carolina Academic Press, 2013.

10. Giles-Vernick, Tamara and James L.A. Webb, Jr., eds. *Global Health in Africa: Historical Perspectives on Disease Control*. Athens: Ohio University Press, 2013.

11. Gunner, L., dina, L., and Moyo, D. *Radio in Africa: Publics, Cultures, Communities*. James Curry, 2012.

12. Honwana, A. *The Time of Youth: Work, Social Change, and Politics in Africa*. Kumarian Press, 2012.

13. Kinyanjui, M. N. *Gender and the informal economy in Urban Africa: from the margins to the centre*. Zed Books, 2014.

14. Little, Peter D. *Economic and Political Reform in Africa: Anthropological Perspectives*. Bloomington and Indianapolis: Indiana University Press, 2014.

15. Mudimbe, V. *Contemporary African Cultural Productions*. CODESRIA, 2013.

16. Ndlovu-Gatshenoi, S. *Coloniality of Power in Postcolonial Africa: Myths of Decolonization*. CODESRIA, 2013.

17. Nugent, P. *Africa since Independence (Revised Ed)*. Palgrave Macmillan, 2012.

18. Oliver, Roland and J.D. Fage. *A Short History of Africa*. London: Harmondsworth, 1962.

19. Renne, Elisha P., ed. *Veiling in Africa*. Bloomington and Indianapolis: Indiana University Press, 2013.

20. Shillington, Kevin. *History of Africa*. New York: St. Martin Press, 1989.

JOURNALS

1. *Journal of African History*
2. *African Studies*
3. *Canadian Journal of African Studies*
4. *Journal of Retracing Africa*
5. *African Economic History Review*
6. *African Affairs*
7. *African Studies Review*
8. *African Studies Bulletin*
9. *History in Africa*
10. *African Historical Studies*
11. *Journal of African Law*
12. *Journal of Africana Religions*
13. *The Journal of Modern African Studies*
14. *Journal of Southern African Studies*
15. *African Languages and Cultures*
16. *Journal of African Cultural Studies*
17. *Islamic Africa*
18. *African Arts*
19. *African Music*
20. *Issue: A Journal of Opinion*

WEBSITES

Africa: History, an annotated guided maintained by the African Studies Center at the University of Pennsylvania: http://www.africa.upenn.edu/About_African/ww_hist.html.

History and Cultures of Africa, maintained by the Columbia University Libraries: http://library.columbia.edu/locations/global/africa.html.

African National Congress: South Africa's National Liberation Movement: http://www.anc.org.za/index.php.

United Nations Development Programme (UNDP) in Africa: http://www.africa.undp.org/content/rba/en/home.html.

The Story of Africa: Africa from the Dawn of Time: http://www.bbc.co.uk/worldservice/africa/features/storyofafrica/.

Exploring Africa: http://exploringafrica.matrix.msu.edu/index.php.

Internet African History Sourcebook: http://www.fordham.edu/halsall/africa/africasbook.asp.

Documents from the Organization of African Unity: http://web.archive.org/web/20001211022400/http://www.law.uc.edu/Diana/oaudocs.html.

All Africa- All the time: http://allafrica.com/.

Africa Confidential: http://www.africa-confidential.com/news.

Africa Science News: http://www.africasciencenews.org/en/.

African Union: a united and strong Africa: http://www.au.int/en/.

African Newspapers: http://www.world-newspapers.com/africa.html.

Africa: Carefully Selected News, Travel, Information & Lifestyle: http://www.africa.com/.

Reuters Africa: http://af.reuters.com/.

Afrol News: African Online News: http://afrol.com/

African Gender Institute: http://agi.ac.za/

African Studies Association: http://www.africanstudies.org/

NEPAD: transforming Africa: http://www.nepad.org/

Arts in Africa: http://www.artsinafrica.com/

VIDEOS

1. A Day in the Life of a Village in Africa, Documentary, 2002, 60 min., DVD.

2. Africa: A Voyage of Discovery with Basil Davidson, Programs 1-8, 448 min., 1984, VHS.

3. Black Gold, Documentary, 2006, 78 min., DVD.

4. Congo: White King, Red Rubber, Black Death, Documentary, 2003, 84 min, DVD.

5. Portrait of Africa Tapestry Video; Paramount Pictures; produced by Dann Moss, 1989. Hollywood, Calif. : Paramount Pictures, 56 min., videocassette.

6. Africa a history denied / Time-Life Video and Television presents; written, produced & directed by David Dugan, c1995. Alexandria, Va. : Time-Life Video and Television.

7. Doing Good Open University. New York, [2013], c2012. N.Y. : Films Media Group. Streaming video file (58 min.).

8. The Our Africa website is an evolving collection of videos of life in Africa, http://www.our-africa.org/.

9. How to Rob Africa: http://topdocumentaryfilms.com/how-to-rob-africa/.

10. An African Journey: http://topdocumentaryfilms.com/an-african-journey/.

11. Journey of Man: A Genetic Odyssey: http://topdocumentaryfilms.com/journey-man-genetic-odyssey/.

12. The Beautiful Game (documentary), 2012. Directed by Victor Buhler.

13. Africa in defiance of democracy, New York, N.Y. : Films Media Group, [2005] 56 mins, http://digital.films.com/PortalViewVideo.aspx?xtid=29500.

14. Africa as an Investment. New York, N.Y. : Films Media Group, [2012], c2007 19 mins, http://digital.films.com/PortalViewVideo.aspx?xtid=48318.

15. A Son of Africa. California Newsreel (Firm). New York, N.Y. : Films Media Group, [2013], c1996. 28 mins, http://digital.films.com/PortalViewVideo.aspx?xtid=49763.

16. Africa. Part One The Uncovered Continent / International Center for G. New York, N.Y. : Films Media Group, [2013], c1993. 26 mins, http://digital.films.com/PortalViewVideo.aspx?xtid=53114.

17. Africa calling appeal for understanding / Octapixx Worldwide (Firm) New York, N.Y. : Films Media Group, [2008], c2004. 57 mins, http://digital.films.com/PortalViewVideo.aspx?xtid=39458.

18. A Fresh Look at the Democratic Republic of the Congo, Zambia, and South Africa, New York, N.Y: Films Media Group, [2010], c2010. 57 mins http://digital.films.com/PortalViewVideo.aspx?xtid=41989.

19. West Africa, New York, N.Y. : Films Media Group, [2011], c2009. 48 mins, http://digital.films.com/PortalViewVideo.aspx?xtid=43767.

20. Linking Africa The Future Is Digital / German United Distributors. New York, N.Y. : Films Media Group, [2012], c2011. 52 mins, http://digital.films.com/PortalViewVideo.aspx?xtid=48291.

CPSIA information can be obtained
at www.ICGtesting.com
Printed in the USA
FFOW03n0528130116
20329FF